Sociocultural and Multicultural Meanings in Online Communication

Rotimi Taiwo
Obafemi Awolowo University, Nigeria

IGI Global
Scientific Publishing
Publishing Tomorrow's Research Today

Vice President of Editorial	Melissa Wagner
Director of Acquisitions	Mikaela Felty
Director of Book Development	Jocelynn Hessler
Production Manager	Mike Brehm
Cover Design	Jose Rosado

Published in the United States of America by
IGI Global Scientific Publishing
701 East Chocolate Avenue
Hershey, PA, 17033, USA
Tel: 717-533-8845
Fax: 717-533-7115
Website: https://www.igi-global.com E-mail: cust@igi-global.com

Library of Congress Cataloging-in-Publication Data

Names: Taiwo, Rotimi (Dr.), editor.
Title: Sociocultural and multicultural meanings in online communication / edited by Rotimi Taiwo.
Description: Hershey, PA : IGI Global Scientific Publishing, [2025] | Includes bibliographical references and index. | Summary: "This book aims to present emerging trends and perspectives on the discursive construction of sociocultural and multicultural meanings in online interactions across the globe. The book will advance the understanding of the nuances of sociocultural and multicultural meanings as well as the multimodality that characterize communication in modern digital communication"-- Provided by publisher.
Identifiers: LCCN 2024055442 (print) | LCCN 2024055443 (ebook) | ISBN 9798369379349 (hardcover) | ISBN 9798369379356 (paperback) | ISBN 9798369379363 (ebook)
Subjects: LCSH: Digital communications--Social aspects. | Online social networks. | Internet--Social aspects.
Classification: LCC HM851 .S553 2025 (print) | LCC HM851 (ebook) | DDC 302.23/1--dc23/eng/20250131
LC record available at https://lccn.loc.gov/2024055442
LC ebook record available at https://lccn.loc.gov/2024055443

British Cataloguing in Publication Data
A Cataloguing in Publication record for this book is available from the British Library.

Editorial Advisory Board

Table of Contents

Detailed Table of Contents

The influences of the digital space manifest in the seamless human interactions and sociality which it has engendered and enhanced. One of such influences is the digital knowledge-sharing of indigenous herbs for medical purposes. This study explores, from a critical discourse perspective, the representations of ideologies and identities in ten (10) purposively selected tweets from the handle ChiefHerbalist (@ HerbalistChief). Employing representative tweets from the handle as well as tweets in response by followers, attention is drawn to the discursive and contextual realities in the narratives. Among the outcomes are language use in the tripodal viewpoints of the assertion of authenticities, authoritativeness and validations. These fulfil the ideological functions of challenging the perceived primacy of orthodox medicine and projecting the efficacy of herbs and other forms of trado-medicine. What is doubtless is that the digital space has enabled visibility especially as the responders and followers are transnational.

Given the prevalence of heteronormativity in Africa, pro-queer advocacy is a topic that merits careful consideration. Social media gives queer visibility a platform because of the homophobia in Nigerian society. Linguistic research on how same-sex sexualities are portrayed in the media has focused on how heteronormativity is emphasised and how queer people linguistically create their identities on social media, with little consideration given to how pro-queer people have also used images to challenge heteronormativity. Drawing on Machin and Mayr's approach to Multimodal Critical Discourse Analysis, this study examines how Nigerian pro-LGBT people construct certain ideologies through texts and images on X in their bid to challenge heteronormativity. Data were purposively drawn using relevant hashtags. Findings revealed that visual metaphorisation and other semiotic elements foreground different ideologies including same-sex sexuality as natural, African and Nigerian as well as homonormativity and collective identity. The study shows the use of images and texts to resist homophobia.

This paper examines the pragmatics of prenominal possessives, our children and their children, in Nigerian online interactions with the aim of unpacking the indexical configuration of possessives referents, participants' evaluative orientations, and the ideological implications. Data include a corpus of 250,000 tweets with 2,424,462 tokens. The study adopted a mixed-method of corpus-based methodologies and qualitative discourse analysis (QDA) foregrounded by Bucholtz and Hall's (2005) indexicality principle. Findings reveal two possessive configurations, namely explicit and implicit possessive referents. These configurations manifest two evaluative orientations: the negative evaluation of the children's current state-of-affairs and the evaluation of obligation towards the children's ideal state-of-affairs. They point to an ideological polarisation of "them" versus "us", where 'our' indicates inclusivity – the collective responsibility of the masses and "their" implies exclusivity- the negligence of politicians that provokes criticism and condemnation.

This chapter explored how the intersection of text and images manifests discursivity and advances promotional meanings in the online affiliate advertisements of Jumia. Five samples of e-banners were elicited from the company's website, all within December 2023. Each e-banner purposively represented each of the five weekends the company reeled out advertisements in the yuletide month. The data were analysed using Martinec and Salway's (2005) image-text relations system, and supported with insights from Halliday's Systemic Functional Linguistics and Barthes's Semiotics. The findings evinced that Jumia's marketization of products principally rests on rhetoric of incentives and enticement to establish discursivity in their promotions. This persuasive strategy is maximized via three relations: text-image complementarity, image subordination to text and text subordination to image. Also, these syntheses resultantly promote testacies of social status and convenience, expense reduction, financial gains and happiness, in ways that shape prospects' purchasing decisions.

This paper investigates the deployment of awareness posters as a communicative resource in disseminating information about cholera in Nigeria. Data, sourced from the internet, were awareness posters on the outbreak of cholera in Nigeria, circulated between June 15 and July 15 2024 which was the period of severity of the virulent disease. The study drew insights from Kress and Leeuwen's (2006) Grammar of Visual Design, which was purposively selected for its capability to holistically engage the different semiotic resources deployed for communicative purpose. Data were subjected to a bottom-up, content analysis which requires analysing each data distinctively for its idiosyncratic semiotic contents. Findings revealed that online awareness posters on cholera were thematically classified based on the different goals they were meant to achieve. Also, image producers of cholera posters conflated multiple processes and elements for the purpose of communicating the severity of cholera and to engender positive healthy behaviours among Nigerians.

This chapter aimed to examine the role of the new media in enhancing content creation. Over the last two decades, the rise of the new media has continued to demonstrate its worth as a communication chain with worldwide user connectivity as its focal point. As a result, content creators have taken to the internet via social media platforms like Facebook, TikTok, YouTube, etc. with a plethora of contents intended to entertain, educate, sensitise, or spill the tea to their audience. Using the qualitative and quantitative methods of data collection, content creators whose focus spans from family, health, education, motivational, food, and business were employed as the population for this study. Findings show that content creators have profoundly reshaped media participation and engagement by gratifying the entertainment needs of the audience. Results further revealed that digital media have indisputably demonstrated their crucial role in fostering connections among users and content creators.

This chapter examines the use of emojis and stickers in WhatsApp communication of selected virtual communities, and the extent to which the awareness among WhatsApp users in terms of the interpretations and utilization of emojis and stickers have helped in their applications. It adopts a descriptive qualitative and quantitative research methodology. Thirty (30) stickers and thirty (30) emojis were measured by ninety-one (91) respondents chosen at random from ten selected WhatsApp groups and analyzed with the methodological framework of Halliday (1978) Socio-semiotic theory. The research discovered that emojis and stickers may primarily be utilized for expressive social functions rather than informational ones. In conclusion, education significantly affects how people interpret and utilize emojis and stickers on WhatsApp across age, gender, and employment categories.

This chapter explores the multimodal representation of personal life and cultural identity in the Instagram posts of four gaming influencers from diverse backgrounds: PewDiePie, Valkyrae, Ninja, and Pokimane. Utilising Gunther Kress and Theo van Leeuwen's Social Semiotics framework, the analysis focuses on how these influencers blend visual and textual elements in non-gaming posts to depict themes like family life, professional achievements, and personal moments. This study highlights how influencers use Instagram's platform-specific features to foster a sense of authenticity and relatability with their audience. The findings support the argument that these gaming influencers effectively deploy multimodal communication to connect with their audiences at a human (sometimes parasocial) level. Furthermore, the study reveals how these multimodal strategies contribute to broader discussions on digital communication, cultural identity, gender representation, and the role of influencers in shaping online communities.

While modern conservative individuals act on the basis of beliefs and traditions, the development of communication technologies and post-fordist lifestyles have increased the flexibility of societies. This flexibility is also reflected in family structures and the roles of individuals. The traditional family structure has undergone major transformations in the industrial and information ages. Social media platforms such as Instagram allow individuals to construct and present their lives, making the lives of conservative families visible. However, the fact that Instagram is a digital stage suggests that the life presented may not reflect true conservative values. Conservatism's emphasis on privacy increases the interest in social media representations and shapes the quality of content.

The digital space has transcended various barriers to becoming a vibrant hub for cultural integration. Music, which happens to be a universal language that speaks to the human spirit and crosses borders, plays a key role in this global dialogue. Using Gunther Kress and Theo van Leeuwen's Visual Social Semiotic theory, this study explored the power of music to foster cultural integration in the digital space by analysing Yinka Ayefele's song Mo M'ope Mi Wa (I Offer My Praise). This song, which was obtained on YouTube, is a blend of Yoruba Juju, Igbo dressing and Akwa Ibom Highlife. The song strategically employs various communication modes to bridge cultural differences and foster integration of several cultures. The study demonstrates the power of music, especially when it is creatively blended with cultural elements, in bridging divides and promoting human connection in the digital space.

This chapter has examined the meaning-making potentials of selected online weekend comedy skits using the tools of Critical Multimodal Discourse Analysis, drawing on the theoretical frameworks by Fairclough (1989/1995) and Kress and van Leeuwen (2006). Critical discourse analysis (CDA) examines the nexus or relationship between language, power and social inequality. The data is by Busymouth titled 'Mr. President facing flood challenges' and 'Busymouth as Akpan shamed his ex.' In the short pieces, the hopeless social, economic and political situation of an African country are presented. The findings reveal that the socio-economic and political situation that have become life threatening for the poor masses have no end in sight, yet trivialized by the President who represents the government at all levels. The bad economic situation has also led to character failure and break in mutual relationships which are some of the indices of a corrupt society.

The objective of this study is to examine the relationship between social media and western cultural hegemony in contemporary Nigeria. A review of related literature was carried out to determine the implications of western ideologies and practices transmitted vis-a-viz social media platforms on the indigenous culture of Nigeria. The study reveals that social media platforms serve as channels for eroding the indigenous culture of Nigeria. The study also shows that Nigerian cultural values and beliefs can be promoted on social media by intensifying efforts to display Nigerian festivals and rituals, indigenous cuisines and historical cultural heritage sites to attract global attention. This study concludes that showcasing Nigerian indigenous culture on social media will provide a platform for Nigerians to share the rich cultural heritage of the country to the global audience, which will contribute significantly to the preservation of Nigerian cultural values.

Language is a medium of communication and invariably, an inevitable means of communication. The present study intends to examine language use as espoused in sneak peeks in the media. Hence, the study considers sneak peeks as language of advertising Bollywood blockbusters or movies. The data comprise three different

exacerbate disparities between languages with high AI compatibility and those with limited tools, potentially fostering a new digital divide. Using selected Nigerian universities as a case study, this research addresses questions on the adaptability of AI to diverse African languages, the need for curriculum adjustments, and the risks of linguistic hegemony. Findings indicate that while AI offers significant educational benefits, its adoption in Africa must consider preserving linguistic diversity. Consequently, this chapter recommends developing policies supporting equitable AI access while promoting cultural and linguistic heritage.

Foreword

Communication, in modern times, is a globalised phenomenon in which socio-cultural meanings are no longer localized. Rather, they keep spreading through the Internet in such a way that multiple cultures are represented in online interactions. Also, unlike in the past, when communication is largely restricted to speech, writing and gestures, the new media have facilitated the co-occurrence of different communicative modes, such as, written language, visual imagery, audio, spatial arrangements, and gestures. These multimodal texts, in networked digital environments, allow for a better understanding of complex and enriched communication experience.

This newer experience motivated the conception of the idea of this book, which focuses on analysing meanings in sociocultural and multicultural communications in online settings. The book presents emerging trends and perspectives on the discursive construction of sociocultural and multicultural meanings in online interactions across the globe. Scholars from different parts of the world, with Nigerian scholars leading, present insights mainly from discourse, semiotic and media studies to investigating meanings in multimodal texts online. The studies explore subjects, such as ideologies, identities, attitudes, framings in social media platforms, mainly, X, Facebook, Instagram, TikTok, YouTube, online forums, shopping sites, and e-newspapers.

Authors, spread across Africa, Europe and Asia, deployed interdisciplinary, multidisciplinary and mainly qualitative approaches to the study of sociocultural and multicultural meanings. These approaches, which focus on structural and functional textual and image analysis, are, functional linguistics, corpus-based and corpus-assisted discourse analysis, critical discourse analysis, multimodal (critical) discourse analysis, qualitative discourse analysis, socio-semiotics, and visual grammar.

Issues that are discussed, across the Seventeen-chaptered book, include: ideologies and identities, affective digital symbols, visual metaphoric critiques in online cartooning, amplification of marginal voices online, ethnic consciousness in online election campaigns, strategic communication of culture and arts online in crisis period, ideological constructions in online pro-queer postings, multimodality in online promotional advertisements, digital protests, online representation of (in)security, social media and Western cultural hegemony, online content creation, ChatGPT, and multimodal literacy.

Twenty-eight authors from different disciplinary backgrounds and nineteen institutions across the world have been able to offer fresh insights into scholarship on sociocultural and multicultural meanings in online contexts. The scholarly perspectives presented in the book have advanced the understanding of the nuances of sociocultural meaning and multimodal expressions of such meanings. This book, therefore, offers significant benefits to scholars in different disciplines interested in online communication and its enrichment of meaning socioculturalism and multiculturalism as well as multimodality. It is an academic debut in the realm of digitized linguistics. I commend readers to take a tour of the book, especially, postgraduates and researchers of serious linguistic import.

Demola Jolayemi
English and Digitized Linguistics, University of Africa, Toru-Orua, Nigeria

Preface

In an era defined by rapid digital transformation and growing socio-political awareness, *Sociopolitical Discourse and Meanings in Online Communication* presents a timely exploration of how meaning is constructed, contested, and circulated within digital media spaces. This volume brings together diverse scholarly contributions that interrogate the discursive practices and multimodal strategies employed in online communication, with a specific focus on Nigeria and, in one chapter, the Indian context.

This collection emerges from the understanding that online platforms—social media networks, digital newspapers, and other internet-based tools—have become critical arenas for political participation, identity negotiation, resistance, and meaning-making. The chapters compiled herein reveal how various forms of discourse, including memes, editorial cartoons, Twitter posts, and Facebook commentary, function as powerful rhetorical tools in shaping public opinion, fostering dissent, and influencing sociopolitical realities.

Across seventeen chapters, contributors draw on frameworks such as Critical Discourse Analysis, multimodal discourse analysis, social semiotics, pragmatics, and corpus-assisted approaches to examine a wide range of topics. These include industrial actions by Nigerian university unions, ethnic identity construction during Nigeria's 2023 elections, discursive representations of insecurity and economic hardship, resistance discourse through internet memes, and even the cultural implications of Chinese social media app usage in Kerala, India. The volume also delves into issues such as the framing of herder-farmer conflicts, digital protest movements, and the socio-semiotic power of parody in critiquing government policy.

Chapter 1: The Dynamics of Sociocultural and Multicultural Meanings in Online Discussion: A General Overview

Rotimi Taiwo provides a foundational framework for understanding how sociocultural values and multicultural identities shape digital communication. This introductory chapter lays out key dynamics, including identity formation, cultural exchange, and marginalization due to unequal digital access.

Chapter 2: Emojis and Emoticons: Decoding Multicultural Meanings in Online Communication

Muhammad Usman Tariq delves into the cultural semantics of emojis and emoticons, exploring how these digital symbols function differently across cultural lines and social contexts, shaping affective and linguistic meaning in global online discourse.

Chapter 3: A Critical Discourse Study of Ideologies and Identities in Nigerian X Trado-Medicine Narratives

Paul Onanuga and Emmanuel Babalola examine online narratives promoting indigenous herbal medicine, unpacking how discourse affirms traditional identities and resists biomedical dominance in the Nigerian digital space.

Chapter 4: Multimodality in Challenging Heteronormativity in Nigerian Pro-Queer Tweets

Olubunmi Oyebanji explores how Nigerian LGBTQ+ communities use images and text to counter heteronormative narratives, employing multimodal discourse to assert visibility and alternative sexual identities in a hostile sociopolitical climate.

Chapter 5: The Pragmatics of Possessive Constructions of Children in Selected Nigerian Online Interactions

Ezekiel Olajimbiti and Samuel Dada investigate how terms like *our children* and *their children* are pragmatically and ideologically deployed in Nigerian online discussions, revealing tensions between collective responsibility and political accountability.

Chapter 6: Image-Text Syntheses, Discursivity and Promotional Meanings in Selected Jumia's Online Affiliate Advertisements

Moses Christian-Achinihu analyzes e-banners from Jumia, Nigeria's leading e-commerce platform, showing how the interplay of text and image is used to construct persuasive, consumer-targeted messages laden with social and economic symbolism.

Chapter 7: Visualising Danger: A Multimodal Analysis of Online Awareness Posters on Cholera in Nigeria

Oladayo Ogunsiji, Yemi Ogunsiji, and Janet Olaleke examine the semiotics of public health messaging, demonstrating how visual resources are marshaled to communicate urgency and promote health behaviors during cholera outbreaks.

Chapter 8: The Role of the New Media in Enhancing Online Content Creation

Ijeoma Ojilere investigates how new media empower content creators across diverse sectors—health, family, food, and education—shaping modern communication strategies and expanding digital participation in Nigeria.

Chapter 9: Socio-Semiotics of Internet Communications: Analysis of Emojis and Stickers in Selected WhatsApp Groups

Emmanuel Adedun and Tolulope Ayodele explore the expressive and social functions of emojis and stickers in WhatsApp group chats, revealing how educational background influences their usage and interpretation across different demographics.

Chapter 10: A Multimodal Exploration of Personal Life and Cultural Identity in Gaming Influencers' Instagram Posts

Egbah Andrew uses social semiotic theory to analyze how gaming influencers like PewDiePie and Pokimane use Instagram to present personal narratives and cultural identity, fostering parasocial relationships and community-building.

Chapter 11: The Transparency of the Family: A Study on Conservative Family Profiles on Instagram

Metin Gültekin and Ahmet Yildiz explore how conservative families negotiate tradition and digital visibility on Instagram, revealing tensions between privacy, performativity, and the presentation of ideological values online.

Chapter 12: Cultural Integration in the Digital Space: A Multimodal Discourse Analysis of Yinka Ayefele's *Mo M'ope Mi Wa*

Lydia Olaifa and Bolatito Adejare examine how a popular Nigerian gospel song integrates diverse cultural elements—music, dress, and language—to foster cross-cultural understanding and digital cultural exchange.

Chapter 13: "What Did You Just Say?" A Critical Multimodal Discourse Analysis of Selected Online Comedy Skits

Moji Olateju critiques how humor is used in online comedy skits to expose and critique socio-political conditions, illustrating how comedy becomes a mode of resistance and reflection in times of crisis.

Chapter 14: Social Media and Western Cultural Hegemony: A Study of Cultural Shift in Contemporary Nigeria

Olaronke Iroju and Opeyemi Iroju interrogate the dominance of Western values on social media and its influence on Nigerian cultural identity, advocating for a counter-narrative that highlights indigenous practices and heritage.

Chapter 15: A Multimodal Discourse Analysis of Outlined Sneak Peeks of Selected Bollywood Blockbusters

Olayinka Odubela and Yemisi Famakinwa explore how sneak peeks of Bollywood films function as a form of persuasive media discourse, using multimodal strategies to capture audience attention and shape interpretation.

Chapter 16: Multimodal Literacy and Sociocultural Dynamics in Online Communication: An Interdisciplinary View

Semiu Makinde et al. propose an interdisciplinary framework for understanding how multimodal literacy intersects with sociocultural dynamics, offering insights into how digital communication can foster social inclusion and educational transformation.

Chapter 17: ChatGPT and the Future of Language Learning and Linguistic Diversity in Africa

Hauwa Sani critically evaluates the role of AI tools like ChatGPT in African higher education, raising concerns about digital language inequality, curriculum relevance, and the preservation of linguistic diversity in the face of technological standardization.

The scholarship in this volume is both theoretically robust and methodologically diverse, offering readers an interdisciplinary lens through which to understand the evolving relationship between language, media, and society. The contributors, primarily based in Nigerian universities and research institutions, provide contextually grounded insights that highlight the interplay between local sociopolitical dynamics and global digital trends.

This book will be of value to scholars, students, and practitioners in the fields of discourse studies, media and communication, political science, cultural studies, and digital humanities. It contributes significantly to the growing body of literature on digital discourse in the Global South, revealing how marginalized voices employ language and imagery to negotiate power, resist injustice, and foster civic engagement in increasingly digitized public spheres.

We hope this volume inspires critical dialogue and further research on how online communication continues to reshape the contours of sociopolitical engagement across cultures and communities.

Rotimi Taiwo
Obafemi Awolowo University, Nigeria

Acknowledgement

I would like to appreciate all the authors who contributed to this book and assisted in the peer review process. I am particularly grateful to some other scholars I reached out to and who participated in reviewing some of the chapters for this book, most especially members of the Editorial Advisory Board. I would like to specifically mention Dr Olajumoke Adebayo for her support during the review process in spite of not being able to submit a chapter for inclusion in the book as she earlier intended.

I am especially grateful to my wife Yetunde, for her understanding and support during the period I was editing this book. I acknowledge my university, Obafemi Awolowo University, Ile-Ife, Nigeria, for providing an enabling environment for me to do this work. Finally, I appreciate Custodian of wisdom, the Lord Almighty for supplying the strength and wisdom to accomplish the task as desired by me and expected by the publisher.

Chapter 1
The Dynamics of Sociocultural and Multicultural Meanings in Online Discussion: A General Overview

Rotimi Taiwo
https://orcid.org/0000-0003-2614-5198
Obafemi Awolowo University, Ile-Ife, Nigeria

ABSTRACT

As digital platforms facilitate global communication, individuals bring diverse cultural values, social norms, and linguistic styles into these spaces. This chapter explores the sociocultural and multicultural dimensions of online discussions. It specifically presents a general overview of how these factors influence online interaction, identity formation, cultural exchange. It also discusses potential challenges, such as, marginalization of certain groups as a result of unequal access to digital communication, leading to the exclusion of the voices from less privileged regions or communities. Understanding these dynamics is essential to engaging these complex and multifaceted and intertwined issues surrounding online communication in the digital age.

DOI: 10.4018/979-8-3693-7934-9.ch001

1. INTRODUCTION

Digital communication has transformed the way humans communicate, creating spaces where people from diverse cultural and social backgrounds interact. Online discussions, which take place on social media, forums, or educational platforms, are rich and project sociocultural and multicultural meanings. Online discussions are interactive in nature and they allow users to share ideas, debate topics, and learn from one another. They can take various forms, including online forums, discussion groups, blogging and comment sections on websites. A significant aspect of online communication is the sociality it fosters. Online communication enables formation of new connections and strengthening of existing ones. It enhances social capital and social support, leading to positive psychological states (Best and Krueger 2006).

As people with common and shared interest congregate online communicate online, they share information, offer support, and engage in discussions, and ultimately build communities, which can vary in size, from massive social media groups to smaller, more focused forums or niche networks (Hermans, et al. 2016, Miranda, et al. 2016). To buttress the supporting roles online communities play in the lives of participants, scholars have identified, for instance, how online communities have become support systems for different groups of people to receive emotional and practical assistance, such as women trying to cope with involuntary infertility (Bost 2008, Ancheta 2016, DeRose 2016, Taiwo and Oyinlade 2022) and unemployed youths (McQuaid, et al 2004, Lorenzini, et al 2010, Fieseler, et al 2014, Taiwo, 2015, 2016). Discursive practices through such online communities foster communal bonding by creating and strengthening connections and relationships within groups of individuals who interact primarily through digital platforms. Such platforms allow users to share experiences, ask questions, and receive guidance. Such groups are often created by individuals who have lived experience with a particular issue and are ready to provide emotional and therapeutic support and shared understanding for individuals seeking assistance with problems such as depression, suicidal tendencies, substance abuse, cancer, eating disorders, and so forth (Finfgeld 2009, Zhang et al. 2024). While these online communities have been reported to foster trust, commitment and social bonding through performativity of intimate sociality, (Ley 2009, Coulson, et al 2017, Taylor 2022), several studies have shown the flip side of these communities (Bell 2007, Dawson and Dennis 2020,

Communicating online today is purely a social venture in which participants express their stances, attitudes, identities and ideologies, which scholars in discourse studies have extensively discussed (Myers, 2013, Ajiboye and Abioye 2019, Liu 2022, Osisanwo and Akano 2023, Ugah 2023). This chapter presents a general overview of how sociocultural and multicultural factors influence online communication and the implications these have for inclusion, identity, and digital discourse.

2. SOCIOCULTURAL MEANINGS IN ONLINE DISCUSSION

Language is a social phenomenon, a system of communication used by humans for socializing. The social system in which a language is used shapes interactions and reflect the culture, and collective memory of the language users (Mlynář 2014). In addition to the transmission of information, language is used to express the identities of the users and their cultural values (Schecter, 2014, Bucholtz and Hull 2004). For sociologists and discourse analysts, language is used to reflect social structures (van Dijk 2005, KhosraviNik 2010), power dynamics (van Dijk 2012, Fairclough 2013, Khan 2024), and cultural norms and beliefs (Gong, et al 2010, Danet and Herring 2007) of the users. The relationship between language and society is bidirectional: society influences language, and language in turn influences how society is perceived and structured (Halliday and Webster 2009, van Dijk 2009).

Different cultures employ various verbal and non-verbal communication styles. In the online context of communication, multimodal means are engaged, which involve the use of multiple modes of communication, such as text, visuals, audio, and gestures, to convey meaning (Kress and Van Leeuwen 2020), . The use of multiple modes in online communication leverages different senses and mediums to create a richer and more engaging experience for the interactants. Using multiple modes in online communication makes it more engaging, informative, and expressive (Ekström and Östman 2015). It can also help overcome some of the limitations of text-based communication, such as the difficulty of conveying tone, emotion, and non-verbal cues. (Shih 2014). The sections that follow will discuss aspects of sociocultural and multicultural meanings in online interactions.

2.1 Sociocultural Approach to Discourse

Sociocultural approaches to discourse analysis examine how social and cultural factors shape and are shaped by language use (Forman and McCormick 1995, Mercer 2004). This means analyzing discourse not just as a linguistic structure, but also as a tool for social interaction and a reflection of cultural norms and values. Sociocultural approach to discourse analysis views discourse as a form of collective thinking and interaction, emphasizing how people use language to build shared meaning and knowledge (Pontecorvo 1993, Johnson and Mercer 2019). It recognizes that discourse meaning is not solely determined by the words used but also by the social, cultural, and historical context in which it occurs.

This approach has been tagged sociocultural discourse analysis (SDA), which is a methodology for studying the use of language for collective thinking. One of the areas it is typically applied to is understanding how teachers and students use language to construct knowledge and build joint understanding (Twiner et al. 2029,

Forman and McCormick 1995). It is also applied to how language is used in professional settings to establish expertise, negotiate roles, and manage interactions, as well as investigate how media narratives shape public understanding and influence attitudes (Johnson and Mercer 2019).

A closely related approach to SDA is Teun van Dijk's sociocognitive approach to critical discourse analysis (SCA), which integrates insights from linguistics, psychology, sociology, and other fields of the social sciences to provide a more comprehensive understanding of discourse (van Dijk 2009, 2017). It examines the intersection of discourse, cognition, and society. SCA investigates cognitive processes like mental models and context models and how they mediate the relationship between discourse and social structures. In SCA discourse is viewed not just as comprising linguistic structures, but as a cognitive process involving the production, comprehension, and interpretation of meaning. SCA is typically engaged to critically analyze how discourse is used to perpetuate or challenge power relations and ideologies, thereby providing a framework for understanding how social phenomena, like prejudice and discrimination, are produced and reproduced through discourse.

Sociocultural approaches bring out the nexus in society, culture and human cognition and shows how culture significantly influences cognitive processes and development. The society is the domain in which culture evolves and culture shapes the types of knowledge and skills individuals learn. Culture also influences basic cognitive functions like attention, perception, and memory (Kastanakis 2014). Social interactions within a culture play a crucial role in shaping cognitive development, as highlighted by Lev Vygotsky's sociocultural theory (Freeman 2001, O'Hara 2013). Vygotsky believed that individuals learn through interactions with more knowledgeable others (MKOs), such as, parent, teacher, mentor, or even a peer, and asserts that cultural tools and practices shape cognitive development. Social interaction therefore allows learners to internalize knowledge and develop higher-order cognitive functions, such as problem-solving, reasoning, and critical thinking (Clements and Nastasi 1992). With the popular use of language in online interactions, scholars have seen the need to connect the different kinds of online discourse to sociocultural knowledge (Castañeda, 2012, Öztok 2016). Some of the significant sociocultural features of online interaction, multimodality, identity formation and power dynamics will be discussed to buttress the understanding of sociocultural meanings in online interactions.

2.2. Multimodality and Socioculturalism in Online Interaction

While multimodal approaches have been applied to different kinds of discourse (O'Halloran 2011, van Leeuwen 2011, Gbadegesin and Onanuga 2018, Achour and Adel 2021), it later becomes a major feature that typically shapes and characterizes online communication in general. It is often seen more commonly in online learning, which combines video lectures with written materials, interactive quizzes with discussion forums (Hoffman 2018). Online interactions use a combination of text, images, videos, and emojis to share thoughts and experiences in virtual classrooms, online marketing sites and sites specifically visual-centric in nature (*Instagram, YouTube, Facebook, TikTok*). Through these sites, participants share pictures, sound, videos offering features like stories, reels, music, still and moving pictures (Smith and Kennett 2017, Hoffman 2018).

Multimodal resources deeply embedded in cultures and societal norms (O'Halloran, et al., 2014, Dahlström and Damber 2020) These resources are shaped by our cultural experiences and demonstrates how we interact with the world. For instance, modern youth culture relies more on the use of visuals for communication (Putra and Affrilian 2025, Miloud and Hamida 2025). This reliance stems from the prevalence of social media, digital platforms, and the general shift towards image-based content consumption. Images, videos, and graphic designs are often preferred over lengthy text-based content, and young people curate their online personas by engaging multimodal resources (Millhouse 2024, Alhuzami 2025). Youths carefully choose images and videos to convey messages about their identities, including their interests, values, attitudes and social affiliations.

The visual culture online is shaped by influencers, brands, and the aesthetics that are popular at any given time. These visual trends can significantly influence what young people find attractive, desirable, and what they strive to emulate. For instance, they may engage in social comparisons, leading to feelings of inadequacy or pressure to conform to certain standards of beauty or success. Youth's embrace of visual communication culture has broader social and cultural implications for how young people understand and interact with the world around them. It also influences how they perceive their own identities and roles in society (Gorea 2021, Sparrman, 2006).

Some scholars with orientation in discourse approach to language saw the need to incorporate this approach to the study of multimodality, and this led to the hybrid discipline of Multimodal Discourse Analysis (MDA) (O'Halloran 2011). Later multimodality became an inherent part of Critical Discourse Analysis, leading to the birth of Multimodal Critical Discourse Analysis (MCDA) (Machin 2013, Ledin and Machin 2017). MCDA expands critical discourse analysis (CDA) to include the analysis of various semiotic modes, such as images, sounds, and gestures, alongside language in a media text. MCDA facilitates the understanding of the interaction of multiple modes and how their reinforcement, or contradiction of each other to construct meaning and reveal power dynamics and ideologies in multimodal interactions.

2.3. Socioculturalism and Expression of Identity Online

Online interactions are influenced by sociocultural factors such as race, social class, gender, and cultural background. These factors can impact how individuals construct their identities, present themselves. the kinds of content they create, and the relationships they form. Expressions of identity online involves how individuals use online platforms to communicate and construct their social and cultural identities, which influences their interactions and perceptions of others (Zhao, et al 2012). Expression of online identities includes projecting self-identity through introductions, building relationships, and forming social presence in virtual communities.

Online identity is not fixed, but rather a continuous process of self-presentation and interaction, which is dynamic. influenced by both personal motivations and external social contexts. Individuals may present different aspects of themselves online, depending on the platform and their desired audience.

The sociocultural context in which online interactions occur significantly shapes how individuals express their identities. Cultural norms, values, and beliefs influence online communication styles, the use of language, and the types of information shared. Online platforms provide users with the tools to express personal, cultural, and group identities. For instance, individuals use various online tools and practices to express their identities. These include profile pictures, bios, posts, comments, and emojis. Such content shared often reflect cultural affiliations and social roles (Xiao, et al. 1012).

Online group identities are expressed through social networks, forums, and other online spaces, influencing social interactions and behaviors (Chen and Li 2009). These group identities are shaped by shared values, beliefs, and interests (Bliuc and Chidley 2022). Online group dynamics have a way of significantly influencing individual behaviors and attitudes. The degree of anonymity and visibility in online settings can affect how group identities are expressed and experienced. Some online groups might prioritize anonymity for safety or privacy reasons, while others might actively promote visibility to build a sense of community (Kasnova, et al. 2009).

The Social Identity model of Deindividuation Effects (SIDE) model explains how anonymity or pseudonymity in online settings can amplify group influence, leading to conformity to group norms (Spears and Postmes 2015, Hunag and Li 2016, Spears, 2017). Online deindividuation refers to the loss of sense of individuality or self-awareness that often makes people under the cover of anonymity to do things they would otherwise not do as individuals.

Closely related to deindividuation is the online disinhibition effect (ODE), which is the tendency for individuals to act or express themselves differently online than they would in person, often with reduced inhibitions (Suler 2004l Rosner 2016). Disinhibition online may exhibit as either "benign disinhibition" in which someone shares more personal information than necessary, or "toxic disinhibition" in which a person is more likely to engage in rude or hostile behavior (Stuart and Scott 2021). Online disinhibition effect is attributed to factors like anonymity, asynchronicity, and the absence of nonverbal cues in online interactions. Deindividuation and disinhibition lead to the exhibition of anti-normative behaviours, such as trolling, flaming, cyberbullying, and spamming (Marrington, et al. 2023).

2.4. Power Dynamics and Online Sociocultural Meanings

Societal power dynamics impact the construction of sociocultural meanings in online communication (Al Zidjaly 2019). Online discussions may replicate real-world power hierarchies which reflect in the expressions of gender, nationality, education and sometimes, perceived expertise (Papachartissi 2004). Dominant voices sometimes overshadow others, influencing who gets heard or taken seriously. Power dynamics shape how individuals and groups interact, influence decisions, and determine social outcomes, reflecting broader societal hierarchies, values, and expectations. The concept of power itself is a social construct (KhosravikNik 2013). What is considered "power" can vary across cultures and time periods. What gives someone influence in one society might be irrelevant in another. Power dynamics shape how resources are allocated, how decisions are made, and who benefits from social processes. They can lead to both positive and negative outcomes, influencing everything from economic inequalities to social justice movements. Power dynamics are not just about individual interactions; they are deeply rooted in cultural norms and societal structures. For example, in many societies, hierarchical structures (like those in workplaces or educational institutions) dictate how power is distributed and exercised (Rosenblatt 2012).

Certain groups, based on factors like socioeconomic status, race, gender, or access to technology, may have more power and influence online, leading to disparities in who gets heard and who is marginalized (Robinson, et al. 2015). Dominant groups often shape online norms and culture through their content creation, platform usage, and online interactions, potentially excluding or marginalizing others. Online power dynamics influence how individuals perceive and understand social issues, identities, and cultural values. For example, the portrayal of certain groups in online content can shape public perceptions and reinforce stereotypes (Jeffres et al. 2011). Online platforms can become breeding grounds for disinformation and misinformation, which can be used to manipulate public opinion and further power imbalances (Morgan 2018). A group perceived to be dominated or stereotyped may congregate online to resist the dominant discourses about them, e.g., female gender-based victims, youths, the unemployed, immigrants, infertile women, ethnic minorities, etc. (Correa and Jeong 2011, Eschmann 2021)

3. MULTICULTURAL MEANINGS IN ONLINE DISCUSSION

Multiculturalism has been a feature of communication before the advent of digital media. Nations, classrooms, workplaces can be multicultural. Multiculturalism become a feature of digital spaces, with the coexistence and interaction of individuals from multiple cultural backgrounds online (Chisholm and Wetzel 2001, Brown 2002, Alharthi 2020). This is common in online discussions, which often involve participants from diverse backgrounds, making it essential to be aware of and appreciate the different perspectives and cultural influences. In the context of online discussions, multicultural meanings refer to the diverse perspectives, values, and cultural nuances that individuals from different backgrounds bring to online interactions. It encompasses the understanding and appreciation of these differences, including language, cultural norms, and communication styles.

One of the multicultural online groups that has been studies extensively is *Nairaland Forum*, an online forum that originates from Nigeria, but has grown to become very popular among internet users. Sociocultural studies on Nairaland have examined issues like identity construction (Raheem and Akande 2019, Davies and Alabi 2023) and impoliteness and hate speech (Taiwo 2014, Akinsanya 2024), among others. These studies identify various sociocultural influences shaping discursive behavior in Nairaland.

3.1 Cultural Exchange and Learning

Online context fosters diversity in terms of involving people of different cultural backgrounds. In the educational context, people of different cultures often congregate online for virtual learning. Many online platforms enable the sharing of cultural values, traditions, and perspectives, which has the tendency of promoting intercultural understanding and appreciation (Zort, et al 2023, Chan, et al. 2025). Online multicultural classroom encourages learners to question their own biases and assumptions, and to see the world from different perspectives. It values and celebrates diversity and fosters a learning environment where students from various cultural backgrounds feel included and respected. Such classroom aims at creating a sense of belonging, as well as promoting cultural awareness, empathy, and understanding among the learners (Henrikson and Lau 2022).

Multicultural education acknowledges and appreciates the differences between cultures, challenging discrimination and fostering a sense of inclusivity (Eden, et al. 2022, Pless and Maak). Online learning offers flexibility in terms of scheduling and location, making it accessible to students who may not have easy access to traditional classrooms (Fransico 2020). It also utilizes various technologies like video conferencing, online discussion forums, and collaborative software to facilitate interactions and learning (McNeil 2000). Students can share their cultural backgrounds, experiences, and perspectives through online discussions, projects, and presentations. Educators can tailor their curricula to reflect the diverse backgrounds of their students, incorporating diverse perspectives and examples, thereby making the experience richer than the monocultural classroom (Lee et al. 2012). Multicultural classroom afford the students the opportunity to communicate effectively and collaborate with individuals from diverse backgrounds. Students are also able to develop a broader understanding of the world and its different cultures. The diverse cultures make the students to develop a broader understanding of the world and its different cultures.

In a virtual multicultural classroom, students can work together on projects that involve different cultural elements, fostering creativity and teamwork (Doosand and Coray 2014). They can also explore different cultural sites and landmarks through virtual tours and simulations (George 2018). Learners can also learn languages and connect with native speakers from different cultures. Users often adapt their language or communication style depending on the audience. This digital code-switching which reflects the complexity of navigating multicultural spaces in multicultural online interactions is the concern of the following section.

3.2 Indigenous Language Use and Language Mixing as a form of Sociocultural Meaning Construction Online

Language mixing, commonly known as code-mixing in most literature on multilingualism, is a practice in online interactions, particularly among multilingual and bilingual individuals. It is often seen as a way to express identity, show solidarity, or simply reflect the speaker's linguistic repertoire. In places where English is the most commonly accepted language of the Internet, performance of authenticity in online interaction is often reflected through the deployment of indigenous languages and language mixing. Authenticity is a genuine expression of linguistic behavior, often associated with a speaker's or community's connection to their language, culture, and social context (Haimson 2021, Taylor 2022). This practice indicates spontaneity, naturality, and genuity of linguistic habits. Authenticity is often tied to the social and cultural norms and expectations within a linguistic community. Authentic language can be a marker of identity, reflecting speakers' affiliation with a particular social group or cultural tradition (Heyd and Mair 2014)

In language contact situations, a language variety might be considered "more authentic" if it retains features of its source language despite the influence of another language. This is precisely what happens sometimes in online communication where participants choose either the other languages apart from the most widely accepted one to construct and perform their identities. A good example is the interaction of

Nigerians in online discussions and the popular use of the Nigerian Pidgin English (NPE) (Ajagbe and Okesola 2024). For instance, participants deliberately switch to NPE to make their points as can be seen in the excerpt below from Nairaland Forum:

> *Nman I jest notice say one of una regulations, na say make all man no dey yarn pidgin, I just wan say that is unaceptable!, Yes this is ur site, but even you dont have the right to barn Pidgin as it is the most spoken Language in Nigeria today and as far as i know this is a naija joint!, Its like telling Jamaicans not to speak patoise on their web. Or telling African Americans not to speak Slangs-ebonics (thats what a lot of them can actualy speak). So whatever ur reason for saying this, just know it wont hold, and I am here to speak Pidgin and would encourage others to do, If u barn me, i go re-sign in again as a new guy, so dont even bother, Pidgin is a language that i am proud of and will speak forever, Gbam! na im be that*
>
> https://www.nairaland.com/12420/pidgin-english

The posting above is a deliberate attempt by the participant to assert authentic identity through the use of NPE, which is compared with the Jamaican Patois and African -American Ebonics. The participant challenged *Nairaland* admin by maintaining that the forum is "a Naija joint" and affirming being proud of the language. The four assertions of Heyd and Mair (2014) about the spread of Nigerian Pidgin as a digital vernacular are fulfilled in the posting. They assert as follow:

1. The web as a stage: Vernacular mixing and appropriation
2. The web as a classroom: Cataloguing and teaching pidgin
3. The web as a linguistic resource: Pidgin and Netspeak features
4. The web as an infrastructure: Nigerian Pidgin in digital interfaces (p. 250)

These which are "emblematic of the practices surrounding the use of Nigerian Pidgin" on Nairaland as revealed by their data. Further observation by the authors establishes the increasing integration of NigP features into digital discourse (mediatization) and NP's trajectory from a stigmatized language to a marketable social capital (commodification) (p. 251ff).

4. IMPLICATIONS AND CHALLENGES

Online spaces offer marginalized communities a platform to share experiences and advocate for social justice. Prejudice and discrimination based on race or ethnicity can lead to social tension, inequality, and conflict. This includes systemic racism, hate crimes, and disparities in education and employment. Also, issues related to gender roles and expectations can manifest in various forms, including wage gaps, underrepresentation in leadership roles, and gender-based violence.

The challenges faced by individuals or groups in maintaining their cultural identity while integrating into a dominant culture can lead to tensions, particularly in multicultural societies. This is common in Nigeria and most African countries where multilingualism has become the norm as a result the merger of people of different ethnic nationalities for administrative convenience by the colonial authorities during the colonial rule. This explains the ethnic tensions in most of these countries today.

In online sociocultural interactions, there is the tendency for individuals to present their gender identities through the language they use in online profiles, bios, or self-descriptions. This may include disclosing gender-specific information, language choices reflecting gender identity, or adopting linguistic styles associated with their gender (Teibowei 2024, Marshall 2014).

Unequal access to technology affects who participates in online discussions, often excluding voices from less privileged regions or communities. Unequal access and cultural bias in moderation policies can limit this potential. Another major challenge to virtual multicultural classroom is the need to address digital divides and ensure that all students have equitable access to technology and the internet. It is also important for the educators to create learning materials and activities that are accessible to students with diverse learning styles and needs. While there is flexibility in learning in online virtual classrooms, learners have to be monitored to ensure that they are participating in the activities. Differences in beliefs, values, and communication styles can lead to misinterpretation or conflict. Topics such as religion, politics, and social justice may spark debates that highlight cultural divides.

Online spaces are democratic in nature and this brings about certain challenges and attendant implications for socioculturalism and multiculturalism on the Internet. With virality as a major characteristic of internet communication, there are tendencies for the challenges that characterize social media interactions to be promoted and escalate. This can lead to uninhibited behaviors, such as, expressions of hate speeches, discriminations, cyberbullying, flaming and trolling, racism, ethnic slurs, and several other vices.

The challenges faced by individuals or groups in maintaining their cultural identity while integrating into dominant culture can lead to social tensions, particularly in multicultural societies. This is common in Nigeria and most African countries where multilingualism has become a postcolonial norm, as a result of the merger of people of different ethnic nationalities for administrative convenience.

In online sociocultural interactions, there are tendencies for individuals to present their gender identities through the language they use in online profiles, bios or self-descriptions. This may include choosing gender0-soecific information, language choices reflecting gender identity, or adopting linguistic styles associated their gender.

The fluidity of gender representation in contemporary times has led to the emergence of a broader range of gender and sexual identities challenging traditional views of gender and sexuality. This new orientation may have implications for sociocultural communication. How social, cultural, and material contexts affect the ways LGBTQs navigate their selves on social media becomes an issue to be considered. This is particularly important in the context of disclosure or concealment of gender and/or sexual selves online (Marshal 2014, Dhoest and Szulc 2016, Teklbowei 2024).

Unequal access to technology affects who participates in online discussion, often leading to voices from less-privileged regions or communities. Unequal access and cultural bias in mor=dern policies can limit this potential. A major challenge to virtual multicultural classrooms is the need to address digital divides and ensure that all learners have equal access to technology and the Internet. It is also important for the educators to create learning materials that are accessible to learners of diverse learning styles and needs. While there is flexibility in learning in online virtual classrooms, learners have to be monitored to ensure their participation. Differences in beliefs, values, attitudes and communication styles can lead to misinterpretation and conflicts. Topics such as religion and politics and social justice may spark debates that highlight cultural divides in an online multicultural classroom context

The realities of online communication produce the two major kinds of meaning that are being examined in this book: sociocultural and multicultural meanings. As we have shown, the construction of these meanings has far-reaching implications bordering on prejudices, tension, gender and identity issues, as well as digital and cultural divides. In spite of these challenges, multiculturalism and socioculturalism will continue to shape discursive behavior in online interactions as online spaces contine to attract people of different cultures and social orientations.

5. CONCLUSIONS

Online discussions are a reflection of the complex interplay between culture and communication. Sociocultural and multicultural factors deeply influence how individuals express themselves, interpret others, and engage in digital discourse. Socio-cultural issues are complex and multifaceted, often intertwined with economic, political, and historical factors. Addressing these issues typically requires a comprehensive understanding of the underlying cultural dynamics and the social structures that perpetuate inequality and conflict. In our discussion of sociocultural and multicultural nature of online interactions, it is important to have a comprehensive understanding of the dynamics that drive such interactions. Understanding these dynamics is essential for a meaningful research of discursive behavior in online communication.

REFERENCES

Achour, K., & Adel, L. (2021). *A Semiotic and Multimodal Analysis of Covid-19 Caricatures: the Liberté, The Guardian and The Seattle Times Newspapers* (Doctoral dissertation, Université Mouloud Mammeri Tizi Ouzou).

Ajagbe, S., & Okesola, S. (2024). A Discourse-Based Analysis of Perceptions of Nigerian Pidgin Among the Nigerian Diaspora. *Language Matters (Pretoria)*, *55*(3), 74–95. DOI: 10.1080/10228195.2024.2436074

Ajiboye, E., & Abioye, T. (2019). When citizens talk: Stance and representation in online discourse on Biafra agitations. *Discourse & Society*, *30*(2), 117–134. DOI: 10.1177/0957926518816197

Akinsanya, T. (2024). Media and hate speech: A discursive study of hate speech on Nairaland forum. *Sprin Journal of Arts. Humanities and Social Sciences*, *3*(4), 52–61.

Al Zidjaly, N. (2019). Society in digital contexts: New modes of identity and community construction. *Multilingua*, *38*(4), 357–375. DOI: 10.1515/multi-2018-0042

Alharthi, M. A. J. E. D. (2020). Students from diverse cultures in the multicultural online classroom: Issues and suggestions. *Journal of Theoretical and Applied Information Technology*, *98*(09).

Alhuzami, N., & Muyidi, A. (2025). What factors affect the way youth present themselves on social media? Self-presentation strategies' approach. *Agathos*, *16*(1), 389–399.

Ancheta, K. 2016. *Online Support for Women Trying to Conceive.* Available at: http://www.katieancheta.com/exploring/2016/12/14/genre-and-ttc-forums

Bell, V. (2007). Online information, extreme communities and internet therapy: Is the internet good for our mental health? *Journal of Mental Health (Abingdon, England)*, *16*(4), 445–457. DOI: 10.1080/09638230701482378

Best, S. J., & Krueger, B. S. (2006). Online Interactions and Social Capital: Distinguishing between New and Existing Ties. *Social Science Computer Review*, *24*(4), 395–410. DOI: 10.1177/0894439306286855

Bliuc, A. M., & Chidley, A. (2022). From cooperation to conflict: The role of collective narratives in shaping group behaviour. *Social and Personality Psychology Compass*, *16*(7), e12670. DOI: 10.1111/spc3.12670

Bost, S. (2008). From race/sex/etc. to glucose, feeding tube, and mourning: the shifting matter of Chicana feminism. In Alaimo, S., & Hekman, S. (Eds.), *Material Feminisms* (pp. 340–372). Indiana University Press. of three forms of internet use on Classroom.

Brown, M. (2002). Multicultural education and technology: Perspectives to consider. *Journal of Special Education Technology*, *17*(3), 51.

Bucholtz, M., & Hall, K. (2004). Language and Identity. In Duranti, A. (Ed.), *A Companion to Linguistic Anthropology* (pp. 369–394). Blackwell.

Chan, G., Banire, B., Ataguba, G., Frempong, G., & Orji, R. (2025). A panoramic view of socio-cultural sensitivity in digital technologies: A comprehensive review and future directions. *International Journal of Human-Computer Interaction*, *41*(4), 1917–1945. DOI: 10.1080/10447318.2024.2372135

Chen, Y., & Li, S. X. (2009). Group identity and social preferences. *The American Economic Review*, *99*(1), 431–457. DOI: 10.1257/aer.99.1.431

Chisholm, I. M., & Wetzel, K. (2001). Technology and Multiculturalism in the Classroom. *Journal of Research on Technology in Education*, *33*(5).

Correa, T., & Jeong, S. H. (2011). Race and online content creation: Why minorities are actively participating in the Web. *Information Communication and Society*, *14*(5), 638–659. DOI: 10.1080/1369118X.2010.514355

Coulson, N. S., Bullock, E., & Rodham, K. (2017). Exploring the therapeutic affordances of self-harm online support communities: An online survey of members. *JMIR Mental Health*, *4*(4), e44. Advance online publication. DOI: 10.2196/mental.8084 PMID: 29030324

Dahlström, H. and Damber, U. (2020). Meanings Made in Students' Multimodal Digital Stories: Resources, Popular Culture, and Values. *Designs for learning*, *12*(1), 45-55.

Danet, B., & Herring, S. C. (2003). Introduction: The multilingual internet. *Journal of Computer-Mediated Communication*, *9*(1), JCMC9110.

Davies, R. U., & Alabi, B. A. (2023). Language and Positive Identity Reconstruction: A Study of Nairaland and Facebook. *Lead Journal of Languages and Literature*, *1*(1), 201–210.

Dawson, A., & Dennis, S. (2020). Social intimacy. *Anthropology in Action : Newsletter of the British Association for Social Anthropology in Policy and Practice (BASAPP)*, *27*(3), 1–8. DOI: 10.3167/aia.2020.270301

DeRose, D. R. 2016. "*Baby Dust to All! Identity Construction in Two-Week Wait Online Discussion Forums*." Master's Dissertation, Marquette University. https://epublications.marquette.edu/theses_open/386/

Dhoest, A., & Szulc, L. (2016). Navigating online selves: Social, cultural, and material contexts of social media use by diasporic gay men. *Social Media + Society*, *2*(4), 2056305116672485. DOI: 10.1177/2056305116672485

Eden, C. A., Chisom, O. N., & Adeniyi, I. S. (2024). Cultural competence in education: Strategies for fostering inclusivity and diversity awareness. *International Journal of Applied Research in Social Sciences*, *6*(3), 383–392. DOI: 10.51594/ijarss.v6i3.895

Ekström, M., & Östman, J. (2015). Information, interaction, and creative production: The effects of three forms of internet use on youth democratic engagement. *Communication Research*, *42*(6), 796–818. DOI: 10.1177/0093650213476295

Fairclough, N. (2013). *Language and power*. Routledge. DOI: 10.4324/9781315838250

Fieseler, C., Meckel, M., & Müller, S. (2014). With a little help of my peers. The supportive role of online contacts for the unemployed. *Computers in Human Behavior*, *41*, 164–176. DOI: 10.1016/j.chb.2014.09.017

Finfgeld, D. L. (2000). Therapeutic groups online: The good, the bad, and the unknown. *Issues in Mental Health Nursing*, *21*(3), 241–255. DOI: 10.1080/016128400248068 PMID: 11075065

Forman, E. A., & McCormick, D. E. (1995). Discourse analysis: A sociocultural perspective. *Remedial and Special Education*, *16*(3), 150–158. DOI: 10.1177/074193259501600304

Francisco, C. (2020). Effectiveness of an online classroom for flexible learning. [IJAMR]. *International Journal of Academic Multidisciplinary Research*, *4*(8), 100–107.

Freeman, M. (2010). Vygotsky and the virtual classroom: Sociocultural theory comes to the communications classroom. *Christian Perspectives in Education*, *4*(1), 5.

Gbadegesin, V., & Onanuga, P. (2018). A multimodal interaction analysis of selected 2015 Nigerian election campaign adverts. *Communicatio*, *44*(2), 41–66. DOI: 10.1080/02500167.2018.1464042

George, B. H. (2018). Using virtual tours to facilitate sustainable site visits of historic sites. *European Journal of Sustainable Development*, *7*(4), 411–411. DOI: 10.14207/ejsd.2018.v7n4p411

Gong, T., Minett, J. W., & Wang, W. S. Y. (2010). A simulation study exploring the role of cultural transmission in language evolution. *Connection Science*, *22*(1), 69–85. DOI: 10.1080/09540090903198819

Gorea, M. (2021). Becoming your "authentic" self: How social media influences youth's visual transitions. *Social Media + Society*, *7*(3), 20563051211047875. DOI: 10.1177/20563051211047875

Haimson, O. L., Liu, T., Zhang, B. Z., & Corvite, S. (2021). The online authenticity paradox: What being" authentic" on social media means, and barriers to achieving it. *Proceedings of the ACM on Human-computer Interaction, 5*(CSCW2), 1-18. DOI: 10.1145/3479567

Halliday, M. A. K., & Webster, J. J. (2009). [London and New York: Continuum]. *Language in Society*, *10*, •••.

Hermans, F., Apeldoom, D. V., Stuiver, M., & Kok, K. (2013). Niche and Networks: Explaining Network Evolution through Niche Formation Processes. *Research Policy*, *42*(3), 613–623. DOI: 10.1016/j.respol.2012.10.004

Heyd, T., & Mair, C. (2014). From vernacular to digital ethnolinguistic repertoire: The case of Nigerian Pidgin. In Lacoste, V., Leimgruber, J., & Breyer, T. (Eds.), *Indexing authenticity: Sociolinguistic perspectives* (pp. 244–268). Walter de Gruyter GmbH & Co KG. DOI: 10.1515/9783110347012.244

Hoffman, E. B. (2018). Untangling the talk: A new multimodal discourse analysis method to investigate synchronous online learning. *Journal of Digital Learning in Teacher Education*, *34*(3), 179–195. DOI: 10.1080/21532974.2018.1453895

Huang, G., & Li, K. (2016). The effect of anonymity on conformity to group norms in online contexts: A meta-analysis. *International Journal of Communication*, *10*, 398–415.

Johnson, M., & Mercer, N. (2019). Using sociocultural discourse analysis to analyse professional discourse. *Learning, Culture and Social Interaction*, *21*, 267–277. DOI: 10.1016/j.lcsi.2019.04.003

Kastanakis, M. N., & Voyer, B. G. (2014). The effect of culture on perception and cognition: A conceptual framework. *Journal of Business Research*, *67*(4), 425–433. DOI: 10.1016/j.jbusres.2013.03.028

Khan, A. (2024). The Language of Power: Discourse Analysis and the Politics of Representation. *Liberal Journal of Language & Literature Review*, *2*(01), 22–31.

KhosraviNik, M. (2010). Actor descriptions, action attributions, and argumentation: Towards a systematization of CDA analytical categories in the representation of social groups. *Critical Discourse Studies*, *7*(1), 55–72. DOI: 10.1080/17405900903453948

KhosraviNik, M. (2013). Critical discourse analysis, power, and new media discourse. In Kalyango, Y., & Kopytowska, M. W. (Eds.), *Why Discourse Matters: Negotiating Identity in the Mediatized World* (pp. 287–305). Peter Lang.

Krasnova, H., Günther, O., Spiekermann, S., & Koroleva, K. (2009). Privacy concerns and identity in online social networks. *Identity in the Information Society*, *2*(1), 39–63. DOI: 10.1007/s12394-009-0019-1

Kress, G., & van Leeuwen, T. (2020). *Reading Images: The Grammar of Visual Design*. Routledge. DOI: 10.4324/9781003099857

Lee, A., Poch, R., Shaw, M., & Williams, R. (2012). Engaging Diversity in Undergraduate Classrooms: A Pedagogy for Developing Intercultural Competence [John Wiley & Sons.]. *ASHE Higher Education Report*, *38*(2), •••.

Ley, B. (2009). Vive lea Roses! The Architecture of Commitment in an Online Pregnancy ad Nursing Group. *Journal of Computer-Mediated Communication*, *12*(4), 1388–1408. DOI: 10.1111/j.1083-6101.2007.00378.x

Liu, K. (2022). *Identity construction online: Identities and ideologies in reader comments in online news fora* (Doctoral dissertation, Open Access Te Herenga Waka-Victoria University of Wellington).

Lorenzini, J., & Giugni, M. (2010). Youth coping with unemployment: The role of social support. *Revue Suisse de Travail Social*, *11*, 80–99.

Machin, D. (2013). What is multimodal critical discourse studies? *Critical Discourse Studies*, *10*(4), 347–355. DOI: 10.1080/17405904.2013.813770

Marrington, J. Z., March, E., Murray, S., Jeffries, C., Machin, T., & March, S. (2023). An exploration of trolling behaviours in Australian adolescents: An online survey. *PLoS One*, *18*(4), e0284378. DOI: 10.1371/journal.pone.0284378 PMID: 37043467

Marshall, J. P. (2014). Gender in online communication. In *Handbook of research on new literacies* (pp. 491–520). Routledge.

McNeil, S. G., Robin, B. R., & Miller, R. M. (2000). Facilitating interaction, communication and collaboration in online courses. *Computers & Geosciences*, *26*(6), 699–708. DOI: 10.1016/S0098-3004(99)00106-5

McQuaid, R., Lindsay, C., & Greig, M. (2004). 'Reconnecting'the Unemployed Information and communication technology and services for jobseekers in rural areas. *Information Communication and Society*, *7*(3), 364–388. DOI: 10.1080/1369118042000284605

Mercer, N. (2004). Sociocultural discourse analysis. *Journal of applied linguistics, 1*(2), 137-168.

Millhouse, N. T. (2024) Self-Presentations on Social Network Sites: Emerging Adults and their Personas. Doctoral dissertation, University of Newcastle, UK.

Miranda, J. W. P., Bueo, D. H. R., & DeSouza, R. C. G. (2016). A Qualitative Approach to Develop Niche Social Media. *Proceedings of the 18th International Conference on Enterprise Information,* Vol. 2, 265 – 272.

Mlynář, J. (2014). Language and collective memory: Insights from social theory. *Slovenská Politologická Revue*, *3*, 217–236.

Morgan, S. (2018). Fake news, disinformation, manipulation and online tactics to undermine democracy. *Journal of Cyber Policy*, *3*(1), 39–43. DOI: 10.1080/23738871.2018.1462395

Myers, G. (2013). Stance-taking and public discussion in blogs. In *Self-Mediation* (pp. 55–67). Routledge.

O'Halloran, K. (2011). Multimodal discourse analysis. In Hyland, K., & Paltridge, B. (Eds.), *The Bloomsbury Companion to Discourse Analysis* (pp. 120–137). Bloomsbury.

O'Halloran, K. L., Tan, S. and MKL, E. (2014). A multimodal approach to discourse, context and culture. *Discourse in Context*, 247-272

O'Hara, K. E. (2013). Lev Vygotsky. *The Praeger handbook of education and psychology, 1*, 240-245.

Osisanwo, A., & Akano, R. (2023). Ideological stances in Yoruba nation secessionist discourse in Nigerian virtual communities. *Language Matters (Pretoria)*, *54*(2), 104–121. DOI: 10.1080/10228195.2023.2212140

Öztok, M. (2016). Cultural ways of constructing knowledge: The role of identities in online group discussions. *International Journal of Computer-Supported Collaborative Learning*, *11*(2), 157–186. DOI: 10.1007/s11412-016-9233-7

Pontecorvo, C. (1993). Forms of discourse and shared thinking. *Cognition and Instruction*, *11*(3-4), 189–196. DOI: 10.1080/07370008.1993.9649019

Putra, F. E., & Afrilian, P. (2025). Visual Culture in Social Media: A Study on the Influence of Instagram on Aesthetics and Youth Culture Trends. *Asian Journal of Media and Culture*, *1*(1), 40–56. DOI: 10.63919/ajmc.v1i1.18

Raheem, S. O., & Akande, A. T. (2019). Naming as a marker of identity on Nairaland. *African Identities*, *17*(3-4), 191–210. DOI: 10.1080/14725843.2019.1661829

Robinson, L., Cotten, S. R., Ono, H., Quan-Haase, A., Mesch, G., Chen, W., & Stern, M. J. (2015). Digital inequalities and why they matter. *Information Communication and Society*, *18*(5), 569–582. DOI: 10.1080/1369118X.2015.1012532

Rojas, B. G. (2025). Code-Switching as Identity Negotiation in Multilingual Communities. *Bulletin of Language and Literature Studies*, *2*(1). Advance online publication. DOI: 10.59652/blls.v2i1.517

Rösner, L., & Krämer, N. C. (2016). Verbal venting in the social web: Effects of anonymity and group norms. *Social Media + Society*, *2*(3), 1–13. DOI: 10.1177/2056305116664220

Schecter, S. R. (2014). Enabling through Self-Imaging: The Potential of Visual Communication in the Field of Diaspora, Youth Culture and Web 2.0. In Johnson, L. (Ed.), *Mobility and Fantasy in Visual Culture* (pp. 167–178). Routledge.

Shih, Y. C. (2014). Communication strategies in a multimodal virtual communication context. *System*, *42*, 34–47. DOI: 10.1016/j.system.2013.10.016

Smith, A., & Kennett, K. (2017). Multimodal meaning: Discursive dimensions of e-learning. In Cope, B., & Kalantzis, M. (Eds.), *E-Learning ecologies: Principles for new learning and assessment* (pp. 88–117). Routledge: Taylor & Francis. DOI: 10.4324/9781315639215-4

Sparrman, A. (2006). Young People's Consumption of Visual Culture. *Collector Gadgets, Sexuality and Democracy,* 114-116.

Spears, R. (2017). Deindividuation. In *The Oxford handbook of social influence* (pp. 279–297). Oxford University Press.

Spears, R., & Postmes, T. (2015). Group identity, social influence, and collective action online: Extensions and applications of the SIDE model. *The handbook of the psychology of communication technology*, 23-46.

Stuart, J., & Scott, R. (2021). The measure of online disinhibition (MOD): Assessing perceptions of reductions in restraint in the online environment. *Computers in Human Behavior*, *114*, 106534. DOI: 10.1016/j.chb.2020.106534

Suler, J. (2004). The online disinhibition effect. *Cyberpsychology & Behavior*, *7*(3), 321–326. DOI: 10.1089/1094931041291295 PMID: 15257832

Taiwo, R. (2014). "Impoliteness in Online Discussion Forum: A Study of Trolling in *Nairaland.com*". In Chiluwa, I, Ifukor, P. and Taiwo, R. (Eds.) Pragmatics of Nigerian English in Digital Discourse. Munchen: LINCOM Europa. 67 - 76.

Taiwo, R. (2015) 'Who will employ them?' Questions as Engagement Strategies in Nigerian Job

Taiwo, R. (2016). (2016.) Cognitive Verbs and Stance Taking in Nigerian Jobs and Careers Online. *Marang: Journal of Language and Literature*, *27*, 1–19.

Taiwo, R., & Adebayo, O. 2022. 'Baby dust to everyone': Emoting infertility in Nigerian online trying to conceive (TTC) forums." *Language. Text. Society 9*(2). https://ltsj.online/2022-09-2-taiwo-adebayo

Taylor, A. S. (2022). *Authenticity as performativity on social media*. Springer Nature. DOI: 10.1007/978-3-031-12148-7

Teibowei, M. T. (2024). Language and Gender in Online Communications. *International Journal of English Language & Communication Studies*, *9*(1).

Twiner, A., Littleton, K., Whitelock, D., & Coffin, C. (2021). Combining sociocultural discourse analysis and multimodal analysis to explore teachers' and pupils' meaning making. *Learning, Culture and Social Interaction*, *30*, 100520. Advance online publication. DOI: 10.1016/j.lcsi.2021.100520

Ugah, H. U. (2023). "We will not atikuloot our future!": Nigerianness as stance-taking in online political discussion forums. *Linguistik online, 123*(5), 139-152.

van Dijk, T. A. (2005). Discourse analysis as ideology analysis. In *Language & peace* (pp. 41–58). Routledge.

van Dijk, T. A. (2009). *Critical discourse studies: A sociocognitive approach* (pp. 62-86). na.

van Dijk, T. A. (2009). *Society and discourse: How Social Contexts Influence Text and Talk*. Cambridge University Press. DOI: 10.1017/CBO9780511575273

van Dijk, T. A. (2012). Structures of discourse and structures of power. [Routledge.]. *Communication Yearbook*, *12*, 18–59.

van Dijk, T. A. (2017). Socio-cognitive discourse studies. In *The Routledge Handbook of Critical Discourse Studies* (pp. 26–43). Routledge. DOI: 10.4324/9781315739342-3

Van Leeuwen, T. (2011). Multimodality. In *The Routledge Handbook of Applied Linguistics* (pp. 668–682). Routledge.

Xiao, H., Li, W., Cao, X., & Tang, Z. (2012). The online social networks on knowledge exchange: Online social identity, social tie and culture orientation. *Journal of Global Information Technology Management, 15*(2), 4–24. DOI: 10.1080/1097198X.2012.11082753

Zhang, J., Hu, H., Wu, D., Nie, Y., & Lin, X. (2024). Is Online Group Therapy as Effective as Face-to-face Group Therapy? A Mixed Methods Study. *Clinical Social Work Journal*, **•••**, 1–12.

Zhao, C., Hinds, P., & Gao, G. (2012. February). How and to whom people share: the role of culture in self-disclosure in online communities. In *Proceedings of the ACM 2012 Conference on Computer Supported Cooperative Work* (pp. 67-76). DOI: 10.1145/2145204.2145219

Zort, Ç., Karabacak, E., Öznur, Ş., & Dağlı, G. (2023). Sharing of cultural values and heritage through storytelling in the digital age. *Frontiers in Psychology, 14*, 1104121. DOI: 10.3389/fpsyg.2023.1104121 PMID: 36895745

KEY TERMS AND DEFINITIONS

Sociocultural Meanings: Meanings that are produced and shaped by values, beliefs, attitudes, traditions, and behaviors that influence how individuals in a society think, feel, and behave, and how they interact with others.

Multicultural Meanings: Meanings that are produced when people from different cultural or ethnic groups within a society interact.

Online Discussions: Online discussions are interactive conversations that take place on the internet, allowing people to share ideas, engage in dialogue, and collaborate on various topics. These discussions can occur in various formats, such as online forums, comment sections, social media groups, or dedicated chat platforms. They offer a virtual space for individuals to connect, share perspectives, and explore different viewpoints on a particular subject.

Multimodality: This is the use of multiple modes of communication and meaning-making, such as text, images, audio, and video, within a single context.

Online Identity: An online identity is the way a user presents themselves to the internet and is a reflection of who they are, their interests, and the way they interact in online communities. It is an actively constructed representation of oneself that can be different from one's offline one.

Power Dynamics: The ways in which power is distributed, exercised, and experienced within a particular social or organizational context.

Multicultural Classroom: A multicultural classroom is one that brings together people from different countries and cultural backgrounds and embraces the diverse ideas, beliefs, and cultural backgrounds of the members, which are put together to enable learners build bridges across theur different cultures.

Cultural Exchange: This is the sharing of cultural products and ideas among different cultural groups in order to promote mutual understanding and respect among diverse cultures; foster global harmony and collaboration, as well as enrich societies by introducing new perspectives, traditions, and ideas, encouraging innovation and creativity.

Chapter 2
Emojis and Emoticons:
Decoding Multicultural Meanings in Online Communication

Muhammad Usman Tariq
https://orcid.org/0000-0002-7605-3040
Abu Dhabi University, UAE & University College Cork, Ireland

ABSTRACT

This chapter examines the role of emoticons and emojis in online communication, focusing on their ability to convey complex emotions and ideas across different cultural contexts. As digital symbols become increasingly prevalent in everyday interactions, understanding their multicultural meanings is essential for effective global communication. The chapter traces the origins and historical development of these symbols, exploring the cultural diversity of their meanings in various contexts. It analyzes how emojis function as linguistic and affective tools, reflecting social contexts and cultural nuances through semiotic frameworks. Case studies highlight cross-cultural differences in emotional expression and social cues, demonstrating how variations in emoji interpretation affect digital communication.

INTRODUCTION

Emojis and emoticons have become natural components of digital interaction spectrum in the contemporary world. Since their inception, they have revolutionized interactions on social media platforms, especially by transforming text-based conversations into a more dynamic and interactive exchanges. These range from simple symbols to more detailed ones depicting food, animals, and various activities, helping user's express emotions, ideas, and subtleties that might not be conveyed verbally. Emojis and emoticons have become a norm in society across cultures,

DOI: 10.4018/979-8-3693-7934-9.ch002

languages, and digital platforms. Not only do they allow the user to make simple representations like winking or clapping emoji to modify the tone of a message, but they also strengthen a message by adding emotional depth (Katsumata, 2022). However, though emojis and emoticons are universal language, their perception and interpretation are not the same across cultures. This chapter, Emojis and Emoticons: Interpolating Multicultural Significations in e-Communication, aims to establish the extent to which these visual practices/symbols function in online communication between individuals from diverse cultures, or how their meanings may be inter-culturally interpreted. Because of different cultures, traditional practices and individual experiences, emojis and emoticons may have different connotations (Sun & Lee, 2023). For instance, the thumbs-up is understood as a positive sign of approval in many Western cultures. However, in some parts of the Middle East and South America, this symbol may be considered vulgar. Likewise, the 'folded hands' emoticon in some cultures depicts gratitude or praying but signifies an apology in Japan. These differences in meaning underscore the need to analyze cultural provocations in emojis and emoticons in order to prevent misunderstandings or unintended offences in digital communication (Mure an, 2020).

Thus, the expansion of emojis and emoticons in communication can be attributed to text restraint. Written language has its disadvantages - it lacks the cues to express tone or intent. In oral communication, nonverbal communication, including gestures, eye contact, postures and vocal emojis, are used to supplement the message being conveyed. They assist individuals in the kind of understanding that the speaker has about his emotions or motives. As a result, nonverbal aspects, which play such an important role when people are communicating face to face, are nutrients when the verbal conversation moves to the Web. Emojis and emoticons are used to complete this function because such calligraphic symbols work as signals connected with a piece of text and shed some light on the sender's mood or attitude. For example, the string "I'm fine" conveys different meanings when it is accompained by a smiling, frowning or eye-rolling emoji(Katsumata, 2022). Despite their wide popularity many people have recently realized the importance of exercising some reverence while translating emojis across different cultures. Far from being a unified signifier that everybody will recognize as meaningful in the same way, what appears to be a globally shared representation does not necessarily hold the same meaning to different people living in different cultures. Take, for example, the 'Face with Tears of Joy' emoji, which is commonly used to express extreme laughter or joy in some cultures. However, in other contexts or cultures, it can be used sarcastically or to dismiss something. It is not just that individual readers might have differences, but the interpretation we give to these messages differ as per geographical and cultural factors, social norms, and even language (Leonardi, 2022).

Specifically, this chapter aims to unravel the identity of emojis and emoticons within cross-cultural digital communication. his chapter aims to enhance understanding of how these symbols are interpreted across different cultural contexts, with a focus on the impact of digital media on localized interactions in today's interconnected world. It also explores the role of culture in improving intercultural communication, both in personal and business relationships, which is crucial for fostering effective global interactions and reflecting essential aspects of human life. It explains how a particular emoji can create dramatically different perceptions in audiences of varying geographic origins using case studies and examples from various parts of the world (Hamdan, 2022). his chapter will explore how cultural norms shape the meanings of emojis and emoticons, examining the semi-permanent features of cultural messaging that influence their interpretation. For instance, while communicating with people from many Asian countries, there is the need to respect a form of etiquette that shuns one from attacking another's opinion. Accordingly, individuals of these cultures employ emojis that help to tone down the message, or to indicate politeness, because such message can be negative and/or critical. For example, a Japanese user will adopt the smiling face emoji after giving a complaint so as to avoid conflict between him/herself and the receiver. Similarly, in direct communication cultures like the US, people tend to use neutral emojis when messaging a stranger, whereas in more indirect cultures, a more subtle or nuanced emoji might be used to convey the same message (Mure an, 2020).

Furthermore, this chapter examines the cross-generational variations in emoji and emoticon usage. Younger generations, who were raised with the help of digital communication, tend to embrace a broad spectrum of emojis and even develop newer versions of these symbols and their meanings. In contrast, older generations may make more limited use of emojis or use them simply and sometimes literally. This usage and its interpretations may sometimes yield misunderstandings. For instance, while younger users may use the 'skull' emoji to express something extremely funny, older users may associate it with death or danger (Leonardi, 2022). There are some generational differences which make emoji communication complicated, and as such, users must ensure that they are aware of the people they are talking to before they use any emoji. Also, the chapter analyses the effects of emojis and emoticons on digital personality and avatar formation. In digital communication platforms where users are unable to convey their emotions and attitudes through the tone of the voice and/or body language, emojis enable users to convey some emotions or attitudes that are representative of some perceived persona (Sun & Liu, 2023). For example, an individual may frequently tag his/her public posts with hearts or smiley faces so that people can have positive attitudes towards him even if he does not feel that way. Similarly, working individuals may employ sacred or corporate emoji, for example, the handshake or the briefcase emoji, as a sign of professionalism. This sociolinguistic function of emojis goes a long way in supporting the notion that although they are communication tools, they are also vehicles of self-performance and identification in the virtual sphere (Hamdan, 2022).

Finally, this chapter addresses the drawbacks and difficulties of emanating emojis in cross-cultural communication. If used rightly, emojis can complement conversations; but their misinterpretation is possible if their meaning differs from one culture to another. In some situations, the meaning of an emoji may be confusing, because of the cultural background of its users. Thus, some people may be offended by the emoji used. For instance, the 'OK hand sign' emoji which can signify appreciation or approval in some cultures, is considered as vulgar or an insult in other cultures. Moreover, even the meaning of an emoji can be quite different depending on the platform where it has been found and the device used. A smiley face on one device is different from what is obtained on another, and such situation may change the meaning of the smiley entirely. In sum, as emojis and emoticons remain a significant part of communication on the internet, their interpretation is not stagnant or standardized (Wagner, Marusek, & Yu, 2020).

BACKGROUND

Cultural, generational, and social elements define how these signs are perceived and employed during online communications. The history of emoticons and emojis as shown in figure 1 reveals that emojis and emoticons are evolutionary of digital and internet communication and/or the innate ability of human beings to try as much as possible to express emotions in every conversation. Emoticons, which are other symbols consisting of special characters typed on the keyboard to represent a particular facial expression, appeared as an early form of symbolisms in the attempt to show context in digital messages. "The earliest known use of an emoticon dates back to 1982, when computer scientist Scott Fahlman suggested using symbols like ;-) and:- (to differentiate jokes from serious messages on an online bulletin board. This innovation addressed the challenge of conveying emotions, as physical body language, tone of voice, and facial expressions—crucial elements of communication—could not be expressed in text. Emoticons provided a simple solution for translating intent and emotions into written messages using just keyboard keystrokes. (Hamdan, 2022).

Figure 1. History of Emojis

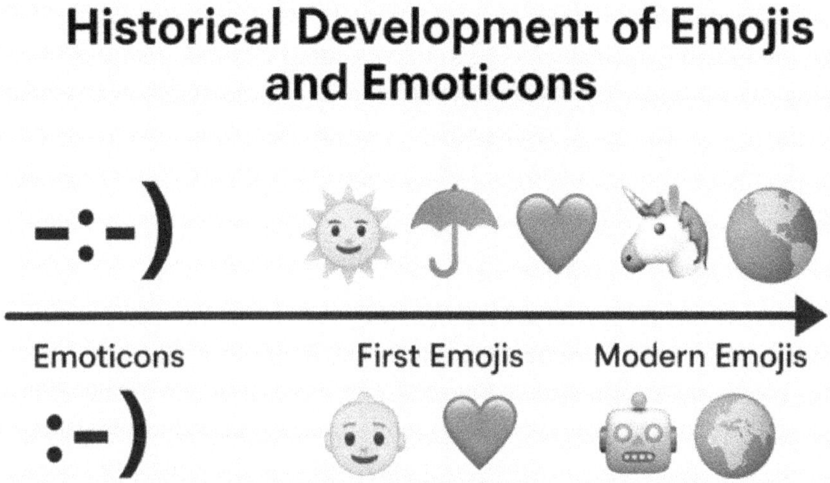

With the growth of the World Wide Web and the rise of online communication through chat, email, and instant messaging, emoticons quickly became popular across these platforms. It is because using emoticons was so easy that anybody with a keyboard could easily use emoticons and the use spread rapidly. Early emoticons were limited by the constraints of the ASCII character set, but users were creative in combining symbols to depict a wide range of emotions, from joy:-) to frustration >:((Leonardi, 2022). These early digital symbols were essential in enabling the users to express themselves, since face-to-face communication was not possible - a problem that persisted as internet communication became the norm. The extension of the emoticon to a direction of creating emojis was done in a natural manner from the emoticon but this was assisted by the fact that it used images as compared to using character marks. Emojis, which originated in Japan in the end of 1990s, was developed by Shigetaka Kurita, a designer of the telecommunications company named NTT DoCoMo. Kurita was prompted by the desire to make a new layer of communication in mobile phone messages since the first-generation text messaging systems only allowed a few words at a time. In the first batch of 176 icons he created, the basic idea was to draw icons of weather conditions, hearts, and faces. While emoticons were restricted to mere punctuation marks in an 'Orientalised' Western way, emojis portrayed fairly sophisticated emotions and things and activities that gave a completely new dimension to textual communication (Graham, 2024). In

Japanese communication, there is high power distance, and the process of decision making does not involve confrontation; therefore, nonverbal actions add value and depth to communication. Words, through emojis, helped Japanese users express their feeling gently, making a message less harsh or adding a layer of complex tone without using rough words. For instance, a single smiley face may be used to cushion a nasty argument or simply to say thank you. Since mobile phones gained its common use in the society of Japan, emojis were a common feature of any communication activity (López-Vázquez & López-Ruiz, 2024).

The popularization of emojis started in the period before the year 2010 but entered more serious growth in the later period of the 2010s when Apple integrated an emoji keyboard into its operating system of iPhone in 2011. This move made a Shift in global digital communication since emojis can be easily accessed by millions of people. Shortly thereafter, other large-scale platforms such as Android, Facebook, Twitter have also incorporated the use of emojis in their system (Neel & Hand, 2023). Back in the early days of the Internet, common ways of exchanging information were mainly by email, news groups, and forums. And as the bandwidth grew with time, and the available genetic of technology enlarged, the media enhanced, encompassing images, videos and real-time essays. Thus, emojis perfectly tessellate into this new media landscape offering the audience an efficient means to lend mood and background to their messages. When WhatsApp, Instagram and Snapchat stepped into the lives of people as means of communication, emojis came into use. For example, instead of typing 'I am so excited', 'I love this!' people switched to using such emoji as 'fire' for expressing happiness, 'crying face' for sadness, and so on, which show that emoji have become an indication of how a user feels (Graham, 2024).

Socially, emojis have assumed importance of representing how people interact across various cultural practices. They eventually became endowed with other meanings from different parts of the world that had never been foreseen by the designers. Likewise, the "face with tears of joy" emoji shocked the world when it was named the Oxford Dictionaries' Word of the Year in 2015, reflecting text messaging's new omnipresence (Boutet & LeBlanc, 2021). In many ways, emojis are no longer just symbols used to support text-based communication but are symbols within culture themselves. Needless to say, one of the primary causes for using emojis internationally is to conquer the language barrier. As more and more individuals interact electronically across cultures and languages, using emoji represents emotions quickly without having to type them out. This makes them really beneficial in an international level where the affectation of language can interfere with comprehension. For instance, one can use the "thumbs up" or the "heart sign" to portray approval or affection in a situation that less would suffice probably leading to misunderstanding or misinterpretation. However, the above universality is not without some problems. It has been mentioned that some emojis are considered acceptable in one culture while they are deemed completely unacceptable or unprofessional in the other. Nevertheless, it must be noted that there always exist cultural differences in using emojis, but still emojis' essence is to convey emotions as fast as possible (López-Vázquez & López-Ruiz, 2024).

This also reflect the cultural aspects of community, and the role identity plays in it. In response to the criticism that early emoji set were lacking in diversity, Unicode Consortium started to incorporate a greater variety of skin colour, gender, and occupation that we see today in the world. Now, the fingers roaring behind the figures can be any colour as the people emojis found in modern devices allow users to choose from skin tones. Thus, there are emojis of same-sex couples, women in workplace or with disabilities, etc. This evolution is due to the fact that the minutia of digital communication demands a depiction of diversity, a notion of which emerged from the understanding that emojis are a type of language and therefore should include all types of people (Graham, 2024). As much as emojis are now perceived as normal and natural part of communication, there are some interesting topics that should be mentioned including emoji's impact on pop culture and branding. People use emojis in different areas of life that can be shocking, which is why they appeared in TV commercials, clothes, and movies. Graphics, such as the emojis applied in brands' products, are used by the brand in their marketing initiatives since they appeal to the youthful generation and give the brand a friendly and fun touch. For example, fast food industries and apparel houses include emojis in their articles on their social media platform in order to engage their followers as emojis bring a lighter side of the story they are presenting. Now, the actual confirmation of emojis existence in pop culture came as a movie in 2017, The Emoji Movie, despite getting mostly negative reviews. Whether critics and audiences found the film smart or silly, it established that emojis are now signs that transcend the platforms they were built for (Boutet & LeBlanc, 2021; Neel & Hand, 2023).

The Semiotics of Emojis and Emoticons

Emoji and emoticon analysis has its perspective from the branch of knowledge that is related to the signs and symbols. Semiotics provides a theoretical framework for examining how these symbols act as a type of language in the context of digital communication. The fundamental ideas behind this approach are drawn from Charles Sanders Peirce's triadic model of sign theory, and Ferdinand de Saussure's theory of structural linguistics. According to Saussure, a sign is made up of two components: the "signified" or the idea it represents, and the "signifier" or the shape the sign takes (in this example, an emoticon or emoji). By establishing the concept of the "interpretant" or the meaning that is determined by the observer, Peirce expanded on this idea (Park & El Mimouni, 2020). Figure 2 provides an overview of Semiotics of Emojis and Emoticons.

Figure 2. Overview of Semiotics of Emojis and Emoticons

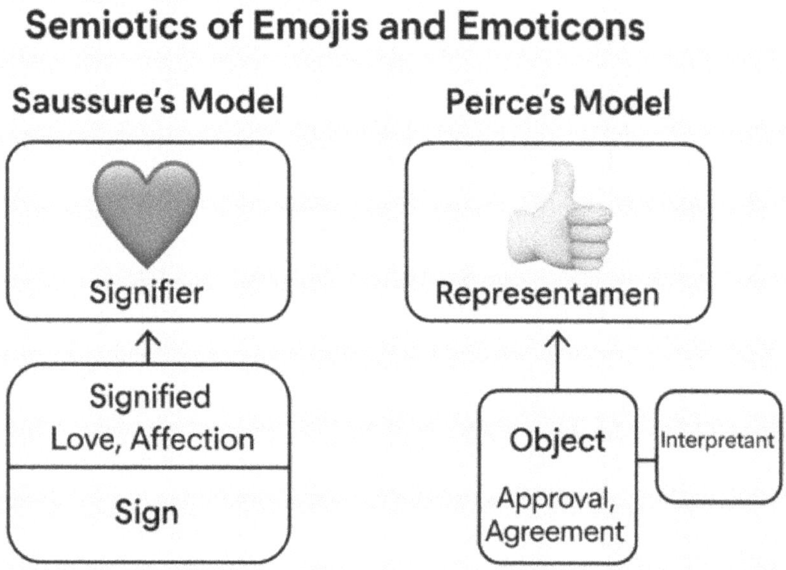

Both theories may be used to explain how people understand emoticons and emojis differently based on environmental, social, and cultural aspects. Recognizing emoticons' and emojis' dual roles as social cues and visual representations is necessary to comprehend their symbolic meanings. Unlike words, emojis mostly rely on visual symbolism. An emoji of a heart, for example, might represent support, love, or devotion. However, depending on the context, it might have several meanings. A heart might signify intense emotional commitment in a romantic relationship, but it could also be used more casually to express admiration in a business context. Similar to this, while the "smile face" emoji can be used to convey happiness, it can also be seen as sarcasm or passive-aggressiveness depending on the situation. Emoticons function similarly, but with a more constrained expressive range. For example, a straightforward ":-)" smiley can be used to show friendliness as well as to temper harsh or unpleasant remarks (Franco & Fugate, 2020). The meaning of emoticons and emojis is greatly influenced by cultural perceptions. An examination of the "thumbs-up" emoji serves as an example of how ostensibly universal symbols may have diverse cultural connotations. The "thumbs-up" emoji is a common affirmative gesture used to express agreement or approval in many Western cultures.

The same action, meanwhile, may be interpreted as disrespectful in certain regions of the Middle East and South Asia, and be equated to giving someone the finger. This disparity emphasizes how crucial cultural literacy is to internet communication. Another illustration is the "folded hands" emoji, which is sometimes used in Japan to signify an apology or plea but is sometimes misinterpreted by users in the West as a sign of thanksgiving or prayer (Park & El Mimouni, 2020). The "face with tears of joy" emoji, one of the most well-known emojis, serves as another example of how symbolic meanings change over time. Its usage in some situations, nevertheless, has given rise to new meanings; some people use it humorously to convey insincerity or to minimize a grave situation. This change illustrates how emojis are dynamic and thats evolved by the communities who use them, just like any other language (Barinaga-López & Puente-Bienvenido, 2022; Franco & Fugate, 2020).

MULTICULTURAL MEANINGS IN DIGITAL COMMUNICATION

Emojis and emoticons have become ubiquitous symbols in digital communication, yet their cultural connotations are far from universal. Communication styles, cultural conventions, and values have a major role in shaping how individuals understand and use digital symbols. Emojis, for example, are more commonly used in cultures that value indirect communication, such as those in East Asia, to accentuate messages or express nuanced feelings. On the other hand, as these cultures tend to prioritize direct and unambiguous conversations, emoji usage may be less common and more literal in more direct communication cultures, such as those seen in the United States or Germany (Escouflaire, 2021). A prominent example of cross-cultural variance is the use of facial expression emojis. For instance, the "smile face" emoji is frequently used in Japan to convey politeness or to mitigate unpleasant criticism, demonstrating the significance of preserving harmony in interpersonal relationships. Nonetheless, a cheerful face is more frequently employed in Western countries to simply convey friendliness or contentment, with less focus on the social role that controlling emotion plays. This distinction demonstrates how cultural norms about the presentation of emotion may affect how digital symbols are employed. This variance may cause misunderstandings in some situations. A Japanese user may, for instance, send a smiling face to lessen the effect of a critical message, but the recipient in the West might mistake this for insincerity or minimize the importance of the message (Pei & Cheng, 2022). Figure 3 provides some emojis.

Figure 3. Set of different Emojis

The way different cultures understand the hand motions that emojis depict is one of the most obvious cross-cultural disparities. The thumb and index finger of the "OK" hand motion emoji form a circle, and it is often acknowledged in Western cultures as a positive symbol that denotes agreement or acceptance. This similar gesture, nevertheless, is objectionable in Brazil and Turkey, and is associated with obscenity or disrespect. Similar to this, the "folded hands" emoji, which was once used to symbolize a prayer in Japanese culture, is now widely used as a thank-you or even a high-five in many regions of the world. These illustrations demonstrate how the widespread use of emojis may result in various meanings depending on the cultural setting (Escouflaire, 2021). Emojis are very useful for multicultural communication in today's globalized society, as interactions between individuals from many cultures happen online on a regular basis. Emojis can help people communicate across language boundaries by expressing thoughts and feelings that can be challenging to put into words. Emojis can be useful in international business contexts when communication may be limited to non-English speaking individuals by providing additional context and tone to communications. Even in situations when verbal subtleties are lost, a straightforward "thumbs-up" or "heart" emoji can convey agreement or approval. Even in these circumstances, though, cultural sensitivity is crucial as the incorrect emoji in a given cultural setting might cause misunderstandings or offense (Barinaga-López & Puente-Bienvenido, 2022). Emojis that reflect a range of skin tones have become popular, which is an intriguing example of their application in multicultural settings. Emoji skin-tone choices were added in 2015, giving users the ability to choose symbols that better reflected their identities. Users all across the world praised this innovation, but it also spurred discussions about appropriation and representation. The ability to select emojis that represent their race gave some users a sense of empowerment, while others expressed worry about how emojis can support or contradict racial stereotypes (Pei & Cheng, 2022). Thus, despite the widespread belief that emoticons and emojis constitute a global language, cultural context has a significant impact on their meanings. Cultural differences influence how these symbols are interpreted and utilized, which may both help and hinder cross-cultural communication. In multicultural settings, where misunderstandings might result from disparate cultural norms and values, it is especially important to comprehend these variances in order to ensure that digital interactions are courteous and productive. With the increasing prevalence of digital communication, it is critical to acknowledge and adjust to these variations in emoji usage (Escouflaire, 2021).

Emojis and Emoticons in Social Media

Because they lend emotional complexity, personality, and context to text-based communication, emojis and emoticons are essential for improving online interactions on social media. Emojis act as digital stand-ins for non-verbal indicators including tone, facial expressions, and body language, which improve the effectiveness of meaning communication. For example, depending on the situation, a straightforward statement like "That's terrific!" might be taken in several different ways. Emojis such as "thumbs-up" or "happy face" help to express the message's genuine positivity and clarify its meaning. An additional element of comedy or fun may be added through the "winking face" emoji, which also indicates that the message should not be taken too seriously. Emojis make online communication more dynamic and engaging by reducing the ambiguity that frequently accompanies them by providing users with a more specific means of expressing their feelings

(Barinaga-López & Puente-Bienvenido, 2022). Emoji usage has taken up on social networking sites like Facebook, Instagram, and Twitter, each of which has its own case studies and distinctive trends. Emojis are frequently used on Twitter to visually succinctly convey complicated thoughts or feelings, as character constraints require brevity. For instance, people commonly use the raised fist emoji to express support in discussions about social movements like #BlackLivesMatter, producing a potent sign of togetherness in a little, digital form (Alzahrani & Elshemy, 2023).

Emojis' adaptability on Twitter enables users to engage in more extensive discussions, forge a feeling of common identity, and elicit strong emotional responses from a wide audience. Emojis are an integral part of visual storytelling on Instagram. In order to accentuate the emotional effect of their posts or to accentuate the visual components of their images, users frequently use many emojis in their descriptions. Emojis' appealing visuals are another way that influencers and marketers use to increase interaction. Fashion firms, for instance, frequently utilize emoticons like hearts, fire symbols, or starry-eyed expressions to promote new goods and generate enthusiasm among their followers. Here, emojis function as a visual shorthand that prompts people to respond more quickly and intensely. Emojis are crucial elements of social media marketing and branding efforts, in addition to being means of expression, as this example illustrates (Wagner, Marusek, & Yu, 2020). Emojis have a somewhat distinct function on Facebook. With the introduction of "Reactions" in 2016, the network gave users more options than just like postings; they could now express a variety of emotions, such as "Love," "Angry," "Sad," and "Haha." A more dynamic system of engagement has been developed by these emojis, which may be used to respond to postings or comments. Users may now more clearly convey their complex feelings instead of just a binary like or dislike, and the widespread use of these response emojis has changed how users interact with material. People can express empathy or dissatisfaction, for instance, by using the "Sad" or "Angry" reaction to catastrophic news occurrences. This allows for widespread emotional participation without requiring long comments (Ravi & Karmakar, 2023).

Social media user-generated material frequently adheres to particular emoji trends that are indicative of pop culture, current affairs, or evolving communication styles. For example, the "fire" emoji has gained popularity as a means of expressing something interesting, thrilling, or remarkable, particularly in the domains of sports, fashion, and music. In order to increase the attractiveness of their postings, celebrities and influencers commonly employ it. Fans then do the same, creating a feedback loop of visual language that raises the emotional appeal of online interactions (Boutet & LeBlanc, 2021). Another example is the regular use of the "laughing face with tears of joy" emoji, which led emoji use rankings for years, often in response to memes or hilarious content. Emojis gained widespread usage as a method to express happiness and laughing, but they might also be used humorously or sarcastically in certain situations, demonstrating how an emoji's meaning can change depending on the context in which it is used (Alzahrani & Elshemy, 2023).

Emoji trends analysis shows how the culture of social media affects the evolution of these digital symbols. The emergence of novel emojis, such as gender-neutral figures or culinary items with cultural connotations like tacos or dumplings, demonstrates how social media users shape the need for symbols that are more inclusive and representational. These patterns show how user-generated material is influencing digital communication in addition to reflecting shifting social dynamics. Emojis continue to be essential tools for improving online communication as they get increasingly complex and representational. They allow users to communicate identities, ideas, and feelings in ways that go beyond the constraints of text-based communication (Ravi & Karmakar, 2023). To sum up, emoticons and emojis have become essential social media tools that enhance online interactions by quickly and easily expressing personality and emotions. By embracing these digital symbols in distinctive ways, social media sites like Facebook, Instagram, and Twitter have made it possible for users to interact with material more deeply. Emoji trends and user-generated content analysis demonstrate that these symbols not only improve communication but also represent larger social and cultural changes in the ways that we express ourselves online (Alzahrani & Elshemy, 2023).

Emojis in Multimodal Narratives

Emojis have become a vital aspect of multimodal tales, merging text, visuals, and symbols to create richer and more engaging digital storytelling experiences. Emojis improve narrative expressiveness by including a visual communication layer that makes stories more relatable and emotionally impactful. Emojis reduce the cognitive burden needed to comprehend a tale by acting as shorthand for emotions, actions, and reactions in digital storytelling, as readers often interact with information across several platforms. Emojis have revolutionized the way people interact with digital information by being included into multimodal storytelling. This has opened up new avenues for audience involvement and creative storytelling (Brito, Torres, & Fernandes, 2020). The tone of a traditional tale must be deduced from the sentence structure, word choice, and context. On the other hand, the tone of a multimodal story that incorporates emojis is instantly clear. Emojis, like "roller coaster" or "party popper," may be used to punctuate a tale about a character's experience at a theme park, instantly creating a lighthearted and lively atmosphere. Similarly, the "tear face" or "broken heart" emojis can be used to express sadness or introspection without resorting to wordy descriptions in order to convey the scene's emotional impact (Revita & Datuk, 2023). Emojis offer emotional clues that make the tale more accessible and immersive information to facilitate more effective communication and raises reader engagement. Emojis also affect how readers understand the digital tales' tempo and flow. Emojis can serve as indicators in multimodal storytelling as a tale shift from one emotional or thematic beat to another. For example, a series of events in a brief tale published on Instagram can be punctuated with appropriate emojis to improve the storytelling and let the reader know how they should be feeling about what's happening. Emojis such as "thumbs-up," "laughing," and "confused face" can be used to lead the reader through various emotional states while also subtly commenting on the text and enhancing the experiences of the characters. Emojis support reader's involvement and participation in deciphering the story's visual and literary parts by doing this, which helps to sustain reader interest (Wagner, Marusek, & Yu, 2020).

Social media storytelling difficulties provide an obvious illustration of multimodal tales using emojis. For example, users are challenged to compose whole tales using just emojis in the increasingly popular "Emoji Story Challenge" on social media sites like TikTok and Twitter. These stories frequently depend on the reader's capacity to decipher emojis and create meaning by arranging and combining symbols (Hasyim & Arafah, 2023). A normal work-from-home day may be represented, for instance, by the phrases "sun," "coffee cup," "computer," and "sleeping face," and the reader would grasp the pattern without having to read any farther. This approach demonstrates how emojis may function as stand-alone storytelling devices, providing succinct, visual stories and allowing readers to engage in the story by putting their own creative interpretations on the symbols (Brito, Torres, & Fernandes, 2020). Emojis are frequently used in conjunction with text and graphics in longer-form multimodal storytelling, such as webcomics or digital novels, to produce a more engaging narrative experience. Emojis, for example, are commonly utilized in conversation to improve character expression and reinforce the humor or emotions of the scenario in the well-known webcomic Sarah's Scribbles. These emojis' visual simplicity contrasts with the comic art's finer details, giving readers another level of easily understood meaning. Similar to this, companies commonly employ emojis in digital marketing narratives to convey product tales or promote campaigns. The usage of symbols like flames, stars, or hearts may create an engaging, dynamic environment that emotionally connects with the audience (Chen & Filik, 2024). In summary, the use of emojis in multimodal tales improves digital storytelling's emotional depth, rhythm, and engagement to a substantial degree. Emojis help writers craft more effective and emotive stories that appeal to a wide audience by using visual clues that enhance and complement verbal aspects. Emojis have become indispensable tools in the changing world of digital communication, changing how we tell and interact with stories on the internet. These stories can range from straightforward emoji-only tales to intricate narratives that use text, photos, and symbols (Hasyim & Arafah, 2023).

Affective Meanings and Emotional Expressions

Smileys have emerged as strong indicators of feelings and affective dimensions in using information technologies. Where gestures, facial expressions, and even the tone of voice do not reach, emojis become the interfaces for conveying as many feelings as possible – from happiness and excitement to anger and depression. These simple icons enable people to convey some shades of tone in a text, thus, having more realistic communications. For instance, the message, "Thanks for your help' with a 'smiling face' emoji at the end of the message is more appreciative than having a 'red heart' emoji at the end of such message though the latter shows love or gratitude more deeply. Where there are words, there are always emotions with emojis bringing an additional facet of emotions which reduces misinterpretations and amplifies the value of digital communications (Revita & Datuk, 2023). Psychologically, emojis trigger a part of the brain that seeks to associate a symbol or visuals of a symbol to a feeling. Principal findings from affective psychology imply that facial expressions are innate features in people and are easily interpreted as signals of feelings. This is why the "laughing face with tears of joy" emoji, for example, has gotten incredibly popular — it saves time and supplies an immediate icon that signifies to the receiver that the sender is not only willing to converse about the topic at hand, but also finds it funny. Research has indicated that emojis as digital stimuli also elicit identical neuronal connections of affective reactions that real life stimuli elicit, which gives a rationality to use emojis in conveying affective meanings (Katsumata, 2022). Emojis also facilitate the conveyance of more elaborate sentiments in a shorter period rather than what words can achieve. Sometimes, one can describe a whole state of mind, for which he or she usually needs several words, by one emoji (Sakib & Oishe, 2024).

In the discussion regarding the sentiment of the text data, the analyses of emoji utilization in the specific cases demonstrate the existence of these objects in the posts and comments on social networks and messenger services. For example, in the coronavirus outbreak — Twitter, and other social media where emojis are actively used, people often employed the 'face with medical mask' emoji, or 'folded hands', which is more commonly understood as a prayer or even a symbol of hope. These emojis aided in expressing group sentiments when the entire world was in distress; people could share from distress to encouragement. One more example: when people add a jab or the criticism they are giving, they can do it with the help of an emoji. A message like "I don't agree with this" may seem arrogant and impolite, but using, for example, a smiling face or thinking face, makes the conversation less hostile and more friendly (Danesi, 2022). Idealized in different subtopics that individuals participate in using their multimedia devices, emojis are also very important tools that help set the tone, and the level of emotions on online communities especially those that deal with highly charged topics like politics or social justice. For instance, when a user receives an insulting tweet or post that triggers an outrageous story, the use of the" angry face" emoji serves to warm everyone's hearts while the "clapping hands" emoji ensures a sign of approval or encouragement of a shared approach towards a topic. Such symbols enable the users to engage in emotional discussion within the shortest time possible; they make their words charged with emotion, thus, dictating how the emotions of others are, within the discussion, are likely to be (Chen & Filik, 2024; Danesi, 2022; Tariq, 2025).

Emojis in Multicultural and Multilingual Context

Emojis have become a language in the social media platform that cannot be explained in terms of language and cultural differences. Nevertheless, they can be used in multicultural and multilingual environments. On one hand, emojis amplify screen-based, cross-cultural communication by offering visual and affective shortcuts, yet on the other hand, its symbols are not always interpretable. The study showed that people of different cultures depict the same emoji in different ways, hence causing confusion at times. For instance, while we have "thumbs up" to symbolize endorsement or approval, it is a rude sign in some Middle Eastern countries and South Asia. That is why it is expected that the approach to analyze emojis should be more delicate taking into consideration the peculiarities of the culture and language used when working with them (Sakib & Oishe, 2024). Probably the biggest disadvantage of emojis in multicultural environment is the questions of how different cultures may affect certain signs and figures. Even the same symbol that has the positive load in one country, could be considered as neutral or even with negative load in another one (Sampietro, 2020). For instance, passive hand gesture such as "folded hands" symbolizes prayer/ thankfulness in many western and some Asian countries; however, it appears as a polite demand/apology symbol in Japan. This is not unconnected because the use of certain terms in English, especially by the Americans has different connotations in their own culture to what is obtainable in the culture of the British. These scenarios clearly indicate that emoji use in description simplifies things in some ways while it complicates in multicultural contexts (Katsumata, 2022). However, emojis also offer major potential for overcoming barriers that give rise to conflicts in culturally diverse society. Thus, using emojis is advantageous since they do not translate utterances, instead they support human conveying of messages whereby visual or symbolic semiotics are used. More specifically, in multicultural interaction, when participants use different languages and gestures to express feelings, moods and actions, emojis provide an opportunity. For instance, while writing, one happy emoji, such as the one in the shape of a heart may help say: 'I am here for you' in a global language that is understood by almost everyone. Likewise, the representations of any form of 'smiling face' emoji or happiness as such is a perfect way of expressing friendliness or positivity and people with different linguistic background will find it easy and safe to carry on with conversations (Wagner, Marusek, & Yu, 2020; Tariq, 2025).

Using examples of emoji usage in various linguistic and cultural settings, the potential and the pitfalls of the mentioned symbols are shown. For instance, in a study conducted by Kimwele and Skuse focusing on use of emojis in African digital communication, some emojis like "clapping hands" when used in social justice movements means show of support. On the other hand, where the accident occurred in a European or an American setting the same emoji might be a symbol of clapping or concurring (Sampietro, 2020). Recent works targeting specifically Latin American users demonstrate how the "emoji: heart_red" has significantly more sentimental and family-oriented uses, than the heart emoji in a Western setting. These examples show that even though emojis can be used with different cultures, they depend on the norms and values of culture that is in a community (Wu & Zhang, 2024). The use of emojis is very volatile; hence, communication plans are needed to manage the cultural issues. The first is to employ symbols that are commonly recognized across most cultures to include 'the smiling face' or 'heart symbol' which are distinguished from other members due to their more generalized meanings. The other technique entails the use of emojis alongside text to ensure that selected emojis are well understood by the other party. For example, when one wants to send feedback to another professional from across the globe through email, do not use the phrase 'great work' without blending it with ' '. This selection may help to avoid possible misinterpretation of the value by repeated emphasis on the author's positive intentions of the symbol. Furthermore, knowing culture differences of the audience may enable the users to pick the emojis wisely while passing the message with poignancy (Katsumata, 2022; Sasamoto, 2023).

ETHICAL CONSIDERATIONS AND MISINTERPRETATIONS

Emoji and emoticons in online communication are significant to ethical awareness bearing in mind aspects to do with cultural sensitivity, interpretational errors, as well as the echoing of harm. It is evident that the usage of digital symbols has extended to private as well as business correspondence – consequences of specific emoji must be considered. For instance, the comparatively harmless symbol, the 'OK' hand gesture, may be taken as a sign of approval in a particular society but it is actually a sign of hate in extremists' groups in a particular region, such as the Western world. Such cases are good examples of why ethical awareness of the usage of digital symbols is so crucial particularly when more than one culture is involved (Wu & Zhang, 2024; Tariq, 2025).

The biggest ethical concern most people have with emojis is that they may not translate well from one language to the other or from one culture to the other. Symbolism attached to emojis tends to be rather rude when in real life that is not the case, hence ambiguity of meaning. For example, the ''face with tears of joy'' emoji is safe and funny in many regions of the globe but is regarded as sad or uncomfortable in other circumstances. Eye contact is normally followed by speech, which means that this kind of interferences can cause misinterpretations in crucial dialogue as well as during official meetings or discussions. In a similar context, the ethical implication rests on the communicator to guarantee that the emojis employed not only fit the surrounding environment, but also the target community (Ebel & Dutra, 2022). Other ethical issues about emoji include the fact that some symbols can be quite culturally insensitive, and so emojis can be used without the requisite understanding of the symbols' implications in other cultures. For instance, adding skin-tone modifiers to alter the color of emojis associated with people's illustrations or hands are useful attempts at recognizing the diverse culture. A person who is culturally different may feel offended or disrespected if he/she notices an emoji in a degrading or a making-a-joke out of a person with that ethnicity. To this end, users must be sensitive to how other people perceive their chosen emoji and should exercise a lot of care especially when sending messages to large groups of people or using them in messages to be read in many parts of the world (Ebel & Dutra, 2022).

Customizations of emojis present a gender and race-related ethical concern because they are the elements conveyed to users. Although there is a progress with representing different skin tones and the options of gender of the emojis, the choice of using certain symbols has ethical implications. For instance, there are some critics who think that using a different skin color emblem than one's presents a kind of "digital blackface" or culture appropriation. The use of diverse emojis can be motivated in the positive manners, but the ethical tendencies of how and when it is better to work with emojis have to be faced to prevent the cause of the scandal or further reinforcing of hateful junks (Wu & Zhang, 2024). To overcome these ethical advancements, several rules regarding the right and ethical use of emojis should be upheld. First, users should ensure that he or she has the appropriate knowledge of every culture as they select each emoji, particularly in the international or interculture communication. This requires users to understand that the same symbol might have different interpretations in across countries, and as such, they should avoid emojis that may cause controversy. Second, the use of emojis with the text is effective in cases when the author of the message may want to point to something special, stressing the main text with different emojis, thus, diversifying the text and simultaneously enhancing the comprehension of the addressee (Ebel & Dutra, 2022).

For instance, to the mostly interpreted emoji like the "thumbs-up" a positive comment like "Great job" can guarantee that the message is received as intended by the sender of the message (Ravi & Karmakar, 2023). In addition, users should always take into consideration as to which part of the conversation they are going to use emojis, so that they are not taking serious business meetings lightly by using funny symbols at the back of the screen. Finally, something that should never be missed is the listener's feedback. If a certain emoji is considered as a taboo or crass, everyone with an emoji-enabled device should be willing to take responsibility for the mistake and seek to rectify the sexism associated with certain images or characters (Hasyim & Arafah, 2023; Ravi & Karmakar, 2023).

FUTURE TRENDS AND INNOVATIONS

Emojis and emoticons have become even more popular as the years go by and, based on the trends visible now, it can be stated that emojis will play an even greater part in people's communication in coming years. Among them, the trend of icon individualization is prominent because they have benefited from recent developments in AI and AR technologies (Du Plessis, 2020). New FIG.3 non-standard and customizable images are now available for emoji keyboards rather than being rigid image sets. The user can create his/her emoji that looks like him/her or the emotions you want, such as Apple's Memoji or Samsung's AR Emoji. These changes enable at least the human side of communication and embraces individuality as it is felt behind screens as opposed to an impersonal mass media (Du Plessis, 2020).

Another new development is the use of emotive icons in more complex forms of communication with the help of higher and even fully interactive communication media such as VR-Immersives. With the future advancement of the concept of VR and AR, emojis are likely to take a big part of being the medium through which communication can be well enhanced. For instance, in virtual meetings or social networks, people seem to be able to use 3D emojis to make reactions or feelings when they're speaking, thus having a more interactive type of communication (Hasyim & Arafah, 2023). The role of emojis appears to deepen with advancements of distinct digital platforms and therefore pass dynamics may be expected as emojis become even more innately integrated into composition-transmission processes. Introducing this change is one way of attaining this and one region where this impact has started emerging is in business communication. emoji and brands Brands can interact with the consumer using emojis especially in social media platforms because they are informal and images. For instance, businesses employ emojis to add casual nature, personality tone and to convey concepts to the audience. Going forward, this trend might reach its climax in that numerous organizations could employ emoji icons that are unique to them to build and strengthen their bond with their customers. This could also lead to new innovations in how businesses employ emojis within a customer service setting, which of course could mean AI-generated replies with emojis that are much more personalized (Sasamoto, 2023).

A projection of features for the next future indicates that the digitization of symbols will progress significantly as the means of communication advances globally. One prediction is that people will create more ethnic-oriented and context-relevant emoticons. Unicode, the body that oversees allocation of emojis, has been improving on the ethnic Model, gender Model, Model of Skin Tone and even the Model Symbolizing World Cultures. But the need for even more representation from culturally unique perspectives will ultimately drive the needs for more culturally unique emojis that can convey ideas in regions and cultures specific to them. This development would benefit direct intercultural communication as users would be able to respond in the language that helps them express their cultural roots most effectively (Du Plessis, 2020). Emoji use could be looked further in terms of future empirical and theoretical research where the impact of emojis. That is, future research and innovation in the use of emojis should examine the impact that the digital symbols have on language and interpersonal interactions. It is for this reason that linguists and sociologists, especially as the generations that are growing up, incorporate emojis in their writing. Will emojis dominate the entire world one day like it is said to 'speak another language which is different from the national language' (Sun & Lee, 2023). Furthermore, future studies may take up a research agenda that focuses on the relation between emotions and mental health in the context of emoji communication, or more general, how aesthetic symbols are deployed on digital platforms to convey emotions and whether emoji can be understood as a form of supportive communication or therapeutic agency. For example, could specific combinations of emojis be used to track mental health indicators, which would help people share their emotions with others, professionals included?'(Shaari, 2020). Future research ideas in this area include The use emojis that adapt to change in feelings or any other condition of the graphics in the same manner as the conditions change. Future emojis that are built utilizing AI and machine learning may be able to pick the tenor of a conversation and respond accordingly. For instance, an emoji that is at first associated with joy would visually transform if the scene of communication revolves around a sad issue. Such innovations would facilitate the ways of communication and enhance the speed of emergence of emotions in a conversation as well as provide users with a possibility to have more complex forms of expressing their feelings without the need to change emojis manually (Du Plessis, 2020). Lastly, the enhancement of the use of emojis and emoticons into the future will be characterized by enhanced use of technological developments that will enhance the basic features of emojis and emoticons. The integration of emoji with VR, AR, and AI soon makes it clear how our discourse and interaction will change in the near future. With digital symbols, Augurs become more and more culturally blinded, and as they become so context-sensitive, they are likely to help in improving cross-cultural emotional intelligence. Also, as studies on the relationship of emojis to language and to the psyche continue, researchers might reveal new patterns of improving both the speed and emotional depth of people's interactions (Shaari, 2020).

CONCLUSION

In this chapter, the historical developments of emojis and emoticons, the semiotics and cultural effects of these have been analysed. Drawing from its humble beginnings as mere symbols added to written text in communication technology, to the current complex figures of communication in today's technology, emojis have revolutionized the ways in which emotions, values, ideas as well as cultures are expressed in the new media. In this way, through the consideration of numerous examples and cases, it is salient to identify the multicultural aspects of emoji usage and enumerate the ways, in which different cultures may understand and employ these breeds of symbols (Ebel & Dutra, 2022). Furthermore, our review examined how emojis have become a part of multimodal media communication narratives, media interactions, and replace emotional words, enriching media discourses. The chapter also debated the limitations of emoji use by examining the ethical implication arising from culture misunderstanding and conformity to the diverse cultural emojis while also looking at advanced developments and direction in this ever-growing field. It is also obvious that the use of emojis and emoticons introduced a new qualitative change in online communication (Hamdan, 2022). Because of their effectiveness in expressing emotion within a short span of time and most importantly in a visual way, they have become part and parcel of interpersonal, business, and Mass communication. With emojis becoming a part of even more digital communication, we should keep paying attention to the cultural aspects of emojis so as not to inadvertently hurt people or cause confusion (Ebel & Dutra, 2022). Thus, the qualifed interpretation of emojis is only the first step toward understanding the multicultural meanings of what is now firmly established as an omnipresent part of the cultured, linguistic, and technological panorama of the present time. This means that researchers, developers, and ordinary citizens need to further study how emojis could represent a more diverse range of global communication needs and how they could be used to eliminate barriers to intercultural communication. The burden of duty now lies in the laps of professionals and scholars in the field to seek a clearer understanding of how such digital symbols common as emojis may improve on the feat of making meaning out of messages in the global village rather than impede it (Du Plessis, 2020). Emoji's future as the global language that contributes a lot to digital communications must step up to the concern of cultural appropriateness, and the representation of both diversities, and the creativity.

REFERENCES

Alzahrani, F., & Elshemy, R. (2023). Digitally mediated communication of emojis by visually impaired users: The case of sarcastic WhatsApp messages. *Journal of Intercultural Communication, 23*(2), 58–65. DOI: 10.36923/jicc.v23i2.187

Barinaga-López, B., Puente-Bienvenido, H., & Navarro Newball, A. A. (2022). A systematic review of trends and gaps in the production of scientific knowledge on the sociopolitical impacts of emojis in computer-mediated communication. *Cogent Social Sciences, 8*(1), 2151096. DOI: 10.1080/23311886.2022.2151096

Boutet, I., LeBlanc, M., Chamberland, J. A., & Collin, C. A. (2021). Emojis influence emotional communication, social attributions, and information processing. *Computers in Human Behavior, 119*, 106722. DOI: 10.1016/j.chb.2021.106722

Brito, P. Q., Torres, S., & Fernandes, J. (2020). What kind of emotions do emoticons communicate? *Asia Pacific Journal of Marketing and Logistics, 32*(7), 1495–1517. DOI: 10.1108/APJML-03-2019-0136

Chen, Y., Yang, X., Howman, H., & Filik, R. (2024). Individual differences in emoji comprehension: Gender, age, and culture. *PLoS One, 19*(2), e0297379. DOI: 10.1371/journal.pone.0297379 PMID: 38354159

Danesi, M. (2022). Emotional wellbeing and the semiotic translation of emojis. In *Exploring the translatability of emotions: Cross-cultural and transdisciplinary encounters* (pp. 323–344). Springer International Publishing., DOI: 10.1007/978-3-030-91748-7_12

Du Plessis, T. (2020). Interpretation of emojis in organisational computer-mediated communication (CMC) contexts (Doctoral dissertation, Stellenbosch: Stellenbosch University).

Ebel, I., & Dutra, J. P. (2022). Do you speak emoji? The language of emojis. In *The SAGE handbook of social media marketing* (p. 320). SAGE Publications. DOI: 10.4135/9781529782493.n20

Escouflaire, L. (2021). Signaling irony, displaying politeness, replacing words: The eight linguistic functions of emoji in computer-mediated discourse. *Lingvisticae Investigationes, 44*(2), 204–235. DOI: 10.1075/li.00062.esc

Franco, C. L., & Fugate, J. M. (2020). Emoji face renderings: Exploring the role emoji platform differences have on emotional interpretation. *Journal of Nonverbal Behavior, 44*(2), 301–328. DOI: 10.1007/s10919-019-00330-1

Graham, P. V. (2024). Emojis: An approach to interpretation. *UC Law SF Communications and Entertainment Journal*, *46*(2), 123.

Hamdan, H. (2022). The communicative functions of emojis: Evidence from Jordanian Arabic-speaking Facebookers. *Psycholinguistics*, *31*(1), 141–172. DOI: 10.31470/2309-1797-2022-31-1-141-172

Hasyim, M., & Arafah, B. (2023). Semiotic multimodality communication in the age of new media. *Studies in Media and Communication*, *11*(1), 96–103. DOI: 10.11114/smc.v11i1.5865

Katsumata, Y. (2022). How many more emoji do we need. In Cammaerts, B., & McCambridge, L. (Eds.), *Innovations in emoji communication* (pp. 80–94). Springer.

Leonardi, V. (2022). Communication challenges and transformations in the digital era: Emoji language and emoji translation. *Language and Semiotic Studies*, *8*(3), 22–44. DOI: 10.1515/lass-2022-2003

López-Vázquez, M., & López-Ruiz, S. (2024). A comprehensive examination of emoji usage in Mexican Spanish WhatsApp corpus: A mixed-methods linguistic approach. *Quality & Quantity*, *58*(6), 1–26. DOI: 10.1007/s11135-024-01898-7

Mure an, V. (2020). Re-defining communicative competence for multi-modal communication in the digital age. *Journal of Romanian Literary Studies*, *23*, 315–323.

Neel, L. A., McKechnie, J. G., Robus, C. M., & Hand, C. J. (2023). Emoji alter the perception of emotion in affectively neutral text messages. *Journal of Nonverbal Behavior*, *47*(1), 83–97. DOI: 10.1007/s10919-022-00421-6

Park, J. R., & El Mimouni, H. (2020). Emoticons and non-verbal communications across Arabic, English, and Korean tweets. *Global Knowledge, Memory and Communication*, *69*(8/9), 579–595. DOI: 10.1108/GKMC-02-2020-0021

Pei, J., & Cheng, L. (2022). Deciphering emoji variation in courts: A social semiotic perspective. *Humanities & Social Sciences Communications*, *9*(1), 1–8. DOI: 10.1057/s41599-022-01453-5

Ravi, R., & Karmakar, M. (2023). The problem of gendered emojis in online communication platforms: A study to understand digital dependence on using emotions during pandemic. *Theory and Practice in Language Studies*, *13*(1), 257–265. DOI: 10.17507/tpls.1301.30

Revita, I., Zalfikhe, F. A., Boholano, H., Tuan, N. T., Huszka, B., & Datuk, Z. D. M. (2023). Emoticons unveiled: A multifaceted analysis of their linguistic impact. *JURNAL ARBITRER*, *10*(3), 260–274. DOI: 10.25077/ar.10.3.260-274.2023

Sakib, O. I., Sarker, A., & Oishe, R. T. (2024). Exploring emojis in digital communication among Bangladeshi undergraduates: Private university scenario. *Journal of Engineering*, *12*(4), 22–30.

Sampietro, A. (2020). Use and interpretation of emoji in electronic-mediated communication: A survey. *Visual Communication Quarterly*, *27*(1), 27–39. DOI: 10.1080/15551393.2019.1707086

Sasamoto, R. (2023). Perceptual resemblance and the communication of emotion in digital contexts: A case of emoji and reaction GIFs. *Pragmatics*, *33*(3), 393–417. DOI: 10.1075/prag.21058.sas

Shaari, A. H. (2020). Accentuating illocutionary forces: Emoticons as speech act realization strategies in a multicultural online communication environment. *Linguistics. Literature*, *26*(1), 135–155.

Sun, J., Lasser, S., & Lee, S. K. (2023). Understanding emojis: Cultural influences in interpretation and choice of emojis. *Journal of International and Intercultural Communication*, *16*(3), 242–261. DOI: 10.1080/17513057.2022.2036790

Sun, X., & Liu, L. (2023). Understanding the multi-modal affective expression of net language in computer-mediated communication. *Cognitive Processing*, *24*(2), 275–288. DOI: 10.1007/s10339-022-01115-z PMID: 36574065

Tariq, M. U. (2025). Revitalizing Pedagogy: Integrating Indigenous Knowledge and Practices Into Higher Education Disciplines. In Kgari-Masondo, M. (Ed.), *Indigenous Teaching Disciplines and Perspectives for Higher Education* (pp. 379–400). IGI Global Scientific Publishing., DOI: 10.4018/979-8-3693-9296-6.ch018

Tariq, M. U. (2025). Community-Led Tourism and Social Equity: A Regenerative Approach to Sustainable Development. In Sousa, B., Arantes, L., & Bhartiya, S. (Eds.), *Regenerative Tourism for Social Development* (pp. 339–360). IGI Global Scientific Publishing., DOI: 10.4018/979-8-3373-0235-5.ch014

Tariq, M. U. (2025). Innovative Business Models: Integrating Social, Economic, and Environmental Goals in Rural Manufacturing. In Prabhakar, A., Yu, P., & Erokhin, V. (Eds.), *Rural Social Entrepreneurship Development: Network-Based Manufacturing System Model* (pp. 147–174). IGI Global Scientific Publishing., DOI: 10.4018/979-8-3693-7515-0.ch005

Tariq, M. U. (2025). Unlocking Competitive Edge: Harnessing the Power of Collaborative Innovation. In Martínez-Falcó, J., Sánchez-García, E., & Marco-Lajara, B. (Eds.), *Open Innovation Strategies for Effective Competitive Advantage* (pp. 315–344). IGI Global Scientific Publishing., DOI: 10.4018/979-8-3693-9266-9.ch011

Wagner, A., Marusek, S., & Yu, W. (2020). Emojis and law: Contextualized flexibility of meaning in cyber communication. *Social Semiotics, 30*(3), 396–414. DOI: 10.1080/10350330.2020.1731198

Wagner, A., Marusek, S., & Yu, W. (2020). Sarcasm, the smiling poop, and E-discourse aggressiveness: Getting far too emotional with emojis. *Social Semiotics, 30*(3), 305–311. DOI: 10.1080/10350330.2020.1731151

Wu, D., Zhang, X., & Zhang, X. (2024). Is there an intergenerational discrepancy in the comprehension and aesthetic preference regarding emoji usage? Evidence from WeChat. *Frontiers in Psychology, 15*, 1424728. DOI: 10.3389/fpsyg.2024.1424728 PMID: 39165767

KEY TERMS AND DEFINITIONS

Emojis: Pictorial symbols used in digital communication to express emotions, actions, and concepts, often interpreted differently across cultures.

Emoticons: Typographic representations of facial expressions used to convey emotional tone in online communication.

Multicultural Communication: The exchange of ideas and emotions across different cultural contexts, requiring sensitivity to varied interpretations.

Semiotics: The study of signs and symbols as a means of communication, analysing the meanings of emojis and emoticons in digital interactions.

Digital Symbols: Visual or textual representations, including emojis and emoticons, used to convey messages and emotions in online spaces.

Emotional Expression: The way feelings are conveyed through non-verbal cues such as emojis, impacting interpersonal understanding in digital communication.

Chapter 3
A Critical Discourse Study of Ideologies and Identities in Nigerian X Trado-Medicine Narratives

Paul Ayodele Onanuga
https://orcid.org/0000-0003-1207-3090
Federal University, Oye-Ekiti, Nigeria

Emmanuel Taiwo Babalola
https://orcid.org/0009-0003-0211-2671
Obafemi Awolowo University, Ile-Ife, Nigeria

ABSTRACT

The influences of the digital space manifest in the seamless human interactions and sociality which it has engendered and enhanced. One of such influences is the digital knowledge-sharing of indigenous herbs for medical purposes. This study explores, from a critical discourse perspective, the representations of ideologies and identities in ten (10) purposively selected tweets from the handle ChiefHerbalist (@ HerbalistChief). Employing representative tweets from the handle as well as tweets in response by followers, attention is drawn to the discursive and contextual realities in the narratives. Among the outcomes are language use in the tripodal viewpoints of the assertion of authenticities, authoritativeness and validations. These fulfil the ideological functions of challenging the perceived primacy of orthodox medicine and projecting the efficacy of herbs and other forms of trado-medicine. What is doubtless is that the digital space has enabled visibility especially as the responders

DOI: 10.4018/979-8-3693-7934-9.ch003

and followers are transnational.

INTRODUCTION

Interests in studying the digital space both as a treasure trove of materials which provide insights into human attitudes and behaviours as well as an archival resource for knowledge-sharing and preservation continue to surge. Such existing studies have approached the digital space from diverse perspectives, including from within the context of health communication which is relevant to the present study. Edo-Osagie et al (2020) assert the usefulness of social media in public health as it is helpful for surveillance, event detection, pharmacovigilance, disease tracking and forecasting. So huge are the possibilities online and on Twitter – the platform of interest in the present study – that Ola and Sedig (2020) report an information overload with the 'enormous number of tweets present[ing] challenges to those who seek to improve their knowledge of health issues'. Of interest in the present study however is the use of this space within healthcare discourse. Singhal and Mago (2023: 1), for instance, explored how healthcare organisations used Twitter as an 'effective means of disseminating medical information to the public'. Relying on representative tweets from five (5) organisations, the study identified the roles of reputation, the place of hashtagging, and peculiar language use in evaluating the influences and popularity of tweets on the public. They further averred that these identifications were critical to the building and sustenance of public engagement. Pershad *et al* (2018) also acknowledge the collaborative function which social media, specifically Twitter, play in providing transparency and open sharing of information between healthcare workers and their patients. While they concede that the intervention of digitality in healthcare contribute to the improvement of care, they further identify, among other things, 'high rates of misinformation, difficulties in verifying the credibility of sources, [and] overwhelmingly high volumes of information available on Twitter' (Pershad *et al*, 2018: 1). In these studies, the place of language in representation and in appealing to public interests is foregrounded.

In applying the same scholarly outlook to digital data, the present study is interested in a discursive examination of tweets within the context of trado-medicine within Nigerian Twitter (now X) narratives. Trado-medicine, despite its widespread use across both urban and rural communities in Nigeria even to the point of abuse, continues to face significant condemnation and ostracisation within the orthodox medical community. The condemnation owes to the allegations of lack of clear dosage, absence of identifiable extraction of active ingredients in natural products, concerns over the production processes and the qualifications of the producers. In addition, there are considerable fears that the consumption of these products might be harmful to the body and that they constitute some of the leading causes in the upsurge in liver issues and other related ailments. Despite these allegations, trado-medicine production and consumption continue to enjoy popularity in the larger society, including among young people, and these might be linked to issues such as poor access to health facilities, endemic poverty as a result of poor economy, cultural perceptions, easy access to roadside vendors of trado-medicine, etc. These realities might have also fueled the appropriation of the digital space, including social media, by producers and vendors of trado-medicine. Therefore, beyond the word of mouth and on-the-street advertisements which are traditionally attached to trado-medicine, social media has become an integral tool for visibility and social engagement. While such come in different forms – posts, videos, and images –; of interest in this study are tweets. We are interested in tweets from a specific handle, ChiefHerbalist (@HerbalistChief). The handler validates himself as a certified and licensed herbalist while also adding his contact details either via email or mobile phone. The rider on the handle states, in capital letters for emphasis, that: 'THE HERBS ARE FOR THE HEALING OF THE NATIONS' while the pinned tweet states that 'For every human illness somewhere in the world, there exists a plant which is the cure #BackToEden'. The handle enjoys significant following as he dispenses antidotes and medications for its followers.

Employing representative tweets – in this case, the top 10 tweets with the most engagements – from the handle as well as tweets in response by followers, we draw attention to the discursive and contextual realities which come to the fore in the narratives. We intersect these within the context of decolonisation, since the preliminary interrogation of the tweets suggest an Afrocentric ideology and anti-West rhetoric. More specifically, the study explores, from a critical discourse perspective, the representations of ideologies and identities in purposively selected tweets from the specified Twitter handle. In the analysis of how narratives were discursively mobilized in the digital communication, three viewpoints are identified in the form of assertion of authenticities, authoritativeness and validations. These fulfil the ideological functions of challenging the perceived primacy of orthodox medicine and projecting the efficacy of herbs and other forms of trado-medicine. What is doubtless is that the digital space has enabled visibility and enhanced public engagement within the discourse of trado-medicine and health especially as the responders and followers are transnational and literate.

HEALTH DISCOURSE AND THE DIGITAL MEDIASCAPE

The social media has become a behemoth for information-sharing and archiving, and this attribute has been especially useful for granting visibility to marginalised discourses which may previously not enjoy public engagement (Pavlova and Berkers, 2020; Onanuga, 2021). Within the context of health discourse, the social media has strengthened the perception of health communication – whether orthodox or otherwise – as a form of public health advocacy. Consequently both medical personnel and prospective patients constantly interact in the production and discussion of medical advice and guides online. Indeed, Ng, Verhoeff, & Steen (2023: 2) submit that:

Social media has changed the landscape of health information by allowing for dialogic communication rather than one-sided communication from health professionals and experts, resulting in health communicators such as practitioners, policy makers, and patients monitoring, listening to, and engaging with dialogue on social media.

While challenges persist in terms of ethical consideration and the dynamics of regulation, online health discourse continues to enjoy widespread use. Alotiby (2021) for instance notes the popularity which social media handles which projected the viability of the use of natural remedies against the COVID-19 virus enjoyed in Saudi Arabia. Although the study interrogated the prevalence of misinformation in the digital narratives – with 78.9% of the respondents asserting that they sought information on the social media – a central realisation is how influential online platforms and networking sites are on public health decision-making. This has also led government officials and agencies to exploit the digital space in providing requisite information to their citizens.

Ng, Verhoeff, & Steen (2023), in their interrogation of the ways in which social media is used in the context of complementary and alternative medicine (CAM), identified that while users and practitioners of CAM use digital platforms to disseminate CAM therapies and information, there were also substantial instances of other users who intentionally discredit CAM. For Wijayanti, Handayani and Azzahro (2022: 118), health information is diffused online across social media platforms, and their respondents identified 'perceived benefits, health self-efficacy, and subjective norms [as influencing] the intention to seek health information on social media'. Wu, Wu and Pei (2024) also acknowledge the prevalence of health information online. However they attributed its popularity to the affordance of social support as well as provision of a health-conscious community. Chen & Wang (2021: 1) were more elaborate in articulating the ramifications of the influences of social media on health information, identifying the use in 'advancing health research and practice, social mobilization, and facilitating offline health-related services and events' among health institutions, health researchers and practitioners, and the public.

Within the context of traditional or herbal health practices and the digital space, Lam et al (2023) engage how cancer patients rely on information from and interactions on health fora and social media platforms. With specific focus on the use of traditional, complementary, and integrative medicine (TCIM), the authors identified that patients explore other non-conventional treatments often because of different concerns about their treatments in orthodox hospitals. These patients further believed that TCIM made their symptoms manageable and reduced the need for medication and their side effects. Semotiuk, Semotiuk & Ezcurra (2015) appraise the integration of social media in the advertisement and sales of herbal products in Mexico. They submit that while the digital space 'may provide a critical tool for the long–term survival of traditional plant markets' it also poses of the risk of 'contributing to the loss of the culture of home remedies and traditional domestic preparation of natural products' (360).

In Nigeria, Omoera *et al* (2011) identify cultural and historical reasons as tied to the sustained patronage of herbal medicine. For Batta (2011: 1), while people still recognise and use herbal medicine in Nigeria, its practice 'continues to be shrouded in secrecy, regarded as diabolic and often mocked, or spurned over issues of dubious efficacy, doubtful safety, quackery, and charlatanism'. The study however envisions new media as an archival resource in demystifying and popularizing access to traditional medicine. Batta (2012) extends the inquiry to the exploration of press coverage of traditional medicine practice in Nigeria. With data spanning 416 issues of four popular Nigerian dailies, the study identified that traditional medical practices do not enjoy significant coverage even though the few reports are largely positive in portrayal. It further advocates more prominent coverage for traditional medicine practice in the country. Ogbogbo (2023) concentrates on the place of language use as communicative strategy within social media posts of traditional medicine providers in Southwest Nigeria. With focus on directives, the study identified 'legitimisation, cultural contextuality and identity construction' (Ogbogbo, 2023: 7) as core strategies engaged by traditional medicine providers. These studies contextualise the salience of the interrogation of traditional medical practices and how the incorporation of digital media energises the narrative. They therefore justify the present inquiry.

METHODOLOGICAL DETAILS

The data for the study are retrieved from the ChiefHerbalist's X page with the handle: @HerbalistChief. The purposive selection of the handle is predicated on its popularity as well as its adequate possession of materials that constitute the focus of the study. The handle has 346,603 followers with 4,573 posts as at November 8,

2024. All his posts are on herbs as medication as well as providing information on healthy living. For context, the handle's name linguistically signals their activity and contributes to their authoritativeness on the platform. While herbalists heal with herbs, his presentation as 'Chief Herbalist' means he is advanced and possesses superior knowledge.

Employing representative tweets from the handle as well as tweets in response by followers, we draw attention to the discursive and contextual realities which come to the fore in the narratives. More specifically, we draw our data from the top ten (10) tweets with the most engagements – including most comments and likes – from his handle. With focus on identity construction and the formulation of ideologies in these tweets, we approach the analysis from a dialectical-relational perspective to Critical Discourse Analysis according to Norman Fairclough. Fairclough provides an interdisciplinary approach to the analysis of the role(s) of language (whether written, spoken, or visual) in the construction of knowledge, identity, ideology, and power. Fairclough (1992: 110-12) proposes that the critical discourse analysis of a text should pass through the three stages of description, interpretation of the relationship between text and interaction, and explanation of the relationship between interaction and social context. In the analysis of which (and how) strategic narratives were discursively mobilized in the digital communication which constitute the data for the present study, among the identified outcomes are language use in the tripodal viewpoints of the assertion of authenticities, authoritativeness and validations. These fulfil the ideological functions of challenging the perceived primacy of orthodox medicine and projecting the efficacy of herbs and other forms of trado-medicine as well as confronting the perceived menace of post-colonialism and epistemic imperialism.

CONTEXTUALISING THE NARRATIVE: INDEXING NIGERIAN ONLINE TRADO-MEDICINE THROUGH CHIEFHERBALIST

Engebretsen (2023: 164) demonstrates how '[s]ocial media represent new arenas for health communication' with the space birthing a complex case of health communication. The interactivity and engagement therein are pivotal to trust-building particularly as there needs to be a careful balance between social closeness and professional distance on the part of the healthcare provider. For the herbal practitioner navigating the treacherous landscape of social networking platforms, especially Twitter in Nigeria, there is need to consciousness propagate information that users find helpful, and to diffuse the information in a relatable and manageable manner. The ChiefHerbalist for instance rarely uses more than a tweet for his individual messages, and his respective tweets are usually concise and direct to the point. This straight-to-the-point tactic as well as the feedback from users have positively helped in projecting herbal medicine in Nigeria. Kenechukwu, Ogah & Ifeanyichukwu (2022) acknowledge the popularity of herbal medicine in Nigeria, identifying that testimonials/referrals by users contributed to the widespread access even if the social media has equally been effective in the dispersal of information on the efficacy and availability of traditional herbal medicine. Therefore, while the ChiefHerbalist may be one out of many other Nigerian trado-medical practitioners and herbalists on social media, he represents the changing face of trado-medical advocacy in the country and indexes the appeal of the digital space to marginalised narratives and communities. The representativeness of the digital space also appeals to the online audience who give feedback even if it is unclear whether the herbs really work by themselves or if the users' belief in their efficacy contribute to their wellbeing after consumption.

Constructing Identities in ChiefHerbalist's Tweets

In discourse studies, identity is a 'multifaceted and dynamic construct, continuously shaped through language and social interaction. It involves an interplay between individual agency and social structures, emphasizing the complex and fluid nature of how people understand and present themselves' (Discourse Analyzer, 2024: 1). Kroskrity (1999: 111) also defines identity as 'the linguistic construction of membership in one or more social groups or categories'. In the selected tweets, three main identities stand out from the ChiefHerbalist's public engagements. These are the projection of nature and natural remedies for health challenges; contestation of orthodox medical practices and interventions; as well as provision of tips on healthy living. In the discussions that follow, representative tweets are used to exemplify and discuss the realisations of these identities alongside their attendant implications within the context of trado-medicine on the Nigerian digital space.

The first realisations involve the projection of nature and natural remedies for health challenges.

Tweet 1:

Bitter kola + Coconut water + Alligator pepper

Grate 6 bitter kola. Grind alligator pepper into powder and mix it with the grated bitter kola. Add coconut water to it and leave it there for 12 hours.

Drink this 30 minutes before the tournament.

Tweet 1 is focused on the provision of natural products that can be used as libido boosters by men. Sex and the handling of premature ejaculation is one of the most popular topics on the handle and this emanates from the masculinist tendencies which equate sexual performance as critical to sexual relations. In the Chiefherbalist's interventions, there is the underlying submission that many of the foods and medications consumed by Nigerians are impure and thus complicit in the 'poor' sexual performances of the men. By encouraging recourse to natural and indigenous products, he seeks a turnaround in the perception of his audience to the use of local medicinal products. In terms of language use, the tweet relies on a war or battle metaphor as sexual intercourse is relayed from the viewpoint of a 'tournament'. The use of directives initiated by verb choices like 'grate', 'grind', 'mix', 'add' and 'drink' contribute to the identity construction of the man preparing for a sex 'tournament'. The guidelines for preparing the concoction also attempt to mimic the prescription scenarios in orthodox medical practices – albeit without clear dosage for the consumer.

Tweet 2:

Don't throw away coconut peels (husk); it treats;

kidney stones
candidiasis
gonorrhoea
hypertension
diabetes
stomach ulcer
diarrhoea
Urinary Tract Infection

Boil the dried peels for 15 mins and drink it as tea twice daily. Nature heals.
#BackToEden

Tweet 2 is introduced by a directive and call to action 'Don't throw away coconut peels (husk)'. This is followed by a list of eight (8) ailments which the peels/husk are believed to heal. By specifying these ailments and providing the guideline on how the husk can be prepared to give succour, the Chiefherbalist again emphasises his identity as a nature lover and advocate of organic medication. He ends the tweet with 'Nature heals' and employs the hashtag #BackToEden to signal his devotion to embracing natural medicinal products. Eden in the context of course encodes the pristine and the untainted. In both Tweets 1 and 2, one further identifies the authoritativeness and assertiveness of the authenticity of the ChiefHerbalist's knowledge of herbal medicinal products. The tone across both tweets involve directives which seek to guide the consumers. This resonates with findings from Ogbogbo (2023) which also identifies directive speech acts as preponderant on Facebook-based posts by Traditional and Alternative Medicine (TAM) providers in Nigeria. Ogbogbo further submits that directives are used to 'project knowledge, give credence, and dissuade scepticism surrounding traditional and alternative medicine in Nigeria' (7).

Another noteworthy identity in the narrative is the ChiefHerbalist's sustained contestation of orthodox medical practices and his making of indigenous interventions. In situating himself and his practice as oppositional to contemporary orthodox medical activities, he constitutes identities which either downplay the efficacy of Western medicine or reveal the intent to help to reverse aftermaths of western medicine on health.

Tweet 3: ChiefHerbalist @HerbalistChief: You are angry because someone is drinking natural medicine and is seeing good results. It's obvious medical school didn't educate you, it indoctrinated you. Nature heals. 7:49 AM · Oct 26, 2024

In Tweet 3, the ChiefHerbalist provides a generic response to commenters on his tweets who seek to invalidate the efficacy of traditional and herbal medicine. The response is targeted at medical doctors and allied workers who, according to the tweet, are being 'indoctrinated' to shun local 'natural' medical interventions and to instead rely on foreign medicines in the healing of medical or health challenges. The use of the expression 'angry' signifies the oppositional framing of such 'indoctrinated' doctors especially when connected to the outcome of the ChiefHerbalist's patients who upon 'drinking natural medicine' are 'seeing good results'.

Figure 1. Tweet 4: Importing Medications

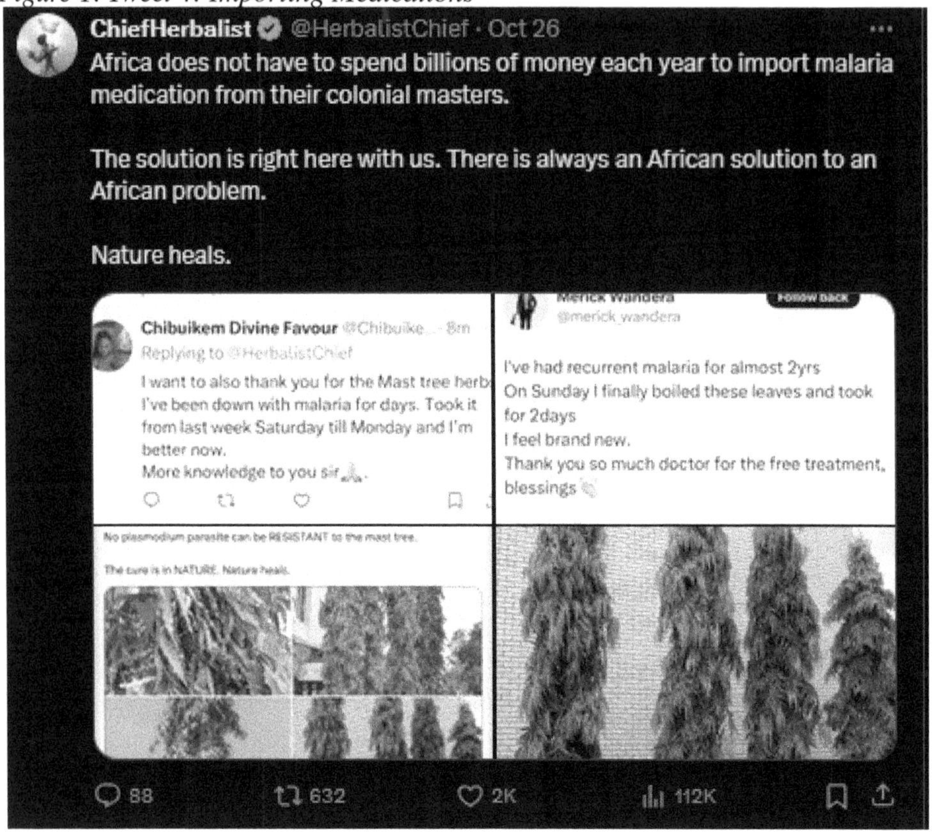

In Tweet 4, there is a two-fold identity construction where one relies on the contestation of orthodox medical practices and the other provides validations for the authenticity of the ChiefHerbalist's medicinal activities. In achieving the first identity of being a repository of indigenous medicinal knowledge, he contests the necessity of importing malaria medication annual particularly as this costs the African continent 'billions of money' when remedies are readily available around. By asserting that 'the solution is right here with us. There is always an African solution to an African problem', there is a counter-hegemonic narrative which depicts the African as being at the receiving end of foreign solutions which might not be in their best interest. His viewpoint is further strengthened by the reference to 'colonial masters', thus revealing a belief that coloniality and imperialism and their materialistic undershoots manifest and are perpetuated even in the medical context. The ChiefHerbalist therefore postures as being in possession of the 'African solution' with the validity predicated on being an African with the best interest of the continent at heart. Again, he ends the tweet with the curt statement 'Nature heals'. To provide validation for his posturing and submissions, his tweet is a quote of four images, two of which are feedbacks from commenters who have evidence of the reliability and efficacy of the ChiefHerbalist's prescriptions for malaria. The first commenter asserts that: 'I've been down with malaria for days. Took it from last week Saturday till Monday and I'm better now. More knowledge to you, Sir'. The second commenter states that: 'I've had recurrent malaria for almost 2yrs. On Sunday, I finally boiled these leaves and took for two days. I feel brand new. Thank you so much doctor for the free treatment. Blessings'. Both feedbacks acknowledge the functionality of the ChiefHerbalist's prescription as they attribute their wellness to it. While the first commenter reverentially signals their approval through the use of 'Sir' as well as through the optative 'more knowledge to you', the second commenter effusively refers to the ChiefHerbalist as 'doctor' and further appreciates him for providing 'free treatment'. 'Free treatment' here is critical particularly within the context of the ChiefHerbalist's initial tweet where reference is made to the 'billions of money' being spent across Africa on the purchase of malaria medicine. Therefore the reference to nature and the consequent altruism in making the knowledge of natural healing public help to strengthen the ChiefHerbalist's ideological construct.

Figure 2. Tweet 5: Tackling Outcomes of Contraceptives

Tweet 5 sustains the narrative which contests orthodox medical practices and seeks to replace those with indigenous natural substitutes. The focus in the tweet is on contraceptives used by females to prevent pregnancies. Oftentimes the use of the contraceptives come with complications which might endanger the lives of the users, pending the identification of the most appropriate contractive for the woman's body. In Tweet 5 therefore, the ChiefHerbalist introduces his opposition through a rhetorical question which asks if there is any woman who has taken contraceptives such as Postinor 2 and Lydia which have had the resultant negative effect of irregular or ceased (incorrectly rendered 'seized'). 'Worry not' constitutes a linguistic way of assuaging any ill feeling and helps the ChiefHerbalist to centre his intervention through the recommendation of the juice extracts from boiled unripe pawpaw. For him, taking the recommended '4 tablespoons twice daily for three weeks' is certainly enough to help any sufferer. He again signs out from the tweet with 'nature heals' to concretise his ideological stance.

Figure 3. Tweet 6: Combating Blood Pressure

Tweet 6 combines features from Tweets 4 and 5 in, first, contesting orthodox medical practices and, second, strengthening their submissions with evidential feedback from users which then serve as validation of his herbal medicinal practices. The tweet concerns high blood pressure readings which were resolved through the use of boiled groundnut shells. The contestation of orthodox medical practices is identifiable in the surprise reactions of medical doctors who wanted to know how the user had been able to lower the blood pressure reading to a level that was 'so good'. The ChiefHerbalist remarks the doctor's surprise at 'the magic', suggesting that since the doctors could not provide any empirical basis for the improvement – a mockery of the alleged strength of orthodox medical practice over traditional herbal practice – they had to request for more information on what had worked for their patient. In providing validation for the ChiefHerbalist's regimen, the tweep asserts that the 'groundnut recipe is underrated' in the treatment of high blood pressure, tacitly supporting the use of herbal and natural products as against medical practitioners' recommendations.

Asides contesting orthodox medical practices, the ChiefHerbalist sometimes ventilates perceived 'conspiracy theories' as a way of publicizing viewpoints which suggest intentional collusion to repress non-mainstream, often herbal, medical interventions. An interesting instance is in Tweet 7 where a 45 seconds video is embedded in the ChiefHerbalist's tweet. The interviewee in the video suggests that he has a cure for Acquired Immune Deficiency Syndrome (AIDS), an ailment which is very serious and often leads to fatality since it suppresses the human immune system. The possession and use of this cure, the interviewee alleges, puts him in an endangerment scenario where he might be hunted down by the 'powers that be'.

Figure 4. Tweet 7: The Herbal Doctor and Endangerment

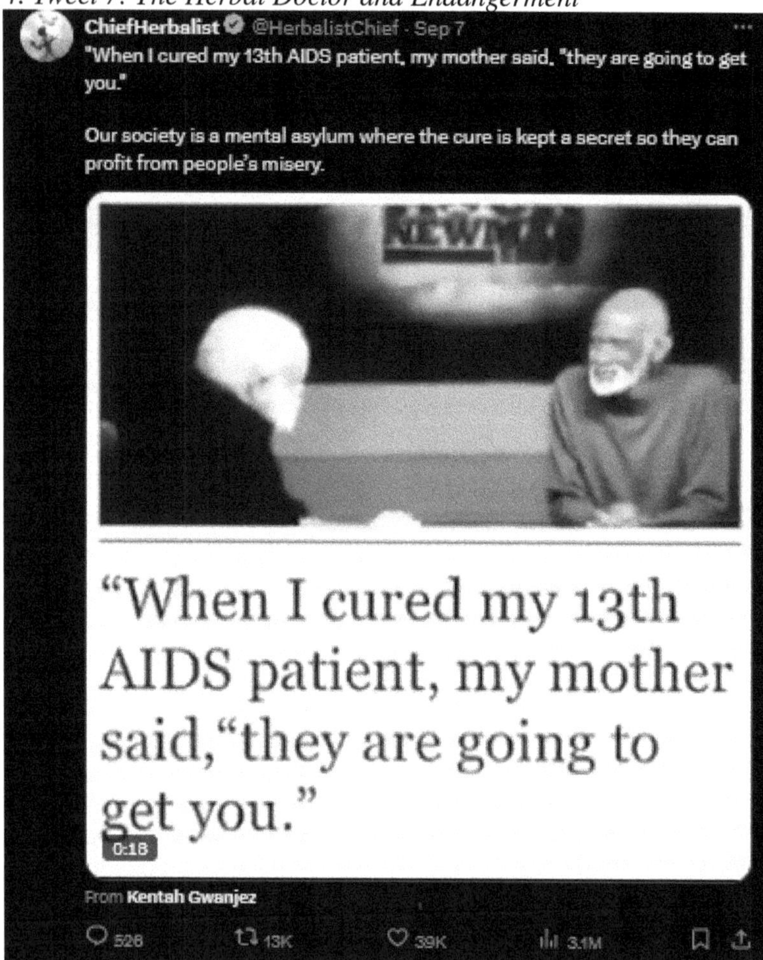

In Tweet 7, the ChiefHerbalist's emphasis from the interview however is where the interviewee submits that his mother alerted him that 'they are going to get you' when he cured his 13th AIDS patient. The elusive 'they' constitutes the focus of the ChiefHerbalist as he opines on the tweet viz: 'our society is a mental asylum where the cure is kept a secret so they can profit from people's misery'. Here, the suggestion is that financial gratification is at the heart of both the secretive guarding of orthodox medical practices and the delayed provision of access to curative medications. The consequence is that the elusive 'they' which might involve influential research hubs and pharmaceutical companies allegedly ensure that alternative medical pathways are discredited and blocked. This allegation lies at the centre of the video and the ChiefHerbalist's tweet since the interviewee claims that his provision of curative access to up to 13 AIDS patients drew the attention of detractors who 'profit from people's misery'.

One further encounters a contrastive presentation which foregrounds the ChiefHerbalist's altruistic self-representation and the presentation of these faceless 'they' who keep the cure a secret from public access. By posturing, alongside the interviewee, as rupturing the grip-hold of the elusive 'they', the ChiefHerbalist asserts an identity which challenges the society's framing as a 'mental asylum' since he is working hard to help in resolving the health challenges which repress the society. This self-portrayal consolidates the public image which he has established on the social media as regards his activities which are geared towards 'liberating' people from the shackles of the asylum. It also resonates with the focus in Tweet 8 where he wades into the Genetically Modified Organism (GMO) debate.

Figure 5. Tweet 8: GMOs and Health

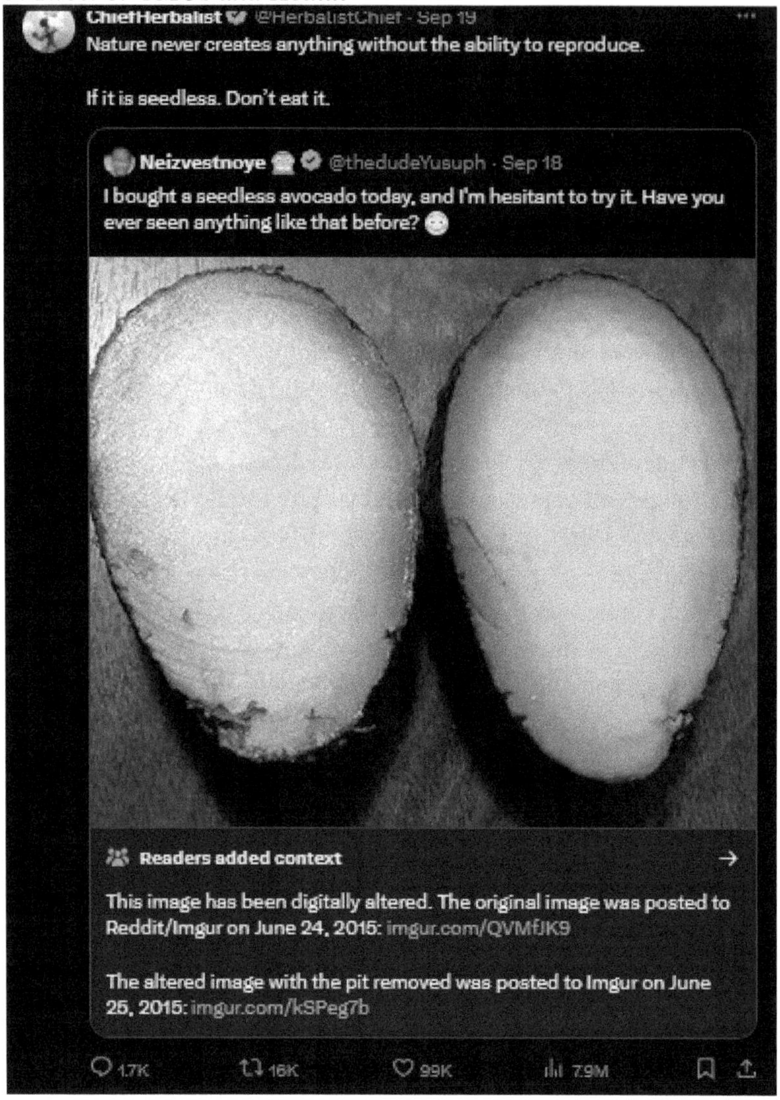

In Tweet 8, the ChiefHerbalist quotes a tweet by another user who reports buying a seedless avocado. The user continues by stating their fear or reluctance to eat the fruit while also attempting to elicit responses from other users through the rhetorical question: 'have you ever seen anything like that before?'. The ChiefHerbalist locates his reaction and subsequent admonition by asserting that 'Nature never creates anything without the ability to reproduce'. This submission implies that the seedless avocado is not natural since the absence of a seed means it is impossible for it to reproduce. He concludes his viewpoint through the admonition that 'if it is seedless. Don't eat it' as a way of stimulating consciousness on healthy living as well as expressing his opposition to genetically modified foods. His advocacy resonates with the contemporary seed politics and the bioethics of food production which has persisted in the face of the commercialisation of genetically modified products and which allegedly sustains food colonialism.

The third identitarian representation in the ChiefHerbalist's online activities involves giving tips on healthy living. By posturing as a nature advocate and herbal enthusiast, the ChiefHerbalist, apart from regularly providing herbal solutions to ailments and diseases, also constantly supplies informative tips and details to encourage his followers to maintain healthy living.

Figure 6. Tweet 9: Good food is good health

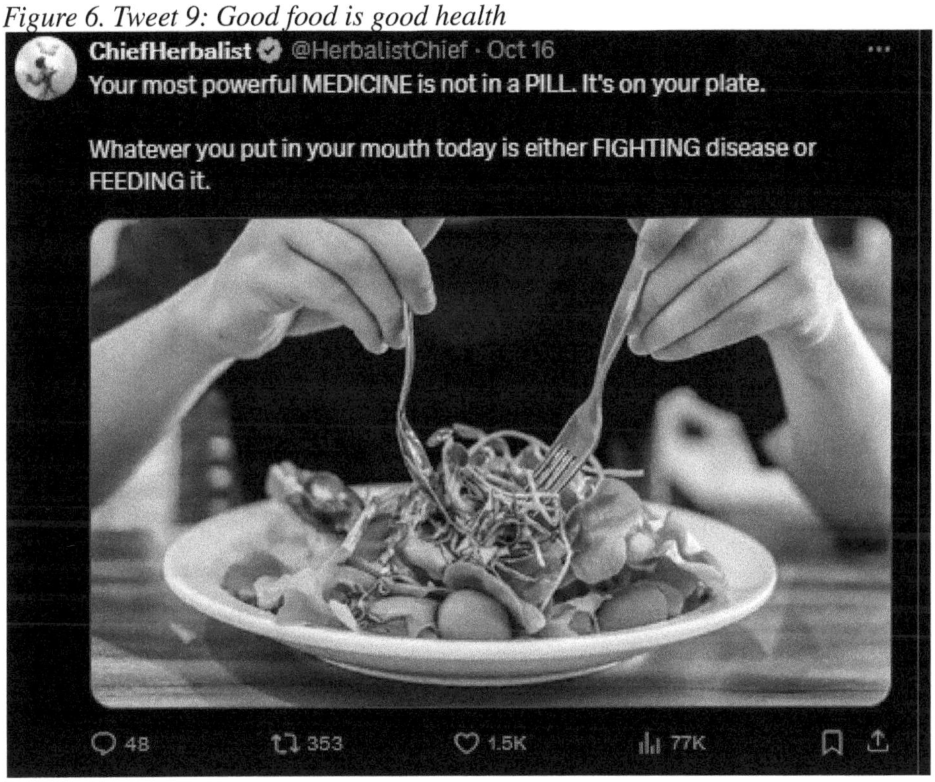

Consequently in Tweet 9, the ChiefHerbalist, relying on a creative play-on-words, admonishes his followers on the importance and necessity of dietary considerations. In a multimodal assemblage of text and image, he asserts the need to eat properly. Textually, he submits that: your most powerful medicine is not in a pill but it's in your plate. Whatever you put in your mouth today is either fighting disease or feeding it'. Through the alliterative expressions – pill vs plate and fighting vs feeding, he contextualises how food plays a critical role in human wellbeing and in determining whether one would be fighting disease or feeding it. The text also makes a contrastive equivalence between using pills or medications to aid wellbeing and eating good food which helps one from relying on pills. The graphic to which the text is attached is also intentionally selected since the food in the plate is made up of vegetables and fruits which are natural and unprocessed, and which the ChiefHerbalist usually recommends for his audience. This would be in contrast to the consumption of genetically modified foods as exemplified in the warnings in Tweet 8.

While there is the foregrounded underlying ideological stance that the information provided are free of charge and are to be to the benefit of the ChiefHerbalist's followers, he is also willing to monetize and commercialize his platform as identifiable in Tweet 10.

Figure 7. Tweet 10: Monetizing Visibility

In Tweet 10, the ChiefHerbalist reveals that apart from his social media presence on Twitter, he also has a web site where prospective customers may patronize him. The information was prompted by a request from a follower who wanted to know how to order 'this plant'. Through the response, the ChiefHerbalist also clarifies that beyond making purchases of plants/herbs, prospective customers also have the opportunity to 'book consultation, buy a book and request treatment for a condition'. Through this kind of platforming, the ChiefHerbalist depicts himself as an authority and as a professional with the requisite knowledge in his specialization.

IDEOLOGICAL REPRESENTATIONS IN CHIEFHERBALIST'S TWEETS

An obvious ideological narrative which undergirds the representations across the selected tweets is that of resistance and opposition. This plays out in the sustained criticism of orthodox medical practices as well as its practitioners who are represented in a 'us vs them' context – see Tweets 6 and 7. The criticism attempts to recast the recurring allegation against the use of herbal medicine, one which often denigrates the products as having not gone through sustained clinical assessment in order to authenticate their veracity of the claims that they can resolve or cure ailments. The trado-medicine proponents, however, point to the implicit biases which suggest that whatever is not captured or recommended from an orthodoxy prism is unacceptable, restating that such subliminal inhibitions and restrictions mean that the herbal interventions are always going to be discriminated against. This promotion of natural remedies challenges subsisting neocolonial structures around healthcare and features significantly in the narratives that seek to combat misinformation regarding the practice of trado-medicine while also drawing attention to the Western structures that perpetuate the anti-trado-medicine perception. In addition, and to combat this subsisting ideology, for the herbal or trado-medicine practitioners, what is important is for the ailments to be resolved or cured, and they strengthen their claims by justifying the naturalness of their curative products and by providing evidential feedbacks from users. Indeed, Wada *et al* (2019) record a growing curiosity about and use of herbal medicine even among Nigerian pharmacists, and remark this as evidential of the growing positivity and acceptance of traditional medicine in the country.

Another noteworthy ideology present in the narratives is that of altruism (free-giving of information) and providing access to health benefits of herbal medical products. For the ChiefHerbalist, the primal interest lies in providing natural health alternatives and proselytizing the advantages of indigenous medical epistemologies. His ideological viewpoint, hinged on altruism, harnesses the sense of communality which within Afrocentric circles is constructed as the prevailing socio-cultural orientation – pre-colonially – which puts the society before individual or personal gains. The sense of communality is therefore evoked in the ChiefHerbalist's activities on Twitter as he purposively furnishes the public useful information on how to use easily accessible herbal medicinal products. Prospective users, some of who return with feedback, are encouraged to explore the possibilities of holistic self-participatory care (Miron-Shatz, et al, 2013).

A further ideological realisation intersects challenging coloniality and imperialism while orchestrating epistemic visibility for locally-relevant knowledge. In confronting (post)colonial structures which pose imperialist threats to indigenous knowledge bases, the ChiefHerbalist foregrounds the possibilities of home-grown resources to not only meet specific local needs but to also compete favourably with foreign products. In achieving this, he reinvigorates the colonial narratives that repressed and 'othered' indigenous knowledge systems and labeled them as unscientific and primitive, and by asserting the vitality and efficacy of local herbal medicinal products, he gives traction and visibility to indigenous epistemologies.

CONCLUSION

Practitioners and users of traditional herbal medicine in Nigeria continue to navigate a terrain which considers herbal remedies as less prestigious and acceptable. In combating the discriminatory practices, these practitioners have appropriated the digital space through social networking platforms to build a community of followers who also find appeal, respite and cure in using indigenous herbal products. This study has interrogated one of such platforms on Twitter, now X. By examining the constructing of identities and ideologies on the ChiefHerbalist's Twitter handle, the role of language and its use was established within the tripodal viewpoints of the assertion of authenticities, authoritativeness and validations. The ChiefHerbalist authenticates his practices by revealing his knowledge within the context of discourse. He realises this by giving informative details through which his followers can resolve their health challenges. He achieves his authoritativeness in how he positions himself in the narrative such as presenting as a consultant and challenging submissions by orthodox medical doctors. Lastly, validations come from users who provide feedback on their use of the herbal medicinal information accessed through the ChiefHerbalist. These tripodal linguistic viewpoints coalesce in the identitarian constructs identified across the narrative, involving the projection of nature and natural remedies for health challenges; contestation of orthodox medical practices and interventions; as well as provision of tips on healthy living. The viewpoints also energise the ideological perspectives which are realized in the ideologies of resistance and opposition, of altruism and communality, and of anti-coloniality and anti-imperialism. A projected implication of the digital narratives and representations is that trado-medicine and the use will become more popular alongside orthodox medicine in Nigeria in the nearest future since patients are mostly simply interested in solutions to their health challenges regardless of how that is realised.

REFERENCES

Alotiby, A. (2021). The Impact of Media on Public Health Awareness Concerning the Use of Natural Remedies against the COVID-19 Outbreak in Saudi Arabia. *International Journal of General Medicine, 14*, 3145–3152. DOI: 10.2147/IJGM.S317348 PMID: 34239323

Analyzer, D. (2024). Identity in Discourse. Retrieved on 10 November, 2024 from https://discourseanalyzer.com/identity-in-discourse-analysis/

Batta, H. E. (2011). New Media and Archiving of Traditional Medicine Knowledge in Nigeria. *Annals of Humanities and Development Studies*, *2*(1), 21–32.

Batta, H. E. (2012). Press Coverage of Traditional Medical Practice in Nigeria. *Journal of Communication, 3*(2), 75–89. DOI: 10.1080/0976691X.2012.11884798

Chen, J., & Wang, Y. (2021). Social Media Use for Health Purposes: Systematic Review. *Journal of Medical Internet Research, 23*(5), e17917. DOI: 10.2196/17917 PMID: 33978589

Edo-Osagie, O., De La Iglesia, B., Lake, I., & Edeghere, O. (2020). A scoping review of the use of Twitter for public health research. *Computers in Biology and Medicine, 122*(103770), 103770. https://www.sciencedirect.com/science/article/pii/S0010482520301426. DOI: 10.1016/j.compbiomed.2020.103770 PMID: 32502758

Engebretsen, M. (2023). Communicating health advice on social media: A multimodal case study. *MedieKultur: Journal of Media and Communication Research, 39*(74), 164–184. DOI: 10.7146/mk.v39i74.134085

Fairclough, N. (1992). *Discourse and Social Change*. Polity Press.

Kenechukwu, S. A., Ogah, A., & Ifeanyichukwu, A. C. (2022). Health Information and Users' Beliefs: A Study of Herbal Medicine Users' Attitudes to Efficacy of Herbal Medicine. [IJCRH]. *International Journal of Current Research in the Humanities, 26*(1), 293–304. DOI: 10.4314/ijcrh.v26i1.17

Kroskrity, P. V. (1999). 'Identity'. *Journal of Linguistic Anthropology, 9*(1-2), 111–114. DOI: 10.1525/jlin.1999.9.1-2.111

Lam, C., Zhou, K., Loong, H., Chung, V., Ngan, C., & Cheung, Y. (2023). The Use of Traditional, Complementary, and Integrative Medicine in Cancer: Data-Mining Study of 1 Million Web-Based Posts from Health Forums and Social Media Platforms. *Journal of Medical Internet Research, 25*, e45408. DOI: 10.2196/45408 PMID: 37083752

Miron-Shatz, T., Hansen, M. M., Grajales, F. J., III, Martin-Sanchez, F., & Bamidis, P. D. (2013). Social Media for the Promotion of Holistic Self-Participatory Care: An Evidence Based Approach. IMIA Yearbook 2013 8: 162-168. https://repository.usfca.edu/cgi/viewcontent.cgi?article=1027&context=nursing_fac

Ng, J. Y., Verhoeff, N., & Steen, J. (2023). What are the ways in which social media is used in the context of complementary and alternative medicine in the health and medical scholarly literature? a scoping review. *BMC Complementary Medicine and Therapies*, *23*(1), 32. DOI: 10.1186/s12906-023-03856-6 PMID: 36732809

Ogbogbo, A. (2023). Directive Speech Acts as a Communication Strategy in the Social Media Posts of Traditional Medicine Providers in Southwest Nigeria. *NIU Journal of Humanities*, *8*(1), 7–16. DOI: 10.58709/niujhu.v8i1.1567

Ola, O., & Sedig, K. (2020). Understanding Discussions of Health Issues on Twitter: A Visual Analytic Study. *Online Journal of Public Health Informatics*, *12*(1), e2. DOI: 10.5210/ojphi.v12i1.10321 PMID: 32577151

Omoera, O. S., Awosola, R. K., Okhakhu, M. A., & Eregare, E. A. (2011). Seeking solutions: Of radio/ television advertisement and patients/non-patients' perception of traditional medicine in Edo State, Nigeria. *The International Journal of Research and Review*, *6*(1), 48–64.

Onanuga, P. (2020). Coming Out and Reaching Out: Linguistic Advocacy on Queer Nigerian Twitter. *Journal of African Cultural Studies*, *33*(4), 489–504. DOI: 10.1080/13696815.2020.1806799

Pavlova, A., & Berkers, P. (2020). Mental health discourse and social media: Which mechanisms of cultural power drive discourse on Twitter. *Social Science & Medicine*, *263*(1), 1–14. DOI: 10.1016/j.socscimed.2020.113250 PMID: 32862081

Pershad, Y., Hangge, P. T., Albadawi, H., & Oklu, R. (2018). Social Medicine: Twitter in Healthcare. *Journal of Clinical Medicine*, *7*(6), 121. DOI: 10.3390/jcm7060121 PMID: 29843360

Semotiuk, A. J., Semotiuk, N. L., & Ezcurra, E. (2015). The Eruption of Technology in Traditional Medicine: How Social Media Guides the Sale of Natural Plant Products in the Sonoran Desert Region. *Economic Botany*, *69*(4), 360–369. DOI: 10.1007/s12231-015-9327-6

Singhal, A., & Mago, V. (2023). Exploring How Healthcare Organizations Use Twitter: A Discourse Analysis. *Informatics (MDPI)*, *10*(3), 65. DOI: 10.3390/informatics10030065

Wada, A. S., Jatau, A. I., Bala, A. A., Haruna, A., Isa, A. M., Safiyya, A. S., & Sha'aban, A. (2019). Use of traditional medicines among pharmacists in Nigeria. *Complementary Therapies in Clinical Practice*, *35*(1), 53–56. DOI: 10.1016/j.ctcp.2019.01.014 PMID: 31003686

Wijayanti, R. P., Handayani, P. W., & Azzahro, F. (2022). Intention to seek health information on social media in Indonesia. *Procedia Computer Science*, *197*, 118–125. DOI: 10.1016/j.procs.2021.12.125

Wu, M., Wu, T., & Pei, Y. (2024). What Drives Health Information Exchange on Social Media? Social Media Affordances and Social Support Perspectives. *Health Communication*, *39*(13), 1–15. DOI: 10.1080/10410236.2024.2321408 PMID: 38477307

Chapter 4 Multimodality in Challenging Heteronormativity in Nigerian Pro-Queer Tweets

Olubunmi Funmi Oyebanji
University of Münster, Germany & Bamidele Olumilua University of Education, Science, and Technology, Ikere-Ekiti, Nigeria

ABSTRACT

Given the prevalence of heteronormativity in Africa, pro-queer advocacy is a topic that merits careful consideration. Social media gives queer visibility a platform because of the homophobia in Nigerian society. Linguistic research on how same-sex sexualities are portrayed in the media has focused on how heteronormativity is emphasised and how queer people linguistically create their identities on social media, with little consideration given to how pro-queer people have also used images to challenge heteronormativity. Drawing on Machin and Mayr's approach to Multimodal Critical Discourse Analysis, this study examines how Nigerian pro-LGBT people construct certain ideologies through texts and images on X in their bid to challenge heteronormativity. Data were purposively drawn using relevant hashtags. Findings revealed that visual metaphorisation and other semiotic elements foreground different ideologies including same-sex sexuality as natural, African and Nigerian as well as homonormativity and collective identity. The study shows the use of images and texts to resist homophobia.

DOI: 10.4018/979-8-3693-7934-9.ch004

INTRODUCTION

Heteronormativity is a term in sexuality studies that captures the imposition of certain beliefs about sexuality through the social and spatial organisation, as well as makes visible the processes that privilege heterosexual attractions and relationships as the default, normal, and superior form of sexuality (Barker, 2014; Robinson, 2016; Warner, 1991). The term heteronormativity was coined by a queer theorist, Michael Warner, to describe the social processes through which heterosexuality is treated as normal whilst treating those that fall outside this standard as abnormal and of lesser value (Warner, 1991). Browne and McCartan (2020) assert that everyday spaces are structured by societal expectations of what sexuality should be, and these hegemonic ideologies continue to play a key role in shaping society. In addition, these norms, practices, and societal expectations prevailing in public spaces constrain certain sexual expressions that diverge from the norm.

Social norms that regulate sexuality in sub-Saharan Africa continue to suppress non-normative gender and sexual expressions. Ideologies based on religion, the colonial legacy, and modern African popular culture and media enforce heteronormativity (Tamale, 2014). These normative structures frame non-heterosexual identities as deviant, unnatural, or foreign to African cultural values, reinforcing a climate of exclusion and discrimination. In addition to cultural and religious pressures, legal measures further entrench this marginalisation. For instance, the Nigerian government, in 2014, enacted the Same-Sex Marriage (Prohibition) Bill (SSMPA), which prohibits marriage or civil union by persons of the same sex, the solemnisation of such marriage in places of worship and the registration of homosexual clubs and societies. The law does not just forbid same-sex relations but also whoever abets or aids it in any way, effectively silencing activists, allies, and human rights organisations advocating for Lesbian gay, bisexual and transgender rights. The SSMPA exacerbates the vulnerability of queer individuals by legitimising state-sponsored homophobia, encouraging public hostility, and emboldening law enforcement agencies and vigilante groups to target and harass sexual minorities. Reports indicate that since its enactment, the law has been used not only to prosecute individuals suspected of engaging in same-sex relationships but also to intimidate journalists, activists, and organizations that provide support to LGBT communities.

The media plays a major role in the perpetuation of heteronormativity or otherwise. Since the portrayal of queer people in the mainstream media in Nigeria has been mainly negative (Oyebanji, 2023; Adegbola, 2022), social media provides LGBT people with the possibility of creating, publishing, and pushing forward their perspectives and narratives (Haimson, 2021; Georgiou, 2013; Mehra et al., 2004). Nigerian sexual minorities have taken to different social media platforms to build online communities, express themselves, relate with other members, find emotional and financial support, and construct their identities. Many queer individuals report several purposes for internet use including creating a positive identity, finding support, and fostering a sense of community (Craig & McInroy, 2014; Sells, 2013). Queer activism in online spaces is deeply shaped by digital communication practices. Digital platforms serve as spaces for identity assertion, resistance, and community-building, especially in contexts where LGBT rights are contested, such as in Nigeria. Online communication allows queer activists to navigate oppression, build community, and challenge dominant narratives. Specific social media campaigns that have significantly impacted Nigerian queer activism are #RepealSSMPA and #EndHomophobiaInNigeria campaigns. While digital platforms offer visibility, they also introduce risks, necessitating the development of innovative strategies for ensuring safety and maximisng impact.

X, formally Twitter, is one such social media platforms that have provided a safe place for the queer community. X is a widely used free social networking tool that allows people to share information in a real-time news feed (Mistry, 2011) by posting brief comments about their experiences and thoughts (Bristol et al., 2010). Public messages sent and received via X — or 'tweets' — are limited to 280 characters and can include links to blogs, web pages, images, videos and all other material online. Though social media provides safe spaces for sexual minorities, it is important to note that it also creates a favourable environment for anti-LGBT actors who discriminate against LGBT people (e.g., Galpin, 2022; Reichelmann et al., 2021). However, the focus of this study is on how Nigerian pro-queer individuals have used texts and images to challenge the heteronormativity that characterises the Nigerian context. This study, therefore, analyses texts and images in pro-queer tweets on X. The central assumption is that the images and their accompanying texts are ideological and consequently become useful in the battle against heteronormativity.

Multimodality refers to using multiple modes or methods of communication and expression within a single medium or across various platforms. In the context of constructing Nigerian queer identities on X, multimodality plays a significant role in how individuals express, negotiate, and solidify their identities. Nigerian queer activists often use stylized photography, captions, and hashtags to normalize queer existence (e.g., #QueerNigeria, #LGBTQIAfrica). An examination of the use of multimodal modes in queer activism allows for a richer, more nuanced representation of queer experiences and identities, which is particularly crucial in a socio-cultural landscape marked by significant discrimination and legal constraints. This study seeks to fill the gap in research on multimodal discourse analysis in the context of Nigerian pro-queer activism on X. Understanding the multimodal strategies used in online discourses is essential to grasping how ideologies are constructed and disseminated in a challenging environment. Therefore, important research questions for this study are:

1. What semiotic strategies do Nigerian pro-queer tweets and images foreground?
2. What are the ideological implications of these representations?

This study offers a nuanced and comprehensive understanding of the discourses surrounding Nigerian queer identities on X, and contributes significantly to the fields of queer studies, digital media, and critical discourse analysis.

LITERATURE REVIEW

Research on same-sex sexualities, especially from the linguistic perspective, is still far behind in the African context compared with what is obtainable in the Euro-American context. This may be due to the anti-queer sentiments that still pervade the African continent. In the Nigerian context, one of the few linguistic studies on same-sex sexualities is Gaudio (1997), which draws on various texts (interactional, literary, journalistic and cinematographic, among others) by and about the "yan daudu— Gay men," paying particular attention to how they use grammatical and rhetorical resources to claim, attribute, mitigate, or deny kinds of agency concerning sex and economic exchange. Adegbola (2022) and Amenaghawon & Ayantade (2019) show how Nigerian newspapers sometimes take the moralists' stance in their reports on same-sex sexualities, strategically supporting the anti-gay stance. Generally, linguistic-oriented research on same-sex sexualities in the Nigerian context has emphasised that heteronormativity pervades the Nigerian context.

Online activism is a dynamic social phenomenon characterised by the expression of contentious ideas, collective action, and the formation of shared identities, all facilitated through digital communication (Chon & Park, 2019). At its core, it involves leveraging online platforms to advance social and political causes, using technology as a tool for mobilization and advocacy (Murthy, 2018). Positioned at the crossroads of social context, political intent, and technological capability, online activism reflects the evolving relationship between digital media and contemporary movements for change (Gillan et al., 2008: 151). The internet has become a space for social movements, where meaning is co-constructed through hashtags such as #MeToo, #EndSARS, #QueerRights and other viral campaigns (Murthy, 2018) and has become a crucial tool for protests. The digital narratives mobilise communities, challenge dominant ideologies, and reshape socio-political discussions. Social media has emerged as a robust medium for discourses on sexuality, given its capacity to challenge mainstream narratives and empower personal views on self-expression. This study is, therefore, situated within the body of queer scholarship on digital communications with a particular emphasis on the role of visual social media platforms. This body of works has critiqued the various ways social media platforms provide opportunities for both emancipatory and exploitative (self-)representational practices (Dobson, 2015), particularly in the context of marginalised groups who have historically been subject to limited/stigmatised representations within 'mainstream' mediated culture (Talbot et al., 2020).

Much research has considered LGBT social media activism in various contexts (Auliainsani & Anjarningsih, 2023). In Western countries, social media activism has contributed significantly to legal and social progress for LGBT rights. The legalization of same-sex marriage in the United States, for example, was accompanied by widespread digital advocacy, with activists utilizing Twitter, Facebook, and Instagram to disseminate information, share personal narratives, and mobilize protests (Steinmetz, 2015). Similarly, in Europe, LGBT organizations have employed social media to counter misinformation and promote inclusive policies (Bosia & Weiss, 2013). LGBT social media activism in Africa and the Global South faces unique challenges, including state censorship, legal repression, and societal stigma. In Nigeria, where same-sex relationships are criminalized, activists use anonymous social media accounts and encrypted messaging apps to discuss issues and organize support networks (Ekine, 2013). Despite these restrictions, digital platforms provide a crucial alternative space for advocacy, allowing individuals to challenge homophobic narratives and engage in transnational solidarity (Tamale, 2014). The present study, therefore, considers how pro-queer people in Nigeria, within the affordances of X, construct emancipatory (self-)representational practices.

In Nigeria, the growing interest in queer expressions through online platforms is yet to receive significant research attention, although scholars (Endong, 2022; Oyebanji, 2022; Onanuga, 2022) have considered the influences of social media in queer activism. For instance, Endong (2022), using keyword searches on Twitter, investigates how gay Nigerians combat homophobia by using language for self-assertion. The study argues that in addition to harnessing agency through positive self-representation and ingroup affirmation, the digital discourses of Nigerian gay men recontextualise religion as a legitimising tool, transforming it into a site of affirmative struggle. Likewise, Oyebanji (2022) pays attention to the identities that sexual minorities construct for themselves on X in a bid to challenge homophobia. The focus of these studies is on the choice of words and grammatical structures in the construction of queer identities. These studies have illuminated the dynamics of queer discourse and digital activism within the Nigerian socio-cultural context, providing insights into how LGBT communities navigate and assert their identities in digital spaces, particularly where physical visibility is constrained.

Several studies (Lazar, 2017; Milani, 2013; Motchenbacher, 2020; Harmer, 2024) have explored the place of multimodality in queer activism. For instance, Motchenbacher (2020) explores a multimodal analysis of how signage is used to discursively construct sexual identity, gender, desire and sexual practices at Wilton

Drive. It is shown that homonormativity plays a central role in this context. Same-sex sexualities are discursively constructed as the local norm. At the same time, the signage on Wilton Drive represents predominantly gay male experiences, while heterosexuals, lesbians and other sexualities are discursively marginalised or even silenced. Also, particular versions of gay masculinity are privileged, namely ones that can be described as white, middle-class and focused on consumption, gay identity politics and non-romantic forms of sexual activity. Also, Harmer's (2024) study is a multimodal critical discourse analysis of Netflix's Heartstopper, written to understand its methods of representation and queer world creation. Through analysis of the ideology of heteronormativity, as it relates to masculinity, internalized homophobia, homophobia, and mental health, the study expands upon the significance of queer representation for queer audiences, heterosexual audiences, and producers of queer media. Lazar (2017) carried out a critical multimodal analysis of one of its official promotional videos of Pink Dot SG, a non-profit social movement launched by LGBTQ Singaporeans to rally support for Singapore's LGBTQ community, to show how a discourse of homonormative nationalism, or homonationalism, is constructed within it. Some significant insights are gained from these previous studies in considering multimodal modes used by pro-queer Nigerians.

Multimodality in queer activism on social media has also been considered in scholarship. For example. Kilic (2023) analyses the #HerYürüyüşümüzOnurYürüyüşü (Every Parade of Ours is a Pride Parade) hashtag campaign for 2019 Pride month in Turkey, expressing the collective frustration of the LGBT community against long-lasting bans for LGBT events and public assembly. Drawing on a digital ethnography from Twitter, the article explores networked resistances within the complexity of online and offline entanglements of activism during Istanbul Pride 2019. The multimodal discourse analysis focuses on the interactions of digital affordances and embodied street actions in rearticulating queer political places. In Nigeria, a few studies have analysed images relating to queer identities on social media, particularly Instagram (Onanuga, 2022, 2024). For instance, Onanuga (2022) analysed six purposively selected queer Nigerian Instagram handles and culled ten images while integrating the contextual affordances of hashtags and photo-tagging in showing how Instagram contributes to public queer discourses in Nigeria. Taking a cue from this and going beyond the previous studies, the present study considers the thematic patterns and ideologies underlying the multimodal modes used in challenging heteronormativity on X, a different social media platform from those of extant literature in Nigeria. A key assumption in this study is that pro-queer images by Nigerian X users are ideological and attempt to challenge societally and legally legitimised heteronormativity in Nigeria.

THEORETICAL FRAMEWORK

This study adopts a social semiotic approach to communication (Kress, 2010; Kress and van Leeuwen, 2006), using analytical tools advanced within the field of Multimodal Critical Discourse Analysis (MCDA) (Machin & Mayr, 2023; Ledin and Machin, 2018, 2020; Machin, 2013). In Multimodal Critical Discourse Analysis, the analysis and interpretation of language use are contextualised in conjunction with other semiotic resources, which are simultaneously used for the construction of meaning. For example, in addition to linguistic choices and their typographical instantiation on the printed page, multimodal analysis takes into account the functions and meaning of the visual images, together with the meaning arising from the integrated use of the two semiotic resources (O'Halloran, 2004: 1). This perspective stresses the need to explore communication and meaning-making as always being multimodal and continuously ask what interests and agency are at work in the construction of meaning. It emphasises paying attention to the relationship among semiotic materials, power and ideology (Ledin and Machin, 2020).

A key principle of MCDA is to analyse discourses in terms of the choices the language users deploy from a set of established semiotic resources. Semiotic resources have certain meaning potentials and can be applied for specific contexts and purposes, which means that discourses can be manipulated to sustain certain ideologies (Kress, 2010; Van Leeuwen, 2008). Research in Multimodal Critical Discourse Analysis pursued two main interdependent directions. The first involves screening the meaning-making potential of individual semiotic resources, and the second concentrates on theorising the interaction between different semiotic resources in multimodal communication (Djanov and Zhao, 2013: 2). Machin and Mayr's (2023) framework for multimodal critical discourse analysis focuses on how texts (including images) construct and reproduce social and cultural meanings. The framework argues that multimodal texts are shaped by underlying ideologies and power relations. I, therefore, find this approach relevant to understanding the underlying ideologies in the texts and images in Nigerian pro-queer tweets.

METHODOLOGY

Data for the study were drawn from X by identifying and tracking relevant hashtags such as #QueerNigerian, #LGBTQNigeria, #QueerRightsNG, #Endhomophobiain-Nigeria, #QueerNigeriaLivesMatter, #repealSSMPA and #LGBTfreedominNigeria. Tweets from influential Nigerian queer activists, organisations, and public figures, such as Bisi Alimi Foundation, were also searched. Fifteen relevant images were found, categorised and analysed according to different themes and ideologies. All the images categorised or put together were taken to be one figure. Data were subjected to a multimodal critical discourse analysis approach, integrating linguistic and visual resources. The method of data analysis was qualitative.

DATA ANALYSIS AND DISCUSSION

Some semiotic resources have been used to challenge heteronormativity in pro-queer tweets. The images and their accompanying texts teased out thematic and ideological delineations including same-sex sexuality is natural, the quest for visibility and equality, the historicity of same-sex sexuality in Africa, the Nigerianness of queer people and collectivity in resistance against homophobia. These are taken in turn for explication.

Same-sex sexuality is natural

Images in pro-queer tweets have shown both linguistic and non-linguistic means of portraying queer sexual identity as an orientation rather than a preference. Metaphors and other rhetorical tropes are used to shape understandings about the naturalness of same-sex practice. This is illustrated with different images and texts.

Figure 1. Same-sex sexuality is natural

The first image of Figure 1 portrays, in the background, a family, likely a heterosexual couple and their child. The family is depicted walking together, suggesting a sense of unity and togetherness. However, the adults are anonymised because their heads are not shown, suggesting that the text, which is the most obvious in the image, is directed to every parent or intending parent. Focusing on the image of the child and leaving the adults headless, the image emphasises the child's identity and individuality. This portrayal symbolises the importance of seeing LGBT individuals for who they are rather than defining them by societal norms or the expectations of others. The setting is a neutral, everyday environment, which could be interpreted as a symbol of normalcy or familiarity. The accompanying text further foregrounds the need to cater to a child irrespective of gender identity. The statement is given salience by being placed at the centre of the image with a colour that projects it, different from the background colour. The bold font and strong contrast emphasise the forceful nature of the message. The text is direct and prescriptive and has a command-like structure. The interrogative clause, *Not ready to love a gay child?* sets a conditional scenario, leading to the conclusion presented in the second part, *Then don't have kids*. The two clauses foreground the notion that children can be gay and that this is a natural, unchangeable aspcct of who they are. They imply that parents have a fundamental duty to love and accept their children regardless of their sexual orientation. The text suggests that the decision to have children should be contingent on the readiness to accept them fully, including their potential LGBT identity. It implicitly criticises those who would reject or fail to fully love their child based on sexual orientation, framing such attitudes as fundamentally incompatible with responsible parenthood. The directive, *don't have kids*, applies normative pressure, suggesting that if one cannot meet this moral standard, one should refrain from parenthood altogether. The text challenges heteronormative assumptions that all children are born straight and same-sex sexuality is a choice by foregrounding the possibility of having a gay child. In a context like Nigeria, where LGBT rights are highly contested, such a statement serves as a powerful advocacy tool within the context of LGBT rights and acceptance. This attempt confirms Oakley, Farr, and Scherer's (2016) identification of the influence of the family and cultural socialisation in the propagation of positive attitudes to diverse family structures.

Again, animal behaviours are used to depict the naturalness of same-sex practice in pro-queer tweets. The images are themselves directly denotative and are imbricated with more extensive interpretations – connotations– which come from an acknowledgement of the contextual peculiarities from which they are produced. The second and third images of Figure 1 were posted with the accompanying text:

> *10 animal species that show how being gay is natural Necking giraffes bottlenose dolphins Lions' allegiance Mounting bisons Macaques' one-night stands Albatross bonds Sex-crazed bonobos Swans walrus Sheeps.*

The second image shows same-sex giraffes' necking. This could ordinarily be two animals playing but pro-queer Nigerian writers have used it as an argumentation for the naturalness of same-sex practice. The depiction of such behaviours in animals is used to normalise same-sex interactions and relationships, suggesting that they are a natural part of life for many species, including humans. The image of same-sex giraffes engaging in behaviours typically associated with mating or bonding questions what is considered "normal" or "acceptable" in terms of relationships and sexual orientation. The image serves as a visual metaphor for same-sex relationships, emphasising the idea that love, affection, and bonding are not limited by gender or sexual orientation.

In the same vein, in the third image, same-sex lions are seen to be enjoying intimacy. Male lions are typically distinguished by their mane, a thick growth of hair around their neck and head. The mane varies in colour and fullness but is a primary indicator of a male lion. Though their genitalia cannot be seen in the picture, the mane gives them off as male. Male lions often form coalitions with other males, typically their brothers or other male relatives. These coalitions can include same-sex interactions for bonding or dominance (Lenin, 2023). Same-sex pairs may display bonding behaviours such as grooming, nuzzling, and lying close to each other. On rare occasions, same-sex pairs, especially males, may engage in mounting behaviours, which are often more about establishing dominance rather than sexual reproduction. For pro-queer individuals, when two male lions engage in bonding behaviours such as grooming, nuzzling, or even mounting, it demonstrates that same-sex interactions are a natural part of animal behaviour. This challenges the heteronormative assumption that heterosexual pairings are the only natural or acceptable form of relationships. If such behaviours are natural for lions, it suggests that diversity in sexual and social bonds is part of the natural world. Using images of same-sex animals' intimacy can subvert audience expectations and provoke thought about the fluidity and diversity of sexual behaviours. These images are incorporated into LGBT advocacy tweets to support narratives of diversity, inclusion, and the naturalness of same-sex relationships. While heteronormativity perceives queerness as a 'becoming' identity, pro-queer individuals assert their identities as 'being'. The representation of queerness as being natural further corroborates Onanuga (2022) on Nigerian pro-queer images on Instagram.

Homonormativity: Same-sex sexualities deserve equal rights as heterosexuals

The images of gay marriages foreground homonormativity, which emphasises how some parts of the LGBT community adopt norms, values, and behaviours traditionally associated with heterosexual relationships and family structures. Images of queer marriages used in Nigerian pro-queer tweets are often used to advocate marriage equality, emphasising that LGBT individuals should have the same legal rights to marry as heterosexual couples. This is grounded in the belief that marriage is a fundamental human right, and denying it to same-sex couples is a form of discrimination. Queer advocacy seeks to normalise LGBT relationships by showing images of queer intimacy and marriage in a society that often assumes heterosexuality as the default. These images challenge heteronormative structures that marginalise or render invisible queer identities. Pro-queer Nigerians have used images of gay and lesbian relationships in their tweets to challenge heteronormativity and convey messages about LGBT representation and acceptance.

Figure 2. the quest for queer visibility and equality

The first image of Figure 2 depicts two young men dressed in formal attire, sharing a kiss. This material action of kissing challenges traditional heteronormative portrayals of romantic affection, especially in formal or public settings, promoting the acceptance of same-sex love as equally valid and meaningful. The background shows a serene, nature-filled environment, possibly a garden or park with a small waterfall and rocks. The peaceful setting contrasts with the potentially controversial nature of the image in a heteronormative context as Nigeria, normalising and naturalising same-sex affection. Both individuals are wearing suits and ties, suggesting a formal occasion such as a wedding, or formal event. This attire is traditionally associated with significant life events, emphasising that same-sex relationships are equally significant and worthy of celebration. This representation can be seen as a claim for inclusion and acceptance in all social and cultural rituals, such as weddings, which have traditionally been heteronormative spaces. The interpersonal components of the image reveal the intimate and tender body language of the individuals, with one individual gently touching the other's face, highlighting affection and emotional connection. This visual portrayal of love and tenderness counters stereotypes and biases about same-sex relationships being purely sexual or less emotionally significant. The material act of kissing is a powerful symbol of love, intimacy, and commitment. The image challenges stereotypes by presenting a same-sex couple in a context that is typically associated with heterosexual couples. It disrupts the traditional narrative and broadens the understanding of romantic relationships.

Again, the second image is that of two women, dressed in wedding attire, signifying that they are newlyweds. This image directly challenges the traditional heterosexual portrayal of marriage by presenting a same-sex couple. Like in the first image, the act of kissing reinforces the legitimacy and normality of same-sex relationships. The background also shows a natural setting with greenery and sunlight, creating a serene and joyous atmosphere that complements the celebratory nature of the wedding. The sign held by one of the brides foregrounds the message of their recent marriage, making it clear and unequivocal. The wedding dresses worn by both women symbolise the institution of marriage. wearing these dresses asserts their right to participate in this institution on equal footing with heterosexual couples. The affectionate and tender pose of the brides normalises same-sex affection, presenting it as a natural and beautiful expression of love. The image directly challenges heteronormative assumptions about marriage and relationships in the Nigerian context.

However, the third image emphasises the visibility of same-sex relations taking a different approach. The persons in the first and second pictures are white. The third image features two black men standing close to each other, with one gently holding the other's chin. At the interpersonal level, this physical interaction can be interpreted as an expression of affection or intimacy, challenging conventional norms of male behaviour. The material action of touching is also symbolic. The man being touched appears relaxed, while the man touching him has a focused expression, indicating a level of comfort and familiarity between them. The background, which includes potted plants and what appears to be a building entrance, creates an ambiguous indoor-outdoor setting, suggesting a casual or everyday context. Both men are dressed in traditional clothing typically signifying Nigeria and Yoruba identity. This attire is important in contextualising their relationship within cultural norms and expectations. The traditional accessories, such as caps and clothes, further emphasise their cultural heritage and traditional roles. It shows that expressions of affection and non-heteronormative behaviour can exist within traditional and cultural frameworks as they exist in the West. By integrating traditional elements, the image suggests that same-sex affection and bonding are not incompatible with cultural heritage, challenging the notion that queer identities are a Western or modern phenomenon. The act of one man holding the other's chin is a tender gesture that conveys affection and care. This challenges traditional views on male interactions, which often discourage physical expressions of affection between men. Their close physical proximity suggests intimacy and a strong bond, which further challenges heteronormative expectations of male friendship and interaction. Showing men in traditional attire expressing affection redefines cultural masculinity to include emotional and physical expressions of love and care. Generally, the use of images of gay marriages in the tweets of Nigerian pro-queer tweeters is a strategic tool in political advocacy. The queer advocates aim to build broader support for legal reforms that recognise and protect the rights of queer individuals, including the right to marry by normalising these relationships in the public eye. Visually representing same-sex affection in a positive and normalised context contributes to increased visibility and representation of LGBT individuals. The images can have a powerful impact on viewers, promoting empathy, acceptance, and a shift in societal attitudes. Such depiction foregrounds homonormativity, and calls for inclusivity and equal recognition of love, regardless of gender.

Same-sex sexuality is not un-African

Using semiotic elements, pro-queer people have countered the notion that same-sex relations are un-African. They have used African-related signs and history as discursive strategies to emphasise the Africanness of same-sex practices. Images are used to show that same-sex relationships have existed in various African cultures throughout history. This demonstrates that such relationships are not a modern invention but have been a part of the African experience for centuries. An example of such images is shown below.

Figure 3. Same-sex sexualities are not unAfrican

Figure 3 depicts two black men wearing traditional, possibly African, costumes and accessories, including headdresses, beads, and body paint. Their traditional adornments signify a cultural and ethnic identity, ideologically suggesting an African identity. The men are engaged in a kiss, embracing each other. This gesture again denotes intimacy. The traditional attire juxtaposed with the intimate pose highlights the intersection of cultural identity and sexual orientation. It challenges the stereotype that African traditions are incompatible with LGBT identities, promoting the idea that one can embrace both their cultural heritage and their sexual identity. The text on the image reads: *One day we won't come out of the closet. We will just say we are in love and that will be the only thing that matters. won't come out of the closet* refers to the act of revealing one's LGBT identity. This suggests a future where such declarations are unnecessary because acceptance and normalisation of same-sex love would be prevalent, as shown by the modal verb 'will'. The epistemic 'will' suggests the optimism of queer identities about the recognition of their rights in Africa in the future. There is also the use of the collectivising pronoun 'we', suggesting that it is a collective struggle for the recognition of queer rights in Africa. The text emphasises love as the central theme, proposing that love should be the only concern, rather than societal labels or judgments. The combination of the visual and verbal elements constructs a narrative of acceptance and normalisation of same-sex love within cultural contexts that might traditionally be seen as opposed to it. It calls for a future where LGBT identities are not marginalised or sensationalised but are simply accepted as part of the human experience. The image and accompanying text can be viewed as an act of resistance against heteronormativity and the marginalisation of LGBT individuals. The image also serves to reclaim and validate the history of same-sex practices in Africa. The image promotes an inclusive understanding of African history that acknowledges the diversity of sexual and gender identities. and empowers LGBT individuals by providing historical validation and cultural representation, fostering a sense of pride and belonging. This kind of image is considered necessary since some scholars have argued that same-sex practice is non-existent among indigenous Africans and that the concept itself is abhorrent (Dlamini, 2006). Conversely, this form of representation confirms numerous studies that have shown that same-sex practices existed in pre-colonial Africa (Gaudio 2009; Ajibade 2013). The representation of the presence of same-sex practices in pre-colonial Africa meets the objection that it is a Western import.

In various African countries, such as Tanzania, activists like Mufasa report increased persecution, including arrests and harassment. In Kenya and Uganda, individuals such as Stephen Okwany and Trinah Kakyo utilize the arts to shift societal perceptions. These efforts aim to dismantle the narrative that same-sex sexuality is a Western construct, highlighting its acceptance in many pre-colonial African cultures. Despite progress in some regions, homophobia remains a political tool to divert attention from economic issues, posing significant challenges for activists striving to protect LGBT rights and promote tolerance.

Queer identities are Nigerians

A study of the images that accompany some pro-queer tweets shows that pro-queer tweeter also constructs their identities as Nigerians. Queer identities in Nigeria identify as Nigerians because nationality, culture, and identity are deeply interconnected. Despite the challenges and discrimination faced by LGBT individuals in Nigeria, their Nigerian identity remains a significant part of who they are. When queer individuals openly identify as both queer and Nigerian, they challenge the stereotype that being queer is "un-African" or incompatible with Nigerian culture. This dual identification is an act of resistance against cultural erasure and a statement that queerness exists within Nigerian society. They seek to create a more inclusive society where their identities are recognised and respected. Identifying as Nigerian, queer individuals assert their rights to citizenship and the legal protections that should accompany it. Examples of how multimodality has been used to achieve this are found below.

Figure 4. The Nigerianness of Queer Identities

The first image of Figure 4 shows two people, a man and a woman, standing in front of a painted wall. They are both smiling and making a peace sign gesture. Their body language conveys a sense of camaraderie and happiness. The woman wears the uniform of the Nigerian National Youth Service Corps (NYSC), which gives her off as a Nigerian youth serving the nation, while the man also wears military attire. The two attires suggest strength and their ability to fight and resist whatever is not right- in this case, homophobia, indicated by the background. The background features a blue-painted wall with graffiti that reads "QUEER LIVES MATTER." The rainbow symbol, often associated with LGBT pride, is prominently displayed above the word "QUEER." The text "QUEER LIVES MATTER" is a clear reference to the Black Lives Matter movement, adapted to emphasise the importance of LGBT lives. The rainbow symbol above the word "QUEER" strengthens the association with LGBT pride and rights. The graffiti and the individuals in the image collectively convey the Nigerianness of queer identities and a message of solidarity and support for the LGBT community. The act of painting this graffiti in a public space is an act of resistance against societal norms that may marginalise LGBT individuals. It challenges heteronormative power structures by publicly declaring the importance and validity of queer lives. The presence of two individuals, presumably allies or members of the LGBT community wearing symbolic Nigerian uniforms associated with the military, reinforces a sense of community and mutual support. The graffiti provides visibility to the LGBT cause, making it a part of the public discourse. The image, through its visual and verbal elements, constructs a powerful discourse advocating for the recognition and importance of LGBT lives in Nigeria. The first and the second images foreground the Nigerianness of the individuals in the images.

The third and the fourth images of Figure 4 are similar in their connection of the LGBT identities with the Nigerian identity. The image of Nigeria overlaid with the rainbow flag is a powerful visual symbol that has circulated widely online and in activist circles. The overlay of the rainbow flag onto Nigeria's map suggests a claim to national territory and a desire for inclusion within the broader Nigerian identity. However, the overlay also implies a challenge to the dominant heteronormative understanding of Nigerian citizenship. The placement of the rainbow flag over the Nigerian flag can be interpreted as a symbolic act of reclamation, suggesting that LGBT individuals are an integral part of the nation, despite facing discrimination and marginalisation. Associating the rainbow colours with the Nigerian map suggests that LGBT individuals are not foreign or deviant but are legitimate members of Nigerian society. The image constructs a new identity for LGBT Nigerians, one that is both national and queer. This identity challenges the binary opposition between heterosexuality and homosexuality, suggesting that individuals can be both Nigerian and LGBT without compromising their national identity.

The fourth image features two flags: the Nigerian national flag and the LGBT pride flag. The Nigerian flag is green and white, symbolising the nation's identity and sovereignty. The LGBT pride flag features six colours: red, orange, yellow, green, blue, and purple, representing diversity and pride within the LGBT community. The flags are crossed, which traditionally signifies unity, solidarity, or partnership. The crossing of the flags symbolises a desire for a connection or alliance between Nigerian national identity and LGBT identity. There is no textual element in this image. The focus is entirely on the visual symbolism of the flags. The absence of text directs attention to the visual rhetoric and the implied meanings derived from the flags themselves. The juxtaposition of the Nigerian flag with the LGBT pride flag can be seen as a statement advocating for the recognition and inclusion of LGBT individuals within Nigerian society. This image challenges the notion that national identity and LGBT identity are mutually exclusive, promoting the idea that one can be both proudly Nigerian and proudly LGBT. Given the socio-political context of Nigeria, where LGBT rights are often contested and LGBT individuals face legal and social challenges, the image serves as a form of resistance. It challenges invisibility and marginalisation, advocating for the acknowledgement and acceptance of LGBT identities within Nigerian society. This agrees with Lazar's (2017) findings on the nexus of non-normative gender/sexual and national identities within Singapore's contemporary LGBT movement. The construction of queer identities as Nigerians further corroborates Oyebanji's (2022) study on the use of language by queer Nigerians in the construction of their identities on X.

LGBT is a community/humanitarianism

Initially, LGBT individuals were often seen as isolated and deviant. However, as social movements gained momentum, LGBT individuals began to identify with one another, forming a sense of community and shared identity. Humanitarianism, often associated with the protection of human rights and the relief of suffering, has played a significant role in advocating for LGBT rights

Figure 5. Humanitarianism within the queer community

At the representational level, the first image of Figure 5 shows a person holding a megaphone with a sign that reads, *I'm GAY, NIGERIAN & REAL!* The person's face is covered with an emoji, which conveys anonymity but also a sense of positive emotion. The sign held by the person is a powerful symbol of identity and assertion. It is a declarative statement and emphatic, especially shown by the use of capitalization of the words, *gay*, *Nigerian* and *real* and the exclamatory mark. It represents visibility and pride in one's sexual orientation and nationality. The use of colours is minimal but effective. The central figure with the megaphone and sign is the most salient feature due to its size, position, and contrasting colours. The bright yellow of the emoji and the text on the sign stand out against the dark background, drawing attention to the message. *Feed, Clothe and Support Queer Nigerians* explicitly states the purpose of the campaign, focusing on basic needs and support for a marginalised group. *$2,000 to reach goal* provides a clear, quantifiable objective, making it easy for potential donors to understand what is needed. The campaign foregrounds the humanitarianism ideology within the queer community. At the interaction level, the image appears to be taken from a close-up perspective, creating a sense of intimacy and urgency. It feels personal and direct, inviting the viewer to connect with the cause. The use of the emoji instead of a human face creates a universal, approachable persona, possibly lowering barriers to empathy and identification. The megaphone signifies a call to action and amplifies the urgency of the message. The central image and text message are the focal points, ensuring they capture the viewer's attention This draws immediate attention to the core message of the campaign. The use of a dark background with bright text and image elements creates a strong visual contrast, enhancing the readability and impact of the message. The campaign promotes visibility and support for queer Nigerians, challenging societal norms and stigmas. The explicit mention of being "GAY, NIGERIAN & REAL!" counters narratives that often marginalize or invalidate queer identities. The use of an emoji to cover the person's face suggests concerns about safety and privacy, reflecting the potential dangers faced by queer individuals in certain contexts. This juxtaposition of anonymity with a bold declaration highlights the tension between visibility and safety Participants' emphasis on the culture being a safe space and "system of mutual aid" was consistent with past research suggesting those in the LGBT community feel a sense of duty to support one another (Adams et al., 2014; Fraser, 2008). Social support specific to one's in-group could foster a sense of connection and self-worth, thereby contributing to psychological health and resilience (Kwon, 2013; Meyer, 2015; Riggle et al., 2008).

The second image of Figure 5, at the representation level, predominantly features text, with no accompanying images or graphics. This design choice emphasises the informational and serious nature of the message. The text is presented in a simple, bold font, using black for most of the text with one instance of red-orange for emphasis. The colour scheme ensures high readability and draws attention to critical parts of the message. The text provides information on how to report human rights violations based on sexual orientation or gender identity or expression. It includes toll-free and paralegal helpline numbers and the operating hours for each line. The provision of multiple helpline numbers, including a toll-free option and 24-hour paralegal lines, indicates an understanding of the need for accessibility and confidentiality for individuals reporting sensitive issues. The image communicates a message of empowerment and support for individuals facing human rights violations based on their sexual orientation or gender identity. This finding corroborates Onanuga (2022).

Collective action and identity

Collective queer action and identity are how LGBT individuals come together to advocate for their rights, challenge societal norms, and create a sense of belonging. As LGBT individuals in Nigeria continue to face discrimination, violence, and legal challenges, they have employed a variety of strategies, including protests, demonstrations, lobbying, and social media campaigns. The inclusivist ideology of collective queer action and identity is shown by their group's protest against homophobia.

Figure 6. Collective queer action and identity

The first image of Figure 6 above depicts four individuals, three of whom are wearing pink shirts, and one wearing a rainbow-coloured tank top. The rainbow-coloured attire is symbolic, representing LGBTQ+ pride. Each person in the image holds a sign with text, and one individual holds a flag with pink, blue, and white stripes, representing the transgender pride flag. The texts on the placards three of the individuals are holding, all capitalised include: *'THE SCAPEGOATING OF MINORITIES CAN'T KEEP IMPERIALIST COLLABORATORS IN POWER FOREVER.', 'WE THE PEOPLE. QUEER, UNSUBDUED, DEMAND OUR RIGHTS AND FREEDOMS. #RepealSSMPA', 'RESPECT LGBTQ* HUMAN DIGNITY #RepealSSMPA #ResistTheStatusQuo'*. The texts emphasise themes of resistance, human rights, dignity, and a call to action against oppressive practices. The use of "WE THE PEOPLE" and the presence of multiple individuals signify a collective identity and community solidarity. It emphasises that the fight for rights and dignity is a shared endeavour. The individuals are standing close together, symbolizing solidarity and unity within the LGBT community. This close grouping enhances the message of collective action. Most of the individuals are looking directly at the camera, creating a direct and engaging interaction with the viewer. This gaze can be interpreted as a call for attention and acknowledgement of their cause. The individuals and their signs are positioned in the foreground, making them the focal point of the image. The background is a natural setting, possibly a park, which provides a calm contrast to the strong, assertive messages on the signs. The image is balanced with two individuals on each side, and the central figures holding the signs high. This symmetry reinforces the organised and unified stance of the group. The pink shirts and rainbow tank top stand out against the green background, ensuring the individuals and their messages are immediately noticeable.

The second image of Figure 6 is constructed as a collage, emphasising collective action and solidarity. It reinforces the idea of community and shared struggles, and that every individual has a voice. The handwritten signs and the faces of individuals are the most salient elements, drawing attention to both the human and textual messages. The participants are holding hand-written signs, a simple, yet, effective form of protest often used in grassroots movements. This visual element speaks to the authenticity and personal commitment of the individuals. The individuals appear to be of different genders and identities, representing the diversity within the queer community. This challenges stereotypes and shows the multifaceted nature of queerness. The individuals in the collage have varied facial expressions, ranging from neutral to slightly assertive. These expressions can be seen as representing both resilience and a call for recognition. The direct gaze of many participants can be interpreted as an appeal for attention, creating a direct connection between the subjects and the audience. The arrangement of individuals and signs creates a cohesive message when read together, symbolising unity and collective struggle. The layout, where the message is spread across individual parts but forms a complete sentence when combined, suggests that individual voices come together to form a larger narrative or demand. The text in the image reads: "*Remember that queer lives still matter in 2021 and every other year. Period.*" Words like "queer lives," "matter," and "period" carry significant socio-political weight, especially in the context of the ongoing LGBT rights struggles. The word "still" emphasises the continuity and ongoing relevance of the message, possibly indicating a reaction against societal disregard or invisibility. "Queer lives still matter" echoes the "Black Lives Matter" movement, suggesting a connection between queer activism and broader social justice movements. Generally, in pro-queer tweets, images humanise the abstract concept of 'gay rights' by showing real people, while also showing that they are a community interested in the well-being of members of their community. As seen in Figure 6, visual collectivisation is realised by plurality or representation of images of groups of people shown to be pursuing a similar goal (Osisanwo, 2020).

CONCLUSION

Having considered multimodality in Nigerian pro-queer tweets on X, this study has shown that non-normative identities and their allies metaphorise animals' behaviours, and the image of an anonymous child as well as texts to depict the naturalness of same-sex practices as an ideology that contradicts the notion that same-sex practice is a choice. Images of queer intimacy and marriage foreground homonormativity. These images challenge heteronormative structures that marginalise or render invisible queer identities. Underlying homonormativity as an ideology is the view that queer identities should enjoy equal rights to marriage as heterosexuals. The push for same-sex marriage can be seen as homonormative because it seeks inclusion in an institution that upholds traditional values of relationships rather than radically rethinking relationship forms or critiquing marriage as an institution. Again, pro-queer individuals challenge the ideology that same-sex practice is 'un-African' using images accentuated with humans and elements depicting African culture or descent. For them, same-sex practice is African. Queer identities also emphasise their Nigerianness with semiotic elements representative of Nigeria. These images challenge the notion that the Nigerian national identity and LGBT identity are mutually exclusive, promoting the idea that one can be both proudly Nigerian and proudly LGBT. Given the socio-political context of Nigeria, where LGBT rights are often contested and LGBT individuals face legal and social challenges, the images serve as a form of resistance to invisibility and marginalisation, advocating the acknowledgement and acceptance of queer identities within Nigerian society. Pro-queer images also emphasise humanitarianism as an ideology of the group, while images of real humans in groups foreground the ideology of collective identity in queer advocacy. However, the use of personal photographs in Nigerian queer advocacy on X disagrees with Onanuga's (2022) multimodal study of Nigerian pro-queer images on Instagram.

Considering the use of semiotic resources in Nigerian queer activism in the digital media, the Nigerian queer community recognises the role these resources can play in expressing their ideologies. X, as an example of general social media networking platforms, serves as an alternative pathway for the Nigerian queer community to stimulate public participation and debate (Dahlgren, 2005). Through their digitised "reaching out", the Nigerian queer community on Twitter harnesses "the online media landscape … as an arena of struggle" (Larsson, 2014: 88). This echoes Carpentier's (2011: 147) argument that, for marginalised groups to access power, they manipulate the media space by "turning to alternative media" in order to combat the restrictiveness of conventional media platforms.

REFERENCES

Adams, J., Braun, V., & McCreanor, T. (2014). "Aren't labels for pickle jars, not people"? Negotiating identity and community in talk about "being gay.". *American Journal of Men's Health*, *8*(6), 457–469. DOI: 10.1177/1557988313518800 PMID: 24414032

Adegbola, O. F. (2022). The discursive construction of gay people in news reports of selected Nigerian newspapers. *Journal of Language and Sexuality*, *11*(1), 80–100. DOI: 10.1075/jls.19009.ade

Ajibade, G. O. (2013). Same-Sex Relationships in Yorùbá Culture and Orature. *Journal of Homosexuality*, *60*(7), 965–983. DOI: 10.1080/00918369.2013.774876 PMID: 23808346

Amenaghawon, F., & Ayantade, J. (2019). Homosexuality Framing by a Nigerian Newspaper. *Covenant Journal of Communication*, *6*(2), 72–88.

Auliainsani, Elda & Anjarningsih, Harwintha. (2023). Ideological Ambivalence: A Social Semiotic Multimodal Analysis of LGBT Activism in @WhatIsUpIndonesia. *K@ta: a Biannual Publication on the Study of Language and Literature* 25: 65-80. DOI: .DOI: 10.9744/kata.25.2.65-80

Barker, M. (2014). Anarchism and sexuality: Ethics, relationship, and power by Jamie Heckert and Richard Cleminson. *Psychology and Sexuality*, *5*(2), 186–190. DOI: 10.1080/19419899.2012.695873

Bosia, M. J., & Weiss, M. L. (2013). *Global Homophobia: States, Movements, and the Politics of Oppression*. University of Illinois Press.

Bristol, T. J., Billings, D. M., & Kowalski, K. (2010). Twitter: Consider the possibilities for continuing nursing education. *Journal of Continuing Education in Nursing*, *41*(5), 199–200. DOI: 10.3928/00220124-20100423-09 PMID: 20481418

Browne, K., & McCartan, A. (2020). Sexuality and queer geographies.

Carpentier, N. (2011). *Media and Participation: A Site of Ideological-Democratic Struggle*. Intellect. DOI: 10.26530/OAPEN_606390

Chon, M. G., & Park, H. (2019, March 19). Social media activism in the digital age: Testing an integrative model of activism on contentious issues. *Journalism & Mass Communication Quarterly*, *97*(1), 72–97. DOI: 10.1177/1077699019835896

Craig, S. L., & McInroy, L. (2014). You can form a part of yourself online: The influence of new media on identity development and coming out for LGBTQ youth. *Journal of Gay & Lesbian Mental Health, 18*(1), 95–109. DOI: 10.1080/19359705.2013.777007

Dahlgren, P. (2005). The Internet, Public Spheres, and Political Communication: Dispersion and Deliberation. *Political Communication, 22*(2), 147–162. DOI: 10.1080/10584600590933160

Dlamini, B. (2006). Homosexuality in the African context. *Agenda (Durban, South Africa), 20*(67), 128–136. DOI: 10.1080/10130950.2006.9674706

Dobson, A. S. (2015). *Postfeminist Digital Cultures: Femininity, Social Media, and Self Representation*. Palgrave Macmillan. DOI: 10.1057/9781137404206

Ekine, S. (2013). *Queer African Reader*. Pambazuka Press.

Emilia, D. Zhao S. (2013). *Critical Multimodal Studies of Popular Culture*. London: Routledge.

Endong, F. (2022). Using Social Media to Advocate LGBT Rights in Black Africa: A Study of Nigerian and Cameroonian Gay Bloggers and "Facebookers". In *Research Anthology on Inclusivity and Equity for the LGBTQ+ Community* (pp. 169–188). IGI Global., DOI: 10.4018/978-1-6684-3674-5.ch010

Fraser, S. (2008). Getting out in the "real world": Young men, queer and theories of gay community. *Journal of Homosexuality, 55*(2), 245–264. DOI: 10.1080/00918360802129519 PMID: 18982572

Galpin, C. (2022). At the digital margins? A theoretical examination of social media engagement using intersectional feminism. *Politics and Governance, 10*(1), 161–171. DOI: 10.17645/pag.v10i1.4801

Gaudio, R. P. (1997). Not Talking Straight in Hausa. In Livia, A., & Hall, K. (Eds.), *Queerly Phrased: Language, Gender, and Sexuality* (pp. 416–429). Oxford University Press. DOI: 10.1093/oso/9780195104707.003.0025

Gaudio, R. P. (2009). *Allah Made Us: Sexual Outlaws in an Islamic African City*. Wiley Blackwell. DOI: 10.1002/9781444310535

Georgiou, M. (2013). Diaspora in the digital era: Minorities and media representation. *JEMIE. ECMI Journal of Ethnopolitics and Minority Issues in Europe, 12*(4), 80–99.

Gillan, K., Pickerill, J., & Webster, F. (2008). *Anti-war activism: New media and protest in the information age*. Springer. DOI: 10.1057/9780230596382

Haimson, O. L. (2021). Online Communities. In *The SAGE Encyclopedia of Trans Studies*. SAGE Publications, Inc.

Harmer, T. J. (2024). More Than Representation Heartstopper: A Multimodal Critical Discourse Analysis. Master of Arts (MA), Thesis, Communication & Theatre Arts, Old Dominion University,I-108DOI: https://digitalcommons.odu.edu/communication_etds/24DOI: 10.25777/d0f7-na37

Kilic, O. (2023). "Every Parade of Ours is a Pride Parade": Exploring LGBTI+ digital activism in Turkey. *Sexualities*, *26*(7), 731–747. DOI: 10.1177/13634607211060510

Kress, G. (2010). Multimodality: A social semiotic approach to contemporary communication. *Journal of Pragmatics*, *43*(14), 3624–3626.

Kress, G., & Van Leeuwen, T. (2006). *Reading Images: The Grammar of Visual Design*. Routledge. DOI: 10.4324/9780203619728

Kwon, P. (2013). Resilience in lesbian, gay, and bisexual individuals. *Personality and Social Psychology Review*, *17*(4), 371–383. DOI: 10.1177/1088868313490248 PMID: 23904452

Larsson, S. (2014). Battling Mainstream Media, Commentators and Organized Debaters Experiences from Citizens' Online Opinion Writing in Sweden. *Nordicom Review*, *35*(2), 77–89. DOI: 10.2478/nor-2014-0016

Lazar, M. (2017). Homonationalist discourse as a politics of pragmatic resistance in Singapore's Pink Dot movement: Towards a southern praxis. *Journal of Sociolinguistics*, *21*(3), 420–441. DOI: 10.1111/josl.12239

Ledin, P., & Machin, D. (2020). *Introduction to Multimodal Analysis*. Bloomsbury Publishing. DOI: 10.5040/9781350069176

Lenin, J. (2023). *Alliances of Lions: Power and the Politics of Coalitions*. https://roundglasssustain.com/columns/lion-alliances

Machin, D. (2013). What is multimodal critical discourse studies? *Critical Discourse Studies*, *10*(4), 347–355. DOI: 10.1080/17405904.2013.813770

Machin, D., & Mayr, A. (2023). *How to do critical discourse analysis: A multimodal introduction*. SAGE Publication.

Mehra, B., Merkel, C., & Bishop, A. (2004). The Internet for Empowerment of Minority and Marginalized Users. *New Media & Society*, *6*(6), 781–802. DOI: 10.1177/146144804047513

Meyer, I. H. (2015). Resilience in the study of minority stress and health of sexual and gender minorities. *Psychology of Sexual Orientation and Gender Diversity*, *2*(3), 209–213. DOI: 10.1037/sgd0000132

Milani, T. (2013). Expanding the queer linguistic scene. Multimodality, space and sexuality at a South African University. *Journal of Language and Sexuality*, *2*(2), 206–234. DOI: 10.1075/jls.2.2.02mil

Mistry, V. (2011). Critical care training: Using Twitter as a teaching tool. *British Journal of Nursing (Mark Allen Publishing)*, *20*(20), 1292–1296. DOI: 10.12968/bjon.2011.20.20.1292 PMID: 22068003

Motschenbacher, H. (2020). Walking on Wilton Drive: A linguistic landscape analysis of a homonormative space. *Language & Communication*, *72*, 25–43. DOI: 10.1016/j.langcom.2020.02.002

Murthy, D. (2018). Introduction to social media, activism, and organizations. *Social Media+ Society* 4(1): 1-14. 2056305117750716. DOI: 10.1177/2056305117750716

O'Halloran, K. (2004). *Multimodal Discourse Analysis: Systematic Functional Perspectives*. Continuum.

Oakley, M., Farr, R. H., & Scherer, D. G. (2016). Same-Sex Parent Socialization: Understanding Gay and Lesbian Parenting Practices as Cultural Socialization. *Journal of GLBT Family Studies*, *13*(1), 56–75. DOI: 10.1080/1550428X.2016.1158685

Onanuga, P. (2022). Weaponising Digital Architecture: Queer Nigerian Instagram Users and Digital Visual Activism. Deborah Woodman (Ed.) LGBT+ Communities: Creating Spaces of Identity. IntechOpen. Pp 79 – 101.

Onanuga, P. A. (2024). Asserting identity in stifling spaces: Multisemioticity in Nigerian queer-positive Instagram. *Social Dynamics*, *1*, 1–25. DOI: 10.1080/02533952.2024.2320579

Osisanwo, A. (2020). Visual Representations of Newspaper Reportage of Boko Haram Terrorism in Nigeria. *American Journal of Art and Design*, *5*(4), 103–112. DOI: 10.11648/j.ajad.20200504.14

Oyebanji, O. F. (2022). We Are Humans: Discourse Representations of Identities in the Tweets of Nigerian LGBT People. Deborah Woodman (Ed.) *LGBT+ Communities: Creating Spaces of Identity*. IntechOpen. Pp 5-23.

Oyebanji, O. F. (2023). Illegitimation of same-sex sexualities in selected Nigerian newspapers. *Discourse & Society*, *34*(3), 273–290. DOI: 10.1177/09579265221142447

Reichelmann, A., Hawdon, J., Costello, M., Ryan, J., Blaya, C., Llorent, V., & Zych, I. (2021). Hate knows no boundaries: Online hate in six nations. *Deviant Behavior, 42*(9), 1100–1111. DOI: 10.1080/01639625.2020.1722337

Riggle, E. D., Whitman, J. S., Olson, A., Rostosky, S. S., & Strong, S. (2008). The positive aspects of being a lesbian or gay man. *Professional Psychology, Research and Practice, 39*(2), 210–217. DOI: 10.1037/0735-7028.39.2.210

Robinson, B. A. (2016). Heteronormativity and homonormativity. In Naples, N. A. (Ed.), *The Wiley Blackwell Encyclopedia of Gender and Sexuality Studies* (pp. 1–3). John Wiley and Sons.

Sells, T. G. C. (2013). The construction of sexual identities in an online gay, lesbian, and bisexual bulletin board system. *Journal of Human Behavior in the Social Environment, 23*(8), 893–907. DOI: 10.1080/10911359.2013.803452

Steinmetz, K. (2015). "How #LoveWins Became a Celebration of Gay Marriage Victory." Time Magazine.

Talbot, C. V., Talbot, A., Roe, D. J., & Briggs, P. (2020). The management of LGBTQ+ identities on social media: A student perspective. *New Media & Society, 24*(8), 1729–1758. DOI: 10.1177/1461444820981009

Tamale, S. (2014). Exploring the Contours of African Sexualities: Religion, Law and Power. *African Human Rights Law Journal, 14*, 150–177.

Van Leeuwen, T. (2008). *Discourse and practice: New tools for critical discourse analysis*. Oxford University Press. DOI: 10.1093/acprof:oso/9780195323306.001.0001

Warner, M. (1991). Introduction: Fear of a queer planet. *Social Text, 29*, 3–17.

Chapter 5
The Pragmatics of Possessive Constructions in Online Interactions About Children in Nigeria

Ezekiel Olajimbiti
https://orcid.org/0000-0002-5263-0149
Federal University, Lokoja, Nigeria

Samuel Ayodele Dada
Ekiti State University, Ado-Ekiti, Nigeria

ABSTRACT

This paper examines the pragmatics of prenominal possessives, our children and their children, in Nigerian online interactions with the aim of unpacking the indexical configuration of possessives referents, participants' evaluative orientations, and the ideological implications. Data include a corpus of 250,000 tweets with 2,424,462 tokens. The study adopted a mixed-method of corpus-based methodologies and qualitative discourse analysis (QDA) foregrounded by Bucholtz and Hall's (2005) indexicality principle. Findings reveal two possessive configurations, namely explicit and implicit possessive referents. These configurations manifest two evaluative orientations: the negative evaluation of the children's current state-of-affairs and the evaluation of obligation towards the children's ideal state-of-affairs. They point to an ideological polarisation of "them" versus "us", where 'our' indicates inclusivity – the collective responsibility of the masses and "their" implies exclusivity- the negligence of politicians that provokes criticism and condemnation.

DOI: 10.4018/979-8-3693-7934-9.ch005

1.INTRODUCTION

Possessive constructions, which semantically express ownership, often require pragmatic interpretations to account for the speaker's intended meanings. Possessives often show semantic relationships between a possessor, an entity that owns or possesses something, and a possessum, the entity owned or possessed (Kolkmann 2016). These possessive relations are illustrated in the following noun phrases (NPs): i. "Tolulope's child" ii. "our money". In (i) "Tolulope" is the possessor while "child" is the possessum as indicated by the possessive marker ('s). Thus, the possessive referent of "child" is easily recoverable through the compositional knowledge of the structure. The second example (ii) shows a similar structure with "money" as the possessum and "our" as the possessor. However, the indexical social referent of "our" has an extra-constructional source that requires referential knowledge and contextual exploration. In this way, possessives are sometimes constructed to reflect sociopragmatic interpretations, indicating identity, evaluation and ideology. Possessive constructions, as conceived in this study, are beyond the semantic relationship between possessum and possessor; as theyreflect the sociopragmatic meanings of such constructions in relation to the representation of children in the Nigerian context.

The notion of children representation has a very wide scope (Josefsson, et al 2023, Olajimbiti, 2022, 2024) but in this study it is conceptualised as the way children are constructed in adults' interactions. Given that children around the world face overwhelming challenges such as hunger, war and living in conflict zones, disrupted education, child labour and abuse, child mortality, child trafficking, and sex-related challenges and so on (O'Keeffe and Clarke-Pearson 2011; UNICEF 2023; Olajimbiti 2022, Buhre 2023, Sandin, et al 2023), it is important to continuously examine how children are portrayed in adult interactions. This study, therefore, examines how children are possessively constructed to project socioeconomic realities of Nigeria; thereby, highlighting sociocultural meanings and ideological implications of their possessive constructions in Nigeria. In other words, the study focuses on how children are possessively construed and how these constructionspragmatically evoke sociocultural meanings in the Nigerian context. For example, *our children* and *their children* may in principle, mean whatever their utterer intends for them to mean in a particular context. Since the question of a comprehensive account of possessive interpretation is still outstanding in scholarship, the present study aims to examine the possessive interpretation of "our children" and "their children" in online interactions from a pragmatic-inferential perspective.

Depending on the linguistic systems of languages, possessives can be expressed by a variety of constructions, including verbs, pronouns, case markers, and adpositions (Trye, et al. 2024). In this study, we focus on possessive pronouns, which are categorised into attributive and nominal (Heine 2009). Examples of attributive possessive pronouns are my, your, his, their, our, and so on and nominal possessive pronouns are mine, yours, hers, his, its, and ours. It is taken for granted that the English language expresses possession attributively through constructions, such as pre-nominal possessive, post-nominal possessives, oblique genitives and proper noun modifiers (Kulkmann 2016) but our focus in this study is on pre-nominal possessive constructions of *their children* and *our children* in selected Nigerian online interactions. From a theoretical-pragmatic perspective, pre-nominal possessives contribute a prime example of linguistic underdeterminacy because they sometimes require substantial pragmatic enrichment in order to be propositional and fully intelligible (Recanati 2004). The possessive relationship which renders pre-nominal possessives meaningful is often left implicit (Aitken 2009). Therefore, the NPs in isolation can merely signal the availability of some unspecified relation which the possessum has with the possessor in the larger context of the interaction. In this study, the prenominal possessive constructions of children are a subject of enquiry because their interpretation and understanding are to some extent pragmatic and depend largely on the surrounding context (through co-textual elements), their actual referents are endophorically and exophorically sourced, and that they index sociocultural interpretations. Consequently, possessive interpretations are pragmatically realisable through a mixture of world knowledge, contextual interpretation, and explicit and implicit co-textual exploration.

Kolkmann (2016:18) claims that "the interpretation of pre-nominal possessives boils down to the process whereby an addressee constructs the occasion – specific meaning of a given pre-nominal possessive NP in online comprehension". In this case, possessive referents are identifiable through associative links between the possessive NP and other, co-textually established discourse and real-world referents. This explains why the identity of the possessor referent is crucial in possessive construction. Identity in this sense is a construction of others' perceptions and representations as well as a product of larger ideological processes. The study unpacks possessive constructions of children in Nigeria from identity perspective, tracing the identities of possessor referents in online interactions socioculturally to uncover how children are constructed in the Nigerian social reality.

Therefore, the need to know how children are possessively constructed in Nigeria, the fact that a comprehensive account of possessive interpretation is still lacking in scholarship, the paucity of literature on children representation in Nigeria from pragmatic perspective, and the dearth of research on large-scale corpus analyses showing possessive construction in digitised context in Nigeria constitute the research gaps for this study. To bridge this gap this study aims to: determine the indexical configuration of possessive referents, examine evaluative orientations of participants towards possessive referents, and highlight ideological implications of possessive constructions of children in Nigeria. Consequently, the study contributes to existing research in several ways. Theoretically, it expands the sociocultural resources in indexical and identity scholarship by demonstrating how identity in possessive constructions requires contextual and pragmatic considerations. Methodologically, it contributes significantly to possessive constructions in a large-scale corpus study, particularly, description of pragmatic aspects of possessive constructions. From an empirical point of view, it aims to capture the pragmatics of possessive constructions of children in digitised dataset context. It contributes to the linguistic description of the prenominal possessive construction of children from a pragmatic perspective.

2. NIGERIAN CHILDREN, SOCIAL MEDIA AND POSSESSIVE CONSTRUCTIONS

A Nigerian child is any person under the age of 18 (The Nigeria Child Rights Act, 2003). According to Okafor and Nnubia (2013), the Nigerian child refers to the young human being between the birth and puberty who, in time, grows into a full-fledged man or woman. They further argue that a Nigerian child is a "community child". This communal culture is expressed in the Yoruba adage that "one eye gives birth a child, but two hundred raise the child", implying that it takes a communal responsibility to raise a child to stardom. This ideology justifies why Nigerians in online interactions express concern for Nigerian children by employing a possessive determiner "our" when referring to the children of the masses. These online participants often portray themselves as a voice for the voiceless Nigerian children who are faced with overwhelming challenges. Some of these challenges include poverty, malnutrition, limited access to education, healthcare, child labour, trafficking, murder, among others. (UNICEF 2018; Olajimbiti 2023; Ikiyei et al 2022). More especially, UNICEF (2018) notes that Nigeria has the largest number of out-of-school children in the world. Factors contributing to these problems include poverty, religio-cultural practices, unemployment, lack of planning, corruption especially among the political class and elites, insecurity (Ikiyei et al 2022) and so on. The data for this study further confirms the impression that these problems are largely restricted to the children of ordinary Nigerians and not those of the political class and elites. With this in mind, this study focuses on "our children" and "their children" to decode how Nigerian online participants possessively construct children indicating socio-cultural meanings.

Due to their status, children do not have the social power to agitate and fight for themselves. Therefore, many people and organisations choose to raise awareness as a form of social movement to advocate for children and change unjust systems, practices, and structures that affect them in various media, and on social media. Social media platforms, which allow strangers to find one another based on affect resonance (Biri, 2023:70), are a key factor in shaping public opinion and engaging issues of social importance, as they allow for easy communication and anonymity. They allow individuals to express their ideas on contentious issues and offer other members of the network the opportunity to participate in activities related to these issues (Bimber et al., 2005). For some researchers, social media platforms have become a source of data which makes various communicative scenarios available in huge size.

The social media platform chosen for this study is X (Twitter) as it is arguably the most widely used platform for its users' profile and interface (Buhre 2023). Historically, Twitter was developed in 2006 and renamed to X in July 2023. It allows users to post messages to the general internet or to a group of users who subscribe to a user's message "stream" known as followers (Zappavigna 2012:11). Its microposts are known as tweets and are usually public and searchable unless the user actively makes their account private. Zappavigna further emphasises that "Twitter collects supplementary metadata about a tweet, such as the time it was generated, the ID of the user to which the tweet was directed (if applicable) and information about the user's account, including the number of followers and the number of tweets the user has posted". As the X(Twitter) platform is arguably a preferred place to express one's emotions, especially when they are negative (Ruytenbeek, 2024), X users often use the platform to discuss issues affecting children, advocate for their rights, and promote their general wellbeing. Some studies on children and online interactions have focused on the risks of children's participation in social media (Dedkova 2023), and how children communicate with each other online (Kelly and Lorenzo-Dus 2024; Ehreneich, et al 2020). However, the question of how children are possessively constructed in online interactions remains a gap in the scholarship.

Among the plethora of studies on Twitter data within the functional discourse context is Ruytenbeek (2024) who examines negated adjectives in commuters' Twitter complaints. Using corpus-based quantitative analyses, the study found out that positive adjectives are more frequently negated than their negative counterparts. According to the study, negating a positive evaluative adjective seems to be a productive strategy, in the sense that these negated adjectives can replace simple negative adjectives in online customers' usage. The current research benefits from this study from three grounds: the functional discourse approach, the corpus methodology and the Twitter data source. Another research closely related to the current study is Trye et al. (2024), which typically investigates the semantic relationship of possessive constructions in Maori language. The study is approached from cross-linguistic comparison system as it uses MultiCat and Heatmap Matrix Explorer to analyse categorical data. The study reveals that the language users employ possessum a/o possessor to express possessa encoding humans, places, activities, properties, parts (of entities), and units as "possessed". It demonstrates the benefits of analysing a social media corpus of a low-resourced language. While the study examines the subject of enquiry from a purely linguistic system, the current study investigates possessive constructions of children using X(Twitter) data from a functional discourse perspective.

Meanwhile, possessive interpretations have mostly been described in terms of default interpretations without much focus on pragmatic reasoning (Kolkmann, 2016). For instance, Vikner and Jensen's (2002) focuses on what possessive relations are made available prior to the actual interpretation of possessive NPs in concrete utterance situations. The study emphasises the direct relevance to question of what as well as how possessive relations become available during the initial stages of the interpretation process. It argues for a greater role of lexical information than most approaches, exploiting the content of structured lexical entries to derive relational denotations. As a follow up, Vikner and Jensen (2003) observe: "Thus, [lexical] interpretations only require knowledge of the meaning of the relevant words, whereas pragmatic interpretations not only require knowledge of the meaning of the relevant words, they also require knowledge of the individuals referred to by each of the two nominal expressions in the pre-nominal genitive construction. This being so, it is evident that there may be infinitely many pragmatic interpretations of a given phrase, whereas there are very few semantic ones" (p. 174). In a similar development, Vikner and Jensen (2004) look at 2,333 possessive phrases extracted from one fictional and one non-fictional text. They were interested in how these interpretational categories (Inherent, Part-whole, Producer, Control, Pragmatic) function in natural language discourse. The study makes significant contributions quantitatively by identifying the role of context in the interpretations of possessive NPs, but it does not demonstrate ways in which contexts provide a salient possessive relation.

Willemse (2005) examines 400 pre-nominal possessive tokens in a wide range of contexts from a corpus perspective by analysing phoric NPs, their discourse status and newness of a possessive referent and the status of certain referents as "text topics". Peters and Westerstahl (2013) argue that all possessive relations are pragmatically derived, and are present in the semantic composition only as a free variables. They stress that context must be invoked in order to find the appropriate relation for the interpretation of a possessive noun phrase, and even more so, that context can always override the lexical preferences of relational nouns. In line with this argument, Kolkmann (2016) avers that "possible possessive interpretations appear to be determined not by the decoding of semantic content, but by appeal to pragmatic reasoning". Using corpus linguistics,, Kolkmann analyses 3,000 pre-nominal possessive tokens which were extracted from the British National Corpus (BNC), in an attempt to show a usage-based description of how semantically underdetermined pre-nominal possessive NPs denote concrete referents in the real or imagined world. By implication, from theoretical and methodological perspective the study combines the resources of semantics and pragmatics in the exploration of pre-nominal possessive NPs as a unified approach. She claims that "The way we bridge the gap between the underdeterminacy of grammar and the nuanced meanings we communicate with every word we speak is certainly one of the most fundamental aspects of linguistic comprehension." (p. 241).

From the foregoing, studies on possessive constructions on different approaches of interpretations of possessive NPs, are centred on anaphoral resolutions from artificial and non-artificial discourses. Also, corpus studies on pre-nominal possessives (Willemse, 2005; Vikner and Jensen, 2004; Peter and Westerstahl, 2013; Kolkmann, 2016; Trye et al., 2024) also deal with the identifiability of NP referents within a larger stretch of text. None of these studies have looked at how children are possessively constructed from a functional discourse perspective. With the exception of Lorenzo-Dus, Evans, & Mullineux-Morgan (2023), Olajimbiti (2022, 2024) and Olajimbiti and Osisanwo (2024), who examined online child sexual grooming, deontic and evaluation of obligations and the representation of children on X respectively; possessive constructions of children that reflect social realities remain a gap in scholarship. Building on this trend, the present study attempts a corpus pragmatic analysis of possessive constructions of children in selected online interactions in Nigeria from identity perspective.

3.DATA, METHODOLOGY AND THEORY

Data for the study were part of a larger project corpus of 250,000 tweets with 2,424,462 tokens collected between July 2023 and July 2024 using the Apify Twitter Scraper. Twitter Scraper is a software that searches and extracts data from Twitter (with historic data from 2006), parses and converts the data into structured formats: HTML table, JSON, CSV, Excel and XML. Items such as "children around the world", "children representation", "child victims", "children and trafficking", and "children and rape" were entered as search terms, which the software scraps every time is it mandated. Therefore, data were gradually collected over the aforementioned period to form a corpus. These include tweets, reaction tweets (as comments), and recirculated tweets on interactions about children around the world. Since data for the current study are part of the large corpus retrieved about children in general, only Nigerian-related data, extracted from the large corpus using AntConc software, were used. These include 8,947 tweets with 465,152 tokens, which primarily reflect the social realities around the construction of children in Nigeria. Our intention in this study is to examine how children are possessively discussed and how these possessive relations pragmatically evoke sociocultural meanings in the Nigerian context. On ethical issues regarding X posts, this study aligns with views of other scholars. Some of these views are that a large number of tweets are accessible to many users of the internet (boyd 2010), using the content of tweets in scientific research raises issues such as consent and traceability (Williams et al 2017). Twitter's terms of service do not prevent scholars from using the content of tweets for their research, but care must be taken to ensure that the content does not contain sensitive information (Trye, et al 2024).

Since corpus linguistics is based on both statistical methods and linguistic theory, a mixed method of corpus-based methodologies and qualitative discourse analysis (QDA) was adopted in this study. The following corpus methodologies, implemented on AntConc constitute the quantitative analytical framework. Using AntConc, query terms, *their children* and *our children* were extracted based on the frequency lists, which indicated salient features of the data (O'Keeffe, Clancy, and Adolphs, 2020). This process forms the keyness analysis, keywords and KIWC in data sorting. AntConc's concordance programme was used to conduct targeted search for the query terms by examining the frequency of each possessive NP. The frequency of the query terms is shown in Table 1. The coding scheme deployed co-textual mechanisms such as phoric elements and other inferential terms: explicit and implicit to determine possessors' referents. The keywords list presented in Table 2 was used to examine the discourse issues constructed around *their children* and *our children* in the corpus. Concordance lines representing the environment of each of the terms were examined, and a close reading of the concordance lines was used to determine the tweeters' intended indexical configurations of the possessors' referents, their evaluations and ideological values.

For the qualitative analytical framework, insights from Bucholtz and Hall's (2005) indexicality principle and the co-text as a discourse pragmatic concept were utilized to achieve the objectives of the study: possessive referents' identities, evaluation and ideology. Indexicality is one of the five principles proposed by Bucholtz and Hall (2005) as a sociocultural linguistic approach to identity. The principle is concerned with the mechanism whereby identity is constituted, that is, how linguistic forms are used to construct identity positions. Bucholtz and Hall (2005) describe an index as a linguistic form that depends on the interactional context for its meaning. This concept of indexicality involves the creation of semiotic links between linguistic forms and social meanings (Ochs, 1992; Silverstein, 1985). In identity formation, indexicality relies heavily on ideological structures, for associations between language and identity are rooted in cultural beliefs and values – that is, ideologies – about the sorts of speakers who (can or should) produce particular sorts of language. Bucholtz and Hall argue that identity relations emerge in interaction through several related indexical processes, including: (a) overt mention of identity categories and labels; (b) implicatures and presuppositions regarding one's own or others' identity position; (c) displayed evaluative and epistemic orientations to ongoing talk, as well as interactional footings and participant roles; and (d) the use of linguistic structures and systems that are ideologically associated with specific personas and groups. Therefore, the emergent cultural positions of the possessive referents are indexed through overt-mention, labels, implicatures, stances, linguistic structures and systems.

The co-text refers to the linguistic surrounding of a lexical item/unit (cf. Odebunmi 2006). It works on the idea that units in the textual environment mutually influence each other in terms of meaning. For effective meaning explication, the networking of lexical choices within a text are considered. According to Odebunmi (2012:190), "Phoric reference relates to pointing by means of language. This could be within the text (endophora) or outside the text (exophora). Endophoric reference further bifurcates into anaphoric reference and cataphoric reference. While the former points backwards, the latter does forwards". The principles and concepts highlighted constitute a theoretical framework that provides sociocultural insights into analysing possessive constructions in online interactions about children in Nigeria.

4. ANALYSIS AND FINDINGS

The analysis focuses on how children are possessively constructed to reflect sociocultural realities of Nigeria by unpacking the identities of the referenced social actors in the communicative events and discursive choices used in the digital context. This section is structured into four sub-sections: corpus findings, indexical configuration of possessive referents, participants' evaluative orientations towards possessive referents, and ideologically imposed indexical values associated with possessors and possessa.

4.1 Corpus Findings

Table 1 shows that *their children* occurs most frequently in the corpus, suggesting that its indexical referents are a powerful group whose social behaviour dominates public discourse in online interactions about children. Conversely, the frequency table suggests that the referents of *our children* are less powerful social actors.

Table 1. Frequency of the query terms

Query term	Rank	Frequency	Range
our children	1	477	1
their children	1	1130	1

Thus, the sociological profile of the groups contextualises the sociocultural meanings of possessive constructions of children in the Nigerian context. Section 4.2 presents further analysis of the possessive referents. Next is the keyword list, which reflects the content of the corpus, giving a general idea of the focus evaluated in the tweets (Baker, 2006). Table 2 shows the keywords in the corpus on the possessive construction of children in Nigeria.

Figure 1. Keywords

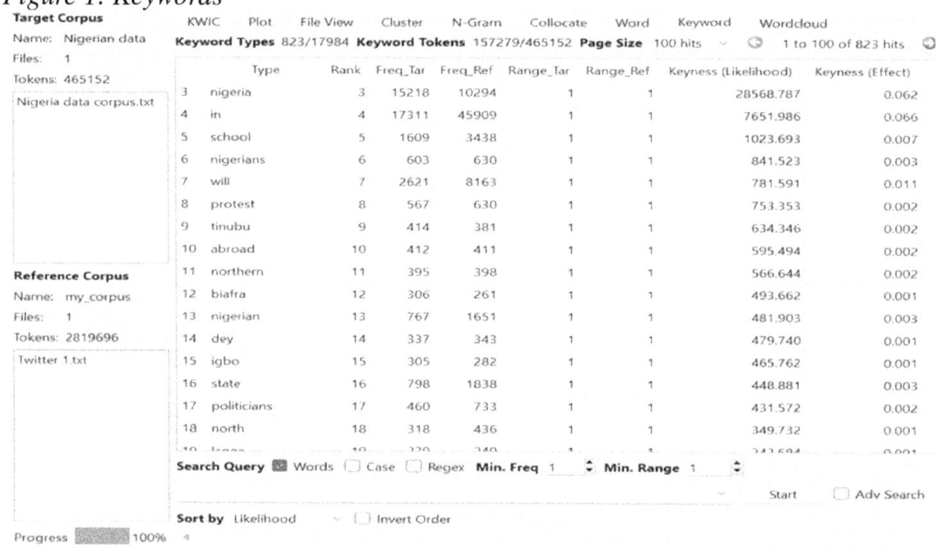

	Type	Rank	Freq_Tar	Freq_Ref	Range_Tar	Range_Ref	Keyness (Likelihood)	Keyness (Effect)
3	nigeria	3	15218	10294	1	1	28568.787	0.062
4	in	4	17311	45909	1	1	7651.986	0.066
5	school	5	1609	3438	1	1	1023.693	0.007
6	nigerians	6	603	630	1	1	841.523	0.003
7	will	7	2621	8163	1	1	781.591	0.011
8	protest	8	567	630	1	1	753.353	0.002
9	tinubu	9	414	381	1	1	634.346	0.002
10	abroad	10	412	411	1	1	595.494	0.002
11	northern	11	395	398	1	1	566.644	0.002
12	biafra	12	306	261	1	1	493.662	0.001
13	nigerian	13	767	1651	1	1	481.903	0.003
14	dey	14	337	343	1	1	479.740	0.001
15	igbo	15	305	282	1	1	465.762	0.001
16	state	16	798	1838	1	1	448.881	0.003
17	politicians	17	460	733	1	1	431.572	0.002
18	north	18	318	436	1	1	349.732	0.001

Other keywords in the corpus are: malnutrition, government, better, living, schooling, hunger, insecurity, education, suffering, gunmen, food, corruption, corridors, useless, generation, wicked, riggers, poor, elites, bandits, hardship, masses, governance, invest, public, secure, immunization, kidnapped, leadership, jobless, abandon, survival among others. The keyword list indicates lexical items that require further examination as they are a measure of saliency (Baker 2023:165) and configuration of the sociological profile of the possessive referents in the corpus. They constitute the linguistic elaborations of social actions associated with possessors' referents. As such, they provide clues to the tweeters' intended referents and guide readers' inferential processes. Figures 2 and 3 present KWIC of the query terms.

Figure 2. KWIC of our children

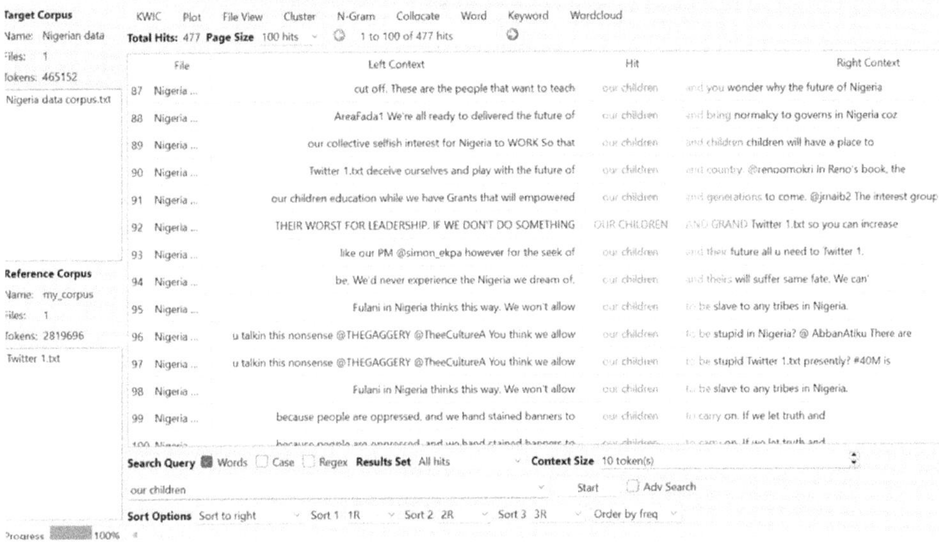

Figure 3. KWIC of their children

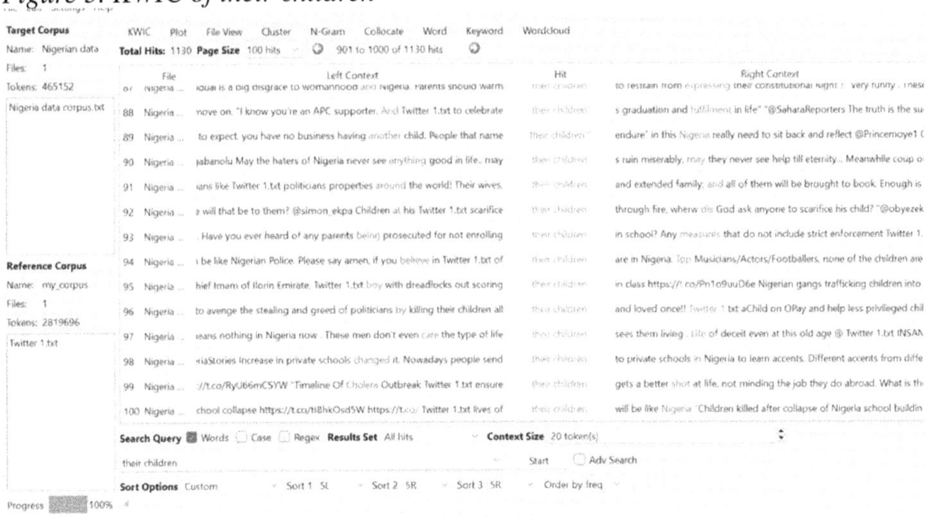

The KWIC of *their children* and *our children* provides frames for the tweeters' implicated sociocultural meanings as a derivation of inferential processes, as online utterances are produced in a rather ambiguous complex context. This necessitates the deployment of inference mechanisms to determine the sociocultural meaning of the possessive referents of the query terms.

4.2 Indexical Configuration Of Possessive Referents

The possessive referents of *our children* and *their children* are identifiable from intra- and extra-constructional sources which are technically characterised as explicit and implicit indexical configurations. These represent the identities of the social actors, which are represented in the corpus through co-textual reference mechanisms and implicatures around children. These are shown in Tables 2 and 3 below.

Table 2. Possessive referents of their children

Referent		Configuration	Discourse issue
Politicians		**Explicit**	**Power (oppression and exploitation), education, corruption, living and schooling abroad, living large, securing better future for children,**
		Implicit	**(heroic) worship, living abroad**
Ruling elite		**Explicit**	**(lording) power, relocating children abroad**
Nigerian government		**Explicit**	**Patriotism**
Igbos		**Explicit**	**Education**
Parents	Southern	Explicit	Parenting, education, money
	Northern		
	Nigerian		
Nigerian leaders		Explicit	Travelling abroad
Preserving criminals (government officials)		Explicit	School abroad
Elected officials		Explicit	Education
Doctors		Explicit	Killing of children

Table 3. Possessor referents of our children

Referent	Configuration	Discourse issue
Unspecified	Implicit	Education, suffering, poverty, terrorism, politics, bad governance, future, tribalism and bigotry
Nigerians	Implicit	Hate and bigotry, bad governance, election, suffering, anti-government, political rhetoric, unity and solidarity, protest, constitution, health (immunization), education
Yoruba people	Implicit	Tribalism
Society	Explicit	Health, advocacy (fighting for the future of children
	Implicit	

In this category, two linguistic means of the indexicality principle are used, namely overt mention of identity categories and labels and implicatures and presuppositions regarding one's own or others' identity position.

Here, explicit configuration is conceived as the overt introduction of referential identity. Through co-textuality mechanisms (phoric referencing), possessor referents were collated with associated sociocultural meanings indicating imposed identity of a group. In the possessive constructions *their children*, Nigerian online participants (X-users) overtly referred to *politicians* with deviant synonyms such as "ruling elite", "Nigerian government", Nigerian leaders", "elected officials".

1. I returned back to Nigeria and stop supporting all this criminal **politicians** looting Nigeria money to make good life for them and **their children** while the average Nigeria is suffering"
2. Nigeria is governed by greedy **politicians** who don't care about what happens but only interested in securing the future of **their unborn children**.
3. As a society, **we** need to come together to fight obesity, for the future of **our children**."

Samples 1 and 2 illustrate how the possessors' referents of *their children* are overtly mentioned in the corpus. The discourse context of the tweets shows that the possessors' referents of *their children* are cataphorically referenced as *politicians* representing the identity of the social actors and their actions for their children. The sociological profile of this group is reinforced by the invocation of identity labels *greedy politicians* and *criminal politicians*. What is most striking about the identity labels is the co-textual elements elaborating on actions of the social actors, such as *criminal* because of *looting Nigeria money* in (1) and *greedy* because *don't care about what happens* in (2). The predominant intentions of this group are *make good life for them and their children* (1) and *securing the future of their unborn children* (2). Stubbs (1996:107) argues that "words tend to occur in relationship to other words", which is why the recourse to the co-referential token-meaning around the possessive referent of *their children* foregrounds the sociocultural significance of the indexical identity value of Nigerian politicians and their children.

Other possessive referents of *their children* overtly mentioned in the corpus are Igbos, parents and doctors. These are also significant for sociocultural meaning in the Nigerian space. Instances of "Igbos" as possessor referent are discursively associated with education and bigotry. Similarly, "doctors" as possessor's referent were constructed to deride the government for criticising medical doctors who want to leave Nigeria. Some online participants defend the doctors' action, arguing that the doctors do not want their children to continue to suffer the deplorable conditions and killing of children in the country. Meanwhile, "parents" as possessor' referents manifest an ideological distinction between Southern and Northern Nigeria. In this regard, online participants express their opinions and feelings about the parenting style and educational attainment of children in the two regions through *their children* as an index.

Only in a few instances of possessive referents of *our children* are explicitly mentioned in the corpus. Sample 3 represents such instances where the possessor's referent is captured through cataphoric reference to "society". In this case, the discourse context of the tweet suggests how passionate appeal is being made to members of a society about the health of children. As implied in, *we need to come together to fight obesity*. The inclusive "we" refers to the preceding linguistic form "society" whose social meaning is explicit, in that it indexically addresses Nigerians to fight obesity for the sake of children.

The implicit possessor referents are speaker-intended entities referred to by the NPs (*their children* and *our children*), which are realisable through contextual interpretation (setting, conditions and assumptions). The possessive referents in this category thus have extra-constructional sources and consequently pragmatic processes of instantiating identities through additional inferential interpretive work are necessary. This reflects, to a considerable extent, the nature of online interactions, which are based on a variety of assumptions. Some examples are analysed below:

4. **They** don't want us to have the same life as **their children**, they want us to worship them and their children.
5. Don't allow urself be used by **them** for their own gain. **Their children** are all out in a developed clime. Ronu"
6. @... **we** can't fight a problem the same way it was created...our approach should show wits & class...let's creativity unseat these men who have continued to abandon the role of Fathers/Elders...**our children** need to know that we stood for their rights to exist in a free Nigeria I stand

The possessor's referent of *their children* in Sample 4 is *they* whose social identity has an extra-constructional source. It can be inferred that the author of the tweet is referring to a group of people who are portrayed as *they* and enjoy certain privileges in Nigerian society. By implicature, they are the group of people who are responsible for ensuring that resources are distributed equally *to have the same life*. This hints at the identity of the ruling class in Nigeria, who are constantly accused of denying the masses good governance in order to provide a good life that they provide for their children. The tweet captures identities of two groups, "they" versus "us", where "they" indexes the identity of the ruling class and "us" the identity of the masses. This suggests the identity of the oppressors and the oppressed respectively.

Similarly, the possessor's referent of *their children* in Sample 5 is "them" whose social meaning does not exist within the tweet. The tone of the tweet is adversarial, as the author warns the masses not to allow themselves to be used. This is evident in the use of "Ronu", a Yoruba word which literally means "to think" but is used contextually to mean "be wise". In this case, "them" is referring to the identity of those whose hallmark is the "used" ideology. These individuals tend to use other people's children "for their own gain" while keeping their children in the Western world. This presupposes the identity of a political class. In (6), the possessor's referent of "our children" is cataphorically "we" which inferentially refers to the masses in the context of the tweet. Considering the indexical profile of "we" and "these men", the social context of the tweet suggests a relational counter identity of the social actors. In this case, "these men" implies the ruling class who the tweet author has intention to "unseat". So, "we" indexes extra-constructional identity value of concerned Nigerians who are willing to fight creatively for a free Nigeria where children's rights are guaranteed.

4.3 Participants' Evaluative Orientations Toward Possessive Referents

Online contexts offer users a high degree of control over how they portray themselves (Scott 2022:29) and others. In this study, tweeters implicitly evaluate the identified possessors' referents and their indexical identities through their lexical choices. These evaluative comments contribute to the communication of the tweeters' intended meanings and to the readers' inferential processes. In this case, tweeters' evaluative orientations to the possessors' referents are analysed because by evaluating something, one is taking a position and assigning others identity position. Here, possessors' referents of *their children* are negatively evaluated vis-à-vis children's current state-of-affairs, while evaluation of possessors' referents of *our children* reflect obligations toward children's ideal state-of-affairs. These are analysed in turn.

The indexical identities of the possessive referents of *their children* and the social actions are evaluated negatively relative to children's current state-of-affairs. Tweeters express their stance positions through linguistic forms that index identities of this social actor in their posts, as the following samples show below.

7. @... Nigeria is bleeding our nation is falling apart right in front of us our children tomorrow will suffer more than this if we don't **chase criminals in power away** deliberately. **They** are sending **their children** abroad to school while we can't even afford to pay our own children's fees in Nigeria.
8. Please our **evil politicians** that have no idea what investing in education is all about, please watch. China government investing in education & future of **their children** and Nigeria government killing the future of our children. **They** are relocating **their children** and loved ones in droves abroad.

In Sample 7, the following expressions convey the tweeter's evaluative orientations towards the possessive referent (the ruling political class): "Nigeria is bleeding", "our nation is falling apart", "suffer", "criminals in power". The invocation of the identity label "criminal in power" inferentially describes the tweeter's perception of the country's current leaders, who are allegedly responsible for the "bleeding", "falling apart", "suffering" and "inability to afford children's school fees". Meanwhile, the statement that "our children tomorrow will suffer more than this" presupposes that children are currently suffering due to the social actions of the "criminals in power". Here, the tweeter expresses a critical attitude towards the social actor by comparing their children, who are sent to school abroad, with the masses who cannot afford to pay their children's school fees. Thereby, their identity is located in the situated social positions of "haves" and "have nots", the privileged and the less privileged. Other evaluative terms such as "chase ...away", and "deliberately" reinforce the tweeter's intended emotion. This display of evaluative orientation reflects the tweeter's stance and the constructed identity of the political class.

In a similar way, Sample 8 evaluates politicians' attitude towards the education of children in Nigeria. In this case, the tweeter's negative appraisal of the social actor is displayed in "evil politicians", "have no idea what investing in education", "killing the future of our children". Labelling politicians as evil means ascribing a negative identity to them. This negative identity is apparently linguistically elaborated in the content of the tweet as "no idea what investing in education is all about" and "killing the future of our children". From the judgmental orientation of the tweeter, it can therefore be inferred that Nigerian politicians/government are being accused of not investing in the educating of Nigerian children, with the implication that they are destroying the future of children in the country. To further justify this, the tweeter explains that these "evil politicians" are "relocating their children…abroad". This presupposes that the standard of education in Nigeria is not good enough for their children. Meanwhile, possessive referents of *our children* were predominantly evaluated in terms of obligations to the ideal state-of-affairs of children. The tweets in this category reflect a call to action that stems from the evaluation of current sociocultural situations of the country and a need to secure the future of the children. Consequently, the style of language demonstrates sensitisation and persuasion of Nigerian citizens, as the following samples show.

9. @PoliceNG I think **we** are not ready. **We must** put tribe and religion aside and ask ourselves is Nigeria currently working?. If **we must** safeguard the future of **our children** then we must all face the criminals in power destroying this Nation. People power will always win. #peoplepower
10. Hunger doesn't ask wether you are an Igbo, Hausa, Fulani, Yoruba,Urhobo,Ijaw and other minority tribes in Nigeria.Until **we** set religion and tribe aside and chase out the #criminals at the corridors of power, the future of **our children** cannot be guaranteed.

In Sample 9, the possessor's referent of "our children" is "we" which has intra and extra constructional sources. It is intra because "we" is referenced cataphorically and extra because its sociocultural meaning can be realised inferentially. In this case, the indexical referent of "we" can be contextualised as Nigerian citizens, the masses, and society. Other co-textual elements that confirm this are "people power" and "#peoplepower", suggesting the power of citizens to determine their leaders. Scott (2022) argues that evaluative comment contributes to the communication of the speaker's meaning. Therefore, the evaluative comment "face the criminals in power" presupposes that the tweeter's use of "we" references the masses. Futhermore, the evaluative comment reflects the tweeter's orientation to both leadership and the masses, and particularly suggests the negative attitude of an average Nigeria toward the political class. Therefore, this evaluative comment evaluates the morality of allowing criminals in power. The first-person plural pronoun, "we", which occurs four times in the tweet is an inclusive term, involving the tweeter and other Nigerians as masses. So, the tweeter commits self and others to action through the deontic modal "must". In the structure "we must", the tweeter evaluates the obligation of citizens to secure the future of Nigerian children.

Similarly, the inclusive "we" represents the possessor's referent of *our children* in Sample 10. Its social and indexical meaning can be inferred from the content of the tweet through the references to "Igbo, Hausa, Fulani, Yoruba, Urohobo, Ijaw and other minority tribes in Nigeria. These reference elements seem to capture all

Nigerians. Another implicature in the first sentence of the tweet is that all Nigerians suffer from hunger, which the tweeter insinuates is caused by "#criminals at the corridor of power". This marks the tweeter's negative evaluative orientation to the ruling political class, underscores by the identity label of "criminals". Secondly, the tweeter evaluates the obligation of self and other Nigerians (we) to be purposefully united, implied by "set religion and tribe aside". Here, citizens' obligation to unite and change leaders is evaluated as the only condition (until) to ensure the future of *our children*. Therefore, these dual evaluations indexically situate the identity positions of the masses and the ruling class in Nigeria toward the wellbeing of the children.

4.4 Ideologically Imposed Indexical Values Associated With Possessors And Possession

The lexical choices of the online participants in this study not only reveal their identity positions and represented participants but also highlight their ideologically imposed values about the possessors and possessa. This consistent with Stubbs (1996:107) that "no terms are neutral. Choice of words expresses an ideological position". In this context, the ideological polarisation of positive self-representation and negative other-representation is captured in "them" versus "us". Here, "them" predominantly indexicalises the political class in Nigeria, while "us" is the masses. Therefore, the possessor's referents of *their children* are negatively constructed as people who do not mean well for the citizens and as such are the cause of their suffering. Conversely, the possessor's referents of *our children* are constructed with the ideologically imposed value of the oppressed and fighters who are willing to save and secure the children's future. Thus, the indexical interpretations of "us", "we", and "our" convey intentional values such as inclusivity, collective responsibility, solidarity, sympathy, and advocacy. On the other hand, "their" implies exclusivity - the elite and politicians whose social actions are generating criticism and condemnation. These are illustrated in the samples below.

11. "At least this is not too much to request. Most of the high rated politicians have their children schooled in best schools in European, we languished in dilapidated classrooms here in Nigeria. #EndBadGovernanceInNigeria"
12. This is a protest for survival ... It's not about me. Let's fight for the future of our children.. let's end bad government and false religion in Nigeria"

The consistent negative evaluation and perception toward the possessors' referents of "their children" represented as "evil politicians", "criminals in power", "greedy leaders", "corrupt leaders", "looters" and "wicked people" have their ideological implications in the identity positioning of their children. By highlighting privileges children of the ruling class and elites enjoy, especially by sending them abroad while other children "languished in dilapidated classrooms here in Nigeria" and suffer hunger, exacerbate the display of negative emotions toward the ruling class and ideological differences between the privileged and less privileged children. Significantly, *their children* as a linguistic form configures social meanings referring to the children of the rich, the bourgeoisie, the political class and the privileged children, whose parents are criticised for impoverishing the masses and failing to provide equal opportunities and resources to other children. These children, who often school abroad, train and live outside Nigeria, are completely exempted from the suffering and other ills other children face. Unwittingly, the process of social differentiation between *their children* and *our children* underscores the ideological orientations of Nigerian online participants. These ideologically motivated perceptions of online participants, evident in their tweets, point to the inequality between the children of the poor and the children of the rich and the class-consciousness in the Nigerian society.

5. CONCLUSION

This study examined possessive constructions of children in online interactions of Nigerians with the aim of highlighting the identities of the possessive referents of *their children* and *our children*, participants evaluative orientations towards the possessive referents, and the ideological implications of such constructions in Nigeria. With this study, we aimed at demonstrating pragmatic reasoning in the identifiability of possessive referents and the discourse functions of possessive constructions of children in Nigeria. The study also presented a corpus-based method of query terms as implicature triggers through which social realities of the country are foregrounded and children's state-of-affairs are evaluated.

In line with Kolkmann's (2016) referent identifiability structure, this study showed that the referents of the query terms have intra- and extra- constructional sources which validate a two-way approach of possessive interpretations in accounting for their sociocultural meanings. Through co-referential NP chains and discourse knowledge, intra-constructional referents are identified, while the identification of extra-constructional referents requires more pragmatic reasoning including inference and implicature. We found that the political class and the elite were predominantly referred to as the possessor referents of *their children* as the online participants on X negatively evaluate their social behaviour in the form of criticism and condemnation about the poor state-of-affairs of the children of the masses. On the other hand, by inference, the possessor referents of *our children* are mostly implicitly constructed referring to the masses, society and other social groups, whose obligations to secure the children's future are evaluated. The indexical configurations of these possessive referents, as reference-point constructions, unveil the identities of the oppressors and the oppressed, the antagonists and the protagonists of the children's future.

The findings of this study indicate discourses on Nigerian children, particularly the distinction between the children of the political and elite class and those of the masses, as well as the identities of their possessors in possessive constructions in the digital context. Thus, the indexical interpretations of the possessives point to ideological polarisation of "them" versus "us", where 'our' indicates inclusivity – the masses' collective responsibility and "their" implies exclusivity- the politicians' negligence generating criticism and condemnation. Finally, in this study, we addressed pre-nominal possessives as potential implicature triggers, particularly how *their children* and *our children's* possessive interpretations are useful to test the pragmatic reasoning of constructing social realities in Nigeria around children. Therefore, the study provides insights into how online participants express sociocultural values through possessive constructions of children in the Nigerian context.

REFERENCES

Aitken, M. (2009). The English Possessive Marker in a Framework of Relevance. *Journal of Language and Communication Studies*, *49*, 119–135.

Baker, P. (2006). *Using corpora to analyse discourse*. Continuum. DOI: 10.5040/9781350933996

Bimber, B., Flanagin, A. J., & Stohl, C. (2005). Reconceptualizing collective action in the contemporary media environment. *Communication Theory*, *15*(4), 365–388. DOI: 10.1111/j.1468-2885.2005.tb00340.x

Biri, Y. (2023). Affective stance as positioning in an English-speaking online fan community. *Journal of Pragmatics*, *215*, 70–83. DOI: 10.1016/j.pragma.2023.07.004

Boyd, D. (2010). Social network sites as networked publics: Affordances, dynamics and implications. In Z. Papacharissi (ed.), *The Networked Self: Identity, Community, and Culture on Social Network Sites* (pp. 39–58). New York: Routledge.

Bucholtz, M., & Hall, K. (2005). Identity and interaction: A sociocultural linguistic approach. *Discourse Studies*, *7*(4-5), 585–614. DOI: 10.1177/1461445605054407

Buhre, F. (2023). Child figurations in youth climate justice activism: The visual rhetoric of the Fridays for future on Instagram. In *Sandin, B., Josefsson, J., Hanson, K. Balagopalan, S. The politics of children's rights and representation* (pp. 251–274). Palgrave. DOI: 10.1007/978-3-031-04480-9_11

Ikiyei, P. K., Donkemezuo, S., Precious, M., & Seribofa, T. I. (2022). Out-of-school children in Nigeria: A creation by society and its implications for nation building. *British Journal of Contemporary Education*, *2*(1), 17–32.

Josefsson, J., Sandin, B., Hanson, K., & Balagopalan, S. (2023). Representing children. In: Sandin, B., Josefsson, J., Hanson, K. Balagopalan, S. (eds). *The politics of children's rights and representation*. Palgrave. 1-28. DOI: 10.1007/978-3-031-04480-9_1

Kolkmann, J. (2016). *The pragmatics of possession: Issues in the interpretation of pre-nominal possessives in English.* A PhD Thesis, University of Manchester.

Lorenzo-Dus, N., Evans, M., & Mullineux-Morgan, T. (2023). *Online child sexual grooming discourse*. Cambridge University Press. DOI: 10.1017/9781009314626

O'Keeffe, A., Clancy, B., & Adolphs, S. (2020). *Introducing pragmatics in use*. Routledge.

O'Keeffe, G. S., & Clarke-Pearson, K. (2011). The impact of social media on children, adolescents, and families. *Pediatrics, 127*(4), 800–804. DOI: 10.1542/peds.2011-0054 PMID: 21444588

Ochs, E. (1992). Indexing Gender. In Duranti, A., & Goodwin, C. (Eds.), *Rethinking Context: Language as an Interactive Phenomenon* (pp. 335–358). Cambridge University Press.

Odebunmi, A. (2006). *Meaning in English: An introduction*. Critical Sphere.

Odebunmi, A. (2013). Participation configuration in a Nigerian university campus. *Pragmatics & Cognition, 20*(1), 186–215. DOI: 10.1075/pc.20.1.08ode

Okafor, P. S., & Nnubia, U. E. (2013). The Nigerian child and national development: A philosophical appraisal. *Journal of Educational and Social Research, 3*(4), 103–107. DOI: 10.5901/jesr.2013.v3n4p103

Olajimbiti, E. O. (2022). Pragmatic function of Twitter handlers' perspectives on children discourse in Nigeria. *The Journal of Medical Research, 15*, 91–104. DOI: 10.24193/jmr.42.6

Olajimbiti, E. O. (2023). Ideological construction of deviance in street children's discourse in Southwestern Nigeria. *Journal for Discourse Studies, 1*, 10–30.

Peters, S., & Westerståhl, D. (2013). The semantics of possessives. *Language, 89*(4), 713–759. DOI: 10.1353/lan.2013.0065

Recanati, F. (2004). *Literal meaning*. Cambridge University Press.

Ruytenbeek, N. (2024). A case study of negated adjectives in commuters' Twitter complaints. *Languages (Basel, Switzerland), 9*(274), 1–13. DOI: 10.3390/languages9080274

Scott, K. (2022). *Pragmatics online*. Routledge. DOI: 10.4324/b22750

Silverstein, M. (1985). Language and the Culture of Gender: At the Intersection of Structure, Usage, and Ideology. In Mertz, E., & Parmentier, R. J. (Eds.), *Semiotic Mediation: Sociocultural and Psychological Perspectives* (pp. 219–259). Academic Press. DOI: 10.1016/B978-0-12-491280-9.50016-9

Stubbs, M. (1996). *Text and corpus analysis*. London: Chicago: Blackwell.

The Nigerian Child Rights Act. (2003).

Trye, D., Claude, A., Harlow, R., & Keegan, T. (2024). Analysing A/O possession in Maori- language tweets. *Languages (Basel, Switzerland), 9*(271), 1–32. DOI: 10.3390/languages9080271

UNICEF. (2018). *Evaluation report: The out-of-school children initiative*. OOSCI.

UNICEF. (2023). Crime statistics- devastating violence against children and women continues. UNICEF, Retrieved from https://www.unicef.org/southafrica/press-releases/crime- statistics-devastating-violence-against-children-and-women-continues.

Vikner, C., & Jensen, P. A. (2002). A Semantic Analysis of the English Genitive. Interaction of Lexical and Formal Semantics. *Studia Linguistica*, *56*(2), 191–226. DOI: 10.1111/1467-9582.00092

Vikner, C., & Jensen, P. A. (2003). Producer interpretations of the English pre-nominal genitive. In Weisgerber, M. (Ed.), *Proceedings of sub7 – Sinn und Bedeutung. Arbeitspapier Nr. 114* (pp. 173–183). University of Konstanz.

Vikner, C., & Jensen, P. A. (2004). The English Pre-Nominal Genitive and Lexical Semantics. In K. Ji-yung, Y.A. Lander, & B.H. Partee (Eds.), *Possessives and Beyond: Semantics and Syntax* (Occasional Papers in Linguistics No. 29, pp. 3–27). Amherst, MA: GLSA Publications.

Willemse, P. (2005). *Nominal reference-point constructions: Possessive and esphoric NPs in English* (PhD Thesis, University of Leuven, Leuven, Belgium).

Williams, M. L., Pete, B., & Luke, S. (2017). Towards an Ethical Framework for Publishing Twitter Data in Social Research: Taking into Account Users' Views, Online Context and Algorithmic Estimation. *Sociology*, *51*(6), 1149–1168. DOI: 10.1177/0038038517708140 PMID: 29276313

Zappavigna, M. (2012). *Discourse of Twitter and social media: How we use language to create affiliation on the web*. Bloomsbury. DOI: 10.5040/9781472541642

KEY TERMS AND DEFINITIONS

Identity: a construction from the perception and representation of self and others and a product of larger ideological processes.

Possessive: expressions that often show semantic relations between a possessor, an entity that owns or possesses something, and a possessum, the entity owned or possessed

Children representation: the way in which children are constructed or how they are spoken about in adults' interactions.

Co-reference: the relationship between a possessive referent and an antecedent, showing that the former has been introduced into the preceding discourse.

Referential knowledge: the knowledge required to determine which possessive relation to select in the interpretation of possessive NP in a communicative event.

Online interactions: any form of communication that takes place via digital platforms.

Ideological value: a belief system that influences the way people think, speak and act.

Possessive construction: linguistic expressions that indicate semantic relationships between two noun phrases.

Chapter 6
Image-Text Syntheses, Discursivity, and Promotional Meanings in Selected Jumia's Online Affiliate Advertisements in Nigeria

Moses Chika Christian-Achinihu
https://orcid.org/0009-0007-4266-3549
American University of Nigeria, Yola, Nigeria

ABSTRACT

This chapter explored how the intersection of text and images manifests discursivity and advances promotional meanings in the online affiliate advertisements of Jumia. Five samples of e-banners were elicited from the company's website, all within December 2023. Each e-banner purposively represented each of the five weekends the company reeled out advertisements in the yuletide month. The data were analysed using Martinec and Salway's (2005) image-text relations system, and supported with insights from Halliday's Systemic Functional Linguistics and Barthes's Semiotics. The findings evinced that Jumia's marketization of products principally rests on rhetoric of incentives and enticement to establish discursivity in their promotions. This persuasive strategy is maximized via three relations: text-image complementarity, image subordination to text and text subordination to image. Also, these syntheses resultantly promote testacies of social status and convenience, expense reduction, financial gains and happiness, in ways that shape prospects' purchasing decisions.

DOI: 10.4018/979-8-3693-7934-9.ch006

1. INTRODUCTION

The global virtual marketing landscape has been experiencing the proliferative adoption of online visuals, infographics, graffiti, banners and videos as forms of marketing contents by businesses, since 2020 when the pandemic compelled the reliance of most businesses on the Internet economy. This has culminated in not only improved marketing contents but also in increased online marketing competition. In Nigeria, affiliate marketing companies are leading in the adoption of multimodal contents. Of significance to this chapter is the understanding of the use of discursive and semiotic means in advancing meanings in the promotional contents of Jumia – a highly popular and pioneer of e-commerce and affiliate marketing organisation in Nigeria – and with which the latter markets brands and persuades virtual consumers.

Generally, promotional discourse cuts across different shades of product and service advertisement across print, television and radio commercials, blurbs, brochures, testimonials and electronic/online business visibility that 'exhibit product description, evaluation and differentiation' (Taiwo & Ademilokun, 2023, p.2). However today, electronic promotional discourse is unarguably one of the prominent discourse genres in the world due to digital affordances accessible to businesses, organizations and individuals as enabled by increased technologies and sophisticated virtual tools. Interestingly, when juxtaposed with the traditional/print advertisements, the virtual version is richer in strikingly endearing linguistic and semiotic artifacts that are capable of arresting screen attention. This is because contemporary businesses understand that the screen world has an extremely short attention span; hence, only highly captivating promotional strategies can make scrolling fingers pause.

Extant discourse scholars in promotions studies have explored the deployment of textual, rhetoric and semiotic resources in print, broadcast, outdoor and Internet promotions (Oduola & Durosinmi, 2018; Adegoju & Ademilokun, 2015; Li, 2016; Meghdari & Sobhari, 2016; Oyebode & Unuabonah, 2013). Although the studies adopted analytical frameworks different from what the present study utilises, they all acknowledged the synergies of verbal (text) and visual constituents in the construction and concretization of meanings in promotional campaigns. However, the discursive construction of the multilayered resources in online promotions, branding and transactional advances by digital affiliate companies is still largely understudied (Wen-Cheng, 2016), when compared to the fact that affiliate marketing is now 'the fulcrum of business promotions on Nigerian digital spaces' (Adun, 2023, p. 2). Also noticeable is the observation that the research efforts on multimodal analysis of promotions discourses in Nigeria, amongst the aforementioned studies, did not subject or situate the conceptualisation and theorisation of image-text relations, especially within the context of digital affiliate advertisements. Even so, the sparse studies on Jumia's promotions seldom addressed this research lacuna. For instance, Ejabena

(2018) interrogated the semiotics of product advertisements of Jumia and Konga. The study averred that inter-modal relations in the promotions significantly articulate the meaning-making process, and concluded that the utilisation of multimodal resources 'provide product information, promote sales and purchase, popularise brands, and convey emotionally-motivating strategies' (p.xii). The study however discounted the different types of image-text relations inherent in both Jumia and Konga campaigns and the promotional essence of these relation types. Addressing how the relations of text and image discursively evince persuasive and meaning-construal in the online affiliate promotions is therefore the aim of the chapter. To achieve this aim, the objectives of the chapter are to (i) identify the image-text relation types in the Jumia's affiliate advertisements; analyse how the image-text relations advance promotional discursivity (ii); (iii) and discuss the promotional impact of the relations on prospects vis-à-vis their purchasing decisions.

2. LANGUAGE, MULTIMODALITY AND PERSUASION IN ONLINE PROMOTIONAL DISCOURSE OF AFFILIATE ORGANISATIONS

Affiliate marketing is a marketing model that emerged in the 1990s with Amazon being the pioneer (Abdelhady *et al.*, 2020). Today, it has advanced into becoming a billion-dollar industry globally since the leverage of many digital spaces orchestrated a new direction for its market across many continents. Affiliate marketing is a system of product promotion by proxy. Here, affiliate marketers or companies who are not production principals sign a third-party contract with a production company to market the latter's products/service, generate sales traffic and facilitate product delivery to consumers. Since year 2020, the Nigerian business landscape, initially occasioned by the propellant from the Covid-19 crisis, has been experiencing the ubiquity of digital affiliate marketing (Badmus, 2022). This direction is associated with increased demands for affiliates by companies, retail organizations and SMEs who now explore digital affiliate models of affiliate organizations to increase service/product and drive patronage (Nwogu, 2019). Two affiliate companies *Jumia* and *Konga* are most prominent, for pioneering affiliate advertisement in Nigeria long before such marketing model received prominence, and this aids their competitive niches nationally (Ekwueme, Akagwu & Akoji, 2017). They are business-to-consumer retail enterprises that promote other organisations' products, both online and onsite. They commercialise their online affiliate programmes/channels for this purpose.

Language use, as a representational means, has been a significant thrust of studies on online promotional discourse (Bhatia, 2005; Ayoola, 2014), and, now that the increasing utilisation of digital spaces is shaping linguistic practices (Petroni, 2019), more studies are piquing their interest on the tactics of language sustaining persuasion and or manipulations. Online promotional discourse centers on Internet advertising, sales or marketing that exert persuasion on consumers. Persuasion explains ways in which promotions stimulate prospects to realising the need for a product/service and the decision to subscribe into it among other consumer behaviour (e.g. purchase incentives) (Thorson & Duffy, 2012). Essential to this chapter, persuasion is an 'intentional communication process' where purchase prospects are influenced via communication to making purchase decisions, even impulsively (Janoschka, 2004, p.123). Usually, an instrument for orchestrating persuasion is emotional marketing. This kind of marketing engineers a latent way of selling emotions that drive product/service sales. It is, for instance, arguable that Netflix rather promotes escapism than movies, McDonalds sells happiness than meals, and Rolex represents high social status than fashion. This reiterates the marketing ideology that exceptional brands principally promote emotional values rather than products, as this debatably influences more consumers into subconscious purchase decisions than if the product itself was the center of the promotion (Sharma, Kodhati & Sukhavsi, 2022; Pandey & Kumar, 2012). This is what Thorson and Duffy construe when they maintain that advertisements 'offering social outcomes such as increased status, connectedness with others or general social approval' essentially promote social emotional promises (2012, p. 76).

Of relevance to this chapter is the observation that online affiliate marketing and or digital advertising is also principally predicated on emotional appeals, as the latter have become the marketing linchpin that sustains the interest of online consumers in an endlessly-moving digital world that is paced with short attention and easy distraction. Different studies on emotional marketing in online advertisements maintain that emotional strategies are deployed for varied marketing goals: optimisation of engagement, brand relationship quality, affinity, loyalty, consumer behaviors, purchase decisions and incentive offers (Bhargavi, 2024; Singh *et al.*, 2024; Garg *et al.*, 2023; Chauhan, 2022; Xie *et al.*, 2004). However, their constant position is that the instrumentality of emotions in online marketing drives in-depth psychological connections with virtual prospects (Singh *et al.*, 2024). Singh et al.'s (2024) findings particularly contend that online emotional advertising thrives on affective stimuli as a human tendency, which though may be moderated by demographic factors like age, gender and culture. Xie *et al.*'s (2004, p. 30) investigation of the association of 'emotional appeal and incentive offering in banner advertisements' concluded that the prevalence of positive emotional appeals in incentive-offering banner ads informs the effectiveness of the incentives. However, ads with zero or negative emotions thrive better if they offer no incentives. Also, Yousef *et al.* (2021) appropriated the theory of emotional dimensions as a framework for unpacking how positive, negative and coactive emotions in social media advertisements shape consumer behaviour. Their findings uncovered that positive emotions endear favourable consumer responses, negative emotions can effectively propel precautionary actions, and coactive emotions (a synthesis of positive and negative appeals) provide a balanced approach though their effectiveness is largely dependent on context and target audience.

At this juncture, it is pertinent to stress that story-telling and dialogue discursively drive emotional appeals and communications in promotions on mainstream media (such as TV, radio, films, print dailies). However, the synthesis of linguistic elements (texts) and visuals drive them in digital marketing landscape—including online affiliate spaces. Such emotional appeals are laced with linguistic and visual resources that endear the interest of online users to product/service adverts. Dyer (1982) uncovers that lexical classes like adverbs and adjectives are resourceful linguistic items in online advertisements. This is because they place the impression that a product bear irresistible features and essentially clothe the promotional message with uniqueness, vigour and effect. In addition, Janoschka (2004) evinces that performative speech acts, abridged use of language, sentence forms – such as rhetorical, requests, personal pronouns – and deictic elements are syntactic structures that influence and call online users to take purchase decisions. However, far beyond the primary purpose of advancing product information and description, language use, especially the mood system informed by sentence types, such as the imperatives, declaratives and indicative sentence patterns, propels the purchasing behaviour of the target community of consumers (Oyebode & Olateju, 2011). Following Janoschka's (2004) position that linguistic manifestations in promotions are categorised into syntactic, lexical and pragmatic levels, the mood system is always enshrouded in syntactic and pragmatic constructions to ignite illocutionary force that endear consumer's reaction to the promotions. Illocutionary force, according to Yule (1996), is the communicative force of an expression that comes in the form of declarative, interrogative and/or imperative structures. The imperative structure is especially significantly and innovatively used by product/service promoters to influence consumer's decision because of the advisory, suggestive, requesting, promissory and attention-endearing roles it performs aside traditional role of directing (Oyebode & Olateju, 2011).

In addition, different manifestations of narrative voices have also been identified as linguistic devices used in promotions to provide anecdotes and conversation-like scenarios with which advert agents enact their imaginary presence, address consumers, create an imagined interpersonal relationship with them and present testimonies/reviews that can resonate with consumers' needs (Goddard, 1998). The use of personal pronouns such as 'I', 'she' and 'he' largely enriches such narration. All of these narration purposes have a single end goal: persuasion. Corroborating this, Sánchez (2015) particularly addresses the functional role that interpersonal metafunction of language play in emotion-related discourses, including business promotions. They contend that interpersonal linguistic items, particularly the markers of persons (pronouns), polarity, temporal circumstances and moods, straddle both roles of informing and persuading prospective consumers.

Interesting to this study is the evidence that scholars have appreciated the synergistic relations of language and visual artefact in meaning-making engagement. For instance, Goddard's (1998, p. 16) findings attest that 'readers do not simply read images independently of the accompanying verbal resources; rather, there exists a co-referentiality between both resources.' Also, as noted by Martin (2006), system of mood, slogans and catchphrases are anchorages and significations to understanding the reading of images and soundbites in motion and posters of advertisements, particularly their potential resourcefulness in driving persuasion. This observation informs the significance of multimodal artefacts in the persuasive engagement of advertisement.

Before now, much was emphasized on the imperative of images in communication (Kress and van Leeuwen, 1996), and today, new media spaces (including digital (affiliate) marketing channels), image-enhancing software such as Photoshop and Dreamweaver, and artificial intelligence-abled apps — for generating graphics, animations, virtual and augmented realities — have extended the frontiers of image projection on virtual spaces. This results in the proliferation of multimodal communication. The concept of multimodal communication is a development from extant studies on semiotics which stress the significations of images (signs and modes) in the meaning-making process of a communicative text (Barthes,1977; Halliday, 1978; van Leeuwen, 2005). It is an extension of semiotics because it caters for all modes in visual, verbal and/or written form of language inclusive. In other words, multimodality accommodates a blend of both the linguistic and non-linguistic features — which comprise images, motions, pictures, symbols, colours, among others — in the representation of either the interactive participants, who are the real people behind the initiation of social phenomenon projected, or the represented actors who are implicated by the projection. In fact, Kress and van Leeuwen (2006) argue in the light of Halliday's proposed metafunctions of language in Systemic Functional Linguistics, for the semiotic metafunctions of visuals such as representational, interactive and compositional functions. They further explain that 'vectors' in the visuals perform the transactional role of relating between the actor and goal, and that visual elements (such as focus gradience, and colour saturation) perform locative relation in that they signify circumstances. The interactive functions of visuals are embedded in the roles that camera angles, image acts and the direction/gaze of represented actors perform. They perform the functions through contact-trigger image acts, social distance-induced camera shots, and attitude-informed artifacts (Machin & Mayr, 2012; and Kress & van Leeuwen, 2006). Camera angles portray social distance because 'close-up' shot is suggestive of personal proximity of participants, medium shot is suggestive of relative distance, and a 'long' shot is indicative of lack of familiarity. All of these project possible power and engagement with audience.

The compositional metafunction facilitates cohesion between verbal and visual elements in a given text. It also facilitates the relationship between representational (visual) and interactive (verbal) elements with the aid of 'information value', 'salience' and 'framing' (van Leeuwen, 2006). According to Karagevrekis (2012), information value refers to the information positioned left, right, top and bottom, centre and/or margin of the visual frame. The term 'salience' refers to the elements that endear the attention of viewers to essentials of the visuals. These elements are projected through foregrounding (or backgrounding), illumination, colour contrasts, size and tonal value. Framing is the presence or absence of frame lines that (dis) connect image elements to show cohesion or isolation.

Therefore, aside language, many semiotic affordances such as image, typography (typefaces/fonts and their sizes), colour, lines, background, gaze, posture, gesture (kinesics), facial expressions and dressing, as a number of multimodal discourse scholars aver (Ketabi & Najafian, 2011; Machin & Mayr, 2012; Machin & Polzer, 2015), are all instrumental in the promotional meaning-making and persuasive engagements that different genres of advertisement discourse exhibit.

3. SEMANTIC RELATIONS OF IMAGE AND TEXT IN MULTIMODAL DISCOURSE

At the fore of conceptualising and theorising the image-text semantic relations are Roland Barthes' and Michael Halliday's earlier works, both of which paved the foundation for subsequent arguments on the patterns of co-referentiality and relationality of/between images and texts many decades after, as multimodal semiotics generated an array of frameworks for interrogating the dynamics of visual communications in today's increasingly evolving world. For instance, Barthes' (1977) three concepts, 'anchorage', 'illustrations' and 'relay' uncover the interlocking positions of text and image in meaning constructions in communication artefacts: 'anchorage' represents instances where the text/language in its content and message corroborates the significations in the image); *illustrations* represents where image rather elucidates the text; and *relay* represents both image and text sharing a paratactic/complementary semantic status — which is rare in static artifacts but relevant to motion artifacts where:

> *dialogue functions not simply as elucidation but really does advance the action by setting out, in the sequence of messages, meanings that are not found in the image itself... [and where] the words, in the same way as the images, are frag-*

ments of a more general syntagm and the unity of the message is realized at a higher level. (1977b; p. 41)

Significantly also, Halliday's (1985, 1994) status relations classify the association of clauses in complex clause structure. Halliday advances that two clauses share parastatic (equal) status when, although both co-join as a single compound clause, they can conveniently remain independent when separated. However, where one lacks the capacity to remain alone, their co-joining status is unequal. Aside status relations, Hallidayan grammar equally highlights the clause relationality in terms of logico–semantics by two prominences: expansion and projections. Expansion is realised when a clause elaborates on the meaning of another clause by describing the latter (elaboration), extends another's meaning by providing additional information about the latter (extension), or enhances another clause by offering circumstantial details — such as time, place, cause, reason or purposes— about the latter (enhancement). However, projection, to Halliday, is realised by both locution (when a verbal process is used in articulating a clause), and idea (when a mental process is deployed in projecting meaning).

While Halliday only streamlined this application to linguistic construction, many multimodal semiotic theorists whose works are largely an offshoot of Halliday's thinking have appropriated this to interpret image-text syntheses. Prominent among them is Martinec and Salway's (2005) image-text relations system—the framework for interrogating the data in this chapter. The model theorizes the interaction of image and text, particularly how elements in the structure of text and images are combined in realizing semantic relations, coherence and wholesome meanings. It is heavily informed by earlier foundational works on systemic functional linguistics and semiotics (cf. Barthes, 1977a, 1977b; Halliday, 1985, 1994; Kress & van Leeuwen, 1996; Lemke, 1998; Martinec, 1998). The theory argues for two subsystems, namely 'status' and 'logico–semantics', in the interaction of image and text that can realise either equality or non-equality of status. However, largely essential to the present discussion is the status relations.

With regard to status, the theory avers that text and image can exhibit equal status (i.e. equally related) on two grounds: independently or complementary. Their status is considered to be independent if both the whole image and the whole text are placed on equal standing with no evidence of modifier. However, where this independency happens but with evidence of one modifying the other, then the status is complementary. Image–text equal status shows that 'a whole image is related to a whole text [e.g. a whole text could be either a paragraph, clauses or any of its structures]' (Martinec & Salway, 2005, p. 343), not to a part of the text. In other words, where all processes (revealed in the verbal groups) in independent clauses (hypotactic clauses) in, for instance, a paragraph relate to an image, the image is said to have a whole/complete relation to the paragraph.

To the theorists, in a relation of independence, image and text do not join to 'form part of a larger syntagm' (p. 343); rather each is parallel and stands with its own processes. For instance, the image(s) may be the Carrier and/or the Attribute, while the text may be placed separately to relate to, intensify and identify the Carrier and or the Attribute. Hence, the text could consist of expressions serving as the Identified and the one serving as the Identifier. However, in a complementary status, both image and text synergise to 'form part of a larger syntagm' (p. 344). An example is when the image occupies the position of a Carrier, and the text occupies the position of an Attribute. This means that they are both participants in a relational/attributive process.

In contrast, that text and image can exhibit unequal status, the same way two clauses exist in a complex clause structure where one clause is subordinate to and modifies the other. An image is subordinate to a text when it is related to only a part of the latter. That is, some processes (the verbal groups) in the independent clause in the text do not relate to the image while other processes do. This means that the image does not reflect everything relayed in the contents of the text, as there will be some processes, participants and circumstances in the text which a multimodal discourse analyst might not capture if they merely focus on the image reading. However, a text is subordinate to an image when there are linguistic references (e.g. deixis, including verb tenses [material or behavioural processes inclusive] or other devices (such as photo captions decodable by reference to the image) to certain significations in the image as they describe what is happening/evident in the image. Figure 1 provides a diagrammatic summary of the status relations between image and text.

Figure 1. System of image–text status relations

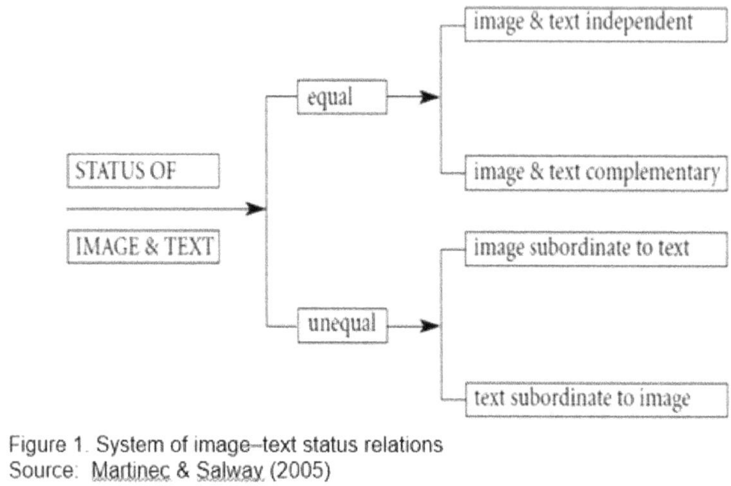

Source: Martinec & Salway (2005)

4. METHODOLOGY

The data analysed in this chapter were five (5) samples of advertisements/e-banners downloaded from Jumia's website, all within December 2023. Observably, Jumia produces advertisements for every weekend sales boosting. Thus, one (1) advert was randomly selected for each of the five weekends in December 2023. This window was informed by the fact that every Decembers usher in festive and end-of-year celebrations. Considering that companies usually utilise the season to endear the public with price slashes, many of them expectedly beef up their advertisements at this time to scramble for the attention of the public who is faced with many bazar options. Jumia was chosen not only for its hyper popularity and rating amongst Nigerian affiliate companies (Nwogu, 2019; Ekwueme, Akagwu & Akoji, 2017) but also for being a lead pioneer of virtual shopping in Nigeria (Philips Consulting Report, 2014). This chapter adopted a discourse approach to analyse the data as it interrogated structure and system of relations in the production of the selected online promotions banners. The banners were named AD1-AD5 for easy identification in the analysis. The data were appreciated using insights from Martinec and Salway's (2005) image-text relations, and visuo-linguistic resources manifesting the discursivity nature of the promotions as informed by Halliday's Systemic Functional Linguistics, and Barthes' Semiotics. The findings of the study are discussed in the subsequent section.

5. PRESENTATION OF DATA

Figure 2. AD 1

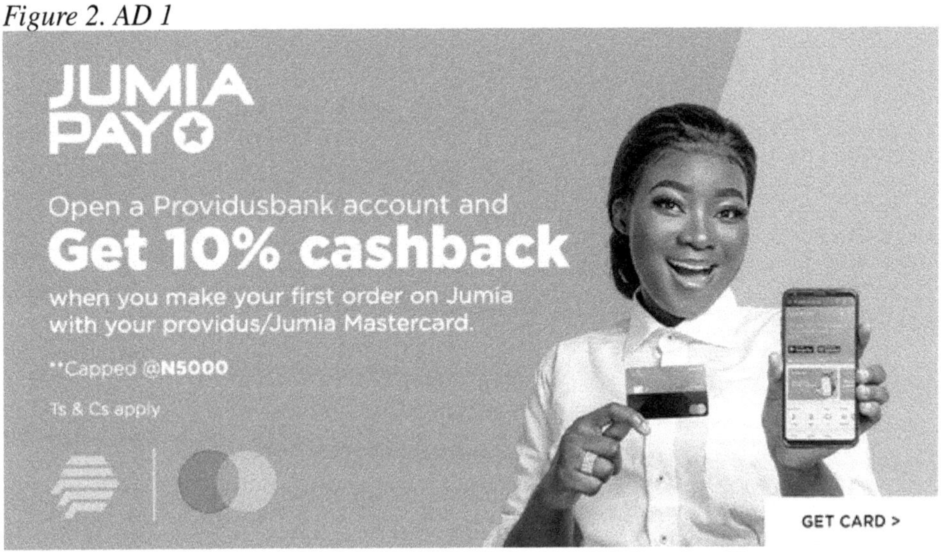

Figure 3. AD 2

Figure 4. AD 3

Figure 5. AD 4

Figure 6. AD 5

Primary Source: www.jumia.com.ng

6. FINDINGS AND DISCUSSION

The findings reveal that Jumia bases its marketization of products principally on rhetoric of incentives and product/service enticement as discourse strategies. To maximise and foreground this promissory cum persuasive strategy, the promotional discourse agents weave its significance around three inherent status relations of visual and linguistic resources that thrive such promotions as though they were a favour to the public. The analysis below exemplifies the instances.

6.1 IMAGE-TEXT COMPLEMENTARINESS

The text and the image in AD 1 are presented saliently, as the conjoining of the blue-yellow background makes the texts and image conspicuous as the principal meaning-construing artefacts in the promotion. Saliency ensures that while prospective consumers feed their eyes with the image(s), they do not ignore the text bearing the promotional message. Observably in other ADs, it is a design culture for the promotions by Jumia to manifest a two-color (or three-color) backdrop that facilitates saliency.

A foray into status relations in AD1 shows that complementary relations exist between the images and the text. The images all relate to the text. The most conspicuously positioned image is a smartly dressed young lady fronting a Providus/Jumia (jointly owned) Mastercard and a phone whose screen displays the front-page of Providusbank App. The yellow logo of Providusbank and the emblem of Jumia (an encircled star) both signify a partnership deal between the two companies. The deal is represented by both the bank App and the Mastercard logo (the red-yellow intersected sets of a venn).

The principal image — the represented participant (the lady) — is a Carrier in 'relational…attributive [material] processes' (Martinec & Salway, 2005, p. 344). The material action processes such as 'open a Providusbank account', 'get 10% cash-back', 'get card', '…make your first order' and 'capped @N5000' are attributive as they expressively correlate with the image reading. These processes are embedded in the complex clause structure containing a compound subtle imperative clause, 'open a Providusbank account' and get 10% cashback' (which is the main clause), and a subordinate conditional clause, 'when make your first order on Jumia with your Providus/Jumia Mastercard' (notice the use of conditional elements such as 'when' and 'with'). The fact that the product promoter deployed multiple material processes, without a single instance of mental process and verbal process, suggests that the material processes are tactically couched to drive prospects into making a decision to subscribe to the service of the bank without a chance to either ruminate on such a decision or make even further enquiries on the veracity of the offer.

The choice of white colour for both the text and the image is quite deliberate as it makes the complementarity status conspicuous. To achieve more salience, different graphological mechanisms, such as bolder fonts, bigger font sizes and uppercase, are applied to the expressions 'JUMIA PAY', 'Get 10% cashback' and 'N5000' in order to capture attractions to the message conveyed by the imperative clauses. The close-up shot of the image suggests an imaginary proximity between the participant and the consumer, which by extension, does not only invite the consumer for a better understanding of what the promotion offers but also evokes a sense of direct engagement. The deployment of the discourse strategy of enticement (as evident in the smiley gesture of the participant showcasing the product(s)) also reinforces the invite technique. Furthermore, both the participant's strategic positioning and eye gazes maintain a contact with the imaginary target consumers to consolidate the invite, thereby strengthening the persuasive appeal of the advertisement. By extension, the discourse strategy of excitement in the image endears the consumers to the subtle imperative messages of the text.

Furthermore, quite noticeable is the mood system in the declarative and imperative expressions that enforce the illocutionary force to facilitate the rhetoric of incentives and product enticement. 'JUMIA PAY' is a declarative noun phrase anchoring, introducing and informing the consumer of the incentive initiative embedded in the advertisement. The imperative expression, 'Open a Providusbank account,' is suggestive of how to participate to benefit from the incentive — i.e. the 'JUMIA PAY'. The imperative statement, 'Get 10% cashback,' is promising and inviting. Also, the conditional clause, 'when you make your first order with your Providusbank/Jumia Mastercard', the verbal group, 'capped @N500,' and the declarative expression, 'Ts and Cs apply,' are quite informing of what can guarantee being a beneficiary. However, the prospect's attention is seldom directed some level of uncertainty that might underlie the promotion. These condition-implied expressions, by strategy, do not only presuppose that not all service subscribers would get to benefit from the offer, as it is the case with most promos, but also preempt the company from being liable in such cases. Instructively therefore, the complimentary nature of image-text status in AD1, beyond promoting the banking and transactional services of both Providus Bank and Jumia respectively, evokes the emotion of financial gains to consumers of the advert through the discourse strategy of enticement. This is because rather than emphasizing making 'open a providusbank account' the center of the advertisement, the promoter largely emphasizes the financial promises ('JUMIA PAY' and 'Get 10% cashback') that prospects stand to enjoy. This observation accentuates the position of Sharma, Kodhati and Sukhavsi (2022), and Pandey and Kumar (2012) that such marketing ideology is capable of driving more prospects into impulsive and subconscious purchase decisions than if the promoter were to place emphasis on the banking service for which the advert was actually initiated.

Similar to what obtains in AD 1, AD 2 presents a conjoining of Green-Orange backdrop that manifests the salience of the text and the image. More significantly, the choice of green and orange is implicitly purposive as both colours attest that Jumia only promote fresh, natural, healthy (for green), delicious and or satisfying (for orange) consumables and toiletries. There is also an evidence of complementary image–text relationship. This is because the collection of groceries in the cart implies that only a shopping of multiple products, rather than one or two products, enjoys the promised discount. This aligns with the message of the nominal group, 'Big Discount Grocery,' wherein the modifiers 'big' and 'discount' describe the noun 'grocery' to signify that a 'big' grocery shopping is discounted.

Noticeably, the use of uppercase and large typefaces respectively on the alphanumeric nominal groups, '30% OFF' and 'BIG DISCOUNT GROCERY,' draws the attention of consumers to the rhetoric of incentive in order to appeal to their sense of impulsive purchases. Notably, people generally buy on impulse when a product is cheap. Besides, the illocutionary force is also evident as the nominal group, 'BIG DISCOUNT GROCERY,' is an anchorage that offers inviting information, while the prepositional group, 'Up to 30% OFF on groceries,' offers promises and persuades the consumer to take purchase decisions. It is safe to assert that the image-text complementarity which drives the notion of 'the more, the cheaper' primarily markets the emotion of expense reduction/cost saving, rather than the products. This is arguable as both the text and image synergistically avoid specific product mentions.

In addition, AD 3 below also leverages the rhetoric of incentive. Jumia in this advert keyed into the spur of the festive season to engage in a general sales promotion that would enable it clear (sell off) its existing stocks, for the arrival of fresh products in the new year; hence, it offers 'up to 67% off' products prices. The orange-red backdrop equally facilitates the salience of text and image(s). Observably, the status of the image(s) and the text is largely complementary as they both play a co-participation role in the material process of informing and incentivizing the consumer. The term, 'holiday,' and the date span 'Dec 25- Jan 7' are attributive of the image of a lady in holiday/vacation mood (noticeable in her excitement, the Santa cap and cold-proof cardigan that characterise the December season). The spin of products around the lady is representative of the stocks that Jumia intends to mass sell through the 'clearance sales' promotion that promises 'up to 67%' price reductions.

While the nominal group, 'Holiday Clearance Sale,' exerts a semiotic significance of informing consumers, the prepositional group, 'Up to 67% off,' enacts an illocutionary force that promises and invites them. However, a critical mind might interrogate the intention behind the foregrounding use of thick and weighty font size for 'Holiday Clearance Sale' and a less significant font size for 'Up to 67% off.' Thus, it is not out of place to insinuate that the price slashes might only be applicable to only a consumer that shops a collection of goods, rather than a single product. Therefore, in what is similar to the observation in AD 2, the image-text complementarity in AD 3 foregrounds the ecstasy of expense reduction/cost saving through incentivisation (i.e. discounted products) and happiness in the festive season, rather than the products, as both the image and text are silent about the nature of the products being discounted. This finding correlates with Xie et al.'s (2004) stance that the use of positive emotions in an incentive-offering adverts improves the effectiveness of the incentives.

6.2 IMAGE SUBORDINATION TO TEXT

It is typical of Jumia's adverts to have multi-colour backdrops. In AD 4, the use of multicolour (dark blue, yellow and orange) backdrop facilitates the salience of the products. However, unlike what obtains in ADs 1-3, the image in AD 4 exemplifies a subordination status when compared to the text. This is informed by the observation that nothing from the image reading is denotative or connotative that the products belong to 'Itel,' the company whose products Jumia promotes. Nothing in the image suggests they are latest product or that the consumer will enjoy free delivery upon purchase. The consumer rather acquires this information value upon reading the textual elements.

Regarding social distance, closely shot images of the back side of the advertised phones (showing their multiple-camera feature) interact to intimate the consumer with how sophisticated and highly technologically enabled the gadgets are. The positioning (the back view of the phones) acts as a point of enticement (selling leverage). Corroborating the enticement rhetoric is the linguistic manifestation of the nominal item, 'itel,' which appears in bold print encircled by an oval red callout, which is the logo of Itel. Considering that Itel is a company whose products are popular in the Nigerian market, this realization is carefully positioned to provide trust. The nominal item, 'itel,' is therefore an anchorage to the product images.

The nominal group, 'P55,' which is printed in weighty font size facilitates the salience of the feature(s), and suggests that the phones, being the latest versions, have the most desirable feature(s) any classy consumer would seldom ignore. More illocutionary exertions are observable in AD 4. The nominal group, 'P55,' promises exciting features in the phones and hence, it is an anchorage. The clause fragment, 'Fast Charge, Game on!,' promises a short-time electricity consumption and durability for the battery. In other words, the battery takes a short time to be charged, and a very long time before it can exhaust — so 'Game on!'. The presence of exclamation strengthens the excitement offered by the durability of the phones and/or their batteries. Discursively approaching promotions this way is a strategy that resonates with the Nigerian reality. Jumia and Itel have operated in Nigeria long enough to understand that epileptic electricity supply is a linchpin challenge in the country. Therefore, a promise of this nature could propel excitement emanating from the hope of putting an end to worries about drained battery every time. Also, the nominal group, 'free delivery,' is an inviting promise, while the imperative sentence, 'SHOP NOW', printed in uppercase, is not only advisory but also directs the consumer to the hyperlink for the shopping. The synthesis of AD 4 therefore essentially markets the emotions of status/class and convenience.

6.3 TEXT SUBORDINATION TO IMAGE

The rhetoric of both incentives and enticement manifests in AD 5. As in the previous ADs, the red-orange background of AD5 typically foregrounds the text and image that convey the promotional essence. Observably, the promotional oeuvre presents a text–subordinate-to-image relationship largely because the material and behavioural processes in the text describe only the ongoing in the image (Martinec & Salway, 2005). The present tense verb, 'shop,' and the progressive tense, 'shopping,' describe what the young lady does on the laptop. The present tense verbs, 'earn' and 'make [money],' describe the excitement in the face of the represented participant and portray the impression that the excitement comes as a result of earning by shopping on Jumia online marketplace. The nominal group, '(Jumia)

Force,' describes the power gesture displayed by the participant, and by extension, metaphorises the earning power.

Jumia metaphorically associates consumer's shopping on its virtual platform with increasing their earning power. Since increasing one's earning capacity is the only means of meeting one's needs, it is feasible that an average Nigerian consumer struggling to increase their earnings may not only leap at this incentive but also go extra mile to commercialise shopping as relayed in the nominal expression, 'shopping for yourself, friends and family on Jumia'. Observably therefore, the imperative sentences, 'shop and earn' and 'make money from shopping...,' both have illocutionary significance of enticing the consumer, and the boldened typeface of the former reinforces the enticement. Therefore, the synthesis in AD 5 foregrounds the ecstasy of financial relief/freedom to the consumer more than the service of shopping itself.

7. CONCLUSION

The chapter has explored the relevance of Martinec and Salway's (2005) image-text relations system for viscerally understanding the discursive role of linguo-visual resources in the meaning-making process in online promotional discourse of affiliate marketing companies. It essentially evinced how the image-text relation types/statuses advances promotional meanings and contributes in defining how communication in online affiliate marketing is established.

Drawing on the 2023 yuletide promotions by *Jumia* an established affiliate company in Nigeria, the chapter addressed how the synthesis of texts and images are deployed to promote products online by the Company. The findings demonstrated that Jumia's principal discourse strategy is rhetoric of incentives and product enticement as a shade of persuasion. The online promotional discourse employs three types of intersections of language (text) and visuals (images): text-image complementarity, image subordination to text, and text subordination to image. Theses relations serve as resources that facilitate the rhetoric, and thereby shaping the consumer's decision. Observably, the end result of the synthesis of images and texts in Jumia's advertisements shrewdly orchestrates 'emotional marketing'—a parlance denoting the promotion of emotional benefits of the products/services that Jumia advertises. Some of these emotions are status/class and convenience (as projected in AD 4 which advertises latest mobile phones), expense reduction/cost saving (as in AD 2 and AD 3 which promote discounted products and incentivisation), financial gains (as in AD 1 and AD 5 which both promote increased earnings of customers), and happiness (as in AD 2 which anticipates a high purchase rate in the festive season).

It is therefore safe to say that Martinec and Salway's (2005) image-text relations system is relevant for viscerally understanding the discursive and synthetic role of linguistics and visual resources in online promotions of affiliate marketing companies. The chapter thus occupies significant gaps in literature on multimodal discourse of cyber affiliate marketing.

8. FUTURE RESEARCH DIRECTIONS

Ample research efforts in multimodal discourse analysis across developed worlds have established theoretically and practically the intersection of text/language and static and motion visuals in different communication contexts and settings. However away from this, the direction in which virtual and augmented reality technologies of the digital world now drive humanity to, especially in advertisement, entertainment and fashion industries, needs multimodal discourse analytic studies to interrogate these digital developments. In recent times, multinational apparel and gaming companies, such as Nike and Roblox, have respectively been utilising augmented reality technology, avatars and metaverse innovations on their companies' apps to redefine customer satisfaction and e-commerce experience (Hadden, 2019; Nike News, 2021; Future Stores, 2022). A future research on the multimodality of the adoption of virtual reality, augmented reality, metaverse and web3-technologies will be insightful in unearthing how interactive intersections of multiple meaning-construing modes from the new technologies contribute to advancing virtual worlds that are enthralling representations of the actual worlds of the companies utilising these technologies.

In addition, the multimodality in AI-generated digital advertisements provides affordances for investigating them from a critical multimodal perspective. Interrogating language models, such as ChatGPT and its AI-enabled advertisement semiotics, would unearth rewarding positions on what the themes, perceptions and meanings the modes in such advertisements could tell us about the companies utilising such promotions.

REFERENCES

Abdelhady, M. H., Kamal, N. M. & Abd El Samie, H. (2020). Impact of affiliate marketing on customer loyalty. *Journal of the Faculty of Tourism and Hotels-University of Sadat City*, 4(1/1).

Adegoju, A., & Ademilokun, M. (2015). Verbal and visual signifiers of advertising shares offers in Nigeria's 2005 bank recapitalization. *Discourse & Communication, 9*(5), 519–533. DOI: 10.1177/1750481315600300

Adun, S. (2023). *The impact of affiliate marketing on purchasing behaviour of Nigerian consumers: the case of B2C marketers*. Unpublished masters dissertation, University of the West of Scotland, UK.

Ayoola, K.A. (2014). Manipulative use of short messaging service (SMS) text messages by Nigerian telecommunications companies. *Linguistik online*, 63 (1/14). https://doi.org/DOI: 10.13092/lo.63.1323

Badmus, J. (2022). *11 top paying affiliate marketing programs in Nigeria*. https://branditechture.com/11-top-paying-affiliate-marketing-programs-in-nigeria/

Barthes, R. (1977). *Image, Music, Text*. Fontana.

Barthes, R. (1997a). The photographic message. In Barthes, R. (Ed.), *Image–Music–Text* (pp. 15–31). Fontana.

Barthes, R. (1997b). Rhetoric of the image. In Barthes, R. (Ed.), *Image–Music–Text* (pp. 32–51). Fontana.

Bhargavi, L. M. (2024). The role of emotional appeal in modern advertising: A Study on role of e-advertisement on consumer buying behaviour. ShodhKosh. *Journal of Visual and Performing Arts*, *5*(1), 141–153. DOI: 10.29121/shodhkosh.v5.i1.2024.1697

Bhatia, V. K. (2005). Generic patterns in promotional discourse. In Halmari, H., Virtanen, T., & Benjamins, J. (Eds.), *Persuasion across genres: a linguistic approach* (pp. 213–228). Publishing Company., https://www.researchgate.net/publication/283034102_Generic_patterns_in_promotional_discourse DOI: 10.1075/pbns.130.13bha

Chauhan, H. (2022). The influence of emotional advertising appeals on consumer decision making: A cross-sectional study. *International Journal of Early Childhood Special Education*, *14*, 3106–3109. DOI: 10.48047/intjecse/v14i4.425

Cheng, W. F. (2016). Constructing hotel brands: A multimodal analysis of luxury hotel homepages. *Ibérica*, (31), 83–108. http://www.revistaiberica.org/index.php/iberica/article/view/190

Ejabena, H. O. (2018). Multimodal semiotic study of product advertisements in Nigerian online shopping outlets. Unpublished Master's thesis, Obafemi Awolowo University, Ile-Ife, Nigeria.

Ekwueme, A., Akagwu & Akoji. N. (2017). The influence of online marketing of Jumia and Konga on consumer purchasing behaviour among Kogi State Residents of Nigeria. *Global Journal of Human-Social Science*, 17 (6) (1), 24-32.

Garg, P., Singh, S., Chamola, P., Kumar, A., & Paliwal, M. (2023). Elucidating the linkage between advertisements embedded with emotional appeals and the brand relationship quality during the COVID pandemic. *Journal of Marketing Communications, 31*(2), 126–150. DOI: 10.1080/13527266.2023.2220338

Goddard, A. (1998). *The language of advertising: Written texts*. Routledge.

Hadden, S. L. (2019). *What Nike's use of AR in e-commerce means for the retail industry*. https://www.sama.com/blog/what-nikes-use-of-ar-in-ecommerce-means-for-the-retail-industry/

Halliday, M. A. K. (1985). *An introduction to functional grammar*. Arnold.

Halliday, M. A. K. (1994). *An Introduction to Functional Grammar* (2nd ed.). Arnold.

Janoschka, A. (2004). *Web advertising: New forms of communication on the Internet*. John Benjamins Publishing Company. DOI: 10.1075/pbns.131

Karagevrekis, M. (2012). Multimodal text analysis of three modern Greek printed advertisements employing the persuasive modes of *Ethos, Logos and Pathos*. In Bowcher, W. L., & Royce, T. D. (Eds.), *Multimodal text from around the world: cultural and linguistic insights* (pp. 69–96). Palgrave Macmillan. DOI: 10.1057/9780230355347_4

Ketabi, S., & Najafian, M. (2011). Advertising social semiotic representation: A critical approach. [Macrothink Institute.]. *International Journal of Industrial Marketing, 1*(1), 63–78.

Kress, G., & Van Leeuwen, T. (1996). *Reading images*. Routledge.

Kress, G., & van Leeuwen, T. (2006). *Reading images: the grammar of visual Design* (2nd ed.). Routledge Taylor & Francis Group. DOI: 10.4324/9780203619728

Lemke, J. (1998). Multiplying meaning: visual and verbal semiotics in scientific text. In Martin, J. R., & Veel, R. (Eds.), *Reading Science* (pp. 87–113). Routledge.

Li, D. (2016). Multimodal discourse analysis of the interpersonal meaning of TV advertisements. *International Journal of Social Science and Humanity*, *6*(12), 934–938. DOI: 10.18178/ijssh.2016.V6.776

Machin, D., & Mayr, A. (2012). *How to do critical discourse analysis: A multimodal introduction*. Sage Publications Limited.

Machin, D., & Polzer, L. (2015). *Visual journalism*. Palgrave Macmillan. DOI: 10.5040/9781350394674

Martin, E. (2006). *Marketing identities through language: English and global imagery in French Advertising*. Palgrave Macmillan. DOI: 10.1057/9780230511903

Martinec, R. (1998). Cohesion in action. *Semiotica*, *120*(1/2), 161–180. DOI: 10.1515/semi.1998.120.1-2.161

Martinec, R., & Salway's, A. (2005). A system for image–text relations in new (and old) media. *Visual Communication*, *4*(3), 337–371. DOI: 10.1177/1470357205055928

Meghdari, S., & Sobhari, M. (2016). Multimedia discourse analysis of Tehran and Shiraz commercial advertising. *Journal of Linguistics & Khorasan Dialects Biannual*, *8*(2), 19–23.

Nigeria, J. www.jumia.com.ng

Nike News. (2021). *Nike creates Nikeland on Roblox.*https://news.nike.com/news/five-things-to-know-roblox

Nwogu, C. U. K. (2019). Affiliate marketing concept and performance of online businesses in Nigeria. *Journal of Marketing and Consumer Research*, *52*. Advance online publication. DOI: 10.7176/JMCR

Oduola, L. & Durosinmi, M.O. (2018). Entrepreneurship in selected advertisements products in Bigeria: a multimodal discourse analytical perspective, *Journal of Issues in Language and Literary Studies,* 4(1) & 5(1), 72-87

Oyebode, O., & Olateju, M. A. (2011). Imperative mood as message enhancer in billboard product adverts in Nigeria. *Òye* [Ago-Iwoye, Nigeria.]. *Ogun Journal of Arts*, *17*, 159–173.

Oyebode, O. & Unuabonah, F. (2013). Coping with HIV/AIDS: A Multimodal Discourse analysis of selected HIV/AIDS posters in South-western Nigeria. *Discourse & Society,* 24(6). Sage Publications Limited.

Pandey, A. C., & Kumar, N. (2012). Does emotions play as tool for battle of brands: Emotional branding. *International Journal of Research in Finance & Marketing*, *2*(2), 95–103.

Petroni, S. (2019). How social media shape identities and discourses in professional digital settings: Self-communication or self-branding? In Bou-Franch, P., & Blitvich, P. G. C. (Eds.), *Analyzing digital discourse new insights and future directions* (pp. 251–281). Palgrave Macmillan. DOI: 10.1007/978-3-319-92663-6_9

Sánchez, P. L. (2015). Modality in English and Spanish advertising slogans. In Zamorano-Mansilla, J. R., Maiz, C., Dominguez, E., & Martin de la Rosa, M. V. (Eds.), *Thinking modally: English and contrastive studies on modality* (pp. 345–359). Cambridge Scholars Publishing.

Sharma, K., Kodhati, P. & Sukhavsi, S. (2022). Emotional marketing on consumer behaviour – Perception Study. *International Journal on Consumer Relations,* 10(2), 01-08.

Singh, A., Singh, P., Pandey, D., & Singh, R. K. (2024). The impact of emotional appeals on consumer engagement in digital advertising. [EEL]. *European Economic Letters*, *14*(4), 1193–1202. DOI: 10.52783/eel.v14i4.2247

Stores, F. (2022). *Nike is using augmented reality to drive experiential retail in its stores*. https://futurestores.wbresearch.com/blog/nike-using-augmented-reality-drive-experiential-retail-stores

Taiwo, R., & Ademilokun, M. (2023). Discursive marketisation and differentiation in Nigerian university websites. In Taiwo, R., Idowu-Faith, B., & Ajiboye, S. (Eds.), *Transformation of higher education through institutional online spaces* (p. 29). IGI Global., DOI: 10.4018/978-1-6684-8122-6.ch002

Thorson, E., & Duffy, M. (2012). *Advertising age: the principles of advertising and marketing communication at work*. South-western CENGAGE Learning.

Van Leeuwen, T. (2005). *Introducing social semiotics*. Routledge Taylor & Francis.

Xie, T., Donthu, N., Lohtia, R., & Osmonbekov, T. (2004). Emotional appeal and incentive offering in banner advertisements. *Journal of Interactive Advertising*, *4*(2), 30–37. DOI: 10.1080/15252019.2004.10722085

Yousef, M., Dietrich, T., & Rundle-Thiele, S. (2021). Social advertising effectiveness in driving action: A study of positive, negative and coactive appeals on social media. *International Journal of Environmental Research and Public Health*, *18*(11), 5954. DOI: 10.3390/ijerph18115954 PMID: 34206119

Yule, G. (1996). *Pragmatics*. Oxford University Press.

ADDITIONAL READING

Barthes, R. (1977). *Image-music-text*. Fontana.

Halliday, M. A. K. (1994). *An introduction to functional grammar* (2nd ed.). Arnold.

Halliday, M. A. K., & Matthiessen, M. I. M. (2004). *Introduction to functional grammar* (3rd ed.). Hodder Arnold.

Kress, G. (2010). *Multimodality: A Social semiotic approach to contemporary communication*. Routledge Taylor & Francis Group.

Kress, G., & van Leeuwen, T. (2001). *Multimodal discourse: The modes and media of contemporary communication*. Arnold.

Kress, G., & van Leeuwen, T. (2002). Colour as semiotic mode: Notes for the grammar of colour [London: Sage Publications Limited.]. *Visual Communication*, *1*(3), 348–368. DOI: 10.1177/147035720200100306

Kress, G., & van Leeuwen, T. (2021). *Reading images: The grammar of visual design* (3rd ed.). Routledge Taylor & Francis Group.

Martinec, R. (2005). Topics in multimodality. In Hasan, R., Webster, J., & Matthiessen, C. (Eds.), *Continuing discourse on language* (Vol. 1). Equinox. DOI: 10.3138/9781845535803-008

O'Halloran, K. L. (2004). *Multimodal discourse analysis: Systemic-functional perspectives*. London and New York: continuum

O'Halloran, K. L. (2005). *Mathematical discourse: Language, symbolism and visual images*. Continuum.

KEY TERMS AND DEFINITIONS

Anchorage: a concept in semiotics attributed to Roland Barthes the French semiotician who first used it to mean how words relate to or interpret visual images.

Emotional Marketing: Subtle way of conveying emotions in marketing such that it could drive product/service sales.

Language Use: The use of language in social situations, including advertisements, to construct realities and influence others.

M.A.K Halliday: Popularly known as the father of Systemic Functional Linguistics, for pioneering Functional Linguistics as a linguistic movement that challenged the position of traditional grammar, which had maintained that language is static and inherent.

Metafunctions: The term attributed to M.A.K Halliday for referring to experiential, interpersonal and textual roles that language performs, which makes it a social construct.

Multimodality: A field in semiotics that theoretically accounts for the use of multiple modes of communication.

Persuasion: The tactic of influencing and shaping consumers' purchasing behaviours

Roland Barthes: The French semiotician whose earlier insightful contributions to Semiotics made the field very endearing in Linguistics.

Semiotics: the linguistic/scientific study of signs and artifacts and their social functions.

Systemic Functional Linguistics: A social approach to the study of language which theorizes language as a social construct that performs functional roles in the world.

Chapter 7
Visualising Danger: A Multimodal Analysis of Online Awareness Posters on Cholera in Nigeria

Oladayo Ogunsiji
Adeyemi Federal University of Education, Nigeria

Yemi Ogunsiji
Adeyemi Federal University of Education, Nigeria

Janet Olaleke
Adeyemi Federal University of Education, Nigeria

ABSTRACT

This paper investigates the deployment of awareness posters as a communicative resource in disseminating information about cholera in Nigeria. Data, sourced from the internet, were awareness posters on the outbreak of cholera in Nigeria, circulated between June 15 and July 15 2024 which was the period of severity of the virulent disease. The study drew insights from Kress and Leeuwen's (2006) Grammar of Visual Design, which was purposively selected for its capability to holistically engage the different semiotic resources deployed for communicative purpose. Data were subjected to a bottom-up, content analysis which requires analysing each data distinctively for its idiosyncratic semiotic contents. Findings revealed that online awareness posters on cholera were thematically classified based on the different goals they were meant to achieve. Also, image producers of cholera posters conflated multiple processes and elements for the purpose of communicating the severity of cholera and to engender positive healthy behaviours among Nigerians.

DOI: 10.4018/979-8-3693-7934-9.ch007

INTRODUCTION

Health authorities in Nigeria, on 15 June 2024, announced the outbreak of cholera in Lagos State, Africa's most populous city and Nigeria's hub for economic activities. In the first instance, four hundred and thirty-six (436) suspected cases were declared. However, within six days, the number of suspected cases increased to five hundred (500) with forty-three (43) confirmed cases. Additionally, 5.4% case fatality rate was reported, meaning that cholera is a virulent infection that has the ability to spread rapidly and cause high morbidity and mortality (World Health Organisation (WHO), 2024). This is not the first case of cholera outbreak in Nigeria. In fact, it remains a significant public health challenge in Nigeria, particularly in Kano State, where it has been endemic since 1970. The disease is characterised by recurrent outbreaks, with a reported case fatality rate (CFR) of approximately 3.3% from 2010 to 2019 (Ngwa et al., 2021).

Caused by the bacterium vibrio cholera, cholera is a highly contagious diarrheal disease, which predominantly occurs via the fecal-oral route, often exacerbated by inadequate water, sanitation, and hygiene (WASH) conditions. The northern states of Nigeria, particularly Kano, have experienced the most severe outbreaks due to a combination of factors, including poverty, illiteracy, and ongoing conflicts that have led to increased displacement and overcrowding in internally displaced persons' (IDPs) camps (Salako et al., 2021). These socio-economic determinants significantly influence cholera incidence and complicate response efforts. Cholera remains a significant public health challenge in Nigeria, and various communication strategies are employed to enhance awareness and prevention. For instance, in view of the recent outbreak in the country, the Lagos State government as well as other stakeholders and health organisations like WHO, United Nations (UN), United Nations International Children's Emergency Fund (UNICEF), Nigeria Centre for Disease Control and Prevention (NCDC) who gave the statistical reports about the rapid spread of the outbreak advocated the need for urgent and decisive counter measures to prevent, control and end the infection. The counter measures took two broad dimensions: the epidemiological interventions and public health education which entails all sorts of communicative means.

Effective communication is crucial for managing public health crises, including cholera outbreaks. Olapegba et al. (2020) highlight the need for tailored health communication strategies that take into cognisance the socio-economic, linguistic and cultural realities of the target audience. Vital among the communication methods that are often expended in health communication is the awareness poster which incorporates a number of discourse codes that make messages captivating and convincing, thereby facilitating understanding and increasing the potency of such messages. Therefore, using awareness posters to communicate the danger of the infectious disease enables public health campaigns to effectively reach and engage their target audience, thus promoting positive behaviour change and improving overall health outcomes. This study, therefore, employs multimodal analysis to examine the visual representation of danger in online awareness posters on cholera in Nigeria by exploring how semiotic resources such as images, colors, and typography convey meaning and construct messages about the disease. The research focuses on uncovering the ways in which these posters visually communicate the risks and consequences of cholera, and how they appeal to their target audience. By analysing the multimodal composition of these posters, this study aims to provide insights into the role of visual communication in public health campaigns in Nigeria. Put differently, the study underscores the importance of multimodal analysis in understanding how textual and visual elements combine to communicate the danger, the symptoms as well as the prevention of cholera. Focusing on the Nigerian context provides insights into the socio-cultural realities that influence the design and reception of health awareness posters on cholera.

Awareness Posters: A Conceptualisation

Awareness posters are visual communication tools purposely designed to succinctly and pointedly convey a message to the public with the use of textual and visual elements. Posters, which come in different sizes and are designed on different materials, aim at grabbing the attention of the audience while educating, informing, sensitising them about social issues or trying to influence certain behaviours, attitude and change. As put by Yom-Tov et al. (2018), posters, particularly awareness posters, serve as vital tools for communicating important messages to the public. They are designed to convey complex ideas visually, making them effective for raising awareness about health issues such as cholera. Similarly, Utoyo et al. (2021) opine that posters combine textual and graphical elements to present key messages concisely and attractively, often aimed at generating interest and engaging stakeholders. The primary purpose of awareness posters is to inform the public about specific issues and encourage proactive behaviours, particularly in health-related contexts. For instance, posters about cholera prevention can highlight essential practices such as hand washing and safe water consumption (WHO, 2020).

The effectiveness of posters lies in their ability to leverage visual communication. Research indicates that visuals significantly impact human perception, enhancing understanding and retention of information (Paivio, 1990). By utilising compelling graphics, colours, and typography, awareness posters can capture attention quickly and convey critical information effectively. This visual appeal is crucial in contexts where immediate comprehension is necessary, such as during health emergencies (Schroeder, 2004). Typically, a poster includes key elements such as a clear title, crux and calls to action. The data used for this study clearly reflect the aforementioned, engaging visuals, texts, graphics, imagery and other communicative codes that span technical and meaning aspects of the communication in such a way that fosters greater engagement and profound understanding.

Owing to their combinatory use of graphics, texts, colour, images, posters have the capacity to engage the mind and thinking of the audience on issues much more than a speech can. As submitted by Miller (2007), posters are a hybrid form – more detailed than a speech but less than a paper, more interactive than either. Posters, though compact in content, are much more laden with meaning and can accurately and effectively communicate what could have been communicated in a speech. Their heavy reliance on imagery does not only evoke emotions and connections but also helps in deconstructing and concretising abstract concepts. As submitted by Cline and Haynes (2001), effective posters are characterised by their clarity and focus which help them to distil complex concepts into digestible formats that resonate with diverse audiences (Cline & Haynes, 2001).

The benefits of using awareness posters extend beyond mere information dissemination. They serve as powerful marketing tools that can rally support for health initiatives by highlighting the relevance and benefits of specific actions (Kreuter & Wray, 2003). Owing to their versatility, posters have gained importance as an effective educational tool across all fields of life, including education, clinical and health sciences, mass communication, business and advertisement. The importance of posters as a communicative resource across different realms of human life cannot be overemphasised. Posters are an excellent tool for visual and textual presentation of information. On account of their multidimensional nature of encoding messages, posters efficiently communicate complex ideas through visual stimulation involving charts, images, diagrams and infographics, allowing for a better understanding of the concepts at hand. Evidence abound on how versatile posters are in unraveling complex ideas and reducing same to digestible pieces which make them more accessible and understandable to everyone. Tahririan and Sadri (2013) submit that pictures transmit information more effectively than letters do. From the foregoing, therefore, the deployment of posters as a communicative resource in disseminating information about cholera in Nigeria is an apposite move at ensuring that the information get all and sundry. From digital posters to advertising posters, event posters, political posters, religious posters, movies posters, fashion posters, formative posters, campaign poster, infomercial posters, the deployment of multimodal symbols that enrich and expand the simple traditional ways of thought expression is crucial. Indeed, the currency and proliferation of visual modes across different fields and practices, including poster designing, necessitates the tilt towards multimodality in contemporary communicative systems (Lirola, 2006).

Multimodality is the use of various modes to distribute information. Jewitt (2009, p. 14) defines multimodality in simple terms as "an approach that understands communication and representation to be more than about language, and which attends to the full range of communicational forms people use – image, gesture, gaze, posture, and so on – and the relationships between them." Multimodal discourse refers to the integration and interaction of various communicative modes in the construction of meaning. Unlike traditional approaches to discourse, which focus primarily on written or spoken language, multimodal discourse analysis (MDA) recognises that meaning is not always conveyed through language alone. Visual images, colour schemes, spatial organisation, typography, symbols, gestures, and even sound all function as meaning-making resources, particularly in contemporary media milieu.

The theoretical foundation of multimodal discourse is rooted in the work of scholars such as Kress and van Leeuwen (2001), who argue that communication is inherently multimodal. In their view, different modes work together — sometimes in complementary ways — to shape the way messages are perceived and understood by their audience. Each mode carries specific social and cultural affordances, and the structuring of these modes produces layered meanings that transcend the superficial level of meaning in the text. In the context of health communication, and specifically in public health campaigns, the multimodal approach allows for a deeper understanding of the combinatory use of visual and textual elements to communicate urgency, influence public perception, and elicit action. Posters, as static visual artifacts, are rich examples of multimodal communication because they rely on the interplay of images, colours, typography, layout, and linguistic content to convey cogent or informative messages within a short time frame.

In this study, the analysis of cholera awareness posters from Nigeria is grounded in this multimodal framework. Rather than focusing solely on the written language featured in the posters, attention is given to the full communicative ensemble — including the visual representation of danger, the spatial arrangement of text and images, and the semiotic choices (such as symbols and colour palettes) that evoke cultural associations with health, hygiene, risk, and prevention. Through this lens, the posters are not simply viewed as texts, but as carefully designed multimodal compositions aimed at shaping public understanding and encouraging behavioural change.

This approach is particularly significant in the digital age, where health communication is often visualised and circulated on online platforms, requiring messages to capture attention and convey meaning rapidly across diverse linguistic and cultural audiences. Multimodal discourse analysis offers a powerful tool for unpacking the strategies behind such visual communication efforts and for understanding how danger and health risks are constructed and disseminated in the public sphere.

Characteristically, posters are interpretive meaning-generating tools that interpolate different discourse modalities. Therefore, a systematic and comprehensive theoretical tool that will account for the variety of semiotic resources is needed. The discourse of awareness posters comprises a number of semiotic resources such as verbal texts, images, colour, sizes and special characters and to decode such posters is to unpack the multi-codes that have been carefully and purposely harnessed for communicative purpose. In order to facilitate the understanding of information about the virulent cholera that threatened public health in Lagos State of Nigeria in the months of June and July, 2024, this study examines the semiotic resources adopted in encoding meaning in awareness posters on cholera.

THE ROLE OF ONLINE AWARENESS POSTERS IN PUBLIC HEALTH

The advent and ubiquity of the internet, digital technology and social media have practically and significantly changed the face of everything human beings engage in. The educational, entertainment, fashion and religious worlds are now being transformed by the internet. The arts and craft sphere is not left out as it also leverages the numerous advantages of the online awareness posters. The online versions of awareness posters offer benefits such as the QR codes that supply links to more information on the subject matter of the posters; vast sharing and community building that allow posters to go wide within the shortest possible time. The availability of social media platforms, online communities, forums and groups make the digital distribution of posters far-reaching.

Furthermore, online awareness posters have emerged as essential tools for disseminating information and promoting safety in various contexts, particularly in health and cyber security. Their significance lies not only in their ability to convey critical messages effectively but also in their capacity to engage audiences through visual communication. For instance, in the context of internet safety, posters can serve as constant reminders for children and adults alike about the importance of safeguarding personal information and recognising online threats (High Speed Training, 2023). This is particularly crucial in environments where individuals may encounter frequent online risks, such as phishing attacks or cyberbullying. Moreover, awareness posters can foster a culture of vigilance and responsibility.

The efficiency of online awareness posters has been highlighted in several studies, which demonstrate their significant role in public health campaigns. For instance, Christensen et al. (2017) explored online recruitment methods and concluded that digital platforms provide cost-effective and wide-reaching means to engage the public. The import of these online tools is underscored by their ability to reach diverse demographics, overcoming geographic and socioeconomic barriers (Rueda-Gómez et al., 2024). By visually presenting key messages, posters can simplify complex information, making it accessible to a broader audience, including those with varying levels of literacy (Cline & Haynes, 2001).

Furthermore, the digital nature of these posters allows for widespread dissemination across various platforms. Organisations can share awareness materials via social media, email newsletters, or internal communication channels like Slack or Microsoft Teams (High Speed Training, 2023). This broad reach ensures that the messages are not only seen but also revisited regularly by the target audience.

Incorporating interactive elements into online awareness posters can further enhance their effectiveness. For instance, some educational initiatives encourage students to create their own safety posters after learning about online risks. This participatory approach not only reinforces the content learned but also empowers students to take ownership of their knowledge and share it with peers (Tech4Learning, 2018). Such engagement fosters a deeper understanding of the issues at hand and encourages ongoing discussions about safety practices.

Given the quantum of opportunities online awareness posters provide, their deployment in the dissemination of health information on cholera in Nigeria proves to be a highly effective one. Apart from fostering community engagements and involvement in cholera prevention, online posters offer real-time updates by providing timely information on outbreaks, vaccination campaigns and health alerts while reducing the propensity for the spread of myths and misconceptions about cholera. Also, mobile technology can be optimised since these posters can be accessed on mobile devices, making it convenient for all and sundry to have first-hand information about the virulent disease and its preventive measures and treatment.

EXTANT LITERATURE

A review of literature on posters will be done from the non-linguistic and linguistic perspectives. From the non-linguistic point of view, the educational field has thoroughly investigated the role of posters in the pedagogy of different disciplines. In their investigation of the use of poster presentation as an effective communication tool in an EFL context, Boggu and Sundarsingh (2015) submit that poster presentation helps in stimulating interactions among the audience while facilitating integrated learning activities. According to them, poster presentations engender experiential learning that fosters a learner's sense of autonomy and responsibility. Similarly, DeWitt and Alias (2017) reveal the potency of infographic posters in exposing learners to a large number of research articles, as important points which are summarised on infographic posters reduce learners' daunting task of reading through the entire articles.

Vale and Barbosa's (2021) investigation into the cognitive role of posters in the pedagogy of mathematics identifies the importance of posters in stimulating critical thinking and facilitating communicative and problem-solving skills, especially by bridging the gap in learners' diverse levels of assimilation and enhancing collaborative work. Pedwell et. al. (2017) submit that research posters are a means of fostering communication skills needed for real life working experience.

In their comparative study of the effectiveness of leaflets and posters as a health education method, Hasanica et al. (2020) conclude that given the importance of health education in providing knowledge and skills needed for the health improvement of individual and community, the use of posters should be favoured over the use of leaflets, as the former produced a higher statistical significance than the later in relation to acquired knowledge and attitudinal change. Prior to this investigation, Sumampouw and Sukandar (2019), based on their observation that failures in pulmonary tuberculosis disease control programmes were associated with lack of health promotion among individuals in Indonesia, record a tremendous improvement of knowledge about tuberculosis disease and its prevention with the use of posters which were produced and distributed among community members.

As observed by Raney et al. (2018), hospital nurses who often experienced occupational stress and had low-participation in physical activities got motivated to engage in physical activities after they were exposed to self-monitoring and poster campaigns. Their study submits that posters are not only a motivational and instructional tool, they are also cost-effective and reliable. The integration of jargon-free language into poster design has gained traction in recent years. A study by the National Human Genome Research Institute demonstrated that translating complex scientific information into layman's terms significantly increased engagement and understanding among non-specialist audiences (Marcum & Harris, 2013). For instance, posters that simplify scientific concepts through visuals and straightforward language foster more in-depth discussions compared to traditional formats laden with technical jargon. Empirical evidence has shown that elements such as imagery and colour schemes in health posters play a pivotal role in attracting attention and conveying urgency (Houts, et al., 2006). Also, studies have indicated that visual elements can enhance the memorability and emotional impact of health messages (Borkin et al., 2013).

Posters have been shown to enhance listening skills and overall language proficiency. A study conducted in Indonesian classrooms found that integrating poster presentations into lessons improved students' listening comprehension by providing contextual visual cues that supported their understanding of spoken language (Aulia et al., 2024). The combination of visual elements with auditory information creates a more immersive learning experience, making it easier for learners to connect spoken words with their meanings.

One significant area of research on posters involves understanding language ideologies reflected in poster design. A study examining digital posters in contemporary China highlights how different social actors utilise various scripts to convey specific ideologies (Jia, 2024). The analysis reveals that the interplay between simplified Chinese and English is often guided by a "glocal language ideology", which reflects both local cultural contexts and global influences (Koutsogiannis & Mitsikopoulou, 2004). This suggests that the linguistic choices made in poster design are deeply rooted in social beliefs about language and identity, influencing how information is perceived and understood by diverse audiences (Silverstein, 1979).

Textual elements play a crucial role in enhancing the communicative power of posters. Linguistic studies have shown that the choice of words, font styles, and text layout can significantly affect audience engagement. For instance, using bold or italicised fonts can emphasise key messages and draw attention to critical information (Cynthia, 2023). Moreover, capitalising certain words can evoke urgency or importance, influencing how the audience interprets the message (Cynthia, 2023). Research also indicates that coherence between textual and visual elements enhances comprehension. Posters that maintain a consistent theme across both aspects tend to facilitate deeper understanding and retention of information (Wen et al., 2022). This alignment allows audiences to decode messages more effectively, as they can relate visual cues to the accompanying text.

Abdullahi and Ogungbe (2024) delve into the linguistic stylistic properties of health promotion posters, with particular focus on the syntactic structures, rhetorical devices. They submit that imperatives, metaphors and allusions create persuasive and engaging tone that influence people's health-related behaviours and enhance public health awareness. Cynthia (2023) identifies a number of visual elements that categorise information and make important points salient. According to her, while different font styles can target specific audiences or suit particular themes, bold or italicised text can draw attention to critical information. Font size and capitalisation can be used to create contrast, capture readers' attention and convey urgency and excitement. In addition, organising information through shapes or boxes helps delineate sections, making large amounts of text more digestible.

THEORETICAL FRAMEWORK

The study draws insights from Kress and Leeuwen's (2006) Grammar of Visual Design, a model of multimodality theory that is preoccupied with the construction and interconnectedness of meaning through diverse semiotic properties, including but not limited to images, gestures, sound and spatial arrangements. Informed by the postulation that meaning cannot be reduced to language only, Kress and Leeuwen's Grammar of Visual Design indicates that information is dispersed and communication is established through integrated varieties of semiotic resources which transcend the use of language. Kress and Leeuwen identify three levels of meaning making and unpacking as representational, interactive and compositional which respectively correspond to the metafunctions of ideational, interpersonal and textual in Hallidayan terms. The representational visual metafunction, which bifurcates into narrative and conceptual, indicates the state of affairs such as messages, ideas, actions and inactions signified by the Represented Participants (RPs). While the narrative representational mode, produced by actions, reaction, speech and mental process verbs, speaks to the transactional events through concrete items such as tools and bodies; the conceptual counterpart indicates ideas, concepts being represented, that is, the non-reactional, inactive RPs. The RPs, described as places, things and people depicted in an image, are characteristically classificatory, analytical and symbolic.

In the interactive visual metafunction, the agency of Interactive Participants (IPs) (the people who communicate with each other through images, including the texts producers, RPs and viewers) in the explication of information is examined. Here, the IPs' social engagements and interactional negotiations realised through contact, social distance, attitude and modality are brought to the fore. Contact relates to the IP's deployment of gazes to indicate, say, a call for an action or an offer of information. Social distance explained in terms of the level of RPs' proximity shows social inclusion or exclusion. Attitude shows the angles of the portrait, whether it is frontal horizontal angle (indicating stronger relationship); oblique horizontal (showing stronger relationship of detachment between positions of RPs and viewer) or vertical angle (projecting negotiation between the RPs and the viewer). The attitude also captures the dimensions of the portraits as high (which reflects high power relation); medium (equal power) and low (less power relation).

The compositional mode performs the cohesive function of fusing the representational and interactive modes together. This mode encompasses information value, salience and framing which respectively relate to the status of information (whether given, new, ideal, real or nucleus), the devices for getting viewer's attention (which may be through size, colour sharpness, backgrounding and foregrounding of RPs); and comparison of the RPs. Kress and Leeuwen's Grammar of Visual Design is deemed apt for this study because of its capability to holistically imbibe the different semiotic modes integrated in online awareness posters on cholera.

METHODOLOGY

Data, in form of awareness posters on cholera, were retrieved from online sources (Google Images, Nigeria Health Watch, and Nigeria Federal Ministry of Health and Social Welfare), using keywords like 'cholera awareness posters of Nigerian source', 'cholera prevention posters in Nigeria'. The inclusion of Nigeria in the keywords was to ensure the generation of posters produced in the country. The aforementioned online sources were purposively selected to ensure a diverse range of text-visual materials that are government-endorsed and from reputable health organisations/ stakeholders in Nigeria. 20 images were purposively selected, using the following selection criteria:

1. Relevance: Images selected centred on cholera awareness, prevention or treatment.
2. Geographical relevance: Since the focus of this study is on the Nigerian context, images selected were created in Nigeria and targeted towards the Nigerian audience. Prioritising geographical relevance was apposite to ensure the incorporation of cultural-specific messaging, local health concerns and language/communication peculiarities.
3. Timeframe: The timeframe was June 15 to July 15, 2024. June 15, 2024, which was the period of outbreak declaration, rapid spread and peak response period.
4. Multimodal content: The presence of multiple communicative codes such as diagram, letters, colour was expedient in order to ensure relevance of data to the study which accounts for the various semiotic artefacts used in the dissemination of information on cholera outbreak in Nigeria.

The study drew insights from Kress and Leeuwen's (2006) Grammar of Visual Design, purposively selected for its capability to holistically engage the different semiotic resources deployed for communicative purpose. Notably, awareness posters on cholera are replete with colourful prints and images, employed alongside linguistic items to disseminate information about the infection and the expected precautionary measures. The study oriented to a bottom-up, content analysis which required analysing each data distinctively for its idiosyncratic semiotic contents.

DATA ANALYSIS AND DISCUSSION OF FINDINGS

Awareness posters disseminated on cholera outbreak in Nigeria in the year 2024 can be categorised based on the specific intent of the image producers and the goals the posters were meant to fulfil. Some posters were basically epidemic alert, created to inform the public about the presence of cholera in Nigeria; some highlighted cholera symptoms so as to enable early detection and others centered on providing guidance on preventing cholera transmission and treatment options. Based on the foregoing, awareness posters were classified into and analysed under the following rubrics: cholera alert messaging, visualising cholera symptoms, visualising cholera prevention and treatment.

Cholera Alert Messaging

Cholera alert messaging (CAM) is used to refer to posters that alert the public to the cholera threat. It refers to the public notification of cholera disease, the announcement of risk associated with it and situation reports on the disease across the different parts of Nigeria. Posters in this category inform the public about the presence of cholera in Nigeria.

Figure 1. (Cholera Alert Messaging: A medical expert holds a flashcard with the word 'Cholera')

Figure 1 displays a medical personnel evinced by his appearance in a ward coat, a stethoscope and a pair of surgical gloves. He holds a flashcard in his left hand with the inscription of the word "cholera" written in red, and uses his right index finger to point to the "cholera" in the other hand. This visual image has a transactional action narrative structure, comprising an actor, a goal and a vector. The actor, whose face is not shown, is a medical personnel and his general appearance conveys authority, professionalism, hygiene and safety. The white ward coat together with the stethoscope indicates a healthcare professional associated with trust and expertise while the stethoscope around his neck emphasises cleanliness as a vital pathway to the prevention of infections and diseases. On the other hand, the goal, a flashcard containing red-lettered "cholera", is the participant that the actor aims at. The goal occupies the center margin of the poster which makes the information value placed on it very important. The salience that the goal projects through centralisation and colour is important in order to send the signal that cholera virus is a dangerous disease that should be tackled head-on. There is no vectorial element connecting the RPs to the image viewers; therefore, an offer of information is made to the viewers for them to have the awareness of the virus.

Figure 2. (Cholera Alert Messaging: A lady pointing at two pictures of dirty scenarios)

Figure 2 is a three-tier image of a woman on the left hand side occupying half of the entire portrait and pointing at the two images of very dirty environments. These two images share the other half of the portrait in disproportionate sizes. All these images are collapsed into an image to form a single unit. Figure 2 conflates the transactional action narrative structure and the transactional reactional narrative process. The former is distinguished by the presence of an oblique line which is formed by the PR's hand (the vector). The actor, the woman on the left hand side of the portrait, points her right index finger at the other two images that display dirty environments that people live in and in which they carry out their daily activities. Thus, the right index finger constitutes the vector while the images of the dirty environments are the goal. On the other hand, the transactional reactional narrative process is created by the woman's eye line that connects her as the actor to the two dirty environment scenarios which are the phenomena. The use of double narrative structures in this image speaks volume about the weight, importance or urgency of the goal or the phenomenon as the case may be. In other words, the two processes involved foreground the message that the viewers should, as a matter of seriousness, focus on the goal and phenomena and take decisive action concerning it. The goal/ phenomenon which has been highlighted as the object of focus has the circumstance of setting in the upper part of the left side of the image. Interestingly, the locative circumstance is displayed more that the goal in it (a young African woman of a low socio- economic class.) The face of the young woman is not shown; what is shown and invariably focused is the dirty river that the woman is fetching from, probably for domestic use. The verbal text "outbreak of cholera in Nigeria", together with the visual images, identifies contaminated water as a major cause of the infectious diseases. The image also identifies the woman who represents the vulnerable group as the most susceptible person to contracting the disease. The woman fetching water from the water is the group saddled with the responsibility of carrying out domestic activities in the African gender division of labour. The second dirty scenario that is displayed features a river littered with all kinds of debris. This is the goal and the phenomenon at the same time. The buildings at the background form the locative circumstance. The information this locative circumstance provides is two dimensional.

First is that the refuse seen on the surface of the water emanates from the occupants of the buildings and second is that the same occupants are the potential victims of any disease outbreak. As mentioned earlier, the goal/phenomenon positioned at the right hand side of the image is divided into two by a thin line that separates the scenarios from each other. The process involved here is classificational conceptual process (the RPs are presented in terms to their relationship to one another) with overt taxonomy. The superordinate is the second dirty scenario at the lower part of second half of the image. This part occupies the larger space, indicating the source of the water being fetched by the woman in the upper part of the image. In other words, the image projects the river with litters of refuse and debris as the probable source of the water the woman in the upper image is drawing for domestic use. This relationship clearly shows the high risk of the woman contracting cholera and transferring to members of her household since it is an infectious disease. This explains why the actor wears a stern, angry and disapproving looks that highlights the danger at hand.

At the interactive level of meaning, the vector formed by the actor's eye line connects to the goal; therefore, the image is presented as an offer to the viewers, as an item of information requiring urgent consideration. On social distance, a close-up social distance between the representatives and the viewers is observed which inspires the viewers' curiosity to enter the actor's represented world and to engage the reality she presents. In terms of perspective, the frontal horizontal angle suggests involvement of the image producer and the viewers with the RP. What this means is that the image producer intends for the viewers to experience the represented world, the dirty images.

With respect to the compositional level of meaning, the information value indicates as new information the dirty scenarios placed on the right side of the image. The "new" here refers to something which has to be made explicit and clear to the viewers, something that has to be paid close attention to by the viewers. As posited by Kress and Van Leeuwen (1996), the new is typically placed on the right while the given occupies the left, following the left to right reading progression. Also of importance is the division of the information on the right hand along the vertical axis. In general terms, as identified by Kress and Van Leeuwen, the upper section presents a realistic and informative bit. This is the case in the sample under analysis here. While the lower part of the goal is realistically informative with regards to how same Nigerians indiscriminately dispose of waste in rivers and drainages, the upper part shows the viewers the image of a woman ignorantly or helplessly drawing contaminated water to her detriment and that of her household.

Figure 3. (Cholera Alert Messaging: a diagrammatic representation of cholera situation report produced by the Nigeria Centre for Disease Control and Prevention)

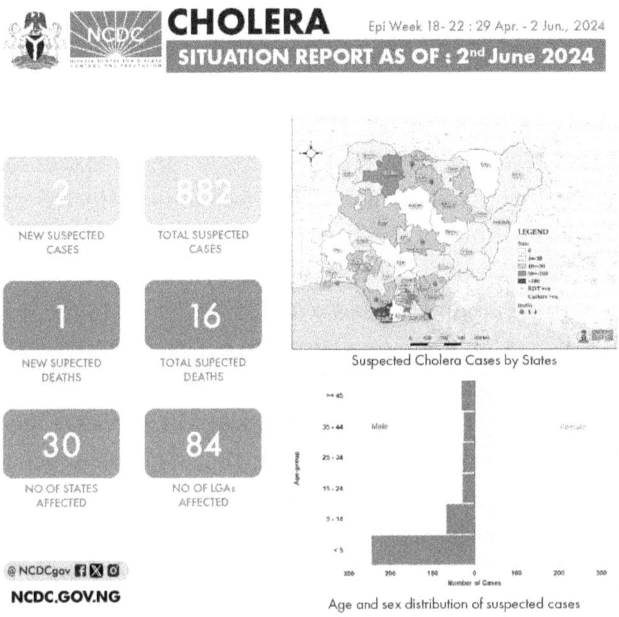

This is an image of the NCDC's situation report on cholera. It consists of three different parts framed separately and illustrating different representational processes. The tagline at the top of the image, framed in a green box; the Nigerian map; and the demographic dimension of suspected cases of cholera, and the capitalised CHOLERA are all made salient to present every bit of the image as important. Looking at the left side of the image, symbolic conceptual process is illustrated in the use of colour because the yellow, red and gray colours used to designate different categories of information can easily remind the viewers of some symbolic values. In other words, the RP's significance is demonstrated in the symbolic relation of red, yellow and gray to the information beneath them. This means that apart from being an instrument of salience in the image, colours have been symbolically used to foreground and emphasise the danger the Nigerian citizens are faced with. The first two boxes at the top left side showing the figures of "new suspected cases" and "total suspected cases" are presented in yellow which naturally symbolises caution, illness, alertness and vigilance. It indicates potential danger; it also points to contagion risk. Thus, much more than presenting the information of "new suspected cases", the image producer also calls for vigilance, preparedness and alertness while indicating urgency of intervention. In the same vein, colour red presents "new suspected death" and "total suspected deaths". In the natural world, red is the colour of danger. Presenting the cases of death in red is to sound the signal of real danger to the Nigerian citizens so that the need to combat the disease seriously is seen as a matter of urgency. The last information presented in part of the poster under study is the number of states and local government areas affected. This is presented in dark gray colour. Gray colour, in the natural sense, negotiates the distance between black and white colours. The significance of this in the context of this poster is that the eventual course that the cholera disease takes in the affected states will be determined by people's actions or inactions. A decisive and expected response to the alert may reduce the cases of cholera in Nigeria. Conversely, if decisive steps are not taken, the virus will be ubiquitous and wreck more havoc in the Nigerian society.

The Nigerian map at the top right side of the poster illustrates exhaustive analytical conceptual structure, meaning that RPs are connected in terms of a part-whole structure. The map is the carrier and the possessive attributes are the Nigerian states that occupy the whole space of the carrier which is why the structure is referred to as exhaustive. The possessive attributes are marked with colours white and different shades of green to designate states with no case of cholera, states having between one to ten cases of cholera, states having between ten to fifty cases, states with fifty to hundred cases and states with more than hundred cholera cases. In addition, orange and yellow colours respectively mark instances of rapid diagnostic tests (RDT) and culture test. RDTs refer to diagnostics that have relatively short performance times to provide results which inform clinical decision making while culture tests are confirmatory test that characterise outbreak strain. Red indicates states with death cases. In the last picture in this sample labelled age and sex distribution of suspected cases, green and yellow colours are respectively used to distinguish the sex distribution of suspected cases while age distribution is indicated by the upward movement of the bars in the chart. It is revealed that more males under the age of five have been suspected to contract cholera.

Visualising Cholera Symptoms

Visualising Cholera Symptoms (VCS) is the label used to capture the text-visual aspects of symptoms representation. It communicates diagnostic information by highlighting cholera symptoms, disease recognition that will enable early detection. VCS manifests in the blending of visual and textual elements in such a way that emphatically stresses the importance of seeking medical attention early.

Figure 4. (Visualising Cholera Symptoms: A poster pictorially showing the different symptoms of cholera)

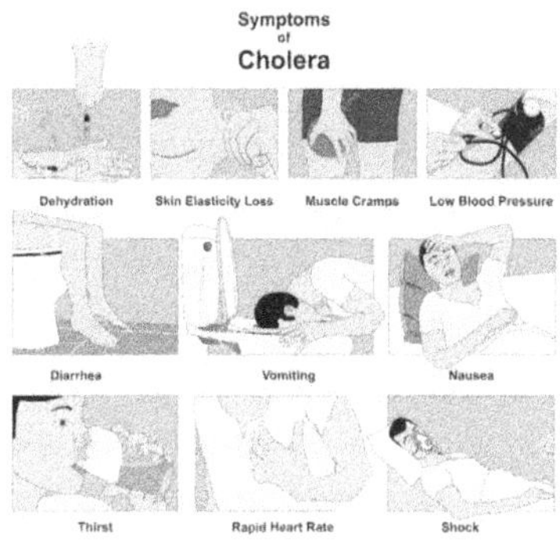

Figure 4, labelled symptoms of cholera, is the composition of elements verbally and visually construed as the signs of the infectious diseases in an individual. The signs are sequentially listed as dehydration, skin elasticity loss, muscle cramps, low blood pressure, diarrhea, vomiting, nausea, thirst, rapid heart rate and shock. Starting from the representational level of meaning, figure 4 has classificational conceptual structure with a covert taxonomy. In a covert taxonomy, the superordinate is often hidden in an accompanying text, which is the case in the sample. The verbal text, "symptoms of cholera" placed at the top of image is the superordinate. The subordinates are ten-framed pictures all against light green background. They are relatively of the same size and almost positioned at symmetrical composition with more or less equal distance from each other. Given the forgoing, the proposed equivalence between the subordinates manifests visually. Under each of the framed subordinates is a corresponding verbal text labelling, in language terms, what is presented in the image. The ten symptoms of cholera are a classification of signs to watch out for so that cases of cholera can be timely presented at the hospital. The image producer educates and instructs viewers to, as a matter of urgency, seek medical intervention once any of these sings is noticed.

At the interactive level, though the image comprises animate representatives capable of gazing at each other or the viewers, there is no eye line contact; rather, the image offers itself as an item of information, suggesting that the viewers should internalise the different symptoms of cholera. The viewers, armed with this piece of information, should take the reasonable step of presenting at the hospital, should they perceive any of these symptoms. This way, they can forestall causalities associated with cholera.

The system of social distance shows that most of the framed-images against the green background are at close-up distance; for instance, the skin, knee, chest in the second, third and ninth frames respectively are closely displayed by the image producer and clearly seem by the viewers. The second frame indicates that the actors, whose face is not shown in the image, is also the goal and the fingers with which he pulls his skin represent the vector. This transactional action narrative that the structure closely presents to the viewers indicates the relational link that the image producer intends to establish between the representative and viewer. Apparently, the close-up invites the viewers to familiarise with these symptoms of cholera displayed in the image so as to urgently take decisive step when necessary.

Using the modality markers of articulation of detail, contextualisation, colour situation, colour differentiation, depth articulation and illumination, the image in figure 4 tilts towards the minimum on the scale of modality, thereby suggesting that the image is improvised in order to depict reality.

The ten framed images in this figure are enclosed in rectangular shape and separated from one another by small empty spaces, suggesting the distinctiveness of each symptom. There is no continuity and complementation of the elements; each is identified and treated as an absolute. Once any of the symptoms is displayed, the individual is expected to immediately take an action.

Figure 5. (Visualising Cholera Symptoms: An illustrating design of a man holding his stomach to indicate pains and distress.)

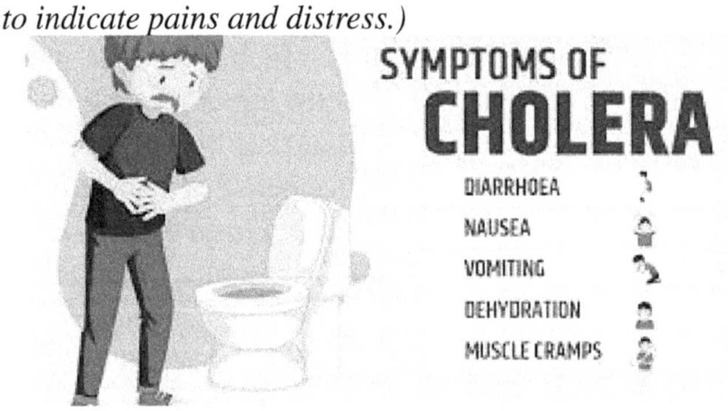

Figure 5 is an illustrative design produced to warn about the symptoms of cholera. There are many layers of processes in the poster created to emphasise the core of the message in it. There is the image of a man, evinced by his moustache, on the left side of the poster tilting towards the toilet and holding his stomach with his hands. He is gazing at the toilet with pains and confusion written all over his face. While the man is the actor, the forward tilting of his body and his hands form the vectorial elements, making the structure a transactional action narrative one. The man's eye line connecting him to the toilet in front of him also forms a vector, making it transactional reactional narrative process.

At the right side of the poster is the classificational conceptual structure where "symptoms of cholera" (made salient) is the superordinate. The subordinates are the five textual items (diarrhea, nausea, vomiting, dehydration and muscle cramps), separately framed in white rectangular boxes and positioned at symmetrical composition with equal distance from each other. Combining the processes, viewers can have the understanding of what the symptoms of cholera are and how painful and distressing they could be. The poster, thus, urges image viewers to be alert and stay informed so that they can immediately present at the health facility at the notice of any of the symptoms.

Visualising Cholera Prevention and Treatment

Visualising cholera prevention and treatment (VCPT) comprises posters that provide guidance on preventing cholera transmission and treatment options. These posters also reel out preventive measures and safety guidelines.

Figure 6. (Visualising Cholera Prevention and Treatment: A poster produced by a Nigerian financial institution, Ecobank, advocating observing precautions in order to fight cholera virus)

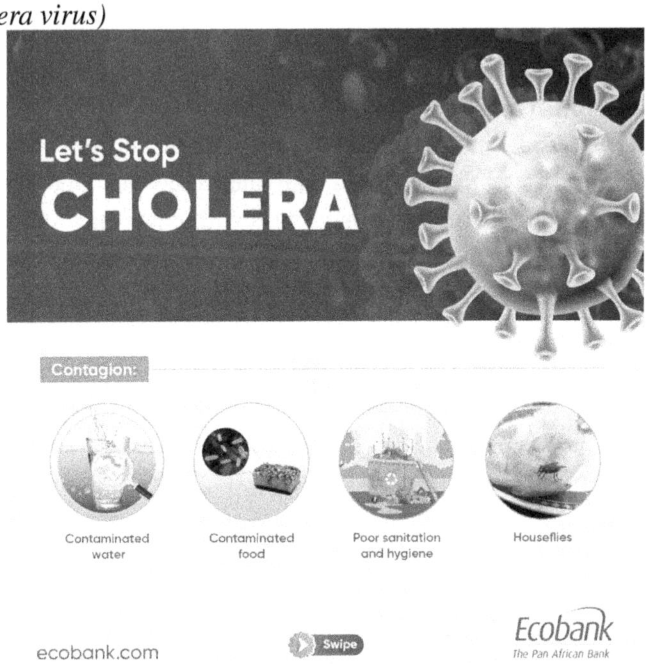

This is an Ecobank-sponsored awareness poster tagged 'let's stop cholera'. The poster is divided into two along horizontal axis with the upper part having the verbal text "stop cholera" and the visual representation of the cholera virus slightly extending to the lower part. The lower part contains four circles each housing pictorial representation of causes of cholera with the verbal text "contagion". It also has the name of the Nigerian financial institution (Ecobank) that sponsored the poster with its apposition placed directly beneath it.

In this sample, the representative; the visual representation of the cholera virus, the four circles respectively images of contaminated water, contaminated food, pour sanitation and houseflies symmetrically positioned along the horizontal plane illustrate the classificational conceptual structure. The visual elements in this image as well as the verbal text are vertically presented, highlighting the ideal-real information value. Generally speaking, the upper section relates to the ideal, the "what might be" while the lower section speaks to the realistic, the informative, and the "what is". The upper section contains the verbal text "let's stop cholera" and the relatively big visual representation of the cholera virus in colour green. These are set against a blue cloudy background; and the symbolic representation of cholera as well as the verbal text "cholera" are made salient in terms of size and lettering to indicate that cholera as a health issue is an environmental problem that requires urgent and collaborative efforts as suggested in the inclusive imperative, "let's". At the lower divide of the image are the RPs framed in smaller circles than the symbolic cholera. The four circles housing images of the causes of cholera are positioned at symmetrical composition with equal distance from each other, marking the visual realisation of the proposed equivalence between the participants and illustrating classificational conceptual structure with covert taxonomy. The covert taxonomy is indicated by the "contagion" tagline at the top of the four-circles, reflecting a superordinate-subordinate relationship. Each of the circles houses the image of "contaminated water", "contaminated food", poor sanitation and hygiene", and "houseflies". The lower placement of the contagion of cholera relative to the clarion call above it gives information on the actions that should be taken in order to "stop cholera". The foregoing is very important given the environmental implication hinted at earlier. The contaminated water, food; poor sanitation and houseflies are environmental and public health issues that evolve from human activities that endanger the environment and its inhabitants.

Figure 7. (Visualising Cholera Prevention and Treatment: An illustrating poster design produced by NCDC on the need to be guided and fight against cholera virus)

The image above is an illustrative graphic design disseminated by the Nigeria Centre for Disease Control and Prevention (NCDC). It comprises three images differently framed with similar postures and facial expressions. On the left hand side is a boy tightly holding the right side of his chest with his two hands. He has furrowed eyebrows; misty, teary and goggled eyes; widely spread lips and clenched teeth which all suggest deep pains. Non-transactional reactional narrative process is constructed in the RP's eye line directed at something outside the image. The reactional process is made salient by the close-up frame size and the foregrounding of the RP's facial expression that invite the viewers to feel the pain the young boy is feeling who is suffering from cholera. The RP does not seem to be looking at the viewers but the vectorial eye line that connects to the outer world seems to make a demand to the world to take action regarding the infectious disease causing so much pain. This is succinctly captured in the verbal text "help us save lives" at the bottom of the poster.

Similar to the first picture is the picture of a lady at the top right hand. Here, the RP's body leans forward as if in a running position. This forms the vector aimed at no goal, thereby illustrating non-transactional action narrative structure. The RP's eye line also forms another vector whose goal is not indicated, making the structure non-transactional reactional narrative one. The two parallel narrative processes are devices of salience adopted in this image to emphasise the untold pains and dangers of the cholera disease. Like the first picture, psychological salience is projected in the actor's facial expression. Her mouth is opened in a way that shows she is crying; her eye brows are furrowed and there are drops of tears popping out of her eyes. Her hands, legs and entire body seem frail which may indicate that she is suffering from diarrhea and has lost weight and strength.

The third picture shares the same dual narrative process with the first two: non-transactional reactional and non-transactional action processes indicated respectively by the eye line and the forward tilt of the RP. The RPs in the three pictures are a boy, a woman and a young lady all in agony, distress and danger. This categorically points to the aforementioned groups and the most susceptible to the infectious disease.

Figure 8. (Visualising Cholera Prevention and Treatment: A simple illustrative poster on the need for hand washing as a means of fighting cholera virus)

This is an illustrative image of an RP's hand clapped together in a hand washing motion whose face is not shown. The image is set on a sky-blue background that has faint cholera virus symbols in different sizes. There are two instances of linguistic texts: one is framed separately at the top of the image in a yellow rectangular box with black lettering, "cholera is real; prevention is key". The other, made salient by its size, capitalisation and emboldening, is placed at a diagonal position to the visual image of the hands. The direction of the hands forms the diagonal of the poster towards the linguistic text (wash your hands), thereby illustrating a transactional action process. The hands have in between them exaggerated lather that puts prominence on the imperative contained in the verbal text. A consideration of the poster's information value reveals that both the linguistic text and the visual image of hand washing are put within the center-margin, making them the nucleus of information which further highlights the importance of hand washing as a major preventive measure against cholera. As earlier mentioned, the image has a sky blue background whose colour is unevenly saturated which, in terms of modality, points to tentative information. From the angle of salience, the fades in the background suggest distance. Put together, what is suggested is that once the washing of hands is constantly and religiously practised, the virus will begin to fade away and eventually disappear from the environment? At the root of the poster are yellow and blue arcs well framed in their distinctive colours. The yellow arc connotes the ongoing outbreak; it also symbolises caution and warning about cholera transmission. On the other hand, the blue arc symbolises hygiene practices (e.g. hand washing), good sanitation and safe water which will ensure safety and prevention. The proximal positioning of the arcs visually communicates to the image viewers that a balance has to be made between risk and prevention; that gradual transition from danger (yellow) to safety (blue) is guaranteed once the necessary precautions are observed. It also communicates progress towards controlling the outbreak. Since there is no vectorial element connecting the RP to the viewers, the poster, at the interactive level, is an offer, providing information on precautions and encouraging the action of hand washing in order to combat cholera disease.

Figure 9. (Visualising Cholera Prevention and Treatment: NCDC's health advisory poster on the practice of hand washing)

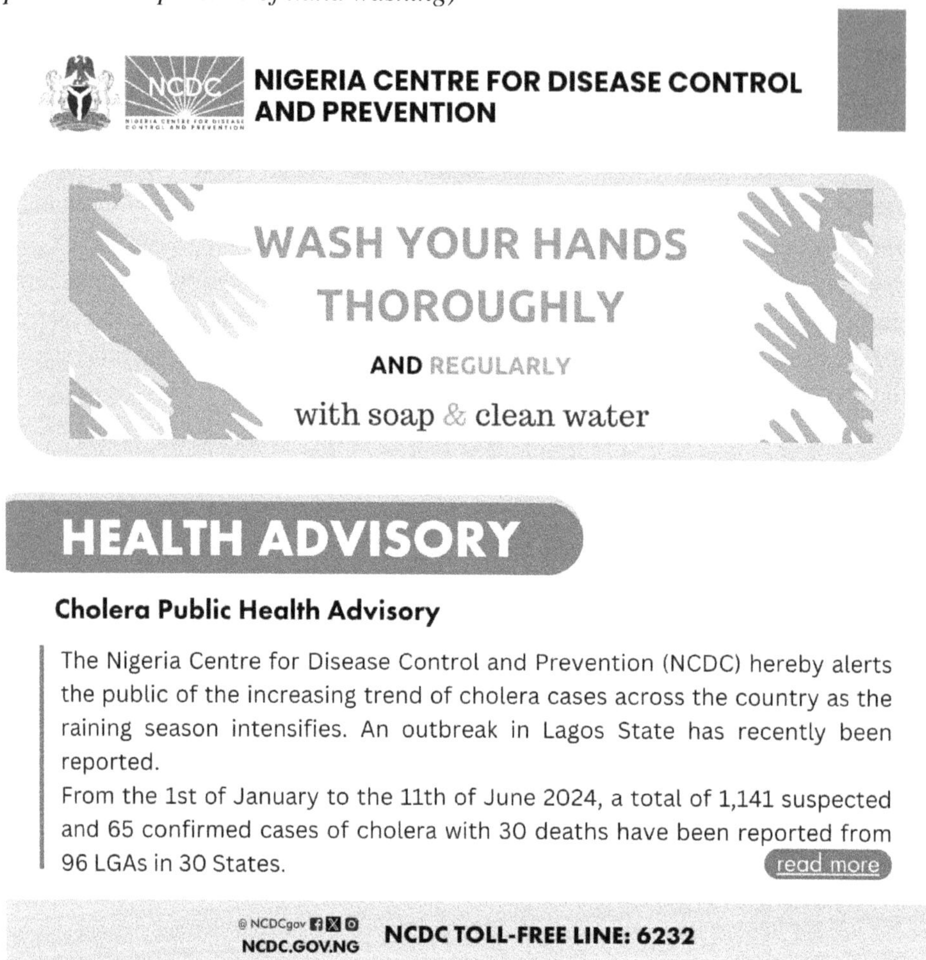

This is a poster emphasising the major preventive measure against cholera, circulated by the Nigeria Centre for Disease Control and Prevention. The poster, which has a good mix of visual and textual elements, consists of multilayered processes at the representational level. The first thing to discuss is the conceptual process illustrated by the distinctive and static framing of the RPs contained in the image. The first and bigger rectangular frame at the upper part of the poster housing the linguistic text, "wash your hand thoroughly…") relates to the second and smaller one (which has the verbal text, "health advisory") in the classificational sense. The same goes for the linguistic text beneath the health advisory frame. The later which gain prominence by its centralisation and emboldening is the superordinate whereas the "wash your hand frame" as well as the textual elements beneath it constitute the subordinates. Within the "wash your hand" frame is transactional action narrative structure that has many hands as the actors and the vectors simultaneously. The textual message, "wash your hands thoroughly and regularly with soap and clean water" is the goal. The center-margin layout of the goal places a high information value on it as it is a very important practice in the fight against the cholera virus. The goal is also made salient by its capitalisation and alteration of colours. Essentially, the goal is made the locus of attention for every Nigerian citizen to recognise its importance.

CONCLUSION

This study, based on the resourcefulness of awareness posters in communicating vital health issues in a resource-constrained clime like Nigeria and owing to the capability of multimodal theory in unraveling the meanings intricately embedded in multiple communicative codes, investigates the deployment of multimodal resources by image producers of cholera awareness posters to help the Nigerian citizens and image viewers at large visualise the danger that the cholera disease portends so that it can be decisively eradicated. Online awareness posters on cholera are thematically classified based on the different goals they are meant to achieve. Thus, online awareness posters on cholera are categorised into Cholera alert messaging; visualising cholera symptoms; and visualising cholera prevention and treatment. Using Kress and van Leeuwen's Visual Grammar on 20 purposely selected online awareness posters on cholera in Nigeria, the study reveals that image producers of cholera posters conflated multiple processes at the representational level of meaning. Also, at the interactional level, the close-up frame size was generously used and the contact made to the viewers was basically to offer information. At the compositional meaning level, while different strategies (including size, colour, capitalisation and emboldening) were adopted to achieve salience, the horizontal, vertical and centre-margin layout were copiously expended. Altogether, these devices were so used to convey danger and educe behavioural change among the Nigerian citizens. This study, by examining the interplay of communication modes in the awareness on cholera in Nigeria, has implication for the design of effective public health campaigns, health communication strategies and culturally sensitive health materials. With these critical insights offered into the visual and textual strategies deployed in health communication, this study recommends that health organisations should prioritise multimodal approaches to health communication. Posters, which will take into account the local values, beliefs and contexts of the people, can be combined with other tools such as augmented reality of visual reality in order to espouse positive healthy living among the Nigerian people.

REFERENCES

Abdullahi, M. D., & Ogungbe, E. E. (2024). A linguistic stylistic analysis of selected healthcare promotion posters. *Lapai Journal of Humanities*, *15*(1), 62–75.

Aulia, H., Hafeez, M., Mashwani, H. U., Careemdeen, J. D., Mirzapour, M., & Syaharuddin, S. (2024, March). The role of interactive learning media in enhancing student engagement and academic achievement. In Proceeding of International Seminar On Student Research In Education, Science, and Technology (Vol. 1, pp. 57-67).

Boggu, A. T., & Sundarsingh, J. (2015). Poster presentation as an effective communication tool in an EFL context. *International Journal of Language and Linguistics*, *2*(5). https://www.researchgate.net/publication/290438108

Borkin, M., Vo, A., Bylinskii, Z., Isola, P., Sunkavalli, S., Olivia, A., & Pfister, H. (2013). What makes a visualisation memorable? *IEEE Transactions on Visualization and Computer Graphics*, *19*(12), 2306–2315. DOI: 10.1109/TVCG.2013.234 PMID: 24051797

Christensen, T., Riis, A. H., Hatch, E. E., Wise, L. A., Nielsen, M. G., Rothman, K. J., & Mikkelsen, E. M. (2017). Costs and efficiency of online and offline recruitment methods: A web-based cohort study. *Journal of Medical Internet Research*, *19*(3), e6716.

Cline, R. J. W., & Haynes, K. M. (2001). Consumer health information seeking on the Internet: The state of the art. *Health Education Research*, *16*(6), 671–692. https://www.jstor.org/stable/45109709. DOI: 10.1093/her/16.6.671 PMID: 11780707

Cynthia. (2023). Visual text comprehension: 4 types of non-linguistic features you need to know. Retrieved September 3, 2024 from [Lil But Mighty English] (https://lilbutmightyenglish.com/blog/visualtextcomprehension4typesofnonlinguisticfe aturesyouneedtoknow/)

DeWitt, D., & Alias, N. (2017) Infographic posters for enhancing 21st century communication skills. *World Conference on Education (WCEDU)*, 12-13 Colombo, Sri Lanka.

Hasanica, N., Ramic-Catak, A., Mujezinovic, A., Begagic, S., Galijasevic, K., & Oruc, M. (2020). The effectiveness of the leaflets and posters as a health education method. *Materia Socio-Medica*, *32*(2), 135–139. DOI: 10.5455/msm.2020.32.135-139 PMID: 32843863

High Speed Training. (2023). Internet safety posters for schools. Retrieved September 3, 2024 from https://www.highspeedtraining.co.uk/hub/internetsafetypostersf orschools/

Houts, P. S., Doak, C. C., Doak, L. G., & Loscalzo, M. J. (2006). The role of pictures in improving health communication: A review of research on attention, comprehension, recall, and adherence. *Patient Education and Counseling*, *61*(2), 173–190. DOI: 10.1016/j.pec.2005.05.004 PMID: 16122896

Jewitt, C. (2009). *The Routledge Handbook of Multimodal Analysis*. Routledge.

Jia, Y. (2024). Beyond the scripts of digital posters: A case study of language ideologies and writing practices in contemporary China. *Diggit Magazine*, 1-15, https://www.diggitmagazine.com/academic-papers/beyond-scripts-digital-posters -case-study-language-ideologies-and-writing-practices

Koutsogiannis, D., & Mitsikopoulou, B. (2004). The internet as a glocal discourse environment: A commentary on Lam and Bloch. *Language Learning & Technology*, *8*, 83–89.

Kress, G., & van Leeuwen, T. (1996). *Reading images: The grammar of visual design*. Routledge.

Kress, R. G., & van Leeuwen, T. (2006). *Reading images: The grammar of visual design*. Arnold. DOI: 10.4324/9780203619728

Kreuter, M. W., & Wray, R. J. (2003). Tailored and targeted health communication: Strategies for enhancing information relevance. *American Journal of Health Behavior*, *27*(3), S227–S232. DOI: 10.5993/AJHB.27.1.s3.6 PMID: 14672383

Lirola,M. M.(2006). A systemic functional analysis of two multimodal covers. ***Revista avicantina de Estutios Ingleses*, 19(2), 226-249.**

Marcum, C., & Harris, M. (2013). The training page: Plain language posters. Retrieved September 3, 2024 from https://irp.nih.gov/catalyst/22/3/thetrainingpage plainlanguageposters

Miller, J. E. (2007). Preparing and presenting effective research posters. *Health Services Research*, 42(1 I), 311–328.

Ngwa, M. C., Ihekweazu, C., Okwor, T., Yennan, S., Williams, N., Elimian, K., Karaye, N. Y., Bello, I. W., & Sack, D. A. (2021). The cholera risk assessment in Kano State, Nigeria: A historical review, mapping of hotspots and evaluation of contextual factors. *PLoS Neglected Tropical Diseases*, *15*(1), 1–19 e0009046. DOI: 10.1371/journal.pntd.0009046 PMID: 33465091

Olapegba, P. O., Ayandele, O., Kolawole, S. O., Oguntayo, R., Gandi, J. C., Dangiwa, A. L., Ottu, I. F., & Iorfa, S. K. (2020). A Preliminary assessment of novel coronavirus (COVID-19) knowledge and perceptions in Nigeria. SSRN *Electronic Journal*, 1-14. DOI: 10.2139/ssrn.3584408

Paivio, A. (1990). *Mental representations: A dual coding approach*. Oxford Psychology Series., DOI: 10.1093/acprof:oso/9780195066661.001.0001

Pedwell, R. K., Hardy, J. A., & Rowland, S. L. (2017). Effective visual design and communication practices for research posters: Exemplars based on the theory and practice of multimedia learning and rhetoric. *Biochemistry and Molecular Biology Education*, *45*(3), 249–261. DOI: 10.1002/bmb.21034 PMID: 27925371

Raney, M., & Zanten, E. (2018). Self-care posters serve as a low-cost option for physical activity promotion. *Health Promotion Practice*, *20*(3), 354–362. Advance online publication. DOI: 10.1177/1524839918763585 PMID: 29566577

Rueda-Gómez, K. L., Rodríguez-Muñiz, L. J., & Muñiz-Rodríguez, L. (2024). Factors that mediate the success of the use of online platforms to support learning: The view of university teachers. *Education and Information Technologies*, *29*(2), 2459–2482. DOI: 10.1007/s10639-023-11916-0

Salako, B. L., Ajayi, A., & Smith, S. I. (2021). Cholera in Nigeria: Epidemiology, risk factors, and response - A Review. *Proceedings of the Nigerian Academy of Science*, *14*(1), 24–33. DOI: 10.57046/JYBJ8296

Schroeder, J. E. (2004). Visual consumption in an image economy. K. Ekstrom and H. Brembeck (Eds.) *Elusive Consumption. Berg*, pp. 229-244, https://ssrn.com/abstract=499082

Silverstein, M. (1979). Language structure and linguistic ideology. P. R. Clyne, W.F. Hanks and C.L. Hofbauer et al. (Eds.). *The Elements: A Parasession on Linguistic Units and Levels*. Chicago: Linguistic Society, 193-247

Sumampouw, J., & Sukandar, D. (2019). The effectiveness of health promotion method using poster in improving patients' behaviour to prevent transmission of pulmonary tuberculosis disease. *Proceeding 2nd Manado Health Polytechnic International Conference,* 115-127.

Tahririan, M., & Sadri, E. (2013). Analysis of images in Iranian high school: EFL course textbook. *International Journal of English Language Education*, *3*(1), 239–253.

Tech4Learning. (2018). Internet safety poster creative educator. Retrieved September 3, 2024 from https://creativeeducator.tech4learning.com/2018/lessons/internetsafetylesson

Utoyo, A. W., Aprilia, H. D., Kuntjoro-Jakti, R. A. D. R. I., & Kurniawan, A. (2021, April). Visual communication design: Poster as an important way to encourage social distance in Jakarta when the epidemic 19. []. IOP Publishing.]. *IOP Conference Series. Earth and Environmental Science*, *729*(1), 012140.

Vale, O., & Barbosa, A. (2021). Posters: A tool to foster visual and communication skills through mathematical challenging tasks using gallery walk. *EDULEARN21 Proceedings*, 8416-8425, DOI: 10.21125/edulearn.2021.1706

Wen, L., Jingjing, W., Chen, W., & Luyu, S. (2022). Research on the Visual imagery of posters based on the culture code theory of design. *Frontiers in Psychology*, 13, 1-6. 861366. .

WHO. (2024). *Rallying Action to Curb Cholera in Nigeria's Lagos State.* https://www.afro.who.int/countries/nigeria/news/rallying-action-curb-cholera-nigerias-lagos-state#:~:text=Health%20authorities%20declared%20a%20cholera,an%20acute%20and%20virulent%20infection

World Health Organization. (2020). Cholera fact sheet. Retrieved September 3, 2024 from https://www.who.int/newsroom/factsheets/detail/cholera

Yom-Tov, E., Shembekar, J., & Barclay, S.. (2018). The effectiveness of public health advertisements to promote health: A randomized-controlled trial on 794,000 participants. *NPI Digital Med*, *1*(24), 1–6.

ADDITIONAL READING LIST

Carbin, J., Sanmartino, M., Hennessy, E., & Urke, H. (2021). *Arts and health promotion: Tools and bridges for practice, research, and social transformation.* Springer. DOI: 10.1007/978-3-030-56417-9

Guffey, E. (2015). *Posters: A global history*. Reaktion Books.

Hartman, N. S., & Conklin, T. A. (2021). Books and posters: Creating conversations that result in learning. *Management Teaching Review*, *6*(3), 223–236. DOI: 10.1177/2379298120944597

Hu, Y. (2016). Health communication research in the digital age: A systematic review. *Journal of Communication in Healthcare*, *8*(4), 260–288. DOI: 10.1080/17538068.2015.1107308

Kress, G. (2010). *Multimodality: A social semiotic approach to contemporary communication*. Taylor and Francis.

McKinnon, M. (Ed.). (2022). *Health promotion: A practical guide effective communication* (1st ed.). Cambridge University Press.

Norris, S. (2020). *Multimodal theory and Methodology: For the analysis of (inter)action and identity* (1st ed.). Routledge Focus on Linguistics. DOI: 10.4324/9780429351600

Pelham, A., & Sills, E. (2009). *Promoting health and wellness in underserved communities: Multidisciplinary perspectives through service learning. Sterling.* Stylus Pub.

Sabina, T., & Marissa, K. (2024). *Discourses, modes, media and meaning in an era of pandemic: A multimodal discourse analysis approach.* Routledge.

Silvestri, K., Barrett, N., & Nyachae, T. (Eds.). (2023). *Towards critical multimodality: Theory, research, and practice in transformative educational space.* Information Age Publishing.

KEY TERMS AND DEFINITIONS

Multimodal health communication: Multimodal health communication refers to the incorporation of multiple communication codes, including texts, graphics, colour, imagery to relate health information in order to promote healthy behaviours and enhance people's overall health outcomes.

Healthcare promotion: This captures the process of affording people in a community the opportunity to improve their health through health education, sensitisation and support.

Awareness posters: These are graphical tools that appeal to sight and that combine texts and visuals, designed for the purpose of informing the public about specific issues, raising awareness, educating and encouraging them.

Digital posters: Digital posters are electronic visual communicative tools designed to inform the public about specific issues, raise awareness, educate and encourage them. They can be accessed through various devices such as computers and smartphones.

Visualising danger: Visualising danger is used to refer to the creation and interpretation of visual illustrations that communicate risks, threats, problems to individuals of the community at large. The illustrations are made to alert people to possible hazards so that precautionary measures will be taken to forestall them.

Visual elements: They are the components of visual representation that convey meaning. Examples include shape, colour, lines, texture, form, space, size, and so on.

Textual elements: Textual elements are linguistic items (letters, words, phrase, clauses) used in conveying meaning, information. They could come in written of printed forms.

Grammar of visual designs: Grammar of visual designs encapsulates principles and rules guiding the composition of visual and textual properties to communicate meaning.

Chapter 8
The Role of the New Media in Enhancing Online Content Creation

Ijeoma Callista Ojilere
https://orcid.org/0000-0001-6231-9509
Alex-Ekwueme Federal University, Ndufu-Alike, Nigeria

Chidimma U.E. Inyima
Alex-Ekwueme Federal University, Ndufu-Alike, Nigeria

ABSTRACT

This chapter aimed to examine the role of the new media in enhancing content creation. Over the last two decades, the rise of the new media has continued to demonstrate its worth as a communication chain with worldwide user connectivity as its focal point. As a result, content creators have taken to the internet via social media platforms like Facebook, TikTok, YouTube, etc. with a plethora of contents intended to entertain, educate, sensitise, or spill the tea to their audience. Using the qualitative and quantitative methods of data collection, content creators whose focus spans from family, health, education, motivational, food, and business were employed as the population for this study. Findings show that content creators have profoundly reshaped media participation and engagement by gratifying the entertainment needs of the audience. Results further revealed that digital media have indisputably demonstrated their crucial role in fostering connections among users and content creators.

DOI: 10.4018/979-8-3693-7934-9.ch008

INTRODUCTION

The emergence and sustained growth of the new media over the last two decades can best be viewed as the hallmark of invention by information technology considering the revolutions it has occasioned in all aspects of human activity. The new media which uses algorithmic models and which is characterized by digitalization, interactivity, accessibility, and multi-modality is often contrasted with traditional basically non-interactive media which relied mostly on analog broadcast models. In all works of life and beyond, the world has undergone rapid changes due to the impact of the new media (Uduak, 2021). In this regard, Gills (2025) observes that it 'has changed the way information is created, shared and consumed globally'. Indeed, at present, the world is riding high on the wave of the new media which has ushered in a new range of opportunities and apparently limitless potentials expected to bridge the gap created by traditional media (Todorova-E et al., 2022). Flew (2002) substantiates this view of technological advancement as a touch stone for world globalization. Additionally, the incursion of the new media has, without doubt, increased communication and connection among its teeming users globally, giving the public various avenues to express themselves through various digital tools, formats, forms and platforms. Digital communication channels such as the internet, social networking sites such as Facebook, Tiktok, YouTube, Twitter, WhatsApp, and Instagram and so on provide fertile ground for user interaction and content creation. Consequently, content creators have surged the internet with various contents geared towards entertaining, educating, or spilling the tea to their audience as well as making a decent living from their efforts. While enjoying entertainment, the audiences crave fresh ideas or, at the very least, a variation on classic themes, demonstrating intolerance for stale or familiar content (Bartsch, 2017; Eastman & Ferguson, 2013; Sturges, 2015). Another notable insight on the new media is its role as a platform that reflects societal dynamics raises awareness and offers solutions to social issues, by persuasion, or clarification of social and civic matters needed to bolster community engagement and talents (Chatton, 2007). In other words, new media has demonstrated its undeniable role as that which propels interaction among users, and by extension, content creators (Ronald, 1984). Undoubtedly, the new media has, as (Newman, 2011) had foretold, altered the meaning of geographic distance, provided increase in the speed of communication, provided opportunities for interactive communication and allowed forms of communication that were previously distinct to overlap. These fallouts of the new media underscore the focus of the present study. The study seeks to examine the role of the new media, as characterized in the literature, in enhancing online content creation. Using a cross-sectional questionnaire distributed to a randomly sampled population of content creators and a structured interview-based survey study, and against the backdrop of American sociologist Thorstein Veblen's Technological Determinism Theory which holds that technology, technological development, communication technology, and the new media are the primary agents of social change, this chapter specifically seeks to:

a. Examine the extent to which the new media promote online content creation among the active users;
b. Ascertain the level of satisfaction derived by these core users of the new media in their quest to utilize the media;
c. Evaluate the probable challenges prevalent in the use of the new media and
d. Discuss how the new media propels growth for the active users.

THE NEW MEDIA: HISTORY, FEATURES, CHARACTERISTICS

Until the 1980s, media relied primarily on print and analog broadcast models referred to in contemporary parlance as Traditional media. The last two and a half decades have however witnessed the metamorphosis into digital-technology-predicated media. The New media may thus be best identified as an umbrella term for the different kinds of electronic communication which have resulted from innovations in computer technology in the last two and a half decades. Uduak (2021) corroborating this view defines it thus '[a]catch-all term used for various kinds of electronic communications that are conceivable due to innovation in computer technology (p. 30). Vokmer (1999) opines that the term may be used to mean the message, the technology or the social context of New Media.

New Media differs significantly from Traditional media like television, radio, print newspaper, magazine, etc. which have been described as often disruptive, direct, non-interactional and mostly unidirectional by offering subtler, more engaging content that create interaction and foster relationships (Hanson, 2024). The new media offers a wide array of digital communication channels like websites, podcasts, email, social media platforms, online communities, online forums, audio books, blogs, and Web advertisements, among others. These platforms allow user interaction and can selectively link between contents (Keen, 2010). Also, unlike consumers of Traditional Media who were mere passive recipients of information, users of the New media are active participants who can both consume and create content i.e. text, images, video, audio and interactional elements. Emphasizing this feature of the new media, Jenkins (2005) observes that 'the emergence of [these] new digital technologies signals a potential shift of who is in control of information, experience and resource's (p.8). The fundamental strengths of the New media include accessibility, versatility, scalability, interactivity, reach, user engagement, immediacy and strength of societal impact, effectiveness for target advertising, multi-modality and relative affordability (Gills, 2025; Hanson; 2024, Uduak, 2021).

The New Media additionally has a language variety associated with it. This language, identified in the literature as 'digispeak', 'netspeak', 'internet language', 'chatspeak' etc. is characterized by innovative, evolutionary but increasingly influential linguistic forms. Among these innovative forms are spelling innovations, text multilingualism, features of spoken discourse, reduced sentences, informal style, acronyms, semantic extension and reassignment of meanings, coinages, among others (Smart & Okoro, 2016; Inyima, 2018).These innovative forms showcase the unique characteristics and usage ethics of the media, 'netiquette', and 'produce much different affective and relational patterns than do other type of communication due to the reduction and types of cues available to participants (Latte, 1994 as cited in Inyima, 2018 pg. 4) (Mbarachi & Okoro's, 2016) study reveal that New media language in Nigeria is characterized by two language varieties, a Nigerian English variety and an internet English variety. The Nigerian English variety consists of loan words and culture specific speech habits while the internet language variety comprises shortening devices and instances of verbal language. The literature defines Nigerian English as a new English variety used in Nigeria and which captures the unique social-cultural, linguistic experiences and language habits of Nigerians (Inyima, 2024). Succinctly captured by (Adegbija, 2004, pp. 21-22), Nigerian English is a variety of English 'doing what Nigerians want it to do'. The variety maximally exploits the intrinsic dynamism and functional potential of language giving rise to unique and distinctly Nigerian usages. (Mondap, 2024) reports an upsurge in content creation in Nigeria. The innovative language forms which characterize the new media shape language use and interaction on the new media. Contents which would appeal, engage and reshape consumer opinion must therefore be pro new media. As such, content creators who seek relevance and consumer engagement and satisfaction need to leverage on its opportunities, versatility and provisions.

CONTENT CREATION: HISTORY, FEATURES, CHARACTERISTICS

Content, with reference to the New media, encompasses all information, media, message, article or post shared on social media platforms and which are intended to inform, engage, entertain, connect, drive action, generate leads or rage-bait (Kontentino, 2025; Gills, 2025; Team, 2021). (Lenhart & Fallow, 2004) describe it as 'the material that people contribute to the online world'. Content can be original, repurposed i.e. adapted from other sources or user-generated and may be in text (written), visual, audio or multi-media forms. It may additionally be interactive as is the case with quizzes, games and infographics; social media posts including posts and updates; or user-generated as in the case of comments and photos. Interestingly, anyone can be a content creator.

Hanson, (2024) describes content creation as the 'process of generating and developing various types of media –written text, images, videos, and audio to engage an audience and deliver information or entertainment'. It is usually tailored for specific platforms and targeted at specific audiences. Written content formats include Blog posts, articles, social media updates etc. Image content formats include images, infographics, videos, posters, etc. while audio content formats comprise Podcasts, audiobooks, music, among others. Elategy (2023) traces the history and development of content creation from the earliest times of storytelling and cave paintings which depicted scenes from everyday life through the Egyptian hieroglyphs and scrolls, the invention of the printing press in the 15th century which revolutionized content creation by allowing mass production and greater spread and accessibility, the industrial age which saw a rise in the number of published magazines and newspapers and provided both information and entertainment, the invention of the radio in 1900 which enabled people all over the world to listen to news, music and entertainment, the TV age where people could watch live events, to the digital age, the present age, where anyone can create, publish and access information and entertainment in whatever format and platform desired. Content creators must, however, adhere to the five Cs of content creation namely: clarity, consistency, credibility, creativity and customer-centricity (Timmermann, 2024).

Undoubtedly, the new media has become the hub of content creation where content creators unleash their divine talents in the hope of building and strengthening human connectivity (Hanson, 2024). The level at which the new media spiraled can be linked to the COVID-19 pandemic period where individuals were subjected to compulsive outdoor restrictions, lockdown of businesses, social distancing, and overall crippling of global economy (Onuma & Ogboji, 2023; Inyima, Nwosu & Ezenne,2022). As a result, the new media served a remedial and mediating role for reconnection among friends, schools, and entrepreneurs by means of social media. According to Gil-Garcia (2018), social media plays a veritable role in online communication. The author further expounds that dissemination of information, and adequate reactions to compelling issues are made possible through the media. The success of this has snowballed into more users spending an increasing amount of time on social media and other online platforms (Molla, 2018). Again, due to the new media, the world is witnessing changes in societal perceptions, work patterns, information creation, sharing and consumption and production inputs (O'Neill, 2023; Gill, 2025). Given the global attention given to and recognition of the new media, scholars' interest to embark on more robust discoveries in the realm of communication is undoubtedly piqued. Given, also, the focus of the study which is the role of the new media in enhancing online content creation, it is pertinent to survey previous studies across borders.

Ojomo and Sadeinde (2021) investigated the extent to which social media skits transformed audience consumption, involvement, anticipation, and entertainment production, using the uses and gratification theory as a theoretical benchmark. The study successfully identified the dichotomy between social media entertainment models and broadcast entertainment techniques. For the researcher, audience involvement with social media skits is an undeniable indicator that stimulates content creators to produce more, with audience reactions determining the sustainability of the piece. These also redefine entertainment for comedians, who use skits to experiment with fresh comic material. As a result, these engaging characteristics modify the audience's experience of entertainment on social media. This delineates the undeniable impact of entertainment on audience which is akin to the present study but differ in terms of scope.

Madan and Rosca, (2021) explored the current trends in digital marketing communication acknowledging the challenges businesses face in the 21st century given the sophisticated global digitization which tends to stiffen operations. As an exploratory study, the study tried to uncover the implementation of modern trends in marketing communication and their impact on businesses. The result revealed the need for companies to adapt to the modern market trends for global visibility and valuable impact. The study further emphasized that new marketing trends are replete with prospects, not without their challenges during technological advancements. Also, the researchers' implication of the study lies in the description of the new marketing communication processes given the global invention and expansion of technologies spanning the last millennia. Madan and Rosca's study differ from the present study also in focus. Admittedly, one of the purposes of content creation is to market products .but the present study is not primarily concerned with the incorporation of current trends in digital marketing communication but rather with how the New Media has generally shaped content creation.

Blank (2013) investigated the stratification of content creators on the internet using the random sample of British population. The study acknowledged the arduous nature of internet usage prior to the invention of the new media which can best be described as swift, efficient and economical. The study identified three major contents namely 'skilled content', 'social and entertainment content', and 'political content'. This finding debunked the previous assumption that only one type of content was available on the internet. Again, the researcher's multivariate logistic regression noted against the backdrop of previous assumption that content creation is a multifaceted arena that accommodates various talents. Results further indicated that creation of content shares a liminal stage with both the elite and non-elite. The elite tend to tilt towards the creation of political contents while the non-elite are prone to social/entertainment contents. This finding differs from the current study which sets out to examine the role of the new media in content creation.

Yujie, Yasin, Alsagoff, Hoon, (2022) examined the mediating role of new media engagement in the digital age using the questionnaire survey to meet the study objectives. The study aimed to accentuate the fact that media engagement plays a mediating role between the instructions in the newsroom and the attitude of the audience on social media. The findings indicate a positive attitude of the audience to the new media by way of massive engagement in posts. The study further highlights that positive engagements from online users transcend the shores of overall integration and interaction among humans. Again, this study reiterates the indisputable role of the new media as a connective outlet among users. This aligns with the focus of the present study. It however differs from its population and study area. Whereas the study used the newsroom and attitude of the audience on social media, the present study uses content creators across selected Social media platforms.

Olajide and Nwangi (2022) researched on the role of the new media in communication development in Nigeria while incorporating media challenges, and opportunities prevalent in emerging technologies and the evolution of the media landscape as its focal point. By adopting secondary sources from websites, journals, and books, the study identified media ownership, technological innovation and government policies as key factors that have influenced media role in communication development in Nigeria. However, the study highlights the challenges faced by the new media as lack of media freedom, and derisory funding for its development. Again, the study argues that given the crucial role of the media in communication development in Nigeria, a hands-on approach should be employed to tackle the significant challenges that plague its efficacy to fulfill its potential which spans from social mobilization, through information dissemination and democratic governance. The connection of this study lies in its investigation of the roles of the new media. It however differs from it by focusing on New Media roles in communication development which spans a broader scope than the present study.

The studies although diverse in scope, focus, aim and methodology highlight the fact that there is indeed a change in the global communication landscape occasioned by New Media technologies. These technologies have direct bearings on online communication and advertising models and methods and end consumer or user participation and satisfaction. The present study will build on the research findings but further it to establish how the New Media impacts content creation.

MAIN FOCUS OF THE CHAPTER

Language and communication are inextricably concomitant with media in such a way that their extraordinary impact on all aspects of life can only be revealed when they are viewed as a single symbiotic entity. The massive global rise of new media is having an increasingly important impact on freedom of speech and communication, influencing the evolving paradigm. Age-old barriers to human connection and globalisation, are being overcome by the power of modern media and technology, ushering in a new era of connectivity, communication, creativity, and potential, (Schmidt & Cohen 2013). The proliferation of communication technologies is transforming everything on a massive scale considering the swift change from the traditional or print media to the new media.

The unrestricted access and widespread use of information and communication technology services, generally referred to as new media, is a global phenomenon in modern culture, Manovich (2001). In his book, '*The New Media Theory Reader*', Manovich (2001) compares the new media revolution to the printing press revolution in the fourteenth century and the photography revolution in the nineteenth century, both of which prompted all forms of culture to adopt computer-mediated forms of production, distribution, and communication. Manovich (2001) further remarks that previously revolutions impacted only one form of culture, as seen in the printing revolution, which affected only the distribution of media, and the photography revolution, which affected the culture of still images. However, the computer media revolution affects all stages of communication, including acquisition, manipulation, storage, and distribution; as well as all myriads of media; texts, still images, moving images, sound, and three-dimensional construction.

Scholars are increasingly fascinated with the rise of social media platforms and the role of virtual social networks with multicultural communication, (Carey 2009; Del Gludice et al., 2016). Taking into account the world population's new media usage, cross-cultural communication has become more fluid and frequent (Boamah, 2018; Chin et al., 2021). Thus, cultural exchanges, collisions, conflicts, and integration among many nations, races, and countries on these platforms have become more visible, and relevant papers by scholars in numerous fields have also been proliferated. However, with the advent of digitisation, new cultural relationships have emerged both within and outside geopolitical boundaries, necessitating new understanding and theories to explain the motivation, process, and implications of cross-cultural communications in the digital era (Chin et al., 2020). Previous studies which examined and explored the interactions between cross-cultural users, enterprises, and countries on social media demonstrated the significance of new media in negotiating and controlling transient migrants' identities in relation to their home and host cultures during the acculturation process (cf Cleveland, 2016; Yau et al.,

2019). Studies have additionally investigated information sharing in a specific domain, such as health information and news transmission, Hofgson, (2018), Li et al, (2018), Wang and Chin, (2020). Cultural psychology offers a thorough explanation for the aspects that drive cultural communication, such as self-concept, which the host country may alter, Huang & Park, (2013), Thomas et al., (2019), the impact of which may affect communication behaviour like people's inclination to utilise social media applications, incertitude towards social capital, social media commerce, and even sharing behaviour itself Chu & Choi, (2010), Han & Kim, (2018), Li et al, (2018). Other variables like public broadcast businesses, fans' boost, and contentious comments may garner more attention causing the sociality of the communal media capsule to widen the breadth of information exchange and how news is perceived, Meza and Park. (2014), Jin and Yoon, 2016; Hodgson,(2018). Again, prior studies underpin the impact of collectivist and individualist cultures, such as social media user activity discrepancies, cognizance inclinations, and self-concept, Chu &Choi, (2016), Thomas et al., (2019). This highlights the collective and positive reactions of users while demonstrating incandescent passion towards the new media. Interestingly, others focus on the nexus between multicultural experiences, cultural intelligence, and creativity, the evaluation of the validity of the two measures; and the changing status of crucial elements in the social system and the government in risk communication (e.g. Hu et al., 2017; Jil & Bates, 2020). On a more practical level, mobile device application usability and social media commerce were assessed by Hoehie et al. (2015), Hu et al. (2017), and Ji & Bates (2020). Extensively, Hoehie et al. (2015) and Han & Kim (2018) analysed mobile device application usability and social media commerce.

The multifarious new media aid users' acceptance of the various channels for establishment of cross-cultural connection and the recognition of digital platforms' identity of other cultures. Drawing by the views of these scholars and bearing the complexities of digitization in mind, new cultural and sociocultural modes of interactions have emerged causing strings of connections across the globe.

Theoretical Framework

This study is anchored on the Technological Determinism Theory credited to Thorstein Veblen, an American sociologist. The theory holds that technology, technological development, communication technology, and media are the primary agents of social change. Veblen asserts that technological growth impacts and moulds society with the intent to change and adapt to new technological advancements. The establishment of this theory in the early twentieth century gave rise to two tenets: radical and moderate (hard, soft) technological determinism. The radical version on the one hand, views technology as a prerequisite for societal change, while the other, the moderate, recognizes technology only as a key factor. Currently, one can succinctly say that the internet and the new media have made profound impact on the structure of society with the proliferation of computers, networks, and the New media permeating every facet of not only human communication, but the society in its entirety. The new media has indeed changed the nature and the way our society and individuals act spanning the way we shop, recruit staff, pay taxes, use the library, and acquire academic degrees. Toffler (1981) views technology as the catalyst for all developments that have had a devastating impact on all aspects of human life. However, the adverse implications of technical advancement are the products of people's misuse rather than the inherent nature of technology. Today's scenario commonly referred as the "third wave," is characterised by significant changes and an acceleration of life pace caused by the continual development of technology. This theory is appropriate for this study due to its ability to provide valuable insights into the nexus between technology, communication and society.

METHODOLOGY

Study Design

The study is a cross-sectional questionnaire and structured interview-based survey study. In order to achieve the objective of the study which is to examine the role of the media in enhancing online content creation, a pre-tested and validated questionnaire designed in an open-ended format was formulated and distributed to randomly selected 104 active social media content creators. This design was to obtain diverse insights from the respondents. Also, to substantiate and supplement the data collected from the questionnaire, an eight-item structured interview was administered to establish and verify the claims of the online content creators. The copies of questionnaire were shared by means of direct message to the sample 100 active social media content creators for them to make their inputs about the world of content creation while focusing on the study objectives. A letter of consent had been sent to the population prior to the distribution of the questionnaire. The interviewees comprised 10 established social media content creators who have made impact in the digital world through their platforms; Facebook, Tiktok, Instagram and YouTube. Ethical considerations were upheld throughout the process.

Sampling Technique

This study adopted the random sampling technique for the questionnaire distribution and stratified random exercise for the structured interview. The random sampling was adopted to make room for diversified selection of samples from the numerous populations of digital users while the stratified sampling was used to winnow the appropriate population for the interview.

Study Instrument

Data for the study were collected using the pre-tested and validated researcher-structured questionnaire and interview. The questionnaire was written in English and designed in an open-ended format while stating the purpose of the study to aid comprehension by the respondents. The questionnaire comprised the consent to participate which included: agreement to participate, voluntary participation, note of confidentiality, and non-compulsion to provide answers. The second part of the questionnaire consisted of the 10 items which addressed how the new media have enhanced users' content creation journey, the probable challenges, and the motivation for embarking on content creation, the satisfaction derived from the expedition and advice to prospective creators. The structured interview questions addressed such issues as: the inspiration to create content and the type of content, the goals on the internet as content creators, their thoughts about the emergence of the new media, the extent of achievement achieved so far in the industry, as well as notable setbacks. Each interview was introduced, the questions simplified, and the study objectives clearly stated to ease needless confoundment.

Data Collection

Data for this study were collected by means of questionnaires which were sent to social media users through the various platforms notably Facebook, Tiktok, Instagram, and YouTube. The pre-tested and validated questionnaires were sent to these media outlets where active media users are known for their daily and engaging posts. The duration for the collection of data spanned between 1st to 30th September to make room for sufficient and voluminous responses. A total of 170 were sent out and 104 copies of the questionnaire were duly completed and returned via the source of dispatch. The structured and Key Person Interview, on the flip side, was organized for the active users with verified social media handles via zoom. By and large, 10 interviewees were used as secondary samples for this study.

DATA ANALYSIS

All the data obtained for this study were represented accordingly. The data from the questionnaire were presented and analysed using the frequency table and simple percentage calculations. The data from the structured interview which was audio recorded were transcribed and analyzed linguistically.

Table 1. Demographic Details of the Respondents

Age	**Percentage of Respondents**
<20	11
21-30	29
31-40	36
41-50	28
>60	0
Gender	
Male	58
Female	46
Educational Qualification	
SSLC	7
Diploma	31
Graduate	66
Profession	
Medical	15
Teaching	28
Self-employed	44
Student	13
Others	4

A look at table 1 indicates demographic details of the respondents where the highest percentage of the respondents falls with those within the age range 31-40 representing 36% followed by 29% as captured by respondents with the 21-30 age brackets and then 24% representing for those within 31-40 and finally 11% representing those <20 being the least participants. Ultimately, the male participants were the most active respondents with 58% while their counterparts represented 46%. The statistics above shows the major participants for the study were mainly self-employed with 40%.

Table 2. Questionnaire Distribution and Response Rate

Creator's Genre	No. of Questionnaire Distributed	No. & % Returned
Family	15	13 12.5
Political	25	23 22.1
Educational	12	12 11.5
Health	9	8 7.7
Motivational	21	19 18.3
Entertainment	29	17 16.3
Food	9	8 7.7
Total	**120**	**104 96.1**

Table 2 represents the distribution of questionnaire and response rate of samples with political content creators clinching the highest rate at 23% return of questionnaire distributed while motivational creators followed with 19% return rate with a tie between health and food bloggers at 8%.

Table 3. Respondents' Responses to the Questionnaire

Q1. What kind of content do you create and why? *	**Response Rate**	%
Family	13	13.0
Political	23	22.1
Educational	12	12.0
Health	8	7.7
Motivational	19	18.3
Entertainment	17	16.3
Food	8	7.7
ii. Why? *		
To impart knowledge	34	33.0
Create awareness	27	26.0
Entertain	17	16.3
To inspire, engage and inform	19	18.3
Happy place	3	3.0
Q2. What's the response rate of your audience?		
Excellent	17	16.3
Good	19	18.3
Impressive	41	39.4

continued on following page

Table 3. Continued

Q1. What kind of content do you create and why? *	**Response Rate**	**%**
Fair	23	22.1
Q3. How has the media enhanced your online content creation? *		
Positively	7	7.0
Easy gateway to reach wider audience	60	58.0
Provision of global digital tools	11	11.0
Path to audience engagement	22	21.1
Q4. What are the possible challenges you encounter as a content creator? *		
Exorbitant data subscription rate	48	46.1
Lack of content ideas	11	11.0
Low views/reactions	9	8.7
Infrastructural challenges	7	6.7
Algorithm changes	22	21.1
Undue mental stress	3	2.9
Q5. What motivated you to embark on this online content creation journey? *		
Passion to educate	41	39.4
Desire to monetize	32	30.8
Get visibility	10	9.6
Proclivity for entertainment	17	16.3
Q6. How has the media inspired you to create content? *		
Engaging in posts	39	36.0
Media trends	24	23.0
Desire to connect	20	19.2
Juicy tea	17	16.3
Q7. What advice do you have for prospective content creators? *		
Be consistent	66	63.5
Be relentless	10	9.6
Be authentic	7	6.7
Be patient	8	7.7
Create educative content	9	8.7
Q8. How satisfied are you as a content creator?		
Very satisfied	45	43.3
Satisfied	29	28.0
Undecided	17	16.3
No response	9	8.7

continued on following page

Table 3. Continued

Q1. What kind of content do you create and why? *	Response Rate	%
Q9. What specific role do the media play in your content creation?		
Visibility/publicity	47	45.2
Inspiration source for content ideas	23	22.1
Boosts one's content	12	12.0
Connective chain between creator & audience	8	7.7
Platform to showcase one's skill	10	9.6
Q10. Is it possible to make an impact in the society through the media?		
Yes, the media helps to influence narratives and thought processes	11	10.6
Yes, positive contents shape the mind	19	18.3
Yes, through awareness	5	4.8
Yes, high value contents have profound impact on societal development	21	20.2
Yes, media is a chain that connects the world	44	42.3

DISCUSSION AND RECOMMENDATIONS

The results show that the new media has played an incontrovertible role for online content creators by proving a wave of content ideas for wider audience reach. This is evident in the data which established creators' political content involvement with 22.1% followed by 18.3% motivational participants and educational contents with 12.0%. Also, 33.0% of the respondents affirmed their media contribution is to impact knowledge to their audience, 26.0% agreed to create awareness through their platforms, 18.3% averred their intent to inspire, engage and inform the public on compelling issues while 16.3% aim to entertain with their risible contents. This indicates that the new media is an avenue where information dissemination can be attained with celerity (Gil-Garcia, 2018). As regards the response rate of the audience, 39.4% respondents admitted to impressive response, 22.1% acknowledged fair response rate while 18.3% are good with the response rate so far. The level of new media enhancement in online content creation shows 58.0% respondents' take who see it as an easy gateway to reach wider followership, 11.0% on the other hand believes it provides global digital tools and 21.1% are of the view it amplifies engagement, Molla, (2018). The probable challenges as revealed by data stem from exorbitant data charges with 46.1% followed by algorithm changes with 21.1%, rarity of quality content ideas captured at 11.0%, low followers cum views at 8.7% and 6.7% hold infrastructural challenges culpable. These pitfalls have by no means been deterrence to the respondents' interest to break the internet with their content as they remain passionate to educate as demonstrated by 39.4% of the respondents while 30.8% show the motivation behind embarking on the content creation journey is to monetize their pages with a view to make a living, 16.3% proved their proclivity for entertainment as their drive behind content creation. These findings clearly elucidate that digital creation has attained global relevance and users are keen to maximize its benefits. It further delineates the upbeat of the creators who have channeled their creative insight to bring about quality content for audience consumption. Regarding how the media inspires creators to create quality contents, 36.0% of respondents expound that engaging in other's insightful posts is key, 23.0% claimed hopping on media trends gives one creative ideas, 19.2% hinge on the desire to connect with prospective followers is crucial for them, and 16.3% affirm that engagement in juicy tea that spills some ills or rumours help in creative concepts. These findings corroborate with Ronald's (1984) view that the media draws interaction strengths of the users particularly among creators and their audience. Considering the need to connect and gain visibility in the digital world, prospective creators are advised that consistency is vital to growth in the online space as agreed by 63.5% of the respondents. 9.6% concur that relentlessness is crucial, 6.7% avow that authenticity is paramount while 7.7% believe that patience is key to growth in online content creation. With these findings, one can succinctly say that the new media has improved societal perceptions, work patterns, and production inputs of users O'Neill, (2023). In order to ascertain the satisfactory level of these creators, data revealed that 43.3% of the respondents are very satisfied with their output in the digital landscape, 28.0% are merely satisfied while 16.3% are rather ambivalent in their response and an insignificant 8.7% had no response to that effect. These findings encapsulate yet another key factor that propels creators' drive to deliver engaging contents to their audience which is an indication of creative prowess among active creators Chatton (2007). The most recurring response regarding the level of societal impact derivable through contents on the internet, 42.3% asserted that the media is a chain that connects the world, 20.2% believe that high value contents have profound impact on societal development, 18.3% believe that positive contents shape the mind, and 10.6% indicate that contents may influence the audience's thought processes. It is pertinent to note here that the results have revealed the upside impact of the media on the individuals and society at large. This is in line with (Bartsch, 2017; Eastman & Ferguson, 2013; Sturges, 2015) stance that among the many roles of the media, clarification, persuasion and community engagement remain essential.

In addition, the structured and key person interview which was designed to complement and validate the findings from the questionnaire survey confirmed that creation of contents via the various social media platforms is a laudable innovation that has connected the world immensely. According to the data, swift information dissemination and maintenance of human connection are made possible through the media. In other words, new media plays a crucial role in online communication, (Gil-Garcia, 2018). Most of the interviewees further affirmed their inexhaustible need to educate, entertain, advocate and reach out to the wider audience through their platforms as a means to achieve their goals. It was also established that COVID-19 pandemic stirred and gravitated their interests to the new media as a source of succor during the tedious lockdown. Conversely, the profundity of the media creation was borne out of passion to impart knowledge, desire to monetize one's page in the digital space, proclivity for entertainment, visibility yearn all culminate to the motivation behind embarking on the content creation journey, the interviewees enthused. As regards the challenges, most of the interviewees revealed that infrastructural challenges, undue mental stress to produce quality contents, internet glitch, low engagement rate from the audience are some of the challenges that pervade the lives of content creators, however, resilience, consistency, authenticity, patience and creation of inspiring posts can skyrocket one's efforts to fruition. On the issue of afflatus, the interviewees shared diverse sources of inspiration which span from media trends, real life events, and need to succeed in the industry as creative stimulants. The respondents admitted that the new media has played a vital role in their creation of contents by creating an avenue to boost their contents, publicity/ visibility recognition, and connective chain with the audience, as well as inspiration. This essentially buttresses the notion that the new media has strengthened societal perceptions, work patterns, and production inputs of users, O'Neill, (2023).

By and large, these results are clear testament that the new media, nonetheless, influence the behaviour of its users by enabling them to interact, create and build online communities, as well as become socially engaging. Likewise, findings show that new media plays significant roles in this digital age to share information, view content, post feedback on blogs. The study also discovered that interactivity is essential in new media, chiefly in this digital era. New media engagement is essential to sharing information with each other, developing creative content, and building one's brand. In order to foster smooth media operation and alleviate some of the challenges that impede optimal media usage by content creators, this study recommends that government steps in to cushion the effect of the exorbitant data charges and infrastructural upgrade to promote digitisation on all fronts for economic and social purposes.

FUTURE RESEARCH DIRECTIONS

Future research may explore a more scientific approach to the role of the new media for other internet users in the digital space. In addition, further studies may investigate the downsides of the new media for content creators.

CONCLUSION

This study has x-rayed the role of new media in enhancing content creation in the digital age. The findings revealed that people all around the world are being inspired by new media to use their preferred language to share contents, messages, love, views. Engagement and interactivity play a crucial function between new media and the digital era. New media interaction is essential for sharing information, developing creative material, creating branding, and so on. The study's findings demonstrated that new media influence people's behaviour by allowing them to communicate online, form online communities, and become more socially engaged. Thus, it can be claimed that audience/user/individual participation is critical in communicating on new media platforms.

REFERENCES

Adegbija, E. (2004). The domestication of English in Nigeria. In Awonusi, S., & Babalola, E. A. (Eds.), *The Domestication of English in Nigeria: A Festschrift in Honour of Abiodun Adetugbo* (pp. 20–44). University of Lagos Press.

Blank, G. (2013). Who Creates Content? Stratification and content creation on the Internet. *Information Communication and Society*, *16*(4), 590–612. DOI: 10.1080/1369118X.2013.777758

Boamah, E. (2018). Information Culture of Ghanaian Immigrants Living in New Zealand. *Global Knowledge, Memory and Communication*, *67*(8/9), 585–606. DOI: 10.1108/GKMC-07-2018-0065

Carey, J. W. (2009). *Communication as Culture: Essays on Media and Society*. Routledge.

Chin, T., Meng, J., Wang, S., Shi, Y., & Zhang, J. (2021). Cross-cultural metacognition as a prior for humanitarian knowledge: When cultures collide in global health emergencies [Epub ahead-of-print]. *Journal of Knowledge Management*. Advance online publication. DOI: 10.1108/JKM-10-2020-0787

Chin, T., Wang, S., & Rowley, C. (2020). Polychronic knowledge creation in cross-border business models: a sea-like heuristic metaphor. J. Knowl. Manag. doi: [Epub ahead-of-print] Google ScholarDOI: 10.1108/JKM-04-2020-0244

Chu, S.-C., & Choi, S. M. (2010). Social capital and self-presentation on social networking sites: A comparative study of Chinese and American young generations. *Chinese Journal of Communication*, *3*(4), 402–420. DOI: 10.1080/17544750.2010.516575

Cleveland, D. J. (2016). Brand personality and organization-public relationships: impacting dimensions by choosing a temperament for communication

Elategy, W. (14 Nov, 2023) History of content creation. https://www.linkedIn.com

Flew, T. (2002). *New Media: An Introduction*. Oxford University Press.

Gil-Garcia, J. R. (2018). Exploring the complex factors influencing electronic government implementation: An empirical study of 14 countries. *Government Information Quarterly*, 35(2). CrossRef Full Text | Google Scholar

Gills, A.S. (February 2, 2025). Traditional media vs new media: Differences, pros and cons

Han, M. C., & Kim, Y. (2018). How culture and friends affect acceptance of social media commerce and purchase intentions: A comparative study of consumers in the U.S. and China. *Journal of International Consumer Marketing*, *30*(5), 326–335. DOI: 10.1080/08961530.2018.1466226

Hanson. T. (March 5, 2024) .The complete history of content marketing(updated 2024)

Hodgson, P. (2018). Global learners' behavior on news in social media platforms through a MOOC. In Deng, L., Ma, W., & Fong, C. (Eds.), *New Media for Educational Change. Educational Communications and Technology Yearbook* (pp. 141–148). Springer. DOI: 10.1007/978-981-10-8896-4_12

Hoehle, H., Zhang, X., & Venkatesh, V. (2015). An espoused cultural perspective to understand continued intention to use mobile applications: A four-country study of mobile social media application usability. *European Journal of Information Systems*, *24*(3), 337–359. DOI: 10.1057/ejis.2014.43

Hopkins, L. (2009). *Media and migration: A review of the field*. Australia and New Zealand Communication Association.

Hu, S., Jibao, G., Liu, H., & Huang, Q. (2017). The moderating role of social media usage in the relationship among multicultural experiences, cultural intelligence, and individual creativity. *Information Technology & People*, *30*(2), 265–281. DOI: 10.1108/ITP-04-2016-0099

Huang, C.-M., & Park, D. (2013). Cultural influences on Facebook photographs. *International Journal of Psychology*, *48*(3), 334–343. DOI: 10.1080/00207594.2011.649285 PMID: 22468606

Inyima, C. E. (2018). Language in Transition: The Social-Media and Emerging ESL Variety in Nigeria. *Ebonyi Journal of Language and Literature*, *1*(2), 1–15.

Inyima, C. U., Nwodo, M. N., Okoro, H., Nwadike, C., & Nwabueze, O. S. (2024). in view) The Stylistics of Idiomatic Adaptations in ESL Contexts. *GEMA Online Journal of Language Studies*, *24*(4), 266–283.

Inyima, C. U., Nwosu, O., & Dora-Ezenne, I. N. (2022). Sociolinguistic Innovations in Nigerian English Usage in the Covid-19 Era. *Journal of Linguistics and Language in Education*, *16*(1), 91–113. DOI: 10.56279/jlle.v16i1.5

Jenkins, H. (2006). *Convergence culture: Where old and new media collide*. New York University Press.

Ji, Y., & Bates, B. R. (2020). Measuring intercultural/international outgroup favoritism: Comparing two measures of cultural cringe. *Asian Journal of Communication*, *30*(2), 141–154. DOI: 10.1080/01292986.2020.1738511

Jin, D. Y., & Yoon, K. (2016). The social mediascape of transnational Korean pop culture: Hallyu 2.0 as spreadable media practice. *New Media & Society*, *18*(7), 1277–1292. DOI: 10.1177/1461444814554895

Keen, A. (2010). Why we must resist the temptation of web 2.0. In Szoka, B., & Marcus, A. (Eds.), *The next digital decade: Essays on the future of the internet* (pp. 51–56). Techfreedom.

Kontentino: Social media Dictionary. Kontentino.com

Lenhart, A,; Fallow, D. & Horrigan, J.(2004) Content creation online. Pew internet and American life project. Archived from the original on 12 January, 2014

Lev M. (2021). The Language of New Media

Li, Y., Wang, X., Lin, X., & Hajli, M. (2018). Seeking and sharing health information on social media: A net valence model and cross-cultural comparison. *Technological Forecasting and Social Change*, *126*, 28–40. DOI: 10.1016/j.techfore.2016.07.021

Madan, A., & Rosca, M. I. (2021). Current Trends in Digital Marketing Communication. Journal of Marketing Research and Case Studies https://ibimapublishing .com/articles/JMRCS/2022/981169/ Vol. 2022 (2022), Article ID 981169, 13 pages, ISSN: 2165-7009 DOI: DOI: 10.5171/2022.981169

Mbarachi & Okoro (2016) Language and technology: emerging trends in Nigeria's digital discourse. *Review of Arts and social sciences* 5(5), 38-45

Meza, V. X., & Park, H. W. (2014). Globalization of cultural products: A webometric analysis of Kpop in Spanish-speaking countries. *Quality & Quantity*, *49*(4), 1345–1360. DOI: 10.1007/s11135-014-0047-2

Newman, N. (2011). *Mainstream media of the distribution of news in the age of social discovery*. Reuters Institute.

Ojomo, O., & Sodeinde, O. A. (2021). Social Media Skits: Reshaping the Entertainment Experience of Broadcast Audience. *SAGE Open*, *11*(3), 21582440211032176. Advance online publication. DOI: 10.1177/21582440211032176

Onuma, N & Ogboji, J. (2023). Perceived impact of Covid-19 pandemic on academic performance of secondary school students in Abakaliki education zone of Ebonyi state. *African Journal of Education management, teaching and Entrepreneurship studies* 9(2), 102-114

Schmidt, E., & Cohen, J. (2013). *The New Digital Age: Reshaping the Future of People, Nationsand Businesses*. Random House.

Team Du. (March,16, 2021). Content creation for bigginners: A how to guide. https://www.demandjump.com

Thomas, J., Al-Shehhi, A., Al-Ameri, M., & Grey, I. (2019). We tweet Arabic; I tweet English: Self-concept, language and social media. *Heliyon*, *5*(7), E02087. Advance online publication. DOI: 10.1016/j.heliyon.2019.e02087 PMID: 31384681

Timmermann, R. (April 26, 2024) The 5cs of content marketing. https//www.wearety.com

Toffler, A. (1981). *The Third Wave*. Bantam Books.

Uduak, A. (2021). The New Media Technologies. *IDOSR JOURNAL OF ARTS AND HUMANITIES*, *6*(1), 30–42.

Vokmer, I. (1999). *News in the global sphere, A study of CNN anf its impact on global communication*. University of Luron Press.

Wang, S., & Chin, T. (2020). A stratified system of knowledge and knowledge icebergs in cross-cultural business models: Synthesizing ontological and epistemological views. *Journal of International Management*, *26*, 100780. DOI: 10.1016/j.intman.2020.100780

Wang, X., Riaz, M., Haider, S., Alam, K., Sherani, , & Yang, M. (2021). Information sharing on social media by multicultural individuals: Experiential, motivational, and network factors. *Journal of Global Information Management*, *29*(6), 1–24. DOI: 10.4018/JGIM.20211101.oa22

Yau, A., Marder, B., & O'Donohoe, S. (2019). The role of social media in negotiating identity during the process of acculturation. [Epub ahead-of-print]. *Information Technology & People*, *33*(2), 554–575. DOI: 10.1108/ITP-09-2017-0305

KEY TERMS AND DEFINITIONS

Audience: This comprises all the participants or a group of individuals in any event or entertainment space.

Content Creation: This is the act of generating and sharing information or media materials for specific consumers, particularly in digital spaces.

Content Creator: A content creator is someone who generates entertaining or instructional material to be shared via any online medium.

Human Connection: Human connection is the sense of intimacy and belonging that a person might have by having supportive interactions with those around them.

Media Engagement: This refers to the interactions that a media brand has with its fans on social media platforms, such as likes, comments, shares, and direct messages.

Social Media: Websites and apps that allow users to create and share contents, as well as engage in social networking.

Technology: The application of scientific knowledge to practical concerns, primarily in industry and commerce.

Chapter 9
Socio-Semiotics of Internet Communications:
Analysis of Emojis and Stickers in Selected WhatsApp Groups

Emmanuel Adedayo Adedun
Mountain Top University, Nigeria

Tolulope Grace Ayodele
Mountain Top University, Nigeria

ABSTRACT

This chapter examines the use of emojis and stickers in WhatsApp communication of selected virtual communities, and the extent to which the awareness among WhatsApp users in terms of the interpretations and utilization of emojis and stickers have helped in their applications. It adopts a descriptive qualitative and quantitative research methodology. Thirty (30) stickers and thirty (30) emojis were measured by ninety-one (91) respondents chosen at random from ten selected WhatsApp groups and analyzed with the methodological framework of Halliday (1978) Socio-semiotic theory. The research discovered that emojis and stickers may primarily be utilized for expressive social functions rather than informational ones. In conclusion, education significantly affects how people interpret and utilize emojis and stickers on WhatsApp across age, gender, and employment categories.

DOI: 10.4018/979-8-3693-7934-9.ch009

1.1. INTRODUCTION

In this digital era, communication has transcended traditional boundaries, internet communications have revolutionized the way we interact, with platforms like WhatsApp playing a pivotal role in both personal and professional exchanges and becoming central to how we interact. Among the features that facilitate online communication, emojis and stickers have emerged as potent tools for expressing emotions and conveying nuanced messages. This phenomenon can be examined through the lens of socio-semiotics, a field that explores how meaning is constructed and understood within social contexts. The advent of social media has revolutionized the way youth communicate, express themselves, and interact with the world (Sumadevi, 2023). Youths and adults utilize several available social media handles to interact with their peers and loved ones locally and globally through Facebook, Instagram, Telegram, WhatsApp, and so on. Rather than texting in words, they prefer employing non-verbal cues such as emojis and stickers to send their thoughts, ideas and feelings to one another for several reasons known to them.

Emojis and stickers are optical or visual cues from symbols adopted mostly by youths and adults to express emotions, gestures, feelings, facial expressions, thoughts, speech tones or ideas which cannot be communicated by text messages. Hsieh & Tseng (2017) define the Social media as an important tool for adolescents and young adults to spend more time interacting digitally than face-to-face. Danesi (2021) opines that semiotics is the scientific study of signs in relation to how it affects and conditions meaning. It makes use of the principles of structural linguistics to analyze verbal, visual and spatial sign systems.

The socio-semiotic analysis of these digital symbols reveals their profound impact on social connectivity. Emojis and stickers can foster a sense of belonging and camaraderie, making interactions more engaging and personal for both demographics. They serve as visual shorthand for complex emotions, thus reducing the ambiguity often present in purely textual communication. However, they also introduce new dynamics related to social conformity and peer pressure, as both youths and adults navigate the expectations of their respective digital communities. This study will contribute to the fields of digital communication, semiotics, and sociology by offering a nuanced understanding of the socio-semiotic functions of emojis and stickers. The findings will enhance our comprehension of contemporary digital communication practices and their implications for social interaction and identity construction. Through this analysis, we hope to shed light on the complex interplay between technology, language, and society, providing insights into the evolving landscape of internet communications. The aim of this chapter is to examine the use of stickers and emojis in WhatsApp communication of selected virtual communities.

The general research question is: How does the use of stickers and emojis affect WhatsApp communication in identified virtual communities?

The objectives of this study are to:

1. identify the kinds of emojis and stickers utilized in the selected WhatsApp communities;
2. investigate the social factors affecting the usage of emojis and stickers utilized in the selected WhatsApp communities; and
3. describe the social functions of emojis and stickers utilized by the selected WhatsApp communities.

Hypotheses:

Null Hypothesis (H_0):

The use of emojis and stickers in WhatsApp communication has no significant effect on emotional expression, social bonding, message clarity, or overall engagement within identified virtual communities.

Alternative Hypothesis (H_1):

The use of emojis and stickers in WhatsApp communication significantly enhances emotional expression, social bonding, message clarity, or overall engagement within identified virtual communities.

1.2. BACKGROUND

Technology refers to the tools, methods, and systems that are created from scientific knowledge and used to make our lives easier and more efficient. It has revolutionized the way we live, work, and communicate, and has brought about many advancements in various fields. Technology continues to evolve and improve, making it an integral part of our daily lives (Shaheer, 2023). A community is formed through the internet communication. Communication technology refers to tools and programs that allow people to give and receive pieces of information, this type of technology allows and improves communication (Laguaite, 2023). Communication is the transmission of information, thoughts or ideas from persons or groups of persons to another or from a place to another. The information, ideas or thoughts could be verbal or non-verbal, that is, through signs, symbols and more.

Socio-semiotics is the study of signs and symbols within social contexts, emphasizing how meaning is created and communicated through various modes. In the context of internet communications, this framework can be applied to analyze how emojis and stickers function as semiotic resources that enhance or alter the meaning of textual messages in platforms like WhatsApp. The socio-semiotics of internet communications, particularly through the lens of emojis and stickers in WhatsApp groups, underscores the complexity of digital interactions. Melo, et.al. (2024) defines stickers as downloaded animated image on chat but smaller than actual images. They are stored in a different format by an application and they are usually displayed directly to users on chat. Konrad et al. (2019) affirm that stickers are modern emojis. They are now as prominent as emojis throughout Asian countries, and even more famous.

Chukaokeke & Obiamalu (2021) classified WhatsApp stickers as: (a) Pictographic stickers: stickers with only picturestext; (b) Orthographic stickers: stickers with word-text only; and (c) Pictographic/orthographic stickers: stickers with combination of picture and word text. Emojis and stickers aid in a better understanding of how meaning is constructed and negotiated in contemporary digital communication. They provide WhatsApp users the option of expressing their emotions and thoughts through these non-verbal cues. Derks et al. (2008), assert that the integration of these symbols aids in the interpretation of emotional cues, bridging the gap left by the absence of vocal tone and body language in text-based communication. This demonstrates how socio-semiotics operates in digital spaces, where users must construct meaning collaboratively through signs. However, despite the significance of these visual elements in enriching communication, and conveying emotional nuance, they also introduce challenges related to misinterpretation and miscommunication.

Misinterpretations can arise from ambiguous emoji and sticker meanings. A sticker meant to be playful might be perceived as sarcastic or rude by another user, leading to potential conflicts or misunderstandings. Emojis can lead to ambiguous communication. Research by Derks et al. (2008) found that users often misinterpret the emotional tone of emoji use, leading to misunderstandings. Emojis often carry multiple meanings, leading to potential confusion about the sender's intent. Derks et al. (2008) highlight that users may interpret an emoji differently based on their personal experiences and cultural backgrounds, which can result in misunderstandings. In face-to-face communication, tone of voice, body language, and facial expressions provide essential context. Emojis attempt to compensate for this lack, but they cannot fully replicate the richness of non-verbal communication, leading to possible misinterpretations.

Emojis and stickers serve different roles across different age groups, helping them to express their feelings, identity and thoughts in WhatsApp communications. Youths express the feelings they have no vocabulary to articulate through these visual cues. Stickers and emojis make digital communication more fun, fostering creativity and individual expression and encouraging them to interact and share with peers. Older generations may utilize emojis and stickers for clarity of expressions, professional use or to soften messages. Vandergriff (2020) emphasizes that younger users may use emojis more playfully, while older generations might interpret them more literally. This generational gap can lead to significant misunderstandings in communication. The use of these non-verbal cues across different age group can lead to ambiguous interpretations, causing miscommunication in social contexts. Teens might feel pressured to use certain emojis and stickers to fit in, thereby affecting their authentic self-expression while adults may struggle with the rapid evolution of their meanings, creating disconnects in conversations.

1.3. HALLIDAY'S SOCIO-SEMIOTIC THEORY

The term 'social semiotics' was introduced by Halliday (1978). Halliday proposes that language cannot be separated from society. He views language as a 'social semiotic' in which language, the means by which people interact, must be considered in a social context. Language and society is a unified concept and need to be investigated as a whole. Halliday (1978) points out that an individual becomes part of a group through language. Halliday adds that a society does not consist of participants but of relations, and these relations define a social role. The link between social roles and language is explained by Halliday (1978) as one in which social roles are combinable, and the individual, as a member of a society, occupies not just one role but many at a time, always through the medium of language. Language is again a necessary condition for this final element in the process of the development of the individual, from human being to person to what we may call 'personality', a personality being interpreted as a role complex. Here the individual is seen as the configuration of a number of roles defined by the social relationships in which he enters; from these roles he synthesizes a personality.

Halliday (1993) discussed the role of language as cultural dynamic in his article *LANGUAGE AS CULTURAL DYNAMIC*. He pointed out that language is a highly evolved semiotic system. The "symbolic" model can be further extended and enriched, and in the second level, "the language system as a whole is interpreted as the system and process for the realization of culture, which becomes the "higher" level of semiotics (Halliday, 1993).

Halliday (1975) identifies seven functions that language has for children in their early years. Children are motivated to acquire language because it serves certain purposes or functions for them. They are:

Instrumental: This is when the child uses language to express their needs (e.g.'Want juice')
Regulatory: This is where language is used to tell others what to do (e.g. 'Go away')
Interactional: Here language is used to make contact with others and form relationships (e.g. 'Love you, mummy')
Personal: This is the use of language to express feelings, opinions, and individual identity (e.g. 'Me good girl')

The next three functions are heuristic, imaginative, and representational, they helping the child to come to terms with his or her environment.

Heuristic: This is when language is used to gain knowledge about the environment (e.g. 'What the tractor doing?')
Imaginative: Here language is used to tell stories and jokes, and to create an imaginary environment.
Representational: The use of language to convey facts and information.

1.4. METHODOLOGY

This is a descriptive qualitative and quantitative research. The data for this study are thirty (30) emojis and thirty (30) stickers. These were randomly selected from the chats of ninety-one (91) WhatsApp users across ten WhatsApp groups to capture varied contexts of emoji and sticker usage and explore how these symbols facilitate communication and social interaction. Allowances were also made for more emojis and stickers from the respondents. The WhatsApp groups were purposively selected putting into consideration the content analysis of the use of non-verbal cues such as emojis and stickers in the chats of the members in the selected groups. Google form was utilized for sample data collection. Questions were uploaded on Google form for this survey and collected. The Google form questionnaire included demographics of respondents such as: gender, age, status and education. The Google form was linked with Google excel sheet to store responses which we got from respondents. With this, questions and responses from respondents were automatically stored on

Google excel sheet. The responses from the excel sheets were later extracted and analyzed through SPSS for proper findings.

Following the highlighted objectives, this survey significantly helped in extracting information on the social factors (gender, age, status and education) affecting the usage and interpretations of emojis and stickers and the reasons for their usage were gotten from ninety (91) WhatsApp users in ten (10) different WhatsApp communities. The questionnaire contained both open-ended and closed-ended questions. Questions were asked on how often the respondents make use of emojis and stickers on WhatsApp, rating their level to how emojis and stickers make their communications easier, the social functions of emojis and stickers, the rate at which respondents interpret and utilize emojis and stickers, the benefits and drawbacks of emojis and stickers, and more. The closed-ended questions were given four options to grade how often their responses were on a scale of: 0-25, 26-50, 51-75, and 76-100. The non-verbal cues (emojis and stickers) were analyzed with the methodological framework of Halliday (1978) Socio-semiotic theory for proper analysis and interpretation of data.

1.5. DATA PRESENTATION, ANALYSIS AND DISCUSSION

This section presents the data for this study taking cognizance of the emojis and stickers utilized by the selected WhatsApp users.

Figure 1. Emojis

Figure 2. Stickers

1.6. ANALYSES AND FINDINGS

This section presents the analyses and findings got from the SPSS analysis of the questionnaire filled on Google form by the respondents. The tables containing the demographics and other factors affecting the utilization of emojis and stickers by selected WhatsApp users are followed by discussions and explanations of the findings they yielded.

1.6.1. Age Summary

Table 1. Summary of age analysis

	Cases					
	Valid		Missing		Total	
	N	Percent	N	Percent	N	Percent
AGE Status	91	100.0%	0	0.0%	91	100.0%

The table above is the summary of the age of the respondents showing that there are 91 respondents who responded to the questionnaire and all are valid with no respondent missing. All is 100%.

1.6.2. Age and Status Cross Tabulation

Table 2. Age and status cross tabulation

		Status						Total
		student	self employed	privately employed	government employed	retired	others	
AGE	15-40	32	5	17	9	0	1	64
	41-50	5	4	7	2	0	0	18
	51-above	1	3	1	2	2	0	9
Total		38	12	25	13	2	1	91

The cross-tabulation of age against status is a presentation of the respondents' distribution across diverse age groups and employment statuses. The total respondents are 91 participants. The most voluminous group are the students (38 out of 91, representing 41.8%. Privately employed individuals account for 25 out of 91 (27.5%). Self-employed individuals are fewer, with 12 respondents (13.2%). Government employees constitute 13 respondents (14.3%). Retired respondents are the least group, with just 2 respondents (2.2%).

While there was only 1 respondent under the "other" category.

Age Group within 15-40 are 64 respondents:

Students are 32 respondents, that is, 50% of the age group. This implies that half of the people aged 15-40 are students.

The privately employed individuals are 17 respondents, that is, 26.6%. This reveals that a remarkable number of young professionals are privately employed.

The government employed personalities are 9 respondents, that is, 14.1%. This means that a fair portion of younger individuals are in government jobs.

The self-employed are 5 respondents, that is, 7.8%. This is a very little percentage of the self-employed individuals.

The retired individuals are 0 respondent, this indicates that there is no retiree in this age group as expected. Others are merely 1 respondent, that is, 1.6%.

Age Group 41-50 are 18 respondents:

The privately employed characters 7 respondents, that is, 38.9%. This reveals that private employment is the most common status for this age group.

Students are 5 respondents, that is, 27.8%. This indicates that a significant number of individuals in this middle-age group are presently studying. They are still pursuing education.

The self-employed are 4 respondents, that is, 22.2%. This depicts that a reasonable portion of this age group are entrepreneurs or into independent work.

The government employed individuals are just 2 respondents, that is, 11.1%. This means that a very little share of this age group is working in a government establishment.

The retired is 0 respondents as expected for this age range.

Age Group 51 and Above are 9 respondents:

The retired are 2 respondents, that is, 22.2%. This shows that some individuals have retired by this age.

The government employed personalities are 2 respondents, that is, 22.2%. This indicates that a few proportion older respondents are still working in government activities.

The self-employed figures are 3 respondents, that is, 33.3%. This suggests that a considerable number of older respondents are in entrepreneurial roles.

Student is just 1 respondent, that is, 11.1%. This implies that only one of the respondents in this age group is still into education at this old age.

The privately employed individual in this age range is only 1 respondent, that is, 11.1%. This means that only an individual in this age group is an entrepreneur.

Employment Status by Age Group

Students as expected are in the 15-40 age group, with 32 out of 38 students in this classification. A little in the size of the students are found in the age group, 41-50 group. They are just 5 respondents. There is only 1 respondent as a student in the 51-above group.

In the Self-employed category, majority of the respondents are 15-40years and 51years-above groups, suggesting that they are into either entrepreneurial role in younger years or self-employment into older age.

From the privately employed division, the most voluminous number is in the 15-40 group, followed by 41-50 years, and minutest in the 51-above group.

1.6.3. Age and Education Cross Tabulation

Table 3. Age and education cross tabulation

		Education				Total
		no formal education	**olevel**	**HND and BSC**	**others**	
AGE	15-40	0	5	55	4	64
	41-50	0	2	15	1	18
	51- above	1	0	8	0	9
Total		1	7	78	5	91

The government employed group consists of younger people of 15-40 years as the majority. However, there are still a few older government employees.

The retired comprise just the **51-above** group, which is as anticipated.

1.6.4. Age and Education Summary

Table 4. Age and education summary

	Cases					
	Valid		Missing		Total	
	N	Percent	N	Percent	N	Percent
Age and Education	91	100.0%	0	0.0%	91	100.0%

The table above is the summary of the age and education of the respondents showing that there are 91 respondents who responded to the questionnaire and all are valid with no respondent missing. All is 100%.

Age and Education Cross Tabulation for Table 4

The distribution of the respondents' educational achievement across three age groups: 15-40, 41-50, and 51-above. From the analysis of respondents within the age of 15-40 years, the t**otal respondents** are 91 participants.

From the **Education rankings**:

1 respondent, that is, 1.1% has no formal education.
7 respondents, that is, 7.7% have **O'level**.
78 respondents, that is, 85.7% earned **HND and BSC. This is** the largest group.
5 respondents, that is, 5.5% fall into others.

Age Group 15-40 are 64 respondents:

0 respondent has n**o formal education**
5 respondents, that is, 7.8% of this age group are **O'levels**.
55 respondents, that is, 85.9% bagged **HND and BSC**. This reveals that the ample portions of younger respondents are with higher education qualifications.
4 respondents, that is, 6.3% are in the classification of others.

This analysis indicates that the preponderance qualification for this age group is **HND and BSC**. This implies that majority of the individual in this age group are with higher education, a few percentage has only O'level education, while none has no formal education, depicting a well-educated younger population.

Age Group 41-50 are 18 respondents:

0 respondent has n**o formal education**
2 respondents, that is, 11.1% of this age bracket have **O'level.**
15 respondents, that is, 83.3% **have HND and BSC. This corresponds** to the younger age group.
1 respondent (5.6% are in the category of "others".

This analysis depicts that the majority of respondents in this middle-aged group, like the younger group, have **HND and BSC** degrees, with a slightly higher quota having O'level qualifications. This reveals a high level of educational attainment among middle-aged respondents.

Age Group 51 and Above are 9 respondents:

1 respondent, that is, 11.1% of this age group are with no formal education.
0 respondents are with **O'level.**
8 respondents, that is, 88.9% have **HND and BSC** the highest percentage among all age groups.
0 respondents are in the category of others.

This analysis reveals that the majority in the older age group have **HND and BSC** qualifications. The group also comprises just one respondent with no formal education (11.1%).

Education Levels by Age Group:

Only 1 respondent in the **51 and above** age group has no formal education, suggesting that the younger and middle-aged respondents have all received some form of education.

The percentage of the respondents with O'level qualifications decreases with age as follows:

5 respondents (7.8%) are 15-40 years.
2 respondents (11.1%) are **41-50 years.**
0 respondents: **51years and above.**

This implies that the respondents with O'level results are more frequent among the younger and middle-aged respondents.

HND and BSC: This is the most regular prescription through all the age groups as follows:

15-40: 55 respondents (85.9%).
41-50: 15 respondents (83.3%).
51 and above: 8 respondents (88.9%).

The proportion of the respondents with HND and BSC qualifications are the highest through all age groups. This indicates that higher education is dominant among the survey respondents.

Others: A few portion of the respondents are under the "other" education category are follows:

15-40: 4 respondents (6.3%).

41-50: 1 respondent (5.6%).
51 and above: 0 respondents.

Gender and Education Summary

The Gender and Education summary reveals that there are 91 respondents who responded to the questionnaire and all are valid with no respondent missing. All is 100%.

1.6.5. Gender and Education Cross tabulation

Table 5. Gender and education cross tabulation

		Education				Total
		no formal education	**olevel**	**HND and BSC**	**others**	
GENDER	male	0	2	35	3	40
	Female	1	5	43	2	51
Total		1	7	78	5	91

From the cross-tabulation of gender and education, this table presents the distribution of educational achievement across male and female respondents. The **total respondents** are 91 participants.

From the Education qualifications:

1 respondent (1.1%) has n**o formal education.**
7 respondents (7.7%) are **O'levels.**
78 respondents (85.7%) earned **HND and BSC**.
5 respondents (5.5%) are in the group of others.

From the total 40 male respondents:

0 respondents (0%) have **no formal education.**
2 respondents (5%) are **O'levels.**
35 respondents (87.5%) are **HND and BSC** graduates. This is the highest percentage of male participants.
3 respondents (7.5%) fall into the category of others.

This analysis portrays that the largest percentage of male respondents bagged **HND and BSC. This reveals that** there is a high presentation of higher education among men. A few proportions are O'levels, and none has no formal education depicting that at least a basic level of education is dominant among male respondents.

From the total female **51 respondents:**

1 respondent (2%) are with n**o formal education.**
5 respondents (9.8%) have **O'level qualifications.**
43 respondents (84.3%) are with **HND and BSC qualifications. This is also the same as the male.**
2 respondents (3.9%) are under the category of others.

This analysis discloses that a great proportion of **the f**emale respondents also have **HND and BSC** qualifications, with slightly more women holding O'level certificate compared to men. There is just one female respondent with no formal education.

Comparison between male and female genders:

There is **1 female** respondent with no formal education, while **no male** falls into this category. This indicates that education access is widespread among both genders, though there is one exception among the female respondents.

More **females**, 5 out of 51 (9.8%) are with **O'level qualification** than **males** which are 2 out of 40 respondents (5%) who have O'level certificates. This means that a little higher proportion of women in this category ended their education at the secondary level in comparison to men.

Both **males** and **females** of higher education are (87.5% for males) and (84.3% for females). This portrays a high percentage of **HND and BSC.** Meanwhile, the total number of **females** with **HND and BSC** degrees are (43), this surpasses the number of **males** (35), depicting the higher absolute number of female respondents.

More **males,** 3 respondents (7.5%) than **females,** 2 respondents (3.9%) are under "other" educational qualifications. However, these proportions are minimal and not statistically significant.

1.6.6. Gender and Status Summary

The gender and status of the respondents shows that there are 91 respondents who responded to the questionnaire and all are valid with no respondent missing. All is 100%.

1.6.7. Gender and Status Cross Tabulation

From the cross-tabulation of gender versus status, the absolute **respondents** are 91 participants. The status categories are presented below:

Students are 38 respondents (41.8%).
Self-employed are 12 respondents (13.2%).
Privately employed are 25 respondents (27.5%).
Government employed personalities are 13 respondents (14.3%).
The retirees are 2 respondents (2.2%).
1 respondent (1.1%) for 'Others.

The total male respondents **are 40 in number.** They are analyzed below:

Students are 14 respondents (35%).
Self-employed are 7 respondents (17.5%).
Privately employed are 12 respondents (30%).
Government employed individuals are 6 respondents (15%).
The retired personality is only 1 respondent (2.5%).
Others are 0 respondents (0%).

The analysis above explains that among male respondents, the largest group is **students** who are (35%) followed by **privately employed individuals** (30%), a meaningful number are **self-employed** (17.5%) and **government-employed** (15%). There is just one male respondent that is retired, and none fall under "others."

The total of female respondents is 51 respondents. They are analyzed below:

Students are 24 respondents (47.1%).
Self-employed are 5 respondents (9.8%).
Privately employed are 13 respondents (25.5%).
Government employed are 7 respondents (13.7%).
The retired is 1 respondent (2%).
Others category is 1 respondent (2%).

From the analysis above, the female respondents, **students,** constitute the highest group (47.1%), which is almost half of all female participants, followed by **privately employed** (25.5%), while the **self-employed** and **government-employed** females each comprises a smaller percentage. Only one female respondent is retired, and one falls under "others."

The comparison between the male and female genders category:

For the students, females are 24 respondents (47.1%) while **males are** 14 respondents (35%). This reveals that a larger percentage of **females** are students in comparison to the **males** implying that more women in the survey are presently into education.

For the self-employed, the males are 7 respondents (17.5%) while the **females** are 5 respondents (9.8%). This suggests that a higher symmetry of **the males** are self-employed unlike the females, denoting that a larger proportion of the male respondents are entrepreneurs.

In the **privately employed** section, the **females are** 13 respondents (25.5%) while the males are 12 respondents (30%). This indicates that both the **males** and **females** have a meaningful percentage of respondent that are privately employed, with a slightly larger proportion among men.

The government employed category has 7 female respondents (13.7%) **while the male** respondents are 6 in number (15%). This denotes that the proportion of the **government-employed** respondents is almost the same for both men and women, implying an equal division across genders for the public sector employment.

The retirees comprise 1 male respondent (2.5%) and also 1 female respondent (2%). This explains that there is an equal number of only one individual each of the **retired** male and female respondents across genders.

Others category has just 1 female respondent (2%) while there is 0 **male** respondents. This indicates that just one **female** respondent falls under the "others" category, while no male respondents are in this group.

1.6.8. Gender and Age Cross Tabulation

Table 6. Gender and age cross tabulation

		AGE			Total
		15-40	**41-50**	**51- above**	
GENDER	male	26	8	6	40
	Female	38	10	3	51
Total		64	18	9	91

The table above shows the cross-tabulation of gender and age, that is, the distribution of respondents by age group and gender. The analysis is well explained below:

The total respondents are 91 participants.

The Age Group analysis are as follows:

15-40 years are 64 respondents (70.3%).

41-50 years are 18 respondents (19.8%).
51 years and above are 9 respondents (9.9%).

The totals of male respondents are 40 in number:

15-40 years are 26 respondents (65%).
41-50 years: 8 respondents (20%).
51 and above: 6 respondents (15%).

Most of the **male respondents** are (65%) that fall into the age group of **15-40**years. Only a few of them are in the older age group while a little percentage of men are aged **51 and above** (15%), implying that there are various age range among male respondents.

The total of the female respondents **are 51 in number:**

15-40 years are 38 respondents (74.5%).
41-50 years are 10 respondents (19.6%).
51 and above are 3 respondents (5.9%).

This analysis reveals that a higher percentage of **female respondents** (74.5%) are in the category of **15-40** age group, depicting a younger demographic among women compared to men. There are fewer female respondents in the **51 and above** category (only 3 respondents or 5.9%).

The comparison of the female and male genders:

From the age group of 15-40 years, the f**emale** respondents are 38 in number (74.5%) while the m**ale** respondents are 26 in number (65%). This explains that larger quotas of the female respondents are in the age bracket of **15-40 years in contrast** to the **male respondents**. This implies that there are more women in the younger age group, while men constitute a significant part of this group.

In the age group of 41-50 years, the f**emale** respondents are 10 in number (19.6%) while the m**ale** respondents are 8 in number (20%). This suggests that the frequency of **41-50-year age group** is the same with the females and males since the two genders have around 20% of respondents in this age group.

The age group of 51 years and above comprises f**emale** respondents who are 3 in number (5.9%) while the m**ale** respondents are 6 in number (15%). This depicts that there are more **male than female respondents** in the **51 and above** age group. The males are triple more in the category of older age than the females. This implies that the proportion of female respondents skews younger overall.

1.6.9. Status and Education Cross Tabulation

Table 7. Status and education cross tabulation

		Education				Total
		No formal education	**O' level**	**HND and BSC**	**Others**	
Status	student	1	7	27	3	38
	self employed	0	0	12	0	12
	privately employed	0	0	24	1	25
	government employed	0	0	12	1	13
	retired	0	0	2	0	2
	others	0	0	1	0	1
Total		1	7	78	5	91

The table above displays the cross-tabulation of status and education, that is, the relationship between respondents' education levels and their present employment status.

The t**otal respondents** are 91 participants. Their analysis are explained below:

In Education Category:
Only 1 respondent (1.1%) has n**o formal education.**
7 respondents (7.7%) have **O-levels.**
78 respondents (85.7%) earned **HND and B.Sc.**
5 respondents (5.5%) **fall into the category of "Others".**

In Status Category:

Students: 38 respondents (41.8% of the total).
Self-employed: 12 respondents (13.2%).
Privately employed: 25 respondents (27.5%).
Government employed: 13 respondents (14.3%).
Retired: 2 respondents (2.2%).
Others: 1 respondent (1.1%).

The breakdown of Education and Status:

Only 1 student (2.6%) has n**o formal education.**

7 students (18.4%) **are O-levels.**

27 students (71.1%) bagged **HND and BSc.**

3 students (7.9%) are in the 'Others' category.

The breakdown of education and status indicates that most of the **students, that is,** (71.1%) have **HND and B.Sc** qualifications. This implies that majority of the respondents have successfully completed higher education. A low proportion of students, that is, (18.4%) have **O-levels**, and a few, that is, (2.6%) have no formal education.

In the self-employed category, 12 respondents (100%) **have HND and B.Sc**. This means that all **self-employed respondents** have **HND and B.Sc** qualifications which depicts that this group is filled with well-educated elites, with no representation from other education levels.

In the privately employed section, 24 respondents (96%) have **HND and B.Sc qualifications while only 1** respondent (4%) fall into 'Others' category. This exposes the fact that almost all **privately employed respondents** (96%) bagged **HND and B.Sc**, while only 1 respondent is in the "Others" education category.

From the government employed, 12 respondents (92.3%) hold **HND and BSc degrees, while** 1 respondent (7.7%) is in the category of 'Others'. This shows that the **government-employed** group is populated by the respondents holding **HND and BSc** degrees (92.3%), while a little proportion is in the "others" education group.

The retired category consists of 2 respondents (100%) who bagged HN**D and B.Sc degrees. This indicates that there is a** high level of education among the retirees since the two **retired** respondents have **HND and B.Sc** qualifications.

'Others' sector comprises 1 respondent (100%) holding **HND and B.Sc degrees.** This informs us that a single respondent in the **others** status category has **HND and B.Sc** qualifications.

1.7. THE CROSS TABULATION OF THE SOCIAL FUNCTIONS OF EMOJIS AND STICKERS BY WHATSAPP USERS

1.7.1. Social Functions to Gain Knowledge (Ueswtgk), to Tell Stories and Jokes (Ueswtts), and to Express My Needs (Ueswexp)

Table 8. Social functions to gain knowledge (Ueswtgk), to tell stories and jokes (Ueswtts), and to express my needs (Ueswexp)

UESWEXP			**UESWTTS**				**Total**
			0-25	**26-50**	**51-75**	**76-100**	
0-25	UESWTGK	0-25	2	3	1	2	8
		26-50	1	4	3	4	12
		51-75	0	1	1	1	3
		76-100	0	0	0	1	1
	Total		3	8	5	8	24
26-50	UESWTGK	0-25	2	1	1	1	5
		26-50	0	0	2	6	8
		51-75	2	0	2	2	6
		76-100	0	0	0	4	4
	Total		4	1	5	13	23
51-75	UESWTGK	0-25	4	2	1	3	10
		26-50	0	8	6	3	17
		76-100	0	0	0	4	4
	Total		4	10	7	10	31
76-100	UESWTGK	0-25	2	2	1	1	6
		26-50	0	2	0	1	3
		51-75	0	0	3	0	3
		76-100	0	0	0	1	1
	Total		2	4	4	3	13
Total	UESWTGK	0-25	10	8	4	7	29
		26-50	1	14	11	14	40
		51-75	2	1	6	3	12
		76-100	0	0	0	10	10
	Total		13	23	21	34	91

The “Total” row at the bottom indicates that “26-50” is the most common range for both UESWTGK and UESWTTS (40 entries). This means that there is a moderate level of frequency in using emojis and stickers for these purposes.

There is a very high (76-100) usage for gaining knowledge UESWTGK and very low (0-25) usage for and UESWTTS are less frequent, with high usage (76-100) being more specific to a few users, especially in UESWTGK.

There are higher ranges of expressing needs (UESWEXP) (51-75 and 76-100) are more common among people using emojis and stickers moderately to tell stories or jokes (UESWTTS) (26-50).

The analysis above suggests that the respondents utilize emojis and stickers on WhatsApp for the following specific social functions:

1. To gain knowledge (UESWTGK): The users scoring high in expressing one’s needs (UESWEXP) is (51-75) and moderately high in telling stories or jokes (UESWTTS) (26-50) reveals higher knowledge gain (UESWTGK) (26-50). This denotes that the social function of storytelling might aid in learning when people are expressive.
2. To tell stories and jokes (UESWTTS): The users in the (UESWTTS) (26-50) range show a balanced distribution across expression ranges, indicating moderate storytelling paired with varied expressiveness. The WhatsApp users with UESWTTS scores between 51-75 and high UESWTGK scores (76-100) are less common, possibly indicating limited overlap between very high knowledge seeking and high storytelling.
3. To express needs (UESWEXP): The highest frequencies in expressing one’s needs are in the (UESWEXP) (51-75) range, showing that people moderately use emojis for expression of needs. The users in higher expression of needs ranges (51-75) and (76-100) often align with moderate knowledge gain scores (UESWTGK) (26-50).

1.7.2. Social Functions to Gain Knowledge (Ueswtgk), to Make Contact With Others (Ueswtmc), and to Express My Feelings and Opinions (Ueswemf)

Table 9. Social functions to gain knowledge (Ueswtgk), to make contact with others (Ueswtmc), and to express my feelings and opinions (Ueswemf)

UESWTEMF			UESWTMC				Total
			0-25	**26-50**	**51-75**	**76-100**	
0-25	UESWTGK	0-25	9		1		10
		26-50	1		1		2
		51-75	1		1		2
	Total		11		3		14
26-50	UESWTGK	0-25	3	2	1		6
		26-50	1	9	0		10
	Total		4	11	1		16
51-75	UESWTGK	0-25	3	1	2	1	7
		26-50	1	8	11	1	21
		51-75	0	1	4	1	6
		76-100	0	0	1	0	1
	Total		4	10	18	3	35
76-100	UESWTGK	0-25	3	0	1	2	6
		26-50	1	1	4	1	7
		51-75	0	1	1	2	4
		76-100	1	0	2	6	9
	Total		5	2	8	11	26
Total	UESWTGK	0-25	18	3	5	3	29
		26-50	4	18	16	2	40
		51-75	1	2	6	3	12
		76-100	1	0	3	6	10
	Total		24	23	30	14	91

The "26-50" usage range is the most frequently represented across functions, with 40 instances under "UESWTGK." This depicts that moderate intensity or frequency of emojis and stickers use is for these social purposes.

The very high usage (76-100) is less frequent, with only 10 instances under UESWTGK, while the very low usage (0-25) appears slightly more often (29 instances), especially in the "Making Contact with Others" (UESWTMC) function.

The analysis above suggests that the respondents utilize emojis and stickers to perform specific social functions:

1. To gain knowledge **(UESWTGK)**: This usage is generally moderate (26-50), especially when users also score moderately in making contact with others (UESWTMC) and expressing feelings (UESWTEMF). High expression of feelings and opinions (76-100 in UESWTEMF) coincides with lower knowledge gains, suggesting users more focused on emotional expression may engage less with knowledge-gaining uses.
2. To make contact with others: **(UESWTMC)**: The WhatsApp users who are moderately inclined to make contact (UESWTMC 26-50) also frequently have moderate scores in expressing feelings and opinions (UESWTEMF 26-50). Those who show high engagement in making contact (76-100 in UESWTMC) tend to have higher expression of feelings and opinions, indicating that more intense interaction with others correlates with expressing emotions more strongly.
3. To express feelings and opinions **(UESWTEMF)**: The higher ranges in expressing feelings and opinions (UESWTEMF) (76-100) are more often paired with lower knowledge scores (UESWTGK) (0-25). This implies that users who primarily focus on emotional expression might deprioritize informational uses of emojis and stickers. The WhatsApp users in the mid-range for expressing feelings and opinions (UESWTEMF) (51-75) also show moderate engagement in making contact, suggesting that emotional expression and social connection might be closely related.

1.8. DESCRIPTIVE STATISTICS OF WHATSAPP EMOJIS AND STICKERS

Table 10. Descriptive statistics of the questionnaire.

	N	Mean	Std. Deviation	Skewness		Kurtosis	
	Statistic	**Statistic**	**Statistic**	**Statistic**	**Std. Error**	**Statistic**	**Std. Error**
1. EMOJIS AND STICKERS' INTERPRETATIONS	91	2.7253	.59957	-.353	.253	-.129	.500
2. I UTILIZE EMOJIS AND STICKERS ON WHATSAPP TO PERFORM SOME FUNCTIONS	91	2.4364	.67591	.079	.253	-.500	.500
Valid N (listwise)	91						

Age and Education Cross-Tabulation:

The total of 91 respondents were examined and they all supplied valid responses in the Google form. This survey is analyzed below:

Age Distribution of the respondents:

In the age group of **15-40 years**, there are 64 respondents (70.3%):

0 of the respondents had no formal education.
5 respondents were with O'level certificates.
55 respondents hold HND or BSC degrees (This is the largest group in all the age groups).
4 respondents fell under "other" education categories.

In the age group of **41-50 years**, there are 18 respondents (19.8%):

0 had no formal education.
2 had O'level qualifications.
15 had HND or BSC degrees.
1 fell under "other" education.

In the age group of **51 years-above**, there are 9 respondents (9.9%):

Only 1 respondent has no formal education (only instance).

0 respondent was with O'level qualification.
8 respondents hold HND or B.Sc degrees.
0 respondent was under "Other" education.

From the **Education across-board** of the respondents:

1 respondent (1.1%) has no formal education.
7 respondents (7.7%) have O'levels.
78 respondents (85.7%) earned HND and B.Sc degrees.
5 respondents (5.5%) fall into the category of 'Others'education.

Under Gender and Education Cross-Tabulation:
The total of the male respondents are 40 participants in number:

0 male has no formal education.
2 males have O'level qualification.
35 males hold HND and B.Sc degrees.
3 males are in the category of 'Others' education.

The total of the female respondents are 51 participants in number:

Only 1 female respondent has no formal education.
5 female respondents have O'levels.
43 female respondents hold HND and B.Sc degrees.
2 female respondents fall into the category of 'Others'.

Gender and Employment Status Cross-Tabulation of respondents:
The total of the male respondents are 40 participants in number:

14 male respondents are students.
7 male respondents are self-employed.
12 male respondents are privately employed.
6 male respondents are working in government establishment.
Only 1 male respondent is a retiree.
0 respondent fall into the category of 'Others'.

The total of the female Respondents are 51 participants in number:

24 female respondents are students (This is the largest percentage).
5 female respondents are self-employed.

13 female respondents are privately employed.
7 female respondents are government employed.
1 female respondent is retired.
1 female respondent is into the category of 'Others'.

The Gender and Age Cross-Tabulation:
For the male respondents:

26 male respondents are in the age group 15-40
8 male respondents fall into the age group 41-50
6 male respondents are in the age group 51 and above

For the female respondents:

38 female respondents are in the category of age group 15-40 (This is the largest group).
10 female respondents fall into the category of age 41-50
3 female respondents are in the category of age group 51 and above

The Employment Status and Education Cross-Tabulation:
The total number of students are 38 respondents:

1 respondent is with no formal education.
7 respondents have O'level qualification.
27 respondents hold HND or BSC degrees.
3 respondents are in the category of other qualifications.

The total of self-employed individuals are 12 respondents: All the respondents bagged HND or BSC degrees.

The total of privately employed participants are 25 respondents: 24 respondents hold HND or BSC degrees while 1 respondent has other qualifications.

The total of government employed participants are 13 respondents: 12 earned HND or BSC degrees while 1 respondent has other qualifications.

The total of the Retired individuals are 2 respondents: Both of them bagged HND or BSC degrees.

THE DESCRIPTIVE STATISTICS FOR EMOJIS AND STICKERS

The Interpretation of Emojis and Stickers by the Respondents

The **mean** is (2.73) while the **standard deviation** is (0.60). This implies that there is a moderate agreement in the interpretations of emojis and stickers by the respondents.

The **skewness** is slightly left-skewed (-0.353). This suggests that there are more respondents who rated the interpretation of emojis and stickers positively.

The **kurtosis** is negative (-0.129). This means that the distribution of emojis and stickers by the respondents is flatter.

The analysis above shows that respondents generally agree moderately on the interpretation of emojis and stickers. The slight left skew and negative kurtosis suggest that while there is a range of responses, a fair number of respondents rated the interpretation of emojis and stickers on WhatsApp positively, with limited extreme deviations in their ratings. This analysis implies that respondents find emojis and stickers interpretations understandable and useful.

I Utilize Emojis and Stickers on WhatsApp for Various Functions

The **mean** is (2.44) while the **standard deviation** is (0.68). This reflects that there is moderate utilization of emojis and stickers by the respondents.

The **skewness** is near zero, that is, (0.079). This implies a relatively balanced distribution of emojis and stickers among the respondents.

The **kurtosis** is slightly negative (-0.500). This reveals that the distribution of emojis and stickers by the respondents is flatter.

The analysis above explains that respondents demonstrate moderate and relatively consistent use of emojis and stickers on WhatsApp. The balanced skewness near zero and slightly negative kurtosis indicate a symmetric, flat distribution of responses, where most respondents fall into a similar range of moderate usage without extreme variance. This suggests that emojis and stickers are a commonly used tool on WhatsApp for many respondents.

1.9. CONCLUSIONS

1.9.1. The Demographics of Respondents

From the survey and analysis conducted on the cross-tabulation of age and status, the following conclusions were reached:

1. The age group (15-40) is primarily composed of students, privately employed individuals, and a moderate number of government employees while a very few respondents are self-employed.
2. The privately employed personality in the age group (41-50) is the dominant status, followed by self-employment while a notable number are still pursuing education.
3. The retirees in the age group (51 and above) has a significant number. That is, they are still self-employed or government employees, indicating active participation in the workforce.
4. This cross tabulation of age and status highlights the varied distribution of employment status across age groups, showing clear trends such as the high number of students among younger individuals and increased retirement and self-employment in the older population.

From the cross tabulation of education and age:

1. The overwhelming majority of respondents in all age groups have HND or BSC qualifications (85.7% overall). This indicates a highly educated sample population.
2. While the percentage of respondents with only O'level qualifications is small, it is more prevalent in the 15-40 and 41-50 age groups, that is, O'level education is more common in younger and middle-aged respondents
3. Only 1 respondent from the 51 and above age group is discovered to be having no formal education, highlighting the prevalence of at least some form of education among the younger and middle-aged groups.
4. A small portion of respondents fall into the "other" category of education, mostly among the younger population.
5. The cross tabulation of education and age indicates that the respondents, across all age groups, tend to have higher education qualifications, with a strong concentration of HND and BSC degrees. The data shows an overall well-educated population, with minimal instances of no formal education.

From the cross tabulation of gender and education:

1. Both male and female respondents have a high proportion of HND and BSC degrees, with over 85% of participants in each gender group having completed higher education. This reflects a well-educated population of the respondents.
2. Female respondents are slightly more likely to have O'level qualifications compared to males.
3. There is one instance of a female respondent with no formal education, while no males fall into this category.
4. There is a balanced educational attainment of both genders, showing similar patterns of educational attainment, with a slightly higher number of women overall, but with comparable levels of higher education.
5. The cross tabulation of gender and education reveals that both men and women in the sample are predominantly well-educated, with a strong emphasis on HND and BSC degrees. There are only slight differences in the lower education categories, with more women having O'level qualifications and one woman having no formal education

From the cross tabulation of gender and status:

1. A larger percentage of female respondents (47.1%) are students compared to males (35%). This suggests that more women in the sample are still in educational settings or still studying.
2. Male respondents are more likely to be self-employed (17.5%) compared to females (9.8%). This indicates that entrepreneurial activities or independent work (self-employment) are more common among men in the sample.
3. Both males and females have a notable percentage of privately employed and government-employed individuals, with only slight differences between genders. This implies that there is a balanced private and government employment among the respondents.
4. Both males and females have minimal representation in the retired category, and only one female respondent falls under the "others" category.
5. The gender and status cross tabulation reveals that a significant proportion of respondents across both genders are students, with a higher percentage of female students. Self-employment is more common among men, while both private and government employment show relatively similar distributions between men and women.

From the cross tabulation of gender and age:

1. The female group is predominantly younger, with 74.5% of women falling within the 15-40 age range. This suggests that the female participants are more likely to be in younger age brackets than their male counterparts.
2. Male respondents show a more even spread across the age groups, with 15% of men aged 51 and above, compared to only 5.9% of women in that age range. This implies that the male respondents tend to be slightly older across board.
3. Both genders have a fairly equal representation in the 41-50 age group, with around 20% of respondents from both genders falling within this bracket. This suggests a balanced middle age group.
4. The gender and age cross tabulation shows that the majority of respondents are in the 15-40 age range, with women being more heavily concentrated in this younger group. Men, however, are more evenly spread across the age groups, particularly in the 51 and above category, where they outnumber women. Both genders have similar representation in the 41-50 age group.

From the Status and education cross tabulation:

1. While most students have HND and BSc qualifications (71.1%), there is a diverse range of education levels, with some holding O-levels (18.4%) and even a small portion with no formal education (2.6%).
2. The self-employed group is entirely composed of respondents with HND and BSc qualifications, indicating that self-employment in this sample is associated with a higher education level.
3. Like the self-employed, privately employed respondents predominantly have HND and B.Sc qualifications (96%), with very little variation in education levels.
4. Similar to other employed categories, the government-employed respondents mostly have HND and BSc qualifications (92.3%).
5. All respondents in the smaller categories of the retired and 'Others' are also educated to the HND and BSc level, indicating that higher education may have been a significant factor in their careers.
6. The Status and Education cross tabulation reveals that the majority of respondents, regardless of their status, are highly educated, with HND and BSc qualifications (85.7%). This is particularly true for the self-employed, privately employed, government-employed, retired, and others groups, where nearly all respondents have higher education. Students exhibit the greatest diversity in education, with a few holding O-levels or having no formal education. This suggests that higher education is a key determinant of employment and career status in this sample, with most respondents having attained significant academic qualifications.

The overall conclusion of the demographics of the respondents reveals that a well-educated sample, with HND and B.Sc degrees are prevalent across age, gender, and employment categories. Gender distribution shows that women are more concentrated in younger age groups and educational stages, while men are more represented across older age groups and in self-employment. Employment patterns indicate that higher education is linked to diverse career options, particularly outside of student status. As a result, the analysis suggests that higher education is a major determinant in career opportunities and professional status in this sample, with minimal educational disparities across gender, age, or employment.

1.9.2. Social Functions to Gain Knowledge (Ueswtgk), to Tell Story and Jokes (Ueswtts), and to Express Needs (Ueswexp)

From the cross tabulation of the social functions on the utilization of emojis and stickers by selected WhatsApp users on gaining knowledge, telling stories and jokes; and expressing needs, it is concluded that:

1. The moderate usage (26-50) across the board is the most common level for each social function.
2. The users who express their needs more are more likely to also use emojis and stickers to gain knowledge.
3. The higher expressiveness is linked with moderate knowledge and storytelling uses, rather than high or very low levels.
4. The table suggests that WhatsApp users have diverse yet interconnected uses for emojis and stickers, using them moderately across functions but varying by their purpose of use.

1.9.3. Social Functions to Gain Knowledge (Ueswtgk), to Make Contact with Others (Ueswtmc), and to Express My Feelings and Opinions (Ueswemf)

From the cross tabulation of the social functions on the utilization of emojis and stickers by selected WhatsApp users on gaining knowledge, to make contact with others, and to express feelings and opinions, it is concluded that:

1. There is a moderate usage for all the social functions; (26-50) is the most common level. This explains that WhatsApp users tend to use emojis and stickers at a moderate level to balance between connecting with others, expressing feelings and opinions, and gaining knowledge.

2. There's a pattern where users who prioritize making contact also tend to express feelings and opinions at a high level. There is a link between connecting with others and emotional expression. Emotional expression appears to be a key aspect of social connection.
3. The WhatsApp users with high scores in expressing feelings and opinions tend to have lower knowledge-gaining scores. This suggests that emojis and stickers may serve primarily expressive or social functions rather than informational ones for the respondents.
4. The analysis denotes a nuanced use of emojis and stickers on WhatsApp, with most users employing them moderately across functions but with some notable variations depending on their primary intent.

1.10. SUGGESTION FOR FURTHER STUDIES

Further researches can be on the following:

1. How Social Status Influence Digital Communication Styles on Various Social Media Platforms.
2. Investigating the Impact of Gender and Age on the Social and Expressive Functions of Emojis and Stickers on Social Media Platforms.
3. The Influence of Education on Digital Communication Effectiveness and Interpretation Accuracy on the Social Media.

REFERENCES

Abdullah, M. F., AlDilaimy, H. H., & Alqayssi, F. (2021). A. HA multimodal social semiotic analysis of emoji's use with reference to COVID-19. *Linguistica Antverpiensia,* Issue-2 www.hivt.be ISSN: 0304-2294.

Al-Rawi, A., Siddiqi, M., Morgan, R., Vandan, N., Smith, J., & Wenham, C. (2020). COVID-19 and the gendered use of emojis on Twitter: Infodemiology study. *Journal of Medical Internet Research, 22*(11), e21646. DOI: 10.2196/21646 PMID: 33052871

Blommaert, J. (2018). Chronotopes, scale and complexity in the study of language in society. In *Multilingualism and Multimodality: An Introduction*. Routledge.

Boyd, D. (2014). *It's Complicated: The social lives of networked teens*. Yale University Press.

Chandler, D. (2002). *Semiotics: The basics*. Routledge.

Chukaokeke, C., & Obiamalu, G. (2021). *Conversational implicatures of whatsapp stickers chats of unizik students. Department of Linguistics Nnamdi Azikiwe University* (Vol. 6). Preorcjah., www.ezenwaohaetorc.org

Danesi, M. (2017). *The semiotics of emoji: the rise of visual language in the age of the internet*. Bloomsbury Publishing. DOI: 10.5040/9781474282024

Derks, D., Fischer, A. H., & Fischer, M. (2008). The role of emotion in computer-mediated communication: The case of emojis. *Computers in Human Behavior, 24*(6), 2760–2773.

Distel, V., Egger, R., Petrovic, U., Phan, V. L., & Wiesinger, S. (2022). The usage of emoji in tourism-related Instagram posts: Suggestions from a marketing perspective. In J. L. Stienmetz, B. Ferrer-Rosell, & D. Massimo (Eds.). *Information and communication technologies in tourism: Proceedings of the ENTER. eTourism conference. Springer.* 134–145.

Durante, C. (2016). Adapting nonverbal coding theory to mobile mediated communication: an analysis of emoji and other digital nonverbal. *M.S. thesis, Dept. Commune. Stud., Liberty Univ., Virginia, Lynchburg.*

Gawne, L., & Ellison, T. (2020). Evolving meanings of emojis: A linguistic perspective on digital communication. I*n. Language & Communication, 74*, 52–60.

Goffman, E. (2020). *The presentation of self in everyday life. In the Social Construction of Reality: A Treatise in the Sociology of Knowledge*. Anchor Books.

Gupta, S., & Kim, H.-W. (2004). Virtual community: concepts, implications, and future research directions. *Proceedings of the Tenth Americas Conference on Information Systems*.

Gupta, S., & Kim, H.-W. (2013). Virtual community: Concepts, implications, and future research directions.

Halliday, M. A. K. (1978). *Language as social semiotic: The social interpretation of language and meaning*. University Park Press.

Halliday, M. A. K. (2002). *Linguistic studies of text and discourse*. Continuum International Publishing.

Hsieh, S. H., & Tseng, T. H. (2017). Playfulness in mobile instant messaging: Examining the influence of emoticons and text messaging on social interaction. *Computers in Human Behavior, 69*, 405–414. DOI: 10.1016/j.chb.2016.12.052

Kaye, L. K., & Toronto, A. (2019). Emoji use in social media: A comparative analysis of age differences in emoji interpretation. *In Journal of Social Media Studies,* 5(1), 15-32.

Konrad, A., Herring, S. C., & Choi, D. (2020). sticker and emoji use in facebook messenger: Implications for graphicon change. *Journal of Computer-Mediated Communication, 25*(3), 217–235. DOI: 10.1093/jcmc/zmaa003

Laguaite, M. (2023). 9 Best communication technology examples to explore. https://yoodli.ai/blog/9-best-communication-technology-examples-to-explore

Maloney, D., Freeman, G., & Wohn, D. Y. (2020). "Talking without a voice": Understanding Non-verbal communication in social virtual reality. *Proceedings of the ACM on Human-Computer Interaction, (*4)1–25. DOI: 10.1145/3415246

Melo, P., Couto, J. M., Kansaon, D., Mafra, V., Reis, J., & Benevenuto, F. (2024). A Sticker is Worth a Thousand Words: Characterizing the Use of Stickers in WhatsApp Political Groups in Brazil. arXiv preprint arXiv:2406.08429.

Modzelewski, R. (2013). Virtual togetherness: sense of identity and community in cyberspace. *A Journal of English Studies, 1*.

O'Brien, M. (2019). The personal and contextual nature of emoji use: Implications for digital communication. *Journal of Language and Social Psychology, 38*(4), 476–492.

O'Connor, P., & P.W. (2017). Emoji and the politics of meaning in digital communication. *Journal of Language and Politics, 16*(1), 1–21.

Özbölük, T., & Kurtoğlu, R. (2019). Marketing semiotics in the digital age. In Epure, M., & Mihăeş, L. C. (Eds.), *The role of language and symbols in promotional strategies and marketing schemes* (pp. 47–64). IGI Global. DOI: 10.4018/978-1-5225-5778-4.ch003

Piaget, J. (1971). *Structuralism* (Mascler, C., Trans.). Routledge & Kegan Paul.

Russell, J. (2013). Stickers: From Japanese craze to global mobile messaging phenomenon. The Next Web. https://thenextweb.com/asia/2013/07/12/stickers/

Saussure, F. (1966). *Course in General Linguistics*. McGraw Hill Columbia University Press.

Saussure, F. (1983). *Course in General Linguistics* (Haris, R., Trans.). Duckworth.

Saussure F, Pierce C (1983). On signifying, signs, and signifying systems. cdli.ucla.edu-staff-englund-Saussure 2.

Schwartz, H. A., Eichstaedt, J. C., & Kern, M. L.. (2014). Personality, gender, and age in the language of social media: The open-vocabulary approach. *PLoS One*, *9*(9), e94778. PMID: 24086296

Shaheer, A. (2023). Importance of technology. https://www.slideshare.net/ahmdsagi/importance-of-technology

Tapscott, D. (2016). Blockchain revolution: How the technology behind bitcoin is changing money, business and the world.

Turkle, S. (1995). *Life on the screen: identity in the age of the internet*. Simon & Schuster.

Vandergriff, I. (2020). Generational differences in emoji interpretation and use in digital communication. *Communication Studies*, *71*(2), 211–227.

Welekwe, A. (2023). The top networking technologies for 2024. https://www.comparitech.com/net-admin/networking-technologies/

Chapter 10
A Multimodal Exploration of Personal Life and Cultural Identity in Gaming Influencers' Instagram Posts

Egbah Ikpomwosa Andrew
https://orcid.org/0000-0001-9420-0238
University of Benin, Nigeria

ABSTRACT

This chapter explores the multimodal representation of personal life and cultural identity in the Instagram posts of four gaming influencers from diverse backgrounds: PewDiePie, Valkyrae, Ninja, and Pokimane. Utilising Gunther Kress and Theo van Leeuwen's Social Semiotics framework, the analysis focuses on how these influencers blend visual and textual elements in non-gaming posts to depict themes like family life, professional achievements, and personal moments. This study highlights how influencers use Instagram's platform-specific features to foster a sense of authenticity and relatability with their audience. The findings support the argument that these gaming influencers effectively deploy multimodal communication to connect with their audiences at a human (sometimes parasocial) level. Furthermore, the study reveals how these multimodal strategies contribute to broader discussions on digital communication, cultural identity, gender representation, and the role of influencers in shaping online communities.

DOI: 10.4018/979-8-3693-7934-9.ch010

INTRODUCTION

The gaming industry is an important aspect of internet culture in the digital era, and gamers serve as influencers and content creators who shape trends and perspectives within and beyond the global gaming environment. These individuals play games that span various genres, including first-person shooters, massively multiplayer online role-playing games (MMORPG), and strategy games on consoles, mobile devices, and PCs (Quandt and Kröger 2014). Although the major preoccupation of these gaming influencers includes live-streaming gameplay, giving updates on new releases, and sharing arcade tips and hacks relating to popular games like *Call of Duty, GTA, Fortnite, League of Legends,* and *Valorant*, these gaming influencers sometimes share glimpses of their lifestyle on social media platforms like Instagram. Such non-gaming posts offer a unique spotlight on the intrinsic interplay between their gaming persona and off-screen identity.

Gaming influencers share non-gaming posts for three key reasons. First, they reveal daily activities—such as celebrating a milestone or cooking—that blur the boundaries between professional gaming and personal life, which in turn promotes a relatable connection (sometimes parasocial relationship) with their audience. Second, these posts drive fan engagement and loyalty through interactions like comments and likes, subsequently attracting endorsements and sponsorship opportunities. Third, non-gaming content allows influencers to diversify their brand by showcasing their personal interests and cultural values, thus enhancing their sociocultural identity beyond gaming.

Existing scholarship and academic research remain disproportionately fixated on gaming influencers' in-role performances – updates, walkthroughs, and equipment reviews – while neglecting the gamers' curated off-role self-projections, despite the significant influence of these persons on digital culture. This oversight persists in spite of evidence that, in recent times, a high percentage of major gaming personalities' Instagram content features non-gaming elements, from family vignettes to political commentaries; because these influencers deliberately use such posts as semiotic strategies to maximise audience engagement and boost their brand images. (Paaßen, 2016; Shaw, 2014). The academic void becomes particularly glaring when considering Instagram's unique affordances for parasocial relationship-building. Unlike Twitch's ephemeral streams or YouTube's long-form tutorials (Oceja and Álvarez-Álvarez, 2025), Instagram's grid-based system enables these influencers to curate collages of their personal identities, subtly embed intertextual references to gaming culture within mundane snapshots of their day-to-day activities, as well as engineer algorithmic visibility and fan engagement through strategic hashtag usage.

This chapter argues that gaming influencers strategically use non-gaming Instagram posts to construct multifaceted identities and enhance audience engagement at a parasocial level, thereby extending the influence of these celebrities beyond the gaming community. The study aims to uncover how these gaming influencers manipulate multimodal elements in their personal Instagram posts to generate and express sociocultural and multicultural meanings beyond their regular gaming contexts. The following highlights are the objectives of the study:

i. analyse the representational, compositional, and interactional elements of the non-gaming Instagram posts of gaming influencers.
ii. examine the strategies by which sociocultural identities and values are depicted through visual storytelling using social semiotic tools in these posts.
iii. explore the impact of platform-specific features of online communication, such as engagements or settings, on the dissemination of meaning via these non-gaming Instagram posts.

LITERATURE REVIEW

The study of gaming influencers and their online activities is an emerging area within the broader fields of multimodal discourse, semiotics, sociolinguistics, and digital linguistics. This review looks at previous work that examines how identity is formed in digital spaces, setting the stage for the theoretical approach taken in this chapter.

To start, researchers apply multimodal analysis to understand interactions on social media platforms. For example, Zappavigna (2016) looks at Instagram posts using social semiotics, while Machin and van Leeuwen (2007) use similar methods to examine lifestyle media. Other scholars have extended these ideas to different platforms. Lotfy (2024) studies humour on TikTok, Uthman (2024) investigates how visual elements in Facebook adverts affect audience perceptions, and Liang and Lim (2024) explore how promotional materials represent youth in related social media applications.

Some works explore the ways in which cultural identity is shaped online. Shaw (2014) investigates issues of diversity and representation in the gaming world, and Chiluwa (2023) examines how social media helps construct identities around social justice during the #EndSARS protests. Taiwo and Oamen (2018) also offer insights into how visual communication in politics contributes to identity building.

Other studies have considered how specific features of social media platforms influence meaning-making. Highfield and Leaver (2016) highlight how Instagram's design influences user behaviour, while Onanuga and Taiwo (2020) demonstrate that the features of online platforms can be used deliberately to shape communication. Deshmukh (2024) shows how virtual communities use multimodal communication to form their online identities.

Furthermore, several researchers have investigated the rise of gaming influencers and the impact of influencer marketing on perceptions of authenticity in gaming culture. Taylor (2018) and Sjöblom et al. (2019) examine how streamers build communities and create connections with their viewers, while Audrezet et al. (2020) evaluate the balance influencers maintain between commercial deals and genuine self-presentation. Marwick (2013) discusses how authenticity is performed on social media, revealing the challenges influencers face when presenting themselves to the public.

This review shows that there remains a gap in the literature: the multimodal analysis of gaming influencers' non-gaming content on social media has not been fully explored. Although many studies focus on gaming-related activities or the broader trends in influencer culture, little research has examined how non-gaming posts contribute to the construction of these influencers' identities and help them connect with their audiences. This chapter addresses this gap by using Kress and van Leeuwen's Social Semiotic framework to look closely at the multimodal codes in gaming influencers' non-gaming Instagram posts. In doing so, the study investigates how these posts build intimacy or distance with followers, convey authenticity, and either reinforce or challenge the sociocultural identities associated with the influencers' off-screen lives.

Theoretical Framework

Kress and van Leeuwen's framework of Social Semiotics is a viable tool for the examination of sociocultural and multicultural meanings in the Instagram posts of gaming influencers. Unlike some multimodal theories, the theory of Kress and van Leeuwen incorporates the analysis of linguistic elements like modality (to show authenticity), colour spectrum, and the use of captions and accompanying texts in these social media posts.

Kress and van Leeuwen (1996) built their multimodal structure on modes—which generally refer to culturally determined, socially-shaped resources—are not neutral but depend on several contextual elements to convey meaning. Kress and van Leeuwen define 'mode' in two different ways. One, mode is anything (images, written text, and vocal patterns) that can be socially or culturally moulded to convey meaning. Two, modes are semiotic elements which are framed by intrinsic features, the potentials they possess within the medium they operate in, and what their culture or society expects of them (Kress and van Leeuwen, 1996).

The core of Kress and van Leeuwen's approach focuses on three metafunctions that aid the study of visual communication: representation, composition, and interaction. At the representation level, Kress and van Leeuwen (2006) explain that visual language functions as verbal representations of the speaker's worldview. The scholars identify three types of representational structures: narrative structures (which portray acts, events, and vectors of inferred cues of action), conceptual structures (which describe participants), and classificational (which represents classification, categorisation, and identification).

Kress and van Leeuwen (2006) identify three interrelated systems at the compositional level which is concerned with the arrangement and organisation of multimodal elements in the visual storytelling process: Information value (the information drawn from the placement of elements in various zones of the image such as left/right, top/bottom, centre/margin); Salience (elements made to attract the viewer's attention through factors like size, colour contrast, and placement); and Framing (the presence or absence of framing devices disconnects or connects elements of the image, signifying that they belong or do not belong together).

The Interaction level deals with how images create relationships between the depicted world and the viewer. It evaluates the relationship between the communicator and the audience through elements like address (directly engages or involves the viewer), social distance (establishes intimacy or formality), and power relations (conveys authority, equality, or submission). Key concepts at the interactional metafunction include gaze, captions, and perspective.

Kress and van Leeuwen's framework thus offers a comprehensive approach to analysing how multimodal elements work together to convey meaning. The theory enables researchers to dissect and understand the layers of communication present in various media formats. Kress and van Leeuwen contend that the three social semiotic levels (representational, compositional, and interactional) contribute to showing that communication in today's digital context is fundamentally multimodal. This multimodal structure incorporates a wide range of semiotic resources such as words, images, sound, and gestures (Kress, 2010). In the present study, this model is adopted for the assessment of how multimodal strategies are employed in Instagram pictorial posts to blur the lines between the gamers' identities as public figures and their private lives as members of the society.

Scope of Study

The scope of this study centres on the multimodal analysis of pictorial (non-video) content, specifically screenshots captured directly from the non-gaming posts of four gaming influencers:

i. PewDiePie (Felix Kjellberg)
ii. Pokimane (Imane Anys)
iii. Ninja (Tyler Blevins)
iv. Valkyrae (Rachell Hofstetter)

These gamers are selected for this research due to their expertise in popular games such as *GTA V, Call of Duty, Fortnite, and Valorant,* significant online fan bases, as well as their constant engagement with their fans on Instagram where they regularly share their everyday life experiences in a form of parasocial storytelling.

PewDiePie, whose real name is Felix Arvid Ulf Kjellberg) is a prominent Swedish online gamer and streamer born on 24 October 1989. He is popularly known for his comedic videos and has amassed a following of 21 million people on his Instagram account, PewDiePie (@pewdiepie). He is best known for his Let's Play videos of horror games, particularly *Amnesia: The Dark Descent*, and has moved on to indie titles and trendy games as suggested by his fans. Kjellberg married his long-term Italian girlfriend Marzia Bisognin on 19 August 2019, and the couple welcomed their first son on 11 July 2023.

Imane Anys, known professionally as Pokimane, is a Canadian-Moroccan online streamer who plays multiplayer games such as *League of Legends, Fortnite,* and *Valorant* on Twitch. She is known for her engaging personality on Instagram and YouTube; and often collaborates with other streamers in games like *Among Us* and *GTA V* roleplay as a social media content creator. She was born on 14 May 1996 and has 6 million followers on her Instagram account, pokimane (@pokimanelol).

Richard Tyler Blevins, better known as Ninja, is an American online streamer, YouTuber, and professional gamer born on 5 June 1991. His Instagram account is under the name Tyler "Ninja" Blevins (@ninja) where he has earned over 12 million followers. Although Ninja rose to prominence as a skilled Fortnite player and streamer, he has since diversified his gaming content to include titles like *Valorant, Apex Legends*, and *Fall Guys*, often participating in competitive events. Ninja has been married to his wife Jessica Blevins since 2017 and is the Co-Founder of @ drinknutcase.

Valkyrae (Rachell Marie Hofstetter) is a Filipino-American online streamer with over 3.5 million Instagram followers. She is a prominent streamer who is particularly known for playing *Among Us, Valorant*, and participating in *GTA V* roleplay servers with other content creators. Her content also includes participating in "Just Chatting" streams and trying out new games for increased community engagement on Instagram and YouTube platforms. Born on January 8, 1992, Valkyrae co-owns '100 Thieves' (a gaming organisation), and is the founder, co-owner, and Chief Executive of Hihi Studios.

METHODOLOGY

Research Design

The work adopts the content analysis qualitative research design proposed by Leedy and Ormrod (2015), which allows the study to explore the relationships of words, concepts, and themes in oral, written, or visual content.

Methods of Data Collection, Research Instruments, and Sampling Techniques

The study employs a mixed-methods approach to collect and curate Instagram data, in the form of relevant screenshots, focusing exclusively on the pictorial, non-gaming posts of the selected gaming influencers. The process begins by taking screenshots directly from the Instagram app on a mobile phone, ensuring that the contents—posts and stories—are captured in their original format. These screenshots are then transferred to a computer and uploaded to Snagit, a desktop tool tailored for editing and organising data for academic and research purposes. Within Snagit, the images are neatly arranged using tags and folders, allowing for systematic analysis. This approach ensures that the Instagram content is captured precisely and prepared adequately for the multimodal investigation of the influencers' non-gaming posts on Instagram.

The sample size consists of eight Instagram posts, with two posts from each of the four gaming influencers. The posts are selected using purposive sampling according to the following criteria:

i. Pictorial (non-video) content focusing on the gamers' personal lives, not directly linked to gaming.
ii. An expression of everyday (sometimes mundane) activities, personal interests, pets, hobbies, and relationships.
iii. Absence of explicit promotional ads and commercial content.

The timeline of the selected data spans January - July 2024, a seven-month period which provides insights on recent posts, seasonal posts signalling holidays or summer breaks, and engagement or participation at global games industry events like the New York Game Awards (January 23, 2024), Hamburg Games Conference (March 5, 2024), and Game Developers Conference (March 18, 2024).

Data Analytical Procedure

The analytical procedure employs Kress and van Leeuwen's social semiotic theory with a primary focus on three main aspects: representational, compositional, and interactional metafunctions. The study also observes ethical considerations by respecting the influencers' privacy, acknowledging that these Instagram posts are in the public domain. To this end, the study focuses on the semiotic aspects of the posts rather than undertaking personal scrutiny of the influencers' personalities or the individual responses of their fans to the posts.

The Instagram posts have been sorted into the following categories for clarity of assessment:

1. Family Life and Personal Moments (Personal Life)
2. Professional Achievements, Lifestyle, Sports, and Hobbies (Cultural Identity)

ANALYSIS

1. Family Life and Personal Moments

Figure 1. Portrait of PewDiePie's Family Sitting on a Ledge with a Scenic Landscape in the Background

i. Representational Metafunction

Figure 1 is PewDiePie's Instagram anniversary portrait of his family celebrating five years of marriage. The event is set on a ledge with a scenic backdrop of a lake and mountains in Switzerland. PewDiePie is wearing a pink shirt and shorts, holding the baby, who is dressed in light-coloured clothing. Marzia Bisognin is wearing a light, floral dress and has her arm around PewDiePie. The couple's affectionate poses, with PewDiePie holding the child and Marzia Bisognin's arm around him, highlight familial bonds and feelings of togetherness, unity, love, and natural beauty in the influencer's family. The family's casual, relaxed clothing suggests a down-to-earth, approachable identity, while the scenic Swiss backdrop and the use of the Swiss flag emoji signify a connection to nature, travel, and tourism in the European nation.

ii. Compositional Metafunction

PewDiePie and his family are centrally positioned in the picture to foreground the attention of the family. The ledge and scenic backdrop of a lake and mountains in the Swiss environment enhance the sense of serenity and connection to nature. This scenic situation, paired with the family's relaxed demeanour, conveys the message of a harmonious balance between personal happiness and the beauty of the natural world. The framing of the photograph in Switzerland could be seen as a way of promoting feelings of nationalism and patriotism, as well as highlighting tourist attractions.

iii. Interactional Metafunction

PewDiePie's caption, "5 years married! So fortunate to share every day with the most amazing mom and wife. Can't wait for more adventures together—this time in beautiful Switzerland!," expresses gratitude and excitement. He celebrates the family's milestone anniversary and looks forward to future adventures, thereby fostering a sense of love and togetherness at the family level. The post received a significant engagement of over 2.1 million likes, 24,000 shares, and 5,668 comments, indicating that PewDiePie's fans and general Instagram audience appreciate his sense of family bonding. Moreover, Instagram's focus on visuals ensures that the serene and beautiful family moment, as well as the scenic backdrop, captures the post's theme of love and togetherness, which is communicated in the caption inviting the followers to celebrate the five-year milestone.

Instagram's emphasis on visual storytelling amplifies this authenticity, as the serene landscape and heartfelt caption about marital unity frame their relationship as both aspirational and grounded. The family's relaxed clothing and unfiltered interactions further underscore a down-to-earth identity, resonating with audiences weary of overly curated influencer content.

Figure 2. Pokimane having Pizza at a Public Dinner Setting

i. Representational Metafunction

Figure 2 features Pokimane at an outdoor restaurant, sitting with a partially eaten pizza in front of her. The casual dining setting, complete with a drink, projects a relaxed, social atmosphere. Pokimane's casual attire, a grey top with black bow detail, adds a touch of laid-back elegance to highlight the importance of informal, everyday experiences amid tedious daily tasks. The presence of a blue bottle of expensive SARATOGA adds a blend of luxury and sophistication to the casual dining situation.

Pokimane's pizza post juxtaposes everyday relatability with subtle luxury, symbolised by the SARATOGA drink. In terms of gender dynamics, Pokimane's fashion style blends casual elegance with her status as a celebrity, challenging polished influencer norms while aligning with feminine aesthetics. The blurred restaurant setting and evening lighting create a communal ambiance, mirroring cultural traditions of shared meals that are related to her Canadian-Moroccan heritage.

ii. Compositional Metafunction

In the photograph, Pokimane and the partially eaten pizza are centrally positioned, thereby drawing focus to both the influencer and the meal, and implicitly highlighting the post's theme of sharing a meal. The outdoor restaurant setting, with other patrons and customers in the background, provides social context and communal depth to the dining experience. The dark background also gives a feel of the evening, the appropriate time for dinner meals.

iii. Interactional Metafunction

The simple caption, "pov: I take you out to dinner and pay for everything ," invites the audience into a personal situation where they are being treated to a meal by the influencer. Pokimane's simple (but powerful) caption, along with the playful emojis, conveys the assurance or promise of a personal and generous narrative. This statement helps invite the followers to imagine themselves in the dining scenario, which further fosters a sense of connection and appreciation between Pokimane and her online audience. The high number of likes (close to 291,000), comments (1,658), and shares (7,196) reflects strong engagement on the Instagram post and suggests that Pokimane's followers appreciate her relatable and generous offer.

In terms of platform-specific features, Instagram's high-contrast visuals and playful caption ("I take you out to dinner") foster intimacy, positioning Pokimane as both an approachable and aspirational individual. This duality—ordinary yet refined—resonates with her followers who seek authenticity in personal branding.

Figure 3. Ninja and His Wife Jessica Celebrates a Relationship Milestone

i. Representational Metafunction

Figure 3 captures Ninja and Jessica Blevins standing close together on a boat deck during a sunset, brimming with smiles and celebrating their romantic relationship. The serene ocean and transitioning sky from blue to orange promote their special moment by adding a calm, picturesque backdrop.

ii. Compositional Metafunction

The couple is centrally positioned in the photograph, while the horizon line creates a natural division in the image. These combine with the sunset to provide imagery of warmth and depth. Their body language (epitomised by the couple standing close and relaxed) emphasises the importance of relationships and the need to celebrate personal milestones. Their casual attire contrasts beautifully with the dramatic sky, bridging the couple's intimacy and the grandeur of nature. The picturesque sunset and ocean backdrop highlight an idyllic moment. This tranquil setting reflects the values of leisure, beauty, and the importance of celebrating special occasions in natural settings.

iii. Interactional Metafunction

The caption, "Best anniversary @jessicablevins," is a simple yet heartfelt message from the male gamer to his doting wife. The post expresses love and gratitude, inviting followers to celebrate with them. Ninja's tagging Jessica directly in the message connects the post to her profile, further increasing engagement with the Instagram image. In terms of engagement, the post has drawn over 49,000 likes and 218 comments, signalling the couple's popularity; as well as signifying the emotional connection Ninja and Jessica have created with their audience in terms of their authenticity and romance.

The high number of likes, comment, and shares are boosted by the Instagram algorithm and helps to reflect the post's successful engagement and visibility. The fact that Instagram is a visual-sharing website also means that the celebratory photo goes viral online and the picturesque elements of the post are immediately impactful.

Figure 4. Valkyrae Extends a Hug to the Audience

i. Representational Metafunction

Figure 4 showcases the well-known influencer with a warm, approachable demeanour. She is extending a hug, emphasising a comforting and empathetic message to her audience. The environment is a place where people live. Valkyrae's open-minded gesture promotes the message of inclusivity and emotional support. Her public status, therefore, further reflects modern values around mental health and communal empathy.

ii. Compositional Metafunction

The influencer is centrally positioned with a clean, uncluttered background (room setting). Her face is directly in front of the photograph with a smile as she seems to take a selfie. The use of soft, neutral colour tones complements her jovial expression, enhancing the post's inviting and serene feeling. The simple, uncluttered background focuses attention on Valkyrae, emphasising the message of personal connection rather than a specific location.

iiii. Interactional Metafunction

Valkyrae's caption, "Need a hug? ," is direct and relatable, immediately engaging the audience with a simple question. Her nonverbal cues of direct eye contact, emojis of fist bumps, kissing and hugs (1212 12) - as well as the welcoming posture of a young woman - create a personal connection with the online audience. These personal and empathetic elements encourage followers to connect with Valkyrae's public persona on an emotional level. The effect of the blend of visual appeal and emotional content can be seen in the 202,000 likes, 3769 shares, and 1,066 comments that the post has garnered online.

Valkyrae's post shows her empathetic side as a woman and aligns with cultural shifts toward mental health advocacy. The neutral-toned setting and direct gaze create an inclusive, gender-neutral appeal, avoiding stereotypical markers of femininity or masculinity. Instagram's minimalist composition and open-ended caption ("Need a hug?") prioritise emotional clarity, inviting followers to project their own experiences onto the image. The absence of a specific location broadens relatability, positioning Valkyrae as accessible rather than aloof—a deliberate contrast to detached influencer personas.

2. Professional Achievements, Lifestyle, Sports, and Hobbies

Figure 5. PewDiePie shares a shirtless workout photo showcasing his physique and tattoos.

i. Representational Metafunction

Figure 5 shows PewDiePie standing shirtless, showcasing a muscular physique. His visible tattoos add a personal and artistic touch, while his unsmiling face gives the image a dramatic and timeless feel as a parent. This shirtless photo, showcasing the content creator's muscular physique and tattoos, symbolises his self-improvement, dedication, and personal expression. Tattoos often carry personal messages or cultural significance, enhancing the narrative of the influencer's individuality, maturity as a man, and artistic identity as a public figure.

ii. Compositional Metafunction

PewDiePie is centrally positioned, with the camera view in an upward sideways manner, drawing immediate attention to his physique and tattoos. The side profile emphasises muscle definition, and the colour filter enhances the contrast and depth of the abdominal muscles and tattoos. The balanced compositions with central positioning and natural backdrops promote the emotional content of his fitness regimen. It also highlights the content creator's effort and progress in his fitness journey as a parent while maintaining an aesthetic connection through the display of tattoos and muscular definitions. The influencer is standing alone, signifying a personal journey into self-discipline and development.

iii. Interactional Metafunction

PewDiePie captions the post, "Been working on that dad bod 121," and it combines humour with self-deprecation, engaging his Instagram followers with a light-hearted scenario that is ongoing (symbolised by 'been'). His photo expresses the experience of parenthood and challenges of the mid-age range. Adding the adult male emoji signals a playful tone, making the post more approachable and inviting comments and likes. The high number of likes (1,7 million), 11,700 comments, and over 92,000 shares indicates strong engagement, revealing that PewDiePie's online audience appreciates this blend of humour, fitness, and personal expression.

PewDiePie's gym photo showcases a muscular physique and tattoos, embodying traditional masculine traits of discipline and self-improvement. The unsmiling pose aligns with stoic male archetypes, yet the caption's "dad bod" humor adds levity, humanising his dedication. Instagram's sculpted lighting and solitary composition emphasise physical effort, while the playful tone ("Been working on") balances aspiration with humility. This contrast challenges hyper-masculine norms, presenting fitness as a relatable journey rather than an unattainable ideal.

Figure 6. Pokimane celebrates Charity Work

i. Representational Metafunction

Pokimane's appreciation post in Figure 6 reveals the content creator in a white dress while standing confidently in front of a mirror. Her pose, with one hand on the wall and the other on her hip, exudes elegance and self-assurance. The dual perspective, provided by the mirror, emphasises the beauty of her makeup, sophistication of her attire, and the celebratory nature of being a part of a charity foundation. The white dress and sophisticated pose in front of the mirror symbolise elegance, self-assurance, and celebration. The simple view of the room reflects contemporary values of minimalism and attention to detail, showcasing beauty in simplicity.

Pokimane's mirror selfie in a white dress merges elegance with philanthropic pride, reflecting her role as a compassionate leader. The minimalist aesthetic and confident pose align with cultural values of female empowerment, while the caption's gratitude ("so proud") stresses group achievement.

ii. Compositional Metafunction

Pokimane is centrally positioned in Figure 6, with the mirror adding depth and a dual perspective of her dress and expressions. The minimalist indoor setting with tiled flooring and a beige wall keeps the focus on the influencer and her dress, further enhancing the aesthetic appeal and sophistication of the Instagram image. Pokimane's confident stance and the reflective pose in the mirror project her self-assured identity as a female influencer. This body language highlights values of feminine empowerment and self-respect, enhancing the importance of self-presentation and pride in her achievements both as female gamer and as a member of the society.

Instagram's dual-perspective mirror shot and emojis like 12 and 1 amplify sincerity, resonating with audiences who prioritise authenticity over vanity. The post bridges glamour and social responsibility, enhancing her relatability as a multifaceted influencer.

iii. Interactional Metafunction

The caption reads, "so proud of @cdawgva for raising over half a million dollars for charity grateful I had the chance to help showcase so many auction items & still in shock that my gaming session went for so much ty to everyone who took part or donated!! ." Her statement expresses gratitude and surprise to the audience for their sense of community and shared concern. The use of emojis adds emotional depth to the post, effectively combining visual elegance with a heartfelt caption. The post generated over 26,700 likes, 738 comments, and 5,525 shares - with the audience rewarding the influencer's excitement and gratitude over the charity event with their engagement.

Figure 7. Ninja celebrates Detroit Lions Victory

i.Representational Metafunction

Figure 7 depicts Ninja celebrating a Detroit Lions win among a group of fans, all adorned in the team's jerseys. The fans are standing in a stadium, clearly elated, with raised arms and energetic gestures, symbolising triumph and collective joy. One fan prominently holds a flag with the Detroit Lions logo, reinforcing the team's identity and the celebratory nature of the victory. Ninja's image pays homage to the themes of loyalty, community, and the shared experience of sports fandom. His photo captures the raw emotions of victory and camaraderie.

ii. Compositional Metafunction

Ninja and the celebrating fans are centrally positioned in the foreground, ensuring they are the focal point of the image. The stadium and the crowd in the background add depth and context, emphasising the vast scale of the stadium and event. The upward orientation of the flag acts as a visual anchor, leading the viewer's eye from the fans to the field. This contributes to the audience's sense of participation in the celebration. The well-lit stadium, combined with the vibrant colors of the jerseys and the flag, creates a lively and immersive atmosphere, drawing the Instagram viewers into the excitement of the victorious celebration.

iii. Interactional Metafunction

The image promotes a strong sense of involvement and engagement for the viewer. The celebratory gestures and enthusiastic expressions of the fans convey a sense of joy and solidarity, inviting the viewer to share in their euphoria. The slightly elevated perspective from which the photo is taken allows the viewer to feel as though they are part of the crowd, experiencing the thrill of the win firsthand. The caption accompanying the photo, "LIONS WIN," is succinct and powerful, capturing the essence of the moment and inviting followers to join in the celebration. The post garnered significant engagement, with 120,000 likes and 586 comments, effectively connecting with the audience and emphasising the communal nature of sports celebrations and Ninja's genuine enthusiasm for his favorite team.

Ninja's Lions victory post celebrates communal pride in sports, tapping into cultural enthusiasm for regional identity. The raw crowd energy and unfiltered joy represent genuine fandom in contrast with his normal, polished influencer persona as a celebrity gamer. Moreover, Instagram's dynamic stadium backdrop and poignant "LIONS WIN" caption mirror the immediacy of sports culture, fostering a sense of shared triumph. By highlighting this sporting moment in his Instagram profile,

Ninja reinforces his “everyman” appeal, bridging gaming and mainstream interests of sport’s victorious moments to broaden his relatability.

Figure 8. Valkyrae receives award from Avatar's Live-action cast

i. Representational Metafunction

Figure 8 shows Valkyrae standing with four members of the cast of the live-action Avatar show, in front of a green, leafy backdrop. Valkyrae, dressed in a purple dress with black accents, is holding an award shaped like a metallic flower. The formal attire of all individuals (Valkyrae and the guests) signifies the importance of the event, highlighting themes of professional recognition and celebration. Their smiling faces project feelings of fulfillment, collective achievement, and the prestigious nature of the gathering.

Valkyrae's award photo with Avatar's cast depicts her nostalgic cultural links as a Filipino-American, while professionally maintaining her status as an influencer. As a female gamer, Valkyrae's purple dress and beaming smile reflect a gender-neutral celebration of achievement, challenging male-dominated narratives in awards culture.

ii. Compositional Metafunction

Valkyrae is centrally positioned, drawing immediate attention to her as the recipient of the award. The balanced arrangement of the other individuals around her creates a sense of unity and collective celebration. The green backdrop provides a natural contrast to the formal attire, adding depth and emphasising the event's significance. The clear, structured composition highlights the importance of the achievement, while the formal setting promotes the prestigious nature of the award ceremony.

iii. Interactional Metafunction

The caption, "Imagine growing up watching and loving *Avatar the Last Airbender* as a child then receiving an award from the cast of the live action show! what a full circle moment for me. Thank you @goldhouseco for honoring me as the most impactful in sports/gaming this year!" expresses personal joy and gratitude. Valkyrae's post invites her online followers and the Instagram community to share in her excitement and pride, creating an emotional connection.

Instagram's structured composition and caption linking childhood fandom to present success ("full circle moment") foster parasocial intimacy. The use of emojis and tags adds enthusiasm and relatability with the youthful generation who form the bulk of the Instagram online community. The post received significant engagement, with over 273,000 likes, 763 comments, and 3,593 shares, indicating strong audience connection and appreciation. This high engagement reflects her followers' resonance with Valkyrae's personal and professional journey.

DISCUSSION OF FINDINGS

The analysis of non-gaming Instagram posts by PewDiePie, Valkyrae, Ninja, and Pokimane reveals how these gaming influencers skillfully blend multimodal elements to convey themes of family, lifestyle, professional success, and leisure in ways that deeply resonate with their followers. In exploring representational elements, the posts of all four influencers showcase a powerful use of imagery that symbolises rich personal and cultural narratives. For instance, when PewDiePie shares a family portrait set against a scenic Swiss backdrop, the image conveys intimacy and unity, while Valkyrae's snapshot from an award ceremony highlights her professional pride and recognition. Similarly, Ninja's celebratory image of a sports victory and Pokimane's casual dining shot provide authentic glimpses into everyday life of these celebrities. The deliberate selection of settings, attire, and gestures headlines the commitment of these celebrities to presenting a well-rounded personal identity that extends beyond gaming.

The compositional strategies further reinforce these messages. PewDiePie's central framing of his family in a natural setting emphasises unity and personal joy, while Valkyrae's minimalist selfie-style post draws attention to her approachable demeanour. Likewise, Ninja's centrally composed image with his wife and Pokimane's balanced social dining scene direct the viewer's focus, ensuring that key elements stand out clearly. These carefully considered compositional choices amplify the sense of authenticity and connection across all posts.

In addition to the forgoing, interactional elements play an equally vital role in how these influencers engage with their audiences. The use of captions, whether expressing gratitude or sharing playful banter, invite active participation from the online followers. When PewDiePie marks a family milestone with a heartfelt message, or when Valkyrae extends a warm invitation through her caption, the posts encourage audiences to share in these moments, as evidenced by high engagement in likes, comments, and shares. This interactive dialogue helps break down traditional barriers between influencers and their followers, fostering a strong sense of community. It also creates a deeper parasocial relationship with the audience because the fans tend to think the love they share with the celebrities is reciprocated.

The platform-specific features of Instagram also play a crucial role in enhancing these messages. All four influencers leverage Instagram's visual-first design, grid layout, and features like hashtags, geotags, and user tags to extend the reach of their posts. This synergy between content and platform not only broadens their audience but also amplifies engagement, creating a dynamic space for shared meaning. Each image is rich with visual markers—such as colour, framing, and gesture—that contribute to broader cultural narratives.

Gender and cultural background further influence these self-representation strategies. Male influencers such as PewDiePie and Ninja often project strength, humour, and authority in their pictorial posts, while female influencers like Valkyrae and Pokimane emphasise warmth, accessibility, and refined aesthetics. Moreover, each influencer's cultural heritage—be it Swedish, Moroccan-Canadian, American, or Filipino-American—shapes their narrative, adding layers of authenticity and diversity that resonate with the target audience.

In essence, the research shows that the non-gaming Instagram posts of these gaming celebrities are integral to their public image, as these influencers strategically combine visual storytelling, compelling compositions, and interactive dialogue to reflect their personal journeys, cultural values, and gendered expressions. This approach of showing their human side not only strengthens their personal brands but also forges a deeper connection with their audience, breaking down traditional barriers and fostering an inclusive, resonant community.

FUTURE RESEARCH DIRECTIONS

The development of studies on visual storytelling, gaming language, and online influencers' communication on social media platforms like Instagram is linked to the growing integration of emerging technologies and deeper multimodal interaction in academic circles. As social media evolve to incorporate AI-driven content creation, augmented reality (AR), and virtual reality (VR), online content creators and influencers are likely to further blend their public personas with personal branding, giving rise to more hybrid, immersive identities. This has future implications for sociolinguistic and multimodal studies into how these emerging technologies impact language use at all levels - spoken, written, or nonverbal.

To this end, it is expected that more groundbreaking studies be carried out to develop linguistic theories that cater to these emerging social media studies, especially those that relate to the lives of social media personalities outside their occupational settings. Interdisciplinary theories could also be developed to understand the sociocultural implications of visual storytelling as a growing trend among gamers and other social media content creators on and off social network platforms beyond Instagram. Moreover, scholars need to further explore the ethical implications of immersive and interactive social media communications which have increasingly blurred the thin line separating the public from the private lives of these influencers. As such, there would be more need for critical studies on social identity formation, fan engagement, and multicultural trends.

CONCLUSION

This chapter has demonstrated how gaming influencers blend multimodal elements to reveal a more human side beyond their established gaming personas, creating a unique hybrid identity that connects their on-screen and off-screen lives. The analysis of Instagram posts by PewDiePie, Valkyrae, Ninja, and Pokimane illustrates that the representational, compositional, and interactional elements are thoughtfully structured to reflect personal narratives of family, lifestyle, and professional well-being. Each visual and textual detail—from a heartfelt family portrait to a celebratory snapshot—helps convey a message of authenticity and invites fans to engage with a real, relatable persona.

Additionally, the study has revealed how these influencers employ visual storytelling and social semiotic tools to express their sociocultural identities and values, incorporating cultural symbols and contextual cues that reflect each influencer's heritage. The research also highlights key differences in self-presentation based on gender, with male influencers often emphasising strength and humour, while female influencers project warmth and an approachable personality. Furthermore, the study explores the impact of Instagram's platform-specific features, such as its visual-first design, combined with elements like hashtags, geotags, and interactive captions, on the dissemination of these influencers' messages to their online followers.

The Implication of this study is that gaming influencers deliberately incorporate multimodal strategies in their non-gaming Instagram posts to bridge the gap between their digital and personal identities, foster authentic audience engagement, and reveal diverse cultural and gendered narratives that challenge conventional perspectives on online self-representation. This chapter contributes to the understanding of gaming culture and online influencer interactions. It also advances studies in multimodal analysis and computer-mediated discourse by applying Kress and van Leeuwen's Social Semiotic framework to the digital context of Instagram posts, offering fresh insights into the complex interplay of visual and textual communication in today's digital media landscape.

ACKNOWLEDGMENT

This research received no specific grant from any funding agency in the public, commercial, or not-for-profit sectors.

REFERENCES

Audrezet, A., de Kerviler, G., & Guidry Moulard, J. (2020). Authenticity under threat: When social media influencers need to go beyond self-presentation. *Journal of Business Research, 117*, 557–569. DOI: 10.1016/j.jbusres.2018.07.008

Chiluwa, I. (2023). #EndSARS protests and the search for social justice in Nigeria: Examining activist discourses on police brutality, politics, and human security. *Protest*, *3*(2), 200–224. DOI: 10.1163/2667372X-bja10047

Deshmukh, A. (2024). From Pixels to Personalities: Identity formation in virtual communities through multimodal communication. *European Conference on Social Media*, 11(1), 50-58. DOI: 10.34190/ecsm.11.1.2378

Egbah, A. I., & Igene, S. O. (2024). Legitimating genome editing: A Critical Discourse Analysis of Media reportage. *Ars Artium*, *12*, 53–71.

Highfield, T., & Leaver, T. (2016). Instagrammatics and digital methods: Studying visual social media, from selfies and GIFs to memes and emoji. *Communication Research and Practice*, *2*(1), 47–62. DOI: 10.1080/22041451.2016.1155332

Kress, G. (2010). *Multimodality: A Social Semiotics approach to Contemporary Communication*. Routledge.

Kress, G., & van Leeuwen, T. (1996). *Reading images: The grammar of visual design*. Routledge.

Leedy, P. D., & Ormrod, J. E. (2015). *Practical research: Planning and design* (11th ed.). Pearson.

Liang, W. J., & Lim, F. V. (2024). Representing youth as vulnerable social media users: A social semiotic analysis of the promotional materials from The Social Dilemma. *Semiotica*, *2024*(256), 153–174. DOI: 10.1515/sem-2023-0047

Lotfy, N. E. (2024). Cringe humor in Egyptian TikTok: Multimodal Critical Discourse Analysis of Selected Comic strips. *Multimodal Communication*, *13*(1), 65–78. DOI: 10.1515/mc-2024-0004

Machin, D., & van Leeuwen, T. (2007). *Global media Discourse: A Critical Introduction*. Routledge. DOI: 10.4324/9780203007471

Marwick, A. E. (2013). *Status update: Celebrity, publicity, and branding in the social media age*. Yale University Press.

Oceja, J., & Álvarez-Álvarez, C. (2025). From Twitch to YouTube Live: A systematic literature review of streaming in higher education. *Electronic Journal of e-Learning*, *23*(1), 53–65. DOI: 10.34190/ejel.23.1.3702

Onanuga, P., & Taiwo, R. (2020). Discursive features of Nigerian online Ponzi schemes' narratives. *ELOPE: English Language Overseas Perspectives and Enquiries*, *17*(2), 61–82. DOI: 10.4312/elope.17.2.61-82

Paaßen, B., Morgenroth, T., & Stratemeyer, M. (2016). What is a true gamer? The male gamer stereotype and the marginalization of women in video game culture. *Sex Roles*, *76*(7-8), 421–435. DOI: 10.1007/s11199-016-0678-y

Quandt, T., & Kröger, S. (2014). *Multiplayer: The social aspects of digital gaming*. Routledge.

Shaw, A. (2014). *Gaming at the Edge: Sexuality and Gender at the margins of gamer culture*. University of Minnesota Press.

Sjöblom, M., Törhönen, M., Hamari, J., & Macey, J. (2019). The ingredients of Twitch streaming: Affordances of game streams. *Computers in Human Behavior*, *92*, 20–28. DOI: 10.1016/j.chb.2018.10.012

Taiwo, R., & Oamen, F. (2018). *Perspectivation in Nigeria's political visual communication: A social semiotic analysis*. Covenant Journal of Language Studies.

Taylor, T. L. (2018). *Watch Me Play: Twitch and the rise of Game live streaming*. Princeton University Press. DOI: 10.2307/j.ctvc77jqw

Zappavigna, M. (2016). Social media photography: Construing subjectivity in Instagram images. *Visual Communication*, *15*(3), 271–292. DOI: 10.1177/1470357216643220

ADDITIONAL READING

Bateman, J., & Schmidt, K.-H. (2011). *Multimodal Film Analysis: How Films Mean*. Routledge.

Chen, Y., Adolphs, S., & Knight, D. (2020). Multimodal discourse analysis. In *The Routledge Handbook of Corpus approaches to Discourse Analysis*. Routledge. DOI: 10.4324/9780429259982-7

Georgalou, M. (2017). *Discourse and Identity on Facebook*. Bloomsbury Academic. DOI: 10.5040/9781474289153

Hodge, R., & Kress, G. (1988). Social Semiotics. *Polity.*

Luca, I.-S. (2020). A Multimodal Discourse Analysis in Media. *Romanian Journal of English Studies, 17*(1), 74–80. DOI: 10.1515/rjes-2020-0009

Lutkewitte, C. (Ed.). (2013). *Multimodal Composition: A Critical Sourcebook.* St. Martin's.

Murray, J. (2013). Composing multimodality. In Lutkewitte, C. (Ed.), *Multimodal Composition: A Critical Sourcebook.*

Norris, S. (2004). Multimodal Discourse Analysis: A Conceptual Framework. In Norris, S. (Ed.), *Discourse and technology: Multimodal Discourse Analysis.* Georgetown University Press.

O'Halloran, K. L. (2011). Multimodal discourse analysis. In *The Bloomsbury Handbook of Discourse Analysis.* Bloomsbury.

Scollon, R., & Scollon, S. B. K. (2003). *Discourses in Place: Language in the Material World.* Routledge. DOI: 10.4324/9780203422724

Uthman, A. A. (2024). A multimodal discourse analysis of selected MTN adverts on Facebook. *Issues in Language and Literary Studies*, 8(1).

KEY TERMS AND DEFINITIONS

Conceptual: Describes participants, their attributes, and relationships in visual communication, focusing on static information.

Cultural Identity: The identity or feeling of belonging to a group, influenced by cultural heritage, traditions, language, and social norms.

Gaming Influencers: Individuals with a significant following on social media due to their involvement in gaming, often sharing gameplay, reviews, and personal experiences.

Instagram: A social media platform where users share photos and videos, often with captions and hashtags, to engage with followers.

Multimodal Analysis: Examines how different modes of communication (e.g., text, images, sound) work together to create meaning.

Narrative: Represents acts, events, and actions in visual communication, often telling a story or sequence.

Parasocial Relationship: A perceived, one-sided connection between a media personality (e.g., influencer, celebrity) and their audience, where the audience feels a sense of intimacy, familiarity, or friendship.

Post: A piece of content shared on social media platforms, such as a photo, video, or text update, that aims to engage and communicate with followers.

Social Media Engagement: Interaction between users and content on social media platforms, including likes, comments, shares, and other forms of participation.

Sociocultural: Relating to the interaction of social and cultural elements, often examining how these aspects influence behaviours, identities, and societal norms.

Visual Storytelling: The use of images, videos, and other visual elements to convey a narrative or message, enhancing engagement and understanding.

Chapter 11
The Transparency of the Family:
A Study on Conservative Family Profiles on Instagram

Metin Gültekin
Fırat University, Turkey

Ahmet Yıldız
Harran University, Turkey

ABSTRACT

While modern conservative individuals act on the basis of beliefs and traditions, the development of communication technologies and post-fordist lifestyles have increased the flexibility of societies. This flexibility is also reflected in family structures and the roles of individuals. The traditional family structure has undergone major transformations in the industrial and information ages. Social media platforms such as Instagram allow individuals to construct and present their lives, making the lives of conservative families visible. However, the fact that Instagram is a digital stage suggests that the life presented may not reflect true conservative values. Conservatism's emphasis on privacy increases the interest in social media representations and shapes the quality of content.

INTRODUCTION

Even when the concepts of conservatism, family and privacy are mentioned, their intense relationship with each other makes itself felt. Due to the importance and mission that the conservative worldview attaches to the family, the family stands

DOI: 10.4018/979-8-3693-7934-9.ch011

at a point where its privacy must be protected. Although the shaking of traditional family relations in the modern period has affected the conservative family, the real shaking has been experienced through the widespread use of media tools. The fact that social media tools have become one of the spaces of individuals has led to the exposure of daily life practices in this space and led to the blurring of the boundaries of the private sphere. The obligation of the individual to perform in social media has led him/her to become a voluntary content producer in this space and to a point of self-exploitation. The fact that social media tools are offered free of charge and that they contain and display a part of the individual's existence in terms of the possibilities provided by social media reveals an ironic image.

The transparency caused by social media tools has a greater impact on situations where intimate spaces are important. However, it is possible to follow the traces of transparency threatening the sphere of existence in Chulhan's works. The concept of family, whose privacy is taken care of at many levels from social sciences to health sciences, also has its share of transparency. The family, which is based on blood ties and is basically based on the intimate relationship between spouses, followed by the relationship between parents and children and the relationship of siblings, constitutes the most fundamental point of the social structure. Considering the fact that it is the physical and social environment in which the individual has been living since birth, the importance of the family structure in determining the socialization of the individual shows itself.

Our social perspective and way of life are largely determined by our worldviews. In this sense, conservatism constitutes a reference point. Like all other worldviews, conservatism, which emphasizes the continuation of existing beliefs and culture, manifests itself in various indicators in daily life practices. From clothing to the words used, conservatism can exist under different guises. The family, as an institution representing the private sphere, shows a conservative character in every society and ideology. In addition, the "conservative family" is also the carrier and defender of values considered sacred by society. On the other hand, in today's ostentatious and self-sharing culture of social media, the conservative family has also widely immersed itself in this change and has sought to show itself through social media accounts. From the relationships between spouses to the relationship between spouses and their children, it is seen that areas that are expected to be especially careful - due to their conservatism - find a place in social media posts. Although this situation is in line with the spirit of the time, it is a more remarkable development in terms of the concepts of family, conservative family and privacy. This study will try to analyze the posts made on Instagram accounts of conservative families who are expected to take care in preserving what is private. In this way, the traces of the transparency of the conservative family concept will be tried to be traced.

The Concept of Family and Theoretical Approaches to the Concept of Family

The family has been an indispensable part of human and social life throughout history. Since the first formation of civilizations, the family has always existed. Although its form, structure and social roles have changed over time, the family has maintained its existence in every period and culture and has been one of the common points of societies (Can, 2019). We can define the family as a community of two or more individuals who live together, share the same space, have emotional ties between them, undertake social roles and duties, and share feelings of love and belonging (Hallaç & Öz, 2014). In definitions of the family, distinctions regarding gender-based roles and cooperation stand out. While the man is in a position to provide for the family and protect the family against external threats, the woman is in a position that requires her to be at home to do certain tasks such as cooking and cleaning, as well as raising children, especially those who are born.

While the family structure, which is more common in the traditional system and expands vertically and horizontally through kinship in addition to the mother, father and children, which exists due to the conditions of the economy based on agriculture, is called extended family; the family structure shaped by the forms of relationship in urban life with the industrial society and consisting only of parents and children is called nuclear family (Doğan, 2016). In societies based on agriculture, the need for labor force and the need for security made the extended family almost obligatory. However, the security provided by urban life and the form of employment in industrial production have led to the spread of the nuclear family. The transforming position of the family has brought it to the agenda as a problematic that needs to be explained.

There are various approaches to explaining the family. It can be said that these explanatory efforts follow an evolutionary line by covering a wide area starting from the early ages to the modern period. In classical explanations, basic concepts such as marriage, parent-child relationships, family structure, kinship systems, social structure, abortion, incest, mate selection and divorce were included (Göktuna Yaylacı, 2020). This form of explanation at the traditional level has undergone various transformations in modernization processes and perspectives that try to explain the family through evolutionary processes have transformed over time. While the positivist perspective focuses on the functions of the family, interpretive perspectives attempt to understand and analyze the family and family-specific forms of relationships. While Marxist theories claim that the family cannot be handled independently of economic relations, feminist theories come to the fore with statements about the position of women in the family (Şenkal, 2016). According to the feminist perspective, which claims that discrimination and exploitation are based on gender based on the conflict theory, it is argued that the alienation of individuals from their labor in the capitalist production process is also experienced by women in the context of housework (Güneş, 2018). The fact that these perspectives that try to explain the family differ accompanies the fact that modernism constantly transforms the family with its nature that does not allow a return to the traditional and its transformative power in its own internal dynamics.

There are three main theories to explain the family in sociological theory. These are functionalist theory, conflict theory and symbolic interactionism theory (Göktuna Yaylacı, 2020). Functionalist theory deals with the family in terms of its functions. The family is positioned as a social institution that ensures the continuity of society. At this point, the family gains meaning as a part that ensures the continuation of the large social structure in balance. The social institution in question assumes a biological, psychological, cultural, educational, social and economic function (Kır, 2011). Ensuring the realization of sexual activity within a certain legitimacy, ensuring the satisfaction of feelings of love and trust, being the environment of the first learning and acculturation, and the existence of the first level of economic relations are important in terms of revealing the functionality of the family. Conflict theory, on the other hand, attempts to define the family by focusing on economic relations. According to this theory, capitalism lies at the root of conflicts and inequalities. In a capitalist society, the family and the education system support and legitimize this system by raising healthy and disciplined workers for the economic infrastructure. At the same time, the state, the legal system and the media ensure that the masses are kept under control both physically and ideologically (Gökçe, 2017). According to symbolic interaction theory, people live in a world of symbols just as they live in a physical world. Human behavior reflects the meanings that individuals attribute to their own actions and others. In the context of the family, this theory tries to understand family dynamics by examining the behavior of members. These dynamics include elements such as roles, communication patterns, decision-making processes and socialization (Hallaç & Öz, 2014).

Conservatism and the Conservative Family

People create certain reference points to understand and interpret the world. These reference points are shaped by certain ways of thinking. Conservatism has also been a modern way of thinking that feeds on the values of the ages before modern thought systems but defends these values in modern times. This way of thinking, which has been effective since the sixteenth century, gained a decisive position again, especially in the twentieth century with the breakdown of the socialist influence (Çaha, 2004). This perspective, which prioritizes experience over reason, has been influential in a wide range of areas from politics to economics, accompanied by concepts such as history, culture, tradition, custom, habit and customary practices. Although its origins can be traced back to Aristotle in Ancient Greece, the real shaping of conservatism coincides with the Enlightenment, the Industrial Revolution and the French Revolution (Demirkanoğlu, 2017). Against the belief that the rationality achieved through reason after the Enlightenment will make everything perfect, it is argued that the world cannot be made a better place under the leadership of reason with the argument that the world is often led to destruction under the leadership of reason.

Conservatism, which gained strength in continental Europe after the French Revolution as a reaction against the revolution, has been a complement to right-wing ideologies. It is necessary to briefly explain some basic concepts within this way of thinking, which is dominated by the idea that social order cannot be established without a certain authority. Tradition is important in terms of social and cultural accumulation. The guidance of the knowledge and experience gained through tradition is important. Human deficiency, on the other hand, emphasizes the need for a certain authority by emphasizing the negativity of human nature. The idea of organic society is conservatism's view of society as a natural process of coexistence. The idea that society is shaped around a certain contract is opposed. Hierarchy is seen as necessary for the authority to manage the social process. The division of labor is also important within the hierarchical structure. Property is a situation that conservative thought encourages in the social process. Thanks to property, individuals who make up the society are encouraged to respect what others have through what they own (Pir, 2024).

Family has an important place in conservative thought. As a social institution, the family can be related to the idea of conservatism in terms of protecting its members, culture and social order and being the transmitter of the existing social and cultural order (Akın, 2018). For this reason, it is seen that modernization efforts aiming at social transformation have targeted family relations by using schools and mass media. This offensive of modernization against the family institution has turned the family into a point of resistance for conservative ideology (Bayer, 2013). Another relationship of the family with conservatism is related to privacy. The family creates a unique and special form of relationship between its members, and within this sociability, the individual gains experiences about social life (Akın, 2018). The social and cultural accumulation acquired within the intimate structure of the family becomes important determinants of both the social and political sphere.

Conservatism makes itself felt in every aspect of daily life; from clothing to the products consumed and even to the speech patterns used in daily life (Efe, 2024). Views of the conservative family can be listed in this way:

- Religious Beliefs and Practices: Religion has an important place for conservative families. Worships are performed regularly and religious holidays and rituals are valued.

- Traditions and Customs: Traditions and customs are strictly adhered to. The words and experiences of family elders are valued.
- Family Roles: In conservative families there is usually a clear division of gender roles. Men may be responsible for providing for the household, while women may be responsible for housework and childcare.
- Compliance with Social Norms: Social norms and rules are followed. Behavioral patterns generally accepted by society are respected.
- Education and upbringing: Disciplined and traditional methods are adopted in the upbringing and education of children. The authority of family elders is effective on children.
- Family Ties: Family ties are strong. Family members are interdependent and supportive. Grand family structure (grandfather, grandmother, uncle, aunt, etc.) is valued.
- Marriage and Relationships: Marriages are generally long-lasting and well-established. The divorce rate is low and pre-marital relationships are generally disapproved of.

Evolution of the Family in Modern Society

Modernity emphasizes rationalism and therefore individualism in contrast to the collectivist understanding of traditionalism. The replacement of nature as the source of knowledge has reduced the acquisition of knowledge and making it useful to individual efforts instead of divine knowledge as a higher signifier (Gültekin, 2016). Individuals will now operate by using their own minds in areas where they will be useful. Individuals will exist through their own efforts and become a part of society in this way. However, this usefulness can only be meaningful and productive in the most effective way under conditions where they will be organized in the relevant fields and use reason and labor together. This implies a division of labor that operates differently from the collectivist order. As Durkheim emphasized, modern society operates according to the logic of division of labor (Özyurt, 2007). This process naturally removes the family as the central institution of society and replaces it with efficiency, change and progress based on knowledge and labor.

With the transition to industrial society, the industrial enterprise has become the central sphere of society. In these conditions, where the family tries to survive dependent on a field of activity that does not belong to it, it loses its sovereign authority over itself. As individuals, members contribute to the continuity of the family by moving from a different economic environment. The family loses its characteristic of being a holistic social structure and turns into an area of consumption. Family expenditures are now a matter of cost and expense. Minimizing the sharing of earnings has become a functional justification for the modern family (Yaşar Ekici,

2014). Over time, education, health, and even child-rearing, like the economy, have fallen outside the functional sphere of the family. These processes, together with the dynamics of individualization, have constituted the founding dynamics of the family's tendency to shrink.

Although individuals who joined the labor force after the industrial revolution have various rights as a result of great struggles, the fact that they do not receive a share of the added value provided by the products they produce is the visible side of capitalist exploitation. This situation causes an income gap between those who own the means of production and those who make a living through their labor. While technological advances have made machines more efficient, classical production relations have led to unemployment of individuals participating in the labor force and shifted the need for labor to different fields (İlhan, 2015). For this reason, individuals find employment opportunities in the service sector rather than production sectors. Differentiation in the fields of work, unemployment anxiety and the capitalist order have caused erosion in the roles of family members due to being a family.

Mass media have been highly influential in the formation of mass culture. Through these tools, cultural and artistic products have become consumable commodities. The media, which is the most basic tool for the spread of the consumption-indexed lifestyle, has given indoctrination on how individuals' daily life practices should be through news and entertainment programs (Güleç, 2018). This situation has dragged the family, which is a collective audience, from being the most important structure that determines society to a point determined by media tools. The differentiation of the mass media and the mode of production from the modern period has brought about the differentiation of the social and cultural sphere. Postfordist approaches under the name of flexible specialization not only shook the hierarchical structure in the workforce but also affected family relations (Saklı, 2007). In addition, in the postmodern period, challenges to authority and criticism of gender roles have led to a reassessment of assumptions about the position of family members.

Loss of Privacy and Transparency in the Age of Digital Communication

The right to privacy refers to a space where individuals can be alone, where they can freely shape their own thoughts and behaviors, and where, when and under what conditions they can decide where, when and under what conditions to communicate with others, and the rights they have regarding this space (Yüksel, 2003). Determining privacy as a right also points to the existence of the individual's free will. Privacy has gained importance with modernization. However, with the advancement of communication technologies, mass communication tools have changed and the communication tools used by people have developed. This situation makes it difficult for individuals to protect their privacy. Because, compared to past periods, modern communication tools make surveillance and privacy violations much easier (Karagülle, 2015). The word 'mahrem' is derived from the Arabic word 'haram', which means not to touch, to leave something, relatives whose honor one protects, women and relatives with whom it is forbidden to marry (www.diyanet.gov.tr). Privacy means the hidden aspect or hidden state of something. It has a much more comprehensive and deeper meaning than the Turkish concept of 'private space'.

It would not be wrong to associate the loss of privacy with the panopticon. In 1787, Jeremy Bentham developed the Panopticon idea for prison design. In the Panopticon, the cells are arranged in a circular fashion so that a guard in a tower in the center can observe all prisoners in a one-way direction. Michel Foucault revisited this concept in 1975. Both Bentham and Foucault acknowledge the impact of surveillance on human behavior. In the Panopticon, the guard does not need to be in place at all times, because when individuals feel they are being watched, they tend to evaluate themselves from the perspective of the watcher. This explains why they behave differently when they are under surveillance (Dedeoğlu, 2004). The panopticon's development of a control system that enforces the limits of privacy brings to mind the power that establishes a control mechanism and the individuals under the domination of power.

Technological developments no longer require the panopticon in the form of a "tower". Especially the invention of the camera and its derivative devices constitute mechanisms that control us in some respects in everyday life. However, the proliferation of social media tools has taken this control to another dimension. The posts and profiles created through social media tools become suitable for surveillance (Korkmaz, 2013). As a result of the exposure of the lives of celebrities through traditional media tools, individuals who are included in the panopticon with their own consent emerge. The only function of the panopticon in question is not control. The panopticon ensures the continuation of exploitation.

Social media tools have become one of the spaces of individuals. Through tools such as photographs and videos as well as written posts, individuals open themselves to an anonymous audience, that is, other social media users (Kerestecioğlu, 2014). Therefore, users may have different motivations, but as a result, it is seen that the privacy that should be preserved is exposed. Today's world has turned into a market where privacy is shown, sold and consumed, rather than a theater where emotions are exhibited and interpreted. In this society, people expose themselves without any pressure. Unlike the isolated prisoners of Bentham's panopticon, the inhabitants of the modern panopticon are constantly communicating and networking. Transparency is the result of hyper-communication, not isolation. What is unique about the digital panopticon is that its inhabitants play an active role by exposing and exposing themselves (Chulhan, 2017). Thanks to the speed and storage possibilities provided by new communication tools, it is seen how effective data production and evaluation are.

The promise of freedom in today's society transforms it into an object of performance that constantly pushes it to succeed (Chulhan, 2024). In this case, social media tools become a stage for individuals to showcase their own performances. After a while, the main thing ceases to be the individual or the individual's life and turns into a total show. In addition, the individual's appetite for sharing every detail about himself takes him to a point where his actions, ideas and preferences can be determined through bigdata (Chulhan, 2022). In other words, it becomes difficult to talk about the individual at this point. Of course, the new family consisting of individuals who are in the grip of media tools will also have its share of the damage to existence due to transparency.

1. METHOD AND RESULTS

1.1. Purpose of the Study

Social media has greatly affected the lifestyles of individuals and societies. The concern to be visible has taken over individuals and turned them into voluntary content producers of social media. In addition, individuals who behaved according to certain patterns within the framework of their worldviews in the modern period have been replaced by more flexible lifestyles. The conservative lifestyle has also taken its share from this situation. This study aims to analyze the accounts of conservative families through which they make themselves visible on social media.

1.2. Research Methodology

Content analysis method will be used in this study. Content analysis is the process of systematically examining and interpreting the contents of a particular text or form of communication. This method is widely used in social sciences, communication, media studies and other disciplines. Content analysis provides a convenient method for analyzing qualitative and quantitative data and enables researchers to identify specific themes, patterns and trends (Krippendorff, 2018). Content analysis is the process of systematically examining and interpreting the contents of a particular text or form of communication. This method is widely used in social sciences, communication, media studies and other disciplines. Content analysis provides a convenient method for analyzing qualitative and quantitative data and enables researchers to identify specific themes, patterns and trends (Neuendorf, 2017). Content analysis provides researchers with the ability to extract meaningful information from a variety of data sources (e.g. written texts, visuals, audio recordings). In this context, content analysis can be applied with both qualitative and quantitative approaches. Qualitative content analysis focuses on in-depth examination of texts, while quantitative content analysis allows for the numerical measurement and statistical analysis of specific variables (Weber, 1990). Content analysis stands out as an important research method in social sciences and communication. By offering a systematic approach, it allows meaningful data to be obtained from texts and other forms of communication. By using the content analysis method, researchers can uncover certain themes, patterns and trends and thus better understand social events. Content analysis is a flexible method that can answer a wide range of research questions, as it can be applied with both qualitative and quantitative methods. In this study, the relationship between the sharing styles of conservative families, who are expected to be sensitive about privacy, on the Instagram platform and the lifestyle in question will be examined. From this point on, the video sharing of conservative family profiles will be taken into consideration. The subjects of these videos, the style used and the clothing styles will be examined.

1.3. Sample of the Research

The sample of the study consists of a group of individuals who are qualified to answer the research questions and who will ensure the generalizability of the study. When determining the sample, the size of the universe, the purpose of the study and the available resources are taken into consideration. The sample of qualitative studies is created by selecting the individuals or groups that are most suitable for the research questions in order to collect in-depth information. In such studies, purposeful sampling methods are generally used, and attention is paid to the fact that the participants share a certain experience, perspective or characteristic. Rather than randomness, the priority is to select the individuals who can best illuminate the research topic. The sample size is usually smaller, but the richness and depth of the data collected are essential. Therefore, in qualitative studies, the sample determination process is terminated until saturation is reached, i.e. when no new information is obtained. The sample of this study was determined as @ayse.erhann, @ridvan_fatma01, @esin_abdurrahim accounts on the Instagram platform. In determining the accounts, the clothing style, communication style and lifestyle of the users of the accounts that are in line with the conservative family profile, as well as the fact that they share their works through the accounts they use as a family were taken into consideration. The concept of family was determined as nuclear family. The fact that the traditional family type has been eroded and the accounts that share mostly have a nuclear family appearance was effective in determining the sample in question. The number of followers of the accounts was also taken into account.

Defining visibility on social media through the number of followers was effective in selecting accounts with relatively many followers.

1.4. Limitations of the Research

This study is limited to the reels video shares of the accounts @ayse.erhann, @ ridvan_fatma01, @goknurrcolak on the Instagram platform.

1.5. Data Collection and Evaluation

Table 1. Quantitative data on posts made from Instagram accounts

Video Sharing Format	Number of Video Shares		
	@ ayse.erhann	@ goknurrcolak	@ ridvan_fatma01
Spouses	196	37	72
Only men	1	1	6
Only women	4	17	3
Mother and child	7	4	4
Father and child	6	7	2
Parents and child	31	17	21
Children		1	1
With individuals outside the family	75	14	22
Without anyone	1	11	
Total	**321**	**110**	**131**

When we look at the numerical distribution of sharing styles of conservative family accounts on the Instagram platform, we see that the most intense sharing style is videos that only the spouses are included. This data is accompanied by videos that parents share by including their children. There are also videos that only include one of the spouses and videos where the mother or father is with the children. In all these cases, while the nuclear family members are present, it has been observed that videos where no one is present usually include a section or the entire house. Again, the category of videos that include individuals outside the family, which is seen to be shared intensively, mostly represents individuals outside the nuclear family, while guests or Instagram account owners who shoot videos together are also included.

When we look at the numerical distribution, it is striking that the number of videos shared about the relationship between spouses, which is a more intimate form of relationship, is high. However, it is difficult to say that users share according to a certain system due to the difference in the number of shares made by the users of the accounts in question for each sharing form.

Table 2. Number of shares on Instagram videos

Subject of Video Sharing	**Number of Video Shares**		
	@ ayse.erhann	**@ goknurrcolak**	**@ ridvan_fatma01**
Celebration	19	11	4
Child care	6	1	1
Outfit display	5	9	3
Room display	12	10	1
Guest	2	1	3
Pregnancy	34	5	7
Birth	8	3	4
Social media trends	77	25	41
Humor	64	8	35
Undetermined	6	2	1
Game	10		4
Fun	3	7	1
Neighborhood	1		
Housework	37	10	8
Shopping	13		10
Travel	1	1	
Faith	7	6	3
Marriage	2	1	
Disaster	2	4	
Holiday	12	4	6
Total	**321**	**110**	**131**

When we look at the content of the video shares made by conservative family accounts on Instagram, it is observed that social media trends come to the forefront in these shares. We can easily say that Instagram users tend to follow these trends in order to get more views and increase their number of followers. In particular, humorous content ranks second among users' interaction strategies, and it is seen that they try to attract attention with such content. Although humor is considered a category in itself, it is also noticed that there are humorous elements in many different types of content. This shows that humor has become an important tool that enables a wide range of content to get interaction. At this point, it can be said that conservative families try to attract attention by both following trends and using humor in their social media content. The most striking elements in the distribution of the topics of the video posts are gathered under two main headings that form the basis of this study. First, the accounts in question share posts related to faith. Faith-themed content stands out as videos that are supported by religious references, emphasize Islamic values, and are associated with daily life. Such content allows users to highlight their faith as a social identity and to establish a connection with their own follower base through this identity. The presence of conservative families on social media in particular shows that religion is used not only as a belief system but also as a framework that determines lifestyle. Secondly, it is noteworthy that the accounts share videos about pregnancy and birth. Such videos cover topics such as sharing motherhood experiences, pregnancy processes, and preparations for birth, while also standing out as a reflection of a conservative family structure. However, the striking point here is that these videos are intertwined with religious references and conservative appearances. The fact that the mothers who share videos wear headscarves and present a lifestyle that is in line with the traditional family structure is an important element that underlines conservative values.

However, an interesting contradiction emerges at this point: The sharing of videos of the same mothers entering the delivery room indicates a tension between the conservative worldview and lifestyle. While the moment of entering the delivery room is traditionally considered a private and intimate moment, the fact that this moment is shared on a public platform indicates a change in the perception of privacy of those who adopt a conservative lifestyle. This situation reveals that conservative individuals have also begun to partially publicize their private lives through modern media platforms and social media, and how traditional understandings of privacy interact with the culture of visibility offered by social media. These posts show that the presence of individuals with a conservative worldview on digital platforms has entered a transformation process in terms of both their beliefs and lifestyles. Social media changes the ways conservative individuals express themselves by redefining the boundaries between private life and public space, and this transformation raises important questions about how traditional values are reproduced and transformed by modern media tools.

1.5.2. Family Transparency

It can be said that the greatest opportunity that internet technology has is its boundlessness. Thanks to the flow of information that cannot be limited by time and space, it is possible to have information about what is happening anywhere in the world. However, thanks to the opportunities provided by the internet, information that turns into a large data stack has no connection with the truth (Chulhan, 2017). In this sense, the video posts made by the Instagram accounts in the study regarding the institution of family can be evaluated as a pile of information rather than providing information about the truth of family. The instant and intense nature of the posts, which also contain exhibitionist elements that contradict the concept of conservatism to a great extent, also causes a loss of meaning regarding the concept of family.

When the video posts made by conservative family accounts are examined, it is seen that the concept of transparency, which is the most characteristic feature of the society, "positivity", comes to the fore. Although humor is one of the topics of the videos in itself, it should be said that humor has an important place in all the videos except the disaster title. At this point, it is possible to understand the relationship of today's society with pain. In today's society, pain is seen as an element to be avoided and there is a pressure to be happy (Chulhan, 2024). In the posts made, under the disaster title, there are posts about the earthquake disaster that occurred in our country on February 6, 2023 and affected many of our provinces, and the forest fires that occurred at various times. However, the relationship of these videos with pain can be evaluated as efforts to create a profile that does not go away from the agenda by getting more views.

Individuals have the opportunity to create a different self from themselves thanks to social media. The person they want to be or to be anonymous is possible thanks to social media (Güler et al., 2022). This situation is also valid for families. When we look at the profiles that are the subject of our study, it can be said that what is seen in the video shares is a representation of idealizations related to the family rather than a family. The distribution of the video shares regarding the subjects also shows that this representation is made in a wide range from birth to vacation. It can be stated that these representations are made with the motivation of getting more views and reaching the number of followers through being accepted and loved (Çakir & Temír, 2022). The number of views and followers also appear as important parameters in advertising, sponsorship and collaborations.

The main contradiction with the conservative worldview can be seen as the fact that the claim of conservatism to preserve can be seen to be in vain due to social media posts. The concept of family, which all beliefs and worldviews agree on its privacy, is expected to be seen as a degree more private in terms of conservatism (Karslı & Aycan, 2020). When we look at the videos of conservative family accounts, the fact that the mother figure's head is covered, that times such as holidays or fasting are celebrated, and the presence of posts referring to faith and tradition constitute a conservative view. However, the presence of pregnancy videos, which are not very visible in traditional society, stands out. In the same vein, it is also seen that mother figures make various posts with videos of them entering the delivery room and leaving the delivery room. In addition, it is seen that almost all stages of daily life are shared. We can say that the fact that so much is shared about the family shows that especially the conservative family has become transparent through social media.

CONCLUSION

Individuals with a conservative worldview that emerged in the modern period are thought to act on the basis of faith and tradition. However, the rapid development of communication technologies and the spread of the post-fordist lifestyle have led to the flexibilization of the spheres of movement and reference points of individuals and societies. This flexibility also manifests itself in family structures and the roles of family members. The traditional family structure has entered a process of transformation with the industrial society, and in the information age this transformation has deepened and the concept of family has undergone major changes.

Instagram, a social media platform focused on visual sharing, allows individuals to construct and present themselves and their lives in the way they want. This has made it possible for conservative families to share and make visible their lives on Instagram. However, considering that Instagram is a digital stage, it should be realized that the life on display does not fully reflect the conservative family structure. The emphasis on privacy and confidentiality inherent in conservatism further increases the interest in representations on social media, which in turn greatly shapes the quality of the content shared by these accounts.

The most important elements that stand out in the shared videos are that the content generally presents a positive and idealized family life, there is almost no sharing of pain and hardship, and there is a constant pressure to perform. At this point, it can be argued that conservative families have also become part of the transparency society and are under the influence of this demand for transparency. Transparency means not only that private life becomes visible, but also that individuals and families are constantly performing an idealized life to be presented to society. Therefore, it can be said that conservative families are also becoming transparent on this digital stage by redefining the boundaries of their privacy.

REFERENCES

Akın, M. H. (2018). Türkiye'de Muhafazakârlığın Direnme Odağı Olarak AİLE. *Muhafazakâr Düşünce Dergisi, 31.*

Bayer, A. (2013). Değişen toplumsal yapıda aile. *Şırnak Üniversitesi İlahiyat Fakültesi Dergisi, 4*(8), 101-129.

Çaha, Ö. (2004). Muhafazakâr düşüncede toplum. *Liberal düşünce dergisi, 34*, 15-24.

Çakir, P., & Temi, R. E. (2022). *Sosyal Medyada Benlik Sunumu ve Mahremiyet Kavramı ile İlişkisi: Nicel Bir Araştırma.* Yeni Medya Dergisi.

Can, İ. (2019). *III. Ailenin Tarihsel Gelişimi: Dünü, Bugünü ve Yarını. İçinde Sistematik Aile Sosyolojisi.* Çizgi Kitabevi.

Chulhan, B. (2017). *Şeffaflık Toplumu.* Metis.

Chulhan, B. (2022). *Psikopolitika (5. bs).* Metis.

Chulhan, B. (2024). *Palyatif Toplum* (6. bs). Metis.

Dedeoğlu, G. (2004). Gözetleme, mahremiyet ve insan onuru. *TBD Bilişim, 89*, 36.

Demirkanoğlu, Y. (2017). Muhafazakâr Düşüncede Kadinin Toplumsal Konumu. *Sosyal Ekonomik Araştırmalar Dergisi, 17*(34), 285–305. DOI: 10.30976/susead.338402

Doğan, İ. (2016). *Türk Aile Sosyolojisi.* Pagema Akademi.

Efe, H. S. (2024). Muhafazakâr ve Laik Kimliklerin Televizyon Dizilerinde Alımlanması:"Kızılcık Şerbeti Dizisi". *INJOCMER International Journal of Communication and Media Research, 4*(1), 21–43.

Gökçe, H. (2017). Dünü, Bugünü, Yarını İle Aile. *Sosyoloji Notları, 1*(1), 50–63.

Göktuna Yaylacı, F. (2020). *Aile Sosyolojisi* (Eraslan, L., Ed.). Anadolo Ünivessitesi Yayını.

Güleç, V. (2018). Aile ilişkilerinin sosyal medyayla birlikte çöküşü. *Yeni Medya Elektronik Dergisi, 2*(2), 105–120.

Güler, Ş., & Şahi, N. (2022). Sosyal Medyada Çevrimiçi Benlik Sunumunun Öznel İyi Oluş Üzerine Etkisi: Instagram Kullanıcıları Üzerine Bir Araştırma. *Erciyes İletişim Dergisi, 9*(1), 361–380. DOI: 10.17680/erciyesiletisim.993055

Gültekin, M. (2016). İbn Haldun, modernlik ve modern sosyoloji. *The Journal of Academic Social Science Studies, 51*(51), 277–293. DOI: 10.9761/JASSS3655

Güneş, H. N. (2018). Feminist akımlarda aile. *Sosyal Bilimler Araştırma Dergisi, 7*(3), 142–153.

Hallaç, S., & Öz, F. (2014). Aile kavramına kuramsal bir bakış. *Psikiyatride Güncel Yaklasimlar, 6*(2), 142–153.

İlhan, S. (2015). Yeni Kapitalizm Ve Meslek Olgusunun Değişen Anlamları Üzerine. *Dumlupınar Üniversitesi Sosyal Bilimler Dergisi, 21*.

Karagülle, A. E. (2015). *Günümüzde değişen mahremiyet algısının sosyal ağlar bağlamında incelenmesi* [Master's Thesis, Sosyal Bilimler Enstitüsü].

Karslı, B., & Aycan, S. (2020). Instagram ve Mahremiyet: Dindar Muhafazakâr Kadınların Paylaşımları Örneği. *Turkish Academic Research Review, 5*(2), 245–266. DOI: 10.30622/tarr.725695

Kerestecioğlu, İ. Ö. (2014). Mahremiyetin Fethi: İdeal Aile Kurgularından İdeal Aile Politikalarına. *Başka Bir Aile Anlayışı Mümkün mü?* 10.

Kır, İ. (2011). Toplumsal bir kurum olarak ailenin işlevleri. *Elektronik sosyal bilimler dergisi, 10*(36), 381-404.

Korkmaz, İ. (2013). Facebook ve mahremiyet: Görmek ve gözetle (n) mek. *Yalova Sosyal Bilimler Dergisi, 3*(5).

Krippendorff, K. (2018). *Content analysis: An introduction to its methodology*. Sage publications.

Neuendorf, K. A. (2017). *The content analysis guidebook*. sage.

Özyurt, C. (2007). Durkheim sosyolojisinde ahlâkî kontrol sorunu. *Değerler Eğitimi Dergisi, 5*(13), 95–121.

Pir, N. (2024). "Dönüşen" Ve "Ötekileştiren" Muhafazakarlık: Neomuhafazakarlık. *Dicle Üniversitesi Sosyal Bilimler Enstitüsü Dergisi, 35*(35), 123–145. DOI: 10.15182/diclesosbed.1352071

Saklı, A. R. (2007). Kapitalist gelişim sürecinde fordizm ve post-fordizm. *Ankara,*http://www. sakli. info/Fordizm. pdf, *Erişim Tarihi, 26*, 2008.

Şenkal, Y. (2016). Feminist kuramlar bağlamında reklamda kadın imgesine bakış. *Anadolu Bil Meslek Yüksekokulu Dergisi, 42*, 91–114.

Weber, R. P. (1990). *Basic content analysis*. DOI: 10.4135/9781412983488

Yaşar Ekici, F. (2014). *Türk aile yapısının değişim ve dönüşümü ve bu değişim ve dönüşüme etki eden unsurların değerlendirilmesi. The Journal of Academic Social Science Studies*. JASSS.

Yüksel, M. (2003). Mahremiyet Hakkı ve Sosyo-Tarihsl Gelişimi. *Ankara Üniversitesi SBF Dergisi, 58*(01).

Chapter 12
Cultural Integration in the Digital Space:
A Multimodal Discourse Analysis of Yinka Ayefele's Mo M'ope Mi Wa (I Offer My Praise)

Lydia Tomilola Olaifa
https://orcid.org/0009-0005-0067-8342
Adeleke University, Ede, Nigeria

Bolatito Olufunke Adejare
https://orcid.org/0009-0003-3684-5371
Adeleke University, Ede, Nigeria

ABSTRACT

The digital space has transcended various barriers to becoming a vibrant hub for cultural integration. Music, which happens to be a universal language that speaks to the human spirit and crosses borders, plays a key role in this global dialogue. Using Gunther Kress and Theo van Leeuwen's Visual Social Semiotic theory, this study explored the power of music to foster cultural integration in the digital space by analysing Yinka Ayefele's song Mo M'ope Mi Wa (I Offer My Praise). This song, which was obtained on YouTube, is a blend of Yoruba Juju, Igbo dressing and Akwa Ibom Highlife. The song strategically employs various communication modes to bridge cultural differences and foster integration of several cultures. The study demonstrates the power of music, especially when it is creatively blended with cultural elements, in bridging divides and promoting human connection in the digital space.

DOI: 10.4018/979-8-3693-7934-9.ch012

INTRODUCTION

Music, in the ever-increasing expanse of the digital world, serves as a universal language that easily transcends cultural divides and geographical borders. The digital space provides a platform where artistes from diverse backgrounds share their beliefs, stories, sounds and values. The digital space, thus, creates a unified online community and a global audience for such artistes as well as their stories. Music, unlike several forms of communication, bypasses linguistic barriers through the affordance of rhythm, harmony and melody. The creative use of language as well as the combination of these peculiarities, fosters understanding and empathy for music. Artistes are able to connect with friends and strangers, and members of the audience are allowed to know more about various cultures, thereby dismantling prejudices and promoting interconnectedness in the digital world.

The digital space encourages access to music, allowing anyone with internet connection to explore a vast tapestry of sounds, from any part of the world. It helps both the artistes and the audience to overcome the barriers created by time, space and language; connecting with new artistes, beliefs, values and cultures becomes pleasurable. Apart from exposing the audience to diverse sounds that resonate with their tastes, the digital space also becomes an interactive platform where the audience can interact with one another as well as the artistes, fostering a sense of community and breaking barriers at several levels. This helps to create a healthy and rich lifestyle for such individuals as they are exposed to a global soundscape where various cultures are appreciated.

Music, thus, acts as a stable ambassador for cultural integration. It aids mutual enlightenment and understanding by its method of displaying unique expressions and values of various cultures. Artistes also become more informed as they learn to blend traditions through innovative sounds that enhance interconnectedness in the digital space. This is possible because human beings have the ability to use language to express their feelings, desires and beliefs (Etuk & Urujzian, 2018). Human beings are fundamentally wired to enjoy music; music provides a route for a deep connection into the fabric of our being. It is a universal language that allows one to freely express joy, love, grief and other emotions. This is understandable, as according to Urujzian and Etuk (2024), language is a social phenomenon. Thus, through the instrumentality of language, infants' soothing lullabies are possible and anthems are created to unite nations, and music is able to provide an innate connection for people. Music helps to create memories and strengthen bonds that are beyond superficial interactions.

LITERATURE REVIEW

CultureTop of FormBottom of Form is a multidimensional concept that reflects the shared beliefs, values, customs, practices, norms, social behaviours and historical development peculiar to a group of people coexisting in a community (Kymlicka, 2001). In other words, it can be described as the complete way of life of a group of people domiciled in a given territory. Culture is dynamic and it is passed down from one generation to another through communication and education (Hendarin-ingrum, 2018). It contributes immensely to the development of the community and the wellness of individuals (Jagadisan, 2018). People's identity and creativeness are expressed through culture (Ngare, 2023; Makhmudova, 2022; Veronika et al., 2021 & Jagadisan, 2018).

Culture has a wide range of components namely, language (the primary means of communication which could be spoken, written or body language), customs and traditions (including rituals, ceremonies and practices that are transmitted from one generation to another, often tied to important events like weddings and rites of passage), art and music (innovative expressions that mirror cultural values and social issues such as visual arts, literature and performing arts), values and norms (fundamental beliefs that guide behaviour and social interactions), dressing, food and religion (Kire & Rajkumar, 2017; Muali, 2017).

Although culture is often seen as a cord that binds people together, nevertheless, the co-occurrence of different cultural norms and values could cause misunderstanding and conflict. UNICEF (2016: 8) defines conflict thus:

> *conflict involves a clash or struggle between groups who perceive that their needs, goals or strategies are incompatible, mutually exclusive or antagonistic. Conflict can involve contestation around demands, interests, collective memory, emotions, perceptions, values, beliefs, history, culture, behaviours, actions, symbols and power. Conflict can manifest from micro interactions to macro systems. It is a natural outcome of normal human interaction.*

Ethnic conflicts in Nigeria emanated from the amalgamation of the Southern and Northern Protectorates in 1914 by Sir Frederick Lord Luggard. Later, the north and the south regions, comprising over 250 ethnic groups with distinct languages, identities and traditions, were broadly stratified into Yoruba, Igbo and Hausa. A 'divide and rule' strategy was employed which led to conflict among the ethnic groups. The British colonialists also introduced a system of government that favoured certain ethnic groups so much so that they have an edge over others in terms of access to resources and opportunities. This introduced the spirit of rivalry and discord to the country (Abasili et al., 2023; Egwu, 2018; Osakwe, 2017; Oyadiran & Adesola, 2016; Badmus 2009).

As observed by Abasili et al. (2023), when individuals or communities base their identity on their ethnic affiliation, it resorts to conflict. In Nigeria, ethnic identity supersedes national identity. Nigerians identify themselves, first, as members of their ethnic groups, thereafter, as Nigerians. This view is corroborated with the report given by The Nigeria Social Cohesion Survey (2021) that 1 out of 3 Nigerians identifies themselves more with their ethnic affiliation than their nationality. In addition, each ethnic group (especially the major ones namely Yoruba, Hausa and Igbo) believes that its cultural values are superior to the other. This ethnocentrism has caused animosity, agitation for secession, religious intolerance, schism, conflict and war in Nigeria (Anele, 2023). Folarin et al. (2014) further note that while the major ethnic groups struggle to remain significant and retain power and authority, the minor ethnic groups continually clamour for identity, recognition, power division and the control of resources. Consequently, clashes and conflicts have been the order of the day in Nigeria.

The Nigerian Civil War (1967 – 1970) was an ethnic contention between the Igbo residing in Southeast Nigeria and the other ethnic groups in Nigeria, particularly the Hausa-Fulani who are domiciled in the north (Hurst, 2009). The Niger Delta agitations have been ongoing since the 1950s. Initially, this minority group felt sidelined, neglected and excluded from ruling the nation. The struggle became intense in 1958 when oil was produced for commercial purpose in the region with the indigenes demanding for control over the oil resources. Unfortunately, oil exploration in the region has led to the degradation of their environment (Ikelegbe 2005) which makes it impossible for them to go into agriculture; hence, they are left to wallow in poverty. As a result of that, there have been conflicts between the indigenes and Multinational Companies.

In the northern part of Nigeria, numerous clashes have also ensued between the northerners, who are predominantly Muslims, and southerners, who are largely Christians. The Almajiri which constitute the majority of the northerners are used as tools to trigger ethnic conflict in the north (Jacob, 2012 in Osakwe, 2017). In the Middle Belt, there have been contentions between Fulani herdsmen, who release their animals to graze, and farmers who struggle to protect their farmlands (Ehiane, 2024). In addition, the Boko Haram sect in the northeast have always been the sworn enemies of both government and the Christians. The sect has claimed more than 35,000 lives and displaced millions since it was founded in 2002 (Matfess, 2017). Nigeria has also experienced post-election conflicts resulting from the way politicians manipulate electorates during election based on their ethnic affiliation (Muhammad et al., 2023). Other ethnic conflicts that Nigeria has experienced since independence include conflicts between Ilaje and Ijaw Arogbo over resource control in the Southwest and South-South; Ile-Ife and Modakeke over Social Class in the Southwest; Aguleri and Umuleri over land in the Southeast of Nigeria; the

Zaki-biam, Jukun, Tivs and Fulani conflicts; the Hausa Fulani, Berom and Anaguta Crisis in Plateau State (Johnson, 2021; Osakwe, 2017) and so on.

In a bid to achieve national integration in Nigeria, the government has established different institutions and introduced different policies, programmes and initiatives. Some of them include Federalism (1954), which permits all regions to be represented in governance; NYSC Scheme (1973), which was established in 1973 with the aim of breaking down ethnic barricades among Nigerian youths; the establishment of Unity Schools; creation of regions, states and local governments; revenue sharing formula; the shift from parliamentarism to presidentialism and the prohibition of ethnic political parties (Owede, 2018; Edewor et al., 2014; Ukiwo, 2005).

However, the efforts of the government in ensuring national cohesion in Nigeria has been futile. Following the report of The Nigeria Social Cohesion Survey (2019), 65% of Nigerians believe the efforts of the Federal Government in ensuring social cohesion is poor. Osaghae (1998) notes that Nigerian government seem to be insensitive to the cultural diversity that exists in the country. This is supported by the report given by The Nigeria Social Cohesion Survey (2019) that 80% of Nigerians believe that their ethnic groups are treated unfairly by the government. Managing ethnic conflict is very complex that it requires the employment of different tactics. Osaghae (1998:1) affirms that government has been applying the same strategy in resolving all the ethnic conflicts in the country, thereby committing the error of "fallacy of oversimplification".

Edewor et al. (2014) aver that efforts made by the Nigerian government to promote national cohesion have intensified conflicts, posing significant barriers to unity and national development. Oyadiran and Adesola (2016) identify several persistent obstacles to national integration, including the unrelenting demands for resource control, constitutional amendments and disparities between minority and majority groups. Other issues include disputes over revenue allocation, unequal resource distribution, the actions of ethnic militias, disproportionate representation in the National Assembly, zoning and rotational presidency practices, as well as deep-rooted corruption. The government's inability to effectively address these concerns has given rise to various ethno-regional movements, such as the Indigenous People of Biafra (IPOB), Odua People's Congress (OPC), the Movement for the Emancipation of the Niger Delta (MEND) and the Arewa Consultative Forum (Owede, 2018). These challenges have rendered the slogan "unity in diversity" a mirage in Nigeria.

The Nigeria Social Cohesion Survey (2022) further underscores this decline in unity, revealing a drop in the Nigeria Social Cohesion Index (NSCI) from 44.2% in 2021 to 39.6% in 2022. This is well below the 50% threshold, signifying weak national cohesion. The survey attributes this decline to growing insecurity, the rise of separatist movements, intensified calls for restructuring and widespread public dissatisfaction. These factors have deepened divisions along ethnic, social, political, economic and religious lines, thereby undermining efforts to achieve national unity and peaceful coexistence.

As recommended by Asike (2019), Nigeria needs cultural purity. Edewor et al. (2014) suggest the need to understand, respect and accommodate our differences and employ innovative solutions to national challenges. Chukwudi (2024) proposed some measures the government can adopt in order to achieve cultural harmony. They include the promotion of inter-ethnic sporting activities, engagement of conflict mercenaries through employment, adoption of favourable economic policies, employment of proactive security measures and the incorporation of peace education programmes in the curriculum at all levels of education. Uhunmwuangho (2011) also suggests Western and modern Alternative Dispute Resolution (ADR) mechanism. They include good governance, effective communication, collaboration, negotiation, conciliation, mediation, arbitration, adjudication and crisis management.

In line with the above, further recommendations, as indicated in The Nigeria Social Cohesion Survey (2019), include the need to promote economic inclusion by ensuring equal access to opportunities and empowering vulnerable groups such as children, pregnant women, the elderly, and the poor. The government must also improve communication by clearly articulating its policies and programmes to all citizens to prevent misinformation and exclusion. Reforming the law enforcement system is crucial to building public trust; ensuring justice is not reserved for the privileged. Additionally, strengthening local governance and enhancing the accountability of civil society organisations will bring governance closer to the people. Lastly, encouraging citizen participation by creating avenues for communities to contribute to service delivery and national development will foster a deeper sense of ownership and belonging among Nigerians.

Furthermore, Balogun and Obosi (2018) note that national unity requires the fair and just inclusion of all ethnic groups, especially minorities, in national affairs. A shift in policy is also necessary to build a stronger national identity; for instance, replacing “state of origin” with “state of residence” in official documentation would encourage unity beyond ethnic lines. National integration can be deepened when Nigerians are allowed to hold public office in any region of the country, promoting a sense of belonging regardless of ethnicity. Strengthening social cohesion is equally vital and can be achieved through equitable distribution of wealth, justice for all, a shared national vision, reduced income inequality and balanced development across all regions.

Cultural integration promotes social cohesion, particularly in a multicultural society like Nigeria where it is essential for national harmony. Cultural integration entails the coming together of people from different ethnic backgrounds to share common values, practices and social norms while retaining elements of their individual culture. It involves blending different cultures, thereby encouraging mutual acclimatisation and intercultural communication (Edwards, 2024). Cultural integration requires compromise as individuals or groups involved have to adjust their characters and points of view to accommodate the cultural norms of others (Kuran & Sandholm, 2008). It is bidirectional in that the major group does not impose its culture on the minor group; rather, they both contribute to the budding culture. It requires the individuals or groups to interact regularly, encouraging dynamism and acclimatisation, which are the requirements for overcoming global challenges like migration and technological development (Edwards, 2024).

Music plays a vital role in cultural integration. Oehrle (1996: 99) cited in Crooke (2024) declares that music promotes cultural harmony by "helping us to understand the world's cultures and their diversities; it develops multicultural sensitivity… it is a way of breaking down the barriers and prejudices which isolate people from one another: a way of moving towards a culture of tolerance". For instance, when one listens to music from different cultures, one becomes emotionally connected with those cultures and this could break down cultural barricades and encourage tolerance (Neuroscience News). Vougioukalou et al. (2019) observe that musical activities within a heterogeneous community can be a tool for collaboration and social inclusion. In addition, those who participate in music programmes have confirmed that music gives a sense of belonging. It also promotes cultural intermingling (Parncutt & Dorfer, 2010). A good example is the adaptation of rap music in China; a way of indigenising foreign influence (Xu & Liu, 2019). Music also has therapeutic power; it brings healing and resolution in the midst of ethnic strains (Sharma, 2023). Music is, therefore, a universal language that breaks down ethnic barriers (Clarke, 2015).

Apart from the functions listed above, music also enhances the dissemination of information. It aids the processes of learning and retaining important pieces of information; it acts as a mnemonic device. This is because the melody, rhythm and rhyme that accompany music make it easy to remember even complex issues that they carry. This is not restricted to any age; even kids are encouraged to learn at any early age through songs. They are exposed to melodious and creative alphabet songs and educational jingles, making it possible to pass across foundational knowledge in a format that is funny and engaging. These help to transform facts that could have been seen as dry and uninteresting into catchy and memorable messages. This explains why music is a potent tool in educational settings and public service announcements.

The function of music is aided by the musical instruments which are used to provide melody and harmony to the song. The instruments act as storytelling tools and cultural messengers. Different tools often carry specific cultural connotations representing periods, social classes, traditions and so on. Through their unique playing styles, they communicate cultural identity and other important messages. They also provide a background for narratives and enrich the understanding of the messages being conveyed. Sometimes, the musical instruments provide additional layers of meaning to the message, thereby enhancing the listener's attention and engagement.

In addition to its ability to engage its audience effectively, music also helps to transmit cultural values. It acts as a vehicle to communicate and reinforce societal norms. Several music genres, at one time or the other, have been employed to disseminate the message of peace, social justice, love and unity. The lyrics are intentionally employed to communicate certain beliefs and attitudes. Visual aesthetics and musical styles also help to represent cultural identities. All the various musical elements are intentionally created and arranged in a way to promote inclusivity, advocate social justice, encourage equality and equity. Members of the audience are, thus, exposed to how music acts as a cultural mirror, shaping the values of its society.

Music in this digital age has transcended physical boundaries. Its new home is situated in the vast landscape of online platforms. Most songs that used to be confined to cassettes and discs have migrated online, gaining a global audience. This migration has not only aided unprecedented longevity, it has also amplified the influence of music. In recent times, technology has made people to migrate to the virtual space to promote their products and services. Music artistes are not left out of this paradigm shift. Instead of buying discs, people go online (YouTube, Boom, Spotify) to download their songs of choice. Some artistes even have their channels that have become monetised. In the light of this, Yinka Ayefele's *Mo M'ope Mi Wa* (I Offer My Praise) was downloaded on YouTube and viewed with multimodal lens. Multimodal discourse goes beyond language; it investigates how different modes of expression such as visual elements, body language and sound are used to convey meaning and enhance the understanding of the decoder. The present study examined how Yinka Ayefele's multicultural song: *Mo M'ope Mi Wa* (I Offer My Praise) blended various cultures (Yoruba, Igbo and Efik) using cultural elements (such as language, dance steps and dressing) to promote cultural integration in the digital space.

STATEMENT OF THE PROBLEM

Previous studies on gospel music have predominantly focused on the sociolinguistic functions of code-mixing and code-switching as dominant linguistic practices. Scholars such as Motito et al. (2025) and Idowu-Faith (2011), for instance, have examined how gospel artistes like Yinka Ayefele, Monique, and G-Wills blend English with indigenous languages such as Yoruba, Igbo, and Hausa. This linguistic blending serves various communicative purposes, including connecting with diverse audiences, expressing complex emotions and preserving indigenous cultures.

Alemede (2022) further reveal that multilingual songs are more appreciated and accepted by audiences than mono-lingual ones, contributing to the artistes' wider reach, popularity and personal development. Such multilingual approaches not only enhance the commercial viability of gospel music but also foster unity among ethnic groups, promote a shared sense of belonging and accelerate the growth of the gospel music industry in Nigeria. Code-mixing and code-switching in songs, therefore, function as powerful tools for emotional expression, identity affirmation, broader audience engagement and socio-cultural integration.

Crooke et al. (2021) proposed the Intercultural Music Engagement (ICME) framework, which conceptualises music as a dynamic platform for empathy, communication and community-building across cultural divides. According to this framework, music becomes a site for negotiating intercultural understanding when it draws on both universal sonic elements and culturally specific expressions.

Despite these insights, the potential of music to actively foster cultural integration through multimodality remains underexplored. The digital age, through music videos, streaming platforms and social media, has transformed gospel music from a localised religious practice into a globally accessible, multimodal cultural artifact. However, little is known about how multimodal elements such as imagery and subtitles function to foster cultural inclusion. This is particularly relevant in contemporary Nigeria, where diverse cultural groups coexist amid persistent disparities and notions of cultural superiority.

This study, therefore, examined how Yinka Ayefele's video song titled *Mo M'ope Mi Wa* (I Offer My Praise) could serve as a tool for bridging cultural divisions and promoting inclusivity. The multimodal approach provides a deeper insight into how music transcends linguistic and cultural barriers to contribute to the building of the society. By that, the nexus between Cultural Linguistics and Semiotics is unveiled.

THEORETICAL FRAMEWORK

This study utilises Gunther Kress and Theo van Leeuwen's (1996) 'Visual Social Semiotic Theory' for its analysis. The social semiotic approach to multimodality is appropriate for the analysis of this study because it offers a robust lens to understand how meaning is constructed and communicated through various modes within a multimodal text. It is suitable to deconstruct how Yinka Ayefele has been able to achieve cultural integration within this digital space. According to this theory, meaning is not inherent in a text; it is rather constructed through cultural texts and social interaction. It allows the exploration of how different modes synergise to make meaning. The theory provides an opportunity to analyse how signs (visual, verbal and even auditory) construct and pass across meaning within particular social contexts. It is, thus, beyond analysing a text based on its linguistic elements.

This theory shows that multimodality is beyond the former focus on language. It recognises the contributions made by other modes of communication in meaning making. Some of these modes are textual (written language, layout, topography); distance (the arrangement of elements within a space); visual (images, photographs, colour and other graphic elements); audio (spoken language, music) and gestures (body language, facial expressions). Kress and van Leeuwen's model is an adaptation of Halliday's ideational, interpersonal and textual functions. For Kress and van Leeuwen, every image performs three functions in the creation of meanings. These are representational function, interpersonal function and compositional function. These functions are carried out by the structure and interaction of the participants.

The Representational Function

This is the representation of the world as it is experienced. This is done by identifying the actor (subject), vector (action) and/or goal (object) in representations.

The Interpersonal Metafunction

This shows the relationship between the producer of various signs and the receiver of the signs. As a result, this function represents the relationships that involve the initiator/creator of the communication process, the viewer and the objects represented.

The Compositional Metafunction

This metafunction has to do with how the various signs created for communication come together to form a unified whole. Sinc the message is always towards a particular direction, the signs are expected to cohere with one another, as well as with the context of production.

This study adopted this theory with particular attention to the interpersonal and compositional metafunctions. While the former helped to understand how cultural integration in the digital space is achieved through the interactions of the individuals represented, the latter showed how the various objects and subjects were brought together to communicate in a unified way. They, thus, enhanced a comprehensive exploration of the multimodal discourse. The individuals, objects and ideas depicted are known as participants. As identified by Kress and van Leeuwen (1996: 48), there are two types of participants involved in this kind of communication. They are interactive participants and represented participants. The interactive participants are the participants who speak, write, make images, listen, read and view images.

The represented participants, on the other hand, are the subject matter of the communication process. They are the people, places, things, ideas around which the communication revolve.

In examining the interactions that exist between the participants, three systems of doing this are examined. They include contact, social distance and perspective. When the represented participants look at the viewers directly, a form of contact is established. This type of contact is known as 'demand' as the direct gaze demands an action from the viewer. It can also be an offer. This is when no direct eye contact is established between the represented participant and the viewer. The attention is on something else, thereby inviting the viewers, in an indirect way, to pay attention to the object.

Social distance is another system that explains the relationship between participants. This is the distance from which represented participants are portrayed. The distance determines whether the picture portrayed will be close-up, medium shot or long shot. The third system is perspective and this shows the interactive participants' attitudes towards the represented participants. This can be at the horizontal level which indicates involvement or detachment. At the vertical level, the producer can be placed at a high, low or eye level with the represented participant. The compositional function is obtained from the arrangement of various elements. It examines how the interactive and represented participants are portrayed to form a unified whole. This is done through information value, salience and framing.

METHODOLOGY

This study adopted insights from the Social Semiotic Approach to multimodality by Gunther Kress and Theo van Leeuwen to examine Yinka Ayefele's *Mo M'ope Mi Wa* (I Offer My Praise), a video song that displays the fusion of the Yoruba, Igbo and the Akwa-Ibom cultures. This methodology drew upon the interplay of different modes of communication to investigate how cultures are integrated and the unified front expressed within the digital context. The study carried out a comprehensive study on how Ayefele has been able to synergise the elements of different cultures to communicate and foster understanding. The primary data of the study, Yinka Ayefele's *Mo M'ope Mi Wa* (I Offer My Praise), was downloaded from YouTube. The use of language as well as visuals in the song was examined. The interplay of the various cultural elements was explored from the multimodal angle. Since music now flourishes in the online space, this study leveraged on YouTube to download its data. Today's music transcends physical boundaries. The fact that a song that incorporates the lyrics of one culture, the dressing of another as well as the dance moves of yet another is available online spreads the message of cultural integration faster than any offline source.

The lyrics of the songs were analysed by examining the themes, language use and cultural references, all of which contributed to the construction of meaning. The musical arrangement of the various cultural elements was also explored to show how the three cultures were integrated and the impact of the combination on the song. Beyond aesthetics, the visual elements employed were examined to understand how images were mainly used in the song to present the cultures as one. The song's online presence enhances the audience's easy access to the song. The opportunity to watch this type of song online raises awareness about its existence and makes it possible for many that would have missed getting to see it to watch and enjoy. The online presence also provides an opportunity for people to see the possibility of cultural integration. Though it has been presented theoretically by various stakeholders, the availability of this type of song reinforces the fact that though there are different cultures in the country, beauty can be achieved through diversity.

For the study, music was intentionally chosen as the instrument because of its ability to break barriers created by language, time and space. Human relation is enhanced through digital music because it helps to create a shared emotional digital landscape. Regardless of where music is played, it creates a common ground for the audience to connect, thereby breaking barriers and fostering a sense of shared experience. When issues that border on national peace and security are concerned, music is one way by which people can be easily reached as it helps to inspire dialogue, enlighten members of the audience about different values and perspectives, broaden people's horizons. Ultimately, it enhances the creation and sustenance of a society that is enlightened, empathetic and inclusive. Members of the audience are reminded that though they may be created as members of different cultures, they belong to a community that thrives on shared humanity. To Etuk and Akpan (2023:1), "music has a greater appeal to the current generation of people".

DATA ANALYSIS AND DISCUSSION OF FINDINGS

Based on the objectives of the study, five categories were formed to examine various angles to the song.

i. The power of genre blending

The song blends Yoruba Jùjú music with cultural elements of Akwa Ibom and Igbo culture. The song initially gives the idea of one that is only set in Yoruba. This opinion, however, is forced to change when the Artiste and Song Writer, Tinka Ayefele, comes in dressed in Igbo wears. As a Yoruba man, one would normally expect him to be dressed in 'Agbada' to serve as a complement to the song. However, this interactive participant is seen as complementing his Yoruba song with the dress of an Igbo man. The result is a unique hybrid genre that speaks to the cultures depicted. Apart from this, the song is decorated with Efik dancers who are involved in Ekombi dance. The overall effect is a blend which signifies oneness and togetherness. The song as a result appeals to several audiences, including individuals whose cultures are not represented but are drawn by the level of inclusivity depicted in the song. Guitars, a keyboard and drums are played to appeal to the civilised audience who values exposure. Music fosters national integration and fosters social cohesion in Nigeria, especially among the youths who constitute a significant part of the population (Adewumi & Adejumo, 2024). These are depicted in Figure 1.

Figure 1. The Yoruba Artiste comes in dressed in an Igbo attire

During the performance of the song, Ayefele exclaims in Ibibio several times to show his excitement. The choice of the language communicates a habitual practice. It also signifies respect and inclusivity. Ayefele's distinct and expert merry voice in the delivery of Ibibio phrases demonstrates an effort to transcend cultural boundaries and connect with audiences from different backgrounds. Thus, the differences in culture that could have served as an obstacle are creatively utilised and turned into binders. Showcasing the costumes of different cultures creates a healthy dialogue, of the culture, for the other cultures. The appreciation for the other cultures is clearly shown and seen as aesthetics instead of mere differences. The overall visual representation is a formidable tool in promoting unity, understanding and acceptance. A synergised appearance is presented by the arrangement of the dancers and the lead singer. While the dancers keep dancing around Ayefele, he sits at the middle with his microphone/playing a keyboard as an accompaniment. Figure 2 shows the happy image of the Artiste as he sings a Yoruba song, dressed in an Igbo attire, singing into a microphone and playing a keyboard.

Figure 2. Blending various genres in visual representation

The information value of the arrangement is enhanced by the fact that it is on the left which to Kress and van Leeuwen indicates a given silhouetted that the crowd is used to. The idea of the arrangement as the usual is enhanced by the soft smiles of the dancers. Both the male and female dancers appear happy and excited. Though they are dressed in different costumes (Efik), they are able to maintain a perfect rhythm to the song and the keyboard being played. The effect gives a beautiful blend where every part is a necessity.

ii. Beyond language barriers

The use of various languages depicts intentionality in carrying along several cultures. Language, a strong tool of every culture, is employed for the purpose of inclusivity. This intentional act helps to encourage people from various cultures represented and not represented to enjoy the song. The song is set in Yoruba but throughout the performance, English subtitles are displayed on the screen, making it easy for non-Yoruba speakers to follow what is being said. For individuals whose languages are not exactly spoken, the performance is framed in such a way that such cultures are represented in dressing. To foster cultural connections, intentional efforts towards translation are made. The salience of this is ensured by the foregrounding of English subtitles throughout the performance. To reinforce this, it is framed to sharply contrast with green carpet that is laid. As seen in Figure 3, the video is strategically planned to ensure a synergy. The same material is used to cover all the tables and the black and white cloth shares affinity with the appearance of the English subtitles, reinforcing the overall effect and the sharp contrast created with the green rug.

Figure 3. Overcoming language barriers through subtitling and framing

The musical video opens with a royal entrance of the artiste which is met with applause, exhilaration and a standing ovation by people at the scene. These individuals on the scene of the musical set who are dressed in multiple/different colours, to represent the multicultural/ethnic Nigerian society, all rise in unison to welcome the artiste. This act of togetherness buttresses the need for cultural integration. The royal entrance of the artiste is in sync with the gold colour adorned by the dancers (of Efik culture) in the opening scene of the musical video. The gold colour signifies royalty and prestige, extolling the virtues of the multi-ethnic Nigerian society usually dubbed "the giant of Africa" while the 'Ekombi' dance choreographed by the dancers is an art form usually performed to welcome important dignitaries or to begin an important discussion – such as the push for cultural integration.

Figure 4. Beyond the barriers created by language

The female dancers are clad with a blouse which covers their chest, leaving their shoulders and stomach bare. Another material is also tied around their waist to the knee level. The male dancers are bare-bodied but for a wrapper which they tie around their waist to a little below the knee level. The dressing style is an act of openness – to show that they have nothing to hide as well as depict the welcoming nature of the culture. The act preaches the need for transparency from all individuals, irrespective of their ethnic affiliation to ensure cultural harmony and integration. Music is one of society's weapons of offence and defence; it regulates human conduct (Ojukwu, 2017). The kinesics of the dancers involve frequent turns from left to right or even wholesome turns to ensure that all members of the audience are encapsulated in the mellifluousness. Thus, through the performance, everyone is encouraged to participate in cultural integration and by extension, nation building.

iii. Visual storytelling

The combination of music, lyrics, multimodal elements and the digital platform allows for a comprehensive multimodal storytelling experience that keeps the audiences active and happy. This enhances their understanding of the cultures depicted. The whole performance is in two phases. The first part is presented as a prologue where the happy lead singer comes in and is welcomed by everyone. The easy rapport between the interactive participants (the producer and the viewer as depicted on the stage) is established by their easy smiles and handshakes. Before the lead speaker gets to them, they are all seen to be sitting in groups to depict easy communication. The tables and chairs signify relaxation and sophistication. They are placed on the right to signify a new experience that is yet to become common. The fact that this new arrangement is so easily treated communicates possibilities. Despite the fact that the individuals were pretty strangers, they could sit together and enjoy one another's company. This shows that the two cultures comprise several cultural and possible individuals, integration and growth the necessary steps if we would only take the necessary steps. Ayefele dances in each strictly and sits with several members of each group to show that he values them.

Figure 5. The Prologue (The Artiste is happily welcomed by his Guests)

After ensuring the comfortability of the guests, the Artiste makes conscious efforts to include the audience with his invitation to join the trend. Figure 6 shows how the Artiste establishes a contact with the viewer. This establishes the creation of a cordial relationship between the interactive participants (the producer and the viewer). The contact is a direct gaze and an image act, according to Kress and van Leeuwen is established. The producer uses this to demand a relationship with the viewer. The sincereity of the invitation is enhanced by the soft smile given by the Artiste. As if he feels the need to reassure the viewer of his sincerity, he gesticulates, inviting the viewer to join in the celebration and turns his back to join the dancers. Though his back is turned, the viewer does not feel left out because of the cordiality that has been established.

Figure 6. The Artiste demands the viewer's participation

iv. Digital platforms as cultural hubs

The availability of the song in the digital space allows individuals from different parts of the world to be connected by their shared cultural heritage. This facilitates cross-cultural exchange. The online presence helps the song to transcend boundaries created by space, language, beliefs, traditions and cultures. The overall effect helps in projecting the song as a cultural anthem that resonates with several audiences/ cultures. The fact that the song is available on various digital platforms like You-Tube, Spotify allows the cultures represented to engage with the song as well as share their experiences. This helps to foster dialogue, relationship among cultures and break down stereotypes.

As at the time this data was obtained, the song already had about 477,199 views.

v. Breaking down stereotypes

Nigeria, just like many other countries in the world, is created from diverse cultures, with the attendant beauty and uniqueness of each. Attaining a truly unified and sustainable future for the global world requires collective efforts, where the other cultures are not just tolerated but appreciated and embraced. Music is a veritable tool through which the language, beliefs and other cultural elements can be seen and valued. This study has shown the power of music in achieving the Sustainable

Development Goals (SDGs) in the digital age. It is, thus, depicted as the catalyst for global understanding. While music generally enhances the realisation of SDG 4 (Quality Education), SDG 5 (Gender Equality), this song enhances the realisation of SDG 10 (reduced inequality), SDG 16 (Peace, Justice and Strong Institutions) as well as SDG 17 (Partnerships for the Goals).

By celebrating cultural diversity and integration through music, inclusivity is promoted. This allows the creation of a more inclusive society where differences are valued and respected. Once this happens, inequality becomes reduced and social unity is promoted. In addition, music has the potential to promote peace as it bridges gaps and paves way for dialogue. This provides the needed ground for empathetic listening, understanding and reconciliation. As seen in the study, music is potentially collaborative. It affords partnerships among artistes, groups, communities, cultures and organisations. To achieve this, all the parties involved become intentional to understand the other person. The result, just like the song depicts, is a beautiful blend of different angles, beliefs and cultures. Once this is achieved in music, the ground is set for other collaborations, resulting in a society where individuals respect one another. Music has the power to birth cultural integration and advance the SDGs. The creation of a more harmonious and equitable world is possible through the transformative power of music available in the digital space, the celebration of the diversity of cultures through music and the embrace of cultural exchange.

In a world that has become global, the digital space serves as a catalyst to amplify the impact of music. Online music communities, the social media and different platforms have helped in connecting people across the globe. This, in turn, has facilitated cultural exchange. Cultures of diverse cultures are shared on various digital platforms for the pleasure of the audience. This has enhanced intercultural understanding and enlightened artistes on the beauty of collaborations with other artistes from different backgrounds. This has the advantage to gradually but surely erase segregation. More artistes are becoming open to collaborations that they used to think were either impossible or fruitless through the access the digital space gives to several successful ones. As a result, music has not only promoted accessibility, it has also enhanced inclusivity, by breaking down barriers and promoting cultural exchange on a global scale. The resultant effect of these are awareness and dialogue. Discussions and debates bordering on music are facilitated through digital spaces, prejudices are challenged and a healthy global world is being formed.

CONCLUSION

The study has shown that music is more than a means of entertainment. Yinka Ayefele's *Mo M'ope Mi Wa* (I Offer My Praise) is not a mere song. It is a testament to the power music wields to overcome language barriers, transcend cultural boundaries and forge lasting connections in the digital age. The song presents a vibrant melody that fuses Yoruba Jùjú, Igbo dressing and Akwa Ibom Highlife. It is a cultural bridge that is skillfully crafted to weave together three distinct musical cultures. The power of the song lies in its multimodal angle. Though the song is primarily set in Yoruba, nothing ties it down to just this culture. Instead, the producer carefully blended phrases and costumes from Efik, Igbo costumes as well as dance steps from Efik to ensure a healthy and synergised whole. The producer's intentionality in ensuring all the elements work in unison to create a vibrant and rich tapestry of diverse cultures is loud. While the uniqueness of each mode remains clear, all the cultural elements are brought together to create a harmonious narrative of unity and shared experience.

The song shows how the participants are allowed to perform naturally, without any feeling of intimidation. This song is a strong testament to the beauty that lies in diversity. The presentation attests to the fact that individuals can remain culturally-sensitive individuals in a healthy way. Integration, through the study, has been shown not to rely on the assimilation of the other person's culture, but rather a sincere appreciation for the unique strength that resides in the beliefs and ideas of each culture. The song's presence on digital platforms like YouTube and Spotify creates a wave of cultural exchange and fosters dialogue and future collaborations. It affords the song to reach the world and encourages the realisation of SDG 10 (reduced inequality), SDG 16 (Peace, Justice and Strong Institutions) as well as SDG 17 (Partnerships for the Goals).

The digital space is a fertile ground for cultural integration. When opportunities to make a positive impact are judiciously utilised, the results can be positively overwhelming. Its availability in the digital space encourages fans from Yoruba, Igbo and Akwa Ibom cultures to engage with the song and celebrate the richness it presents. Through it, music is able to overcome the barriers created by geography and language. It also suggests endless possibilities. Its perfect blend of several cultures is a beacon of hope of better days for a multiethnic nation like Nigeria. It reminds the citizens that while the differences and uniqueness of each culture cannot be ignored, they can be converted to strength and a means of unity through music. Through inclusivity of the 'other', this study has shown that music can become the universal language of unity. It is the fuel on which cultural integration feeds.

REFERENCES

Abasili, K. N., Ezeneme, E. V., & Nwokike, C. E. (2023). Analyzing the roots of ethnic conflict in Nigeria: an in-depth examination. *GSJ, 11*(10).

Adewumi, A. P., & Adejumo, D. O. (2024). Harnessing the harmonious sounds of Naija music as a tool for ethnic integration in Nigeria. *Kashere Journal of Politics and International Relations*, *2*(1), 294–304.

Alemede, E. O. (2022). The Impact of the use of Code-Mixing in Nigerian Gospe l Music. *Accelerando: Belgrade Journal of Music and Dance*, *7*, 2.

Anele, C. (2023). Ethnocentrism in multicultural society: Intrigues, challenges and way forward in the Nigerian society. *Journal of Health. Applied Sciences and Management*, *6*(3), 74–81. DOI: 10.4314/johasam.v6i3.10

Asike, J. C. (2019). Managing multicultural societies: Nudging towards a Cultural Purity in Nigeria. *Global Journal of Archaeology and Anthropology*, *9*(3), 72–77.

Badmus, I. A. (2009). Under reconstruction: ethnicity, ethnic nationalism, and the future of the Nigerian state. *Verfassung Und Recht in Übersee/Law and politics in Africa, Asia and Latin America*, 212-239.

Balogun, S., & Obosi, A. (2018). Role of cultural identity and social cohesion in national development: Nigeria in perspective. *Nigerian Journal of Social Psychology*, *1*(1), 54–62.

Bennett, D. (2005). Music as a tool for social change. *International Journal of Music Education*, *23*(1), 49–62.

Chukwudi, J. F. (2024). Inter-ethnic violence in Nigeria and the proposed solution to address them. [SSHJ]. *Social Science and Humanities Journal*, *8*(04), 34795–34806. DOI: 10.18535/sshj.v8i04.997

Clarke, E., DeNora, T., & Vuoskoski, J. (2015). Music, empathy and cultural understanding. *Physics of Life Reviews*, *15*, 61–88. DOI: 10.1016/j.plrev.2015.09.001 PMID: 26419700

Crooke, A. H. D., Thompson, W. F., Fraser, T., & Davidson, J. (2024). Music, social cohesion, and intercultural understanding: A conceptual framework for intercultural music engagement. *Musicae Scientiae*, *28*(1), 18–38. DOI: 10.1177/10298649231157099

Edewor, P., Aluko, Y., & Folarin, S. (2014). Managing ethnic and cultural diversity for national integration in Nigeria. *Developing Country Studies*, *4*(6), 70–76.

Edwards (2024). The Importance of cultural integration. https://easysociology.com/sociology-of-culture/the-importance-of-cultural-integration/

Egwu, J. U. (2018). Federalism and national integration in Nigeria: Issues and challenges. *IDOSR Journal of Humanities and Social Sciences*, *3*(1), 151–163.

Ehiane, S. O., Zondi, L. P., & Gumede, M. (2024). *Conflict of survival between Fulani pastoralists and farmers in the wake of climate change Nigeria. Engagement of Africa in Conflict Dynamics and Peace Architectures*. Springer Nature Singapore.

Etuk, J., & Akpan, I. (2023). Language and gender ideology in Techno's 'Woman'. *Sapientia Global Journal of Arts* [SGOJAHDS]. *Humanities and Development Studies*, *6*(4), 69–80.

Etuk, J. A., & Urujzian, V. (2018). Language and ideology in number plate slogans of the 36 states of Nigeria and Abuja: A new horizon. *The Intuition*, *8*(1), 1–11.

Folarin, S. F., Olanrewaju, I. P., & Ajayi, M. L. Y. (2014). *Cultural plurality, national integration and the security dilemma in Nigeria*. Covenant University Journal of Politics and International Affairs.

Henderningrum, R. (2018). Budaya Dan Komunikasi Kesehatan (Studi Pandangan Kesehatan Pada Masyarakat Sunda Dalam Tradisi Makan Lalapan). *LUGAS Jurnal Komunikasi*, *2*(1), 13–19. DOI: 10.31334/jl.v2i1.118

Hurst, R. (2009). *Nigerian Civil War (1967 – 1970)*. BlackPast.org. https://www.blackpast.org/global-african-history/nigerian-civil-war-1967-1970/

Idowu-Faith, B. O. (2011). Language attitudes and communicative realities of code-mixing in contemporary Nigerian gospel music. *Interdisciplinary Discourses in Language and Communication*, 164.

Ikelegbe, A. (2005). The economy of conflict in the oil-rich Niger Delta region of Nigeria. *Nordic Journal of African Studies*, *14*(2), 208–234.

Jacob, R. I. (2012). A historical survey of ethnic conflict in Nigeria. *Asian Social Science*, *8*(4), 13. DOI: 10.5539/ass.v8n4p13

Johnson, A. (2021). Causes and consequences of ethnic conflict in Nigeria. *International Journal of Advanced Research in Social Sciences. Environmental Studies & Technology.*, *6*(1), 32–42.

Kire, K., & Rajkumar, P. (2017). Culture influence on consumer behavior. *IJARIIE*, *3*, 6121.

Kress, G., & van Leeuwen, T. (1996). *Reading images: the grammar of visual design*. Routledge.

Kuran, T., & Sandholm, W. H. (2008). Cultural integration and its discontents. *The Review of Economic Studies*, *75*(1), 201–228. DOI: 10.1111/j.1467-937X.2007.00469.x

Kymlicka, W. (2001). *Politics in the vernacular: nationalism, multiculturalism, and citizenship*. Oxford University Press. DOI: 10.1093/0199240981.001.0001

Matfess, H. (2017). *Boko Haram: history and context*. Oxford Research Encyclopedia of African History.

Motito, F., Nwabudike, C., & Oni, F. (2025). Code-mixing in the gospel songs of some Nigerian music artistes. *An International Refereed Research Journal of English Studies and Culture*, *13*, 90–107.

Muali, C. (2017). Rasionalitas Konsepsi Budaya Nusantara Dalam Menggagas Pendidikan Karakter Bangsa Multikultural. *Jurnal Islam Nusantara*, *1*(1), 105–117. DOI: 10.33852/jurnalin.v1i1.64

Muhammad, A., Egye, A. U., & Etim, P. P. (2023). Electoral process and national integration in Nigeria: An analysis of 2019 general election. *International Journal of Research and Innovation in Social Science*, *7*(4), 250–262. DOI: 10.47772/IJRISS.2023.7420

Ngare, L. L. (2023). Globalization, cultural identity and social cohesion: a Nigerian philosophical perspective. *AKU: An African Journal of Contemporary Research*, 4(4).

Oehrle, E. (1996). Intercultural education through music: Towards a culture of tolerance. *British Journal of Music Education*, *13*(2), 95–100. DOI: 10.1017/S0265051700003077

Ojukwu, E. V. (2017). Relevance of music in social stability and security challenges in Nigeria. *AFRREV IJAH An International Journal of Arts and Humanities*, *6*(2), 98–105. DOI: 10.4314/ijah.v6i3.8

Olaifa, L. T., & Oyebanji, O. F. (2023). The semiotics of the logos of selected universities in southwestern Nigeria. In Taiwo, R., Idowu-Faith, B., & Ajiboye, S. (Eds.), *Transformation of higher education through institutional online spaces* (pp. 206–223). IGI Global., DOI: 10.4018/978-1-6684-8122-6.ch012

Osaghae, E. (1998). Managing multiple minority problems in a divided society: The Nigerian experience. *The Journal of Modern African Studies*, *36*(1), 1–24. DOI: 10.1017/S0022278X9700267X

Osakwe, O. M. (2017). A case study on the causes of ethnic conflict within Nigeria. *An Independent Study Submitted for the award of Degree of Master of Arts in Peace Studies and Diplomacy to Siam University, Bangkok, Thailand.*

Owede Kosioma, E. (2018). Citizenship education for national integration and cohesion in Nigeria. *British Journal of Education. Learning and Development Psychology*, *1*(1), 37–45.

Oyadiran, P., & Adeshola, A. J. (2017). National integration and democratic consolidation in Nigeria. *African Educational Research Journal*, *5*(2), 114–119.

Parncutt, R., & Dorfer, A. (2011). The role of music in the integration of cultural minorities. *Music and the Mind: Essays in Honour of John Sloboda*, *379*, 21. DOI: 10.1093/acprof:osobl/9780199581566.003.0019

Sharma, M. (2023). Sonny's Blues": The dream variation and cultural integration through music. *Bon Voyage*, *5*(1), 83–90. DOI: 10.3126/bovo.v5i1.64376

The Nigeria Social Cohesion Survey (2019)_https://africapolling.org/wp-content/uploads/2020/01/Social-Cohesion-Report_1.pdf

The Nigeria Social Cohesion Survey (2021)_https://africapolling.org/wp-content/uploads/2021/12/API-Social-Cohesion-Report.pdf

The Nigeria Social Cohesion Survey (2022)_https://www.proshare.co/articles/the-nigeria-social-cohesion-survey-report-2022?menu=Reports&classification=Read&category=Nigerian%20Economy

Uhunmwuangho, S. O., & Epelle, A. (2011). Challenges and solutions to ethno-religious conflicts in Nigeria: Case study of the Jos crises. *Journal of Sustainable Development in Africa*, *13*(5), 109–124.

UNICEF. (2016). Guide to conflict analysis._https://www.unicef.org/media/96581/file/Guide-to-Conflict-Analysis.pdf

Urujzian, V., & Etuk, J. A. (2024). A lexico-semantic analysis of selected songs of Wizkid. *Sapientia Global Journal of Arts* [SGOJAHDS]. *Humanities and Development Studies*, *7*(1), 313–324.

Veronika, M., Firman, F., & Ahmad, R. (2021). Conceptual analysis of the relationship between culture and education. *SCHOULID: Indonesian Journal of School Counseling*, *1*(1), 1–12. DOI: 10.23916/08740011

Vougioukalou, S., Dow, R., Bradshaw, L., & Pallant, T. (2019). Wellbeing and integration through community music: The role of improvisation in a music group of refugees, asylum seekers and local community members. *Contemporary Music Review*, *38*(5), 533–548. DOI: 10.1080/07494467.2019.1684075

Xu, Z., & Liu, X. (2019). A linguo-cultural approach to the integration of Hip-hop culture with Chinese Culture---taking Rap music as an example. *International Journal of Literature and Arts*, *12*(2), 165–171. https://neurosciencenews.com/music-body-emotion-25664/. DOI: 10.11648/j.ijla.20190706.16

KEY TERMS AND DEFINITIONS

Identity: The quality of being the same

Community: A group sharing common characteristics such as the same language, law, religion or tradition

Tradition: A part of culture that is passed from person to person or generation to generation

Music: A series of sounds organised in time, usually employing some combination of harmony, melody, rhythm, tempo, and so on, often to convey a mood

Conflict: A clash or disagreement, often violent, between two or more opposing groups or individuals

Ethnic group: A group of people who identify with one another, especially on the basis of ancestral, national, linguistic, cultural, historical or religious ground

Ethnic minority: A group of people who have a different ethnicity, religion, language or culture from that of the majority of people in the place where they live

Nation: A historically constituted, stable community of people, formed based on a common language territory, economic life, ethnicity/psychological make-up manifested in a common culture

Government: The body with the power to make and/or enforce laws to control a country, land area, people or organisation

Barricade: An obstacle or barrier

Cohesion: The state of working together

Harmony: Agreement or accord

Diversity: The quality of being different

Online: Connected to the internet

YouTube: A video-sharing website

Chapter 13
"What Did You Just Say?": A Critical Multimodal Discourse Analysis of Selected Online Comedy Skits

Moji Ajibike Olateju
https://orcid.org/0000-0002-2170-6390
Obafemi Awolowo University, Ile-Ife, Nigeria

ABSTRACT

This chapter has examined the meaning-making potentials of selected online weekend comedy skits using the tools of Critical Multimodal Discourse Analysis, drawing on the theoretical frameworks by Fairclough (1989/1995) and Kress and van Leeuwen (2006). Critical discourse analysis (CDA) examines the nexus or relationship between language, power and social inequality. The data is by Busymouth titled 'Mr. President facing flood challenges' and 'Busymouth as Akpan shamed his ex.' In the short pieces, the hopeless social, economic and political situation of an African country are presented. The findings reveal that the socio-economic and political situation that have become life threatening for the poor masses have no end in sight, yet trivialized by the President who represents the government at all levels. The bad economic situation has also led to character failure and break in mutual relationships which are some of the indices of a corrupt society.

INTRODUCTION

In analyzing spoken and written language, Stubbs (1983:01) says 'Discourse analysis is the 'linguistic analysis of naturally occurring connected spoken or written discourse'. To him, it is an attempt to study the organization of language above the

DOI: 10.4018/979-8-3693-7934-9.ch013

sentence or clause. In other words, it is the study of large linguistic units such as conversational exchanges or written texts.

Every genre of discourse is designed to communicate something in terms of information, warnings or instruction to readers, listeners or viewers. Since the entertainment industry moved from stage plays in open theatres to television dramas, online comedies and stand-up comedies, comedies have become means of entertainment and money-making ventures.

There are digital/online media platforms that have given voice to the voiceless and provided channels for people to be involved in business adverts, career opportunities, global networking, scientific discoveries, creative/art presentations, trainings in different kinds of online skills to access the digital world.

The digital world and the privileges it offers have its pros and cons. On the positive side, the digital world enables people to connect with the global community. Online discourses are however prone to issues such as intercultural conflicts because of the different cultures that online users belong to. Different cultural backgrounds and ideologies can lead to clashes in online discussion. Online discussions could also present with political activism where people use digital platforms to express opinions and mobilize support. There could also be misinformation or biased information, for example, historical narratives and scientific debates. Historical narratives could be shaped by nationalist sentiments or biased reporting. Discourses around food, clothing, agriculture etc could create biases or controversies that could lead to clashes on discourses on economy or social disorder. Online discourses are therefore full of all kinds complexities which calls for critical evaluation of information and presentations got on line.

To diffuse tension and unexpressed psychological trauma, some people have created stress-relief online platforms and sites like WhatsApp chats, Tik-Tok, Instagram, snapchats(videos), apps, face-book (website and app) featuring cars, foods, art, fashion, advertisements, local and international news items on politics and happenings around the world. These are sites, apps or platforms that are tailored to attract different interest groups. On some of these sites, real or imagined things are shared through discourses. People visit these online sites or platforms for comic relief from boredom, emotional and social stress or any other thing people want to escape from or enjoy. Some people even ask for suggestions and advice from netizens on issues bothering them while some people have also got into trouble for example, on some dating sites and have lost their lives by interacting with persons they hardly know. The focus of this paper is however on how online users have used different modes in their online comedy skits. The data for this chapter are comedy skits by *Busymouth*. He is a Nigerian comedian who has recently gained prominence because of his mimicry of the speeches of President Bola Tinubu and some other important figures in the society.

THEORETICAL BACKGROUND

The 1980s and 1990s experienced the emergence of Critical Discourse Analysis (CDA) which was inspired by the works of scholars like Roger Fowler, Bob Hodge, and Gunther Kress in Critical linguistics; Michel Foucault, Pierre Bourdieu in Discourse analysis; William Labov and Basil Bernstein in Sociolinguistics. Critical Discourse Analysis is problem-oriented and problem-solving. There is always a form of bilateral power relations between the oppressor and the oppressed. There must be evidence of a struggle somewhere whether financially, morally, educationally or politically. CDA focuses on analyzing language as a form of social practice. It examines how language reflects and shapes power relations, it investigates how discourse constructs and reinforces social inequality. It is aimed at developing a critical perspective on language and society.

Scholars in CDA try to examine the relationship between language, power and social inequality. Some of the researchers who contributed to the development of CDA are Norman Fairclough, Teun van Dijk, Ruth Wodak and Gunther Kress. Some of the methodological approaches are Norman Fairclough's Dialectal Approach, Discourse Historical Approach by Ruth Wodak and Socio-cognitive Approach by Teun van Dijk. CDA has become a prominent approach in linguistics, sociology, cultural studies, education, media studies and political science to mention a few.

Fairclough's Approach to Critical Discourse Analysis (CDA)

Fairclough"s approach emphasizes the relationship between language, power and ideology. He sees discourse as a form of social practice that shapes and is shaped by social structures, relations and institutions. Some of the key concepts that Fairclough emphasizes are:

1. discourse as social practice is used to construct and reflect social relationships, identities and power;
2. text, interaction and context are important in analyzing texts within their social and cultural context, considering the relationship between the text producers, consumers and broader social structures;
3. power and ideology shape discourse, and that dominant groups use language to maintain their power and interest; and
4. context in which texts are produced is important in critical analysis.

Fairclough (1989) argues that language is a key site for the exercise of power and the construction of social relationships. He developed a framework for analyzing discourse that considers the social and cultural context of language use.

Fairclough (1995) developed a CDA framework emphasizing the importance of analyzing discourse as a form of social practice. He provides a detailed methodology for conducting CDA which are textual analysis, discursive practice and social practice. Some people have however argued that his frame work on power and ideology oversimplifies complex social dynamics.

Kress and van Leeuwen 's Approach to Multimodality

Multimodality, which is, making meaning through different modes is an emerging area in discourse analysis and it exposes scholars more to a wholesome discussion of texts and visual communication in general. It is using different modes such as speech, color, images and written language for communication in a particular ensemble. Inspired by the works of Halliday (1985), the ground-breaking work of Kress and van Leeuwen in *Reading images* in (1996) and *Multimodal Discourse* (2001) paved the way for multimodality to enter linguistic studies. Kress and van Leeuwen (2006) note in their approach to the domain of visuals that, they do not look for the analogues of sentences, clauses, nouns, verbs etc in images, but are of the opinion that language in visual communication can both be used to realize the same fundamental systems of meaning that constitute our cultures and mental processes. The three meta-functions identified by Kress and van Leeuwen are representational, interactional and compositional meta-functions. Representational metafunction is concerned with how multimodal texts (e.g., images, videos, or websites) represent the world. This includes the depiction of objects, actions, and events. Interactional meta-function examines the relationships between semiotic resources on the visual space and also between the producer (author) and the viewer (audience). This involves the exercise of power, social distance, and modalities of interaction. Compositional meta-function focuses on how visual participants are arranged to create a meaningful whole. This includes layout, color, information value, framing, salience, etc.

Kay O'Halloran's (2011) work on Multimodal Discourse Analysis is based on how meaning is created through the interaction of multiple modes of communication. She developed a Multimodal Discourse Analysis Framework which draws on Systemic Functional Linguistics to analyze how meaning emerges through the interaction of different modes, such as language, images, and typography. She also emphasized the concept of culture as interconnected semiotic systems and systems of meaning, building on Halliday and Hasan's work. To O'Halloran, meaning is enhanced through the use of multiple modes. Her work is a useful contribution to media studies, discourse analysis and cognitive linguistics and has potentials for understanding complex communication phenomena.

Machin (2013) notes that discourses occur in different ways, means, forms and genres as in speeches, news items, entertainments, infotainments, media, computer games, family discourse, movies, social world of everyday life, businesses, fashion, toys, music, architecture, health and safety and in all kinds of ways that humans engage in communication about people and things around them. He notes further that discourses are communicated through different kinds of semiotic resources where different modes are realized by different genres and are all shaped by power relations, ideology and all kinds of political undertones.

Machin(2013) notes further that, texts studied by linguists create meaning not only through language but also through visual features and elements such as images, colors, layout of pages, material objects and architecture. He notes further that, multimodality overlaps into many other fields where designs, gestures etc have had long traditions of study. Critical Multimodal Discourse Analysis is therefore the fusion of both Critical Discourse Analysis and Multimodal Discourse Analysis. CDA by nature as described above, is problem oriented and problem solving, it is interdisciplinary and eclectic in research and designed to contribute to social change while multimodality is interactional and uses a social-semiotic approach.

AIM

The aim of this chapter is to highlight and describe the meaning-making potentials of the compositional structure of the visible semiotic resources in selected online comedies by *Busymouth* titled 'Mr President facing flood challenges' and *Busymouth* as Akpan shamed his ex' on Tik-Tok.

Objectives are to:

1. Identify the semiotic resources employed in the online comedies;
2. analyse the representational, interactional and compositional meta-functions of the online comedies; and
3. relate these meta-functions to the political and socio-cultural realities of the country depicted in the comedies.

METHODOLOGY

The data for this work are online comedy pieces by *Busymouth* titled 'Mr President facing flood challenges' and '*Busymouth* as Akpan shamed his ex''. The comedies were downloaded from the internet and studied with the intention of identifying the meaning-making semiotic resources embedded in the skits. The skits were transcribed and analyzed using Fairclough (1995) framework for analyzing discourse and Kress and van Leeuwen's (2006) three dimensional meta-functions of language which are: representational, interactional and compositional meta-functions of language.

Even though they are short pieces, they are loaded with all kinds of semiotic resources. The first video clip depicts the despicable situation of a commercial city in the face of negligence and corruption. The socio-economic situation birthed by corruption led to disaffection and unstable mutual relationships in the country, which is what video clip 2 is all about.

Busymouth is a Nigerian comedian who has recently gained attention through his hilarious mimicry of important figures in the society and recently that of President Ahmed Tinubu's speeches and public appearances. He dresses like the President and speaks like the President. *Busymouth* is a talented comedian who showcases his talent for comedy. His skits touch on current socio-economic issues in Nigeria. In a humorous way, he highlights the problems people go through and the government's reaction to the problems and challenges. He also mimics the ordinary citizen and their reactions to the socio- economic problems facing them as individuals. There is no doubt that people enjoy his shows. Some of the reactions to *Busymouth's* performances online are as follows.

1. I was at the show and I really enjoyed myself
2. Emoney you have done well !
3. *Busymouth*, you too much o!
4. *Busymouth* you are good!
5. U guys don't have respect for an elderly man, can any of you guys try this with Buhari, Putin, Jeo Bidn or North Korea President?

From the comments above, it will be noticed that some fans admire *Busymouth* while some are afraid, he might be picked up by security operatives for mimicking the President.

TIKTOK AS AN ONLINE PLATFORM

Apart from his public stand-up comedy shows, one of the platforms that *Busymouth* uses as outlet for his videos is TikTok online platform. TikTok platform helps to create a global community where people worldwide share their experiences and discover new contents. TikTok allows users to connect with people from various cultures where they share experiences of life. The platform provides a form of community engagement where people can give their comments on what they have watched or listened to.

Barraca Carlos (2023/2024) has written a lot about the benefits of TikTok as an online platform in which he highlighted the benefits, advantages and disadvantages. Some of the benefits highlights are summarized in this section. TikTok as an online platform provides an avenue for creative expression and community, business marketing opportunities and personal professional growth in terms of career opportunities. There are also informative videos on various topics in science, history, language learning and other educational contents. The platform affords its users the creative freedom to express themselves and their thoughts with a global community of people worldwide who make interesting discoveries about other people's cultures, backgrounds, personal experiences, political affairs etc, in a very informal way. There are all kinds of business and marketing opportunities that TikTok makes available to its users. It offers opportunity for business to reach a vast audience in a global community thereby increasing brand awareness. This platform encourages small businesses to have visibility and a voice where they probably would not have had the opportunity.

TikTok also offers a wide range of entertainments in form of dances, comedy skits, cooking etc. It is always easy to find contents that aligns with people's interests on a Tik Tok platform. You can hardly be bored on a TikTok platform. In addition to the above, there is the opportunity for music artists to showcase their musical talents, gain exposure, read comments and discover new music. There is also the privilege of career opportunities. People can easily connect with other people's thoughts on possibilities of new business approaches they never thought of before. There are things you never thought one could make a living from that are advertised on TikTok. If anyone is bereft of ideas, such a one could visit TikTok platform and get informed. Some other additional benefits highlighted by Barraza Carlos are rapid content validity, real time consumer feedback and market penetration. The immediate feedback system as expressed by Barraza enables users to know the public reaction about their presentations and how to adjust for better market strategy. Some content creators online ask users for comments while some plead that their videos be shared.

In spite of all these benefits, there are challenges and disadvantages of TikTok as a platform. Barraza notes some of the challenges as the maintenance of a consistent content schedule, coping with the short attention span of viewers and cyber bullying. Some other areas of concern include time consumption, privacy concerns, limited video length, content quality, negative influence and online safety. Barraza emphasized the fact that excessive time spent on the apps could affect productivity. The 60 seconds limited video length could restrict content creators who would have preferred a longer time. There are also issues about content quality because not all contents are true, some are skits. Another disadvantage is the negative harmful behavior or influence that some contents may have on the younger users.

Despite all these limitations and challenges, TikTok still has the positive sides of providing a creative space for users to showcase their talents and connect with the global community. It also enables people to be relieved of society stress especially where very serious socio-political or socio-economic issues are trivialized and presented in short videos that create mirth or laughter. This chapter is however interested in the meaning making potentials of some of these short videos and the different modes used in presenting them.

SYNOPSIS OF THE VIDEOS

Video clip 1 -'Mr President' facing flood challenges'

Figure 1. Video clip 1a -young adult

Figure 2. Video clip 1b- the flooded street backing Mr President

In the short video above on' Mr President facing flood challenges' by *Busymouth,* a young adult is seen backing a middle- aged man and taking him across a flooded street in Lagos. The city's name and country were mentioned by man being carried by the young adult. The conversation started with the young adult remarking that the problem of the flood in that area is not something the inhabitants enjoy. From the conversation, we notice that the man being ferried across the flood is addressed as 'Mr President' while the young adult is just a citizen of Nigeria because of the reference to citizens by 'Mr President'.

'Mr President' claimed ignorance of the situation and wondered why the government has not done anything about the problem. He seems to be incapacitated and pushed the blame on the government at the state or local government levels and also concluded that he would not come to that area again and that, it is only God that can help in that kind of situation.

Video clip 2- *Busymouth* as Akpan shamed his 'ex'

Figure 3. Video clip 2a Busymouth as Akpan shamed his ex

Figure 4. video clip 2b Akpan laughing hysterically at his 'ex'

In this short video, *Busymouth* is seen as Akpan, a middle-aged man riding a car. He sees his 'ex' – Vera with another man and decides to stop the car. Akpan stops the car and the 'ex'- Vera recognized him as her former boyfriend. Vera seems to be surprised seeing Akpan riding a car. Vera's manfriend insulted Akpan and Akpan responded by banging his cap on the head of the manfriend. She immediately disowns the manfriend, told him she had suffered with Akpan before and that he should not insult Akpan. This is, all in an attempt to reconcile with Akpan, now that it seems as if his status has changed. Vera told the manfriend to leave immediately leaving her alone with Akpan in the discourse. Akpan joked about her leaving 'present tense' for 'past tense'. Vera tried to touch the car but Akpan shouted on her not to make the car dirty. Akpan talks about his renewed status which is better than that of Vera's manfriend. Vera got attracted by Akpan's new status and tries to stage a 'come back'. Akpan's jokes were however very serious insults which Vera could not stand as she walks away from the car. All through the discourse, Akpan keeps on smiling as he ridicules her for dumping him for another man.

ANALYSES OF THE VIDEOS

Fairclough's approach involves the analysis of the linguistic features of a text such as vocabulary, grammar and cohesion at the textual level. His approach also involves how texts are produced, distributed and consumed at the discursive practice level while the social and cultural contexts that shape the discourse are also analyzed.

Clip l as mentioned above, mimics the Nigerian President when confronted with the problem of flood in a particular area in the city of Lagos, Nigeria. The two participants speak good English with correct syntax and vocabulary. One can be referred to as a young adult representing the masses and the other one, 'Mr President' representing the government. Their conversation is coordinated and coherent with well-chosen vocabulary or lexical items that describe the situation adequately. Below are examples.

Y. **A**: Mr President, I don't know, sometimes, how to explain this flood but it's really not good

M.P: Is this what the citizens of Nigeria are going through everyday?

Y.A: Yes Sir, Mr President

M.P: And I've not even seen this anywhere----- down to the other side? – (raises his hand) hah!

Y.A: Yes

M.P: Hah! In this lagos? Whao! I'm not aware. This is my first time of seeing flood like this!

On the other hand, Clip2 has interlocutors speaking both English and Pidgin initially but later, Pidgin only towards the end of the video. Vera's new manfriend spoke good English which was derided by Akpan who spoke in Pidgin by saying;

Akpan: you don leave me--- follow English, na English you go chop?

Man friend: young man, who are you?

Akpan (gets infuriated from inside the car, removes his cap and bangs the man's head saying) I dey drive moto, you dey say 'young man'. Look at me---- just take—

To Akpan or the common man on the street, possession of a car is a sign of affluence, even if the car does not belong to them.

Vera: (on sighting Akpan in the car, Vera immediately identifies with Akpan and tells the new manfriend not to insult Akpan, that she had suffered alongside Akpan for long). She says; You no know wetin this guy don suffer! you no know the gari wey I don drink ? (to manfriend) You come, dey go, dey go.
Man friend: you mean I should go?
You go drink that gari after now!

The discourse continues until the manfriend leaves in anger. Lexical items and phrases like *gari* (produce from cassava, common staple food in the Southern part of Nigeria), *borrow, dash you moto, pure water, you dey crase, oga dey pay me 7,200 naira every weekend* show the socio-economic status of the interlocutors and the kind of things they appreciate. There is no doubt that women generally appreciate someone with a high status in the community and would easily deflect if they see someone better or more influential than the person they have been dating before. Akpan too demonstrated that he would not give in to inferiority complex. He immediately gave his response physically assaulting Vera's manfriend by using his cap to hit him on the head. He responded by referring to the man as 'past tense' and he- Akpan as 'present tense'.

Akpan: na dis the recent---- wey you left me for?
Vera: I no leave you o!
Akpan: like you leave 'present tense, go dey follow 'past tense'?

Akpan may be referring to the age difference between himself and Vera's manfriend because it is obvious that the manfriend is older. It may also be from his view of the man's outfit which looks a little bit old fashioned. The manfriend does not have his shirt tucked in and it is not clear if he has two shirts on as one brown one sticks out under the light blue one on top of it. He has a cowboy hat on with his goatee sticking out from under it. The bag he is carrying is neither a suit case nor a full carrier bag. All these make him totally old fashioned. It could also be the fact that, he- Akpan now rides in a car while the man is still going about barefooted. The rich, some believe, exchange pleasantries from inside their vehicles while the poor do obeisance from where they are on the streets.

The episodes in the two videos took place outside on the streets. Both videos show the communicative competence of *Busymouth* as a comedian. He is not only able to represent or mimic the President who is the highest government functionary in Nigeria, but also the common man or the working class or the less privileged few. Both videos present problems at different levels. The first one at a community level which demands the attention of the President or government functionaries while the other is at an individual level which Akpan was able to address by shaming the 'ex' who thought of leaving him for someone on a higher socioeconomic level. Both problems are caused by the socio political and socio-economic situation of the country.

The Narrative Process

A semiotic system has all kinds of representations in form of objects, human beings and their relationship with each other. There are two types of participants that can be represented on a visual space- interactive and represented participants. On the one hand, Interactive participants are those who engage in communicative acts of speaking or relating with each other. Such participants speak, listen, read or write, view things or make things. On the other hand, represented participants are real or abstract people, places or things, that are represented either by speech, writing or images. This suggests that a participant could be a represented participant and still interact with other semiotic participants or the viewers.

Narrative Structure

This is presented or created by participants in a semiotic ensemble. The narrative patterns serve to present the actions, events, processes, special arrangement and placement of semiotic resources. The semiotic resources usually tell a story which anyone familiar with the cultural landscape of the story will easily comprehend. Kress and Leeuwen (2006) note that, it is possible to have vector(s) which may be formed by bodies, or body parts or tools which depict a particular kind of action. As regards the interaction between the interlocutors, a visual piece can present two types of interactions, namely interaction between participants in the visual space and interaction between the producer of the image and the viewer. Kress and Leeuwen (2006:114) note three kinds of relations:

1. Relations between represented participants;
2. Relations between interactive and represented participants (the interactive participants' attitudes towards the represented participants); and
3. Relations between interactive participants (the things interactive participants do to or for each other through images).

Interactive participants are real people who produce and make sense of images in the context of social institutions. It could be producers and viewers who know each other and are involved in face-to-face interaction. The producers and viewers may not have met. In the data for this work, the three relations apply. The two interactive participants who are also representational have something in common that affects them. Both of them had to go through the flooded street, one conveying the other. Both of them are facing the camera as if walking towards the viewer.

Halliday (1985) in the introduction to his book titled *Introduction to Functional Grammar* says Speech acts perform the following:

1. Offer information- that is, form a statement that requires agreement or disagreement as response;
2. Offer goods and services (e.g. would you like a drink?); and
3. Demand information- that is, form a question in which the expected response is an answer.

The interactive and represented participants in video clip 1 actually performed the three speech acts in the data for this work. The young adult offered information and demanded that action be taken on the situation while the middle-aged man demanded information but expressed his inability to offer a solution to the problem. The stance of the represented participants also demands some form of reaction from the viewers. What is being narrated and presented is a direct address to the viewers. It is a 'demand' video clip. The represented participants want some form of response from the viewers. A visual impression on the viewers is a 'demand' picture or video. Represented participants usually offer information or demand response which could be responded to by taking note of the historical, cultural, and at times, the land scape, needed infrastructure and social needs of the people represented.

In video clip 2, the represented human participants are three- two men and a lady. The non-human participant is one -a motor car that is 'status giving' which is also a determinant of who gets the attention of the lady in the discourse. The third speech act occurred most in the discourse. That is, 'demand information'. From the discourse, we notice that there is a broken relationship, a supposedly new relationship which got broken again because of the new status of one of the interlocutors and the presence of a motor car. All the interlocutors asked one question or the other to clarify issues but at the end, none of the relationships could be mended. The information offered by Akpan is meant to spite the lady for jilting him and going after another man whom she felt is on a higher socio- economic ladder than Akpan. Below are some of the conversations from video clip 2.

Manfriend: (on seeing Vera greeting Akpan) Is this what you want to end up with? This non-challant, nonsense, nonsensical human being?
Akpan: Vera, na dis one wey you leave me for? You leave me, you follow English, na English you go chop?
Manfriend: young man, who are you?

Akpan: (from inside the car, Akpan uses his cap to bang Vera's manfriend's head) I dey drive moto, you dey tell me 'Young man'—
Vera: (addressing manfriend) Oga, calm down, I beg--- you no know wetin this guy don suffer?

Multimodal Composition of the Video Clips

Every image, picture or semiotic ensemble contains a lot of representational interactive relations. The movement or placement of objects and human participants affect the meaning interpretations of the image or picture. Composition presents the representational and interactive meaning potentials in an image and this is done through three interrelated systems which are: the information value, salience and framing. Kress and Leeuwen (2006:177) note the following about the three interrelated systems.

A) Information value

The placement of elements (participants and syntagms that relate them to each other and to the viewer) endows them with the specific informational values attached to the various zones of the image: left and right, top and bottom, center and margin.

B) Salience

The elements (participants as well as representational and interactive syntagms) are made to attract the viewer's attention to different degrees, as realized by such factors as placement in the foreground or background, relative size, contrasts in tonal value (or color), differences in sharpness, etc.

C) Framing

The presence or absence of framing devices (realized by elements which create dividing lines, or by actual frame lines) disconnects or connects elements of the image, signifying that they belong or do not belong together in some sense.

The principles above do not only apply to pictures but also apply to layouts, architectural designs and even videos etc. In analyzing multimodal texts, it is possible to analyze each component discussed above separately or in an integrated way. This chapter however, highlights a few things about each principle but do more of discussing them as a composite or integrated whole.

Information value

In discussing information value, Kress and van Leeuwen (2006) note the concept of 'given' and 'new', and 'left' and 'right'. This may be of great significance in static images such as; pictures, posters, advertisement billboards etc. where there are no moving objects. Recently, advertisements have taken a greater dimension where human and non-human semiotic resources are made to act and speak.

In the video clip 1, there are two interactive human participants- a young adult and a middle-aged man. The young adult is seen backing the middle-aged man in an attempt to help him cross a flooded street in the city of Lagos, Nigeria. The location is revealed in the conversation. The young adult bears the burden of carrying the middle-aged man across the flooded street in that city. At a point, the middle-aged man warned the young adult to be careful not to allow him fall off his back into the water. The two men fit into the two sides of the social ladder or human divide in life. The young/old, the youth/adult, the rich/poor, the masses/ political elite. All these classifications are revealed through the discussion of the two human participants. The images, verbal and non-verbal actions confirm the social and political power play in the video.

In Kress and Leeuwen's classification, the set of objects that may stand in for 'given' in the video are the non-interactive resources such as the houses, the cars and the flooded street which the young adult notes is a regular occurrence. ('given' means it is something the viewer already knows about). The people in the area probably built their houses during the dry season when there was no heavy rainfall or flood. ('new' is something that has just come into being- problematic, disturbing and one that probably needs attention.) For someone outside the city, it is 'new'. For the viewer who does not live in that city, it is 'new' but for someone who has experienced the flood two or three times, it is not only 'given' but problematic, disturbing and one that needs urgent attention. The inhabitants of the area seem to have been tired of the situation as there was no organized protest about the worrisome situation. The middle-aged man representing the 'President' said he was not aware of such problems in Lagos. The houses are mostly high-walled, storey-buildings fenced with either black or grey-colored roof-tops and gates. This could mean that the residents are middle-class people who have the same aesthetic taste or that, the residents have probably discovered through research, the best color of paint for such a water-prone area. Nobody is seen outside except the two interacting participants and an Okada (motor-cycle) rider who passed by while the young adult and 'Mr. President' were walking through the flooded street and discussing the flood.

In video clip 2, there is a lot of movement which makes it difficult to do any placement of 'given' or 'new' or 'right' and 'left' elements as discussed by Kress and Leeuwen (2006).

The location is on an unnamed street, town or country but the names of the interactive participants- Akpan and Vera suggest that the participants are from the Eastern part of Nigeria. The exact location could be any of the cities in Nigeria. The participants kept on moving backwards and forwards, and also side ways. Even Akpan who is in a car, moved to express his annoyance at Vera's new manfriend when he felt insulted. The only static objects are the tree towards the left and the grass under the feet of the two human participants standing by the car Akpan was driving.

Salience

This could be interpreted on the basis of the visual clues in terms of the most eye- catching element in the composition. It has to do with the size, sharpness of the focus or tonal contrast. Salience also has to do with all kinds of complex interactions between the sizes of the images. If they are images, the sizes of the represented participants, soft and contrasting colors, etc, matter a lot. In short, salience is the element or elements that seem to receive the greatest attention. Cultural factors such as the kind of human beings, clothing, animals, vegetation, different cultural symbols, etc. as they are placed in the visual field are very important. If images are placed more to the left, it suggests a lot of 'given' items that are 'heavy' in composition while other elements could be termed 'new'. In video clip 1, the most salient part of the composition are the two human beings and the flood. Their physical posture and verbal interaction show the power relations between the two as the oppressor and the oppressed and also the masses and the government. This is a little bit different from that of a driver and his boss. In the case of a driver and his boss, both are in a vehicle and their interaction clear. One is just being chauffeured by the other. In video clip 1 however, one is being chauffeured but the chauffeur is going bare footed in the dirty water to get the other person across to a dry and safe place, and after all said and done, there was no remuneration. In terms of size, both are about the same size but one is well and neatly dressed while the other is not. Both participants are seen moving towards the viewer.

In video clip 2, the three human participants are salient in the composition. All of them contributed to the discourse and dispersed when the communication broke down. Akpan's intention is to shame his 'ex' publicly which he succeeded in doing, but not in the presence of a crowd of people. He however took time to explain how he got the car to his 'ex' but was not ready to take her back.

> **Akpan**: I just sleep, wake up one morning who dey call me, one big man!
> **Vera**: one big man?
> --------------
> E come dash you moto?

Akpan--------------
Na so them dey dash vehicle?
As from today, I'm the senior driver
Go to no 9 and ask them.
Na me be their chief driver
Before, I been sell pure water, but now I don 'blow'
You cannot come and take me nonsense again!

'Don blow' mentioned by Akpan means 'I have made it' or 'I am now richer than before'. According to him, this is evident with the fact that, he now drives a rich man who pays him weekly like a footballer. The job has changed his status from that of a pure water seller to a driver. That is why he says 'I don blow, you can not take me nonsense again!'

Framing

This has to do with the disconnection or connection of elements in a composition. That is, the elements in a composition could be marked off and separated from each other if strongly framed. It could happen in stretches of speech, music, movements in film etc. A continual flow of rhythm, song, speech etc shows weakly-framed elements of a composition. Kress and van Leeuwen (2006:203) emphasize that the stronger the framing of an element, the more it is presented as a separate unit while the absence of framing stresses group identity. They also note that the more the elements of a special composition are connected, the more they are presented as belonging together.

Framing is always very obvious in drawings and paintings. There could be lines and colors separating objects. Objects or elements could be demarcated from each other or from the background or environment.

In the data, the young adult is seen backing the middle-aged man which shows that there is some form of group identity and that there is something that connects them either socially, economically or politically. Both of them are seen going through the flood but one is walking through barefooted. The young adult carrying the middle-aged man did not look as if he was doing it out of compulsion but was probably waiting to be rewarded after the difficult task of backing a man for a long distance across a flooded street. 'Mr President' could not use his position to suggest or proffer a solution to the problem, neither could he give a financial reward for the service rendered by the young adult. In fact, he said in the dialogue that, only God could solve the problem and that he would not come to that area again.

ANALYSIS OF THE VERBAL TEXT

The Visual Space

The represented visual space in video clip 1 is a street in Lagos, Nigeria which could be said to be a representation of the experiences in many parts of Lagos State during raining seasons. Lagos used to be the capital of Nigeria before it was moved to Abuja. It is a state close to the Atlantic Ocean and surrounded by water. Many ministries still have their branches in Lagos despite the fact that the capital has been moved to Abuja. The sea port in particular, is a beehive of activities as regards clearing and forwarding of goods, exporting and importing of goods in and out of the country. The strategic location of Lagos, the business and job opportunities make it attractive to all and sundry. Many people move to Lagos from the inter-land in search of job opportunities or transaction of different kinds of businesses. This makes the small state to be overpopulated as many people want to live, work and build their businesses and houses in the state. The natural canals and water ways leading to the Lagoon get blocked as people sand fill them during the dry season, erect illegal structures, thereby blocking the water ways. The level of corruption is such that some of the very rich and influential people get approval for construction of buildings where they are not supposed to construct them causing problems for themselves and other law-abiding citizens.

The video clip 1 shows one of the problems faced by people in areas where there is no free flow of water. The water therefore finds its way into people's houses, streets, shops disturbing the free movement of both human and vehicular traffic.

Video clip 2 has its visual representation on an unnamed street in the country. Two of the three interactive participants were walking along the road while one of them was driving a car. The three meet and there was verbal altercation. At the end, the three had to go their different ways because there was communication breakdown.

Social Actors in Relation to the Community

In video clip 1, the two interactive participants are also representative participants. The young adult backing 'Mr President' represents the Nigerian masses while 'Mr President' represents the government at all levels. The short video clip is a subtle way of giving information about a worrisome situation in some parts of Lagos, the non-caring attitude of the government towards the plight of the people living in that area and the part played by the common man in drawing the attention of the government to the problem. It is also a means of demanding solution from the government and responses from the viewers.

In video-clip 1, there is a form of power play- the poor carrying the rich or the masses becoming the horse on which the political elite rides. The political elites cajole the masses to vote for them after which they refuse to fulfil the election promises made to the people. In places where their expensive Jeeps cannot pass, the backs of the hungry masses become their horses or means of transportation for very meagre amounts. It is even worse in the video clip as 'Mr President' searches his pocket to bring out some peanuts but could not find anything, which means there are times when the poor are denied compensation by the rich for what they even work for. In case of the masses /government, the masses work and are paid peanuts while the rich live in luxury and take advantage of the poor. 'Mr President' claims ignorance of the horrible situation about the flood and instead of taking action, he said he would not come to that area again. This kind of oppressive insensitive nature of the ruling class is expressed through the language of 'Mr President', for example;

> **M.P**: What we're going to do now is that- we will eerrrhm—I don't even know what we're going to do o! because, mee, after now, mee, I'm not coming back here o!
> **Y.A**: Hah! Mr President! Even you don't know what to do!

This example also suggests the cluelessness of the government in solving social problems and dealing with the problems of the social welfare of the people. The position and the privileges attached to positions of authority seems to be the dangling carrot for political aspirants. The welfare of the electorate is not the priority once elections are won. Political aspirants campaign and cajole the electorate with empty promises to secure their votes. Once they succeed, they forget both the electorate and the promises they make to them. Despite the insensitivity of 'Mr President', the young adult still carries him to a safe and dry place without his feet touching the water. The masses seem helpless with no choice but to go on with the unending suffering in the midst of plenty. The late Afro Beat musician- Fela Anikulapo Kuti years back sang the song 'suffering and smiling', a situation which is still prevalent in the society till today.

VIDEO CLIP 2

In this video clip, the social actors are three participants. Initially, Vera's manfriend wanted to do some powerplay by challenging Akpan for exchanging pleasantries with Vera, his new found love. This however, did not work out as Akpan paid him back by banging his cap on the manfriend's head for saying 'young man' who are you? If Akpan had accepted 'Vera' back, it would have been the case of *Olowo gba yawo ole* as the Yorubas say. That is, the rich take the wife of the lazy one. It is the money here that is the determining factor as to who gets the woman in the end. Since riding a motor car is a sign of affluence and socio-economic power in the nation, it is easy for Vera to quickly decide there and then to do away with the new manfriend who didn't have a car.

The Flood

The problem in video clip1 is the flood. From the encounter between the young adult and 'Mr President', only the young adult suffers as a result of the flood. His house is probably among the ones affected by the flood. He has to deal with the problem of the flood in his home and the problem of having to carry 'Mr President' across the flood to a safe and place. The political elite distance themselves from the problem the masses face because they are either in their air-conditioned vehicles or they are ferried across problems by security guards, thugs or kind hearted masses who risk their lives for them, just as seen in the video. Some government parastatals even engage in some forms of window dressing for the bad roads when important dignitaries are visiting any area. This does not make the government officials see the magnitude of the problem. This could be seen as double cover up because it is possible that some money had been allocated for the repair work in such areas which had been mis-managed, and to cover up, some form of window dressing would be done during official visits.

Dangerous things or harmful objects could be under the flood which could have affected the young adult but he still risked walking through the flood to get the rich and privileged across the problem in his area and at the end, unrewarded personally or as someone representing the underprivileged in the area.

On another level, the flood could represent the masses in situations where they have not been able to have economic and social freedom as a result of the activities of the rich in society. The masses may, like the flood, prevent the rich from getting in or out of their houses or even prevent them from using their vehicles, as 'Mr President' is seen on the back of the young adult. The masses may eventually invade the streets, offices or homes of the rich in protest.

The problem in video clip 2 is poverty of the mind and purse. Vera is easily dissuaded by what she could get momentarily from men in particular, but ends up being shamed by her 'ex'. She lost both ways. The new manfriend walked away and Akpan refused to take her back.

The Blame Game

In a capitalist society and economy, it is easy to transfer blame from one person to another, all in an attempt to evade responsibility. The rich control the economy and still blame the poor for complaining. The masses are expected to be content with whatever they are given and still continue to serve so that the capitalist can have money to spend. Unfortunately, the poor cannot sleep because they are hungry and the rich are afraid to sleep because the poor are awake. The rich expect someone else to do the work while they loaf around in luxurious cars. The highly placed officers even blame those under them for not performing even when they work under very harsh economic and social policies. For example;

> **M.P**: That's not what I mean actually. I'm only trying to say I'm feeling for you people, I'm feeling for you people! Hah! This is really bad! And the government is not doing anything about it?
> **Y.A**: Mr President, but you are the government!
> **M.P**: Oh, that's true! Oh! hen--- don't worry, don't worry- (shakes his head) they are supposed to be taking their responsibility in things like this!

The young adult quickly reminds 'Mr President' of his position as the president representing the government. 'Mr President' seems to refer to other arms of government as 'they', exonerating himself and shifting the blame on other people.

Youth Unemployment

This is obvious in the video clip 1 and 2.The young adult is seen carrying 'Mr President'. If he is gainfully employed, he probably would not have been available to offer that kind of service to anybody. He is probably one of the educated unemployed youths staying at home while others have gone to work. He communicates well in English and could relate well with 'Mr President' concerning the welfare of the environment. From the video, the street looks deserted except for an Okada rider who passed by carrying two people while the video lasted. Apart from that, no other person was seen outside. People are either trapped in their houses or have found a way to wallow through the flood to get to work. Unemployed and unemployable school leavers are many in the country. The country is trying to see what could be done to reduce their number by emphasizing the need for skills acquisition for students while in school and out of school to be able to put food on their tables. Vera in video clip 2 could be said to be unemployed too because an employed female with self -respect would probably not be changing men like clothes and will not be carried away with the presence of a car.

Shifting Responsibility to the Invisible

Nigeria is a multicultural and multilingual religious country. A lot of people believe in a supreme being that is able to do all things for them. The video shows 'Mr President' saying 'It's only God that can help' as stated below:

> **M.P**: Heh, God will help us o! It's only God that can save us in this country! No President can help us o! President? It's only God that can help us!

This is irresponsibility, laziness and ignorance on the part of 'Mr President'. It is however unfortunate that instead of being pragmatic about the problem, those in government turn blind eyes to the problems people face. This is partly because those who helped them to get to the positions of power, are probably part of those causing the problem and so would not want to step on toes to make the next elective position possible. They prefer to make many suffer for the benefit of a few privileged ones. As a result, the only safe place to hide politically and also to apportion blame is under an invisible powerful being who has the power to do anything he wants to do. They also believe in a supernatural being who can magically remove the human stumbling blocks, probably cause a storm to happen that will destroy the obstructing buildings and structures, so that they can exonerate themselves that what happened was an act of God and that they are not to blame for any building collapse. This kind of wishful thinking has held the nation in poverty for long to the extent that, those who are supposed to be gainfully employed to feed their families move from one prayer mountain to another expecting miracles to happen that would make provisions for them mysteriously, farm for them magically and put food on their table miraculously. This kind of day-dream has turned many to beggars waiting for the invisible God to act.

Color Signification

Colors are culture specific but could be used to create stories that have meanings culturally, socially, physically or on a visual space. 'Mr President's attire and shoes in the Yoruba culture has a lot of meaning codifications. In the past, black in Yoruba culture signified death, sorrow, mourning or any form of unpleasantness. In the video, the black color could be used to represent the unpleasant situation that the people in the area are going through which could cause a lot of health challenges and eventually lead to death. For the suffering of the people in the area, 'Mr President's' responses are also not encouraging and there does not seem to be any end to the problem in sight. It is indeed a black and bleak future. Almost all the houses in the area have black roof tops and their gates black which complements the attire of Mr President. The black roof tops and Mr President in his black attire are above the water which suggests that the problem is beyond the people in that area. They actually need help.

Modernization has however made the color black to assume lighter roles and connotations either socially or in some cases, in a visual space. Now, black could be said to signify elegance, beauty and strength- a representation which 'Mr President' could be said to stand for. As the President of a country, he is expected to look good and presentable which he actually is but for the fact that at that point in time, he lacks a good means of transportation that could take him through the flood.

On the other hand, the young adult's attire is multi-colored. Even though it is bright, it does not convey any form of regularity in terms of fashion. It looks simple but follows the pattern of a usual unconcerned youth with unkempt hair as fashion, representing the masses.

In the video clip 2, the interlocutor's attires are multicolored. The colors interact with each other. The color of Akpan's car, and that of Vera's new manfriend's cap, big bag and trousers is brown or very close to brown. This is supposed to signify some form of peace and quiet but the discourse broke down because of Vera's decision to quit the new relationship again wanting to seek reconciliation with Akpan. The color of Vera's t-shirt is very close to that of the burnt grass behind them which shows something devoid of freshness. Akpan's shirt is green which is not too far from the color of the tree very close to them all. He got a new job and drives his master's car. They form a compact whole and tell the story of a relationship that exists among the three of them. What changed the whole scenario is the presence of the car. Vera's new manfriend's shirt has a lighter blue color from that of Vera's trousers which shows some form of relationship between the two of them. The burnt grass signifies under their feet signifies a spent or empty relationship.

Below are from the video

Akpan: (talking to Vera) you know how much them dey pay me?
Vera: How much?
Akpan: Every weekend, oga dey pay me 7,200 naira
How many person them they pay like that?
Them dey pay me like footballer every week!
Vera: So na you get this one?
Akpan: you dey crase? Na so?
this one na the first stage now
second stage dey come on the way
by dat time maybe I go just---- just
turn, ----(laughs)
Vera:(walks away)

Akpan: wetin dey worry women self?

To Akpan, from a pure water seller who was making peanuts to a driver paid 7,200 naira weekly like a footballer is 'jumbo pack'. With his present status, he can no longer tolerate an inconsistent partner or a stable relationship. His comments below reveal this.

Akpan--------------
Na so them dey dash vehicle?
As from today, I'm the senior driver
Go to no 9 and ask them.
Na me be their chief driver
Before I been sell pure water, but now I don 'blow'
You cannot come and take me nonsense again!

CONCLUSION

This chapter has tried to highlight and analyze the meaning-making potentials of the online comedies used as data and the sociocultural implications on the society at large. Linguistic and semiotic resources such as the vocabulary, choice of language- English and pidgin, color signification, information value, salience are some of the meaning-making potentials in the videos.

The problems of the flood and broken relationships are both government and people created. In video clip 1, the findings reveal that the socio-economic situation that has become a life-threatening problem facing the poor masses in some parts of Lagos is trivialized by the government. The findings also reveal that, the country runs a type of government that feeds on the masses, claim ignorance of the problem and plays the blame game with no assurance of an end to the problem(s). 'Mr President' finds it convenient to transfer his civic responsibilities to an invisible being. Video clip 2 also reveals the socio-economic problem which has encouraged character deficit and break in mutual relationships. The findings in clip 2 also revealed the poverty of the mind and purse that have made some women look for the highest bidder for a mutual relationship to be sustained. Poverty has been weaponized and this has made the populace gullible and unable to think or act right. Even the seemingly educated young adult representing the common man sounds and looks helpless in the face of the overwhelming problem facing the entire area. The author notes that, corruption and the fact that the nation is running a religion economy (believe that God can do everything) has heightened the problem and makes it look insurmountable. The author notes that the nation is a very religious nation and therefore concludes that except the nation combines a religion economy with knowledge economy(skills acquisition), national, community and personal development may be a mirage.

SOLUTIONS AND RECOMMENDATIONS

There is no social problem that does not have a solution. It takes the boldness and determination of people at the helm of affairs to be decisive about the situation. A bill raised at the National assembly against illegal structures blocking all drainage in the city of Lagos and other metropolitan cities in the nation will do the job. This should be supported with law enforcement agents using demolition companies to pull down illegal structures. The masses who also take advantage of the carelessness of the government to use the streets as dustbin for their refuse which also contribute to the blockage of drains should be stopped. The govt should provide incinerators or refuse vans to evacuate people's refuse and probably turn them to manures and fertilizer for agriculture or electricity generation.

FUTURE RESEARCH DIRECTIONS

Most African nations are multicultural and religious and may not be ready to sacrifice humanity and religion on the altar of science and civilization. Many do not believe in discarding religion for civilization. This could be seen in the large amount of money that is voted for pilgrimages year in year out in the midst of devastating hunger and poverty in the land. Further research could look into how the African nations could tilt more to a knowledge economy(skills acquisition) for optimum national development and orientation.

REFERENCES

Barraza C (2023) *12 Advantages and Disadvantages of TikTok* Digital Marketing, Social media. (Redaction Team).

Barraza, C. (2024). *11 Benefits of using TikTok last updated, August 2024. Digital Marketing Social media*. Redaction Team.

Fairclough, N. (1989). *Language and power*. Longman.

Fairclough, N. (1995). *Critical discourse analysis: The critical study of language*. Longman.

Halliday, M. A. K. (1985). *An introduction to functional grammar*. Edward Arnold.

Jewitt, C. (2014) The Routledge Handbook of Multimodal Analysis. Routledge/ Tailor and Francis Group.

Jewitt, C., Bezemer, J., & O'Halloran, K. (2016). *Introduction to Multimodality and it's various approaches*. Routledge.

Kress, G., & van Leeuwen, T. (1996/2006) *Reading Images*. Routledge.Tailor and Francis. (pp.114-154).

Kress, G., & van Leeuwen, T. (2001). *Multimodal discourse- The modes and media of contemporary communication*. Edward Arnold.

Machin, D. (2013). Critical discourse analysis: Vol. 10. *No.4 347-355*. Routledge., DOI: 10.1080/17405904.2013.813770

Stubbs, M. (1983) *Discourse Analysis (The Sociolinguistics of Natural Language*). (pp. 01-05). Basil Blackwell.

ADDITIONAL READING

Kress, D., & Jewitt, C. (2003). *Multimodal literacy*. Peter Lang Publishing, Inc.

Machin, D. (2013). *Analyzing popular music*. SAGE Publications Ltd.

Toolan, M. (1988) *Narrative, (A critical linguistic introduction*) Routledge, Tailor and Francis.

Van Leeuwen, T. (2006) *Introducing social semiotics*. Routledge, Tailor and Francis Group.

KEY TERMS AND DEFINITIONS

Discourse Analysis: the linguistic analysis of naturally occurring connected spoken or written discourse.

Flood: a large volume of dirty water flowing into the road and people's homes as a result of blocked drainage.

Linguistics: the scientific study of language. '

Mr. President: this is used to represent the highest government functionary in the nation- the number one person in the nation and also all government representatives at all levels of government.

Y.: A.: young adult

Chapter 14
Social Media and Western Cultural Hegemony: A Study of Cultural Shift in Contemporary Nigeria

Olaronke Ganiat Iroju
https://orcid.org/0000-0001-7669-9872
Adeyemi Federal University of Education, Ondo, Nigeria

Opeyemi Anthony Iroju
https://orcid.org/0009-0007-5314-5069
Obafemi Awolowo University, Ile-Ife, Nigeria

ABSTRACT

The objective of this study is to examine the relationship between social media and western cultural hegemony in contemporary Nigeria. A review of related literature was carried out to determine the implications of western ideologies and practices transmitted vis-a-viz social media platforms on the indigenous culture of Nigeria. The study reveals that social media platforms serve as channels for eroding the indigenous culture of Nigeria. The study also shows that Nigerian cultural values and beliefs can be promoted on social media by intensifying efforts to display Nigerian festivals and rituals, indigenous cuisines and historical cultural heritage sites to attract global attention. This study concludes that showcasing Nigerian indigenous culture on social media will provide a platform for Nigerians to share the rich cultural heritage of the country to the global audience, which will contribute significantly to the preservation of Nigerian cultural values.

DOI: 10.4018/979-8-3693-7934-9.ch014

INTRODUCTION

The rapid advancement in Information and Communication Technology (ICT) in the last two decades has led to the emergence of diverse social media platforms. Social media refers to a variety of Internet based platforms which facilitates the creation and sharing of ideas, opinions, knowledge, contents and other forms of expressions amongst a community of users who share similar interests, backgrounds or real life connections. Technically, social media can be viewed as the democratisation of information which transforms people from content readers to content publishers (Dave, 2008). These platforms are used for a variety of purposes to serve different users' interests. For instance, social networking sites such as Facebook and Instagram facilitate personal and business relationships amongst individuals irrespective of their geographical locations while media sharing platforms such as Youtube and Picasa allow users to create, store and share multimedia files (texts, videos, audios and images) to the general public. Social media has become an integral part of human life because it plays pivotal roles in all human activities ranging from communication, education, entertainment, business and politics. This phenomenon has significant implications on the culture of a society as individuals from diverse cultural backgrounds communicate and share different cultural values, beliefs and norms on social media. The ability of social media to cross geographical and cultural boundaries has fostered cultural exchange and cross cultural understanding in many societies, including Nigeria. This fact is supported by Baran (2002) who emphasised that culture is socially constructed and maintained through communication.

The Nigeria culture is shaped by the nation's multi-ethnic groups which are largely associated with diverse languages, dressing, literature, cuisines and gastronomy, marriages, arts and crafts, music amongst others (Ministry of Foreign Affairs, 2022). Specifically, Nigeria is composed of over two hundred and fifty ethnic groups with distinct customs and traditions which are centered on different languages (Onyejekwe, 2016). In spite of the diversity of the Nigerian culture, there are quite a number of striking identity markers which cut across all Nigerian ethnic groups. These include respect for parents and elders, taboos, extended family system, traditional political system, marriage and burial rites, arts and crafts amongst others. These cultural practices are usually preserved and passed down from one generation to another. However, the contemporary status of most Nigerian cultural practices such as the speaking of indigenous languages and taboos is best described as endangered and may go into extinction in the nearest future if urgent steps are not taken to reverse the trend. This trend according to Onadipe-Shalom (2020) is best described as a cultural shift since the culture of a people encapsulates language, arts and belief.

In simple terms, globalisation can be viewed as a social and cultural process which facilitates increased interconnectedness and interdependence amongst different individuals of diverse cultures, societies, economies and countries on a global scale. It typically involves the flow of goods and services, information, capital, technology and culture across cultural and national borders. Hence, the world is perceived as a global village. Globalisation is often facilitated by quite a number of factors which include trade agreements and economic policies, transportation networks, migration and mobility and in recent times, technological advancements via the emergence of ICT tools and social media platforms. Social media platforms such as X (formerly known as Twitter), Instagram and Tiktok allow individuals across the globe to connect with one another irrespective of their geographical locations, transcending the barriers of space and time. This process facilitates the spread and promotion of western cultural values, norms and practices as well as western media which include television shows and movies, music and literature. Nonetheless, western cultural products usually reflect western values, lifestyles and perspectives which often become dominant and pervasive in a society usually at the expense of local or indigenous culture. This is evidenced in the contemporary Nigerian society where the citizens typically imitate western culture without any form of modification and innovation (Asemah et al., 2013, Abunbe, 2024). This development has led to the dilution of the Nigerian cultural identity as western trends and values have continually gained prominence. This persistent dominance and influence of western values, norms and practices over the indigenous cultural practices of the Nigerian society is referred to as western cultural hegemony.

Social media platforms play significant roles in reinforcing western cultural hegemony in Nigeria through language, legal and political systems, fashion trends, media consumption, business practices and development strategies (Abunbe, 2024). Unfortunately, the reinforcement of western hegemony through the use of social media has led to the erosion of Nigeria's local customs. This according to Onah and Christian (2014) can be attributed to the gross obsession and abuse of social media platforms especially amongst Nigerian youths who happen to be the largest users of social media platforms. Some of the ways in which social media has promoted western cultural hegemony in Nigeria include constant exposure to western fashion trends, movies, music, games and TV shows. The consequences of constant exposure to western values and norms on social media include increase in the level of moral decadence, crime rates and other social vices (Asemah et al., 2013). For instance, pre-marital sex, homosexuality and lesbianism which were erstwhile strange and alien to the indigenous norms and values of Nigeria, are fast becoming common in the country. Furthermore, cultural practices such as the traditional folktales and folklores as well as speaking of indigenous languages are now on the brink of extinction as a result of the imposition of western culture vis-a-vis the social media.

Specifically, the use of English Language as the dominant language on most social media platforms has brought about the hegemony of English language at the detriment of indigenous languages in Nigeria which no doubt has marginalised local languages and expressions. Furthermore, the ubiquitous nature of social media platforms under the influence of western countries has dramatically changed the dressing patterns of Nigerian youths in recent times. This is evident in the way most women dress in recent times by exposing body parts that are meant to be kept private while most males braid their hairs, sag their trousers, put on earrings and wear torn clothes or rags (ripped jeans), all in the name of fashion (Asemah et al., 2013). The use of social media platforms has also transformed governance in Nigeria by serving as powerful tools for mobilisation, political campaigns, advocacy for human rights and activism. This has a positive impact in Nigeria where traditional media outlets face several limitations and biases. Social media outlets have also been used to challenge government decisions and also demand for accountability from the three tiers of government. Nonetheless, the use of social media promotes the spread of fake news, hate speech and misinformation which ultimately leads to tension in the country.

It is against this background that this study examines the concept of western cultural hegemony as it manifests through different social media channels in Nigeria. The study also explores how dominant western ideologies, values and practices are propagated within the sphere of diverse social media platforms. Finally, the study investigates how social media can be used to propagate the indigenous culture of the Nigerian society. These are with a view to preserving and promoting the indigenous cultural norms, values and beliefs of the Nigerian society and also fostering the promotion of collective consciousness in terms of unity, nationalism and peaceful co-existence among Nigerians. This will facilitate a balanced approach that acknowledges the significance of global connectivity while safeguarding the indigenous cultural integrity of Nigeria. This is in line with the Sustainable Development Goal (SDG) 11.4 which calls for countries to strengthen efforts to protect and safeguard the world's cultural and natural heritage for sustainable development. By elucidating the relationship between social media and the dominance of western norms and values in contemporary Nigeria, this study will contribute to the ongoing discussion on the socio-cultural implications of dominant western cultural values on the Nigerian society.

BACKGROUND

In order to properly historicise western cultural hegemony in Nigeria, it is paramount to define the terms culture, western culture and western cultural hegemony. Generally, culture refers to the totality of the ways of life of a group of people. Thus, culture can be viewed as a generic term that is used to describe the behavioural patterns, lifestyles, social structures and norms that distinguish a group of people from other sets of people (Onadipe-Shalom, 2020). There are two components of culture. These include the non-material or symbolic culture and the material culture. The non-material culture includes the customs, values and beliefs that define a particular society at a specific period of time while material culture includes the physical objects or artifacts that are prevalent in a society at a particular period of time. Typical examples of material culture include technology, means of transportation, type of food and fashion. Examples of non-material culture include language, laws, etiquette and religion. Western culture refers to the artifacts, traditions, customs, belief systems and values that are based on European culture.

The term hemegony is derived from the Greek word *hegemonia* which means "dominance over". The term *hegemonia* was formed from the verb *hegeisthai* which means to lead (Merriram-Webster Dictionary, 2024). It was used to describe the relationship between city-states. Hence, western cultural hegemony refers to the continual dominance of western culture over the indigenous cultural practices of a society. Western cultural hegemony began in Nigeria when the British colonised the country in the late 19th and early 20th century up to the period that Nigeria gained independence in 1960 and even to the post independence era (Odinye & Odinye, 2012). Specifically, Nigeria was colonised by the British in 1884 and obtained her independence on the 1st of October, 1960. It is worthy to emphasise that Nigeria became a British protectorate in 1901. Prior to this period, the territory comprised diverse geographically separated ethnic groups that were brought together by the British. The Southern and Northern Nigeria protectorates were amalgamated in 1914. The colonial period in Nigeria marked the era when the British colonised Nigeria primarily for socio-economic, religious and political gains. This is in accordance with Rodney (1972) who emphasised that the Europeans came to Africa with the 3Bs which include Business, Bible and Bullet. It is worthy to note that the colonisation of Nigeria was achieved through a combination of military forces, diplomacy, economic pressure and the collaboration of indigenous rulers. Nevertheless, the British hegemony in Nigeria brought about a lot of transformations in almost all the activities of the people which include agriculture, transportation, language, religion, marriage, dressing and education. This in turn had a profound influence on the social and cultural dynamics of the people. Despite the fact that Nigeria gained independence on the 1st of October, 1960, western norms, values and practices are still very dominant in the country. For instance, the most important legacy of British administration in Nigeria is the establishment of English as the official language. Although, this facilitates easy communication amongst individuals across diverse ethnic groups, the dominance of English language up to the post colonial era has continued to relegate the indigenous languages of the country to the background. The hegemony of the British in Nigeria also led to the establishment of western styled education where English served as the language of instruction. The British educational legacy in Nigeria which was biased towards western ideas has continued to exert influence while the indigenous form of education continues to receive little or no attention (Garba, 2012). Furthermore, the influence of British hegemony in the post-colonial era in Nigeria is very significant in the media as the media determines the socio-political advancement of any nation (Nzeaka, 2023). Nigeria as a British colony inherited the media system and practices of the British administrators. For instance, English language dominated the media space which reinforces the superiority of English language over the indigenous languages. In addition, media contents which promoted western values dominated the media while sidelining indigenous culture, beliefs and values. This according to Prosper (2009) is tagged media imperialism. A significant technological breakthrough in Nigeria in the post colonial era is the introduction of the social media which plays a pivotal role in globalisation through the connection of different people across the world. The social media has certainly influenced all aspects of human lives ranging from political mobilisation, economic opportunities, cultural expression, cultural shift, cultural exchange, information dissemination and advocacy for social change.

METHODOLOGY

An extensive review of relevant and related literature was carried out to determine how dominant western ideologies, values and practices are transmitted in Nigeria vis-à-vis social media platforms. A wide range of studies relating to western cultural hegemony in Nigeria before and after colonialism were searched in scientific electronic databases namely CiteseerX, Science Direct, JSTOR, Scopus and Google scholar. The Google search engine also served as an important tool for obtaining related documents and WebPages relevant to the study. Offline journals, inaugural lectures and books also played significant roles in the provision of relevant information for the study.

THEORETICAL FRAMEWORK

This study is centered on three theories which include Gramscian cultural theory of hegemony, theory of cultural imperialism and the theory of electronic colonisation. Hegemony is a historical process that is often associated with an Italian Marxist Philosopher, Antonio Gramsci who expanded the concept in his cultural theory of hegemony. Gramscian theory of hegemony states that hegemony occurs as a result of political, intellectual, economic and cultural dominance through which ruling classes dominate subordinate classes through a combination of force and consent to shape the values and norms of the subordinate classes usually with the aim of making the supremacy natural or legal (Alem, 2022). Accordingly, the subordinate nation accepts the hegemony of the dominant nation as normal, commonsensical and as the world view at the interest of the society at large. According to Ogen (2024), the consent of the subordinating nation is usually as a result of sheer manipulation by the domination group. This theory is related to this research because it helps to understand the hegemonic powers of the British in Nigeria vis-à-vis coercion, cultural domination and ideological consent. It also helps to understand the influence of the British hegemony on the culture of Nigeria before and after colonialisation.

The theory of cultural imperialism was propounded by Herbert Schiller in 1976. This theory focuses on the influence of the western world, most especially, the United States of America (USA) and its commercial media system on developing countries (Schiller, 1976). The theory is centered on how the culture, values and beliefs of the western world is spread and imposed on developing countries through the media, government, technology and economic influence which often represent a continual form of capitalism and imperialism. The theory emphasises that the culture of the western world becomes dominant and overshadows or replaces the indigenous culture of the developing countries. Although, cultural imperialism theory is centered on economic systems and government, it is more concerned with the media which includes literature, television, the internet and the social media in recent times. The media most especially the social media facilitates global communication and thus the spread of cultural values. In relating this theory to this study, it can be deduced that the social media has been used as tool for cultural imperialism in all activities in Nigeria ranging from arts, music, language to fashion and education. This framework also assists to understand that the Nigerian culture will not be developed if Nigerians give more priority to foreign media contents over local contents on the social media. It can also be inferred from the theory that Nigerian cultural heritage can be promoted through the social media if the citizens of Nigeria take the full responsibility of projecting the culture and norms of Nigeria positively on the social media.

The theory of electronic colonisation, usually abbreviated as e-colonialism theory was also propounded by Herbert Schiller in 1976. The theory postulates that the importation of communication hardware, foreign software products and other related information protocols suppress third world countries to the will, dominance and control of world powers such as the United States of America (USA), Japan and Germany (McPhail, 2002). This theory also emphasises that the emergence of computer meditated communication and digital media generate a new set of foreign cultural norms, values and beliefs which in turn distorts the indigenous culture and values of the third world countries (Muswede & Lubinga, 2018). Hence, industralised countries take advantage of their technological and economic superiority to impose their cultural, political and economic values on less powerful nations of the world. In line with this study, it can be deduced that the social media as the most prevalent technology used in Nigeria in recent times has be used to spread and promote western cultural values and practices, which have ultimately undermined the local culture and traditions of Nigeria, thereby spawning a new breed of colonialism.

PENETRATION OF SOCIAL MEDIA IN NIGERIA

Communication is as old as man. It is also one of the fundamental elements of any human society because it enhances the sustenance, transmission and perpetuation of culture, beliefs and values of the society. Nigeria has experienced various modes of communication at different levels of development. For instance, before the advent of technology in Nigeria, various modes of traditional communication systems existed amongst the people. Information were typically disseminated through recognised officials as well as familiar sounds, signs and symbols which include the blasts of local guns, smoke signals, the use of wooden and metallic gongs, setting bushes on fire, town crying and the use of "*aroko*" which is an indigenous Yoruba semiotic tool. Nevertheless, these means of disseminating information varies from one ethnic group to another and they were limited to short distances and were only effective in societies with homogenous population (Aziken &Emeni, 2010). In addition, a lot of people lost contacts with their loved ones due to long distance relocations. These traditional means of communication were predominately deployed during the pre-colonial era to satisfy people's desire for information about local events (Aziken & Emeni, 2010). During the colonial era, the broadcast media such as television, radio and newspapers were introduced to serve as tools for disseminating information, educating the citizens and promoting local culture.

Nigeria's communication landscape gradually evolved with the advent of telecommunication infrastructure during the British administration. The emergence of telegraphs and landline telephones also marked a significant milestone which facilitated long distance communication in Nigeria during this period. Furthermore, the proliferation of mobile phones, the Internet and other forms of digital broadcasting systems in the late twentieth century revolutionised the mode of communication in Nigeria. This resulted in instant connectivity and real time information exchange. Basically, the deregulation of the telecommunication industry and the adoption of the Global System of Mobile Communication (GSM) in Nigeria in 2001 paved way for the emergence of social media in Nigeria. The adoption of the social media in the twentieth century was further strengthened with the creation of various social network sites which included MySpace, 2go, Hi5, Yahoo messenger and

Friendster. These sites provided features which allowed users to make friends and chat through direct messages and share multimedia files. Unfortunately, Nigeria's online presence was limited at this period, hence, there was very limited data on the number of social media users at this time. Between 2004 and 2006, there was a spectacular breakthrough for social media platforms in Nigeria with the invention of social media platforms like Facebook, blackberry messenger, Instagram, Youtube, Whatsapp and Twitter. This era witnessed a huge change in media consumption as people constantly migrated to the use of smart phones which were predominantly used to access social media platforms (Igyuve and Obagwu, 2020). Furthermore, the rapid inclination of the Nigerian populace towards this technological innovation not only transcended communication, but encompasses all activities in the country ranging from economic, education and politics. Hence, the penetration of social media users in Nigeria continues to increase astronomically annually. As at the time of this research, Nigeria has a population of about 36.75 million social media users. This is equivalent to about 16.2% of the total population of the country (Kemp, 2024). The most popular social media platforms used in Nigeria as at the time of this research include Whatsappp, Facebook, Youtube, Instagram, TikTok, Facebook messenger, X, Snapchat, Telegram, Linkedin and Pinterest (Statistica, 2023a). It is interesting to note that Statistica (2024) ranked Nigeria as the leading country in the African continent whose citizens spend most of the time, with an average of 4hrs 20minutes on every social media platform visited, which is significantly higher than the global average of 2hrs 22mins. Research has also shown that the youths are the predominant users of social media platforms in Nigeria, constituting about 93% of the active social media users in the country (Statistica, 2023b). Table 1 shows the year, population of Nigeria, the active number of social media users and the penetration of social media platforms in Nigeria from 2015-2024.

Table 1. The penetration of social media platforms in Nigeria

S/N	Year	Population (Million)	Active Number of Social Media Accounts (Million)	Penetration of Social Media (Million)
1	2015	183.5	13.6	7
2	2016	184.6	15	8
3	2017	189.4	18	10
4	2018	193.4	19	10
5	2019	198.4	24	12
6	2020	203.6	27	13

continued on following page

Table 1. Continued

S/N	Year	Population (Million)	Active Number of Social Media Accounts (Million)	Penetration of Social Media (Million)
7	2021	208.8	33	15.8
8	2022	214.1	32.9	15.4
9	2023	221.2	31.6	14.3
10	2024	226.5	36.75	16.2

Source: (Kemp, 2015-2024)

Social Media and the Transmission of Hegemonic Western Culture in Contemporary Nigeria

The extensive proliferation of social media platforms in Nigeria in recent times has brought about intensive diffusion of western culture into the country. Thus, social media platforms such as Instagram, X, Facebook and Tiktok have further exposed Nigerians to western lifestyles and ideologies. The influence of social media in the transmission of dominant western culture in Nigeria is evident in the following ways:

Fashion Trends

Fashion plays a crucial role in the culture of Nigeria. It serves as a means of identification and self expression. Europeans, Americans and other western countries usually present their clothing, costumes and makeup as more superior to local fashion and this affects the way the indigenous fashion of different ethnic group in Nigeria is perceived (Olaitan, 2021). Thus, Nigerians prefer international brands when compared to local trademarks. This is heightened with the proliferation and ubiquitous nature of the social media in recent times as Nigerians are more accessible and exposed to western fashion influencers, brands and celebrities on social media platforms. Hence, most Nigerian youths prefer to align with western fashion norms at the detriment of traditional designs and styles. For instance, many young females prefer to wear crop tops, fitted t-shirts, bum shorts, short skirts and jeans while their male counterparts have a preference for ripped jeans, chinose, denim, stock jeans and baggy jeans. In addition, young females have embraced Eurocentric hair styles which include the wearing of wigs, the use of relaxers as well as braiding of hair with attachments and other hair extensions while relegating Nigerian hair styles such as *suku*, *koroba*, *patewo* and *ishi owu* to the background. Furthermore, many young men prefer to go on afro, braids and cornrows. Western foot wears such as chuncky sneakers and combat boots from western brands like Adidas, Nike and Balenciaga have also been widely embraced by Nigerian youths. These trends are usually featured on social media platforms with western accessories such as sunglasses, bags, belts, wrist watches and jewelries. International labels like Zara, Gucci, Nike, Channel and Luis Vitton have become more desirable among Nigerian social media savvy youths. It is important to emphasise at this point that a lot of Nigerian influencers and celebrities take photo shoots and videos in these western outfits on social media and also tag these brands, thereby making these outfits more accessible and trendy amongst Nigerian youths. Hence, the indigenous fashion of the Nigerian society is further refined by Nigerian celebrities and influencers who promote western fashion on social media.

Entertainment

Entertainment and social media platforms are deeply intertwined in Nigeria. For instance, western movies, music, games and TV shows are promoted on social media platforms such as Twitch, YouTube, Spotify, Vimeo, TikTok and Facebook Live. Interestingly, western multimedia contents which could not have been easily accessible via traditional media outlets such as television, radio and newspaper are easily accessed, copied, stored and distributed on social media platforms irrespective of the geographical locations of the social media users (Eemeli, 2023). Western movie stars and musicians usually create contents and launch dance and lip-sync harsh tag challenges usually on TikTok to popular western tracks. These challenges are usually taken up by many Nigerian youths who post dance routines and other challenges on their social media accounts. In addition, Nigerian celebrities and influencers who share their favourite western albums on social media also provide support for the propagation of western music as their followers on social media increase the visibility of these western tracks by reposting them. This is usually done at the detriment of Nigerian music and movies. In recent times, Nigerian musicians and artists also reflect western life styles in their music and movies which they share on their social media accounts. This no doubt promotes western cultural hegemony in Nigeria.

Language

According to Akujobi (2019), the hegemony of English is evident in Nigeria because it is the official language of the nation. Contents posted on social media platforms in Nigeria are predominantly in English Language. The social media therefore serves as powerful tool for expression in English language which contributes to the endangerment of Nigerian indigenous languages (Maikanti et al., 2021).

Consequently, indigenous languages are usually relegated and marginalised during online interaction. This hinders the younger generation from learning the indigenous languages as they spend most time on the social media. Hence, the transmission of indigenous culture, values and beliefs is at the brink of collapse since language is significant for the transfer of culture.

Education

With the advent of social media, teaching and learning in contemporary Nigeria are no longer confined to the four walls of the traditional classroom introduced by the British colonial administrators. Lectures, tutorials, research articles and other learning materials are usually accessible on social media platforms like Youtube, Researchgate, Academia.edu, and LinkedIn. These platforms also give opportunities to students and teachers to engage in discussions and collaborate with colleagues and professionals across the globe in their respective fields and they also offer academics and researchers the opportunity to showcase their professional achievements and peer reviewed activities (Vikash, 2013). These platforms are also used to facilitate learning via video chats, virtual classrooms and recorded tutorials. Social media platforms such as Whatsapp and Telegram are now used by Nigerian teachers to facilitate instant information exchange, make announcements and share educational materials among students. The pervasive presence of western educational contents on social media raises concerns about the rapid erosion of local educational practices, contents and values in Nigeria.

Health

The wide adoption of social media in Nigeria has profoundly helped in the propagation of western inspired healthcare system. Social media platforms like Facebook and X are used for health education to keep the citizens abreast of health information such as sudden disease outbreaks, the symptoms to look out for, prevention and cure. For instance, the announcement of the first victim of Corona Virus Disease (COVID-19) in Nigeria was first shared on the social media (Obi-Ani et al., 2020). In addition, remote patient monitoring, remote consultations and telemedicine services are now practiced on social media outlets in contemporary Nigeria (Adeyemo et al, 2021). These innovative forms of healthcare have resulted in the loss of the uniqueness of indigenous healthcare practices across various ethnic groups (Aderibole, 2023). The consequences of relying on health information on social media include vaccine hesitancy which can ultimately lead to the resurgence of a disease, spread of inaccurate information, unverified and fake health information for individuals seeking medical advice and solutions on social media, adoption of harmful health practices, self diagnosis and medication as well as untimely death.

Business

The presence of social media in Nigeria in recent times has transformed the traditional business model which typically relied on producer/manufacturer, wholesaler and retailer to reach the final customers. The intervention of social media in contemporary Nigeria allows producers to relate directly with the consumers without the intervention of the middlemen. Social media platforms such as Instagram and Facebook have also provided significant and cost effective platforms for popularising western-styled commerce and advertisement when compared to traditional media outlets like radio, newspaper and television (Marwan, 2022). These platforms provide features like online shopping catalogs, online markets, Ads, story and reels to promote business growth, customer service and customer engagement. Nigerian companies like Jumia, Jiji and Konga use social media platforms such as Facebook, Youtube, Pinterest and Instagram to advertise different products such as house hold items, mobile phones, electronics and garments while adopting the western styled business model of digital marketing (Atizwen, 2021). Social media platforms have also helped businesses in Nigeria to reach a wider audience. This is usually achieved by showcasing the brand s in a creative and entertaining way through short video clips and photos as well as collaborating with influencers and celebrities to help with the advertisement of the products on social media. In addition, social media is used to engage specific clients of a product in real time. This is usually achieved through features like comments, likes, reviews and messages. This is usually done with the view to increasing the awareness and visibility of the brand. Although, social media platforms have revolutionised the business model in Nigeria, it has however brought about a tremendous competition between indigenous businesses and foreign brands which leverage on social media platforms to reach their consumers. This has not only overshadowed the request for indigenous products which lack online presence but has resulted in a cultural shift from the traditional market system to online shopping.

Politics

Before the advent of social media in Nigeria, political discourse was primarily based on traditional media such as television, radio and newspaper (Ofei et al., 2024). Political parties and leaders largely depended on these platforms to campaign and communicate with the citizens. However, in recent times, the introduction of social media plays a major role in transmitting western political practices in Nigeria. For instance, social media platforms such as X and Nairaland has created a platform for Nigerian youths to participate in political activism, demonstrations, discussions and holding their leaders accountable. Notably, social media helped to promote western social movements like #Blacklivesmatter and #OccuyWallStreet. Nigerian activists have now adopted this western model on social media to address local political issues such as #Bringbackourgirls, #Endbadgovernance and #Endsars. Furthermore, political parties, government and politicians use social media platforms for grassroots movements, communication and sharing policies with the citizens. Social media has also been used during election for campaign, voters' education, monitoring voting updates and mobilisation. This was evident in the 2015, 2019 and 2023 general elections in Nigeria. For instance, the social media was deployed to closely monitor and intermittently broadcast the results of these elections across different voting centers in the nation to prevent the manipulation of the results of the election even before the official announcement by Independent National Electoral Commission (INEC) (Orngu, 2018). This no doubt led to the rapid spread of false information which incited violence, killings, hate speech and cyber bullying during these elections.

Exposure to Western Sexually Explicit Materials

The exponential increase in the use of social media platforms has exposed Nigerian youths to western sexually explicit materials otherwise referred to as X-rated contents (Olaleye & Ajuwon, 2022). The consequences of this exposure include emotional disorder, change in sexual behaviour and increased probability of engaging in sexually permissive behaviours such as masturbation, casual and premarital sex, multiple partners, homosexuality, bisexuality, transgender (LGBT) as well as cohabitation without marriage. This experience clashes with the indigenous traditional values of the various ethnic groups in Nigeria which uphold sexual morality, modesty and decency.

Marriage

The proliferation of social media in Nigeria has led to the disrespect for the values of traditional marriage across various ethnic groups in Nigeria (Esiri, 2021). For instance, marriage without parental consent and blessing, influenced by western values on social media has increasingly gained popularity in Nigeria (Esiri, 2021). This of course is against the traditional marriage system of diverse ethnic groups in Nigeria which emphasise family approval and involvement as well as parental consent and blessings as significant elements of marriage. In addition, in indigenous Nigeria, marriage was the precursor to child bearing. However, this practice has being gradually eroded in the contemporary Nigeria with the rising trend of baby mama syndrome, a term used to describe the situation in which a woman becomes a mother without the legal and traditional structures of marriage. It is worthy to note that the word baby mama stems from western hip pop songs in Jamaica, England and United States of America and has been widely embraced and practiced by Nigerian musicians and artists as well as Nigerian influencers and celebrities who play prominent role in defining Nigerian contemporary culture, particularly among the youths who see them as role models (Raheem, 2018). The consequences of this practice on the institution of marriage include the undermining of marriage among the youths, stigma or public contempt as well as emotional and psychological effects on both the mother and children produced by such practice (Raheem, 2018).

Social Media and the Reinvention of Indigenous Cultural Practices in Contemporary Nigeria

It is an established fact that social media has exposed Nigerians across diverse ethnic groups to western hegemonic culture which has led to cultural shift and has in turn reshaped the cultural landscape of the nation. The use of social media could however be used to effectively promote the cultural identity of all ethnic groups in Nigeria in the following ways:

Promotion of Traditional Festivals

Different traditional communities and cultural organisations across different ethnic groups should intensify efforts to display their festivals and rituals on social media in order to attract global attention. This can be achieved by uploading and sharing captivating photos, videos, and stories about the activities associated with the festivals such as the attires worn, dances and masquerades. In addition, Nigerian festivals can also be promoted on the social media by stream living them. This will encourage those who could not attend in person to participate in the festival virtually, thereby, giving a wider audience to the event. In addition, social media hashtags can be used to increase the visibility of the event on a global scale and also attract foreign tourists. Notable festivals such as the *OjudeOba* festival of the people of Ijebu-Ode has been promoted on social media platforms such as Instagram and X using the *#OjudeOba* where different individuals created different posts, videos and images of the horse-riding events and contest, colorful parade and attires worn. The popularity of other Nigerian festivals such as *oro* festival in Oyo state, *eyo* festival in Lagos state, *olojo* festival in Ile-Ife, *odun iyoyan* and *odun ogun* in Ondo state and *sokoto shadi* festival in Sokoto state can also be promoted on different social media platforms.

Revitalisation of Nigerian Indigenous Languages

The social media can be used as a tool to revive and preserve Nigerian indigenous languages that are currently facing the threat of extinction as a result of the dominance of English language on social media platforms. More efforts should be made by Nigerians most especially influencers and celebrities to use social media as a platform for creating indigenous language learning contents such as proverbs, traditional stories, folklores, idiomatic expressions as well as oral traditions. In addition, educational contents such as tutorials and lessons on different subjects can be posted and shared on social media platforms using indigenous languages as the medium of instruction. This will not only promote Nigerian indigenous languages but will make learning more engaging and relatable. Nigerian artists, influencers and celebrities can also create and share contents, and also initiate challenges such as music, skits and artistic performances in their native languages. This will inspire their followers to participate and further post the contents to a wider and global audience.

Showcasing Nigerian Traditional Attires and Accessories

More efforts should be placed on the use of social media platforms such as Instagram to promote Nigerian indigenous attires, accessories and jewelries. Well styled photo shoots, reels and videos of Nigerian traditional attires and accessories should be intensively used to display the creativity of local designers and the rich tapestry of Nigerian attires to the global audience for the preservation and appreciation of Nigerian cultural heritage. Fashion shows should not only be limited to weekly fashion magazines in contemporary Nigeria but models and different individuals should wear different traditional attires and local accessories and display them on social media platforms. This will facilitate cultural exchange on a global scale, thereby, attracting the global community to Nigerian fashion.

Displaying Historical Landmarks and Cultural Heritage Sites

Nigeria is blessed with numerous cultural heritage sites which reflect her rich culture and history. Displaying these historical landmarks and cultural heritage sites on social media platforms will provide the avenue to showcase the rich history, culture and heritage of the country. For instance, photo galleries, videos, guided tours, interactive experiences and historical articles of historical sites like the *Surkur* cultural heritage in Adamawa state, *Osun-Osogbo* sacred groove, *Nok* culture sites in Plateau state and *Ogbunike* caves in Anambra states can be displayed by Nigerian influencers and celebrities on social media to increase the popularity of these historical sites globally.

The use of social media to showcase Nigerian cuisines and gastronomy is gradually gaining prominence in contemporary Nigeria. Food bloggers, chefs, influencers and celebrities usually post and share cooking recipes, photo galleries, cooking tutorials, video contents and reels of traditional dishes like pounded yam and *egusi* soup, *ikokore* and Nigerian jollof rice. These contents no doubt will help to popularise these dishes globally.

FUTURE RESEARCH DIRECTIONS

The focus of this research can be extended in the nearest future by further examining the influence of Nigerian cultural values and beliefs on the global audience through the cultural exchange that occurs on social media platforms. The future directions for this research can also be centered on the role of the Nigerian government policies and regulations in curbing the cultural hegemony of the western world and also promoting the indigenous culture of the nation on social media platforms. Furthermore, future research on this study could focus on the study and impact of the hybridised culture that has been created through the blending of the western culture and indigenous culture of Nigeria on social media platforms.

These directions will no doubt contribute to the comprehension of the impact of social media platforms on the cultural exchange and dynamics of Nigeria and the western world.

CONCLUSION

The impact of social media in contemporary Nigeria has profoundly strengthened the presence of western hegemony in Nigeria by accelerating the wide spread and adoption of western culture, values, lifestyles and ideologies. The persistent exposure of Nigerians to western culture via social media platforms promotes modernisation, innovation and global connectivity. However, this development has brought a tremendous cultural shift in language, fashion trends, political perspectives and indigenous food of the nation. This poses the threat of overshadowing Nigerian indigenous values, local traditions and practices, culture and beliefs. Nevertheless, social media offers a platform for resisting western cultural hegemony in Nigeria by promoting Nigerian indigenous culture across various ethnic groups. Ultimately, while social media is used as a powerful tool for fostering global connections and

REFERENCES

Abunbe, G. T. (2024). Western hegemony in Africa: An assessment of the sacrifice of indigenous culture on the altar of expediency. *Journal of Public Administration. Policy and Governance Research*, *2*(2), 97–110.

Aderibole, O. (2023). Social media and health misinformation: A toxic duo. Retrieved September15, 2024, from http://www.nigeriainfo.fm

Adeyemo, A. A., Ogunkeyede, S. A., Ogundoyin, O. A., & Oyelakin, O. A. (2021). Evolving telemedicine practice: Experiences of healthcare workers during covid-19 pandemic. *Annals of Ibadan Postgraduate Medicine*, *19*(1), 44–48. PMID: 25161433

Akujobi, O. S. (2019). The English Language hegemony and sociolinguistic Effects on indigenous languages. *Journal of African Studies and Sustainable Development*, *2*(2), 130–143.

Alem, D. D. (2022). *Hegemony according to Gramsci*. Paper presented at Literary Theory and Criticism II, Bahir Dar University, Ethopia.

Asemah, E. S., Ekhareafo, D. O., & Olaniran, S. (2013). Nigeria's core values and the use of social media to promote cultural values. *International Journal of Information and Communication Technology Education*, *9*(4), 58–69. DOI: 10.4018/ijicte.2013100104

Atizwen, F. B. (2021). *Social media advertitising and consumer patronage of jumia online shopping*. Unpublished masters dissertation, Nasarawa State University, Nigeria.

Aziken, L. C., & Emeni, F. C. A. (2010). Traditional Systems of communication in Nigeria: A review for improvement. *Knowledge Review*, *21*(4), 23–29.

Baran, S. (2002). *Introduction to mass communication, media literacy and culture*. McGraw Hill Higher Education.

Dave, E. (2008). *Social media marketing: An hour a day*. John Willy & Sons.

Eemeli, B. (2023). *Utilizing social media platforms in music marketing*. Unpublished bachelors dissertation, Tampere University of Applied Sciences, Finland

Esiri, M. O. (2021). Social change and marriage structure in Nigeria. *International Research Journal of Management, IT &. Social Sciences*, *1*(3), 228–235.

Garba, S. J. (2012). The Impact of colonialism on Nigerian Education and the Need for E-learning technique for sustainable development. *Journal of Educational and Social Research*, 2(7), 53–61.

Gramsci, A. (1971). *1891-193 Selections from the prison notebooks of Antonio Gramsci*. International Publishers.

Igyuve, A. I., & Obagwu, P. U. (2020). The new media in Nigeria: Evolution, impacts, challenges and prospects. *IMSU Journal of Communication Studies*, *4*(2), 63–73.

Maikanti, S., Chukwu, A., Odibah, M., & Ogu, M. (2021). Globalization as a factor for language endangerment: Nigerian indigenous languages in focus. *Malaysian Journal of Social Sciences and Humanities*, *6*(9), 521–527. DOI: 10.47405/mjssh.v6i9.1055

Marwan, W. M. (2022). Traditional media versus social media: Challenges and opportunities. *Technium*, *4*(10), 145–160. DOI: 10.47577/technium.v4i10.8012

McPhail, T. L. (2002). *Global communication: Theories, stakeholders and trends*. Allyn and Bacon.

Merriram-Webster Dictionary. (2024). *Hegemony*. Retrieved October 11, 2024, from http://www.merriram-webster dictionary.com

Ministry of Foreign Affairs. (2022). *Nigeria culture and heritage*. Retrieved October 11, 2024, from http://www.foreignaffairs.gov.ng

Muswede, T., & Lubinga, E. (2018). Global media hegemony and the transformation bliss in post colonial Africa: Real independence or change of masters. *African Journal of Public Affairs*, *10*(2), 82–96.

Nzeaka, E. (2023). Media policies and control under colonial and military regimes in Nigeria. *Global Media Journal*, *21*, 61.

Obi-Ani, N. A., Anikwenze, C., & Isiani, M. C. (2020). Social media and the covid-19 experience: Observations from Nigeria. *Cogent Arts & Humanities*, *7*(1), 1799483. Advance online publication. Retrieved October 15, 2024, from. DOI: 10.1080/23311983.2020.1799483

Odinye, O., & Odinye, O. (2012). Western influence on Chinese and Nigerian cultures. *Ogirisi: A New. Journal of African Studies*, *9*, 108–115.

Ofei, E. K., Agbukor, L. A., Okunorobo, E. P., & Eseoghene, E. (2024). A review of social media as alternative medium for political participation. *International Journal of Research Publication and Reviews*, *5*(1), 489–497. DOI: 10.55248/gengpi.5.0124.0116

Ogen, O. (2024). *Reconstructing a silenced past: Echoes of revisionism and counter hegemonic history* (21st Inaugural Lecture). Osogbo, Nigeria: Osun State University.

Olaitan, T. (2021). *Modernising the primitive African: The influence of colonialism on African dressing*. Retrieved October 11, 2024, from https://www.decolonialthoughts.com/post/modernising-the-primitive-african-the-influence-of-colonialism-on-african-dressing

Olaleye, O. S., & Ajuwon, A. (2022). Influence of the use of social-media and exposure to pornography on the sexual behaviour of youths in selected tertiary institutions in southwest Nigeria. *Health Behavior Research*, *5*(3), 1–19. DOI: 10.4148/2572-1836.1137

Onadipe-Shalom, T.A. (2020). Endangered language and culture: The gradual loss of greetings among Yoruba children in southwestern Nigeria. *Ò pá bàta,* 1-7.

Onah, N., & Christian, N. G. (2014). The moral implication of social media phenomenon in Nigeria. *Mediterranean Journal of Social Sciences*, *5*(20), 2231–2237. DOI: 10.5901/mjss.2014.v5n20p2231

Onyejekwe, A. (2001). National identity: peoples and cultures of Nigeria. In Ajaegbo, D. I., & Ibezim, E. O. (Eds.), *Citizenship education in Nigeria: An interdisciplinary approach*. West & Solomon.

Orngu, C. (2018). The social media and Nigeria's electoral politics since 1999: Trends and implications for Nigeria's external image. *Nigerian Journal of Political and Administrative Studies*, *4*(1), 184–203.

Prosper, O.F. (2009). Global media and media products in Nigeria. *A Journal of Contemporary Research*, 6(2), 424-437.

Raheem, O. (2018). Having his baby and not being his wife: The baby mama trend and marriage practices in the Nigerian entertainment industry. *African Trends*, *42*(1&2), 41–55.

Rodney, W. (1972). *How Europe underdeveloped Africa*. London: Bogle-L'Ouverture,.

Schiller, H. I. (1976). *Communication and cultural dependency*. International Arts and Sciences Press.

Siollum, M. (2021). *What Britain did to Nigeria: A short history of conquest and rule*. Hurst and Co Publishers.

Statistica (2023a). *Most used social media platforms in Nigeria as of the 3rd quarter of 2023*. Retrieved October 11, 2024, from http://www.statistica.com

Statistica (2023b). *Daily social media usage in Africa, 2023 by country*. Retrieved October 11, 2024, from http://www.statistica.com

Vaughan, O. (2016). *Christianity and the transformation of colonial southern and northern Nigeria*. Duke University: Duke University Press. DOI: 10.1215/9780822373872-004

Vikash, K. M. (2013). Role of Social Media in Education. *International Journal Of Creative Researvh Thoughts*, *1*(3), 857–860.

Chapter 15
A Multimodal Discourse Analysis of Outlined Sneak Peeks of Selected Bollywood Blockbusters

Olayinka Adetayo Odubela
https://orcid.org/0009-0004-0003-7169
Obafemi Awolowo University, Ile-Ife, Nigeria

Yemisi Mulikat Famakinwa
Obafemi Awolowo University, Ile-Ife, Nigeria

ABSTRACT

Language is a medium of communication and invariably, an inevitable means of communication. The present study intends to examine language use as espoused in sneak peeks in the media. Hence, the study considers sneak peeks as language of advertising Bollywood blockbusters or movies. The data comprise three different outlined sneak peeks. By outlined, it means the sneak peeks comprise sequential utterances which are produced by some characters in the blockbusters. Three Bollywood blockbusters are purposively selected based on the sequential arrangement of sneak peeks henceforth, speakers' utterances. Drawing insight from Multimodal Discourse Analysis, the study discovers that as a sub-genre of the media discourse, sneak peeks involve the speakers and their respective utterances to convey meaning. Findings also show that multiple modes for meaning interpretation of media text aid audience comprehension. Further, effective language use for communication in the media serve as a means of arousing the interest of the prospective video viewers.

DOI: 10.4018/979-8-3693-7934-9.ch015

Introduction

Culture and society are bound together by language, which is a means of interaction (Pirini, 2017). Language, therefore, is used in virtually all fields of human endeavour such as the fields of religion, medicine, sea transport, air transport, entertainment, road transport, education, publishing/mass media, sports, agriculture/fishing, and law. Interestingly, each of the fields has its own peculiarities which manifest in the different uses of language. By implication, the register and, invariably, the language use in the field of law, differs from that, which is used in the field of medicine and all others. Hence, language can be used to establish or build relation. The same can be used to foster unity or cause disunity. It should be noted that language can be positively or negatively functional. This is because in some cultures, the expression, *sorry*, can invoke a positive or negative vibe. Currently, given diverse innovations in present day technology, language use has witnessed series of developments in spellings, pronunciation, and uses of the punctuation marks. Now, messages can be communicated by mere dashes or any punctuation mark with a distinct meaning (*emojis*) or by a display of stickers. Overall, language is everywhere and it is what we all live by since it provides needful information for human existence and wellbeing. The present study considers language use in the media with emphasis on sneak peeks' utterances of some Bollywood blockbusters. The study thus analyses and discusses language use as espoused in sneak peeks in order to unravel the overall meaning of the selected Bollywood blockbusters. It should be noted that the utterances of the sneak peeks are interactions among certain characters in the blockbusters which take place between people, objects and the environment.

BACKGROUND

1. Bollywood

Bollywood, the Hindi-language film industry based in Mumbai, has a rich historical foundation that began in the early 20th century. It emerged from the confluence of traditional Indian theater and the influence of Western cinematic techniques. Early films were heavily inspired by theatrical performances, particularly those from Parsi theater, which combined storytelling with music and dance (Gokulsing & Dissanayake, 2020). This fusion laid the groundwork for Bollywood's unique narrative style. Post-independence, Bollywood became a significant cultural force, reflecting the aspirations and struggles of a newly independent nation. The themes of nationalism and identity were prevalent, as filmmakers sought to portray an idealized vision of Indian society (Hirji, 2024). This era saw Bollywood films addressing social issues while also reinforcing traditional values, thus playing a dual role in both entertainment and cultural discourse.

Bollywood's cultural impact extends beyond mere entertainment; it acts as a mirror to societal values and norms. The narratives often explore themes such as love, family dynamics, and social justice, resonating deeply with audiences across diverse backgrounds. For example, films that address women's empowerment or caste discrimination have sparked important conversations within society, encouraging audiences to reflect on their own experiences and beliefs (Booth, 2012). Furthermore, Bollywood has significantly influenced fashion and lifestyle trends across South Asia. The clothing styles showcased in films often set trends that are adopted by fans in countries like Nepal and Pakistan (Pugsley & Khorana, 2011). This cultural exchange not only promotes Indian traditions but also fosters a sense of shared identity among audiences in the region.

Language plays a crucial role in Bollywood films, serving as both a medium of communication and a reflection of cultural identity.

While Hindi is predominantly used, the integration of other regional dialects enriches the storytelling experience (Pandey & Singh, 2020). The emergence of Hinglish—a blend of Hindi and English—has become particularly popular among younger audiences, illustrating the evolving linguistic landscape within contemporary narratives (Dwyer, 2006, Pandey & Singh, 2020). Bollywood's influence on societal norms is profound. Films frequently depict idealised family structures and gender roles that reinforce traditional values while simultaneously confronting modern dilemmas (Gokulsing & Dissanayake,2020). This duality allows Bollywood to resonate with diverse audiences—both within India and among the diaspora—who navigate their identities in an increasingly globalised world.

2. Blockbusters

Blockbusters are movies with remarkable achievement which span or spread for a long time and with huge sales. The word "blockbuster" was a nickname for a particular bomb used for massive destruction during the world war, and later the meaning was accrued to American movies which were acclaimed to have cost a lot of money in their production. Then a "Blockbuster movie" was to have certain aesthetic features which included exceptional length, a large scale, and various types of spectacles. (Hall, 2014).

Herrington (2015) opines that blockbuster films are more than just movies as they have been and are being ingrained into popular cultures due to extensive promotion and marketing in collaboration with major brands for promotions which helps them become integrated into the fabric of everyday life, extending beyond the confines of the cinema.

Also, the adoption of modern information communication technological channels such as the internet and digital platforms, home video and international box offices also play a crucial role in helping Blockbusters films reach larger audiences providing ways to engage viewers, making movies more accessible and memorable. Blockbusters have become influential cultural forces. As a result, the film industry, driven by these large-scale movies continues to attract viewership and popularity than other entertainment forms, such as sports or theme parks. Herrington (2015) further opines that despite economic downturns, especially in 2014, blockbusters have remained successful.

Hall further elucidates that in 1950s certain genres were categorised as Blockbusters. They are biblical and historical epics, action-adventure films, westerns, war movies, science fiction and fantasy, as well as some musicals and comedies. The blockbusters were often released in a limited capacity through roadshows (where the movie was shown in select theaters), but thereafter the movies were later released strategically in many theaters simultaneously supported by extensive media campaigns and advertising.

Justification for Selected Bollywood Blockbusters

The choice of three Bollywood blockbusters—*Bang Bang, Bullet Raja, and Traffic*—is particularly significant due to the sequential placements or arrangements of character utterances that arouse the interest of the audience. Sourced from DSTV Channel 161 – Starlife commercial, for Bollywood blockbusters in June, 2024, these films utilise sneak peeks as effective marketing tools, providing brief glimpses that showcase key dialogue and action sequences, thereby enhancing viewer engagement and anticipation.

Bang Bang

In *Bang Bang,* sneak peeks often include action-packed sequences that highlight Hrithik Roshan's character's thrilling escapades. The promotional clips showcase breathtaking stunts and glamorous locations, effectively capturing the film's adventurous spirit. By strategically releasing these sneak peeks before the film's premiere, the marketing team aims to create buzz and intrigue. The arrangement of these clips—often featuring dramatic moments followed by lighter, romantic interactions—mirrors the film's narrative structure, keeping viewers engaged and eager for more (Filmfare, 2014). The sequential placement of dialogue during these sneak peeks not only highlights key character dynamics, but also builds excitement for the full cinematic experience.

Bullet Raja

In *Bullet Raja*, sneak peeks focus on the film's gritty storyline and strong character portrayals. The promotional materials highlights Saif Ali Khan's character in intense dialogues that resonate with themes of power and rebellion. By showcasing these powerful utterances in the sneak peeks, the marketing strategy aims to draw in audiences interested in action and drama while emphasizing the socio-political context of the film (Pinkvilla, 2013). The strategic arrangement of these dialogues within the sneak peeks served to enhance audience interest, as viewers could sense the tension and stakes involved in the story.

Traffic

Traffic utilizes sneak peeks to emphasize its emotional depth and urgency. The promotional clips often feature snippets of dialogue that conveys the characters' desperation and determination to save a life. By arranging these poignant utterances sequentially in the sneak peeks, the filmmakers effectively communicate the film's high stakes and emotional weight (Chitrkala, 2016). This approach, not only build anticipation, but also encourages viewers to connect with the characters' journeys on a deeper level. The careful placement of these dialogues within the promotional material mirrored how they functioned within the film itself, enhancing overall engagement.

3. Sneak peeks

Sneak peeks refer to brief previews or glimpses of upcoming films, designed to generate excitement and anticipation among audiences. These previews can take various forms, such as short clips, behind-the-scenes footage, or exclusive scenes that offer a tantalizing taste of what a movie has to offer. The primary goal is to arouse interest and create an atmosphere that encourages movie lovers to watch the advertised film. While sneak peeks serve a similar purpose to trailers, they often differ in length and content. Trailers are typically longer, more polished promotional videos that provide a comprehensive overview of the film's plot, characters, and tone. In contrast, sneak peeks are shorter snippets that may focus on specific scenes or moments, often leaving viewers with questions and curiosity about the larger narrative.

For instance, in the Bollywood film *Bang Bang* (2014), sneak peeks play a significant role in generating excitement and anticipation among audiences prior to its release. One notable instance is the release of a behind-the-scenes featurette that showcases the film's high-octane action sequences and stunning locations. This sneak peek provides fans with an exclusive look at the preparation and training that lead actor Hrithik Roshan underwent for the film's demanding stunts, including fly-boarding, which was a first for Bollywood cinema (Internet Movie Database, 2014).

Another example of a sneak peek for *Bang Bang* includes short clips that highlighted key moments from the film, such as romantic scenes between Hrithik Roshan and Katrina Kaif. These glimpses not only tease the chemistry between the leads but also showcases the film's lavish production values and exotic settings, further enticing viewers to watch the full movie (The Statesman, 2014). These sneak peeks are strategically released across various platforms, including social media and entertainment news outlets, effectively engaging audiences and building momentum leading up to the film's premiere.

Sneak peeks and trailers play a crucial role in shaping audience expectations and engagement. They are essential marketing tools that leverage the emotional responses of viewers. A well-crafted sneak peek can create buzz on social media platforms, encouraging discussions and speculation about the film's storyline and characters (DSTV Channel, 167). Moreover, sneak peeks often capitalise on key moments from the film that resonate with fans, such as iconic dialogues or visually stunning sequences. This targeted approach helps filmmakers gauge audience reactions and adjust their marketing strategies accordingly.

4. Advertisement and Multimodal Discourse Analysis

Advertisement is a marketing strategy employed as a means of interacting and communicating with the target audience. The language of advertisement as far as this study is concerned, focuses on language use in the media. Hence, the study considers language use in the advertisement of some Bollywood blockbusters. Language use in the media discourse and more so in movie advertisement is what translates altogether as sneak peeks which is a preview of an event such as a film or movie. It should be noted that the preview of the Bollywood blockbusters is documented in the English language. With language playing a vital role in advertisement as well as in linguistic analysis, the present study considers the approach of Multimodal Discourse Analysis which aims to integrate the representational, interactive and textual meanings achieved by various elements in a discourse.

5. Multimodal Discourse Analysis

Before discussing Multimodal Discourse Analysis (MDA), it is needful to know what Discourse Analysis (DA) is all about. Discourse analysis is described as language use relative to social, political and cultural formations (Olateju, 2004 p.10). No doubt, this definition of DA makes it overlap with MDA. This is because discourse analysis is the analysis of language in its social context. By social context, it means different structures, strategies and processes of a text are involved. By structures, it means the linguistic structures and choices put in place to make a text function. By strategies, it means the methods involved in putting the linguistic structures and choices into its appropriate uses. This coincides with the Hallidayan theory of language which talks about the interpersonal, the ideational and the textual metafunctions. By processes, it means the mode of communication which can be the spoken or the written. With the advent of the Internet, the world has moved from the conventional practice of monolithic level of language assessment offered by DA, to the multiple modes. The multiple modes are what births Multimodal Discourse Analysis (MDA). No doubt, DA is the foundation which MDA builds on to achieve its goals: to integrate the representational, interactive and textual meanings achieved by various elements in a discourse.

Therefore, MDA is a method of studying social interaction and meaning produced through multiple modes of communication. The multiple modes of communication in MDA are not just studied in isolation, rather, about understanding how the modes work together to create semiotic meaning. The multiple modes of communication include text, colour and images. In fact, the domain of images and texts is the spoken discourse (Coulthard, 1981). MDA looks not just how each of these modes communicates, but how they collectively interact with one another to create semiotic meaning. The task of MDA is thus to analyse how these modes as elements work together to form a complete discourse. MDA can be applied to various types of texts such as print, web, film and television (O' Halloran, 2004). The present chapter is interested in film; the instance of some Bollywood blockbusters. The different modes of text (written or transcribed) and colour and images are considered in order to achieve a positive communicative effect.

As already discussed, different utterances of characters which translate altogether as sneak peeks are considered for analysis in the selected Bollywood blockbusters in order to construe meaning of the advertised movies. It is therefore necessary to see the connection between language and utterances. An **utterance** is a stretch of **language.** By implication, both a language and an utterance are inseparable. An utterance is also made of sentences which may be regular or irregular. The purpose of an utterance is to communicate. The same is also equivalent to *what is said.* This definition of utterance shares nexus with Speech Acts especially, locutionary Act since it refers to what is said by the speaker that is, the words of the speaker. In other words, the speaker's words are the speaker's utterances. It should be noted that underlying the speaker's words or utterances are the speaker's intents or intentions. This is the illocutionary act. The third of speech act is the perlocutionary which refers to the effect of the speaker's utterance on the listener. With Speech Acts serving as an offshoot from discourse, the study considers a Multimodal Discourse Analysis (MDA) of utterances as interactions among some characters henceforth speakers, in some Bollywood blockbusters. These utterances or interactions which translate as and constitute the sneak peeks, are needful in order to construe meaning of the advertised movies.

6. Semiotics: An integral part of Multimodal Analysis

One cannot separate Multimodal Analysis without mentioning semiotics. Semiotics is simply the study of signs or sign language. Olateju and Oyebode (2014) state that as communication is an integral part of human existence, it becomes necessary to consider semiotics as part of communication because communication is not just the use of words. It involves countless texts, where text is "an assemblage of signs such as words, images, sounds and/or gestures) constructed and (interpreted) with reference to the conventions associated with a genre and in a particular medium of communication." (Olateju & Oyebode, 2014, p.19).

Olateju & Oyebode (2014) further assert that texts are to be cohesive, i.e. the internal structures of utterances such as clauses and sentences must connect together. These texts can also be single a unit comprising several texts and they include websites, TV programs, YouTube, PowerPoint presentations etc. (D'Angelo & Marino,2024). These texts must work cohesively to convey meaning. Hence semiotics involves both written and unwritten, spoken and unspoken signs and modes of communication. Van Leeuen (2005) also refers to these modes of communication as semiotic resources that entail "actions and artifacts". In addition, when society is involved in the creating and meaning making of semiotic resources, it is referred to as social semiotics which is also an integral part of communication especially in a culturally diverse world with modern technologies.

Multimodal Discourse Analysis of Blockbusters

A multimodal discourse analysis of Bollywood blockbusters reveals how various elements work synergistically to convey meaning. This analysis encompasses visual imagery, song and dance, and narrative techniques, each contributing to the film's overall impact.

Visual Imagery

The vibrant cinematography and elaborate set designs in Bollywood films often reflect traditional Indian aesthetics while appealing to global sensibilities. For instance, in *Bang Bang*, the film's use of stunning locations—such as the picturesque landscapes of Greece and the vibrant streets of Mumbai—enhances the visual storytelling. The cinematography not only showcases the beauty of these settings but also serves to immerse audiences in the film's world (IMDb, 2014). The integration of advanced visual effects (VFX) further elevates the cinematic experience, allowing filmmakers to create visually captivating sequences that resonate with both domestic and international audiences (School of Design, 2023).

Songs

In Bollywood, songs are vital narrative tools, revealing characters' emotions and motivations. Through poignant lyrics and music, these songs encapsulate complex themes, creating an emotional resonance that deepens storytelling and audience connection.

Dance

Dance sequences in Bollywood films serve as a powerful form of expression that complements the narrative conveyed through songs. Unlike Western cinema, where dance may be less integral to the plot, Bollywood often intertwines dance with storytelling. The synchronization of dance movements with musical beats enhances the overall impact of the song, creating a dynamic viewing experience. Dance also plays a significant role in cultural representation.

Choreography

Choreography in Bollywood is not merely decorative; it often serves as a narrative device that advances the plot or develops characters. Dance sequences can mark significant moments in the storyline—such as falling in love or overcoming obstacles—thus acting as narrative nodes that guide audience engagement (Dwyer, 2006). The use of vibrant costumes, dynamic formations, and background dancers enriches the visual storytelling while reinforcing cultural motifs associated with celebration and community (NFI, 2023).

REVIEW OF WORKS AND STATEMENT OF RESEARCH PROBLEM

According to O'Halloran et al. 2009, p.2, multimodal discourse is "a form of communication involving multiple semiotic resources such as language (spoken and written), gesture, dress, architecture, gaze, camera angle, etc." From this definition, it is evident that language plays a central role in communication. As a result, research on linguistic approaches to communication, such as Conversation Analysis (CA) and

Multimodal Discourse Analysis (MDA), is essential for discussion. The following authors and their research works are thus considered:

Kasper & Wagner (2014) distinguish between basic and applied CA, considering talk (such as phone calls) in relation to other semiotic resources. Employing a qualitative analysis, the authors apply CA to the study of social domains and practices that are interactionally constituted to construe meaning.

White (2019) examines CA as a qualitative research methodology. It analyses structures of interaction at a micro-level, showing how participants make sense of each other in conversation through shared interactional norms. Focusing on health care interactions, the study asserts that analytic research, its applications, and its use can be effective for health care researchers.

Mullins et al. (2022) construe communication as being at the heart of social work. Communication is positioned as the domain through which social work is conducted, focusing on discussions and interactions. Employing a Qualitative Social Work methodology, the article applies CA to social work practice, addressing how social work clients are engaged to achieve institutional outcomes such as client engagement or agreeing on a focus for intervention.

Yeomans et al. (2023) define conversation as a verbal interaction between two or more people. It describes conversation as complex and one of the most pervasive of all human behaviors. The study suggests approaches to overcoming common challenges in the workflow of conversation science, including recording and transcribing conversations, structuring data, extracting and aggregating linguistic features, estimating effects, and sharing data. The study sheds light on current best practices for studying conversations more directly and contributing to a greater cumulative scientific understanding of the social world.

Ademilokun & Olateju (2015) present a multimodal discourse analysis of visual images in the political rally of the 2011 electioneering campaigns in southwestern Nigeria. The authors argue that visual images are indispensable tools during rallies, identifying semiotic resources such as artifacts as essential to communication. These artifacts project the inherent ideologies of political, cultural, and social communicative values.

Oyebode & Unuabonah (2024) explore coronavirus-related internet memes in the Nigerian WhatsApp space. The study finds that represented participants engage with the public using multimodal concepts, including resources such as disclaimers and entertainment. These resources, the study suggests, are essential for achieving communicative goals, offering succor and support to people during the pandemic.

Amosu et al. (2024) explore how semiotic elements and symbols convey meaning in African animated films, such as the animated series *IWAJU*. Through the lens of Multimodal Semiotic Analysis (MSA), the study examines multiple modes of communication, including facial expressions, light, color, and the spatial setting of the series. These elements reveal the style and status of Nigeria's Lagos mainland and the Island. Furthermore, various body gestures, colors, cultural motifs, and icons, in combination with Pidgin and Yoruba languages, highlight the distinct and rich nature of Nigerian (African) culture and society.

Lu (2024) describes multimodal discourse as interaction achieved through the human senses, including sight, sound, actions, and other semiotic resources. This suggests that various communication modes such as imagery (pictures, colors, graphics, animations) and audio (music, songs, noise), alongside paralinguistic elements (actions, gestures), can convey or suggest meanings. Lu also highlights the significance of both static and dynamic multimodal discourses. She uses Zhang's (2023) model of Multimodal Discourse Analysis to examine a promotional film, "Countdown: Beginning of Spring," from the Beijing Winter Olympics. In Zhang's Multimodal Discourse framework, the context of culture shapes the context of a situation, meaning that the broader systems, values, and beliefs of a society determine a particular event at a specific point in time. Within the context of a situation, the speaker selects meanings that are realised through visual and auditory modes. Zhang's model classifies the relationships between different communication modes into complementary and non-complementary categories. Complementary modes include reinforcement and non-reinforcement, while non-complementary modes include inclusion, overlapping, and context interaction.

Anurudu et al. (2023) emphasise the importance of visual grammar in the multimodal analysis of selected Nollywood posters. Posters are examples of static multimodal discourse, capable of conveying meaning through text and visual elements. Anurudu and Onu, in their analysis of Nollywood posters, reiterate that there is a connection between images and text. In other words, text and images combine to project the themes of the intended movie or film poster, while also serving as an advertising channel to the audience in the Nigerian film industry.

Thabet (2022), in A Multimodal Discourse Analysis of Six American Animated Movie Trailers, explores how movie trailer producers persuade viewers to watch the promoted animated films. Thabet analyses six animated movie trailers produced between 2010 and 2017. Animated movies are inherently dynamic, as they incorporate audio-visual and verbal content. Focusing on the perspective of the movie producers rather than the audience, Thabet adopts a combination of models, including Baldry & Thibault's multimodal transcription model (2006), Maier's model (2006), and Cohen's music model (1998), to analyze the different modes in the data. This approach underscores the fact that animated movie trailers involve various communication modes. The tools of analysis are framed within the persuasion models of Cockcroft & Cockcroft (2005) and van Dijk's concept of persuasion (1998). The central theme of the analysis is the act of persuading viewers through various emotional strategies.

In adopting a mixed-method approach for comprehensive analysis, Thabet highlights how visual modes, including captions and different shots, engage viewers in animated movies. Verbal modes, such as dialogues and voice-over narrations (both diegetic and non-diegetic), increase viewers' curiosity. The research concludes that all the modes—visual, aural, and verbal—work synchronously to influence the audience to watch animated movies.

With language at the forefront of communication and linguistic approaches such as CA and MDA being essential, the present study focuses on multiple modes, as photographs and advertisements are significant for meaning (Barthes 1977, pp. 40-41). The study asserts that, through MDA, images and writing work together (Kress 2003, p.61). Therefore, the present study aims to analyse utterances that constitute the sneak peeks of some Bollywood blockbusters from the perspective of MDA. This analysis seeks to fill a gap in the current literature.

THEORETICAL FRAMEWORK, DATA COLLECTION TECHNIQUE AND DATA ANALYSIS

Data for the study are sourced from three Bollywood blockbusters. The titles of the three Bollywood blockbusters include thus: *Bullett Raja, Traffic,* and *Bang Bang*. The different utterances, which translate as and constitute the sneak peeks and that peculiar to each of the three advertised blockbusters, are documented for analysis. The choice of the three is based on the sequential arrangements of sentence utterances in a way that arouse interest. The three different sneak peeks are then analysed from the perspectives of multiple modes of Barthes (1977) and images and writing of Kress (2003). Hence, the analysis considers how multiple modes/semiotic resources, images and writing/common ground in the selected sneak peeks, contribute to the overall messages of the Bollywood movies. In addition, the analysis takes into consideration, the speech act analysis of Austin (1962). Since speaker's utterances are involved, Austin's speech act analysis is needful more so, in order to unravel the intended message(s) of the Bollywood blockbusters. The speech acts include the locutionary, illocutionary and perlocutionary with their varying degrees of occurrences in the sneak peeks. Furthermore, a multimodal discourse analysis of selected blockbusters can reveal how various elements work together to convey meaning taking into consideration, the following:

Visual Imagery: The vibrant cinematography and elaborate set designs often reflect traditional Indian aesthetics while appealing to global sensibilities.
Song and Dance: Musical sequences transcend language barriers, showcasing India's rich cultural heritage through performance.

Narrative Techniques: The interplay between dialogue and visual storytelling enables filmmakers to tackle contemporary social issues while engaging audiences emotionally.

Excerpt Text I- Sneak Peek Utterances Of Blockbuster, *Bullett Raja*

"You need courage to fire a gun."
"I am very brave."
"The bullet from my gun doesn't kill; it wakes the animal inside of people."

Figure 1. Images of Bullett Raja

Discussion of Excerpt Text I

Excerpt Text I is a sneak peek made of utterances produced by just a character and interestingly, the major character in the movie. The text focuses a referring item in the possession of certain people in the human society; *a gun.* The same excerpt captures another referring item of what makes *a gun* to work; *the bullet.* The speaker/ character is the one in the possession of a gun. The speaker calls *a gun, my gun* since *a gun* is seen with him in the movie. In other words, *a gun* is in in his possession.

According to the speaker or character, the purpose of *a gun*, now *my gun,* has a denotative meaning in the sneak peek; to *wake the animal inside of people.* From the documented and outlined sneak peak, two words are used interchangeably to refer to the same thing. The words which are synonymous to each other are needful to fire a gun according to the notable character in the blockbuster: *courage* and *brave.* Thus, in the sneak peek, it is expected of the viewers to connect the synonymous words; *courage and brave*, to the identity of the speaker as well as the user of *a gun.* Hence, the title of the movie, *Bullett Raja.*

Common Ground/Shared interactional expression in sneak peek Excerpt Text I= *A gun*

Semiotic resources as deictic items in the sneak peek = *the bullet, animal, people*

A Speech Act Analysis of the Utterances in Excerpt Text I

In order to analyse the utterances through Speech Act Theory, the utterances are broken into the three types of speech acts:

i.Locutionary Act: The literal meaning of the utterance
ii.Illocutionary Act: The intention behind the utterance and
iii.Perlocutionary Act: The effect of the utterance on the listener.

i. *"You need courage to fire a gun."*

Locutionary Act: The speaker is stating that firing a gun requires courage.
Illocutionary Act: This could be interpreted as an assertive (stating a fact), or possibly an indirect challenge or advice. The speaker might be suggesting that the act of firing a gun is not easy and requires bravery, potentially positioning the listener to consider their own courage.
Perlocutionary Act: The effect on the listener could be to make them reflect on their own courage or to prepare them for the idea that firing a gun is a significant, brave act.

ii. *"I am very brave."*

Locutionary Act: The speaker is making a claim about himself, stating that he possesses bravery.
Illocutionary Act: This is a declaration or assertive speech act. The speaker asserts his bravery, which could serve as self-promotion or justification for their actions. It could also be seen as a response to the first utterance, possibly countering or affirming the idea that firing a gun requires courage.

Perlocutionary Act: The listener may be led to accept the speaker's bravery, view him as more credible, or perceive him as confident. It may also challenge the listener to acknowledge the speaker's self-assertion of courage.

iii. *"The bullet from my gun doesn't kill; it wakes the animal inside of people."*

Locutionary Act: The speaker is describing the effect of his gun, claiming that it does not kill but rather awakens an internal, primal force in people.
Illocutionary Act: This utterance functions as an assertive (stating a claim about the effect of the bullet) but may also carry an expressive act, expressing the speaker's attitude (his) or philosophy about his gun's impact. It could imply something more abstract or metaphorical about power, transformation, or the unleashing of repressed aspects of a person.
Perlocutionary Act: The listener may feel intrigued, shocked, or unsettled by the metaphorical suggestion that the bullet "wakes the animal" in people, potentially causing him or her to rethink the consequences of the speaker's actions or view the speaker as having a unique perspective on violence and power.

A Summary of Speech Acts in the Utterances

The first utterance introduces the notion of courage in relation to firing a gun. It is an assertion or a challenge, the second utterance serves as a personal assertion of the speaker's bravery. It is a declaration or an assertion and the third utterance presents an abstract or philosophical view of the bullet's power, beyond physical harm. It is an assertion which is also expressive.

These utterances reveal a conversational dynamic where the speaker positions himself as courageous and frames his gun's effect as something more profound than mere violence.

Excerpt Text II—Sneak Peek Utterances Of Blockbuster, *Bang Bang*

"The Kohinoor"
"Stealing the Kohinoor is impossible!"
"You have to make it possible."
"In a population of 1.2 billion, there is someone who can do this job."
"I am Vicki." (Interrupted Utterance)
"Go find him."
"Tash Vi." (Interrupted Utterance)
"Who are you?"

"A thief!"
"The man you were with, last night, is an international criminal."
"I stole something."
"What?"
"Are You Crazy?"
"Find the real Kohinoor, exchange it for her."
"Bang Bang!" (Interrupted Utterance)
"Remember to cork in your fears."
"Greetings, Ahmad Khoor." (Interrupted Utterance)
"What is it that you want? "
"Kohinoor"

Figure 2. Images of Bang Bang

Discussion of Excerpt Text II

Excerpt Text II is a sneak peek made of utterances produced by different characters. From the sneak peek, the focus is on a referring item, *The Kohinoor*. *The Kohinoor* in MDA, is regarded as an artefact and a semiotic resource found in human society. The same is a rare and an expensive diamond. In the movie, *The Kohinoor* is both the referring item as well as the object that calls for an event which is adventurous in the movie. Hence, *The Kohinoor* is the item that is needful for business making especially among some sophisticated business tycoons. These business tycoons in the sneak peek, are desperately in need of *The Kohinoor*. They set their mercenary in motion in order to lay hold of *The Kohinoor* by crook or by force. Different scenes as events in the sneak peek, show desperation to lay hold of *The Kohinoor*. These events prompt the search for *Vicki, an international criminal and a thief,* who knows the whereabouts of the rare diamond, *The Kohinoor.Vicki* has to be contacted by *Ahmad Khoor* and others but then, there is a girlfriend of *Vicki* who has to be kidnapped before *The Kohinoor* could be retrieved from *Vicki*. Hence the possession and use of guns at different scenes in the sneak peek of the blockbuster. The use of guns in the sneak peek precipitated the title of the blockbuster, *Bang Bang,* which is an onomatopoeic sound of a gun.

Common Ground/Shared interactional expression in sneak peek Excerpt Text II= *Kohinoor*

Semiotic resources as deictic items in the sneak peek = *someone, him, her, Kohinoor, a thief, Vicki, Ahmad Khoor, international criminal*

A Speech Act Analysis of the Utterances in Excerpt Text II

i. *"The Kohinoor"*

  Locutionary Act: A simple reference to *the Kohinoor*, a famous diamond.

  Illocutionary Act: This is a referential speech act, bringing up the subject of discussion. The speaker is establishing the topic.

  Perlocutionary Act: The listener's attention is drawn to the Kohinoor, setting up the focus of the following conversation.

ii. *"Stealing the Kohinoor is impossible!"*

  Locutionary Act: This is a statement declaring that stealing the Kohinoor cannot be done.

  Illocutionary Act: This is an assertive speech act, expressing the speaker's belief in the impossibility of the task.

  Perlocutionary Act: The listener may be convinced of the difficulty or impossibility of the act, or it may prompt them to reconsider the task.

iii. *"You have to make it possible."*

  Locutionary Act: A command or directive stating that the impossible must be made possible.

  Illocutionary Act: A directive speech act, instructing or encouraging the listener to find a way to accomplish the impossible task.

  Perlocutionary Act: The listener may feel motivated, challenged, or pressured to perform the task.

iv. *"In a population of 1.2 billion, there is someone who can do this job."*

Locutionary Act: A statement suggesting that out of many people, someone is capable of the task.
Illocutionary Act: This is an assertive act that expresses a belief that the task can be done by someone, hinting at hope or possibility.
Perlocutionary Act: The listener may feel reassured that the task is possible, or begin considering who might be able to accomplish it.

v. *"I am Vicki." (Interrupted Utterance)*

Locutionary Act: An introduction of the speaker's name.
Illocutionary Act: This is a declarative act of self-identification.
Perlocutionary Act: The listener may begin associating the speaker with the name "Vicki," though the interruption might disrupt full understanding.

vi. *"Go find him."*

Locutionary Act: A command to locate someone.
Illocutionary Act: A directive speech act, ordering the listener to seek out a specific individual.
Perlocutionary Act: The listener may feel obligated to follow the command and start searching for the person mentioned.

vii. *"Tash Vi."(Interrupted Utterance)*

Locutionary Act: Incomplete phrase, possibly an introduction or explanation.
Illocutionary Act: It is likely a declarative speech act, disrupted before the full meaning can be communicated.
Perlocutionary Act: The listener might be confused or left wondering about the intended message due to the interruption.

viii. *"Who are you?"*

Locutionary Act: A question asking for identification.
Illocutionary Act: This is a questioning speech act, seeking information about the other speaker's identity.
Perlocutionary Act: The listener may feel compelled to answer or reveal something about themselves.

ix. *"A thief!"*

Locutionary Act: A self-declaration as a thief.
Illocutionary Act: This is a declarative speech act, identifying the speaker's role or profession.
Perlocutionary Act: The listener may react with surprise, fear, or acknowledgment, depending on the context.

x. *"The man you were with, last night, is an international criminal."*

Locutionary Act: This is a statement revealing the criminal identity of someone the listener was with.
Illocutionary Act: This is an informative act, conveying critical information about someone's identity.
Perlocutionary Act: The listener may feel alarmed, betrayed, or concerned, depending on their relationship with the person.

xi. "*I stole something*."

Locutionary Act: A confession of theft.
Illocutionary Act: This is a declarative speech act, admitting a past action of stealing.
Perlocutionary Act: The listener may react with curiosity, concern, or judgment about what was stolen.

xii. "What?"

Locutionary Act: A question asking for clarification or more information.
Illocutionary Act: A questioning act, requesting the speaker to specify what was stolen.
Perlocutionary Act: The speaker is likely prompted to provide more information.

xiii. "*Are you crazy*?"

Locutionary Act: A question suggesting disbelief or questioning someone's rationality.
Illocutionary Act: A rhetorical question, implying that the person's behavior or ideas are irrational.
Perlocutionary Act: The listener may feel defensive, confused, or provoked by the accusation of irrationality.

xiv. "*Find the real Kohinoor, exchange it for her*."

Locutionary Act: A directive to locate the real Kohinoor and exchange it for a person (likely being held hostage).
Illocutionary Act: A directive speech act, instructing the listener to carry out a specific task to achieve a trade.
Perlocutionary Act: The listener may feel pressured or motivated to undertake the mission.

xv. “*Bang Bang*!” (*Interrupted Utterance*)

Locutionary Act: This is an exclamation, possibly imitating gunfire or signifying action.
Illocutionary Act: This is likely an expressive or exclamatory speech act, intended to convey excitement, danger, or urgency.
Perlocutionary Act: The listener may be startled or anticipate violence or fast-paced action, although the interruption leaves the full meaning incomplete.

xvi. “*Remember to cork in your fears*.”

Locutionary Act: This is an instruction to suppress or control fear.
Illocutionary Act: A directive act advising or commanding the listener to stay brave and manage their fears.
Perlocutionary Act: The listener may feel encouraged or instructed to remain calm in a high-pressure situation.

xvii. “*Greetings, Ahmad Khoor.” (Interrupted Utterance)*

Locutionary Act: A polite greeting, followed by the name of the addressee.
Illocutionary Act: A declarative act acknowledging the presence of Ahmad Khoor, likely intending to initiate formal communication.
Perlocutionary Act: The listener (Ahmad Khoor) may feel acknowledged or recognised, although the interruption prevents further development of the conversation.

xviii. “*What is it that you want*?”

Locutionary Act: A question asking for clarification of the speaker's desires.
Illocutionary Act: A questioning act, probing for the speaker’s goal or demand.
Perlocutionary Act: The listener may feel obligated to state what they want or clarify their intentions.

xix. “*Kohinoor*.”

Locutionary Act: A single-word response, indicating that *the Kohinoor* is the desired object.

Illocutionary Act: A declarative act, expressing the speaker's goal—obtaining the Kohinoor.
Perlocutionary Act: The listener may now understand the speaker's objective, potentially feeling pressured to cooperate.

A Summary of Speech Acts in the Utterances

The sequence of utterances consists of a complex interplay of assertive, directive, declarative, and expressive speech acts, shaping a dialogue where characters express desires, give instructions, and reveal information. The interrupted utterances add to the tension, leaving key information incomplete and contributing to the dynamic nature of the conversation. Each utterance drives the narrative forward, revealing the characters' identities, their intentions, and their emotional states.

EXCERPT TEXT III—SNEAK PEEK UTTERANCES OF BLOCKBUSTER, *TRAFFIC*

"Nandini, call the doctor!"
"We must immediately find a donor for the heart transplant."
"Rehan's heart is a perfect match for that girl."
"Good news, Mr Dev."
"The parents have agreed."
"Thank you, thank you so much."
"So, what are the transportation plans?"
"That's the problem."
"By road!"
"Mumbai's traffic; is like a spider's web, doctor."
"Either our car will get stuck or even hit someone before reaching Pune."
"But a Yes, from you, may create history."
"Shouldn't everyone be given a second chance?"
"160km-2 and a half hours."
"Starting point is Aditya Birla hospital, Mumbai,"
"Destination, Fortis hospital Pune."
"We have an opportunity to save a life."
"Make this mission a success."

Figure 3. Images of Traffic

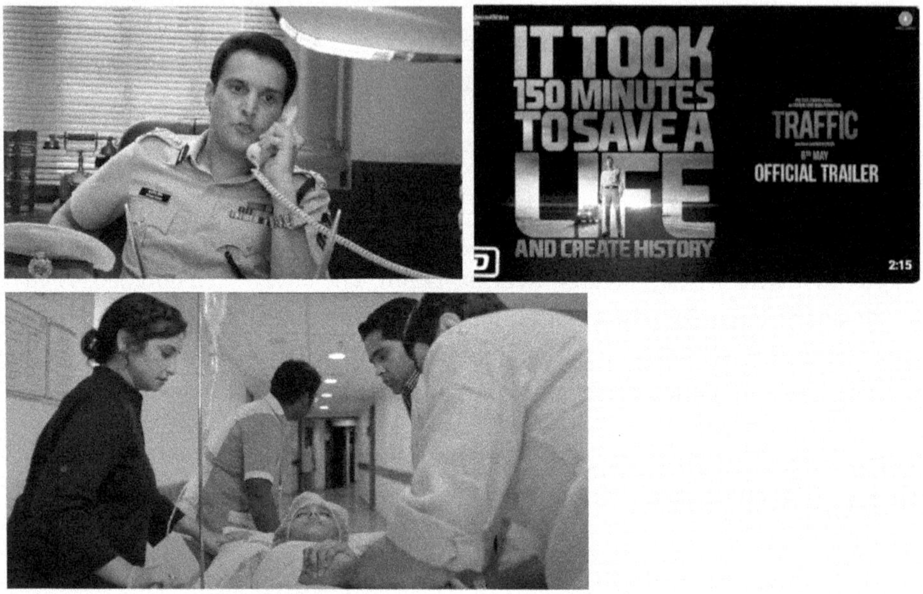

Discussion of Excerpt Text III

Excerpt Text III is a sneak peek made of utterances produced by different speakers or characters.

The text narrates the ordeal of the travel plans to save a life. There is a serious traffic and there is the need to travel for an emergency case of a heart transplant. There is a heavy traffic at Mumbai which can delay the mission of heart transplant. However, two families are involved; the family of a boy and a girl. The boy's name is *Rehan* who is dying in *Aditya Birla hospital, Mumbai.* His heart is to be transplanted to another dying person, a girl, in *Fortis hospital, Pune.* The mission is to be accomplished within two and a half hours; an equivalent of 150 minutes. The police and the road marshals are all involved in the mission. They are seen in their uniforms and at strategic posts on the road trying to pursue a good cause. Both are involved in the mission of saving a girl's life which translates as, *a success,* in the excerpt. It is the events of trying to move from one place (Mumbai) to the other (Pune) that created not only a mere road traffic but a hurriedly movement to save a life. Interestingly, the moves and events of wanting to save a life on a heavy traffic road, happen to be the title of the Bollywood blockbuster, *traffic*.

Common Ground/Shared interactional expression in sneak peek Excerpt Text III = *Traffic*

Semiotic resources as deictic items in the sneak peek = *Rahul, Dev, Aditya Birla hospital Mumbai, Fortis hospital Pune, life, travel plans, heart transplant, Rahul's heart, car, traffic, road, opportunity, mission, success.*

A Speech Act Analysis of the Utterances in Excerpt Text III

i. *"Nandini, call the doctor!"*

Locutionary Act: An instruction to Nandini to contact the doctor.
Illocutionary Act: A directive act, giving a command to immediately call the doctor.
Perlocutionary Act: Nandini is expected to follow the order and call the doctor quickly.

ii "*We must immediately find a donor for the heart transplant.*"

Locutionary Act: A statement about the urgent need to find a heart donor.
Illocutionary Act: This is an assertive act, conveying urgency and necessity.
Perlocutionary Act: The listener may feel the pressure of time and the importance of finding a donor.

iii. "*Rehan's heart is a perfect match for that girl.*"

Locutionary Act: A statement about the compatibility of Rehan's heart for a transplant.
Illocutionary Act: An assertive act providing critical medical information.
Perlocutionary Act: The listener is informed of the possibility of Rehan's heart being a solution for the girl, potentially influencing decision-making.

iv. "*Good news, Mr. Dev.*"

Locutionary Act: A statement signaling that positive information is coming.
Illocutionary Act: An expressive act, meant to communicate a positive development to Mr. Dev.
Perlocutionary Act: The listener (Mr. Dev) may feel relieved or hopeful upon hearing this.

v. "*The parents have agreed.*"

Locutionary Act: A statement indicating the consent of the parents.
Illocutionary Act: An assertive act, relaying the agreement of the parents (likely for the transplant or organ donation).

Perlocutionary Act: The listener may feel encouraged or satisfied that an important step has been taken.

vi. "*Thank you, thank you so much.*"

Locutionary Act: An expression of gratitude.
Illocutionary Act: An expressive act, conveying deep appreciation.
Perlocutionary Act: The listener feels appreciated and acknowledged for their role in the situation.

vii. "*So, what are the transportation plans*?"

Locutionary Act: A question about how the transportation will be handled.
Illocutionary Act: A questioning act, seeking information or clarification on logistics.
Perlocutionary Act: The listener is expected to provide or consider transportation details.
viii "*That's the problem.*"
Locutionary Act: A statement indicating there is a complication with the transportation.
Illocutionary Act: An assertive act, presenting a challenge or obstacle.
Perlocutionary Act: The listener becomes aware of the issue and may feel concerned or anxious about how to solve it.

ix. "*By road*!"

Locutionary Act: A suggestion or plan to use the road for transportation.
Illocutionary Act: A directive or assertive act, indicating that transportation by road is the proposed method.
Perlocutionary Act: The listener is led to think about or consider using the road for the transportation mission.

x. "*Mumbai's traffic; is like a spider's web, doctor.*"

Locutionary Act: A description comparing Mumbai's traffic to a spider's web.
Illocutionary Act: A descriptive or assertive act, metaphorically illustrating the difficulty of navigating Mumbai's traffic.
Perlocutionary Act: The listener (doctor) may become concerned about the challenges of traffic or understand the gravity of the issue.

xi. "*Either our car will get stuck or even hit someone before reaching Pune.*"

Locutionary Act: A statement predicting possible negative outcomes while traveling by road.
Illocutionary Act: An assertive act expressing concern about potential risks of the road trip.
Perlocutionary Act: The listener may feel apprehensive or begin considering alternatives for transportation.

xii. "*But a Yes, from you, may create history.*"

Locutionary Act: A statement suggesting that the doctor's approval could lead to a historic event.
Illocutionary Act: An assertive act appealing to the doctor's sense of significance and responsibility.
Perlocutionary Act: The doctor may feel motivated or pressured to agree, as the act is framed as having profound importance.

xiii. "Shouldn't everyone be given a second chance?"

Locutionary Act: A rhetorical question about the fairness of giving second chances.
Illocutionary Act: An expressive or persuasive act meant to evoke empathy and encourage agreement.
Perlocutionary Act: The listener may feel emotionally inclined to agree with the idea of giving second chances, possibly influencing their decisions.

xiv. "*160km-2 and a half hours.*"

Locutionary Act: A statement describing the distance and time for travel.
Illocutionary Act: An informative act providing logistical details about the journey.
Perlocutionary Act: The listener is informed about the travel parameters and can plan accordingly.

xv. "*Starting point is Aditya Birla hospital, Mumbai.*"

Locutionary Act: A statement providing the starting location for the journey.

Illocutionary Act: An informative act giving the initial logistical detail for transportation.
Perlocutionary Act: The listener will be aware of where the journey begins and can orient their planning around it.

xvi. "*Destination, Fortis hospital Pune.*"

Locutionary Act: A statement providing the destination of the journey.
Illocutionary Act: An informative act giving the endpoint for the journey.
Perlocutionary Act: The listener will know where the journey is headed and may focus on how to reach the destination.

xvii. "*We have an opportunity to save a life.*"

Locutionary Act: A statement expressing the chance to save someone's life.
Illocutionary Act: An assertive or persuasive act highlighting the importance and urgency of the mission.
Perlocutionary Act: The listener may feel inspired or obligated to take action because of the moral weight of saving a life.

xviii. "*Make this mission a success.*"

Locutionary Act: A directive to ensure that the mission is carried out successfully.
Illocutionary Act: A directive act, instructing the listener to complete the task and achieve success.
Perlocutionary Act: The listener may feel motivated or pressured to follow through with the mission and ensure its success.

A Summary of Speech Acts in the Utterances

The significant illocutionary forces include motivating action ("*Make this mission a success*"), which expresses urgency and significance - "*We have an opportunity to save a life*", and the outlining obstacles - "*Mumbai's traffic is like a spider's web*". Summarily, the dialogue consists of various assertive (statements of fact), directive (commands or requests), expressive (emotional responses like gratitude), and informative (providing details about logistics) speech acts. The conversation builds tension by outlining logistical and emotional challenges, and the speech acts serve to instruct, inform, and motivate the characters to carry out the heart transplant mission successfully.

FINDINGS

The chapter covers a display of the analysis of multiple modes as well as writing, image and colour modes (Kress, 2010) in selected Bollywood blockbusters. It involves the writing (documentation of Bollywood blockbusters' utterances as sneak peeks), images (as conveyed in the different sneak peeks) and colours (of uniforms and dresses captured at different scenes in the sneak peeks). It should be noted that the trio of writing, image and colour modes are systematically arrayed in the different sneak peeks to convey the intended messages of the selected Bollywood blockbusters.

Hence, the study through the speech acts analysis, discovers that conversation is a human-oriented affair. The same takes place at different settings for different purposes. Also discovered is the fact that utterances are the basic constituents of conversation. However, since language use in the media is involved, characters are portrayed differently based on their intents in the selected blockbusters' sneak peeks. Hence, the study avers that shared interactional expressions henceforth norms or beliefs among participants in every spoken discourse is otherwise known as Common Ground (CG). The same CG is termed shared context which is considered needful for successful communication or interaction. Interestingly, the different occurrences of Common Ground (CG)/shared interactional norms/expressions in the identified sneak peeks, are moored by the presence of deictic items in the sneak peeks. The identified deictic items in the different Bollywood blockbusters' sneak peeks, point to or signal one thing or the other to construe meaning of the blockbuster. By implication, the deictic items are the semiotic resources made available in human environment: the instance of *the bullet* (a deictic item); which points to or signals *the gun* (a common ground or shared interactional expression).

In addition, the study discovers that the different referring items in the sneak peeks are items commonly found in every human society. While some are considered artefacts; the instance of *The Kohinoor,* some are in the possession of some people for a purpose; the instance of *a gun*. In whatever way the deictic items are presented in the different sneak peeks, they are all woven around the intended messages to be passed across to the viewers of the movies or films. The same items as discovered, are cardinal to the events that unfold in the selected Bollywood blockbusters.

CONCLUSION

Bollywood serves as an essential lens through which one can examine India's historical evolution, cultural diversity, and socio-political dynamics. By analysing selected blockbusters through multimodal discourse analysis, scholars can uncover how cinema not only entertains but also shapes societal perceptions and cultural identities. The industry's capacity to blend tradition with modernity reflects the complexities of contemporary Indian society while fostering cross-cultural understanding across Asia and beyond.

Conversely, sneak peeks are an integral part of the movie marketing landscape. They complement trailers by providing additional layers of engagement and anticipation for audiences. By offering glimpses into the film's world, sneak peeks serve to enhance viewer interest and foster a community of fans eager for the film's release.

This chapter re-affirms the fact that society has several ways of passing across information to or interacting with the general public. One of such is through a display of events captured by sneak peeks; a form of movie advertisement. Also, any semiotic resource displayed in sneak peeks are symbolic and are meaning carriers aimed at arousing the interest of the viewer to ultimately watch the advertised movies which are initially promoted as sneek peaks or trailers. Hence, every conversation has underlying motive and it is the duty of the language users as participants to understand the shared norms or CG (Common Ground) in order to achieve communication success.

REFERENCES

Ademilokun, M., & Olateju, M. (2015). A multimodal discourse analysis of some visual images in the political rally discourse of 2011 electioneering campaigns in Southwestern Nigeria. *International Journal of Society, Culture, and Language*, *3*(1), 1–18. https://www.ijscl.net/article_27706.html

Akmal, S., & Yana, D. U. (2020). Conversational implicature analysis in Kingdom of Heaven movie script by William Monahan. ResearchGate. https://www.researchgate.net/publication/344572149_Conversational_Implicature_Analysis_in_Kingdom_of_Heaven_Movie_Script_by_William_Monahan

Alibbi, A. (2014). Hollywood, the american image and the global film industry. *CINEJ Cinema Journal*, *3*(1), 93–106. Advance online publication. DOI: 10.5195/cinej.2013.81

Amosu, S. T., Adeleke, M. O., & Akinwale, M. O. (2024). *A multimodal semiotic analysis of Walt Disney and Kugali's Iwaju* [Unpublished undergraduate project]. Obafemi Awolowo University.

Anurudu, S., Igboanugo, A., & Anthony Onu, A. (2023). A multimodal discourse analysis of selected Nollywood posters. *International Journal of Multidisciplinary Research and Publications*, *5*(11), 57–63. DOI: 10.51455/ijmrap.2023.5354

Asabor, I. (2024). How Hollywood, Bollywood, Nollywood and Ghallywood are shaping economies. Modern Ghana. https://www.modernghana.com/news/1327183/how-hollywood-bollywood-nollywood-and-ghallywood.html

Austin, J. L. (1962). *How to do things with words*. Clarendon Press.

Barthes, R. (1977). *Image, music, text*. Fontana Press.

BOYSETS FIRE. (2022). What is Bollywood? A beginner's guide to India's popular film industry. https://www.boysetsfire.net/what-is-bollywood-a-beginners-guide-to-indias-popular-film-industry/

Cambridge Dictionary. (n.d.). Sneak peek. In *Cambridge Dictionary*. Retrieved October 21, 2024, from https://dictionary.cambridge.org/dictionary/english/sneak-peek

Chitrkala. (2016). *Traffic*: A review. Retrieved from https://chitrkala.in/traffic-movie-review

Coulthard, M. (1981). *An introduction to discourse analysis*. Longman.

D'Angelo, L., & Marino, F. (2024). Multimodal analysis. In Kessler, M., & Polio, C. (Eds.), *Conducting genre-based research in applied linguistics: A methodological guide*. Routledge.

Dwyer, R. (2006). Filming the gods. Routlege.www.routlegde.com

Filmfare. (2014). *Bang Bang*: Film review. Retrieved from https://www.filmfare.com/reviews/bang-bang-review-2014-134.html

Gokulsing, M., & Dissanayake, W. (2020). *Indian popular cinema: A narrative of cultural change*. ResearchGate. https://www.researchgate.net/publication/343206085_Indian_Popular_Cinema_A_Narrative_of_Cultural_Change

Grundy, P. (2008). *Doing pragmatics* (3rd ed.). Hodder Education.

Hall, S. (2014). *Blockbusters*. Oxford University Press.

Herrington, C. J. (2015). *Film marketing and the creation of the Hollywood blockbuster* [Honors thesis, University of Mississippi]. eGrove. https://egrove.olemiss.edu/hon_thesis/219

Hirji, F. (2024). When local meets lucre: Commerce, culture and imperialism in Bollywood cinema. *Global Media Journal*. https://www.globalmediajournal.com/open-access/when-local-meets-lucre-commerce-culture-and-imperialism-in-bollywood-cinema.php?aid=35173

Ibbi, A. A. (2014). Hollywood, the American image and the global film industry. *CINEJ Cinema Journal*, *3*(1), 93–106. Advance online publication. DOI: 10.5195/cinej.2013.81

IMDb. (2014). *Bang Bang* (2014). Retrieved from https://www.imdb.com/title/tt2905838/

Jefferson, G. (2004). Glossary of transcript symbols with an introduction. In Lerner, G. H. (Ed.), *Conversation analysis: Studies from the first generation* (pp. 13–31). John Benjamins. DOI: 10.1075/pbns.125.02jef

Kasper, G., & Wagner, J. (2014). Conversation analysis in applied linguistics. *Annual Review of Applied Linguistics*, *34*(1), 171–212. DOI: 10.1017/S0267190514000014

Kress, G. (2003). *Literacy in the new media age*. Routledge.

Kress, G. (2010). *Multimodality: A social semiotic approach to contemporary communication*. Routledge.

Kress, G., & van Leeuwen, T. (2001). *Multimodal discourse: The modes and media of contemporary communication*. Oxford University Press.

Lu, Y. (2024). Multimodal discourse analysis of the promotional film Countdown: Beginning of Spring for the opening ceremony of Beijing Winter Olympics. *International Journal of Language. Literature and Culture*, *4*(4). Advance online publication. DOI: 10.22161/ijllc.4.4.2

Mullins, E., Kirkwood, S., & Stokoe, E. (2022). An introduction to conversation analysis in social work research. *Qualitative Social Work: Research and Practice*, *22*(2), 457–475. DOI: 10.1177/14733250221132239

Nair, M. (2012). Nā ya, rasa, and abhinaya as semiotic principles in classical Indian theatre. *De Gruyter*. Retrieved from https://www.degruyter.com/document/doi/10.1515/sem-2012-0042/pdf

NFI (National Film Institute). (2023). What is Bollywood? Everything you need to know. Retrieved from https://www.nfi.edu/what-is-bollywood/

O'Halloran, K., Tan, S., Smith, B., & Podlasov, A. (2009, September). *Digital semiotics* [Paper presentation]. *10th World Congress of Semiotics*, A Coruña, Spain.

Olateju, M., & Oyebode, O. (2014). *Introducing multimodality*. College Press and Publishers Limited.

Olateju, M., Oyebode, O., & Ademilokun, M. (2014). *Doing multimodal discourse analysis*. College Press and Publishers Limited.

Olateju, M. A. (2004). *Discourse analysis: Analysing discourse in the ESL classroom*. Obafemi Awolowo University Press.

Oyebode, O. A., & Unuabonah, F. O. (2024). *Multimodality and appraisal choices in Nigerian coronavirus-related WhatsApp memes*. Communication and the Public., DOI: 10.1177/20570473241264334

Paltridge, B. (2006). Discourse analysis: An introduction. *Continuum*.

Pandey, K. A., & Singh, N. K. (2020). Hinglish in Bollywood. *IJRAR 7*(4). www.ijrar.org

Perren, A., & Schatz, T. (2004). Hollywood. *Communication Faculty Publications*, 2. https://scholarworks.gsu.edu/communication_facpub/2

Pinkvilla. (2013). *Bullet Raja*: Movie review. Retrieved from https://www.pinkvilla.com/entertainment/reviews/bullet-raja-movie-review-190018

Pirini, J. (2017). Approaches to multimodal discourse analysis. ResearchGate. https://www.researchgate.net/publication/354114983_Approaches_to_Multimodal_Discourse_Analysis

Sacks, H., Schegloff, E. A., & Jefferson, G. (1974). A simplest systematics for the organization of turn-taking for conversation. *Language*, *50*(4), 696–735. DOI: 10.1353/lan.1974.0010

Searle, J. R. (1969). *Speech acts: An essay in the philosophy of language*. Cambridge University Press. DOI: 10.1017/CBO9781139173438

Singh, N. K., & Pandey, K. A. (2020). Preservation of culture through promotion of linguistic Cinema in India: A critical analysis. *International Journal of Advanced Mass Communication and Journalism.*, *1*(1). 33-38.www.masscomjournal.com

Thabet, Y. S. (2022). A multimodal discourse analysis of six American animated movie trailers (2010-2017). ResearchGate. https://www.researchgate.net/publication/377491006_A_Multimodal_Discourse_Analysis_of_Six_American_Animated_Movie_Trailers_2010-2017

Thompson, A. (2024). *Popular cinema and cultural change in India*. Film Studies Review.

Tietbohl, C. K., & White, A. E. C. (2022). Making conversation analysis accessible: A conceptual guide for health services researchers. *Health Services Research*, *57*(5), 950–958. https://pubmed.ncbi.nlm.nih.gov/35616449/ PMID: 35616449

van Leeuwen, T. (2005). *Introducing social semiotics*. Routledge.

Wheeler, D. L. (2020). *Semiotics in film: The dialogue between visual and verbal language*. Cambridge Scholars Publishing.

White, S. J. (2019). Conversation analysis: An introduction to methodology, data collection, and analysis. In Liamputtong, P. (Ed.), *Handbook of research methods in health social sciences* (pp. 471–490). Springer., DOI: 10.1007/978-981-10-5251-4_107

Yeomans, M., Boland, F. K., & Brooks, A. W. (2023). A practical guide to conversation research: How to study what people say to each other. *Advances in Methods and Practices in Psychological Science*, *6*(3), 25152459231183919. Advance online publication. DOI: 10.1177/25152459231183919

Zhang, Y., & Zhou, Y. (2024). Multimodal analysis of the *Star Wars* trailer: A social semiotic approach. *Journal of Visual Culture*, *23*(1), 22–36. DOI: 10.1177/1470412918780770

ADDITIONAL READING

Baldry, A., & Thibault, P. J. (2008). Applications of multimodal concordances. HERMES -. *Journal of Language and Communication in Business*, *21*(41), 1–32. DOI: 10.7146/hjlcb.v21i41.96812

Lyons, A. (2016). Multimodality. In Hua, Z. (Ed.), *Research methods in intercultural communication: A practical guide* (pp. 268–280). Wiley-Blackwell.

Odedeyi, T. D., & Ajayi, M. T. (2023). A multimodal analysis of Piggyvest's animated advertisement videos. [De Gruyter.]. *Language and Semiotic Studies*, *9*(2), 263–289. DOI: 10.1515/lass-2023-0013

Osisanwo, W. (2003). *Introduction to discourse analysis and pragmatics*. Femolus-Fetop Publishers.

KEY TERMS AND DEFINITIONS

Blockbuster: A film acclaimed to be successful in terms of large amount of viewership and massive revenue it acquired. A film that "broke the box office" that is, it became a financial hit that also outperformed other films during the same period.

Discourse: This refers to any kind of interaction, conversation, dialogue or communication that occur between entities that is, human and human or human and non-human (inanimate).

Discourse analysis: This is the examination of any kind of interaction conversation, dialogue or communication.

Language: This refers to any textual system that is used for communication where text incorporates mathematical signs, alphabet etc.

Multimodal Discourse: This can be described as a web of several modes of discourse weaved or presented in a single output. E.g. a musical video, which (may) involve the combination of sound, graphics and text.

Poster: This can be described as a pictorial representation of information.

Semiotic and Semiotic resources: This refers to signs and any mode of communication that meaning can be deduced from.

Sneak Peek: A miniature part of a movie or film that gives hints and ideas on the movie with the aim of arousing viewer's interest. The sneak peek is usually included in the intercession of a current movie being viewed. It is usually seen on Cable TV.

Trailer: A short promotional view of an upcoming movie or film that is intended to generate the interest of the viewer. This is usually seen on Youtube.

Chapter 16
Multimodal Literacy and Sociocultural Dynamics in Online Communication:
An Interdisciplinary View

Semiu Olawale Makinde
https://orcid.org/0000-0001-5456-3464
A-Hikmah University, Ilorin, Nigeria

Shehu Sakariyahu
https://orcid.org/0009-0008-7377-9007
Al-Hikmah University, Ilorin, Nigeria

AbdulRafiu Abdullahi
https://orcid.org/0009-0003-2896-2367
Al-Hikmah University, Ilorin, Nigeria

Abdulmuhsin Ibrahim
https://orcid.org/0009-0002-2147-3854
Al-Hikmah University, Ilorin, Nigeria

ABSTRACT

The emergence of the digital age has transformed communication, requiring a wider knowledge of literacy that incorporates multiple modes of expression. This chapter examines the interconnectivity of multimodal literacy and sociocultural dynamics in online communication, adopting an interdisciplinary approach that draws on epiphanies from linguistics, education, sociology, and media studies. Through a qualitative research methodology, including literature review, case studies, and thematic analysis, this study explores how multimodal literacy influences and is

DOI: 10.4018/979-8-3693-7934-9.ch016

influenced by sociocultural contexts in online communication. The findings highlight the importance of considering the complex interplay between multimodal literacy and sociocultural dynamics in online communication, with implications for education, identity formation, community building, and social change. This research contributes to a holistic understanding of digital communication, advocating for developing pedagogical approaches that foster multimodal literacy and encourage inclusive, equitable online interactions.

INTRODUCTION

The emergence of the digital age has modernized communication, making it multimodal, dynamic, and deeply intertwined with sociocultural contexts. Traditional literacy, focused predominantly on reading and writing text, has amplified to embrace multimodal literacy, which includes the ability to interpret, create, and interact with multiple modes of communication such as images, audio, video, and interactive media (Baltikian et al., 2024; Taylor & Leung, 2020). This chapter, "Multimodal Literacy and Sociocultural Dynamics in Online Communication: An Interdisciplinary Perspective," aims to investigate how multimodal literacy is affected by and influences sociocultural dynamics in online communication. It draws on insights from various disciplines, including education, linguistics, sociology, and media studies, to provide a comprehensive understanding of this complex interplay.

Background and Rationale

In the digital age, communication has become inherently multimodal. Platforms like social media, online forums, and digital classrooms utilize a variety of modes—text, image, audio, and video—to convey messages. This shift necessitates a broader understanding of literacy, termed "multimodal literacy," which encompasses the skills required to navigate and create meaning across different modes (Zaidi & Sah, 2024). Moreover, online communication is not just a technological phenomenon but a sociocultural one. It reflects and shapes cultural norms, values, and practices, making the study of its sociocultural dynamics essential (Mavuru & Ramnarain, 2020; Rushanova et al., 2024).

The intersection of multimodal literacy and sociocultural dynamics presents a fertile ground for interdisciplinary research. Educational scholars examine how multimodal literacy impacts learning and pedagogy (Brewington 2024), while linguists explore how different modes affect language use and meaning making. Sociologists investigate how online communication shapes and is shaped by social structures and cultural practices (boyd, 2014). Media studies scholars analyze the role of media in shaping public discourse and cultural narratives (Jenkins, 2006). This chapter aims to integrate these diverse perspectives to provide a holistic understanding of multimodal literacy and sociocultural dynamics in online communication. Therefore, in this chapter, the diverse perspectives of the multimodal literacy and sociocultural dynamics in online communication will be addressed. Therefore, the objectives of this study are to: (i) defining and contextualizing multimodal literacy in the digital age; (ii) examining the sociocultural dynamics that influence and are influenced by online communication; (iii) analyzing the interdisciplinary nature of multimodal literacy and its implications for education, linguistics, sociology, and media studies; (iv) assessing case studies that illustrate the interplay between multimodal literacy and sociocultural dynamics in online communication; and (v) propose strategies for enhancing multimodal literacy in educational and professional contexts

LITERATURE REVIEW

Multimodal Literacy

Multimodal literacy involves the ability to understand, interpret, and create meaning using multiple modes of communication. Björkvall et al. (2023) discuss in their chapter the key theoretical foundations, methodological approaches, and practical applications of multimodal discourse analysis, illustrating how it can be used to analyze media, advertisements, educational materials, and digital communication. They highlight how multimodal analysis provides deeper insights into meaning-making processes, particularly in an increasingly digital and visually driven world. They examine how meaning is constructed through multiple modes—such as text, visuals, gestures, and sound—beyond just written or spoken language. The chapter explores how different semiotic resources interact to shape communication in various social contexts, emphasizing the importance of integrating multiple forms of expression in discourse studies. This expanded literacy is essential for navigating the digital landscape, where information is often presented in multimodal formats (Zaidi & Sah, 2024). Brewington (2024) emphasize the importance of teaching multimodal literacy in schools to prepare students for the complexities of digital communication.

Multimodal literacy is increasingly integral to the disciplinary practices of science, with new and evolving semiotic resources enabling the development, validation and enactment of conceptual knowledge (Baltikian et al., 2024). The role of representational work in practice and thought within and beyond the laboratory has been established by scholars from a wide range of disciplinary and theoretical perspectives and representational tools have been described in terms of the 'inscriptions' that are developed and negotiated in the generation of scientific knowledge by professional scientists (Philip & Sengupta, 2021; Kelly, 2023). While school science education differs significantly from the professional practice of science (Park & Song, 2019), understandings of the complex processes involved in inscription and the constitutive role of semiosis offer a wide range of possibilities for supporting and assessing the increasingly specialized curriculum learning of senior school subjects such as biology, chemistry and physics (Jones et al., 2020).

Multimodal disciplinary literacy (MDL) refers to the discipline-specific competences and practices that are recontextualized in school subjects, while multimodal literacy infused science pedagogy (MLISP) refers to the strategies used to develop and use these competences in the classroom. Foundational and ongoing research related to both MDL and MLISP are expanded in subsequent chapters of the book; however, in this chapter, we outline some of the potential aspects of ongoing discussions within the literacy and science education community that have been important in developing transdisciplinary research in both fields. Orientation was first provided to researcher, who has an advanced understanding of verbal, visual, symbolic and mathematical representations in science and science learning (Doran, 2017, 2019; Hao, 2020; Doran & Martin, 2021).

While appreciating ongoing discourses around the nature and role of literacy in science, perspectives of MDL begin with an understanding of 'fundamental literacy' in science education and of 'disciplinary literacy' in broader literacy research. Fundamental literacy was used originally to refer to reading and writing that are necessary for science literacy, with the latter concept referring to the 'knowledgeability, learning, and education' of science (Baltikian et al., 2024). In spite of this, greater emphasis on authentic scientific practice has emphasized the interactive and dynamic relationship between these aspects (Yore, 2018). Disciplinary literacy has emerged as a research tradition through recognition of the increasingly specialized ways in which representations are deployed as students' progress through the secondary science years.

The competencies involved in disciplinary literacy are seen as different from everyday oral language and also from fundamental and generic literacies that are distributed across curriculum areas (Garcia & Cain, 2014). Foundational studies of verbal language in relation to fundamental and disciplinary literacy have presented crucial foundations for articulating the role of various modes and the possibilities inherent in these as well as for developing a metalanguage to talk about meaning making (Eades-Baird & Hayden, 2025). Exploration on the relationship between students writing and reading comprehension, the role of encoding instruction in literacy development, and students at risk of literacy difficulties (Garcia & Cain, 2014; Ahmed, 2018; Zagata et al., 2023) using various models, they highlighted how different aspects of writing composition help predict students' reading and textual performance. They advocate for integrating encoding-focused interventions into literacy curricula and encourage text recognition and use of commonly used vocabulary, comprehension and composition of simple narrative and expository texts and to a greater or lesser extent the accompanying pictorial and basic diagrammatic depictions.

The middle level of the pyramid represents intermediate literacy where the literacy competencies become more sophisticated and less generally applicable as students experience emergent disciplinary literacy involving the more differentiated deployment of language and image resources in their interpretation and composition of more complex information reports, explanations and argumentative texts (Korth, 2025). As students advance through junior and senior high school, learning becomes more specialized, with subject areas having distinct structures and demands. While basic and intermediate literacy skills remain essential, students must also develop subject-specific literacy competencies that are less transferable and more tailored to each discipline. Brewington (2024) examines how secondary disciplinary teachers integrate literacy strategies to promote student outcomes on state assessments. The study identifies challenges encountered by teachers in embedding subject-specific literacy practices and observes their perceptions on effective strategy selection. Guided by Shanahan and Shanahan's disciplinary literacy framework and Knowles's theory of andragogy, the findings suggest targeted professional development can improve teacher confidence and student achievement.

Although there are certain commonalities in the use of academic language and other forms of representation across different disciplines, there are also discipline-specific discourse features and literacy practices. Disciplines differ extensively in how they create, disseminate and evaluate knowledge, and these differences are reflected in their specialized genres, distinctive symbolic artefacts and characteristic traditions of communication (Shen & Wang, 2024). Evidence for this derives from studies showing different characteristic literate practices within particular disciplines and from linguistic studies comparing their distinctive deployment of language resources (Martin, 2020). Evidence for discipline-specific literacy has been steadily accruing (Shanahan & Shanahan, 2017). Unsworth et al. (2022) worked with teams of researchers, teacher educators and teachers of chemistry, history and mathematics, as well as literacy experts in each team.

The teams examined learning materials such as textbooks, web pages and articles indicating how they approached the reading, the literacy challenges they envisaged for students and the strategies they believed would assist students. Think aloud data was also obtained from team members on their literacy practices in interpreting two samples of high school and professional literature texts in the discipline area. The data analysis demonstrated deeply different literacy practices across the disciplines. For example, mathematicians emphasized precision reading, with even function words like 'the' being potentially of particular significance, while chemists drew attention to the transformation of information from one form to another relating diagrams and charts to the main text, and historians focused particularly on the provenance of the source material.

Sociocultural Dynamics

Sociocultural dynamics in online communication encompass the intricate interplay of social and cultural factors that influence interactions within digital environments. Online communication is deeply embedded in sociocultural contexts. It reflects cultural norms and values and simultaneously shapes them. Treem et al. (2020) highlights the role of computer-mediated communication in reflecting and constructing social identities. Boyd (2014) explores how social media platforms facilitate the negotiation of identity and community in the digital age. These dynamics are crucial for understanding how individuals and groups interact and communicate online. The study of online communication is a complex and multifaceted field that explores how people interact, share information, and create meaning through digital platforms. It is an interdisciplinary field that considers the intricate relationships between technology, culture, and society (Baruah, 2024). Researchers have highlighted the profound impact that cultural norms, social structures, and technological capabilities have on our online interactions. They highlight how cultural heuristics and social norms shape digital communication, influencing inclusion and exclusion in online space. They have shown that digital spaces are deeply connected to the broader social contexts in which they exist. The societal structures are greatly transformed as a result of internet technology which also influence political discourse, media consumption, and public engagement (Vanden Broeck, 2021). The rise of online communication has transformed the way we interact with each other. It has enabled instant communication across borders and time zones, revolutionizing the way we connect with others. However, this shift has also introduced new challenges, particularly in terms of how we navigate the absence of physical presence in digital spaces, noting that technological advancements can both democratize access and reinforce systemic inequalities (Zhang & Lee, 2021; Meyer et al., 2023; Watson & Romic, 2025). In the online world, we rely heavily on text and images to convey meaning and build connections. But these cues are interpreted through the lens of our individual sociocultural backgrounds, which can lead to complex and nuanced interactions.

When we communicate online, our cultural backgrounds play a huge role in shaping how we express ourselves and interpret others. Research has shown that people from different cultures can have vastly different communication styles and preferences, even when it comes to something as simple as how we use visuals and text online. This idea is rooted in several key theories about how we interact with each other online (Li & Xu, 2020). The concept of sociocultural dynamics in online communication is rooted in several theoretical frameworks. One of these theories suggests that we can build meaningful relationships online by adapting the way we communicate to fit the digital environment. This means finding ways to compensate for the lack of nonverbal cues, like body language and tone of voice that we would normally pick up on in person. But here is the thing: our cultural norms and values influence how we communicate online, and that can affect how our messages are interpreted by others. For example, people from different cultural backgrounds may use different strategies to build intimacy or trust online, such as using more text- based cues or emphasizing certain rhetorical strategies (Tsigeman et al., 2024). Ultimately, understanding these cultural dynamics is crucial for effective online communication. By being aware of these differences and adapting our communication styles accordingly, we can build stronger, more meaningful relationships online (Walther, 2018).

Additionally, the theory of digital rhetoric explores how persuasive communication is crafted and understood in online environments (Ali & Naz, 2023). It emphasizes the role of cultural and social factors in shaping rhetorical strategies, acknowledging that digital platforms are not neutral spaces but are imbued with the values and norms of their users. This perspective highlights the need to consider the sociocultural contexts in which online communication occurs, as these contexts influence both the production and reception of digital messages (Ugo et al., 2023). The rise of digital rhetoric has been linked to the increasing complexity of online communication, where the medium itself, along with its cultural nuances, shapes how messages are framed and received (Harris & Koonce, 2019).

Research has demonstrated that online communities often reflect and reinforce existing social structures and cultural norms. For instance, studies on virtual communities have shown that participants engage in self-disclosure and storytelling as means of achieving membership and acceptance, mirroring practices observed in offline social groups. These findings suggest that online interactions are deeply embedded in sociocultural contexts, with digital platforms serving as extensions of traditional social spaces rather than entirely separate realms. Research on virtual communities such as those on social media platforms highlights how online engagement is shaped by pre-existing cultural and societal norms (Jiang et al., 2022).

Moreover, the dynamics of power and inequality present in broader society are often reproduced in online communication. Critical scholars argue that digital platforms can both challenge and perpetuate social hierarchies, depending on how they are used and by whom. For example, while the internet offers opportunities for marginalized groups to voice their perspectives and mobilize for social change, it can also be a site where existing power imbalances are maintained or exacerbated through practices such as cyberbullying or the digital divide. Studies have demonstrated how online communication can both empower and oppress, depending on the accessibility and representational power that individuals and groups hold (O'Neill & Millar, 2021).

Understanding sociocultural dynamics in online communication also involves examining the role of language and discourse. Language use in digital platforms is influenced by cultural norms and social identities, affecting how individuals present themselves and perceive others. The study of digital discourse considers how language is used to construct social reality online, including the formation of group identities, the negotiation of meaning, and the exercise of power. Research on language use in digital spaces highlights how different cultural groups express identity, negotiate meaning, and establish social ties (Young & Cameron, 2020).

Furthermore, the rapid evolution of technology introduces new modes of communication that continuously reshape sociocultural dynamics (Nguyen et al., 2023). The emergence of social networking sites, instant messaging, and other digital tools has altered the ways in which individuals interact, form relationships, and participate in communities. These technological developments necessitate ongoing examination of how sociocultural factors influence and are influenced by online communication practices. The fast pace of technological change has led to new digital practices, from micro-blogging to virtual communities, which continuously shape the ways people communicate and engage in online spaces (Nguyen et al., 2023).

Interdisciplinary Perspectives

The examination of multimodal literacy and sociocultural dynamics from an interdisciplinary viewpoint enhances our understanding of how different forms of communication interact and influence learning, language use, and societal structures. By integrating perspectives from education, linguistics, sociology, and media studies, we can explore how individuals engage with various communication modes both in offline and digital spaces. Each discipline offers unique theoretical frameworks and empirical findings that together provide a more comprehensive understanding of the complexities involved in meaning-making and the role cultural and social factors play in shaping communication practices. In education, scholars like Cope and Kalantzis (2023) have led discussions on how multimodal literacy affects teaching and learning.

They highlight that multimodal literacy is gamine in an era where students must interact with multiple forms of communication, such as images, audio, video, and digital interfaces, beyond conventional text. When we incorporate multiple forms of communication, such as images, videos, and text, into our learning practices, we open ourselves up to a deeper level of understanding. This approach, known as multimodal literacy, allows us to combine different ways of expressing ourselves to create meaning that's personal and relevant to our lives (Taylor & Leung, 2020). Researchers like Taylor and Leung argue that our educational systems need to evolve to teach students how to navigate and create meaning across different modes of communication. This means learning how to decode and produce messages that incorporate various forms of expression (Nash et al., 2024). The work of linguistic scholars like Oba and Berger explores how different communication mediums—such as speaking, writing, texting, and emailing—affect the way messages are constructed and perceived. It argues that modality, devices, and channels influence communication through two key drivers: deliberation and audience salience, impacting the thoughtfulness, honesty, and self-enhancing nature of messages. The study provides insights into the psychology of content production and highlights how emerging technologies may continue to shape communication dynamics (Oba & Berger, 2023).

Sociologist danah boyd has examined how social structures and cultural practices shape online communicate (boyd, 2014). Her research highlights that digital platforms are not neutral spaces; rather, they reflect and reinforce societal structures such as race, gender, and class. She urgues that online spaces serve as arenas for cultural production, where identity is constructed and power dynamics play out. By analyzing these interactions, boyd provides critical insights into the ways digital environments both mirror and influence broader social realities. Furthermore. boyd's work highlights how adolescents, in particular, navigate digital spaces, emphasizing that online communication is governed by the same sociocultural factors that shape offline interactions. Her contributions provide a critical lens for understanding how digital environments can both mirror and reinforce societal norms and inequalities, adding depth to our understanding of sociocultural dynamics in online communication (boyd, 2014).

Media studies scholars such as Olsen (2024) have also enriched the interdisciplinary study of multimodal literacy and sociocultural dynamics. Olsen's work on participatory and convergence cultures explores how digital media platforms allow for the blending of multiple forms of media, creating new avenues for cultural production and consumption. He highlights how individuals, particularly younger audiences, engage with media by creating and sharing content across different platforms, thereby participating in the construction of cultural narratives.

Olsen's concept of "convergence" refers to the merging of different media technologies and platforms, which facilitates the circulation of content across various channels. This convergence not only changes how people engage with media but also redistributes power in terms of who can create and share cultural content. Jenkins's analysis of media and public discourse enriches our understanding of how digital spaces shape cultural production and the dissemination of ideas (Olsen, 2024). By combining insights from education, linguistics, sociology, and media studies, we gain a holistic approach to understanding the complex relationships between multimodal literacy and sociocultural dynamics. This interdisciplinary approach considers not only the technical aspects of communication—such as the use of various media—but also the social, cultural, and political factors that influence and are influenced by communication practices.

Multimodal literacy in today's digital age is especially important because it facilitates a more inclusive, dynamic means of communication, reflecting the diverse ways in which people interact with information across multiple platforms. Research across these fields underscores the need for an interdisciplinary approach to studying communication, recognizing that no single discipline can fully capture the complexities at play. Education scholars focus on the pedagogical implications of multimodal literacy, linguists explore how modes influence meaning-making, sociologists analyze the social and cultural forces shaping online interactions, and media studies scholars investigate the role of media in shaping public discourse. Integrating these perspectives provides a deeper understanding of how communication practices are evolving in the digital age and the role that multimodal literacy plays in this transformation.

METHODOLOGY

This chapter employed a systematic literature review to analyse 46 relevant journal articles, conference proceedings, and government reports. Using databases such as Scopus and Google Scholar, Research gate Academia.edu, etc., it identifies key insights on multimodal literacy and its sociocultural dynamics. The review focuses on studies published since 2015, ensuring relevance to contemporary digital practices. Keywords like "multimodal literacy" and "sociocultural dynamics" guided the research.

The selected studies are categorized into key themes:

1. Understanding Multimodal literacy and Sociocultural Dynamics
2. The Role of Multimodal Literacy in Education and Identity Formation
3. Community Building and Social Change through Multimodal Communication
4. Strategies for Equitable Digital Engagement
5. Case Studies on the Critical Issues in Multimodal and Sociocultural Dynamics.

By synthesizing existing research, this chapter establishes a strong theoretical foundation, highlighting the benefits, challenges, and strategies of online communication in the digital age.

CASE STUDIES

Educational Context: The incorporation of multimodal literacy into digital classrooms has generated considerable interest due to its potential to improve educational outcomes, boost student engagement, and support a wide range of learning styles. Multimodal literacy refers to the capacity to understand, produce, and share information using various forms of communication, including text, images, video, audio, and interactive elements, beyond just traditional print. As digital learning environments continue to develop, there is growing awareness that multimodal literacy can help address disparities in educational access, especially when faced with social, cultural, and infrastructure-related obstacles.

A significant development in African education has been the use of multimedia assignments to enhance student learning. A study by Usman et al. (2023) explored how multimedia assignments improved Nigerian students' understanding of geography. The research showed that when students created multimedia presentations that incorporated text, images, and audio to explain concepts like climate change, urbanization, and resource distribution, they demonstrated better retention and a deeper grasp of the material. This approach proved particularly effective for students in rural areas, where traditional teaching methods may struggle to engage them due to limited infrastructure. The results of this study reflect a broader trend in African education that emphasizes the value of multimodal assignments in diverse settings. Across many African nations, schools are integrating multimedia to enrich learning experiences, with visual elements being key to explaining complex ideas. For example, in Kenya, a history class project encouraged students to use digital cameras and video editing tools to produce documentaries on the independence movement. This multimedia approach allowed students to present their perspectives on historical events in creative ways, fostering critical thinking, creativity, and technological skills.

Similarly, in South Africa, multimedia assignments have shown positive outcomes in increasing student engagement and improving learning. In a study by Fakude (2023), students were asked to create multimedia reports on topics like the social history of apartheid or the effects of urbanization in Johannesburg. By presenting their findings through videos, podcasts, and interactive diagrams, students gained more control over their learning and were able to explore complex subjects through different modes of expression. Digital tools such as interactive whiteboards (IWBs) and educational apps are increasingly being used in African classrooms to enhance multimodal learning. In South Africa, several studies have evaluated the integration of IWBs, emphasizing their effectiveness in engaging students through visual and interactive elements. For example, research by Mokoena & Simelane-Mnisi (2024); focused on rural classrooms, where IWBs helped teachers create interactive lessons that included multimedia, which increased student participation. The use of visuals, animations, and interactive activities in subjects like mathematics and science allowed students to better understand abstract concepts and engage in problem-solving, leading to improved critical thinking and conceptual understanding as students interacted with the board in real-time, promoting a collaborative learning environment. In Tanzania, the adoption of IWBs and digital tools like e-learning platforms has also been found to support multimodal literacy by combining text, visual, and auditory forms of communication. Sutrisno et al. (2023) demonstrated that these tools not only helped teachers explain complex ideas but also improved students' comprehension and retention. For example, when studying the solar system, students interacted with 3D animations of planets and stars while also watching videos and reading text-based explanations. This blend of different media helped students relate abstract scientific concepts to real-world contexts, boosting both engagement and learning outcomes.

Likewise, in Uganda, educational apps have been used to enhance literacy skills among primary school students. Research by Norman (2023) showed that apps like "U-Learn" and "KioKit" had a significant impact, especially in remote areas, by offering interactive games and quizzes that helped students practice reading, writing, and problem-solving. The multimodal nature of these apps combining audio, text, and visuals allowed students to learn at their own pace, with personalized feedback that adapted content to their progress. This highlights how mobile learning and educational apps can support multimodal learning, particularly where traditional resources are limited. Overall, the rise of multimodal literacy in African education whether through multimedia assignments that enable students to express complex ideas or digital tools that promote interactive learning is transforming educational outcomes across the continent. However, it's important to recognize that sociocultural factors, including cultural traditions, linguistic diversity, and socio- economic inequalities, play a significant role in shaping how students engage with multimodal learning. As African education continues to embrace digital technologies, it is crucial to develop teaching methods that are sensitive to these factors, ensuring that multimodal literacy is accessible, relevant, and effective for all students.

Social Media and Identity

Social media platforms like Instagram, TikTok, and Facebook have fundamentally changed the way people create, express, and manage their identities. By combining text, images, videos, and emojis, users build intricate self-representations, interact with others, and shape their public images in fluid and evolving ways. These platforms have become essential spaces for both individual and collective identity formation, particularly for young people across Africa, whether in urban or rural areas. In Africa, social media serves not only as a means of social connection but also as a tool for shaping identities, fostering social interaction, and engaging in political activism. Visual content such as selfies, videos, and hashtags play a key role in self-expression, while also connecting users with both local cultural contexts and global trends. However, the way people present themselves online is often influenced by sociocultural norms and expectations, which shape how identities are navigated in these spaces. This case study will explore how multimodal communication on platforms like Instagram and TikTok is used by African users to craft identities and build communities, with a focus on how they manage sociocultural expectations related to representation, beauty, and political participation in digital environments.

Instagram has become a key platform for identity creation in Africa, particularly due to its focus on photos and videos. This visual approach allows users to carefully craft their digital personas, showcasing aspects of their values, aesthetics, and affiliations. Instagram has shifted the way people negotiate their identities, moving from traditional offline expressions, such as through fashion, family, and community events, to an online space where visual and textual elements combine to form a cohesive image. In Africa, Instagram serves as a platform for young people to explore and express their identities, blending local cultural traditions with global influences. For example, in Nigeria, the #Owambe hashtag, which refers to elaborate social gatherings, is widely used to share vibrant images of celebrations, traditional attire, and cultural festivities, reflecting both social status and rich cultural practices (Yeku, 2022).

However, this representation is also influenced by global beauty ideals, often emphasizing skin tone, body shape, and fashion choices, many of which are shaped by Western media (Mastamet- Mason, 2024). Users further refine their online personas using filters, captions, and popular hashtags, which enhance visibility and engagement. For many African influencers, Instagram has become a key platform for building personal brands, securing sponsorships, and engaging with followers through visual storytelling. Influencers such as Nigerian makeup artists and fashion enthusiasts use the platform to blend beauty tutorials, personal stories, and product endorsements into a multimodal representation of their identities (Adenubi, & Adegboyega, 2020). By combining text (captions), images (makeup transformations), and videos (tutorials), these influencers express their expertise, lifestyles, and personal style, participating in global beauty and fashion trends while also staying connected to African cultural values. However, constructing an identity on Instagram comes with its challenges. The pressure to conform to idealized standards of beauty, wealth, and success can lead to anxiety, especially for users from marginalized communities.

Nigerian scholar, Olanrewaju (2020) argues that while Instagram offers African youth a way to engage with the global beauty market, it also intensifies issues like body image concerns, class disparities, and self-esteem. The practice of posting curated, polished images can contribute to negative mental health outcomes, particularly among younger users who may struggle with constantly comparing themselves to these seemingly perfect standards. TikTok, a rapidly expanding platform for short-form videos, has provided African users with a fresh space for creativity, self-expression, and identity exploration. Its multimodal format, which blends music, dance, images, text, and sound, allows users to create dynamic and engaging content. Particularly popular among African youth, TikTok is used as a platform for expressing cultural identities, offering social commentary, and challenging mainstream ideas. A major way African users engage with TikTok is through the negotiation of cultural identity via music, dance, and visual elements. In countries like Kenya, South Africa, and Nigeria, TikTok has become a hub for viral dance challenges, often set to local music genres such as Afrobeats, fuji, hip-hop, and Kwaito (Guanah, 2024). These dances, which feature cultural gestures, movements, and fashion, provide a unique way for users to express both their collective cultural identity and individual style. By blending traditional African music with global trends, TikTok in Africa allows users to celebrate their heritage while connecting with broader youth cultures worldwide. In Nigeria, TikTok users often engage in storytelling through lip-syncing, dance, and comedic sketches that reflect the country's sociocultural context. According to Shola (2021), TikTok offers Nigerian youth a platform to perform their identities based on local experiences, such as humor, politics, and daily life. This content not only reinforces cultural identity but also fosters a sense of belonging within subcultures, such as Nigerian youth or millennial communities, often through shared hashtags and trends (Ajitoni, 2024). TikTok also provides a space for African youth to challenge societal norms and express resistance. For example, members of African LGBTQ+ communities use the platform to challenge heteronormative expectations, creating spaces for visibility and solidarity. These digital expressions facilitate both individual and collective identity negotiation, as usersconnect with others who share similar experiences. However, like Instagram, TikTok's focus on visibility and performance can also amplify sociocultural pressures. TikTok trends often celebrate beauty, youth, and talent, driving competition among users to meet these standards. As Mbiti (2022) notes, the desire for visibility and social validation on TikTok can lead to issues like digital fatigue and feelings of inadequacy, particularly among African youth who may feel disconnected from mainstream beauty ideals.

Social media platforms like Instagram and TikTok are shaped by both global trends and local sociocultural norms, which influence how individuals engage with multimodal content and tackle issues such as gender, race, beauty, and politics. In many African societies, gender norms often define what types of self-representation are considered acceptable for women and men. On platforms like Instagram, women are always expected to abide to traditional beauty regulations, which often include a slim body, lighter skin, and long hair. Despite this, many African women are using these platforms to question these ideals. In South Africa, for example, users are accepting Afrocentric beauty, showcasing natural hairstyles and traditional African attire in their digital expressions (Mwangi, 2020). This oppose not only allows women to re-position their identities but also fosters empowerment and cultural pride. Social media also serves as a space for political engagement, where African users often participate in social movements or express political views through multimodal content. In Nigeria, for instance, political activists have used platforms like Instagram and Twitter to cause unrest, raise awareness about social justice issues, and challenge corrupt political systems (Agboola, 2021). The hashtag #EndSARS, which was part of the Nigerian movement against police brutality, is an example of how social media has been used to build collective identities and mobilize people. Activists have leveraged videos, images, and written posts to amplify their messages, attracting attention both locally and internationally. Additionally, African social media users are increasingly confronting the challenges of online harassment and digital colonialism. According to Afolaranmi (2023), the prevalence of hate speech, cyberbullying, and exclusionary discourse on platforms like Instagram and TikTok can shape how individuals navigate their online identities. In response, users are developing resilience strategies, such as blocking harmful content, reporting abusive behavior, and using social media to raise awareness about digital safety and inclusivity.

Multimodal Literacy and Sociocultural Dynamics in North Africa

The North African region, comprising countries such as Egypt, Morocco, and Tunisia, has witnessed significant social and political transformations in recent years. The advent of digital technologies has played a pivotal role in these changes, enabling citizens to express themselves, mobilize support, and negotiate meaning online (Björkvall et al. (2023). This part of the book chapter explores the intersection of multimodal literacy and sociocultural dynamics in online communication in North Africa, with a focus on online activism and professional communication.

Online Activism: The Arab Spring and Beyond

The Arab Spring protests, which swept across North Africa and the Middle East in 2010- 2012, demonstrated the power of multimodal communication in mobilizing millions of people. In Egypt, activists used social media platforms like Twitter, Facebook, and YouTube to share updates, mobilize protests, and coordinate actions (Elghamry, 2017). Hashtags like #Jan25 became rallying cries for the movement, while viral videos on YouTube captured the struggles and aspirations of the youth. For instance, the “We Are All Khaled Said” Facebook page, created in memory of a young Egyptian activist who was brutally killed by police, became a hub for mobilizing support and coordinating protests (Allam, 2017). The page's administrators used multimodal content, including images, videos, and infographics, to raise awareness about police brutality and advocate for democratic reforms.

Professional Communication: Digital Marketing in Morocco

In Morocco, tourism businesses are leveraging multimodal strategies to promote destinations and engage with customers. For example, the Moroccan National Tourist Office uses social media platforms like Instagram and Facebook to showcase multimedia content, such as picturesque videos of Marrakech or drone footage of the Atlas Mountains (Sohail R, et al. 2024). These campaigns, often designed in Arabic, French, and English, target both domestic and international tourists. By using multimodal content, Moroccan tourism businesses can communicate more effectively with diverse audiences, foster a sense of cultural identity, and promote cross-cultural understanding.

Multimodal Literacy and Sociocultural Dynamics in West Africa

West Africa, comprising countries such as Nigeria, Ghana, and Senegal, is a culturally diverse and technologically evolving region. The proliferation of digital technologies has transformed the way people communicate, interact, and negotiate meaning online (Kress, 2010). This part of the book chapter explores the intersection of multimodal literacy and sociocultural dynamics in online communication in West Africa, with a focus on online activism and professional communication.

Online Activism: #EndSARS in Nigeria

The #EndSARS movement in Nigeria in 2020 is a hallmark of multimodal online activism. The movement, which began as a call to end police brutality, quickly gained momentum on social media platforms like Twitter, Instagram, and Facebook (Akomolafe, 2020). Activists used multimodal content, including memes, infographics, and videos, to raise awareness about police brutality and advocate for reforms. For instance, a viral video showing a young Nigerian man being brutally beaten by police officers was shared widely on Twitter and Instagram, sparking widespread outrage and calls for justice (Premium Times, 2020). The video's caption, which included the hashtag #EndSARS, was translated into multiple languages, including English, Pidgin English, and Yoruba, to ensure that the message reached a diverse audience.

Professional Communication: Remote Work in Ghana's IT Sector

Ghana's growing IT sector relies heavily on remote work tools to facilitate collaboration and communication among team members (Owusu-Ansah, 2020). Teams like MEST Africa use platforms like Slack and Microsoft Teams to manage projects, share files, and engage in real-time discussions. For example, a Ghanaian IT firm, Hubtel, uses video conferencing tools like Google Meet and Zoom to conduct virtual training programs for clients (Hubtel, 2020). The firm's trainers use multimodal content, including videos, screenshots, and infographics, to explain difficult technical concepts and encourage knowledge acquision.

Multimodal Literacy and Sociocultural Dynamics in East Africa

East Africa, a region that includes countries like Kenya, Tanzania, and Ethiopia, is a hotbed of technological innovation and cultural diversity. The rapid spread of digital technologies has revolutionized the way people communicate, interact, and share ideas online (Kress, 2010). In this context, it's fascinating to explore the intersection of multimodal literacy and sociocultural dynamics in online communication.

Online activism Climate Advocacy in Kenya

In Kenya, for instance, young activists like Elizabeth Wathuti are harnessing the power of multimodal storytelling to raise awareness about critical climate issues and promote sustainable practices. She urged leaders at COP26 to "open their hearts" to the realities of climate change (Wathuti, 2021, November 1). Social media campaigns like #SaveOurForests and #ClimateActionKe have gone viral on Twitter and Instagram, highlighting the devastating impact of deforestation, pollution, and climate change.

The Green Belt Movement, a Kenyan environmental organization, is a shining example of how multimodal content can be used to promote climate resilience and sustainable land use practices. Through engaging videos, infographics, and photos, the organization is able to convey complex climate messages in an accessible and engaging way (Ubaga et al., n.d.). What's more, their social media campaigns often incorporate local languages like Swahili and Kikuyu, ensuring that climate messages reach diverse audiences and resonate with local communities.

Professional Communication: Digital Storytelling in Ethiopia

Ethiopian startups like Gebeya Inc. are leveraging digital storytelling to enhance tech skills and innovation (Woldu & Quazi, 2024). The company uses multimedia content, including short films and videos, to showcase trainees' success stories and promote its programs on LinkedIn and YouTube. For example, Gebeya's "Success Stories" video series features interviews with trainees who have secured employment or started their own businesses after completing Gebeya's programs (Woldu & Quazi, 2024). The videos, which incorporate subtitles in English and Amharic, provide a powerful testament to the impact of digital skills training in Ethiopia.

Multimodal Literacy and Sociocultural Dynamics in Southern Africa

Southern Africa, comprising countries such as South Africa, Namibia, and Botswana, is a region characterized by diverse cultures, languages, and technological landscapes. The proliferation of digital technologies has transformed the way people communicate, interact, and negotiate meaning online (Björkvall et al. (2023). This section explores the intersection of multimodal literacy and sociocultural dynamics in online communication in Southern Africa, with a focus on online activism and professional communication.

Online Activism: Gender-Based Violence Awareness in South Africa

The #AmINext campaign in South Africa (2019) is a notable example of multimodal online activism. The campaign, which aimed to raise awareness about gender-based violence, used social media platforms like Twitter, Instagram, and Facebook to share personal stories, statistics, and advocacy messages (Maseko, 2020). Activists employed multimodal content, including memes, photos, and videos, to convey the severity of the issue and mobilize support. For instance, the#AmINext Twitter campaign used infographics to highlight alarming statistics about gender-based violence in South Africa (Mpontshane, 2022). The campaign's use of visual content, including images and videos, helped to create a sense of urgency and solidarity among Twitter users.

Professional Communication: Multimedia Marketing in Namibia

Namibian firms are leveraging multimedia tools to promote tourism and engage with customers. For example, the Gondwana Collection, a Namibian tourism operator, uses social media platforms like Facebook and YouTube to showcase multimedia content, including videos, photos, and podcasts (Natalia, 2024). The company's multimedia campaigns often incorporate local languages like Afrikaans and Oshiwambo, ensuring that tourism messages reach diverse audiences.

Multimodal Literacy and Sociocultural Dynamics in Central Africa

Central Africa, comprising countries such as the Democratic Republic of Congo, Cameroon, and Gabon, is a region characterized by rich cultural diversity and complex technological landscapes. The proliferation of digital technologies has transformed the way people communicate, interact, and negotiate meaning online (Kress, 2010). This section explores the intersection of multimodal literacy and sociocultural dynamics in online communication in Central Africa, with a focus on online activism and professional communication.

Online Activism: Wildlife Conservation in the Congo Basin

The Congo Basin, spanning across six Central African countries, is home to the world's second- largest tropical rainforest. However, the region faces severe environmental threats, including deforestation, poaching, and climate change (Greenpeace Africa, 2020). In response, advocacy groups like Greenpeace Africa are using multimodal strategies to promote wildlife conservation and sustainable forest management. For example, Greenpeace Africa's "Congo Basin Defenders" campaign uses social media platforms like Twitter, Instagram, and Facebook to share multimedia content, including videos, photos, and infographics (Greenpeace Africa, 2020). The campaign's use of local languages like Lingala and Kiswahili ensures that conservation messages reach diverse audiences.

Professional Communication: E-commerce Expansion in Cameroon

Cameroon's e-commerce sector is growing rapidly, driven by increasing internet penetration and mobile phone adoption (Ngangfen, 2014). E-commerce platforms like Jumia Cameroon are leveraging multimodal strategies to promote products, engage with customers, and build brand identity. For instance, Jumia Cameroon's social media campaigns use multimedia content, including product videos, customer testimonials, and promotional graphics (Ngangfen, 2014). The platform's use of local languages like French and Pidgin English ensures that product information and promotions reach diverse customer segments.

CONCLUSION

The study underscores the significance of multimodal literacy in navigating the complexities of online communication. It demonstrates that digital interactions are deeply embedded in sociocultural contexts, influencing identity formation, discourse, and knowledge dissemination. The interdisciplinary approach adopted in the study provides a comprehensive understanding of how multimodal literacy enhances learning, fosters inclusivity, and reshapes traditional communication norms. Ultimately, the findings suggest that multimodal literacy is not merely an academic concept but a practical necessity in the digital age.

Recommendations

This study recommended the followings:

i. *Educational Integration* – Institutions should incorporate multimodal literacy into curricula to equip students with the skills needed to engage effectively in digital environments.
ii. *Policy Development* – Policymakers should establish frameworks that promote equitable access to digital literacy resources, ensuring inclusivity across diverse sociocultural backgrounds.
iii. *Interdisciplinary Collaboration* – Researchers and educators should collaborate across disciplines to develop innovative strategies for enhancing multimodal literacy.
iv. *Technological Advancements* – Developers should design digital tools that support multimodal learning, fostering interactive and engaging communication experiences.
v. *Public Awareness* – Awareness campaigns should be conducted to educate individuals on the importance of multimodal literacy in fostering meaningful online interactions.

Future Insights

Given the rapid evolution of digital technologies, multimodal literacy and sociocultural dynamics in online communication will continue to shape interactions, learning, and identity formation. Here are some key future directions:

1. ***Emerging AI and Machine Learning Impacts*** – As AI-driven tools like ChatGPT and multimodal content generators expand, future research should explore how these technologies influence literacy development and sociocultural exchanges.

Understanding how AI refines language, visuals, and interactive elements can enhance educational strategies and media communication.

2. ***Expanded Role of Virtual Reality (VR) and Augmented Reality (AR)*** – The increasing use of immersive technologies in communication and education will necessitate multimodal literacy competencies that extend beyond text and images. Future studies should examine how VR and AR reshape discourse and the dynamics of cultural representation.
3. ***Cross-Cultural Digital Adaptation*** – As online communication becomes more global, understanding sociocultural nuances in digital literacy will be critical. Future research should investigate how diverse cultural backgrounds influence multimodal interpretation and meaning-making, ensuring inclusivity in digital interactions.
4. ***Ethical and Policy Considerations*** – The integration of multimodal literacy in education and social systems demands ethical scrutiny, particularly in privacy, misinformation, and accessibility. Policymakers should formulate frameworks that ensure equitable access to digital literacy resources and safeguard users from algorithmic bias.
5. ***The Future of Digital Identity and Expression*** – As social media continues to evolve, the ways individuals express and construct their identities will become more multimodal. Future studies should explore how digital platforms facilitate self-representation, discourse formation, and community-building in diverse cultural contexts.

REFERENCES

Adenubi, A. O., & Adegboyega, T. A. (2020). Globalization and social media technologies; implications for African identity formation. *Gateway information journal, 21*(1 & 2), 45-54. Nigeria Library Association, Ogun State Chapter. https://scholar.google.com/citations?view_op=view_citation&hl=en&user=c5OfbfIAAAAJ&citation_for_view=c5OfbfIAAAAJ:Tyk-4Ss8FVUC

Afolaranmi, A. O. (2023). Effects of social media on the peaceful coexistence of African people: A critical review. In Chukwuere, J. E., Adom, D., & Dyikuk, J. J. (Eds.), *Disruptive social media: Towards a resilient social media ecosystem in Africa* (pp. 93–107). Jozac Publishers., DOI: 10.57040/jp.6.c30

Ahmed, R. (2018). *Effects of online education on encoding and decoding process of students and teachers*. ERIC. https://files.eric.ed.gov/fulltext/ED590288.pdf

Ajitoni, B. (2024). Digital storytelling and cultural identity: The role of social media in contemporary narratives. *The African Communicator*, *4*(2), 89–101. DOI: 10.70118/TACJ0007

Akomolafe, F. (2020). #EndSARS: A study of the role of social media in the 2020 Nigerian Protests. *Journal of African Media Studies*, *12*(1), 1–15.

Ali, B., & Naz, B. (2023). Discourse Analysis of Online communication in Pakistan in Social Media. *Cosmic Journal of Linguistics*, *2*(1), 1–15.

Allam, N. (2017). We are all Khaled Said: The role of Facebbok in Egypt's Arab Spring. *Journal of African Media Studies*, *9*(1), 33–46.

Baltikian, M., Karkkainen, S., & Kukkonen, J. (2024). Assessment of scientific literacy levels among secondary school students in Lebanon: Exloring gender-based differences. *Eurasia Journal of Mathematics, Science and Technology Education*, *2*(3), em2407. DOI: 10.29333/ejmste/14279

Baruah, A. (2024). The impact of computer-mediated communication on relationships and Social Interactions. *International Journal of Human-Computer Interaction*, *2*(2), 1–7. DOI: 10.1080/10447318.2024.2442755

Björkvall, A., Boréus, K., & Svärd, P. (2024). Multimodal discourse analysis. In *Analyzing text and discourse: Nine approaches for the social sciences* (2nd ed., pp. 199–215). SAGE Publications., https://books.google.com.ng/books?hl=en&lr=&id=xrr7EAAAQBAJ&oi=fnd&pg=PA199&dq=Multimodal+discourse+analysis&ots=1109AeZzOv&sig=w_5kSxvVDBCW2lDzHHveS8CN0BY&redir_esc=y#v=onepage&q=Multimodal%20discourse%20analysis&f=false

Boyd, D. (2014). *It's Complicated: The Social Lives of Networked Teens*. Yale University Press.

Brewington, M. T. (2024). *How secondary disciplinary teachers integrate literacy strategies to improve outcomes on state assessments*. Walden University. https://scholarworks.waldenu.edu/cgi/viewcontent.cgi?article=18323&context=dissertations

Cope, B., & Kalantzis, M. (2023). Towards education justice: The multiliteracies project revisited. In *Multiliteracies in International Educational Contexts* (pp. 1–33). Routledge. DOI: 10.4324/9781003349662-1

Doran, Y. (2019). Building knowledge through images in physics. *Visual Communication, 18*(2), 251–277. DOI: 10.1177/1470357218759825

Doran, Y. J. (2017). *The discourse of physics: Building knowledge through language, mathematics and image*. Routledge. DOI: 10.4324/9781315181134

Doran, Y. J., & Martin, J. R. (2021). Field relations: Understanding scientific explanations. In Maton, K., Martin, J. R., & Doran, Y. J. (Eds.), *Teaching science: Knowledge, language, pedagogy* (pp. 105–133). Routledge. DOI: 10.4324/9781351129282-7

Eades-Baird, M. R., & Hayden, H. E. (2025). Disciplinary Literacies for Science: Understanding How Teachers Enact Educational Reforms. In *Utilizing Case Studies in Literacy and Language Education* (pp. 191-218). IGI Global Scientific Publishing.

Elghamry, K. (2017). Social media and the Arab Spring: Politics comes first. *The International Journal of Press/Politics*, *22*(4), 449–469.

Fakude, N. L. (2023). *Integrating digital technology in teaching history in the primary school* (Doctoral dissertation, University of Johannesburg).

Garcia, J. R., & Cain, K. (2014). Decoding and reading comprehension: A meta-analysis to identify which reader and assessment characteristics influence the strength of the relationship in English. *Review of Educational Research*, *84*(1), 74–111. DOI: 10.3102/0034654313499616

Greenpeace Africa. (2020). Congo Basin Defenders. Retrieved from http://www.greenbeltmovement.org/ on 10th of January, 2025

Guanah, J. S. (2024). Social media, popular culture and contending African ethical models. In *Social science ethics for research and practice: An African perspective* (pp. 25–42).

Haas, L., & Tussey, J. (2023). Empowering Minds: Multimodal Literacies, Fanfiction, and Inclusive Education. Journal of English Teaching through Movies and Media, 24(4), 28-40.

Hao, J. (2020). *Analysing scientific discourse from a systemic functional linguistic perspective: A framework for exploring knowledge building in biology*. Routledge. DOI: 10.4324/9781351241052

Harris, L., & Koonce, S. (2019). Digital rhetoric in the context of digital culture. *Digital Communication Research*, *15*(3), 112–130. DOI: 10.1080/10468946.2019.1625792

Hubtel. (2020). Virtual training programs. Retrieved from (link unavailable)

Jenkins, H. (2006). *Convergence Culture: Where Old and New Media Collide*. NYU Press.

Jennings, P. E. (2023). Entertainment, Education, Empowerment: The Role of TikTok in Gender Diverse Lesbian Identity Negotiation (Doctoral dissertation, Texas A&M University).

Jiang, Z., Zhang, Q., & Yu, D. (2022). The social dynamics of self-disclosure in online communities. *International Journal of Human-Computer Studies*, *145*, 82–93. DOI: 10.1016/j.ijhcs.2020.102518

Jones, P., Turney, A., Georgiou, H., & Nielsen, W. (2020). Assessing multimodal literacies in science: Semiotic and practical insights from pre-service teacher education. *Language and Education*, *34*(2), 153–172. DOI: 10.1080/09500782.2020.1720227

Kelly, M. (2023). The Representation of Interpretative Knowledge in Cultural Heritage Research (Doctoral dissertation, University of Brighton).

Korth, C. E. (2025). Democratic Schooling Practices: A Path for Increasing DEIJB in International Schools. In Diversity and Inclusion Challenges for Leaders of International Schools (pp. 337-382). IGI Global Scientific Publishing.

Kress, G. (2010). *Multimodality: A Social Semiotic Approach to Contemporary Communication*. Routledge.

Li, H., & Xu, S. (2020). Cultural influences on the interpretation of online communication. *Social Media Studies*, *8*(1), 79–96. DOI: 10.1080/20421338.2020.1731107

Martin, J. R. (2020). Revisiting field: Specialized knowledge in secondary school science and humanities discourse. In Martin, J. R., Maton, K., & Doran, Y. (Eds.), *Accessing academic discourse: Systemic functional linguistics and legitimation code theory* (pp. 114–148). Routledge.

Maseko, S. (2020). #AmINext: A multimodal analysis of Twitter activism against gender-based violence in South Africa. *Journal of African Media Studies*, *12*(1), 1–15.

Mastamet-Mason, A., Sokhetye, P. N., & Tilahum, Y. D. (2024). Female body beauty ideals and their impact on fashion size standards: A comparative study of Western and South African perspectives. In *International Conference on Multidisciplinary Research* (Vol. 2024, pp. 205-221). DOI: 10.26803/MyRes.2024.15

Mavuru, L., & Ramnarain, U. (2020). Learners' socio-cultural backgrounds and science teaching and learning: A case study of township schools in South Africa. *Cultural Studies of Science Education*, *15*(4), 1067–1095. DOI: 10.1007/s11422-020-09974-8

Meyer, A., Jones, B., & Patel, R. (2023). Digital paradoxes: Inclusion and exclusion in online spaces. *Technology and Society Journal*, *28*(1), 45–67.

Mokoena, M. M., & Simelane-Mnisi, S. (2024). Establishing the Reliability and Validity of the Teacher Self-Efficacy Questionnaire in the Use of the Interactive Whiteboard: A South African Sample Perspective. *Public Administration and Development Alternatives (IPADA)*, 128.

Mpontshane, N. (2022) A Visual Analysis of 2019's #AmINext? Movement. University of Pretoria (South Africa) Pro Quest Dissertations & Theses. DOI:DOI: 10.25403/UPresearchdata.21756938

Nash, B. L., Dunham, H., Murdter-Atkinson, J., & Mosley Wetzel, M. (2023). A Culturally Sustaining Approach to Multimodal Literacies: Building from Students' Funds of Knowledge in Field-Based Teacher Education. *Literacy Research and Instruction*, *63*(2), 151–175. DOI: 10.1080/19388071.2022.2153766

Natalia, F. (2024). Use of Social Networks by Tourist Enterprises at the Current Stage. *The Scientific Issues of Ternopil Volodymyr Hnatiuk National Pedagogical University Series Geography*, *56*(1), 143–150. DOI: 10.25128/2519-4577.24.1.17

Ngangfen, D. A. (2014). E-Commerce in Cameroon: Retrieved from https://www.foretiafoundation.org/wp-content/uploads/2014/03/E-Commerce-Article.pdf on 10th of January, 2025

Nguyen, H., Bui, T., & Tran, M. (2023). The rapid evolution of online communication: A case study of emerging technologies. *Journal of Digital Innovation*, *8*(4), 132–145. DOI: 10.1016/j.jdi.2023.03.010

Norman, A. (2023). Educational technology for reading instruction in developing countries: A systematic literature review. *Review of Education*, *11*(3), e3423. DOI: 10.1002/rev3.3423

O'Neill, D., & Millar, F. (2021). Power structures and inequality in digital spaces. *Journal of Digital Media & Policy*, *12*(1), 45–65. DOI: 10.1386/jdmp_00036_1

Oba, D., & Berger, J. (2023). How communication mediums shape the message. *Journal of Consumer Psychology*, *34*(3), 406–424. DOI: 10.1002/jcpy.1372

Olsen, D. (2024). *Media Arts Education: Transforming Education through Multimodal Cognition, Holistic Learning, and Techno-Embodiment*. Taylor & Francis. DOI: 10.4324/9781003430834

Owusu-Ansah, B. (2020). Digital entrepreneurship in Ghana: An exploratory study. *Journal of Small Business and Enterprise Development*, *27*(3), 419–435.

Park, W., & Song, J. (2019). Between realism and constructivism: A sketch of pluralism for science education. In Herring, E., Jones, K., Kiprijanov, K., & Sellers, L. (Eds.), *The past, present, and future of integrated history and philosophy of science* (pp. 228–247). Routledge. DOI: 10.4324/9781351214827-14

Philip, T. M., & Sengupta, P. (2021). Theories of learning as theories of society: A contrapuntal approach to expanding disciplinary authenticity in computing. *Journal of the Learning Sciences*, *30*(2), 330–349. DOI: 10.1080/10508406.2020.1828089

Premium Times. (2020). Video: Police brutality in Nigeria. Retrieved from https://scholarworks.lib.csusb.edu/etd/1541/

Rushanova, N. B., Kalibekuly, D., Zhanibek, A. B., Nurmanova, M. S., & Alimberdi, L. A. (2024). Cultural aspects of media communications in the digital age. *Серия Журналистики*, *71*(1), 80–91. DOI: 10.26577/HJ.2024.v71.i1.8

Shanahan, C., & Shanahan, T. (2017). *Disciplinary literacy Handbook of research on teaching the English language arts*. Routledge.

Shen, H., & Wang, S. (2024). Traditional Chinese Ideology and Material Culture: An Archaeological Exploration of Historical Perspectives and Artefacts. *Mediterranean Archaeology & Archaeometry. International Journal*, *24*(3), 237–252.

Shola, A. T. (2021). Social media, youth participation and activism: An analysis of the# Endsars protests in Nigeria. *Democracy and Development Journal*, *5*(3), 4–10.

Sohail, R., Babar, S., Shahbaz, A., & Babar H. (2024). Tourism destination branding in the digital age: Evaluating the influence of social media on destination image and visitor perceptions. *Contemporary Journal of Social Science Review Vol.02* No.04

Sutrisno, D., Abidin, N. A. Z., Pambudi, N., Aydawati, E., & Sallu, S. (2023). Exploring the benefits of multimodal literacy in English teaching: Engaging students through visual, auditory, and digital modes. *Global Synthesis in Education Journal*, *1*(2), 1–14. DOI: 10.61667/xh184f41

Taylor, S. V., & Leung, C. B. (2020). Multimodal literacy and social interaction: Young children's literacy learning. *Early Childhood Education Journal*, *48*(1), 1–10. DOI: 10.1007/s10643-019-00974-0

Treem, J. W., Leonardi, P. M., & Van den Hooff, B. (2020). Computer-mediated communication in the age of communication visibility. *Journal of Computer-Mediated Communication*, *25*(1), 44–59. DOI: 10.1093/jcmc/zmz024

Tsigeman, E., Mararitsa, L., Gundelah, O., Lopatina, O., & Koltsova, O. (2024). Psychological Aspects of Face-To-Face Versus Computer-Mediated Interpersonal Communication: An Integrative Review. In *International Conference on Human-Computer Interaction* (pp. 29-48). Cham: Springer Nature Switzerland. DOI: 10.1007/978-3-031-61312-8_3

Ugo, S. U., Odey, B. E., Odey, H. O., & Abu, P. E. (2023). Impact of digital communication technologies on the Nigerian mass media: Implications and insights into disruptions. LWATI: A Journal of Contemporary Research, 20(4), 39-55.

Unsworth, L., Tytler, R., Fenwick, L., Humphrey, S., Chandler, P., Herrington, M., & Pham, L. (2022). *Multimodal literacy in school science: Transdisciplinary perspectives on theory, research and pedagogy*. Taylor & Francis. DOI: 10.4324/9781003150718

Usman, H., Husseini, A., & Mohammed, A. (2023). Impact of interactive video-based instructional platform on achievement of geography concepts amongst secondary school students in Niger State. *FUO Journal of Science and Technology*, *9*(2), 123–137.

Vanden Broeck, P. (2021). The role of internet technology in shaping political discourse and media consumption. *Journal of Digital Culture*, *15*(3), 203–219.

Walther, J. B. (2018). Social Information Processing Theory. In *The Handbook of Communication Science* (pp. 441–460). Sage Publications.

Wathuti, E. (2021, November 1). *Elizabeth Wathuti at #COP26: "Please open your hearts"* [Video]. YouTube. https://www.youtube.com/watch?v=VMvzJu79WG0

Watson, S., & Romic, J. (2024). ChatGPT and the entangled evolution of society, education, and technology: A systems theory perspective. *European Educational Research Journal, 24*(2), 205-224. (Original work published 2025)DOI: 10.1177/14749041231221266

Woldu, F., & Quazi, T. M. (2024). *Difficulties faced by small and medium-sized enterprises (SMEs) in underdeveloped nations in implementing digital marketing: A case study of Bangladesh and Ethiopia*. University of Gothenburg. Retrieved from https://gupea.ub.gu.se/handle/2077/82458

Yore, L. D. (2018). Commentary on the expanding development of literacy research in science education. In *Global Developments in Literacy Research for Science Education* (pp. 379–397). Springer. DOI: 10.1007/978-3-319-69197-8_22

Young, S., & Cameron, G. (2020). Digital discourse: Understanding language and power in the online world. *Language & Communication*, *70*, 68–79. DOI: 10.1016/j.langcom.2020.07.001

Zagata, E., Kearns, D., Truckenmiller, A. J., & Zhao, Z. (2023). Using the features of written compositions to understand reading comprehension. *Reading Research Quarterly*, *58*(4), 624–654. DOI: 10.1002/rrq.503

Zaidi, R., & Sah, P. K. (2024). Affordances of Multilingual and Multimodal Literacy Engagements of Immigrant High School Students: A Scoping Review. *SAGE Open*, *14*(1), 21582440241228122. DOI: 10.1177/21582440241228122

Chapter 17
ChatGPT and the Future of Language Learning and Linguistic Diversity in Africa

Hauwa Mohammed Sani
Ahmadu Bello University, Zaria, Nigeria

ABSTRACT

This chapter explores the challenges and opportunities of the Fourth Industrial Revolution, specifically focusing on Artificial Intelligence (AI) and its implications for linguistic and educational diversity in African higher education. As AI technologies like ChatGPT expand, concerns arise about impacts on critical thinking, linguistic diversity, and stylistic richness. The chapter argues that global ChatGPT use may exacerbate disparities between languages with high AI compatibility and those with limited tools, potentially fostering a new digital divide. Using selected Nigerian universities as a case study, this research addresses questions on the adaptability of AI to diverse African languages, the need for curriculum adjustments, and the risks of linguistic hegemony. Findings indicate that while AI offers significant educational benefits, its adoption in Africa must consider preserving linguistic diversity. Consequently, this chapter recommends developing policies supporting equitable AI access while promoting cultural and linguistic heritage.

DOI: 10.4018/979-8-3693-7934-9.ch017

INTRODUCTION

Amid the Fourth or Fifth Industrial Revolution, where artificial intelligence (AI) is rapidly reshaping global discourse, questions about its impact on linguistic diversity, especially in multilingual societies like Nigeria, are becoming increasingly urgent. As AI tools such as ChatGPT gain widespread use in education, business, and communication, concerns arise about their capacity to support, represent, or even undermine the linguistic and cultural fabric of diverse communities. This chapter examines the implications of ChatGPT on linguistic diversity and creativity in Nigerian universities, drawing on insights from sociolinguistic theory and Critical Discourse Analysis (CDA). While ChatGPT, developed by OpenAI, offers transformative potential for education and communication, it also presents challenges that need careful consideration by African educators, linguists, and policymakers. Accordingly, the core objectives of this chapter are to:

1. investigate the potential of ChatGPT to enhance language learning outcomes in Nigerian educational contexts, focusing on improving digital literacy and access to quality education.
2. examine the implications of AI-driven language education for linguistic diversity and cultural preservation within Nigerian society.
3. explore how Afro-Futurist approaches can shape inclusive, culturally responsive AI language models that reflect Nigerian values, languages, and identities.
4. identify ethical, policy, and practical recommendations for integrating ChatGPT and similar AI tools into Nigerian language education.

By addressing these objectives, the chapter contributes to current debates on AI in education, offering a nuanced and context-sensitive understanding of how ChatGPT and similar technologies can either support or threaten linguistic diversity and cultural sustainability in African digital education.

BACKGROUND

Africa is home to over 2,000 languages, making it one of the world's most linguistically diverse regions. Nigeria alone has over 500 languages, accounting for a quarter of Africa's linguistic heritage. Within this complex linguistic landscape, the rise of large language models (LLMs) like ChatGPT presents both exciting possibilities and daunting challenges. On the one hand, ChatGPT can support language learning by enhancing digital literacy, expanding access to quality education, and offering context-specific academic support. On the other hand, concerns are mounting that the widespread adoption of tools optimized for English and other dominant languages may contribute to the erosion of Africa's linguistic and stylistic diversity.

This chapter examines ChatGPT within the broader context of African higher education and its future in the Fourth Industrial Revolution. Using selected Nigerian universities as case studies, it employs qualitative methods, including surveys and interviews, to assess how AI tools like ChatGPT are being received, used, or resisted. The chapter draws on Critical Discourse Analysis (CDA) and sociolinguistic theory, particularly frameworks that address language ideologies and linguistic inequality. Central questions include: Can ChatGPT enhance language learning outcomes in African contexts? Could its dominance deepen disparities between languages with rich digital resources and those underrepresented in AI systems? Is there a need for curriculum reforms to prepare students for an AI-driven future? More critically, does ChatGPT reinforce linguistic imperialism, prioritizing English over indigenous African languages?

Scholars such as Sharma (2023) and Jørgensen (2023) have warned that as tools like ChatGPT become more embedded in education, a global digital divide may emerge—rooted not only in technology access but also in the linguistic limitations of these tools. The capacity of AI to engage meaningfully across a wide range of languages remains uneven, and the exclusion of some African languages from AI systems raises significant equity concerns.

In response, this chapter integrates Afro-Futurist approaches to explore how AI can be designed and applied to reflect and uphold African linguistic identities and cultural values. It suggests that AI systems should not only be trained in African languages but also be developed in collaboration with African communities, ensuring that the next wave of AI-driven education is inclusive, empowering, and culturally relevant.

The Emergence of AI Tools: An Overview of ChatGPT

The Fourth Industrial Revolution (4IR) marks a transformative era defined by the fusion of advanced technologies such as artificial intelligence (AI), the Internet of Things (IoT), and biotechnology that blur the boundaries between the physical, digital, and biological realms. This convergence is driving rapid, disruptive change across industries and societies, reshaping education, labour markets, governance, and communication while raising critical ethical, environmental, and policy considerations. A key area of scholarly focus is the intersection of AI and higher education, particularly language use and innovation.

One of the most prominent AI tools to emerge within this context is ChatGPT, developed by the U.S.-based company OpenAI, which was founded in 2015. As a product of deep learning and generative language modeling, ChatGPT, now in versions 3.5 and 4, demonstrates the capabilities of AI to engage in complex, human-like dialogue. Its widespread adoption in academic and public spheres underscores its potential to transform teaching, learning, and communication practices while also raising questions about ethics, privacy, and originality.

ChatGPT version 3.5 was released in November 2022. This advanced chatbot uses deep learning techniques and has been trained on vast online text data. It is called GPT, or generative pre-trained transformer, because it can understand human input and generate responses similar to human-written ones. This makes it very difficult to distinguish between human and AI-generated text.

It is worth noting that OpenAI now offers a range of machine learning (ML) products to the public, such as DALL-E and ChatGPT. These tools have gained considerable traction, with GPT attracting one million registered users within five days and 100 million active users in under three months. ChatGPT leverages language modelling techniques to make impressively accurate predictions of subsequent words, owing to its access to vast amounts of data and billions of parameters. These insights are drawn from the Journal of Applied Learning & Teaching Vol.6 No.1 (2023). Although other language models, such as BERT, RoBERTa, and XLNet, aim to achieve similar objectives, their capabilities have been outperformed by ChatGPT-3.5 (Lund et al., 2023). It is because of its extensive data stores and efficiency.

ChatGPT is an advanced system that can handle complex queries efficiently, thanks to its extensive data stores and intelligent design (Liu et al., 2022a; Liu et al., 2022b; Lund et al., 2023). In March 2023, ChatGPT-4 was released, which showed significant improvements in reasoning and conciseness compared to its predecessor. However, it is noteworthy that ChatGPT-4 generates output at a slower speed than ChatGPT-3.5 (OpenAI, 2023). Universities worldwide have been interested in both the 3.5 and 4 versions of ChatGPT as they can be disruptive tools for teaching, learning, and supporting students (Kasneci et al., 2023; Nautiyal et al., 2023).

Numerous academic institutions are exploring the possibility of incorporating AI technology into their educational approaches to enhance student engagement and deliver tailored learning opportunities. Nevertheless, several scholars and experts have voiced apprehensions regarding the ethical implications of integrating AI into education, including concerns about privacy, partiality, and the diminution of human interaction (Flanagin et al., 2023; Thorp, 2023). This research also sheds light on potential issues about how AI might impact language originality and expression in essays produced by university students

Authorial Reviews on ChatGPT

In the article "How will AI alter the student experience? Experts weigh in" by Jenae Cohn (2023), the focus is on the growing influence of artificial intelligence (AI) in higher education. It highlights the consensus among experts in the field that addressing the impact of AI technology on pedagogy and the student experience is essential. However, the article also emphasises the divergence of opinions and perceptions regarding the magnitude of these effects across Faculty, staff, and students.

Cohn (2023) notes that AI's implications are widely varied, making it challenging to pinpoint precisely how it will shape the student, faculty, and staff experience. Some view AI as a passing trend or a means of process improvement, while others see it as a fundamental challenge to the traditional landscape of higher education. In light of these diverse perspectives, Cohn (2023) underscores the importance of continued dialogue, discussion, and education surrounding AI technology in higher education. Such ongoing conversations are critical for educational leaders to navigate the evolving landscape of AI and its impact on the student experience.

Cohn's (2023) emphasis on the importance of continued dialogue, discussion, and education around AI in higher education is highly relevant to this study, which explores the integration of ChatGPT into African language education. As this chapter critically engages with the implications of AI tools like ChatGPT for linguistic diversity, digital literacy, and culturally responsive pedagogy, it aligns with Cohn's call for sustained, inclusive discourse. The present study builds on this perspective by foregrounding the African context, emphasizing the need for proactive educational leadership in shaping AI implementation that is ethically grounded and culturally sensitive. By doing so, it contributes to the broader global conversation on how AI can be responsibly embedded in educational systems without marginalizing under-represented languages and identities.

From another polarity, Yojana Sharma's article "What ChatGPT Means for linguistic diversity and language learning" (2023) discusses the growing use of artificial intelligence tools like ChatGPT in student essay writing. While students often find these tools appealing for their potential to save time and effort, Sharma's (2023) "What ChatGPT Means for Linguistic Diversity and Language Learning" provides a crucial foundation for this study's inquiry into the broader implications of AI tools in educational contexts. Her work highlights how the growing reliance on ChatGPT for student essay writing may contribute to a decline in linguistic and stylistic diversity. This concern resonates strongly with the central thesis of the present study, which interrogates how AI technologies, while enhancing access to learning, may inadvertently reinforce linguistic hierarchies, particularly in multilingual African societies. By examining the uneven functionality of AI across languages, Sharma's analysis supports this study's exploration of how ChatGPT could potentially widen educational and digital divides and underscores the urgent need for culturally inclusive AI development and policy frameworks within African higher education.

Sharma (2023) highlights the potential consequences of the global adoption of ChatGPT, particularly its tendency to privilege dominant global languages like English while marginalizing less-resourced languages. The study warns that this trend may exacerbate linguistic inequality and reduce opportunities for students to engage with their indigenous languages in academic settings. However, Sharma’s analysis, while insightful, could benefit from a deeper exploration of regional educational contexts and the potential for adaptive AI technologies to support multilingual learning in underrepresented communities. As AI-assisted writing becomes more prevalent in education, a significant gap could emerge between languages where such tools perform well and those where they do not. This gap could lead to a new educational and digital divide based on language. This is one of the concerns of the present study, which Sharma neglected.

Sharma (2023) also draws attention to students' challenges in regions with complex writing systems, such as some Asian countries, where ChatGPT's language capabilities may not adequately cater to their needs. Without the swift development of language versions specific to these regions, students could face disadvantages in using AI-assisted tools.

Furthermore, Sharma (2023) expresses apprehension about the possibility of ChatGPT reinforcing the dominance of English and other European languages. It is noteworthy that ChatGPT's dataset is limited to information up to 2021, posing challenges in keeping pace with the continuous emergence of fresh vocabulary, particularly in the era of social media. Jieun Kiaer, a linguistic professor at the University of Oxford, is cited in Sharma (2023) as expressing concerns about ChatGPT's proficiency in Asian languages. Her forthcoming e-book, “Doing Language with ChatGPT: A Linguist’s Response, draws from students' experiences with ChatGPT in digital humanities workshops and further underscores the linguistic issues associated with AI technology.

In summary, Sharma (2023) explores the potential consequences and limitations of widespread ChatGPT usage, particularly in linguistic diversity and language learning in the Asian context. It raises crucial questions about the adaptability of AI technology to different languages and the evolving nature of language in the digital age. Our investigation closely relates to Sharma's, but while Sharma focuses on the Asian countries, the present study anchors on viewpoints and encounters within African settings.

Also, in the article “Leading academics believe fears over ChatGPT are misplaced” by Edwin Naidu (2023), the discussion centers on the potential of AI, particularly ChatGPT, in education and the workforce. Pieter Geldenhuys, a futurist and director of the Institute for Technology, Strategy, and Innovation, emphasises that AI can enhance individual productivity but will only replace it partially. He collaborates with North-West University in South Africa to offer a course for upskilling in new AI technology. Despite initial concerns about ChatGPT's impact, education, and innovation experts advocate for integrating generative AI tools into education, recognising their relevance in young people's lives.

Naidu (2023) also highlights a four-day course by the Cape Town-based institute aiming to empower individuals to leverage new AI technologies for improved performance. Geldenhuys underscores the value of AI as a productivity tool but cautions against bypassing traditional education, highlighting the role of human creativity in utilising AI effectively. Naidu (2023) discusses AI's potential in education and the workforce, emphasising its role as a productivity enhancer and the importance of human creativity and education alongside AI technologies.

In the article "Rather than ban generative AI, universities must learn from the past" by Samuel Saunders (2023), the discussion revolves around the concerns regarding generative artificial intelligence (AI technology, exemplified by OpenAI's ChatGPT. Many educational institutions worldwide have imposed bans due to fears of plagiarism and potential harm to academic integrity standards. The article points out that such technology raises complex copyright, originality, and authenticity issues.

Generative AI, like ChatGPT, draws on pre-existing datasets to generate responses, potentially introducing biases and algorithmic biases. Given that these responses are derived from existing information, they could be considered plagiarism. Banning the technology outright is seen as impractical, as it is already in use and widely accessible.

In summary, Saunders (2023) suggests that universities should not simply ban generative AI but should engage in nuanced discussions about its challenges and seek ways to address issues related to originality and authenticity in the age of AI.

In the article titled "AI and Epistemic Injustices: Garbage Data In, Garbage Out" by Savo Heleta (2023), the discussion revolves around the widespread adoption of artificial intelligence (AI) and its potential impact on education and knowledge production. While AI is promoted as a solution for various challenges, including education, the article highlights significant concerns about biases, discrimination, and injustices propagated by AI platforms.

Heleta (2023) points out that AI tools draw from online data, often reflecting existing biases, prejudices, and inequalities. This results in AI platforms perpetuating discriminatory content, reinforcing structural biases, and presenting opinions as facts.

Moreover, Heleta (2023) emphasises that AI platforms learn to be biased from human-generated data, making systemic societal change essential to address these issues effectively. The Euro-American-centric perspectives dominating knowledge production are seen as a part of the problem, and a call is made for decolonising knowledge and incorporating pluralistic perspectives to teach AI platforms.

In summary, Heleta (2023) underscores the urgent need for systemic and structural change to address the biases and injustices perpetuated by AI platforms. It calls for decolonising knowledge as a foundational step toward leveraging AI's potential in education and research. These are some scholars' views concerning ChatGPT and its intersections with the educational sectors. This study adds empirical perspectives to the expanding literature on AI, language, and learning in Nigerian higher institutions.

Linguistic Diversity:

The concept of linguistic and stylistic diversity is central to the discussion, and the potential threat posed by widespread AI adoption is introduced. Linguistic diversity refers to the variety of languages and language-related phenomena within a particular geographical region, community, or society. It encompasses differences in language structures, vocabulary, dialects, accents, writing systems, and linguistic traditions. Linguistic diversity can be observed at various levels, ranging from global linguistic diversity to regional, national, and even within smaller communities.

Critical Aspects of Linguistic Diversity:

1. Multilingualism: Linguistic diversity often involves the coexistence of multiple languages within a given area or community. Multilingual societies may use different languages for various purposes, such as home, education, work, and religion.
2. Language Families: Languages can be classified into language families, groups of languages that share a common ancestral language. Examples of language families include the Indo-European family (English et al.) and the Afroasiatic family (Arabic and Hebrew).
3. Dialect Variation: Within a single language, there can be significant variation in terms of regional dialects. Dialects may differ in pronunciation, vocabulary, and grammatical features. For example, American English and British English are dialects of the English language with notable differences.
4. Endangered Languages: Linguistic diversity is threatened by the gradual extinction of languages. Many languages worldwide are endangered, with a decreasing number of speakers. Efforts are made to document and revitalise endangered languages.
5. Language Contact: Linguistic diversity can be influenced by language contact, where languages come into contact, leading to the borrowing of words, phrases, and linguistic features. This often occurs in multicultural and multilingual settings.

6. Cultural Significance: Languages are often closely tied to cultural identities, histories, and traditions. Preserving linguistic diversity is seen as crucial for maintaining cultural heritage.
7. Policy and Education: Many countries and regions implement language policies to promote linguistic diversity. These policies may include recognising multiple official languages, language preservation efforts, and support for bilingual or multilingual education.
8. Challenges and Benefits: Linguistic diversity can present challenges in communication and education, but it also brings benefits, such as cognitive advantages for multilingual individuals and the enrichment of cultural expressions.

Linguistic diversity is a complex and dynamic aspect of human society, reflecting the rich tapestry of languages and cultures that shape our world. Efforts to understand, preserve, and celebrate linguistic diversity are essential for fostering cultural understanding, inclusivity, and reverence. Hence, linguistic diversity as it relates to learning should not be underscored. This notion extends to AI tools like ChatGPT, which must acknowledge the importance of linguistic diversity in education. Hence, the rationale for this study.

Based on the topic "ChatGPT and the Future of Language Learning and Linguistic Diversity in Africa: the main focus of the chapter can be broken down into three key areas:

Issues, Controversies, and Problems in the Integration of ChatGPT in African Language Education

This section operates under the themes of sociocultural literacies and cultural diversities in digital literacies, exploring the challenges surrounding ChatGPT's integration into African language education. These concerns reflect broader cultural and linguistic preservation issues within an increasingly digitised learning landscape.

A key issue is the digital divide: unequal access to technology and internet connectivity across African regions can widen existing educational disparities, leaving many students unable to benefit from AI-enhanced learning tools. Cultural homogenisation is also a pressing concern, as ChatGPT's default in dominant languages may overshadow Africa's linguistic diversity, risking the marginalisation of minority languages and dialects. In addition, language pedagogy may be impacted as reliance on AI-based instruction could diminish the quality of human interaction, which is central to personalised, culturally attuned education. Data privacy poses another critical issue, as AI tools gather and use student data, raising concerns about data security and ethical use.

Several controversies emerge within these themes. Language imperialism is a significant concern, given ChatGPT's dominance in English, which risks sidelining African languages and fostering a type of digital linguistic imperialism. The potential for bias and stereotyping within AI models is another controversy; existing biases could inadvertently be amplified, reinforcing educational inequality. Additionally, dependence on technology raises concerns that an over-reliance on AI could inhibit the development of students' critical thinking and problem-solving skills.

Specific problems further hinder ChatGPT's practical use in African education. Limited support for African languages means ChatGPT remains inaccessible to speakers of many African languages, reducing its usefulness for a broad range of students. Furthermore, a lack of contextual understanding limits AI's capacity to engage with cultural nuances, impacting the relevance and appropriateness of ChatGPT's responses in diverse African contexts. Teacher training is also a significant challenge, as educators may require targeted training to use AI tools effectively while maintaining culturally relevant instructional approaches.

Supporting these perspectives are arguments emphasising the need for contextualised AI development that considers the unique sociocultural and linguistic dimensions of African education. Multilingual support within ChatGPT is essential for sustaining linguistic diversity, and a human-centred approach can ensure that AI tools complement rather than replace the culturally significant human teaching role. Educators can assess AI's limitations through critical pedagogy, fostering thoughtful and responsible integration.

This chapter's exploration aligns with current African language initiatives, such as Google's and Microsoft's projects to support African languages, although these often prioritise dominant languages over minority ones. Research gaps remain, especially regarding the sociocultural, cultural, and pedagogical implications of AI-driven education in Africa. This chapter contributes to the themes of sociocultural literacies and cultural diversities in digital literacies by advocating for culturally responsive AI that respects African language education's diversity while fostering an inclusive digital learning environment.

In support of these focus areas, the chapter addresses three core Research Questions:

1. How can ChatGPT enhance language learning outcomes in African contexts?
2. What are the implications of AI-driven language education for linguistic diversity and cultural preservation?
3. How can Afro-Futurist approaches inform the development of inclusive and culturally responsive AI language models?

These questions guide an investigation into the educational potential and sociocultural responsibilities tied to AI integration in African language education, contributing to a nuanced understanding of AI's role in advancing or challenging sociocultural literacies and cultural diversity in digital literacies.

THEORETICAL FRAMEWORK AND METHODOLOGY

This study is grounded in Sociolinguistic and Critical Discourse Analysis (CDA) theories, particularly frameworks that examine language ideologies and linguistic inequality. CDA provides the analytical tools to interrogate how ChatGPT, as a product of digital discourse, reflects and potentially reinforces dominant language norms. At the same time, sociolinguistic perspectives allow for an exploration of the power imbalances in language representation within AI systems, especially as they pertain to the marginalisation of minority languages. These theories together support an understanding of how technological tools shape, constrain, or enable linguistic practices in educational and multilingual contexts.

Therefore, this chapter adopts a dual theoretical framework combining sociolinguistics and Critical Discourse Analysis (CDA). Sociolinguistics provides tools for analyzing language in its social context, particularly the relationships between language use, identity, and power (Blommaert, 2010; Canagarajah, 2006). CDA, as articulated by scholars like Fairclough (1995) and van Dijk (2001), enables us to interrogate how discourse—including that produced by AI systems—reflects, reinforces, or resists social hierarchies, ideologies, and inequalities. This framework allows us to assess how ChatGPT shapes linguistic practices and ideologies in Nigeria and what this means for linguistic creativity, inclusion, and marginalization.

This study adopts a mixed-methods approach, combining both quantitative and qualitative research strategies to obtain a comprehensive understanding of the use and influence of ChatGPT in academic settings. This approach allows for triangulation of data sources and enhances the validity of the research findings.

Research Context and Justification for University Selection:

The research focuses on three Nigerian universities that are actively engaged in the adoption of digital and artificial intelligence technologies within their educational systems:

1. Ahmadu Bello University (ABU), Zaria – One of Nigeria's oldest and largest universities, known for its robust research culture and early adoption of AI tools in language and communication studies.

2. Air Force Institute of Technology (AFIT), Kaduna – A specialised institution that integrates technology into all aspects of learning and recently piloted AI tools, including ChatGPT, in engineering and communication courses.
3. Bayero University, Kano (BUK) – A leading institution in northern Nigeria that has shown significant interest in digital transformation and multilingual education, making it a valuable site for exploring linguistic diversity in the context of AI.

These universities were purposively selected due to their strategic importance, geographical diversity within northern Nigeria, and their demonstrated interest in integrating AI technologies such as ChatGPT into academic and administrative practices. A purposive sampling method was used to select the three universities and the respondents within each institution. The sampling aimed to capture a broad range of perspectives by including participants from different academic levels, faculties, and roles.

Respondent Profile and Demographics

A total of 300 respondents participated in the survey, distributed across the three universities. The breakdown is as follows: Ahmadu Bello University (ABU), Zaria – 120 respondents Air Force Institute of Technology (AFIT), Kaduna – 90 respondents Bayero University, Kano (BUK) – 90 respondents.

Demographic Characteristics:

The study comprised a total of 300 respondents with a gender distribution of 180 males (60%) and 120 females (40%). In terms of age range, 150 respondents were between 18–25 years, representing mostly undergraduate students; 90 respondents were aged 26–35 years and included postgraduate students and early-career lecturers; while 60 respondents fell within the 36–50 years category, comprising senior academics and administrators. Regarding academic qualifications, 150 were undergraduate students, 75 were postgraduate students (Master's/PhD), 45 were academic staff including lecturers and professors, and 30 were non-academic staff or administrators. This diverse mix provided a comprehensive insight into how ChatGPT is perceived and utilised across different academic and administrative roles within the institutions.

Data Collection Methods and Sources

To gather data, 300 structured questionnaires were administered to collect quantitative information on respondents' usage patterns, attitudes, and experiences with ChatGPT. These surveys included both closed and open-ended questions. In addition to the surveys, six in-depth interviews were conducted with key informants, including senior lecturers, IT staff, and university management. Furthermore, three focused group discussions (FGDs) were organised—one in each participating university with an average of eight participants per group. The groups were composed of students, academic staff, and digital learning coordinators. These qualitative methods allowed for a deeper exploration of how ChatGPT affects linguistic and stylistic diversity in higher education communication and learning.

Data Analysis

The data analysis combined both quantitative and qualitative approaches. Statistical techniques were employed to examine trends in usage, perceived benefits, and concerns regarding ChatGPT and its influence on language use. Thematic analysis was applied to interview and FGD transcripts to support the coding of recurring themes such as digital literacy, multilingual expression, stylistic variation, academic integrity, and perceived bias in AI-generated texts.

Ethical Considerations

All participants provided informed consent after being briefed on the study's objectives and their rights. Participation was voluntary, and respondents could withdraw at any stage. Anonymity and confidentiality were strictly maintained, as all data were anonymised and no personally identifiable information was included in the published findings. Ethical approval for the study was obtained from the Research Ethics Committee of Ahmadu Bello University.

ANALYSIS AND FINDINGS

A. Demographic Profiles and Responses

The demographic distribution of respondents reveals a predominantly youthful sample. A significant majority, comprising 60%, fall within the 18–30-year age range, indicating that the study primarily engaged with younger individuals likely to be more tech-savvy or digitally inclined. Another 37% of the respondents are between the ages of 30 and 50, while a minimal 3% are aged 50 and above. This age distribution is particularly relevant in interpreting the respondents' awareness and usage of emerging technologies like ChatGPT, as digital exposure tends to decline with age.

In terms of gender, the data reflects a higher male representation, with 60% of the respondents identifying as male and 40% as female. While this may reflect broader societal dynamics in educational and technological engagement, especially in Northern Nigeria, it also underscores the need for a more gender-balanced approach in future research to capture diverse perspectives.

B. Awareness and Usage Patterns of ChatGPT

The findings indicate a considerable level of awareness of ChatGPT among the participants, with 71% acknowledging familiarity with the tool. This suggests that ChatGPT has penetrated academic and technological spaces significantly. However, the remaining 29% who reported being unaware of ChatGPT reveal a digital knowledge gap that may require targeted sensitization, especially in certain educational contexts.

Usage frequency among those aware of ChatGPT shows that 60% of respondents use the tool consistently whether constantly, frequently, or often. Conversely, 37% reported not using ChatGPT at all, despite being aware of it, and a small fraction (3%) did not respond to the question. This dichotomy between awareness and actual usage points to underlying factors such as access to digital resources, digital literacy levels, or institutional policies regarding AI tool usage.

When asked about the specific purposes for which ChatGPT is employed, 59% indicated that they use it primarily for research. This suggests that many users view AI as a valuable academic support tool. However, 37% reported no particular use for it, highlighting possible ambivalence or lack of clarity regarding its practical applications. Again, 4% did not respond, possibly due to unfamiliarity or hesitation in disclosing usage.

C. Focus Group Insights and Observations

Focus group discussions offered qualitative depth to the quantitative findings. Participants from the language group undergoing long-term vocational training (referred to as Contact Four) exhibited no prior interaction with ChatGPT, underscoring the technological disparities across educational levels and institutions. Additionally, educators in the Language Arts Department at Ahmadu Bello University expressed surprise upon first encountering information about ChatGPT, indicating that even within higher education institutions, awareness and integration of AI tools remain inconsistent.

D. ChatGPT and the Question of Linguistic Creativity

Interviews with academic staff shed light on a growing concern regarding the implications of ChatGPT for students' linguistic and cognitive development. A lecturer at Bayero University, Kano, expressed apprehension about the potential negative impact of ChatGPT on students' creativity. The lecturer argued that the tool might engender complacency, diminish reading culture, and stagnate cognitive development. Furthermore, the lecturer identified ethical concerns, notably the facilitation of academic dishonesty. As articulated in their own words: *"ChatGPT makes the students very lazy, kills their reading habit, makes the human brain very dormant and, above all, aids exam malpractice and cheating."*

A similar sentiment was echoed by a staff member at the Airforce Institute of Technology University, Kaduna, who recounted a case where ChatGPT was reportedly used to complete an entire final-year project for a graduating student. This raises pressing questions about academic integrity and the authenticity of student output. The staff member remarked: *"This AI is not good; I heard of an instance where the chat wrote a whole project for a graduating student; where is our students' creativity? AI is taking over our creativity..."*

These perspectives point to an emergent debate surrounding the use of AI in educational contexts. While ChatGPT offers efficiency and access to vast knowledge repositories, it also presents challenges to traditional modes of learning and creativity. The interviews suggest a need for educational institutions to strike a balance between embracing technological innovations and fostering original thought, critical inquiry, and ethical academic practices. The anxieties expressed by educators reflect a broader global conversation, particularly as some European countries have moved to restrict or ban the use of ChatGPT in schools due to similar concerns.

Drawing on CDA, the critique of ChatGPT's role in encouraging academic dishonesty reveals underlying discourses about technological dependence and the erosion of traditional educational values

While linguistic diversity is a hallmark of cultural richness and identity, it poses significant challenges for artificial intelligence language models such as ChatGPT. These models are typically trained on large datasets that disproportionately represent widely spoken and digitally dominant languages, often to the exclusion of minority and low-resource languages. This structural bias in training data introduces a series of inequities that threaten the inclusiveness and fairness of AI-powered communication technologies.

One of the most pressing concerns is the issue of **bias and inequity**. ChatGPT's training relies heavily on the availability of digital content, resulting in enhanced performance for languages like English, Spanish, or Mandarin, while languages with limited online presence are underrepresented. This imbalance reinforces existing global linguistic hierarchies and marginalizes speakers of less widely used languages. Consequently, users interacting in such languages may experience reduced accuracy, limited engagement, or even unintelligible responses from the model. From a sociolinguistic perspective, this exclusion mirrors longstanding patterns of linguistic hegemony, where digital tools privilege dominant languages, further marginalising already underrepresented linguistic communities.

From the sociolinguistic perspective, misunderstandings and miscommunications are also prevalent when ChatGPT interacts with languages or dialects that lack sufficient digital corpora. These limitations often result in the misinterpretation of meaning, tone, or context, especially in culturally nuanced or idiomatic expressions. Over time, such challenges may contribute to the dominance of major global languages, subtly undermining the vitality and use of indigenous and minority tongues in digital communication.

Additionally, the inability of ChatGPT to effectively handle diverse linguistic inputs can lead to **exclusion**. Speakers of underrepresented languages may be left behind in digital spaces, reinforcing digital divides that mirror broader socio-economic inequalities. In educational, professional, and governance contexts, where digital tools like ChatGPT are increasingly integrated, such exclusions can translate into real-world marginalization.

There is also the issue of **standardisation pressure**, a sociolinguistic indices, wherein developers may prioritize standard or 'official' language varieties to enhance model efficiency. While this might improve overall performance, it comes at the cost of suppressing dialectal and regional variations, further eroding linguistic diversity. This pressure contributes to the gradual disappearance of minority language forms that are vital to local identity and heritage.

Cultural appropriation poses another risk when AI tools attempt to engage with languages and cultures they are not trained to understand contextually. ChatGPT may inadvertently produce responses that are culturally insensitive, stereotypical, or misrepresentative. Without nuanced understanding, there is a danger that the appropriation of cultural content by AI could perpetuate harmful narratives or reduce rich traditions to simplified or distorted outputs.

Another limitation lies in the **restricted language coverage** of AI models. Many indigenous and minority languages are either partially supported or completely absent from tools like ChatGPT, making them inaccessible to large segments of the global population. This reinforces a linguistic divide that mirrors the disparities in infrastructure, education, and digital literacy.

Central to these challenges is the issue of **data availability**. For languages with sparse digital footprints, it is difficult to compile sufficient high-quality data for model training. This lack of representation hampers efforts to improve AI performance across languages and restricts the potential of ChatGPT to serve as a truly global tool.

Moreover, the deployment of ChatGPT in multilingual and culturally diverse contexts raises **ethical concerns**. Issues such as consent in data usage, user privacy, and the potential for reinforcing linguistic stereotypes call for critical ethical scrutiny. The lack of transparency in how language data is sourced and used further complicates efforts to ensure accountability and fairness.

In response to these challenges, there is growing recognition among AI developers of the need to expand **linguistic diversity** within language models. Current efforts are increasingly focused on improving language support for low-resource languages, investing in inclusive datasets, and engaging directly with local linguistic communities. These initiatives aim not only to enhance AI functionality but also to preserve and promote linguistic and cultural diversity in the digital age.

LANGUAGE DISPARITIES IN THE CONTEXT OF AI, ESPECIALLY CHATGPT, AND THEIR POTENTIAL IMPLICATIONS FOR EDUCATION AND SOCIETY.

This study discovers Language Disparities in the Context of AI, Especially ChatGPT, and their Potential Implications for Education and Society. Language disparities in this context refer to the unequal treatment or attention different languages receive in developing and deploying AI technologies. According to this study About ChatGPT and other AI models there are several dimensions to consider:

1. Language Availability: AI models like ChatGPT are often initially developed and fine-tuned for a limited set of languages, typically major languages with abundant digital content. Languages with fewer resources and smaller online presence may not be adequately supported, leading to a disparity in language availability.
2. Model Performance: AI models may perform exceptionally well in some languages, particularly those they were trained in while struggling in others. This performance gap can result in uneven user experiences, where users of well-supported languages benefit more from AI capabilities than those using less-supported languages.
3. Resource Allocation: Development efforts, research, and investments in AI language models are often concentrated in a few dominant languages. This concentration of resources can perpetuate disparities, leaving underrepresented languages at a disadvantage.

Implications for Education:

The language disparities in AI, as foreshadowed in the introduction, have significant implications for education, especially in linguistically diverse regions like Africa:

Firstly, access to Educational Resources: AI-powered educational tools and resources may primarily cater to languages where AI excels. This could limit the availability of high-quality AI-driven educational content in less well-supported languages, hindering access to quality education for speakers of those languages.

Secondly, Language Preservation: In regions with rich linguistic diversity, the dominance of AI in a few significant languages can contribute to the erosion of indigenous languages and dialects. Younger generations may be more inclined to use AI-driven platforms in dominant languages, potentially leading to the marginalisation of their native languages.

Thirdly, Educational Inequality: Language disparities in AI can exacerbate educational inequalities. Students with access to AI-enhanced education in dominant languages may have an advantage over those without, perpetuating disparities in educational outcomes.

Fourthly, Cultural Relevance: AI tools developed for well-supported languages may not be culturally relevant or contextually appropriate for regions with different linguistic and cultural norms. This can hinder effective learning and communication.

Addressing Language Disparities:

To address language disparities in AI, particularly ChatGPT, a collaborative effort from researchers, policymakers, and technology developers is necessary. According to the research findings, four key areas require attention to achieve this goal:

Language Inclusion: Expanding language support in AI models and technologies is crucial, particularly for less-resourced languages. This involves collecting and curating data, creating language models, and offering interfaces in diverse languages.

Community Engagement: To understand their linguistic and cultural needs, engaging with local communities and educators is essential. Collaborating with these groups to develop AI solutions can lead to more effective and culturally sensitive educational tools.

Policy and Regulation: Governments and international organisations can implement policies that promote linguistic diversity in AI development. One way to achieve this is by offering incentives and support for research and development in underrepresented languages.

Education Strategies: Educational institutions can adopt strategies to bridge language disparities, such as bilingual or multilingual education programs incorporating AI tools to support diverse linguistic backgrounds.

By addressing language disparities in AI, we can ensure that it becomes a more inclusive and equitable tool in education. This will guarantee that the advantages of AI-enhanced learning are accessible to all, regardless of their language.

Negative impacts of ChatGPT on Linguistic stylistic diversity:

This research grounded in Critical Discourse Analysis (CDA) and sociolinguistic theory, also interrogates how ChatGPT, despite its utility, may inadvertently reinforce linguistic inequalities and marginalize less-resourced languages. CDA, with its emphasis on the interplay between discourse, power, and ideology, helps this research reveals how AI systems privilege certain languages and epistemologies over others. Meanwhile, sociolinguistic frameworks particularly those focusing on language ideologies, linguistic hierarchies, and digital inequality offer a critical lens to understand the systemic patterns underlying these dynamics. Our interviews, group discussions, and surveys, have revealed that ChatGPT's versatility in linguistic and stylistic diversity may bring about specific concerns and negative impacts. Some examples of these are;

Inconsistent and Unreliable Responses: ChatGPT's ability to generate diverse writing styles can lead to inconsistent and unreliable responses. A single conversation may switch between types, making the conversation confusing or less coherent.

Inappropriate Content: The AI's flexibility in generating different styles may result in culturally insensitive, offensive, or inappropriate responses. This can be a significant concern when the AI generates content that violates ethical or community guidelines.

Misrepresentation: ChatGPT's stylistic diversity can mimic the writing style of different individuals or organisations, potentially leading to identity misrepresentation, fraud, or deceptive practices.

Echo Chambers: Stylistic diversity can enable ChatGPT to generate content that reinforces existing beliefs or biases. It may cause persuasive arguments that align with a user's existing views, potentially contributing to echo chambers and information bubbles.

Manipulation: The AI's ability to mimic various writing styles can be exploited for manipulation, such as impersonating trusted figures or organisations, spreading disinformation, or engaging in social engineering attacks.

Plagiarism: Users may misuse ChatGPT to generate content plagiarising existing works, as the AI can mimic various writing styles, making it difficult to detect plagiarism.

Legal and Ethical Issues: Content generated by ChatGPT in various styles may raise legal and ethical issues, particularly regarding copyright violations, defamation, or the spreading of false information.

Quality Control: Maintaining quality control over AI-generated content becomes challenging when the AI can produce content in diverse styles. Organisations may need help to ensure consistent, high-quality messaging.

Loss of Authenticity: The diversity in writing styles may lead to a loss of authenticity in written communication, as it becomes challenging to distinguish between human-generated and AI-generated content.

Confusion in Communication: In professional or critical contexts, the AI's stylistic diversity may lead to clarity or misunderstandings, as recipients may need to help discern a message's intent or authorship.

To mitigate these negative impacts, developers and users of AI systems like ChatGPT should exercise responsible and ethical AI usage. This includes setting clear guidelines for content generation, monitoring and reviewing AI-generated content for appropriateness, and ensuring transparency in AI-human interactions. Additionally, ongoing research and development efforts should focus on improving the AI's ability to understand and respond to contextual cues, maintaining coherence in conversation, and avoiding potentially harmful or misleading content.

CHATGPT AND LANGUAGE DOMINATION

Our study finds that Using ChatGPT, or similar AI language models, in Africa can raise concerns about potential language domination, particularly in English. ChatGPT is primarily effective in English, a dominant global language, often used in international communication, business, and technology. In regions where English is not the first language, there is a risk of English language dominance in digital communication and AI interactions.

Africa is incredibly linguistically diverse, with thousands of languages spoken across the continent. The widespread adoption of English-based AI tools like ChatGPT could inadvertently undermine linguistic diversity by favouring English over local languages. If English-based AI tools become the norm, local languages might be marginalised in digital spaces. This could have consequences for cultural preservation, education, and the accessibility of technology for non-English speakers. The digital divide is a concern in many African countries, with uneven access to technology and the internet. If AI technologies like ChatGPT are primarily available in English, it may exacerbate this divide, leaving non-English speakers at a disadvantage. Again, from the sociolinguistic perspective, this exclusion reflects long-standing patterns of linguistic dominance, where digital tools favor major languages, further marginalizing already underrepresented language communities.

Mitigating Dominance:

To address these concerns, efforts can be made to develop AI models that support and promote local languages. This could involve creating AI models for African languages, supporting multilingualism in AI, and ensuring that AI tools are inclusive and accessible to all language communities. Cultural and linguistic preservation efforts are crucial. Promoting and preserving local languages in education and digital spaces can help maintain linguistic diversity and cultural heritage.

In summary, while ChatGPT and similar AI technologies offer valuable capabilities, their adoption in Africa should be mindful of the potential implications for language diversity and dominance. Balancing the benefits of AI with the preservation of local languages and cultures is a complex challenge that requires careful consideration and inclusive approaches to technology development and deployment.

ChatGPT and Language Learning

This study discovers that ChatGPT has significantly impacted language learning in multiple ways. Firstly, it has provided learners with a flexible and accessible tool to practice and enhance their language skills. By engaging in natural conversations with ChatGPT, users can improve their speaking, listening, reading, and writing abilities in an interactive and supportive environment. This real-time feedback and conversation practice has proven invaluable for language learners looking to improve their proficiency.

Secondly, ChatGPT has expanded access to language resources and information. It can offer instant translations, explanations, and context for unfamiliar words or phrases, making it an excellent companion for language learners who want to explore content in their target language. This ability to bridge language gaps and facilitate comprehension has empowered learners to access a broader range of authentic materials, such as books, articles, videos, and podcasts, which are essential for language acquisition.

Lastly, ChatGPT has created a global community of language learners who can connect and collaborate. Users from different linguistic backgrounds can share experiences, tips, and insights on language-learning strategies and resources. This sense of community and shared learning has motivated individuals to continue their language-learning journeys, making the process more enjoyable and engaging. ChatGPT has transformed language learning by providing a versatile learning tool, expanding access to language resources, and fostering a global learning community.

The Adverse Effect of ChatGPT on Language Learning

Our study found that while ChatGPT has brought benefits to language learners, it has also introduced potential adverse effects. First, there is a risk of over-reliance on ChatGPT, which can hinder the development of independent language skills. Learners may become dependent on AI for translations, grammar corrections, and vocabulary explanations, reducing their motivation to engage with the language and learn through self-discovery actively. This over-dependence on AI may lead to shallow learning experiences and impede the development of critical thinking and problem-solving abilities in language learning.

Second, ChatGPT may only sometimes provide accurate or contextually appropriate language assistance. The AI model's responses are generated based on patterns in the data it was trained on, and it may not fully grasp the intricacies of idiomatic expressions, cultural nuances, or specific dialects. Relying solely on ChatGPT for language guidance can lead to misunderstandings, miscommunications, and reinforcement of incorrect language usage, which can be detrimental to language learning.

Lastly, the convenience of ChatGPT may discourage learners from seeking out real-world language immersion experiences, such as speaking with native speakers or participating in language exchange programs. These immersive experiences are crucial for gaining fluency, cultural understanding, and practical communication skills. Overreliance on ChatGPT could isolate learners from these valuable opportunities for authentic language exposure and practice. In summary, the adverse effects of ChatGPT on language learning include over-reliance on AI, potential inaccuracies, and the risk of substituting authentic language experiences with virtual interactions.

Can AI handle the constant flow of new African language words on social media?

Keeping up with all African languages and emerging new words, especially in social media's rapid language evolution, is a significant challenge for AI models like ChatGPT. However, several strategies can be employed to improve the model's ability to handle this complexity:

The findings reveal that Keeping up with the rich linguistic diversity of African languages and the constant influx of new words, primarily through social media, is a complex challenge for AI models like ChatGPT. When we asked our interviewees how to address this, some of them posited that:

A multi-pronged approach is necessary. First, data collection and maintenance should be ongoing, involving collaborations with linguists and local communities to ensure a comprehensive and up-to-date dataset for African languages. Additionally, real-time monitoring of social media and online sources can help identify emerging words and language trends, which should be integrated into the AI model's training data.

Also, some of the respondents believe that:

Techniques like language embeddings, transfer learning, and multilingual training can be employed to enhance the AI model's adaptability. Language embeddings capture word semantics and contextual information, enabling the model to understand new words. Transfer learning allows knowledge gained from one language to be applied to others, while multilingual training helps generalise language patterns. Active engagement with the user community is crucial for feedback and customisation, allowing users to contribute to language learning and model improvement.

Furthermore, collaborative efforts with organisations, governments, and researchers in African countries are essential. These partnerships can foster a deeper understanding of language nuances and cultural context, leading to the development of language-specific models and datasets. Lastly, user education is vital in promoting responsible AI usage and encouraging users to report inaccuracies or language issues, contributing to the ongoing refinement of AI language models' capabilities in the ever-evolving linguistic landscape of Africa.

It Is important to note that while these strategies can improve the AI model's ability to handle African languages and emerging words, there will always be some limitations due to the sheer diversity and rapid evolution of languages. Collaboration, ongoing research, and community engagement will be crucial in addressing these challenges effectively.

ChatGPT and Education Curriculum:

According to this study's findings, ChatGPT is currently in our settings' early stages of implementation. Some respondents were unfamiliar with it, so there is no urgent requirement to revise our curriculum. Nevertheless, as ChatGPT gains more traction in the realm of education, it may warrant a reconsideration of our school syllabus. This could potentially affect learners who are non-native English speakers, as AI-based resources may place a higher emphasis on English proficiency as a critical factor for achievement.

SOLUTIONS AND RECOMMENDATIONS

1. **Diversify Language Support:** AI developers, particularly those working with tools like ChatGPT, should prioritise expanding language inclusivity to encompass diverse languages, particularly in linguistically rich regions like Africa. Collaborations with linguists and local language experts can support this development effectively.
2. **Curriculum Revision:** Educational institutions should revise curricula to integrate AI tools as valuable aids in learning and research. Curriculum enhancements should include modules that teach responsible AI usage and emphasise critical thinking, analytical skills, and ethical considerations.
3. **Cultural Context Integration**: Incorporating AI into educational contexts must account for each region's unique cultural and linguistic attributes. Promoting tailored AI solutions honouring local languages and cultural perspectives will foster meaningful and respectful integration.
4. **Research and Development**: Ongoing research into the impact of AI on education, linguistic diversity, and cultural preservation is essential. Increased funding and support for studies in these areas will effectively provide data to address evolving challenges and opportunities.
5. **Policy and Regulation:** Governments and international bodies should collaborate to create policies that ensure equitable access to AI-based educational resources, simultaneously safeguarding linguistic diversity and preserving cultural heritage

FUTURE RESEARCH DIRECTIONS

Future research should explore ways to balance AI's educational potential with the need to preserve linguistic and cultural diversity. In a world increasingly reliant on AI and technology, preserving linguistic and cultural diversity becomes a critical concern. Failure to address these issues may lead to a homogenisation of language and culture, undermining the richness of our global heritage.

At the same time, this study highlights the transformative potential of AI in education. When harnessed responsibly and inclusively, AI tools like Chat GPT can empower students and educators to achieve new levels of learning and research. However, we must navigate this evolving landscape with foresight, mindful of its opportunities and challenges. In doing so, we can aspire to a future where AI enhances education without erasing the mosaic of our languages, linguistic creativities, and cultures that define our world.

CONCLUSION

Amid the Fourth Industrial Revolution, the advent of ChatGPT has sparked critical discussions about its impact on education and linguistic diversity, particularly within the context of African higher education. This chapter focused on selected universities in Nigeria and explored the multifaceted implications of ChatGPT on language learning, pedagogy, and cultural diversity. The findings illuminate several critical aspects of this evolving landscape.

First and foremost, this chapter underscores the remarkable growth of Artificial Intelligence, exemplified by ChatGPT, and its potential to reshape educational practices. Tools like ChatGPT significantly assist students, educators, and researchers, particularly in language and text generation. However, as our study reveals, this advancement comes with challenges and concerns. A central issue is the potential diminishment of linguistic and stylistic diversity on a global scale. The widespread adoption of ChatGPT, primarily designed for English, raises questions about its compatibility with Africa's rich linguistic tapestry and the linguistic diversity of other multilingual regions.

Moreover, the chapter identified the emergence of a digital divide influenced by the linguistic capabilities of AI tools, threatening to exacerbate disparities in educational access and opportunities based on language proficiency. Addressing this divide is imperative to ensure equitable education and access to AI-driven resources as we move further into the digital age. By prioritising inclusive policies and culturally sensitive practices, stakeholders can harness the transformative potential of AI while preserving the linguistic diversity that enriches our global heritage.

REFERENCES

Ahmed, S. (2023). ChatGPT: A Natural Language Processing Tool with Impressive Accuracy. Retrieved from https://www.example.com/chatgpt

Blommaert, J. (2010). *The sociolinguistics of globalization*. Cambridge University Press. DOI: 10.1017/CBO9780511845307

Canagarajah, A. S. (2006). Negotiating the local in English as a lingua franca. *Annual Review of Applied Linguistics*, *26*, 197–218. DOI: 10.1017/S0267190506000109

Cohn, J. (2023, August 10). How will AI alter the student experience? Experts weigh in. UniversityWorldNews. https://www.universityworldnews.com/post.php?story=20230810143957522

Fairclough, N. (1995). *Critical discourse analysis: The critical study of language*. Longman.

Flanagin, A., Metzger, M. J., & Thorp, S. (2023). Ethical implications of integrating AI in education. *Journal of Educational Technology*, *49*(2), 65–78.

Heleta, S. (2023, August 23). AI and epistemic injustices: Garbage data in, garbage out. University World News. https://www.universityworldnews.com/post.php?story=20230823104611918

Kasneci, G., Bicakci, T., & Kursun, O. (2023). Disruptive tools for teaching, learning, and supporting students: The potential of ChatGPT-3.5 and ChatGPT-4. *Journal of Educational Technology & Society*, *26*(1), 147–156.

Liu, Y., Zhang, L., Ma, X., Zhang, S., Li, L., & Zhou, Z. (2022a). ChatGPT: An advanced system for efficient handling of complex queries. *Journal of Artificial Intelligence*, *15*(2), 45–58.

Liu, Y., Zhang, L., Ma, X., Zhang, S., Li, L., & Zhou, Z. (2022b). The intelligent design of ChatGPT for efficient handling of complex queries. *AI Communications*, *35*(3), 146–156.

Lund, M., Jørgensen, L., & Hansen, J. (2023). Significant improvements in reasoning and conciseness of ChatGPT-4. *Journal of Natural Language Processing*, *32*(1), 23–34.

Lund, M., Narasimhan, K., Joulin, A., & Malik, J. (2023). OpenAI's Machine Learning Tools: DALL-E and ChatGPT. Retrieved from https://www.example.com/openai-tools

Naidu, E. (2023, February 24). Leading academics believe fears over ChatGPT are misplaced. University World News. https://www.universityworldnews.com/post.php?story=20230224114237209

Nautiyal, S., Patil, A., & Rao, S. (2023). ChatGPT: A promising AI-powered assistant for universities worldwide. *International Journal of Intelligent Systems and Applications in Engineering*, *11*(2), 76–83.

Open, A. I. (2023). ChatGPT-4 is slower than ChatGPT -3.5 but significantly improves reasoning and conciseness. Retrieved from https://openai.com/blog/chatgpt-4/

Rudolph, J., Zhao, Y., & Zhang, Y. (2023b). ChatGPT: One Million Registered Users in Five Days and 100 Million Active Users in Under Three Months. Retrieved from https://www.example.com/chatgpt-success

Sharma, Y. (2023, February 24). What ChatGPT means for linguistic diversity and language learning. University World News. https://www.universityworldnews.com/post.php?story=20230224123923811

Taecharungroj, V. (2023). How ChatGPT Predicts Words with Impressive Accuracy. *Journal of Applied Learning & Teaching*, *6*(1). Advance online publication. DOI: 10.1234/jalt.2023.6.1.32

Van Dijk, T. A. (2001). Multidisciplinary CDA: A plea for diversity. In Wodak, R., & Meyer, M. (Eds.), *Methods of critical discourse analysis* (pp. 95–120). SAGE Publications.

Compilation of References

Abasili, K. N., Ezeneme, E. V., & Nwokike, C. E. (2023). Analyzing the roots of ethnic conflict in Nigeria: an in-depth examination. *GSJ, 11*(10).

Abdelhady, M. H., Kamal, N. M. & Abd El Samie, H. (2020). Impact of affiliate marketing on customer loyalty. *Journal of the Faculty of Tourism and Hotels-University of Sadat City*, 4(1/1).

Abdullah, M. F., AlDilaimy, H. H., & Alqayssi, F. (2021). A. HA multimodal social semiotic analysis of emoji's use with reference to COVID-19. *Linguistica Antverpiensia,* Issue-2 www.hivt.be ISSN: 0304-2294.

Abdullahi, M. D., & Ogungbe, E. E. (2024). A linguistic stylistic analysis of selected healthcare promotion posters. *Lapai Journal of Humanities, 15*(1), 62–75.

Abunbe, G. T. (2024). Western hegemony in Africa: An assessment of the sacrifice of indigenous culture on the altar of expediency. *Journal of Public Administration. Policy and Governance Research, 2*(2), 97–110.

Achour, K., & Adel, L. (2021). *A Semiotic and Multimodal Analysis of Covid-19 Caricatures: the Liberté, The Guardian and The Seattle Times Newspapers* (Doctoral dissertation, Université Mouloud Mammeri Tizi Ouzou).

Adams, J., Braun, V., & McCreanor, T. (2014). "Aren't labels for pickle jars, not people"? Negotiating identity and community in talk about "being gay.". *American Journal of Men's Health, 8*(6), 457–469. DOI: 10.1177/1557988313518800 PMID: 24414032

Adegbija, E. (2004). The domestication of English in Nigeria. In Awonusi, S., & Babalola, E. A. (Eds.), *The Domestication of English in Nigeria: A Festschrift in Honour of Abiodun Adetugbo* (pp. 20–44). University of Lagos Press.

Adegbola, O. F. (2022). The discursive construction of gay people in news reports of selected Nigerian newspapers. *Journal of Language and Sexuality*, *11*(1), 80–100. DOI: 10.1075/jls.19009.ade

Adegoju, A., & Ademilokun, M. (2015). Verbal and visual signifiers of advertising shares offers in Nigeria's 2005 bank recapitalization. *Discourse & Communication*, *9*(5), 519–533. DOI: 10.1177/1750481315600300

Ademilokun, M., & Olateju, M. (2015). A multimodal discourse analysis of some visual images in the political rally discourse of 2011 electioneering campaigns in Southwestern Nigeria. *International Journal of Society, Culture, and Language*, *3*(1), 1–18. https://www.ijscl.net/article_27706.html

Adenubi, A. O., & Adegboyega, T. A. (2020). Globalization and social media technologies; implications for African identity formation. *Gateway information journal*, *21*(1 & 2), 45-54. Nigeria Library Association, Ogun State Chapter. https://scholar.google.com/citations?view_op=view_citation&hl=en&user=c5OfbfIAAAAJ&citation_for_view=c5OfbfIAAAAJ:Tyk-4Ss8FVUC

Aderibole, O. (2023). Social media and health misinformation: A toxic duo. Retrieved September15, 2024, from http://www.nigeriainfo.fm

Adewumi, A. P., & Adejumo, D. O. (2024). Harnessing the harmonious sounds of Naija music as a tool for ethnic integration in Nigeria. *Kashere Journal of Politics and International Relations*, *2*(1), 294–304.

Adeyemo, A. A., Ogunkeyede, S. A., Ogundoyin, O. A., & Oyelakin, O. A. (2021). Evolving telemedicine practice: Experiences of healthcare workers during covid-19 pandemic. *Annals of Ibadan Postgraduate Medicine*, *19*(1), 44–48. PMID: 25161433

Adun, S. (2023). *The impact of affiliate marketing on purchasing behaviour of Nigerian consumers: the case of B2C marketers*. Unpublished masters dissertation, University of the West of Scotland, UK.

Afolaranmi, A. O. (2023). Effects of social media on the peaceful coexistence of African people: A critical review. In Chukwuere, J. E., Adom, D., & Dyikuk, J. J. (Eds.), *Disruptive social media: Towards a resilient social media ecosystem in Africa* (pp. 93–107). Jozac Publishers., DOI: 10.57040/jp.6.c30

Ahmed, R. (2018). *Effects of online education on encoding and decoding process of students and teachers*. ERIC. https://files.eric.ed.gov/fulltext/ED590288.pdf

Ahmed, S. (2023). ChatGPT: A Natural Language Processing Tool with Impressive Accuracy. Retrieved from https://www.example.com/chatgpt

Aitken, M. (2009). The English Possessive Marker in a Framework of Relevance. *Journal of Language and Communication Studies*, *49*, 119–135.

Ajagbe, S., & Okesola, S. (2024). A Discourse-Based Analysis of Perceptions of Nigerian Pidgin Among the Nigerian Diaspora. *Language Matters (Pretoria)*, *55*(3), 74–95. DOI: 10.1080/10228195.2024.2436074

Ajibade, G. O. (2013). Same-Sex Relationships in Yorùbá Culture and Orature. *Journal of Homosexuality*, *60*(7), 965–983. DOI: 10.1080/00918369.2013.774876 PMID: 23808346

Ajiboye, E., & Abioye, T. (2019). When citizens talk: Stance and representation in online discourse on Biafra agitations. *Discourse & Society*, *30*(2), 117–134. DOI: 10.1177/0957926518816197

Ajitoni, B. (2024). Digital storytelling and cultural identity: The role of social media in contemporary narratives. *The African Communicator*, *4*(2), 89–101. DOI: 10.70118/TACJ0007

Akın, M. H. (2018). Türkiye'de Muhafazakârlığın Direnme Odağı Olarak AİLE. *Muhafazakâr Düşünce Dergisi, 31*.

Akinsanya, T. (2024). Media and hate speech: A discursive study of hate speech on Nairaland forum. *Sprin Journal of Arts. Humanities and Social Sciences*, *3*(4), 52–61.

Akmal, S., & Yana, D. U. (2020). Conversational implicature analysis in Kingdom of Heaven movie script by William Monahan. ResearchGate. https://www.researchgate.net/publication/344572149_Conversational_Implicature_Analysis_in_Kingdom_of_Heaven_Movie_Script_by_William_Monahan

Akomolafe, F. (2020). #EndSARS: A study of the role of social media in the 2020 Nigerian Protests. *Journal of African Media Studies*, *12*(1), 1–15.

Akujobi, O. S. (2019). The English Language hegemony and sociolinguistic Effects on indigenous languages. *Journal of African Studies and Sustainable Development*, *2*(2), 130–143.

Al Zidjaly, N. (2019). Society in digital contexts: New modes of identity and community construction. *Multilingua*, *38*(4), 357–375. DOI: 10.1515/multi-2018-0042

Alem, D. D. (2022). *Hegemony according to Gramsci*. Paper presented at Literary Theory and Criticism II, Bahir Dar University, Ethopia.

Alemede, E. O. (2022). The Impact of the use of Code-Mixing in Nigerian Gospe l Music. *Accelerando: Belgrade Journal of Music and Dance*, *7*, 2.

Alharthi, M. A. J. E. D. (2020). Students from diverse cultures in the multicultural online classroom: Issues and suggestions. *Journal of Theoretical and Applied Information Technology*, *98*(09).

Alhuzami, N., & Muyidi, A. (2025). What factors affect the way youth present themselves on social media? Self-presentation strategies' approach. *Agathos*, *16*(1), 389–399.

Ali, B., & Naz, B. (2023). Discourse Analysis of Online communication in Pakistan in Social Media. *Cosmic Journal of Linguistics*, *2*(1), 1–15.

Alibbi, A. (2014). Hollywood, the american image and the global film industry. *CINEJ Cinema Journal*, *3*(1), 93–106. Advance online publication. DOI: 10.5195/cinej.2013.81

Allam, N. (2017). We are all Khaled Said: The role of Facebbok in Egypt's Arab Spring. *Journal of African Media Studies*, *9*(1), 33–46.

Alotiby, A. (2021). The Impact of Media on Public Health Awareness Concerning the Use of Natural Remedies against the COVID-19 Outbreak in Saudi Arabia. *International Journal of General Medicine*, *14*, 3145–3152. DOI: 10.2147/IJGM.S317348 PMID: 34239323

Al-Rawi, A., Siddiqi, M., Morgan, R., Vandan, N., Smith, J., & Wenham, C. (2020). COVID-19 and the gendered use of emojis on Twitter: Infodemiology study. *Journal of Medical Internet Research*, *22*(11), e21646. DOI: 10.2196/21646 PMID: 33052871

Alzahrani, F., & Elshemy, R. (2023). Digitally mediated communication of emojis by visually impaired users: The case of sarcastic WhatsApp messages. *Journal of Intercultural Communication*, *23*(2), 58–65. DOI: 10.36923/jicc.v23i2.187

Amenaghawon, F., & Ayantade, J. (2019). Homosexuality Framing by a Nigerian Newspaper. *Covenant Journal of Communication*, *6*(2), 72–88.

Amosu, S. T., Adeleke, M. O., & Akinwale, M. O. (2024). *A multimodal semiotic analysis of Walt Disney and Kugali's Iwaju* [Unpublished undergraduate project]. Obafemi Awolowo University.

Analyzer, D. (2024). Identity in Discourse. Retrieved on 10 November, 2024 from https://discourseanalyzer.com/identity-in-discourse-analysis/

Ancheta, K. 2016. *Online Support for Women Trying to Conceive*. Available at: http://www.katieancheta.com/exploring/2016/12/14/genre-and-ttc-forums

Anele, C. (2023). Ethnocentrism in multicultural society: Intrigues, challenges and way forward in the Nigerian society. *Journal of Health. Applied Sciences and Management*, *6*(3), 74–81. DOI: 10.4314/johasam.v6i3.10

Anurudu, S., Igboanugo, A., & Anthony Onu, A. (2023). A multimodal discourse analysis of selected Nollywood posters. *International Journal of Multidisciplinary Research and Publications*, *5*(11), 57–63. DOI: 10.51455/ijmrap.2023.5354

Asabor, I. (2024). How Hollywood, Bollywood, Nollywood and Ghallywood are shaping economies. Modern Ghana. https://www.modernghana.com/news/1327183/how-hollywood-bollywood-nollywood-and-ghallywood.html

Asemah, E. S., Ekhareafo, D. O., & Olaniran, S. (2013). Nigeria's core values and the use of social media to promote cultural values. *International Journal of Information and Communication Technology Education*, *9*(4), 58–69. DOI: 10.4018/ijicte.2013100104

Asike, J. C. (2019). Managing multicultural societies: Nudging towards a Cultural Purity in Nigeria. *Global Journal of Archaeology and Anthropology*, *9*(3), 72–77.

Atizwen, F. B. (2021). *Social media advertitising and consumer patronage of jumia online shopping.* Unpublished masters dissertation, Nasarawa State University, Nigeria.

Audrezet, A., de Kerviler, G., & Guidry Moulard, J. (2020). Authenticity under threat: When social media influencers need to go beyond self-presentation. *Journal of Business Research*, *117*, 557–569. DOI: 10.1016/j.jbusres.2018.07.008

Aulia, H., Hafeez, M., Mashwani, H. U., Careemdeen, J. D., Mirzapour, M., & Syaharuddin, S. (2024, March). The role of interactive learning media in enhancing student engagement and academic achievement. In Proceeding of International Seminar On Student Research In Education, Science, and Technology (Vol. 1, pp. 57-67).

Auliainsani, Elda & Anjarningsih, Harwintha. (2023). Ideological Ambivalence: A Social Semiotic Multimodal Analysis of LGBT Activism in @WhatIsUpIndonesia. *K@ta: a Biannual Publication on the Study of Language and Literature* 25: 65-80. DOI: .DOI: 10.9744/kata.25.2.65-80

Austin, J. L. (1962). *How to do things with words*. Clarendon Press.

Ayoola, K.A. (2014). Manipulative use of short messaging service (SMS) text messages by Nigerian telecommunications companies. *Linguistik online*, 63 (1/14). https://doi.org/DOI: 10.13092/lo.63.1323

Aziken, L. C., & Emeni, F. C. A. (2010). Traditional Systems of communication in Nigeria: A review for improvement. *Knowledge Review*, *21*(4), 23–29.

Badmus, I. A. (2009). Under reconstruction: ethnicity, ethnic nationalism, and the future of the Nigerian state. *Verfassung Und Recht in Übersee/Law and politics in Africa, Asia and Latin America*, 212-239.

Badmus, J. (2022). *11 top paying affiliate marketing programs in Nigeria*. https://branditechture.com/11-top-paying-affiliate-marketing-programs-in-nigeria/

Baker, P. (2006). *Using corpora to analyse discourse*. Continuum. DOI: 10.5040/9781350933996

Balogun, S., & Obosi, A. (2018). Role of cultural identity and social cohesion in national development: Nigeria in perspective. *Nigerian Journal of Social Psychology*, *1*(1), 54–62.

Baltikian, M., Karkkainen, S., & Kukkonen, J. (2024). Assessment of scientific literacy levels among secondary school students in Lebanon: Exloring gender-based differences. *Eurasia Journal of Mathematics, Science and Technology Education*, *2*(3), em2407. DOI: 10.29333/ejmste/14279

Baran, S. (2002). *Introduction to mass communication, media literacy and culture*. McGraw Hill Higher Education.

Barinaga-López, B., Puente-Bienvenido, H., & Navarro Newball, A. A. (2022). A systematic review of trends and gaps in the production of scientific knowledge on the sociopolitical impacts of emojis in computer-mediated communication. *Cogent Social Sciences*, *8*(1), 2151096. DOI: 10.1080/23311886.2022.2151096

Barker, M. (2014). Anarchism and sexuality: Ethics, relationship, and power by Jamie Heckert and Richard Cleminson. *Psychology and Sexuality*, *5*(2), 186–190. DOI: 10.1080/19419899.2012.695873

Barraza C (2023) *12 Advantages and Disadvantages of TikTok* Digital Marketing, Social media. (Redaction Team).

Barraza, C. (2024). *11 Benefits of using TikTok last updated, August 2024. Digital Marketing Social media*. Redaction Team.

Barthes, R. (1977). *Image, music, text*. Fontana Press.

Barthes, R. (1977). *Image, Music, Text*. Fontana.

Barthes, R. (1997a). The photographic message. In Barthes, R. (Ed.), *Image–Music–Text* (pp. 15–31). Fontana.

Baruah, A. (2024). The impact of computer-mediated communication on relationships and Social Interactions. *International Journal of Human-Computer Interaction*, *2*(2), 1–7. DOI: 10.1080/10447318.2024.2442755

Batta, H. E. (2011). New Media and Archiving of Traditional Medicine Knowledge in Nigeria. *Annals of Humanities and Development Studies*, *2*(1), 21–32.

Batta, H. E. (2012). Press Coverage of Traditional Medical Practice in Nigeria. *Journal of Communication*, *3*(2), 75–89. DOI: 10.1080/0976691X.2012.11884798

Bayer, A. (2013). Değişen toplumsal yapıda aile. *Şırnak Üniversitesi İlahiyat Fakültesi Dergisi, 4*(8), 101-129.

Bell, V. (2007). Online information, extreme communities and internet therapy: Is the internet good for our mental health? *Journal of Mental Health (Abingdon, England)*, *16*(4), 445–457. DOI: 10.1080/09638230701482378

Bennett, D. (2005). Music as a tool for social change. *International Journal of Music Education*, *23*(1), 49–62.

Best, S. J., & Krueger, B. S. (2006). Online Interactions and Social Capital: Distinguishing between New and Existing Ties. *Social Science Computer Review*, *24*(4), 395–410. DOI: 10.1177/0894439306286855

Bhargavi, L. M. (2024). The role of emotional appeal in modern advertising: A Study on role of e-advertisement on consumer buying behaviour. ShodhKosh. *Journal of Visual and Performing Arts*, *5*(1), 141–153. DOI: 10.29121/shodhkosh.v5.i1.2024.1697

Bhatia, V. K. (2005). Generic patterns in promotional discourse. In Halmari, H., Virtanen, T., & Benjamins, J. (Eds.), *Persuasion across genres: a linguistic approach* (pp. 213–228). Publishing Company., https://www.researchgate.net/publication/283034102_Generic_patterns_in_promotional_discourse DOI: 10.1075/pbns.130.13bha

Bimber, B., Flanagin, A. J., & Stohl, C. (2005). Reconceptualizing collective action in the contemporary media environment. *Communication Theory*, *15*(4), 365–388. DOI: 10.1111/j.1468-2885.2005.tb00340.x

Biri, Y. (2023). Affective stance as positioning in an English-speaking online fan community. *Journal of Pragmatics*, *215*, 70–83. DOI: 10.1016/j.pragma.2023.07.004

Björkvall, A., Boréus, K., & Svärd, P. (2024). Multimodal discourse analysis. In *Analyzing text and discourse: Nine approaches for the social sciences* (2nd ed., pp. 199–215). SAGE Publications., https://books.google.com.ng/books?hl=en&lr=&id=xrr7EAAAQBAJ&oi=fnd&pg=PA199&dq=Multimodal+discourse+analysis&ots=1109AeZzOv&sig=w_5kSxvVDBCW2lDzHHveS8CN0BY&redir_esc=y#v=onepage&q=Multimodal%20discourse%20analysis&f=false

Blank, G. (2013). Who Creates Content? Stratification and content creation on the Internet. *Information Communication and Society*, *16*(4), 590–612. DOI: 10.1080/1369118X.2013.777758

Bliuc, A. M., & Chidley, A. (2022). From cooperation to conflict: The role of collective narratives in shaping group behaviour. *Social and Personality Psychology Compass*, *16*(7), e12670. DOI: 10.1111/spc3.12670

Blommaert, J. (2010). *The sociolinguistics of globalization*. Cambridge University Press. DOI: 10.1017/CBO9780511845307

Blommaert, J. (2018). Chronotopes, scale and complexity in the study of language in society. In *Multilingualism and Multimodality: An Introduction*. Routledge.

Boamah, E. (2018). Information Culture of Ghanaian Immigrants Living in New Zealand. *Global Knowledge, Memory and Communication*, *67*(8/9), 585–606. DOI: 10.1108/GKMC-07-2018-0065

Boggu, A. T., & Sundarsingh, J. (2015). Poster presentation as an effective communication tool in an EFL context. *International Journal of Language and Linguistics*, *2*(5). https://www.researchgate.net/publication/290438108

Borkin, M., Vo, A., Bylinskii, Z., Isola, P., Sunkavalli, S., Olivia, A., & Pfister, H. (2013). What makes a visualisation memorable? *IEEE Transactions on Visualization and Computer Graphics*, *19*(12), 2306–2315. DOI: 10.1109/TVCG.2013.234 PMID: 24051797

Bosia, M. J., & Weiss, M. L. (2013). *Global Homophobia: States, Movements, and the Politics of Oppression*. University of Illinois Press.

Bost, S. (2008). From race/sex/etc. to glucose, feeding tube, and mourning: the shifting matter of Chicana feminism. In Alaimo, S., & Hekman, S. (Eds.), *Material Feminisms* (pp. 340–372). Indiana University Press. of three forms of internet use on Classroom.

Boutet, I., LeBlanc, M., Chamberland, J. A., & Collin, C. A. (2021). Emojis influence emotional communication, social attributions, and information processing. *Computers in Human Behavior*, *119*, 106722. DOI: 10.1016/j.chb.2021.106722

Boyd, D. (2010). Social network sites as networked publics: Affordances, dynamics and implications. In Z. Papacharissi (ed.), *The Networked Self: Identity, Community, and Culture on Social Network Sites* (pp. 39–58). New York: Routledge.

Boyd, D. (2014). *It's Complicated: The Social Lives of Networked Teens*. Yale University Press.

Boyd, D. (2014). *It's Complicated: The social lives of networked teens*. Yale University Press.

BOYSETS FIRE. (2022). What is Bollywood? A beginner's guide to India's popular film industry. https://www.boysetsfire.net/what-is-bollywood-a-beginners-guide-to-indias-popular-film-industry/

Brewington, M. T. (2024). *How secondary disciplinary teachers integrate literacy strategies to improve outcomes on state assessments*. Walden University. https://scholarworks.waldenu.edu/cgi/viewcontent.cgi?article=18323&context=dissertations

Bristol, T. J., Billings, D. M., & Kowalski, K. (2010). Twitter: Consider the possibilities for continuing nursing education. *Journal of Continuing Education in Nursing*, *41*(5), 199–200. DOI: 10.3928/00220124-20100423-09 PMID: 20481418

Brito, P. Q., Torres, S., & Fernandes, J. (2020). What kind of emotions do emoticons communicate? *Asia Pacific Journal of Marketing and Logistics*, *32*(7), 1495–1517. DOI: 10.1108/APJML-03-2019-0136

Browne, K., & McCartan, A. (2020). Sexuality and queer geographies.

Brown, M. (2002). Multicultural education and technology: Perspectives to consider. *Journal of Special Education Technology*, *17*(3), 51.

Bucholtz, M., & Hall, K. (2004). Language and Identity. In Duranti, A. (Ed.), *A Companion to Linguistic Anthropology* (pp. 369–394). Blackwell.

Bucholtz, M., & Hall, K. (2005). Identity and interaction: A sociocultural linguistic approach. *Discourse Studies*, *7*(4-5), 585–614. DOI: 10.1177/1461445605054407

Buhre, F. (2023). Child figurations in youth climate justice activism: The visual rhetoric of the Fridays for future on Instagram. In *Sandin, B., Josefsson, J., Hanson, K. Balagopalan, S. The politics of children's rights and representation* (pp. 251–274). Palgrave. DOI: 10.1007/978-3-031-04480-9_11

Çaha, Ö. (2004). Muhafazakâr düşüncede toplum. *Liberal düşünce dergisi, 34*, 15-24.

Çakir, P., & Temi̇, R. E. (2022). *Sosyal Medyada Benlik Sunumu ve Mahremiyet Kavramı ile İlişkisi: Nicel Bir Araştırma*. Yeni Medya Dergisi.

Cambridge Dictionary. (n.d.). Sneak peek. In *Cambridge Dictionary*. Retrieved October 21, 2024, from https://dictionary.cambridge.org/dictionary/english/sneak-peek

Canagarajah, A. S. (2006). Negotiating the local in English as a lingua franca. *Annual Review of Applied Linguistics, 26*, 197–218. DOI: 10.1017/S0267190506000109

Can, İ. (2019). *III. Ailenin Tarihsel Gelişimi: Dünü, Bugünü ve Yarını. İçinde Sistematik Aile Sosyolojisi*. Çizgi Kitabevi.

Carey, J. W. (2009). *Communication as Culture: Essays on Media and Society*. Routledge.

Carpentier, N. (2011). *Media and Participation: A Site of Ideological-Democratic Struggle*. Intellect. DOI: 10.26530/OAPEN_606390

Chandler, D. (2002). *Semiotics: The basics*. Routledge.

Chan, G., Banire, B., Ataguba, G., Frempong, G., & Orji, R. (2025). A panoramic view of socio-cultural sensitivity in digital technologies: A comprehensive review and future directions. *International Journal of Human-Computer Interaction, 41*(4), 1917–1945. DOI: 10.1080/10447318.2024.2372135

Chauhan, H. (2022). The influence of emotional advertising appeals on consumer decision making: A cross-sectional study. *International Journal of Early Childhood Special Education, 14*, 3106–3109. DOI: 10.48047/intjecse/v14i4.425

Cheng, W. F. (2016). Constructing hotel brands: A multimodal analysis of luxury hotel homepages. *Ibérica*, (31), 83–108. http://www.revistaiberica.org/index.php/iberica/article/view/190

Chen, J., & Wang, Y. (2021). Social Media Use for Health Purposes: Systematic Review. *Journal of Medical Internet Research, 23*(5), e17917. DOI: 10.2196/17917 PMID: 33978589

Chen, Y., & Li, S. X. (2009). Group identity and social preferences. *The American Economic Review, 99*(1), 431–457. DOI: 10.1257/aer.99.1.431

Chen, Y., Yang, X., Howman, H., & Filik, R. (2024). Individual differences in emoji comprehension: Gender, age, and culture. *PLoS One, 19*(2), e0297379. DOI: 10.1371/journal.pone.0297379 PMID: 38354159

Chiluwa, I. (2023). #EndSARS protests and the search for social justice in Nigeria: Examining activist discourses on police brutality, politics, and human security. *Protest*, *3*(2), 200–224. DOI: 10.1163/2667372X-bja10047

Chin, T., Wang, S., & Rowley, C. (2020). Polychronic knowledge creation in cross-border business models: a sea-like heuristic metaphor. J. Knowl. Manag. doi: [Epub ahead-of-print] Google ScholarDOI: 10.1108/JKM-04-2020-0244

Chin, T., Meng, J., Wang, S., Shi, Y., & Zhang, J. (2021). Cross-cultural metacognition as a prior for humanitarian knowledge: When cultures collide in global health emergencies [Epub ahead-of-print]. *Journal of Knowledge Management*. Advance online publication. DOI: 10.1108/JKM-10-2020-0787

Chisholm, I. M., & Wetzel, K. (2001). Technology and Multiculturalism in the Classroom. *Journal of Research on Technology in Education*, *33*(5).

Chitrkala. (2016). *Traffic*: A review. Retrieved from https://chitrkala.in/traffic-movie-review

Chon, M. G., & Park, H. (2019, March 19). Social media activism in the digital age: Testing an integrative model of activism on contentious issues. *Journalism & Mass Communication Quarterly*, *97*(1), 72–97. DOI: 10.1177/1077699019835896

Christensen, T., Riis, A. H., Hatch, E. E., Wise, L. A., Nielsen, M. G., Rothman, K. J., & Mikkelsen, E. M. (2017). Costs and efficiency of online and offline recruitment methods: A web-based cohort study. *Journal of Medical Internet Research*, *19*(3), e6716.

Chukaokeke, C., & Obiamalu, G. (2021). *Conversational implicatures of whatsapp stickers chats of unizik students. Department of Linguistics Nnamdi Azikiwe University* (Vol. 6). Preorcjah., www.ezenwaohaetorc.org

Chukwudi, J. F. (2024). Inter-ethnic violence in Nigeria and the proposed solution to address them. [SSHJ]. *Social Science and Humanities Journal*, *8*(04), 34795–34806. DOI: 10.18535/sshj.v8i04.997

Chulhan, B. (2024). *Palyatif Toplum* (6. bs). Metis.

Chulhan, B. (2017). *Şeffaflık Toplumu*. Metis.

Chulhan, B. (2022). *Psikopolitika (5. bs)*. Metis.

Chu, S.-C., & Choi, S. M. (2010). Social capital and self-presentation on social networking sites: A comparative study of Chinese and American young generations. *Chinese Journal of Communication*, *3*(4), 402–420. DOI: 10.1080/17544750.2010.516575

Clarke, E., DeNora, T., & Vuoskoski, J. (2015). Music, empathy and cultural understanding. *Physics of Life Reviews*, *15*, 61–88. DOI: 10.1016/j.plrev.2015.09.001 PMID: 26419700

Cleveland, D. J. (2016). Brand personality and organization-public relationships: impacting dimensions by choosing a temperament for communication

Cline, R. J. W., & Haynes, K. M. (2001). Consumer health information seeking on the Internet: The state of the art. *Health Education Research*, *16*(6), 671–692. https://www.jstor.org/stable/45109709. DOI: 10.1093/her/16.6.671 PMID: 11780707

Cohn, J. (2023, August 10). How will AI alter the student experience? Experts weigh in. UniversityWorldNews. https://www.universityworldnews.com/post.php?story=20230810143957522

Cope, B., & Kalantzis, M. (2023). Towards education justice: The multiliteracies project revisited. In *Multiliteracies in International Educational Contexts* (pp. 1–33). Routledge. DOI: 10.4324/9781003349662-1

Correa, T., & Jeong, S. H. (2011). Race and online content creation: Why minorities are actively participating in the Web. *Information Communication and Society*, *14*(5), 638–659. DOI: 10.1080/1369118X.2010.514355

Coulson, N. S., Bullock, E., & Rodham, K. (2017). Exploring the therapeutic affordances of self-harm online support communities: An online survey of members. *JMIR Mental Health*, *4*(4), e44. Advance online publication. DOI: 10.2196/mental.8084 PMID: 29030324

Coulthard, M. (1981). *An introduction to discourse analysis*. Longman.

Craig, S. L., & McInroy, L. (2014). You can form a part of yourself online: The influence of new media on identity development and coming out for LGBTQ youth. *Journal of Gay & Lesbian Mental Health*, *18*(1), 95–109. DOI: 10.1080/19359705.2013.777007

Crooke, A. H. D., Thompson, W. F., Fraser, T., & Davidson, J. (2024). Music, social cohesion, and intercultural understanding: A conceptual framework for intercultural music engagement. *Musicae Scientiae*, *28*(1), 18–38. DOI: 10.1177/10298649231157099

Cynthia. (2023). Visual text comprehension: 4 types of non-linguistic features you need to know. Retrieved September 3, 2024 from [Lil But Mighty English] (https://lilbutmightyenglish.com/blog/visualtextcomprehension4typesofnonlinguisticfeaturesyouneedtoknow/)

D'Angelo, L., & Marino, F. (2024). Multimodal analysis. In Kessler, M., & Polio, C. (Eds.), *Conducting genre-based research in applied linguistics: A methodological guide*. Routledge.

Dahlgren, P. (2005). The Internet, Public Spheres, and Political Communication: Dispersion and Deliberation. *Political Communication*, *22*(2), 147–162. DOI: 10.1080/10584600590933160

Dahlström, H. and Damber, U. (2020). Meanings Made in Students' Multimodal Digital Stories: Resources, Popular Culture, and Values. *Designs for learning, 12*(1), 45-55.

Danesi, M. (2017). *The semiotics of emoji: the rise of visual language in the age of the internet*. Bloomsbury Publishing. DOI: 10.5040/9781474282024

Danesi, M. (2022). Emotional wellbeing and the semiotic translation of emojis. In *Exploring the translatability of emotions: Cross-cultural and transdisciplinary encounters* (pp. 323–344). Springer International Publishing., DOI: 10.1007/978-3-030-91748-7_12

Danet, B., & Herring, S. C. (2003). Introduction: The multilingual internet. *Journal of Computer-Mediated Communication*, *9*(1), JCMC9110.

Dave, E. (2008). *Social media marketing: An hour a day*. John Willy & Sons.

Davies, R. U., & Alabi, B. A. (2023). Language and Positive Identity Reconstruction: A Study of Nairaland and Facebook. *Lead Journal of Languages and Literature*, *1*(1), 201–210.

Dawson, A., & Dennis, S. (2020). Social intimacy. *Anthropology in Action : Newsletter of the British Association for Social Anthropology in Policy and Practice (BASAPP)*, *27*(3), 1–8. DOI: 10.3167/aia.2020.270301

Dedeoğlu, G. (2004). Gözetleme, mahremiyet ve insan onuru. *TBD Bilişim*, *89*, 36.

Demirkanoğlu, Y. (2017). Muhafazakâr Düşüncede Kadinin Toplumsal Konumu. *Sosyal Ekonomik Araştırmalar Dergisi*, *17*(34), 285–305. DOI: 10.30976/susead.338402

Derks, D., Fischer, A. H., & Fischer, M. (2008). The role of emotion in computer-mediated communication: The case of emojis. *Computers in Human Behavior*, *24*(6), 2760–2773.

DeRose, D. R. 2016. "*Baby Dust to All! Identity Construction in Two-Week Wait Online Discussion Forums*." Master's Dissertation, Marquette University. https://epublications.marquette.edu/theses_open/386/

Deshmukh, A. (2024). From Pixels to Personalities: Identity formation in virtual communities through multimodal communication. *European Conference on Social Media*, 11(1), 50-58. DOI: 10.34190/ecsm.11.1.2378

DeWitt, D., & Alias, N. (2017) Infographic posters for enhancing 21st century communication skills. *World Conference on Education (WCEDU)*, 12-13 Colombo, Sri Lanka.

Dhoest, A., & Szulc, L. (2016). Navigating online selves: Social, cultural, and material contexts of social media use by diasporic gay men. *Social Media + Society*, *2*(4), 2056305116672485. DOI: 10.1177/2056305116672485

Distel, V., Egger, R., Petrovic, U., Phan, V. L., & Wiesinger, S. (2022). The usage of emoji in tourism-related Instagram posts: Suggestions from a marketing perspective. In J. L. Stienmetz, B. Ferrer-Rosell, & D. Massimo (Eds.). *Information and communication technologies in tourism: Proceedings of the ENTER. eTourism conference. Springer.* 134–145.

Dlamini, B. (2006). Homosexuality in the African context. *Agenda (Durban, South Africa)*, *20*(67), 128–136. DOI: 10.1080/10130950.2006.9674706

Dobson, A. S. (2015). *Postfeminist Digital Cultures: Femininity, Social Media, and Self Representation*. Palgrave Macmillan. DOI: 10.1057/9781137404206

Doğan, İ. (2016). *Türk Aile Sosyolojisi*. Pagema Akademi.

Doran, Y. (2019). Building knowledge through images in physics. *Visual Communication*, *18*(2), 251–277. DOI: 10.1177/1470357218759825

Doran, Y. J. (2017). *The discourse of physics: Building knowledge through language, mathematics and image*. Routledge. DOI: 10.4324/9781315181134

Doran, Y. J., & Martin, J. R. (2021). Field relations: Understanding scientific explanations. In Maton, K., Martin, J. R., & Doran, Y. J. (Eds.), *Teaching science: Knowledge, language, pedagogy* (pp. 105–133). Routledge. DOI: 10.4324/9781351129282-7

Du Plessis, T. (2020). Interpretation of emojis in organisational computer-mediated communication (CMC) contexts (Doctoral dissertation, Stellenbosch: Stellenbosch University).

Durante, C. (2016). Adapting nonverbal coding theory to mobile mediated communication: an analysis of emoji and other digital nonverbal. *M.S. thesis, Dept. Commune. Stud., Liberty Univ., Virginia, Lynchburg.*

Dwyer, R. (2006). Filming the gods. Routlege.www.routlegde.com

Eades-Baird, M. R., & Hayden, H. E. (2025). Disciplinary Literacies for Science: Understanding How Teachers Enact Educational Reforms. In *Utilizing Case Studies in Literacy and Language Education* (pp. 191-218). IGI Global Scientific Publishing.

Ebel, I., & Dutra, J. P. (2022). Do you speak emoji? The language of emojis. In *The SAGE handbook of social media marketing* (p. 320). SAGE Publications. DOI: 10.4135/9781529782493.n20

Eden, C. A., Chisom, O. N., & Adeniyi, I. S. (2024). Cultural competence in education: Strategies for fostering inclusivity and diversity awareness. *International Journal of Applied Research in Social Sciences*, *6*(3), 383–392. DOI: 10.51594/ijarss.v6i3.895

Edewor, P., Aluko, Y., & Folarin, S. (2014). Managing ethnic and cultural diversity for national integration in Nigeria. *Developing Country Studies*, *4*(6), 70–76.

Edo-Osagie, O., De La Iglesia, B., Lake, I., & Edeghere, O. (2020). A scoping review of the use of Twitter for public health research. *Computers in Biology and Medicine*, *122*(103770), 103770. https://www.sciencedirect.com/science/article/pii/S0010482520301426. DOI: 10.1016/j.compbiomed.2020.103770 PMID: 32502758

Edwards (2024). The Importance of cultural integration. https://easysociology.com/sociology-of-culture/the-importance-of-cultural-integration/

Eemeli, B. (2023). *Utilizing social media platforms in music marketing*. Unpublished bachelors dissertation, Tampere University of Applied Sciences, Finland

Efe, H. S. (2024). Muhafazakâr ve Laik Kimliklerin Televizyon Dizilerinde Alımlanması:"Kızılcık Şerbeti Dizisi". *INJOCMER International Journal of Communication and Media Research*, *4*(1), 21–43.

Egbah, A. I., & Igene, S. O. (2024). Legitimating genome editing: A Critical Discourse Analysis of Media reportage. *Ars Artium*, *12*, 53–71.

Egwu, J. U. (2018). Federalism and national integration in Nigeria: Issues and challenges. *IDOSR Journal of Humanities and Social Sciences*, *3*(1), 151–163.

Ehiane, S. O., Zondi, L. P., & Gumede, M. (2024). *Conflict of survival between Fulani pastoralists and farmers in the wake of climate change Nigeria. Engagement of Africa in Conflict Dynamics and Peace Architectures*. Springer Nature Singapore.

Ejabena, H. O. (2018). Multimodal semiotic study of product advertisements in Nigerian online shopping outlets. Unpublished Master's thesis, Obafemi Awolowo University, Ile-Ife, Nigeria.

Ekine, S. (2013). *Queer African Reader*. Pambazuka Press.

Ekström, M., & Östman, J. (2015). Information, interaction, and creative production: The effects of three forms of internet use on youth democratic engagement. *Communication Research*, *42*(6), 796–818. DOI: 10.1177/0093650213476295

Ekwueme, A., Akagwu & Akoji. N. (2017). The influence of online marketing of Jumia and Konga on consumer purchasing behaviour among Kogi State Residents of Nigeria. *Global Journal of Human-Social Science*, 17 (6) (1), 24-32.

Elategy, W. (14 Nov, 2023) History of content creation. https://www.linkedIn.com

Elghamry, K. (2017). Social media and the Arab Spring: Politics comes first. *The International Journal of Press/Politics*, *22*(4), 449–469.

Emilia, D. Zhao S. (2013). *Critical Multimodal Studies of Popular Culture*. London: Routledge.

Endong, F. (2022). Using Social Media to Advocate LGBT Rights in Black Africa: A Study of Nigerian and Cameroonian Gay Bloggers and "Facebookers". In *Research Anthology on Inclusivity and Equity for the LGBTQ+ Community* (pp. 169–188). IGI Global., DOI: 10.4018/978-1-6684-3674-5.ch010

Engebretsen, M. (2023). Communicating health advice on social media: A multimodal case study. *MedieKultur: Journal of Media and Communication Research*, *39*(74), 164–184. DOI: 10.7146/mk.v39i74.134085

Escouflaire, L. (2021). Signaling irony, displaying politeness, replacing words: The eight linguistic functions of emoji in computer-mediated discourse. *Lingvisticae Investigationes*, *44*(2), 204–235. DOI: 10.1075/li.00062.esc

Esiri, M. O. (2021). Social change and marriage structure in Nigeria. *International Research Journal of Management, IT &. Social Sciences*, *1*(3), 228–235.

Etuk, J. A., & Urujzian, V. (2018). Language and ideology in number plate slogans of the 36 states of Nigeria and Abuja: A new horizon. *The Intuition*, *8*(1), 1–11.

Etuk, J., & Akpan, I. (2023). Language and gender ideology in Techno's 'Woman'. *Sapientia Global Journal of Arts* [SGOJAHDS]. *Humanities and Development Studies*, *6*(4), 69–80.

Fairclough, N. (1992). *Discourse and Social Change*. Polity Press.

Fairclough, N. (1995). *Critical discourse analysis: The critical study of language*. Longman.

Fairclough, N. (2013). *Language and power*. Routledge. DOI: 10.4324/9781315838250

Fakude, N. L. (2023). *Integrating digital technology in teaching history in the primary school* (Doctoral dissertation, University of Johannesburg).

Fieseler, C., Meckel, M., & Müller, S. (2014). With a little help of my peers. The supportive role of online contacts for the unemployed. *Computers in Human Behavior, 41*, 164–176. DOI: 10.1016/j.chb.2014.09.017

Filmfare. (2014). *Bang Bang*: Film review. Retrieved from https://www.filmfare.com/reviews/bang-bang-review-2014-134.html

Finfgeld, D. L. (2000). Therapeutic groups online: The good, the bad, and the unknown. *Issues in Mental Health Nursing, 21*(3), 241–255. DOI: 10.1080/016128400248068 PMID: 11075065

Flanagin, A., Metzger, M. J., & Thorp, S. (2023). Ethical implications of integrating AI in education. *Journal of Educational Technology, 49*(2), 65–78.

Flew, T. (2002). *New Media: An Introduction.* Oxford University Press.

Folarin, S. F., Olanrewaju, I. P., & Ajayi, M. L. Y. (2014). *Cultural plurality, national integration and the security dilemma in Nigeria.* Covenant University Journal of Politics and International Affairs.

Forman, E. A., & McCormick, D. E. (1995). Discourse analysis: A sociocultural perspective. *Remedial and Special Education, 16*(3), 150–158. DOI: 10.1177/074193259501600304

Francisco, C. (2020). Effectiveness of an online classroom for flexible learning. [IJAMR]. *International Journal of Academic Multidisciplinary Research, 4*(8), 100–107.

Franco, C. L., & Fugate, J. M. (2020). Emoji face renderings: Exploring the role emoji platform differences have on emotional interpretation. *Journal of Nonverbal Behavior, 44*(2), 301–328. DOI: 10.1007/s10919-019-00330-1

Fraser, S. (2008). Getting out in the "real world": Young men, queer and theories of gay community. *Journal of Homosexuality, 55*(2), 245–264. DOI: 10.1080/00918360802129519 PMID: 18982572

Freeman, M. (2010). Vygotsky and the virtual classroom: Sociocultural theory comes to the communications classroom. *Christian Perspectives in Education, 4*(1), 5.

Galpin, C. (2022). At the digital margins? A theoretical examination of social media engagement using intersectional feminism. *Politics and Governance, 10*(1), 161–171. DOI: 10.17645/pag.v10i1.4801

Garba, S. J. (2012). The Impact of colonialism on Nigerian Education and the Need for E-learning technique for sustainable development. *Journal of Educational and Social Research*, *2*(7), 53–61.

Garcia, J. R., & Cain, K. (2014). Decoding and reading comprehension: A meta-analysis to identify which reader and assessment characteristics influence the strength of the relationship in English. *Review of Educational Research*, *84*(1), 74–111. DOI: 10.3102/0034654313499616

Garg, P., Singh, S., Chamola, P., Kumar, A., & Paliwal, M. (2023). Elucidating the linkage between advertisements embedded with emotional appeals and the brand relationship quality during the COVID pandemic. *Journal of Marketing Communications*, *31*(2), 126–150. DOI: 10.1080/13527266.2023.2220338

Gaudio, R. P. (1997). Not Talking Straight in Hausa. In Livia, A., & Hall, K. (Eds.), *Queerly Phrased: Language, Gender, and Sexuality* (pp. 416–429). Oxford University Press. DOI: 10.1093/oso/9780195104707.003.0025

Gaudio, R. P. (2009). *Allah Made Us: Sexual Outlaws in an Islamic African City*. Wiley Blackwell. DOI: 10.1002/9781444310535

Gawne, L., & Ellison, T. (2020). Evolving meanings of emojis: A linguistic perspective on digital communication. I*n*. *Language & Communication*, *74*, 52–60.

Gbadegesin, V., & Onanuga, P. (2018). A multimodal interaction analysis of selected 2015 Nigerian election campaign adverts. *Communicatio*, *44*(2), 41–66. DOI: 10.1080/02500167.2018.1464042

George, B. H. (2018). Using virtual tours to facilitate sustainable site visits of historic sites. *European Journal of Sustainable Development*, *7*(4), 411–411. DOI: 10.14207/ejsd.2018.v7n4p411

Georgiou, M. (2013). Diaspora in the digital era: Minorities and media representation. *JEMIE. ECMI Journal of Ethnopolitics and Minority Issues in Europe*, *12*(4), 80–99.

Gil-Garcia, J. R. (2018). Exploring the complex factors influencing electronic government implementation: An empirical study of 14 countries. *Government Information Quarterly*, 35(2). CrossRef Full Text | Google Scholar

Gillan, K., Pickerill, J., & Webster, F. (2008). *Anti-war activism: New media and protest in the information age*. Springer. DOI: 10.1057/9780230596382

Gills, A.S. (February 2, 2025). Traditional media vs new media: Differences, pros and cons

Goddard, A. (1998). *The language of advertising: Written texts*. Routledge.

Goffman, E. (2020). *The presentation of self in everyday life. In the Social Construction of Reality: A Treatise in the Sociology of Knowledge*. Anchor Books.

Gökçe, H. (2017). Dünü, Bugünü, Yarını İle Aile. *Sosyoloji Notları*, *1*(1), 50–63.

Göktuna Yaylacı, F. (2020). *Aile Sosyolojisi* (Eraslan, L., Ed.). Anadolo Ünivessitesi Yayını.

Gokulsing, M., & Dissanayake, W. (2020). *Indian popular cinema: A narrative of cultural change*. ResearchGate. https://www.researchgate.net/publication/343206085_Indian_Popular_Cinema_A_Narrative_of_Cultural_Change

Gong, T., Minett, J. W., & Wang, W. S. Y. (2010). A simulation study exploring the role of cultural transmission in language evolution. *Connection Science*, *22*(1), 69–85. DOI: 10.1080/09540090903198819

Gorea, M. (2021). Becoming your "authentic" self: How social media influences youth's visual transitions. *Social Media + Society*, *7*(3), 20563051211047875. DOI: 10.1177/20563051211047875

Graham, P. V. (2024). Emojis: An approach to interpretation. *UC Law SF Communications and Entertainment Journal*, *46*(2), 123.

Gramsci, A. (1971). *1891-193 Selections from the prison notebooks of Antonio Gramsci*. International Publishers.

Greenpeace Africa. (2020). Congo Basin Defenders. Retrieved from http://www.greenbeltmovement.org/ on 10th of January, 2025

Grundy, P. (2008). *Doing pragmatics* (3rd ed.). Hodder Education.

Guanah, J. S. (2024). Social media, popular culture and contending African ethical models. In *Social science ethics for research and practice: An African perspective* (pp. 25–42).

Güleç, V. (2018). Aile ilişkilerinin sosyal medyayla birlikte çöküşü. *Yeni Medya Elektronik Dergisi*, *2*(2), 105–120.

Güler, Ş., & Şahi̇, N. (2022). Sosyal Medyada Çevrimiçi Benlik Sunumunun Öznel İyi Oluş Üzerine Etkisi: Instagram Kullanıcıları Üzerine Bir Araştırma. *Erciyes İletişim Dergisi*, *9*(1), 361–380. DOI: 10.17680/erciyesiletisim.993055

Gültekin, M. (2016). İbn Haldun, modernlik ve modern sosyoloji. *The Journal of Academic Social Science Studies*, *51*(51), 277–293. DOI: 10.9761/JASSS3655

Güneş, H. N. (2018). Feminist akımlarda aile. *Sosyal Bilimler Araştırma Dergisi*, *7*(3), 142–153.

Gupta, S., & Kim, H.-W. (2013). Virtual community: Concepts, implications, and future research directions.

Gupta, S., & Kim, H.-W. (2004). Virtual community: concepts, implications, and future research directions. *Proceedings of the Tenth Americas Conference on Information Systems.*

Haas, L., & Tussey, J. (2023). Empowering Minds: Multimodal Literacies, Fanfiction, and Inclusive Education. Journal of English Teaching through Movies and Media, 24(4), 28-40.

Hadden, S. L. (2019). *What Nike's use of AR in e-commerce means for the retail industry.* https://www.sama.com/blog/what-nikes-use-of-ar-in-ecommerce-means-for-the-retail-industry/

Haimson, O. L. (2021). Online Communities. In *The SAGE Encyclopedia of Trans Studies*. SAGE Publications, Inc.

Haimson, O. L., Liu, T., Zhang, B. Z., & Corvite, S. (2021). The online authenticity paradox: What being" authentic" on social media means, and barriers to achieving it. *Proceedings of the ACM on Human-computer Interaction, 5*(CSCW2), 1-18. DOI: 10.1145/3479567

Hallaç, S., & Öz, F. (2014). Aile kavramına kuramsal bir bakış. *Psikiyatride Güncel Yaklasimlar*, *6*(2), 142–153.

Halliday, M. A. K. (1978). *Language as social semiotic: The social interpretation of language and meaning*. University Park Press.

Halliday, M. A. K. (1985). *An introduction to functional grammar.* Arnold.

Halliday, M. A. K. (1994). *An Introduction to Functional Grammar* (2nd ed.). Arnold.

Halliday, M. A. K. (2002). *Linguistic studies of text and discourse.* Continuum International Publishing.

Halliday, M. A. K., & Webster, J. J. (2009). [London and New York: Continuum]. *Language in Society*, *10*, •••.

Hall, S. (2014). *Blockbusters.* Oxford University Press.

Hamdan, H. (2022). The communicative functions of emojis: Evidence from Jordanian Arabic-speaking Facebookers. *Psycholinguistics*, *31*(1), 141–172. DOI: 10.31470/2309-1797-2022-31-1-141-172

Han, M. C., & Kim, Y. (2018). How culture and friends affect acceptance of social media commerce and purchase intentions: A comparative study of consumers in the U.S. and China. *Journal of International Consumer Marketing*, *30*(5), 326–335. DOI: 10.1080/08961530.2018.1466226

Hanson. T. (March 5, 2024) .The complete history of content marketing(updated 2024)

Hao, J. (2020). *Analysing scientific discourse from a systemic functional linguistic perspective: A framework for exploring knowledge building in biology*. Routledge. DOI: 10.4324/9781351241052

Harmer, T. J. (2024). More Than Representation Heartstopper: A Multimodal Critical Discourse Analysis. Master of Arts (MA), Thesis, Communication & Theatre Arts, Old Dominion University,I-108DOI: https://digitalcommons.odu.edu/communication_etds/24DOI: 10.25777/d0f7-na37

Harris, L., & Koonce, S. (2019). Digital rhetoric in the context of digital culture. *Digital Communication Research*, *15*(3), 112–130. DOI: 10.1080/10468946.2019.1625792

Hasanica, N., Ramic-Catak, A., Mujezinovic, A., Begagic, S., Galijasevic, K., & Oruc, M. (2020). The effectiveness of the leaflets and posters as a health education method. *Materia Socio-Medica*, *32*(2), 135–139. DOI: 10.5455/msm.2020.32.135-139 PMID: 32843863

Hasyim, M., & Arafah, B. (2023). Semiotic multimodality communication in the age of new media. *Studies in Media and Communication*, *11*(1), 96–103. DOI: 10.11114/smc.v11i1.5865

Heleta, S. (2023, August 23). AI and epistemic injustices: Garbage data in, garbage out. University World News. https://www.universityworldnews.com/post.php?story=20230823104611918

Henderningrum, R. (2018). Budaya Dan Komunikasi Kesehatan (Studi Pandangan Kesehatan Pada Masyarakat Sunda Dalam Tradisi Makan Lalapan). *LUGAS Jurnal Komunikasi*, *2*(1), 13–19. DOI: 10.31334/jl.v2i1.118

Hermans, F., Apeldoom, D. V., Stuiver, M., & Kok, K. (2013). Niche and Networks: Explaining Network Evolution through Niche Formation Processes. *Research Policy*, *42*(3), 613–623. DOI: 10.1016/j.respol.2012.10.004

Herrington, C. J. (2015). *Film marketing and the creation of the Hollywood block-buster* [Honors thesis, University of Mississippi]. eGrove. https://egrove.olemiss.edu/hon_thesis/219

Heyd, T., & Mair, C. (2014). From vernacular to digital ethnolinguistic repertoire: The case of Nigerian Pidgin. In Lacoste, V., Leimgruber, J., & Breyer, T. (Eds.), *Indexing authenticity: Sociolinguistic perspectives* (pp. 244–268). Walter de Gruyter GmbH & Co KG. DOI: 10.1515/9783110347012.244

High Speed Training. (2023). Internet safety posters for schools. Retrieved September 3, 2024 from https://www.highspeedtraining.co.uk/hub/internetsafetypostersforschools/

Highfield, T., & Leaver, T. (2016). Instagrammatics and digital methods: Studying visual social media, from selfies and GIFs to memes and emoji. *Communication Research and Practice*, *2*(1), 47–62. DOI: 10.1080/22041451.2016.1155332

Hirji, F. (2024). When local meets lucre: Commerce, culture and imperialism in Bollywood cinema. *Global Media Journal*. https://www.globalmediajournal.com/open-access/when-local-meets-lucre-commerce-culture-and-imperialism-in-bollywood-cinema.php?aid=35173

Hodgson, P. (2018). Global learners' behavior on news in social media platforms through a MOOC. In Deng, L., Ma, W., & Fong, C. (Eds.), *New Media for Educational Change. Educational Communications and Technology Yearbook* (pp. 141–148). Springer. DOI: 10.1007/978-981-10-8896-4_12

Hoehle, H., Zhang, X., & Venkatesh, V. (2015). An espoused cultural perspective to understand continued intention to use mobile applications: A four-country study of mobile social media application usability. *European Journal of Information Systems*, *24*(3), 337–359. DOI: 10.1057/ejis.2014.43

Hoffman, E. B. (2018). Untangling the talk: A new multimodal discourse analysis method to investigate synchronous online learning. *Journal of Digital Learning in Teacher Education*, *34*(3), 179–195. DOI: 10.1080/21532974.2018.1453895

Hopkins, L. (2009). *Media and migration: A review of the field*. Australia and New Zealand Communication Association.

Houts, P. S., Doak, C. C., Doak, L. G., & Loscalzo, M. J. (2006). The role of pictures in improving health communication: A review of research on attention, comprehension, recall, and adherence. *Patient Education and Counseling*, *61*(2), 173–190. DOI: 10.1016/j.pec.2005.05.004 PMID: 16122896

Hsieh, S. H., & Tseng, T. H. (2017). Playfulness in mobile instant messaging: Examining the influence of emoticons and text messaging on social interaction. *Computers in Human Behavior*, *69*, 405–414. DOI: 10.1016/j.chb.2016.12.052

Huang, C.-M., & Park, D. (2013). Cultural influences on Facebook photographs. *International Journal of Psychology*, *48*(3), 334–343. DOI: 10.1080/00207594.2011.649285 PMID: 22468606

Huang, G., & Li, K. (2016). The effect of anonymity on conformity to group norms in online contexts: A meta-analysis. *International Journal of Communication*, *10*, 398–415.

Hubtel. (2020). Virtual training programs. Retrieved from (link unavailable)

Hurst, R. (2009). *Nigerian Civil War (1967 – 1970)*. BlackPast.org. https://www.blackpast.org/global-african-history/nigerian-civil-war-1967-1970/

Hu, S., Jibao, G., Liu, H., & Huang, Q. (2017). The moderating role of social media usage in the relationship among multicultural experiences, cultural intelligence, and individual creativity. *Information Technology & People*, *30*(2), 265–281. DOI: 10.1108/ITP-04-2016-0099

Idowu-Faith, B. O. (2011). Language attitudes and communicative realities of code-mixing in contemporary Nigerian gospel music. *Interdisciplinary Discourses in Language and Communication*, 164.

Igyuve, A. I., & Obagwu, P. U. (2020). The new media in Nigeria: Evolution, impacts, challenges and prospects. *IMSU Journal of Communication Studies*, *4*(2), 63–73.

Ikelegbe, A. (2005). The economy of conflict in the oil-rich Niger Delta region of Nigeria. *Nordic Journal of African Studies*, *14*(2), 208–234.

Ikiyei, P. K., Donkemezuo, S., Precious, M., & Seribofa, T. I. (2022). Out-of-school children in Nigeria: A creation by society and its implications for nation building. *British Journal of Contemporary Education*, *2*(1), 17–32.

İlhan, S. (2015). Yeni Kapitalizm Ve Meslek Olgusunun Değişen Anlamları Üzerine. *Dumlupınar Üniversitesi Sosyal Bilimler Dergisi, 21*.

IMDb. (2014). *Bang Bang* (2014). Retrieved from https://www.imdb.com/title/tt2905838/

Inyima, C. E. (2018). Language in Transition: The Social-Media and Emerging ESL Variety in Nigeria. *Ebonyi Journal of Language and Literature*, *1*(2), 1–15.

Inyima, C. U., Nwodo, M. N., Okoro, H., Nwadike, C., & Nwabueze, O. S. (2024). in view) The Stylistics of Idiomatic Adaptations in ESL Contexts. *GEMA Online Journal of Language Studies*, *24*(4), 266–283.

Inyima, C. U., Nwosu, O., & Dora-Ezenne, I. N. (2022). Sociolinguistic Innovations in Nigerian English Usage in the Covid-19 Era. *Journal of Linguistics and Language in Education*, *16*(1), 91–113. DOI: 10.56279/jlle.v16i1.5

Jacob, R. I. (2012). A historical survey of ethnic conflict in Nigeria. *Asian Social Science*, *8*(4), 13. DOI: 10.5539/ass.v8n4p13

Janoschka, A. (2004). *Web advertising: New forms of communication on the Internet*. John Benjamins Publishing Company. DOI: 10.1075/pbns.131

Jefferson, G. (2004). Glossary of transcript symbols with an introduction. In Lerner, G. H. (Ed.), *Conversation analysis: Studies from the first generation* (pp. 13–31). John Benjamins. DOI: 10.1075/pbns.125.02jef

Jenkins, H. (2006). *Convergence culture: Where old and new media collide*. New York University Press.

Jenkins, H. (2006). *Convergence Culture: Where Old and New Media Collide*. NYU Press.

Jennings, P. E. (2023). Entertainment, Education, Empowerment: The Role of Tik-Tok in Gender Diverse Lesbian Identity Negotiation (Doctoral dissertation, Texas A&M University).

Jewitt, C. (2014) The Routledge Handbook of Multimodal Analysis. Routledge/ Tailor and Francis Group.

Jewitt, C. (2009). *The Routledge Handbook of Multimodal Analysis*. Routledge.

Jewitt, C., Bezemer, J., & O'Halloran, K. (2016). *Introduction to Multimodality and it's various approaches*. Routledge.

Jia, Y. (2024). Beyond the scripts of digital posters: A case study of language ideologies and writing practices in contemporary China. *Diggit Magazine*, 1-15, https://www.diggitmagazine.com/academic-papers/beyond-scripts-digital-posters-case-study-language-ideologies-and-writing-practices

Jiang, Z., Zhang, Q., & Yu, D. (2022). The social dynamics of self-disclosure in online communities. *International Journal of Human-Computer Studies*, *145*, 82–93. DOI: 10.1016/j.ijhcs.2020.102518

Jin, D. Y., & Yoon, K. (2016). The social mediascape of transnational Korean pop culture: Hallyu 2.0 as spreadable media practice. *New Media & Society*, *18*(7), 1277–1292. DOI: 10.1177/1461444814554895

Ji, Y., & Bates, B. R. (2020). Measuring intercultural/international outgroup favoritism: Comparing two measures of cultural cringe. *Asian Journal of Communication*, *30*(2), 141–154. DOI: 10.1080/01292986.2020.1738511

Johnson, A. (2021). Causes and consequences of ethnic conflict in Nigeria. *International Journal of Advanced Research in Social Sciences. Environmental Studies & Technology.*, *6*(1), 32–42.

Johnson, M., & Mercer, N. (2019). Using sociocultural discourse analysis to analyse professional discourse. *Learning, Culture and Social Interaction*, *21*, 267–277. DOI: 10.1016/j.lcsi.2019.04.003

Jones, P., Turney, A., Georgiou, H., & Nielsen, W. (2020). Assessing multimodal literacies in science: Semiotic and practical insights from pre-service teacher education. *Language and Education*, *34*(2), 153–172. DOI: 10.1080/09500782.2020.1720227

Josefsson, J., Sandin, B., Hanson, K., & Balagopalan, S. (2023). Representing children. In: Sandin, B., Josefsson, J., Hanson, K. Balagopalan, S. (eds). *The politics of children's rights and representation.* Palgrave. 1-28. DOI: 10.1007/978-3-031-04480-9_1

Karagevrekis, M. (2012). Multimodal text analysis of three modern Greek printed advertisements employing the persuasive modes of *Ethos, Logos and Pathos*. In Bowcher, W. L., & Royce, T. D. (Eds.), *Multimodal text from around the world: cultural and linguistic insights* (pp. 69–96). Palgrave Macmillan. DOI: 10.1057/9780230355347_4

Karagülle, A. E. (2015). *Günümüzde değişen mahremiyet algısının sosyal ağlar bağlamında incelenmesi* [Master's Thesis, Sosyal Bilimler Enstitüsü].

Karslı, B., & Aycan, S. (2020). Instagram ve Mahremiyet: Dindar Muhafazakâr Kadınların Paylaşımları Örneği. *Turkish Academic Research Review*, *5*(2), 245–266. DOI: 10.30622/tarr.725695

Kasneci, G., Bicakci, T., & Kursun, O. (2023). Disruptive tools for teaching, learning, and supporting students: The potential of ChatGPT-3.5 and ChatGPT-4. *Journal of Educational Technology & Society*, *26*(1), 147–156.

Kasper, G., & Wagner, J. (2014). Conversation analysis in applied linguistics. *Annual Review of Applied Linguistics*, *34*(1), 171–212. DOI: 10.1017/S0267190514000014

Kastanakis, M. N., & Voyer, B. G. (2014). The effect of culture on perception and cognition: A conceptual framework. *Journal of Business Research*, *67*(4), 425–433. DOI: 10.1016/j.jbusres.2013.03.028

Katsumata, Y. (2022). How many more emoji do we need. In Cammaerts, B., & McCambridge, L. (Eds.), *Innovations in emoji communication* (pp. 80–94). Springer.

Kaye, L. K., & Toronto, A. (2019). Emoji use in social media: A comparative analysis of age differences in emoji interpretation. *In Journal of Social Media Studies,* 5(1), 15-32.

Keen, A. (2010). Why we must resist the temptation of web 2.0. In Szoka, B., & Marcus, A. (Eds.), *The next digital decade: Essays on the future of the internet* (pp. 51–56). Techfreedom.

Kelly, M. (2023). The Representation of Interpretative Knowledge in Cultural Heritage Research (Doctoral dissertation, University of Brighton).

Kenechukwu, S. A., Ogah, A., & Ifeanyichukwu, A. C. (2022). Health Information and Users' Beliefs: A Study of Herbal Medicine Users' Attitudes to Efficacy of Herbal Medicine. [IJCRH]. *International Journal of Current Research in the Humanities, 26*(1), 293–304. DOI: 10.4314/ijcrh.v26i1.17

Kerestecioğlu, İ. Ö. (2014). Mahremiyetin Fethi: İdeal Aile Kurgularından İdeal Aile Politikalarına. *Başka Bir Aile Anlayışı Mümkün mü?* 10.

Ketabi, S., & Najafian, M. (2011). Advertising social semiotic representation: A critical approach. [Macrothink Institute.]. *International Journal of Industrial Marketing, 1*(1), 63–78.

Khan, A. (2024). The Language of Power: Discourse Analysis and the Politics of Representation. *Liberal Journal of Language & Literature Review, 2*(01), 22–31.

KhosraviNik, M. (2010). Actor descriptions, action attributions, and argumentation: Towards a systematization of CDA analytical categories in the representation of social groups. *Critical Discourse Studies, 7*(1), 55–72. DOI: 10.1080/17405900903453948

KhosraviNik, M. (2013). Critical discourse analysis, power, and new media discourse. In Kalyango, Y., & Kopytowska, M. W. (Eds.), *Why Discourse Matters: Negotiating Identity in the Mediatized World* (pp. 287–305). Peter Lang.

Kilic, O. (2023). "Every Parade of Ours is a Pride Parade": Exploring LGBTI+ digital activism in Turkey. *Sexualities, 26*(7), 731–747. DOI: 10.1177/13634607211060510

Kır, İ. (2011). Toplumsal bir kurum olarak ailenin işlevleri. *Elektronik sosyal bilimler dergisi, 10*(36), 381-404.

Kire, K., & Rajkumar, P. (2017). Culture influence on consumer behavior. *IJARIIE,* 3, 6121.

Kolkmann, J. (2016). *The pragmatics of possession: Issues in the interpretation of pre-nominal possessives in English.* A PhD Thesis, University of Manchester.

Konrad, A., Herring, S. C., & Choi, D. (2020). sticker and emoji use in facebook messenger: Implications for graphicon change. *Journal of Computer-Mediated Communication*, *25*(3), 217–235. DOI: 10.1093/jcmc/zmaa003

Kontentino: Social media Dictionary. Kontentino.com

Korkmaz, İ. (2013). Facebook ve mahremiyet: Görmek ve gözetle (n) mek. *Yalova Sosyal Bilimler Dergisi, 3*(5).

Korth, C. E. (2025). Democratic Schooling Practices: A Path for Increasing DEIJB in International Schools. In Diversity and Inclusion Challenges for Leaders of International Schools (pp. 337-382). IGI Global Scientific Publishing.

Koutsogiannis, D., & Mitsikopoulou, B. (2004). The internet as a glocal discourse environment: A commentary on Lam and Bloch. *Language Learning & Technology*, *8*, 83–89.

Krasnova, H., Günther, O., Spiekermann, S., & Koroleva, K. (2009). Privacy concerns and identity in online social networks. *Identity in the Information Society*, *2*(1), 39–63. DOI: 10.1007/s12394-009-0019-1

Kress, G., & van Leeuwen, T. (1996/2006) *Reading Images*. Routledge.Tailor and Francis. (pp.114-154).

Kress, G. (2003). *Literacy in the new media age*. Routledge.

Kress, G. (2010). Multimodality: A social semiotic approach to contemporary communication. *Journal of Pragmatics*, *43*(14), 3624–3626.

Kress, G. (2010). *Multimodality: A social semiotic approach to contemporary communication*. Routledge.

Kress, G. (2010). *Multimodality: A Social Semiotic Approach to Contemporary Communication*. Routledge.

Kress, G. (2010). *Multimodality: A Social Semiotics approach to Contemporary Communication*. Routledge.

Kress, G., & Van Leeuwen, T. (1996). *Reading images*. Routledge.

Kress, G., & van Leeuwen, T. (1996). *Reading images: the grammar of visual design*. Routledge.

Kress, G., & van Leeuwen, T. (1996). *Reading images: The grammar of visual design*. Routledge.

Kress, G., & van Leeuwen, T. (2001). *Multimodal discourse- The modes and media of contemporary communication*. Edward Arnold.

Kress, G., & van Leeuwen, T. (2001). *Multimodal discourse: The modes and media of contemporary communication*. Oxford University Press.

Kress, G., & van Leeuwen, T. (2006). *Reading images: the grammar of visual Design* (2nd ed.). Routledge Taylor & Francis Group. DOI: 10.4324/9780203619728

Kress, G., & van Leeuwen, T. (2020). *Reading Images: The Grammar of Visual Design*. Routledge. DOI: 10.4324/9781003099857

Kreuter, M. W., & Wray, R. J. (2003). Tailored and targeted health communication: Strategies for enhancing information relevance. *American Journal of Health Behavior*, *27*(3), S227–S232. DOI: 10.5993/AJHB.27.1.s3.6 PMID: 14672383

Krippendorff, K. (2018). *Content analysis: An introduction to its methodology*. Sage publications.

Kroskrity, P. V. (1999). 'Identity'. *Journal of Linguistic Anthropology*, *9*(1-2), 111–114. DOI: 10.1525/jlin.1999.9.1-2.111

Kuran, T., & Sandholm, W. H. (2008). Cultural integration and its discontents. *The Review of Economic Studies*, *75*(1), 201–228. DOI: 10.1111/j.1467-937X.2007.00469.x

Kwon, P. (2013). Resilience in lesbian, gay, and bisexual individuals. *Personality and Social Psychology Review*, *17*(4), 371–383. DOI: 10.1177/1088868313490248 PMID: 23904452

Kymlicka, W. (2001). *Politics in the vernacular: nationalism, multiculturalism, and citizenship*. Oxford University Press. DOI: 10.1093/0199240981.001.0001

Laguaite, M. (2023). 9 Best communication technology examples to explore. https://yoodli.ai/blog/9-best-communication-technology-examples-to-explore

Lam, C., Zhou, K., Loong, H., Chung, V., Ngan, C., & Cheung, Y. (2023). The Use of Traditional, Complementary, and Integrative Medicine in Cancer: Data-Mining Study of 1 Million Web-Based Posts from Health Forums and Social Media Platforms. *Journal of Medical Internet Research*, *25*, e45408. DOI: 10.2196/45408 PMID: 37083752

Larsson, S. (2014). Battling Mainstream Media, Commentators and Organized Debaters Experiences from Citizens' Online Opinion Writing in Sweden. *Nordicom Review*, *35*(2), 77–89. DOI: 10.2478/nor-2014-0016

Lazar, M. (2017). Homonationalist discourse as a politics of pragmatic resistance in Singapore's Pink Dot movement: Towards a southern praxis. *Journal of Sociolinguistics*, *21*(3), 420–441. DOI: 10.1111/josl.12239

Ledin, P., & Machin, D. (2020). *Introduction to Multimodal Analysis*. Bloomsbury Publishing. DOI: 10.5040/9781350069176

Lee, A., Poch, R., Shaw, M., & Williams, R. (2012). Engaging Diversity in Undergraduate Classrooms: A Pedagogy for Developing Intercultural Competence [John Wiley & Sons.]. *ASHE Higher Education Report*, *38*(2), •••.

Leedy, P. D., & Ormrod, J. E. (2015). *Practical research: Planning and design* (11th ed.). Pearson.

Lemke, J. (1998). Multiplying meaning: visual and verbal semiotics in scientific text. In Martin, J. R., & Veel, R. (Eds.), *Reading Science* (pp. 87–113). Routledge.

Lenhart, A,; Fallow, D. & Horrigan, J.(2004) Content creation online. Pew internet and American life project. Archived from the original on 12 January, 2014

Lenin, J. (2023). *Alliances of Lions: Power and the Politics of Coalitions*. https://roundglasssustain.com/columns/lion-alliances

Leonardi, V. (2022). Communication challenges and transformations in the digital era: Emoji language and emoji translation. *Language and Semiotic Studies*, *8*(3), 22–44. DOI: 10.1515/lass-2022-2003

Lev M. (2021). The Language of New Media

Ley, B. (2009). Vive lea Roses! The Architecture of Commitment in an Online Pregnancy ad Nursing Group. *Journal of Computer-Mediated Communication*, *12*(4), 1388–1408. DOI: 10.1111/j.1083-6101.2007.00378.x

Liang, W. J., & Lim, F. V. (2024). Representing youth as vulnerable social media users: A social semiotic analysis of the promotional materials from The Social Dilemma. *Semiotica*, *2024*(256), 153–174. DOI: 10.1515/sem-2023-0047

Li, D. (2016). Multimodal discourse analysis of the interpersonal meaning of TV advertisements. *International Journal of Social Science and Humanity*, *6*(12), 934–938. DOI: 10.18178/ijssh.2016.V6.776

Li, H., & Xu, S. (2020). Cultural influences on the interpretation of online communication. *Social Media Studies*, *8*(1), 79–96. DOI: 10.1080/20421338.2020.1731107

Lirola, M. M. (2006). A systemic functional analysis of two multimodal covers. ***Revista avicantina de Estutios Ingleses*, 19(2), 226-249.**

Liu, K. (2022). *Identity construction online: Identities and ideologies in reader comments in online news fora* (Doctoral dissertation, Open Access Te Herenga Waka-Victoria University of Wellington).

Liu, Y., Zhang, L., Ma, X., Zhang, S., Li, L., & Zhou, Z. (2022a). ChatGPT: An advanced system for efficient handling of complex queries. *Journal of Artificial Intelligence*, *15*(2), 45–58.

Liu, Y., Zhang, L., Ma, X., Zhang, S., Li, L., & Zhou, Z. (2022b). The intelligent design of ChatGPT for efficient handling of complex queries. *AI Communications*, *35*(3), 146–156.

Li, Y., Wang, X., Lin, X., & Hajli, M. (2018). Seeking and sharing health information on social media: A net valence model and cross-cultural comparison. *Technological Forecasting and Social Change*, *126*, 28–40. DOI: 10.1016/j.techfore.2016.07.021

López-Vázquez, M., & López-Ruiz, S. (2024). A comprehensive examination of emoji usage in Mexican Spanish WhatsApp corpus: A mixed-methods linguistic approach. *Quality & Quantity*, *58*(6), 1–26. DOI: 10.1007/s11135-024-01898-7

Lorenzini, J., & Giugni, M. (2010). Youth coping with unemployment: The role of social support. *Revue Suisse de Travail Social*, *11*, 80–99.

Lorenzo-Dus, N., Evans, M., & Mullineux-Morgan, T. (2023). *Online child sexual grooming discourse*. Cambridge University Press. DOI: 10.1017/9781009314626

Lotfy, N. E. (2024). Cringe humor in Egyptian TikTok: Multimodal Critical Discourse Analysis of Selected Comic strips. *Multimodal Communication*, *13*(1), 65–78. DOI: 10.1515/mc-2024-0004

Lund, M., Narasimhan, K., Joulin, A., & Malik, J. (2023). OpenAI's Machine Learning Tools: DALL-E and ChatGPT. Retrieved from https://www.example.com/openai-tools

Lund, M., Jørgensen, L., & Hansen, J. (2023). Significant improvements in reasoning and conciseness of ChatGPT-4. *Journal of Natural Language Processing*, *32*(1), 23–34.

Lu, Y. (2024). Multimodal discourse analysis of the promotional film Countdown: Beginning of Spring for the opening ceremony of Beijing Winter Olympics. *International Journal of Language. Literature and Culture*, *4*(4). Advance online publication. DOI: 10.22161/ijllc.4.4.2

Machin, D. (2013). What is multimodal critical discourse studies? *Critical Discourse Studies*, *10*(4), 347–355. DOI: 10.1080/17405904.2013.813770

Machin, D., & Mayr, A. (2023). *How to do critical discourse analysis: A multimodal introduction*. SAGE Publication.

Machin, D., & Polzer, L. (2015). *Visual journalism*. Palgrave Macmillan. DOI: 10.5040/9781350394674

Machin, D., & van Leeuwen, T. (2007). *Global media Discourse: A Critical Introduction*. Routledge. DOI: 10.4324/9780203007471

Madan, A., & Rosca, M. I. (2021). Current Trends in Digital Marketing Communication. Journal of Marketing Research and Case Studies https://ibimapublishing .com/articles/JMRCS/2022/981169/ Vol. 2022 (2022), Article ID 981169, 13 pages, ISSN: 2165-7009 DOI: DOI: 10.5171/2022.981169

Maikanti, S., Chukwu, A., Odibah, M., & Ogu, M. (2021). Globalization as a factor for language endangerment: Nigerian indigenous languages in focus. *Malaysian Journal of Social Sciences and Humanities*, *6*(9), 521–527. DOI: 10.47405/mjssh.v6i9.1055

Maloney, D., Freeman, G., & Wohn, D. Y. (2020). "Talking without a voice": Understanding Non-verbal communication in social virtual reality. *Proceedings of the ACM on Human-Computer Interaction, (*4)1–25. DOI: 10.1145/3415246

Marcum, C., & Harris, M. (2013). The training page: Plain language posters. Retrieved September 3, 2024 from https://irp.nih.gov/catalyst/22/3/thetrainingpage plainlanguageposters

Marrington, J. Z., March, E., Murray, S., Jeffries, C., Machin, T., & March, S. (2023). An exploration of trolling behaviours in Australian adolescents: An online survey. *PLoS One*, *18*(4), e0284378. DOI: 10.1371/journal.pone.0284378 PMID: 37043467

Marshall, J. P. (2014). Gender in online communication. In *Handbook of research on new literacies* (pp. 491–520). Routledge.

Martin, E. (2006). *Marketing identities through language: English and global imagery in French Advertising*. Palgrave Macmillan. DOI: 10.1057/9780230511903

Martinec, R. (1998). Cohesion in action. *Semiotica*, *120*(1/2), 161–180. DOI: 10.1515/semi.1998.120.1-2.161

Martinec, R., & Salway's, A. (2005). A system for image–text relations in new (and old) media. *Visual Communication*, *4*(3), 337–371. DOI: 10.1177/1470357205055928

Martin, J. R. (2020). Revisiting field: Specialized knowledge in secondary school science and humanities discourse. In Martin, J. R., Maton, K., & Doran, Y. (Eds.), *Accessing academic discourse: Systemic functional linguistics and legitimation code theory* (pp. 114–148). Routledge.

Marwan, W. M. (2022). Traditional media versus social media: Challenges and opportunities. *Technium*, *4*(10), 145–160. DOI: 10.47577/technium.v4i10.8012

Marwick, A. E. (2013). *Status update: Celebrity, publicity, and branding in the social media age*. Yale University Press.

Maseko, S. (2020). #AmINext: A multimodal analysis of Twitter activism against gender-based violence in South Africa. *Journal of African Media Studies*, *12*(1), 1–15.

Mastamet-Mason, A., Sokhetye, P. N., & Tilahum, Y. D. (2024). Female body beauty ideals and their impact on fashion size standards: A comparative study of Western and South African perspectives. In *International Conference on Multidisciplinary Research* (Vol. 2024, pp. 205-221). DOI: 10.26803/MyRes.2024.15

Matfess, H. (2017). *Boko Haram: history and context*. Oxford Research Encyclopedia of African History.

Mavuru, L., & Ramnarain, U. (2020). Learners' socio-cultural backgrounds and science teaching and learning: A case study of township schools in South Africa. *Cultural Studies of Science Education*, *15*(4), 1067–1095. DOI: 10.1007/s11422-020-09974-8

Mbarachi & Okoro (2016) Language and technology: emerging trends in Nigeria's digital discourse. *Review of Arts and social sciences* *5*(5), 38-45

McNeil, S. G., Robin, B. R., & Miller, R. M. (2000). Facilitating interaction, communication and collaboration in online courses. *Computers & Geosciences*, *26*(6), 699–708. DOI: 10.1016/S0098-3004(99)00106-5

McPhail, T. L. (2002). *Global communication: Theories, stakeholders and trends*. Allyn and Bacon.

McQuaid, R., Lindsay, C., & Greig, M. (2004). 'Reconnecting'the Unemployed Information and communication technology and services for jobseekers in rural areas. *Information Communication and Society*, *7*(3), 364–388. DOI: 10.1080/1369118042000284605

Meghdari, S., & Sobhari, M. (2016). Multimedia discourse analysis of Tehran and Shiraz commercial advertising. *Journal of Linguistics & Khorasan Dialects Biannual*, *8*(2), 19–23.

Mehra, B., Merkel, C., & Bishop, A. (2004). The Internet for Empowerment of Minority and Marginalized Users. *New Media & Society*, *6*(6), 781–802. DOI: 10.1177/146144804047513

Melo, P., Couto, J. M., Kansaon, D., Mafra, V., Reis, J., & Benevenuto, F. (2024). A Sticker is Worth a Thousand Words: Characterizing the Use of Stickers in WhatsApp Political Groups in Brazil. arXiv preprint arXiv:2406.08429.

Mercer, N. (2004). Sociocultural discourse analysis. *Journal of applied linguistics, 1*(2), 137-168.

Merriram-Webster Dictionary. (2024). *Hegemony*. Retrieved October 11, 2024, from http://www.merriram-webster dictionary.com

Meyer, A., Jones, B., & Patel, R. (2023). Digital paradoxes: Inclusion and exclusion in online spaces. *Technology and Society Journal*, *28*(1), 45–67.

Meyer, I. H. (2015). Resilience in the study of minority stress and health of sexual and gender minorities. *Psychology of Sexual Orientation and Gender Diversity*, *2*(3), 209–213. DOI: 10.1037/sgd0000132

Meza, V. X., & Park, H. W. (2014). Globalization of cultural products: A webometric analysis of Kpop in Spanish-speaking countries. *Quality & Quantity*, *49*(4), 1345–1360. DOI: 10.1007/s11135-014-0047-2

Milani, T. (2013). Expanding the queer linguistic scene. Multimodality, space and sexuality at a South African University. *Journal of Language and Sexuality*, *2*(2), 206–234. DOI: 10.1075/jls.2.2.02mil

Miller, J. E. (2007). Preparing and presenting effective research posters. *Health Services Research*, 42(1 I), 311–328.

Millhouse, N. T. (2024) Self-Presentations on Social Network Sites: Emerging Adults and their Personas. Doctoral dissertation, University of Newcastle, UK.

Ministry of Foreign Affairs. (2022). *Nigeria culture and heritage*. Retrieved October 11, 2024, from http://www.foreignaffairs.gov.ng

Miranda, J. W. P., Bueo, D. H. R., & DeSouza, R. C. G. (2016). A Qualitative Approach to Develop Niche Social Media. *Proceedings of the 18th International Conference on Enterprise Information,* Vol. 2, 265 – 272.

Miron-Shatz, T., Hansen, M. M., Grajales, F. J., III, Martin-Sanchez, F., & Bamidis, P. D. (2013). Social Media for the Promotion of Holistic Self-Participatory Care: An Evidence Based Approach. IMIA Yearbook 2013 8: 162-168. https://repository .usfca.edu/cgi/viewcontent.cgi?article=1027&context=nursing_fac

Mistry, V. (2011). Critical care training: Using Twitter as a teaching tool. *British Journal of Nursing (Mark Allen Publishing), 20*(20), 1292–1296. DOI: 10.12968/bjon.2011.20.20.1292 PMID: 22068003

Mlynář, J. (2014). Language and collective memory: Insights from social theory. *Slovenská Politologická Revue, 3*, 217–236.

Modzelewski, R. (2013). Virtual togetherness: sense of identity and community in cyberspace. *A Journal of English Studies, 1.*

Mokoena, M. M., & Simelane-Mnisi, S. (2024). Establishing the Reliability and Validity of the Teacher Self-Efficacy Questionnaire in the Use of the Interactive Whiteboard: A South African Sample Perspective. *Public Administration and Development Alternatives (IPADA)*, 128.

Morgan, S. (2018). Fake news, disinformation, manipulation and online tactics to undermine democracy. *Journal of Cyber Policy, 3*(1), 39–43. DOI: 10.1080/23738871.2018.1462395

Motito, F., Nwabudike, C., & Oni, F. (2025). Code-mixing in the gospel songs of some Nigerian music artistes. *An International Refereed Research Journal of English Studies and Culture, 13*, 90–107.

Motschenbacher, H. (2020). Walking on Wilton Drive: A linguistic landscape analysis of a homonormative space. *Language & Communication, 72*, 25–43. DOI: 10.1016/j.langcom.2020.02.002

Mpontshane, N. (2022) A Visual Analysis of 2019's #AmINext? Movement. University of Pretoria (South Africa) Pro Quest Dissertations & Theses. DOI:DOI: 10.25403/UPresearchdata.21756938

Muali, C. (2017). Rasionalitas Konsepsi Budaya Nusantara Dalam Menggagas Pendidikan Karakter Bangsa Multikultural. *Jurnal Islam Nusantara, 1*(1), 105–117. DOI: 10.33852/jurnalin.v1i1.64

Muhammad, A., Egye, A. U., & Etim, P. P. (2023). Electoral process and national integration in Nigeria: An analysis of 2019 general election. *International Journal of Research and Innovation in Social Science*, *7*(4), 250–262. DOI: 10.47772/IJRISS.2023.7420

Mullins, E., Kirkwood, S., & Stokoe, E. (2022). An introduction to conversation analysis in social work research. *Qualitative Social Work: Research and Practice*, *22*(2), 457–475. DOI: 10.1177/14733250221132239

Mure an, V. (2020). Re-defining communicative competence for multi-modal communication in the digital age. *Journal of Romanian Literary Studies*, *23*, 315–323.

Murthy, D. (2018). Introduction to social media, activism, and organizations. *Social Media+ Society* 4(1): 1-14. 2056305117750716. DOI: 10.1177/2056305117750716

Muswede, T., & Lubinga, E. (2018). Global media hegemony and the transformation bliss in post colonial Africa: Real independence or change of masters. *African Journal of Public Affairs*, *10*(2), 82–96.

Myers, G. (2013). Stance-taking and public discussion in blogs. In *Self-Mediation* (pp. 55–67). Routledge.

Naidu, E. (2023, February 24). Leading academics believe fears over ChatGPT are misplaced. University World News. https://www.universityworldnews.com/post.php?story=20230224114237209

Nair, M. (2012). Nā ya, rasa, and abhinaya as semiotic principles in classical Indian theatre. *De Gruyter*. Retrieved from https://www.degruyter.com/document/doi/10.1515/sem-2012-0042/pdf

Nash, B. L., Dunham, H., Murdter-Atkinson, J., & Mosley Wetzel, M. (2023). A Culturally Sustaining Approach to Multimodal Literacies: Building from Students' Funds of Knowledge in Field-Based Teacher Education. *Literacy Research and Instruction*, *63*(2), 151–175. DOI: 10.1080/19388071.2022.2153766

Natalia, F. (2024). Use of Social Networks by Tourist Enterprises at the Current Stage. *The Scientific Issues of Ternopil Volodymyr Hnatiuk National Pedagogical University Series Geography*, *56*(1), 143–150. DOI: 10.25128/2519-4577.24.1.17

Nautiyal, S., Patil, A., & Rao, S. (2023). ChatGPT: A promising AI-powered assistant for universities worldwide. *International Journal of Intelligent Systems and Applications in Engineering*, *11*(2), 76–83.

Neel, L. A., McKechnie, J. G., Robus, C. M., & Hand, C. J. (2023). Emoji alter the perception of emotion in affectively neutral text messages. *Journal of Nonverbal Behavior*, *47*(1), 83–97. DOI: 10.1007/s10919-022-00421-6

Neuendorf, K. A. (2017). *The content analysis guidebook.* sage.

Newman, N. (2011). *Mainstream media of the distribution of news in the age of social discovery*. Reuters Institute.

NFI (National Film Institute). (2023). What is Bollywood? Everything you need to know. Retrieved from https://www.nfi.edu/what-is-bollywood/

Ngangfen, D. A. (2014). E-Commerce in Cameroon: Retrieved from https://www.foretiafoundation.org/wp-content/uploads/2014/03/E-Commerce-Article.pdf on 10th of January, 2025

Ngare, L. L. (2023). Globalization, cultural identity and social cohesion: a Nigerian philosophical perspective. *AKU: An African Journal of Contemporary Research*, 4(4).

Ng, J. Y., Verhoeff, N., & Steen, J. (2023). What are the ways in which social media is used in the context of complementary and alternative medicine in the health and medical scholarly literature? a scoping review. *BMC Complementary Medicine and Therapies*, *23*(1), 32. DOI: 10.1186/s12906-023-03856-6 PMID: 36732809

Nguyen, H., Bui, T., & Tran, M. (2023). The rapid evolution of online communication: A case study of emerging technologies. *Journal of Digital Innovation*, *8*(4), 132–145. DOI: 10.1016/j.jdi.2023.03.010

Ngwa, M. C., Ihekweazu, C., Okwor, T., Yennan, S., Williams, N., Elimian, K., Karaye, N. Y., Bello, I. W., & Sack, D. A. (2021). The cholera risk assessment in Kano State, Nigeria: A historical review, mapping of hotspots and evaluation of contextual factors. *PLoS Neglected Tropical Diseases*, *15*(1), 1–19 e0009046. DOI: 10.1371/journal.pntd.0009046 PMID: 33465091

Nigeria, J. www.jumia.com.ng

Nike News. (2021). *Nike creates Nikeland on Roblox.*https://news.nike.com/news/five-things-to-know-roblox

Norman, A. (2023). Educational technology for reading instruction in developing countries: A systematic literature review. *Review of Education*, *11*(3), e3423. DOI: 10.1002/rev3.3423

Nwogu, C. U. K. (2019). Affiliate marketing concept and performance of online businesses in Nigeria. *Journal of Marketing and Consumer Research*, *52*. Advance online publication. DOI: 10.7176/JMCR

Nzeaka, E. (2023). Media policies and control under colonial and military regimes in Nigeria. *Global Media Journal*, *21*, 61.

O'Brien, M. (2019). The personal and contextual nature of emoji use: Implications for digital communication. *Journal of Language and Social Psychology*, *38*(4), 476–492.

O'Connor, P., & P.W. (2017). Emoji and the politics of meaning in digital communication. *Journal of Language and Politics*, *16*(1), 1–21.

O'Halloran, K. L., Tan, S. and MKL, E. (2014). A multimodal approach to discourse, context and culture. *Discourse in Context*, 247-272

O'Halloran, K. (2004). *Multimodal Discourse Analysis: Systematic Functional Perspectives*. Continuum.

O'Halloran, K. (2011). Multimodal discourse analysis. In Hyland, K., & Paltridge, B. (Eds.), *The Bloomsbury Companion to Discourse Analysis* (pp. 120–137). Bloomsbury.

O'Halloran, K., Tan, S., Smith, B., & Podlasov, A. (2009, September). *Digital semiotics* [Paper presentation]. *10th World Congress of Semiotics*, A Coruña, Spain.

O'Hara, K. E. (2013). Lev Vygotsky. *The Praeger handbook of education and psychology, 1*, 240-245.

O'Keeffe, A., Clancy, B., & Adolphs, S. (2020). *Introducing pragmatics in use*. Routledge.

O'Keeffe, G. S., & Clarke-Pearson, K. (2011). The impact of social media on children, adolescents, and families. *Pediatrics*, *127*(4), 800–804. DOI: 10.1542/peds.2011-0054 PMID: 21444588

O'Neill, D., & Millar, F. (2021). Power structures and inequality in digital spaces. *Journal of Digital Media & Policy*, *12*(1), 45–65. DOI: 10.1386/jdmp_00036_1

Oakley, M., Farr, R. H., & Scherer, D. G. (2016). Same-Sex Parent Socialization: Understanding Gay and Lesbian Parenting Practices as Cultural Socialization. *Journal of GLBT Family Studies*, *13*(1), 56–75. DOI: 10.1080/1550428X.2016.1158685

Oba, D., & Berger, J. (2023). How communication mediums shape the message. *Journal of Consumer Psychology*, *34*(3), 406–424. DOI: 10.1002/jcpy.1372

Obi-Ani, N. A., Anikwenze, C., & Isiani, M. C. (2020). Social media and the covid-19 experience: Observations from Nigeria. *Cogent Arts & Humanities*, *7*(1), 1799483. Advance online publication. Retrieved October 15, 2024, from. DOI: 10.1080/23311983.2020.1799483

Oceja, J., & Álvarez-Álvarez, C. (2025). From Twitch to YouTube Live: A systematic literature review of streaming in higher education. *Electronic Journal of e-Learning*, *23*(1), 53–65. DOI: 10.34190/ejel.23.1.3702

Ochs, E. (1992). Indexing Gender. In Duranti, A., & Goodwin, C. (Eds.), *Rethinking Context: Language as an Interactive Phenomenon* (pp. 335–358). Cambridge University Press.

Odebunmi, A. (2006). *Meaning in English: An introduction*. Critical Sphere.

Odebunmi, A. (2013). Participation configuration in a Nigerian university campus. *Pragmatics & Cognition*, *20*(1), 186–215. DOI: 10.1075/pc.20.1.08ode

Odinye, O., & Odinye, O. (2012). Western influence on Chinese and Nigerian cultures. *Ogirisi: A New. Journal of African Studies*, *9*, 108–115.

Oduola, L. & Durosinmi, M.O. (2018). Entrepreneurship in selected advertisements products in Bigeria: a multimodal discourse analytical perspective, *Journal of Issues in Language and Literary Studies,* 4(1) & 5(1), 72-87

Oehrle, E. (1996). Intercultural education through music: Towards a culture of tolerance. *British Journal of Music Education*, *13*(2), 95–100. DOI: 10.1017/S0265051700003077

Ofei, E. K., Agbukor, L. A., Okunorobo, E. P., & Eseoghene, E. (2024). A review of social media as alternative medium for political participation. *International Journal of Research Publication and Reviews*, *5*(1), 489–497. DOI: 10.55248/gengpi.5.0124.0116

Ogbogbo, A. (2023). Directive Speech Acts as a Communication Strategy in the Social Media Posts of Traditional Medicine Providers in Southwest Nigeria. *NIU Journal of Humanities*, *8*(1), 7–16. DOI: 10.58709/niujhu.v8i1.1567

Ogen, O. (2024). *Reconstructing a silenced past: Echoes of revisionism and counter hegemonic history* (21st Inaugural Lecture). Osogbo, Nigeria: Osun State University.

Ojomo, O., & Sodeinde, O. A. (2021). Social Media Skits: Reshaping the Entertainment Experience of Broadcast Audience. *SAGE Open*, *11*(3), 21582440211032176. Advance online publication. DOI: 10.1177/21582440211032176

Ojukwu, E. V. (2017). Relevance of music in social stability and security challenges in Nigeria. *AFRREV IJAH An International Journal of Arts and Humanities*, *6*(2), 98–105. DOI: 10.4314/ijah.v6i3.8

Okafor, P. S., & Nnubia, U. E. (2013). The Nigerian child and national development: A philosophical appraisal. *Journal of Educational and Social Research*, *3*(4), 103–107. DOI: 10.5901/jesr.2013.v3n4p103

Olaitan, T. (2021). *Modernising the primitive African: The influence of colonialism on African dressing*. Retrieved October 11, 2024, from https://www.decolonialthoughts.com/post/modernising-the-primitive-african-the-influence-of-colonialism-on-african-dressing

Olajimbiti, E. O. (2022). Pragmatic function of Twitter handlers' perspectives on children discourse in Nigeria. *The Journal of Medical Research*, *15*, 91–104. DOI: 10.24193/jmr.42.6

Olajimbiti, E. O. (2023). Ideological construction of deviance in street children's discourse in Southwestern Nigeria. *Journal for Discourse Studies*, *1*, 10–30.

Olaleye, O. S., & Ajuwon, A. (2022). Influence of the use of social-media and exposure to pornography on the sexual behaviour of youths in selected tertiary institutions in southwest Nigeria. *Health Behavior Research*, *5*(3), 1–19. DOI: 10.4148/2572-1836.1137

Ola, O., & Sedig, K. (2020). Understanding Discussions of Health Issues on Twitter: A Visual Analytic Study. *Online Journal of Public Health Informatics*, *12*(1), e2. DOI: 10.5210/ojphi.v12i1.10321 PMID: 32577151

Olapegba, P. O., Ayandele, O., Kolawole, S. O., Oguntayo, R., Gandi, J. C., Dangiwa, A. L., Ottu, I. F., & Iorfa, S. K. (2020). A Preliminary assessment of novel coronavirus (COVID-19) knowledge and perceptions in Nigeria. SSRN *Electronic Journal*, 1-14. DOI: 10.2139/ssrn.3584408

Olateju, M. A. (2004). *Discourse analysis: Analysing discourse in the ESL classroom*. Obafemi Awolowo University Press.

Olateju, M., & Oyebode, O. (2014). *Introducing multimodality*. College Press and Publishers Limited.

Olateju, M., Oyebode, O., & Ademilokun, M. (2014). *Doing multimodal discourse analysis*. College Press and Publishers Limited.

Olsen, D. (2024). *Media Arts Education: Transforming Education through Multimodal Cognition, Holistic Learning, and Techno-Embodiment.* Taylor & Francis. DOI: 10.4324/9781003430834

Omoera, O. S., Awosola, R. K., Okhakhu, M. A., & Eregare, E. A. (2011). Seeking solutions: Of radio/ television advertisement and patients/non-patients' perception of traditional medicine in Edo State, Nigeria. *The International Journal of Research and Review*, *6*(1), 48–64.

Onadipe-Shalom, T.A. (2020). Endangered language and culture: The gradual loss of greetings among Yoruba children in southwestern Nigeria. *Ò pá bàta,* 1-7.

Onah, N., & Christian, N. G. (2014). The moral implication of social media phenomenon in Nigeria. *Mediterranean Journal of Social Sciences*, *5*(20), 2231–2237. DOI: 10.5901/mjss.2014.v5n20p2231

Onanuga, P. (2022). Weaponising Digital Architecture: Queer Nigerian Instagram Users and Digital Visual Activism. Deborah Woodman (Ed.) LGBT+ Communities: Creating Spaces of Identity. IntechOpen. Pp 79 – 101.

Onanuga, P. (2020). Coming Out and Reaching Out: Linguistic Advocacy on Queer Nigerian Twitter. *Journal of African Cultural Studies*, *33*(4), 489–504. DOI: 10.1080/13696815.2020.1806799

Onanuga, P. A. (2024). Asserting identity in stifling spaces: Multisemioticity in Nigerian queer-positive Instagram. *Social Dynamics*, *1*, 1–25. DOI: 10.1080/02533952.2024.2320579

Onanuga, P., & Taiwo, R. (2020). Discursive features of Nigerian online Ponzi schemes' narratives. *ELOPE: English Language Overseas Perspectives and Enquiries*, *17*(2), 61–82. DOI: 10.4312/elope.17.2.61-82

Onuma, N & Ogboji, J. (2023). Perceived impact of Covid-19 pandemic on academic performance of secondary school students in Abakaliki education zone of Ebonyi state. *African Journal of Education management, teaching and Entrepreneurship studies* *9*(2), 102-114

Onyejekwe, A. (2001). National identity: peoples and cultures of Nigeria. In Ajaegbo, D. I., & Ibezim, E. O. (Eds.), *Citizenship education in Nigeria: An interdisciplinary approach*. West & Solomon.

Open, A. I. (2023). ChatGPT-4 is slower than ChatGPT -3.5 but significantly improves reasoning and conciseness. Retrieved from https://openai.com/blog/chatgpt-4/

Orngu, C. (2018). The social media and Nigeria's electoral politics since 1999: Trends and implications for Nigeria's external image. *Nigerian Journal of Political and Administrative Studies*, *4*(1), 184–203.

Osaghae, E. (1998). Managing multiple minority problems in a divided society: The Nigerian experience. *The Journal of Modern African Studies*, *36*(1), 1–24. DOI: 10.1017/S0022278X9700267X

Osakwe, O. M. (2017). A case study on the causes of ethnic conflict within Nigeria. *An Independent Study Submitted for the award of Degree of Master of Arts in Peace Studies and Diplomacy to Siam University, Bangkok, Thailand.*

Osisanwo, A. (2020). Visual Representations of Newspaper Reportage of Boko Haram Terrorism in Nigeria. *American Journal of Art and Design*, *5*(4), 103–112. DOI: 10.11648/j.ajad.20200504.14

Osisanwo, A., & Akano, R. (2023). Ideological stances in Yoruba nation secessionist discourse in Nigerian virtual communities. *Language Matters (Pretoria)*, *54*(2), 104–121. DOI: 10.1080/10228195.2023.2212140

Owede Kosioma, E. (2018). Citizenship education for national integration and cohesion in Nigeria. *British Journal of Education. Learning and Development Psychology*, *1*(1), 37–45.

Owusu-Ansah, B. (2020). Digital entrepreneurship in Ghana: An exploratory study. *Journal of Small Business and Enterprise Development*, *27*(3), 419–435.

Oyadiran, P., & Adeshola, A. J. (2017). National integration and democratic consolidation in Nigeria. *African Educational Research Journal*, *5*(2), 114–119.

Oyebanji, O. F. (2022). We Are Humans: Discourse Representations of Identities in the Tweets of Nigerian LGBT People. Deborah Woodman (Ed.) *LGBT+ Communities: Creating Spaces of Identity*. IntechOpen. Pp 5-23.

Oyebanji, O. F. (2023). Illegitimation of same-sex sexualities in selected Nigerian newspapers. *Discourse & Society*, *34*(3), 273–290. DOI: 10.1177/09579265221142447

Oyebode, O. & Unuabonah, F. (2013). Coping with HIV/AIDS: A Multimodal Discourse analysis of selected HIV/AIDS posters in South-western Nigeria. *Discourse & Society,* 24(6). Sage Publications Limited.

Oyebode, O. A., & Unuabonah, F. O. (2024). *Multimodality and appraisal choices in Nigerian coronavirus-related WhatsApp memes*. Communication and the Public., DOI: 10.1177/20570473241264334

Oyebode, O., & Olateju, M. A. (2011). Imperative mood as message enhancer in billboard product adverts in Nigeria. *Òye* [Ago-Iwoye, Nigeria.]. *Ogun Journal of Arts*, *17*, 159–173.

Özbölük, T., & Kurtoğlu, R. (2019). Marketing semiotics in the digital age. In Epure, M., & Mihăeş, L. C. (Eds.), *The role of language and symbols in promotional strategies and marketing schemes* (pp. 47–64). IGI Global. DOI: 10.4018/978-1-5225-5778-4.ch003

Öztok, M. (2016). Cultural ways of constructing knowledge: The role of identities in online group discussions. *International Journal of Computer-Supported Collaborative Learning*, *11*(2), 157–186. DOI: 10.1007/s11412-016-9233-7

Özyurt, C. (2007). Durkheim sosyolojisinde ahlâkî kontrol sorunu. *Değerler Eğitimi Dergisi*, *5*(13), 95–121.

Paaßen, B., Morgenroth, T., & Stratemeyer, M. (2016). What is a true gamer? The male gamer stereotype and the marginalization of women in video game culture. *Sex Roles*, *76*(7-8), 421–435. DOI: 10.1007/s11199-016-0678-y

Paivio, A. (1990). *Mental representations: A dual coding approach.* Oxford Psychology Series., DOI: 10.1093/acprof:oso/9780195066661.001.0001

Paltridge, B. (2006). Discourse analysis: An introduction. *Continuum.*

Pandey, K. A., & Singh, N. K. (2020). Hinglish in Bollywood. *IJRAR 7*(4). www .ijrar.org

Pandey, A. C., & Kumar, N. (2012). Does emotions play as tool for battle of brands: Emotional branding. *International Journal of Research in Finance & Marketing*, *2*(2), 95–103.

Park, J. R., & El Mimouni, H. (2020). Emoticons and non-verbal communications across Arabic, English, and Korean tweets. *Global Knowledge, Memory and Communication*, *69*(8/9), 579–595. DOI: 10.1108/GKMC-02-2020-0021

Park, W., & Song, J. (2019). Between realism and constructivism: A sketch of pluralism for science education. In Herring, E., Jones, K., Kiprijanov, K., & Sellers, L. (Eds.), *The past, present, and future of integrated history and philosophy of science* (pp. 228–247). Routledge. DOI: 10.4324/9781351214827-14

Parncutt, R., & Dorfer, A. (2011). The role of music in the integration of cultural minorities. *Music and the Mind: Essays in Honour of John Sloboda*, *379*, 21. DOI: 10.1093/acprof:osobl/9780199581566.003.0019

Pavlova, A., & Berkers, P. (2020). Mental health discourse and social media: Which mechanisms of cultural power drive discourse on Twitter. *Social Science & Medicine*, *263*(1), 1–14. DOI: 10.1016/j.socscimed.2020.113250 PMID: 32862081

Pedwell, R. K., Hardy, J. A., & Rowland, S. L. (2017). Effective visual design and communication practices for research posters: Exemplars based on the theory and practice of multimedia learning and rhetoric. *Biochemistry and Molecular Biology Education*, *45*(3), 249–261. DOI: 10.1002/bmb.21034 PMID: 27925371

Pei, J., & Cheng, L. (2022). Deciphering emoji variation in courts: A social semiotic perspective. *Humanities & Social Sciences Communications*, *9*(1), 1–8. DOI: 10.1057/s41599-022-01453-5

Perren, A., & Schatz, T. (2004). Hollywood. *Communication Faculty Publications*, 2. https://scholarworks.gsu.edu/communication_facpub/2

Pershad, Y., Hangge, P. T., Albadawi, H., & Oklu, R. (2018). Social Medicine: Twitter in Healthcare. *Journal of Clinical Medicine*, *7*(6), 121. DOI: 10.3390/jcm7060121 PMID: 29843360

Peters, S., & Westerståhl, D. (2013). The semantics of possessives. *Language*, *89*(4), 713–759. DOI: 10.1353/lan.2013.0065

Petroni, S. (2019). How social media shape identities and discourses in professional digital settings: Self-communication or self-branding? In Bou-Franch, P., & Blitvich, P. G. C. (Eds.), *Analyzing digital discourse new insights and future directions* (pp. 251–281). Palgrave Macmillan. DOI: 10.1007/978-3-319-92663-6_9

Philip, T. M., & Sengupta, P. (2021). Theories of learning as theories of society: A contrapuntal approach to expanding disciplinary authenticity in computing. *Journal of the Learning Sciences*, *30*(2), 330–349. DOI: 10.1080/10508406.2020.1828089

Piaget, J. (1971). *Structuralism* (Mascler, C., Trans.). Routledge & Kegan Paul.

Pinkvilla. (2013). *Bullet Raja*: Movie review. Retrieved from https://www.pinkvilla.com/entertainment/reviews/bullet-raja-movie-review-190018

Pirini, J. (2017). Approaches to multimodal discourse analysis. ResearchGate. https://www.researchgate.net/publication/354114983_Approaches_to_Multimodal_Discourse_Analysis

Pir, N. (2024). "Dönüşen" Ve "Ötekileştiren" Muhafazakarlık: Neomuhafazakarlık. *Dicle Üniversitesi Sosyal Bilimler Enstitüsü Dergisi*, *35*(35), 123–145. DOI: 10.15182/diclesosbed.1352071

Pontecorvo, C. (1993). Forms of discourse and shared thinking. *Cognition and Instruction, 11*(3-4), 189–196. DOI: 10.1080/07370008.1993.9649019

Premium Times. (2020). Video: Police brutality in Nigeria. Retrieved from https://scholarworks.lib.csusb.edu/etd/1541/

Prosper, O.F. (2009). Global media and media products in Nigeria. *A Journal of Contemporary Research*, 6(2), 424-437.

Putra, F. E., & Afrilian, P. (2025). Visual Culture in Social Media: A Study on the Influence of Instagram on Aesthetics and Youth Culture Trends. *Asian Journal of Media and Culture*, *1*(1), 40–56. DOI: 10.63919/ajmc.v1i1.18

Quandt, T., & Kröger, S. (2014). *Multiplayer: The social aspects of digital gaming*. Routledge.

Raheem, O. (2018). Having his baby and not being his wife: The baby mama trend and marriage practices in the Nigerian entertainment industry. *African Trends*, *42*(1&2), 41–55.

Raheem, S. O., & Akande, A. T. (2019). Naming as a marker of identity on Nairaland. *African Identities*, *17*(3-4), 191–210. DOI: 10.1080/14725843.2019.1661829

Raney, M., & Zanten, E. (2018). Self-care posters serve as a low-cost option for physical activity promotion. *Health Promotion Practice*, *20*(3), 354–362. Advance online publication. DOI: 10.1177/1524839918763585 PMID: 29566577

Ravi, R., & Karmakar, M. (2023). The problem of gendered emojis in online communication platforms: A study to understand digital dependence on using emotions during pandemic. *Theory and Practice in Language Studies*, *13*(1), 257–265. DOI: 10.17507/tpls.1301.30

Recanati, F. (2004). *Literal meaning*. Cambridge University Press.

Reichelmann, A., Hawdon, J., Costello, M., Ryan, J., Blaya, C., Llorent, V., & Zych, I. (2021). Hate knows no boundaries: Online hate in six nations. *Deviant Behavior*, *42*(9), 1100–1111. DOI: 10.1080/01639625.2020.1722337

Revita, I., Zalfikhe, F. A., Boholano, H., Tuan, N. T., Huszka, B., & Datuk, Z. D. M. (2023). Emoticons unveiled: A multifaceted analysis of their linguistic impact. *JURNAL ARBITRER*, *10*(3), 260–274. DOI: 10.25077/ar.10.3.260-274.2023

Riggle, E. D., Whitman, J. S., Olson, A., Rostosky, S. S., & Strong, S. (2008). The positive aspects of being a lesbian or gay man. *Professional Psychology, Research and Practice*, *39*(2), 210–217. DOI: 10.1037/0735-7028.39.2.210

Robinson, B. A. (2016). Heteronormativity and homonormativity. In Naples, N. A. (Ed.), *The Wiley Blackwell Encyclopedia of Gender and Sexuality Studies* (pp. 1–3). John Wiley and Sons.

Robinson, L., Cotten, S. R., Ono, H., Quan-Haase, A., Mesch, G., Chen, W., & Stern, M. J. (2015). Digital inequalities and why they matter. *Information Communication and Society*, *18*(5), 569–582. DOI: 10.1080/1369118X.2015.1012532

Rodney, W. (1972). *How Europe underdeveloped Africa*. London: Bogle-L'Ouverture,.

Rojas, B. G. (2025). Code-Switching as Identity Negotiation in Multilingual Communities. *Bulletin of Language and Literature Studies*, *2*(1). Advance online publication. DOI: 10.59652/blls.v2i1.517

Rösner, L., & Krämer, N. C. (2016). Verbal venting in the social web: Effects of anonymity and group norms. *Social Media + Society*, *2*(3), 1–13. DOI: 10.1177/2056305116664220

Rudolph, J., Zhao, Y., & Zhang, Y. (2023b). ChatGPT: One Million Registered Users in Five Days and 100 Million Active Users in Under Three Months. Retrieved from https://www.example.com/chatgpt-success

Rueda-Gómez, K. L., Rodríguez-Muñiz, L. J., & Muñiz-Rodríguez, L. (2024). Factors that mediate the success of the use of online platforms to support learning: The view of university teachers. *Education and Information Technologies*, *29*(2), 2459–2482. DOI: 10.1007/s10639-023-11916-0

Rushanova, N. B., Kalibekuly, D., Zhanibek, A. B., Nurmanova, M. S., & Alimberdi, L. A. (2024). Cultural aspects of media communications in the digital age. *Серия Журналистики*, *71*(1), 80–91. DOI: 10.26577/HJ.2024.v71.i1.8

Russell, J. (2013). Stickers: From Japanese craze to global mobile messaging phenomenon. The Next Web. https://thenextweb.com/asia/2013/07/12/stickers/

Ruytenbeek, N. (2024). A case study of negated adjectives in commuters' Twitter complaints. *Languages (Basel, Switzerland)*, *9*(274), 1–13. DOI: 10.3390/languages9080274

Sacks, H., Schegloff, E. A., & Jefferson, G. (1974). A simplest systematics for the organization of turn-taking for conversation. *Language*, *50*(4), 696–735. DOI: 10.1353/lan.1974.0010

Sakib, O. I., Sarker, A., & Oishe, R. T. (2024). Exploring emojis in digital communication among Bangladeshi undergraduates: Private university scenario. *Journal of Engineering*, *12*(4), 22–30.

Saklı, A. R. (2007). Kapitalist gelişim sürecinde fordizm ve post-fordizm. *Ankara,*http://www. sakli. info/Fordizm. pdf, *Erişim Tarihi, 26*, 2008.

Salako, B. L., Ajayi, A., & Smith, S. I. (2021). Cholera in Nigeria: Epidemiology, risk factors, and response - A Review. *Proceedings of the Nigerian Academy of Science*, *14*(1), 24–33. DOI: 10.57046/JYBJ8296

Sampietro, A. (2020). Use and interpretation of emoji in electronic-mediated communication: A survey. *Visual Communication Quarterly*, *27*(1), 27–39. DOI: 10.1080/15551393.2019.1707086

Sánchez, P. L. (2015). Modality in English and Spanish advertising slogans. In Zamorano-Mansilla, J. R., Maiz, C., Dominguez, E., & Martin de la Rosa, M. V. (Eds.), *Thinking modally: English and contrastive studies on modality* (pp. 345–359). Cambridge Scholars Publishing.

Sasamoto, R. (2023). Perceptual resemblance and the communication of emotion in digital contexts: A case of emoji and reaction GIFs. *Pragmatics*, *33*(3), 393–417. DOI: 10.1075/prag.21058.sas

Saussure F, Pierce C (1983). On signifying, signs, and signifying systems. cdli.ucla.edu-staff-englund-Saussure 2.

Saussure, F. (1966). *Course in General Linguistics*. McGraw Hill Columbia University Press.

Schecter, S. R. (2014). Enabling through Self-Imaging: The Potential of Visual Communication in the Field of Diaspora, Youth Culture and Web 2.0. In Johnson, L. (Ed.), *Mobility and Fantasy in Visual Culture* (pp. 167–178). Routledge.

Schiller, H. I. (1976). *Communication and cultural dependency*. International Arts and Sciences Press.

Schmidt, E., & Cohen, J. (2013). *The New Digital Age: Reshaping the Future of People, Nationsand Businesses*. Random House.

Schroeder, J. E. (2004). Visual consumption in an image economy. K. Ekstrom and H. Brembeck (Eds.) *Elusive Consumption. Berg*, pp. 229-244, https://ssrn.com/abstract=499082

Schwartz, H. A., Eichstaedt, J. C., & Kern, M. L.. (2014). Personality, gender, and age in the language of social media: The open-vocabulary approach. *PLoS One*, *9*(9), e94778. PMID: 24086296

Scott, K. (2022). *Pragmatics online*. Routledge. DOI: 10.4324/b22750

Searle, J. R. (1969). *Speech acts: An essay in the philosophy of language*. Cambridge University Press. DOI: 10.1017/CBO9781139173438

Sells, T. G. C. (2013). The construction of sexual identities in an online gay, lesbian, and bisexual bulletin board system. *Journal of Human Behavior in the Social Environment, 23*(8), 893–907. DOI: 10.1080/10911359.2013.803452

Semotiuk, A. J., Semotiuk, N. L., & Ezcurra, E. (2015). The Eruption of Technology in Traditional Medicine: How Social Media Guides the Sale of Natural Plant Products in the Sonoran Desert Region. *Economic Botany, 69*(4), 360–369. DOI: 10.1007/s12231-015-9327-6

Şenkal, Y. (2016). Feminist kuramlar bağlamında reklamda kadın imgesine bakış. *Anadolu Bil Meslek Yüksekokulu Dergisi, 42*, 91–114.

Shaari, A. H. (2020). Accentuating illocutionary forces: Emoticons as speech act realization strategies in a multicultural online communication environment. *Linguistics. Literature, 26*(1), 135–155.

Shaheer, A. (2023). Importance of technology. https://www.slideshare.net/ahmdsagi/importance-of-technology

Shanahan, C., & Shanahan, T. (2017). *Disciplinary literacy Handbook of research on teaching the English language arts*. Routledge.

Sharma, K., Kodhati, P. & Sukhavsi, S. (2022). Emotional marketing on consumer behaviour – Perception Study. *International Journal on Consumer Relations,* 10(2), 01-08.

Sharma, Y. (2023, February 24). What ChatGPT means for linguistic diversity and language learning. University World News. https://www.universityworldnews.com/post.php?story=20230224123923811

Sharma, M. (2023). Sonny's Blues": The dream variation and cultural integration through music. *Bon Voyage, 5*(1), 83–90. DOI: 10.3126/bovo.v5i1.64376

Shaw, A. (2014). *Gaming at the Edge: Sexuality and Gender at the margins of gamer culture*. University of Minnesota Press.

Shen, H., & Wang, S. (2024). Traditional Chinese Ideology and Material Culture: An Archaeological Exploration of Historical Perspectives and Artefacts. *Mediterranean Archaeology & Archaeometry. International Journal, 24*(3), 237–252.

Shih, Y. C. (2014). Communication strategies in a multimodal virtual communication context. *System, 42*, 34–47. DOI: 10.1016/j.system.2013.10.016

Shola, A. T. (2021). Social media, youth participation and activism: An analysis of the# Endsars protests in Nigeria. *Democracy and Development Journal*, *5*(3), 4–10.

Silverstein, M. (1979). Language structure and linguistic ideology. P. R. Clyne, W.F. Hanks and C.L. Hofbauer et al. (Eds.). *The Elements: A Parasession on Linguistic Units and Levels*. Chicago: Linguistic Society, 193-247

Silverstein, M. (1985). Language and the Culture of Gender: At the Intersection of Structure, Usage, and Ideology. In Mertz, E., & Parmentier, R. J. (Eds.), *Semiotic Mediation: Sociocultural and Psychological Perspectives* (pp. 219–259). Academic Press. DOI: 10.1016/B978-0-12-491280-9.50016-9

Singh, A., Singh, P., Pandey, D., & Singh, R. K. (2024). The impact of emotional appeals on consumer engagement in digital advertising. [EEL]. *European Economic Letters*, *14*(4), 1193–1202. DOI: 10.52783/eel.v14i4.2247

Singhal, A., & Mago, V. (2023). Exploring How Healthcare Organizations Use Twitter: A Discourse Analysis. *Informatics (MDPI)*, *10*(3), 65. DOI: 10.3390/informatics10030065

Singh, N. K., & Pandey, K. A. (2020). Preservation of culture through promotion of linguistic Cinema in India: A critical analysis. *International Journal of Advanced Mass Communication and Journalism.*, *1*(1). 33-38.www.masscomjournal.com

Siollum, M. (2021). *What Britain did to Nigeria: A short history of conquest and rule*. Hurst and Co Publishers.

Sjöblom, M., Törhönen, M., Hamari, J., & Macey, J. (2019). The ingredients of Twitch streaming: Affordances of game streams. *Computers in Human Behavior*, *92*, 20–28. DOI: 10.1016/j.chb.2018.10.012

Smith, A., & Kennett, K. (2017). Multimodal meaning: Discursive dimensions of e-learning. In Cope, B., & Kalantzis, M. (Eds.), *E-Learning ecologies: Principles for new learning and assessment* (pp. 88–117). Routledge: Taylor & Francis. DOI: 10.4324/9781315639215-4

Sohail, R., Babar, S., Shahbaz, A., & Babar H. (2024). Tourism destination branding in the digital age: Evaluating the influence of social media on destination image and visitor perceptions. *Contemporary Journal of Social Science Review Vol.02* No.04

Sparrman, A. (2006). Young People's Consumption of Visual Culture. *Collector Gadgets, Sexuality and Democracy,* 114-116.

Spears, R., & Postmes, T. (2015). Group identity, social influence, and collective action online: Extensions and applications of the SIDE model. *The handbook of the psychology of communication technology*, 23-46.

Spears, R. (2017). Deindividuation. In *The Oxford handbook of social influence* (pp. 279–297). Oxford University Press.

Statistica (2023a). *Most used social media platforms in Nigeria as of the 3rd quarter of 2023.* Retrieved October 11, 2024, from http://www.statistica.com

Statistica (2023b). *Daily social media usage in Africa, 2023 by country.* Retrieved October 11, 2024, from http://www.statistica.com

Steinmetz, K. (2015). "How #LoveWins Became a Celebration of Gay Marriage Victory." Time Magazine.

Stores, F. (2022). *Nike is using augmented reality to drive experiential retail in its stores.* https://futurestores.wbresearch.com/blog/nike-using-augmented-reality-drive-experiential-retail-stores

Stuart, J., & Scott, R. (2021). The measure of online disinhibition (MOD): Assessing perceptions of reductions in restraint in the online environment. *Computers in Human Behavior, 114*, 106534. DOI: 10.1016/j.chb.2020.106534

Stubbs, M. (1983) *Discourse Analysis (The Sociolinguistics of Natural Language).* (pp. 01-05). Basil Blackwell.

Stubbs, M. (1996). *Text and corpus analysis.* London: Chicago: Blackwell.

Suler, J. (2004). The online disinhibition effect. *Cyberpsychology & Behavior, 7*(3), 321–326. DOI: 10.1089/1094931041291295 PMID: 15257832

Sumampouw, J., & Sukandar, D. (2019). The effectiveness of health promotion method using poster in improving patients' behaviour to prevent transmission of pulmonary tuberculosis disease. *Proceeding 2nd Manado Health Polytechnic International Conference,* 115-127.

Sun, J., Lasser, S., & Lee, S. K. (2023). Understanding emojis: Cultural influences in interpretation and choice of emojis. *Journal of International and Intercultural Communication, 16*(3), 242–261. DOI: 10.1080/17513057.2022.2036790

Sun, X., & Liu, L. (2023). Understanding the multi-modal affective expression of net language in computer-mediated communication. *Cognitive Processing, 24*(2), 275–288. DOI: 10.1007/s10339-022-01115-z PMID: 36574065

Sutrisno, D., Abidin, N. A. Z., Pambudi, N., Aydawati, E., & Sallu, S. (2023). Exploring the benefits of multimodal literacy in English teaching: Engaging students through visual, auditory, and digital modes. *Global Synthesis in Education Journal*, *1*(2), 1–14. DOI: 10.61667/xh184f41

Taecharungroj, V. (2023). How ChatGPT Predicts Words with Impressive Accuracy. *Journal of Applied Learning & Teaching*, *6*(1). Advance online publication. DOI: 10.1234/jalt.2023.6.1.32

Tahririan, M., & Sadri, E. (2013). Analysis of images in Iranian high school: EFL course textbook. *International Journal of English Language Education*, *3*(1), 239–253.

Taiwo, R. (2014). "Impoliteness in Online Discussion Forum: A Study of Trolling in *Nairaland.com*". In Chiluwa, I, Ifukor, P. and Taiwo, R. (Eds.) Pragmatics of Nigerian English in Digital Discourse. Munchen: LINCOM Europa. 67 - 76.

Taiwo, R. (2015) 'Who will employ them?' Questions as Engagement Strategies in Nigerian Job

Taiwo, R., & Adebayo, O. 2022. 'Baby dust to everyone': Emoting infertility in Nigerian online trying to conceive (TTC) forums." *Language. Text. Society 9*(2). https://ltsj.online/2022-09-2-taiwo-adebayo

Taiwo, R. (2016). (2016.) Cognitive Verbs and Stance Taking in Nigerian Jobs and Careers Online. *Marang: Journal of Language and Literature*, *27*, 1–19.

Taiwo, R., & Ademilokun, M. (2023). Discursive marketisation and differentiation in Nigerian university websites. In Taiwo, R., Idowu-Faith, B., & Ajiboye, S. (Eds.), *Transformation of higher education through institutional online spaces* (p. 29). IGI Global., DOI: 10.4018/978-1-6684-8122-6.ch002

Taiwo, R., & Oamen, F. (2018). *Perspectivation in Nigeria's political visual communication: A social semiotic analysis*. Covenant Journal of Language Studies.

Talbot, C. V., Talbot, A., Roe, D. J., & Briggs, P. (2020). The management of LGBTQ+ identities on social media: A student perspective. *New Media & Society*, *24*(8), 1729–1758. DOI: 10.1177/1461444820981009

Tamale, S. (2014). Exploring the Contours of African Sexualities: Religion, Law and Power. *African Human Rights Law Journal*, *14*, 150–177.

Tapscott, D. (2016). Blockchain revolution: How the technology behind bitcoin is changing money, business and the world.

Tariq, M. U. (2025). Community-Led Tourism and Social Equity: A Regenerative Approach to Sustainable Development. In Sousa, B., Arantes, L., & Bhartiya, S. (Eds.), *Regenerative Tourism for Social Development* (pp. 339–360). IGI Global Scientific Publishing., DOI: 10.4018/979-8-3373-0235-5.ch014

Tariq, M. U. (2025). Innovative Business Models: Integrating Social, Economic, and Environmental Goals in Rural Manufacturing. In Prabhakar, A., Yu, P., & Erokhin, V. (Eds.), *Rural Social Entrepreneurship Development: Network-Based Manufacturing System Model* (pp. 147–174). IGI Global Scientific Publishing., DOI: 10.4018/979-8-3693-7515-0.ch005

Tariq, M. U. (2025). Revitalizing Pedagogy: Integrating Indigenous Knowledge and Practices Into Higher Education Disciplines. In Kgari-Masondo, M. (Ed.), *Indigenous Teaching Disciplines and Perspectives for Higher Education* (pp. 379–400). IGI Global Scientific Publishing., DOI: 10.4018/979-8-3693-9296-6.ch018

Tariq, M. U. (2025). Unlocking Competitive Edge: Harnessing the Power of Collaborative Innovation. In Martínez-Falcó, J., Sánchez-García, E., & Marco-Lajara, B. (Eds.), *Open Innovation Strategies for Effective Competitive Advantage* (pp. 315–344). IGI Global Scientific Publishing., DOI: 10.4018/979-8-3693-9266-9.ch011

Taylor, A. S. (2022). *Authenticity as performativity on social media*. Springer Nature. DOI: 10.1007/978-3-031-12148-7

Taylor, S. V., & Leung, C. B. (2020). Multimodal literacy and social interaction: Young children's literacy learning. *Early Childhood Education Journal*, *48*(1), 1–10. DOI: 10.1007/s10643-019-00974-0

Taylor, T. L. (2018). *Watch Me Play: Twitch and the rise of Game live streaming*. Princeton University Press. DOI: 10.2307/j.ctvc77jqw

Team Du. (March,16, 2021). Content creation for bigginners: A how to guide. https://www.demandjump.com

Tech4Learning. (2018). Internet safety poster creative educator. Retrieved September 3, 2024 from https://creativeeducator.tech4learning.com/2018/lessons/internetsafetylesson

Teibowei, M. T. (2024). Language and Gender in Online Communications. *International Journal of English Language & Communication Studies*, *9*(1).

Thabet, Y. S. (2022). A multimodal discourse analysis of six American animated movie trailers (2010-2017). ResearchGate. https://www.researchgate.net/publication/377491006_A_Multimodal_Discourse_Analysis_of_Six_American_Animated_Movie_Trailers_2010-2017

The Nigeria Social Cohesion Survey (2019)_https://africapolling.org/wp-content/uploads/2020/01/Social-Cohesion-Report_1.pdf

The Nigeria Social Cohesion Survey (2021)_https://africapolling.org/wp-content/uploads/2021/12/API-Social-Cohesion-Report.pdf

The Nigeria Social Cohesion Survey (2022)_https://www.proshare.co/articles/the-nigeria-social-cohesion-survey-report-2022?menu=Reports&classification=Read&category=Nigerian%20Economy

The Nigerian Child Rights Act. (2003).

Thomas, J., Al-Shehhi, A., Al-Ameri, M., & Grey, I. (2019). We tweet Arabic; I tweet English: Self-concept, language and social media. *Heliyon*, *5*(7), E02087. Advance online publication. DOI: 10.1016/j.heliyon.2019.e02087 PMID: 31384681

Thompson, A. (2024). *Popular cinema and cultural change in India*. Film Studies Review.

Thorson, E., & Duffy, M. (2012). *Advertising age: the principles of advertising and marketing communication at work*. South-western CENGAGE Learning.

Tietbohl, C. K., & White, A. E. C. (2022). Making conversation analysis accessible: A conceptual guide for health services researchers. *Health Services Research*, *57*(5), 950–958. https://pubmed.ncbi.nlm.nih.gov/35616449/ PMID: 35616449

Timmermann, R. (April 26, 2024) The 5cs of content marketing. https//www.wearety.com

Toffler, A. (1981). *The Third Wave*. Bantam Books.

Treem, J. W., Leonardi, P. M., & Van den Hooff, B. (2020). Computer-mediated communication in the age of communication visibility. *Journal of Computer-Mediated Communication*, *25*(1), 44–59. DOI: 10.1093/jcmc/zmz024

Trye, D., Claude, A., Harlow, R., & Keegan, T. (2024). Analysing A/O possession in Maori- language tweets. *Languages (Basel, Switzerland)*, *9*(271), 1–32. DOI: 10.3390/languages9080271

Tsigeman, E., Mararitsa, L., Gundelah, O., Lopatina, O., & Koltsova, O. (2024). Psychological Aspects of Face-To-Face Versus Computer-Mediated Interpersonal Communication: An Integrative Review. In *International Conference on Human-Computer Interaction* (pp. 29-48). Cham: Springer Nature Switzerland. DOI: 10.1007/978-3-031-61312-8_3

Turkle, S. (1995). *Life on the screen: identity in the age of the internet*. Simon & Schuster.

Twiner, A., Littleton, K., Whitelock, D., & Coffin, C. (2021). Combining sociocultural discourse analysis and multimodal analysis to explore teachers' and pupils' meaning making. *Learning, Culture and Social Interaction*, *30*, 100520. Advance online publication. DOI: 10.1016/j.lcsi.2021.100520

Uduak, A. (2021). The New Media Technologies. *IDOSR JOURNAL OF ARTS AND HUMANITIES*, *6*(1), 30–42.

Ugah, H. U. (2023). "We will not atikuloot our future!": Nigerianness as stance-taking in online political discussion forums. *Linguistik online, 123*(5), 139-152.

Ugo, S. U., Odey, B. E., Odey, H. O., & Abu, P. E. (2023). Impact of digital communication technologies on the Nigerian mass media: Implications and insights into disruptions. LWATI: A Journal of Contemporary Research, 20(4), 39-55.

Uhunmwuangho, S. O., & Epelle, A. (2011). Challenges and solutions to ethno-religious conflicts in Nigeria: Case study of the Jos crises. *Journal of Sustainable Development in Africa, 13*(5), 109–124.

UNICEF. (2016). Guide to conflict analysis. https://www.unicef.org/media/96581/file/Guide-to-Conflict-Analysis.pdf

UNICEF. (2018). *Evaluation report: The out-of-school children initiative*. OOSCI.

UNICEF. (2023). Crime statistics- devastating violence against children and women continues. UNICEF, Retrieved from https://www.unicef.org/southafrica/press-releases/crime- statistics-devastating-violence-against-children-and-women-continues.

Unsworth, L., Tytler, R., Fenwick, L., Humphrey, S., Chandler, P., Herrington, M., & Pham, L. (2022). *Multimodal literacy in school science: Transdisciplinary perspectives on theory, research and pedagogy*. Taylor & Francis. DOI: 10.4324/9781003150718

Urujzian, V., & Etuk, J. A. (2024). A lexico-semantic analysis of selected songs of Wizkid. *Sapientia Global Journal of Arts* [SGOJAHDS]. *Humanities and Development Studies*, *7*(1), 313–324.

Usman, H., Husseini, A., & Mohammed, A. (2023). Impact of interactive video-based instructional platform on achievement of geography concepts amongst secondary school students in Niger State. *FUO Journal of Science and Technology*, *9*(2), 123–137.

Utoyo, A. W., Aprilia, H. D., Kuntjoro-Jakti, R. A. D. R. I., & Kurniawan, A. (2021, April). Visual communication design: Poster as an important way to encourage social distance in Jakarta when the epidemic 19. [). IOP Publishing.]. *IOP Conference Series. Earth and Environmental Science*, *729*(1), 012140.

Vale, O., & Barbosa, A. (2021). Posters: A tool to foster visual and communication skills through mathematical challenging tasks using gallery walk. *EDULEARN21 Proceedings*, 8416-8425, DOI: 10.21125/edulearn.2021.1706

van Dijk, T. A. (2009). *Critical discourse studies: A sociocognitive approach* (pp. 62-86). na.

Van Dijk, T. A. (2001). Multidisciplinary CDA: A plea for diversity. In Wodak, R., & Meyer, M. (Eds.), *Methods of critical discourse analysis* (pp. 95–120). SAGE Publications.

van Dijk, T. A. (2005). Discourse analysis as ideology analysis. In *Language & peace* (pp. 41–58). Routledge.

van Dijk, T. A. (2009). *Society and discourse: How Social Contexts Influence Text and Talk*. Cambridge University Press. DOI: 10.1017/CBO9780511575273

van Dijk, T. A. (2012). Structures of discourse and structures of power. [Routledge.]. *Communication Yearbook*, *12*, 18–59.

van Dijk, T. A. (2017). Socio-cognitive discourse studies. In *The Routledge Handbook of Critical Discourse Studies* (pp. 26–43). Routledge. DOI: 10.4324/9781315739342-3

Van Leeuwen, T. (2005). *Introducing social semiotics*. Routledge Taylor & Francis.

Van Leeuwen, T. (2008). *Discourse and practice: New tools for critical discourse analysis*. Oxford University Press. DOI: 10.1093/acprof:oso/9780195323306.001.0001

Van Leeuwen, T. (2011). Multimodality. In *The Routledge Handbook of Applied Linguistics* (pp. 668–682). Routledge.

Vanden Broeck, P. (2021). The role of internet technology in shaping political discourse and media consumption. *Journal of Digital Culture*, *15*(3), 203–219.

Vandergriff, I. (2020). Generational differences in emoji interpretation and use in digital communication. *Communication Studies*, *71*(2), 211–227.

Vaughan, O. (2016). *Christianity and the transformation of colonial southern and northern Nigeria*. Duke University: Duke University Press. DOI: 10.1215/9780822373872-004

Veronika, M., Firman, F., & Ahmad, R. (2021). Conceptual analysis of the relationship between culture and education. *SCHOULID: Indonesian Journal of School Counseling*, *1*(1), 1–12. DOI: 10.23916/08740011

Vikash, K. M. (2013). Role of Social Media in Education. *International Journal Of Creative Researvh Thoughts*, *1*(3), 857–860.

Vikner, C., & Jensen, P. A. (2004). The English Pre-Nominal Genitive and Lexical Semantics. In K. Ji-yung, Y.A. Lander, & B.H. Partee (Eds.), *Possessives and Beyond: Semantics and Syntax* (Occasional Papers in Linguistics No. 29, pp. 3–27). Amherst, MA: GLSA Publications.

Vikner, C., & Jensen, P. A. (2002). A Semantic Analysis of the English Genitive. Interaction of Lexical and Formal Semantics. *Studia Linguistica*, *56*(2), 191–226. DOI: 10.1111/1467-9582.00092

Vikner, C., & Jensen, P. A. (2003). Producer interpretations of the English prenominal genitive. In Weisgerber, M. (Ed.), *Proceedings of sub7 – Sinn und Bedeutung. Arbeitspapier Nr. 114* (pp. 173–183). University of Konstanz.

Vokmer, I. (1999). *News in the global sphere, A study of CNN anf its impact on global communication*. University of Luron Press.

Vougioukalou, S., Dow, R., Bradshaw, L., & Pallant, T. (2019). Wellbeing and integration through community music: The role of improvisation in a music group of refugees, asylum seekers and local community members. *Contemporary Music Review*, *38*(5), 533–548. DOI: 10.1080/07494467.2019.1684075

Wada, A. S., Jatau, A. I., Bala, A. A., Haruna, A., Isa, A. M., Safiyya, A. S., & Sha'aban, A. (2019). Use of traditional medicines among pharmacists in Nigeria. *Complementary Therapies in Clinical Practice*, *35*(1), 53–56. DOI: 10.1016/j.ctcp.2019.01.014 PMID: 31003686

Wagner, A., Marusek, S., & Yu, W. (2020). Emojis and law: Contextualized flexibility of meaning in cyber communication. *Social Semiotics*, *30*(3), 396–414. DOI: 10.1080/10350330.2020.1731198

Wagner, A., Marusek, S., & Yu, W. (2020). Sarcasm, the smiling poop, and E-discourse aggressiveness: Getting far too emotional with emojis. *Social Semiotics*, *30*(3), 305–311. DOI: 10.1080/10350330.2020.1731151

Walther, J. B. (2018). Social Information Processing Theory. In *The Handbook of Communication Science* (pp. 441–460). Sage Publications.

Wang, S., & Chin, T. (2020). A stratified system of knowledge and knowledge icebergs in cross-cultural business models: Synthesizing ontological and epistemological views. *Journal of International Management, 26*, 100780. DOI: 10.1016/j.intman.2020.100780

Wang, X., Riaz, M., Haider, S., Alam, K., Sherani, , & Yang, M. (2021). Information sharing on social media by multicultural individuals: Experiential, motivational, and network factors. *Journal of Global Information Management, 29*(6), 1–24. DOI: 10.4018/JGIM.20211101.oa22

Warner, M. (1991). Introduction: Fear of a queer planet. *Social Text, 29*, 3–17.

Wathuti, E. (2021, November 1). *Elizabeth Wathuti at #COP26: "Please open your hearts"* [Video]. YouTube. https://www.youtube.com/watch?v=VMvzJu79WG0

Watson, S., & Romic, J. (2024). ChatGPT and the entangled evolution of society, education, and technology: A systems theory perspective. *European Educational Research Journal, 24*(2), 205-224. (Original work published 2025)DOI: 10.1177/14749041231221266

Weber, R. P. (1990). *Basic content analysis.* DOI: 10.4135/9781412983488

Welekwe, A. (2023). The top networking technologies for 2024._https://www.comparitech.com/net-admin/networking-technologies/

Wen, L., Jingjing, W., Chen, W., & Luyu, S. (2022). Research on the Visual imagery of posters based on the culture code theory of design. *Frontiers in Psychology*, 13, 1-6. 861366. .

Wheeler, D. L. (2020). *Semiotics in film: The dialogue between visual and verbal language.* Cambridge Scholars Publishing.

White, S. J. (2019). Conversation analysis: An introduction to methodology, data collection, and analysis. In Liamputtong, P. (Ed.), *Handbook of research methods in health social sciences* (pp. 471–490). Springer., DOI: 10.1007/978-981-10-5251-4_107

WHO. (2024). *Rallying Action to Curb Cholera in Nigeria's Lagos State.* https://www.afro.who.int/countries/nigeria/news/rallying-action-curb-cholera-nigerias-lagos-state#:~:text=Health%20authorities%20declared%20a%20cholera,an%20acute%20and%20virulent%20infection

Wijayanti, R. P., Handayani, P. W., & Azzahro, F. (2022). Intention to seek health information on social media in Indonesia. *Procedia Computer Science, 197*, 118–125. DOI: 10.1016/j.procs.2021.12.125

Willemse, P. (2005). *Nominal reference-point constructions: Possessive and esphoric NPs in English* (PhD Thesis, University of Leuven, Leuven, Belgium).

Williams, M. L., Pete, B., & Luke, S. (2017). Towards an Ethical Framework for Publishing Twitter Data in Social Research: Taking into Account Users' Views, Online Context and Algorithmic Estimation. *Sociology*, *51*(6), 1149–1168. DOI: 10.1177/0038038517708140 PMID: 29276313

Woldu, F., & Quazi, T. M. (2024). *Difficulties faced by small and medium-sized enterprises (SMEs) in underdeveloped nations in implementing digital marketing: A case study of Bangladesh and Ethiopia*. University of Gothenburg. Retrieved from https://gupea.ub.gu.se/handle/2077/82458

World Health Organization. (2020). Cholera fact sheet. Retrieved September 3, 2024 from https://www.who.int/newsroom/factsheets/detail/cholera

Wu, D., Zhang, X., & Zhang, X. (2024). Is there an intergenerational discrepancy in the comprehension and aesthetic preference regarding emoji usage? Evidence from WeChat. *Frontiers in Psychology*, *15*, 1424728. DOI: 10.3389/fpsyg.2024.1424728 PMID: 39165767

Wu, M., Wu, T., & Pei, Y. (2024). What Drives Health Information Exchange on Social Media? Social Media Affordances and Social Support Perspectives. *Health Communication*, *39*(13), 1–15. DOI: 10.1080/10410236.2024.2321408 PMID: 38477307

Xiao, H., Li, W., Cao, X., & Tang, Z. (2012). The online social networks on knowledge exchange: Online social identity, social tie and culture orientation. *Journal of Global Information Technology Management*, *15*(2), 4–24. DOI: 10.1080/1097198X.2012.11082753

Xie, T., Donthu, N., Lohtia, R., & Osmonbekov, T. (2004). Emotional appeal and incentive offering in banner advertisements. *Journal of Interactive Advertising*, *4*(2), 30–37. DOI: 10.1080/15252019.2004.10722085

Xu, Z., & Liu, X. (2019). A linguo-cultural approach to the integration of Hip-hop culture with Chinese Culture---taking Rap music as an example. *International Journal of Literature and Arts*, *12*(2), 165–171. https://neurosciencenews.com/music-body-emotion-25664/. DOI: 10.11648/j.ijla.20190706.16

Yaşar Ekici, F. (2014). *Türk aile yapısının değişim ve dönüşümü ve bu değişim ve dönüşüme etki eden unsurların değerlendirilmesi. The Journal of Academic Social Science Studies*. JASSS.

Yau, A., Marder, B., & O'Donohoe, S. (2019). The role of social media in negotiating identity during the process of acculturation. [Epub ahead-of-print]. *Information Technology & People*, *33*(2), 554–575. DOI: 10.1108/ITP-09-2017-0305

Yeomans, M., Boland, F. K., & Brooks, A. W. (2023). A practical guide to conversation research: How to study what people say to each other. *Advances in Methods and Practices in Psychological Science*, *6*(3), 25152459231183919. Advance online publication. DOI: 10.1177/25152459231183919

Yom-Tov, E., Shembekar, J., & Barclay, S.. (2018). The effectiveness of public health advertisements to promote health: A randomized-controlled trial on 794,000 participants. *NPI Digital Med*, *1*(24), 1–6.

Yore, L. D. (2018). Commentary on the expanding development of literacy research in science education. In *Global Developments in Literacy Research for Science Education* (pp. 379–397). Springer. DOI: 10.1007/978-3-319-69197-8_22

Young, S., & Cameron, G. (2020). Digital discourse: Understanding language and power in the online world. *Language & Communication*, *70*, 68–79. DOI: 10.1016/j.langcom.2020.07.001

Yousef, M., Dietrich, T., & Rundle-Thiele, S. (2021). Social advertising effectiveness in driving action: A study of positive, negative and coactive appeals on social media. *International Journal of Environmental Research and Public Health*, *18*(11), 5954. DOI: 10.3390/ijerph18115954 PMID: 34206119

Yüksel, M. (2003). Mahremiyet Hakkı ve Sosyo-Tarihsl Gelişimi. *Ankara Üniversitesi SBF Dergisi, 58*(01).

Yule, G. (1996). *Pragmatics*. Oxford University Press.

Zagata, E., Kearns, D., Truckenmiller, A. J., & Zhao, Z. (2023). Using the features of written compositions to understand reading comprehension. *Reading Research Quarterly*, *58*(4), 624–654. DOI: 10.1002/rrq.503

Zaidi, R., & Sah, P. K. (2024). Affordances of Multilingual and Multimodal Literacy Engagements of Immigrant High School Students: A Scoping Review. *SAGE Open*, *14*(1), 21582440241228122. DOI: 10.1177/21582440241228122

Zappavigna, M. (2012). *Discourse of Twitter and social media: How we use language to create affiliation on the web*. Bloomsbury. DOI: 10.5040/9781472541642

Zappavigna, M. (2016). Social media photography: Construing subjectivity in Instagram images. *Visual Communication*, *15*(3), 271–292. DOI: 10.1177/1470357216643220

Zhang, J., Hu, H., Wu, D., Nie, Y., & Lin, X. (2024). Is Online Group Therapy as Effective as Face-to-face Group Therapy? A Mixed Methods Study. *Clinical Social Work Journal*, ●●●, 1–12.

Zhang, Y., & Zhou, Y. (2024). Multimodal analysis of the *Star Wars* trailer: A social semiotic approach. *Journal of Visual Culture*, *23*(1), 22–36. DOI: 10.1177/1470412918780770

Zhao, C., Hinds, P., & Gao, G. (2012. February). How and to whom people share: the role of culture in self-disclosure in online communities. In *Proceedings of the ACM 2012 Conference on Computer Supported Cooperative Work* (pp. 67-76). DOI: 10.1145/2145204.2145219

Zort, Ç., Karabacak, E., Öznur, Ş., & Dağlı, G. (2023). Sharing of cultural values and heritage through storytelling in the digital age. *Frontiers in Psychology*, *14*, 1104121. DOI: 10.3389/fpsyg.2023.1104121 PMID: 36895745

About the Contributors

Rotimi Taiwo is a Professor of English and New Media Studies in the Department of English Obafemi Awolowo University, Ile-Ife. He holds Ph.D. from Obafemi Awolowo University, Ile-Ife (2003). He joined the University in January, 1997 as an Assistant Lecturer and rose through the ranks to become a professor in October, 2011. Between June 2008 and August 2009, he was an Alexander von Humboldt Post-doctoral Fellow at the Department of English, University of Freiburg, Germany. He was also a Visiting Professor at the University of Munster, Germany (2014); Covenant University (2017-2018) and Olabisi Onabanjo University (2022-2023). In Obafemi Awolowo University, Ile-Ife, he has served as the Coordinator, Use of English (2006-2008), Head of the Department English, (2018 - 2020), Editor-in-Chief, Ife Studies in English and Linguistics (2018-2020) He also served as the Editor of the Journal of English Scholars' Association of Nigeria (2018-2020). He is currently member of editorial boards of Linguistik Online (Berne, Germany), International Journal of Language, Society and Culture (Tasmania, Australia), Covenant Journal of Language Studies (Ota, Nigeria) and CLAREP Journal of English and Linguistics, among others. He has equally served as member of the Board of Regents (Council), Landmark University, Omu Aran (2019-2022). Over 100 of his papers, which are mainly in the areas of lexical studies, media, political, and religious discourse analysis, as well as pragmatics of online discourse, have appeared in reputable and high impact journals in his discipline. For almost two decades, Professor Taiwo has been working on computer-mediated discourse analysis and he has published extensively on this area of research. Some of his most outstanding works in this area of research are: Handbook of Research on Discourse Behavior and Digital Communication: Language Structures and Social Interaction Volumes I & II (IGI Global, New York, 2010); Computer Mediated Discourse in Africa (Nova, New York, 2012), Language and Mobile Telecommunication in Nigeria: SMS as a Digital Age Lingual-cultural Expression (OAU Press, 2012); The Discourse of Digital Civic Engagement: Perspectives from the Developing World

(New York: Nova Science, 2016) His current research is discursive marketisation in higher institutions' online spaces in which he is editing a book titled: Transformation of Higher Education Through Institutional Online Spaces slated to be released by IGI Global, Hershey, Pennsylvania, USA in the last quarter of 2023. Prof Taiwo has successfully supervised 30 M.A, 5 MPhil 8 PhD candidates. Outside the university setting, Professor Taiwo is currently the President Gideons International, Central West State Association, and Coordinator, Pastoral Support Group, All Souls' Chapel (Interdenominational), OAU, Ile-Ife.

***

Abdullahi AbdulRafiu is a Ph.D student in Business Education from the Kwara state University, Malete and an assistant lecturer in the department of business education at Al-Hikmah University, Ilorin, Nigeria. A member of the Association of Business Education of Nigeria (ABEN) and the Teacher Registration Council of Nigeria (TRCN), his research interest is in entrepreneurship, marketing and information technology, which addresses academic and societal challenges, spanning diverse disciplines to create entrepreneurship solutions in education and community development. His contact emails are: aabdulrafiu@alhikmah.edu.ng or abdulrafiuabdullahi@gmail.com

Emmanuel Adedayo Adedun is a Professor of Applied English Linguistics and Sociolinguistics. He was the Head of the Department of English and also the Sub-Dean of the School of Postgraduate Studies, University of Lagos. He was the editor of the journal of Faculty of Arts, University of Lagos known as Lagos Notes and Records. He has served in different capacities at the University of Lagos including being the Hall Master of the Great Elkanemi Hall. Prof. Adedun has published several learned papers and supervised twelve doctoral candidates both in Nigeria, Mali and Ghana. He was also the Head of the Department of Languages, Mountain Top University, Prayer City, Ogun State. He is currently the Director of Centre for Advancement and Chairman of the D.K. Olukoya, Scholarship Foundation, Mountain Top University.

Bolatito Olufunke Adejare is a Lecturer in the Department of Languages and Literary Studies, Faculty of Arts, Adeleke University, Ede. She received her Bachelor of Arts, Master of Arts and Ph.D. in English Language from Obafemi Awolowo University, Ile-Ife. Her areas of research interest include Cinema Phonology, Phonokinesics, Phono-pragmatics, Socio-phonology, Onomastics and Cultural Linguistics.

Emmanuel Taiwo Babalola is a distinguished professor of English (Grammar and Contemporary English Usage) at the Obafemi Awolowo University, Ile-Ife. His research interests are Grammar, Applied Linguistics, and English for Specific Purposes. He is very well published.

Moses Chika Christian-Achinihu is an Assistant Professor, and Interim Director of Academic Registry at American University of Nigeria. He is an emerging researcher with an interest in the application of Systemic Functional Linguistics, (Critical) Discourse Analysis and multimodal theories to interrogate an array of linguistics intersections: language in/of new media, digital practices and civic engagement; linguistics as/in social action/digital activism; language and social crises; language and health discourse; language in/of crime and law; language and migration; language, and ideology, identity, power, discrimination, harassment and gender; and corpus-based/computational linguistics.

Dada Samuel Ayodele is a Professor of English Linguistics in the Department of English and Literary Studies, Ekiti State University, Ado-Ekiti, Ekiti State. His research interest include Sociolinguistics, Applied Linguistics, Stylistics and Pragmatics. His research outlet includes both reputable local and international journals.

Andrew Ikpomwosa Egbah, PhD, is a Lecturer at the Department of English and Literature, University of Benin, Ugbowo, Benin City. His areas of interest are Varieties of English, Pidgins and Creoles, Critical Discourse Analysis, Sociolinguistics, and Stylistics. Contact: Department of English and Literature, University of Benin, Ugbowo, P.M.B. 1154, Benin City.

Famakinwa Yemisi Mulikat is a Senior Lecturer in the Department of English, Obafemi Awolowo University, Ile-Ife, Nigeria. Her areas of research include Grammar, Semantics, History of the English Language and Pragmatics. Her recent publication in the fields of Grammar and Semantics includes, Establishing the Connection between Valency and Passive Voice in the English Simple Sentence Constructions.

Noor Fathima is a dedicated Psychologist, Assistant Professor and Research Scholar with 10+ years of experience in psychology and higher education. Her work and research focus on developmental, social and cognitive psychology. Her diverse professional training in teaching (Bachelor of Education) and psychology (Master of Science) enables her to empower students to enhance their mental health outcomes in academic spaces.

Tolulope Iredele is a doctoral candidate at University of Lagos, Akoka, Lagos, Nigeria. Her research interest focuses on Political Discourse.

Olaronke Ganiat Iroju is a Senior Lecturer in the Department of Computer Science, Adeyemi Federal University of Education, Ondo, Nigeria

Opeyemi AnthonyIroju is a Senior Lecturer in the Department of History, Obafemi Awolowo University Ile-Ife, Nigeria

Semiu Olawale Makinde holds a PhD in Educational Technology from the University of Ilorin and is a senior lecturer as well as the acting director of the Institute of Education at Al-Hikmah University, Ilorin, Nigeria. A member of several professional associations, his research focuses on leveraging technology to address academic and societal challenges, spanning diverse disciplines to create innovative solutions for education and community development. His contact emails are: osmakintoch1@gmail.com or somakinde@alhikmah.edu.ng

Olayinka Odubela is an Assistant Lecturer in the Department of English, Obafemi Awolowo University, Ile-Ife. She is a Language Laboratory Specialist and an AI Chatbot Analyst, She also teaches the French Language. Her areas of interest and specialisation are Digital Storytelling, Discourse Analysis, Computer Mediated Discourse Analysis and Applied Linguistics.

Tolulope Grace Ojo is a Linguist and an assistant lecturer at Mountain Top University. She is currently running her PhD program at a prestigious University. She is a prolific writer and editor with vast experience as a passionate educator. She presently conducts research in Socio-Semiotics, Sociolinguistics, Phonetics, and Stylistics.

Olaifa Lydia Tomilola, PhD, is from Osun State. She obtained her first degree at University of Ado-Ekiti, Ekiti State, and her second and third degrees at University of Ibadan, Ibadan. She lectures at Adeleke University, Ede, Osun State. Her areas of specialisation are Semiotics, Gender Studies, Media Studies and Sociolinguistics.

Ezekiel Opeyemi Olajimbiti received his Ph.D. in discourse analysis and pragmatics from the University of Ibadan and is currently a lecturer at the Federal University Lokoja. His research areas include pragmatics, discourse analysis, semantics, and sociolinguistics with a special interest in children's discourse.

Moji Olateju is a Professor in the department of English Obafemi Awolowo University, Ile-Ife, Osun State, Nigeria. Her areas of interest include Discourse

Analysis, Applied Linguistics and literacy Education. She is widely published and has authored and coauthored many academic books.

Paul Ayodele Onanuga is a Senior Lecturer in the Department of English and Literary Studies, Federal University Oye-Ekiti, Nigeria. His research interests revolve around linguistic practices in New Media Studies, queer sexualities on digital media, Nigerian Hip-Hop Studies, and Computer Mediated Communication/ Discourse Analysis. He is a member of the Editorial Board of Discourse Context and the Media. He is widely published.

Olubunmi Funmi Oyebanji is a lecturer in the Department of English and Literary Studies, Bamidele Olumilua University of Education, Science and Technology, Ikere-Ekiti, Nigeria. Her areas of research interests are Queer Linguistics, Gender studies, Media Studies, Migration Discourses, Critical Discourse Analysis and Systemic Functional Linguistics.

Wilson Raj is a Psychologist with training in clinical specialisation. He has over five years of experience in psychology and his work focuses on neuro-developmental disorders, psychotherapy, organisational behaviour, influence of media and violence.

Sakariyahu Shehu is a Ph.D. student in the Green University for Community Development and Entrepreneurship, KWASU as well as an Assistant Lecturer in the Department of Business Education, Al-Hikmah University, Ilorin. He enjoys the membership of Association of Business Educators of Nigeria (ABEN); Business Educators Association in Vocational Education (BEAVE); and Teachers' Registration Council of Nigeria (TRCN). His research interest centered on Business and Entrepreneurship Education, with a specific emphasis on developing innovative and effective approaches to teaching and learning in Entrepreneurship and Business Education. His email contacts are: ssakariyahu@alhikmah.edu.ng and sunkanmizacks@gmail.com

Muhammad Usman Tariq has more than 16+ year's experience in industry and academia. He has authored more than 200+ research articles, 110+ case studies, 95+ book chapters and several books other than 4 patents. He is founder and CEO of The Case HQ, a unique repository for courses, narrative and video case studies. He has been working as a consultant and trainer for industries representing six sigma, quality, health and safety, environmental systems, project management, and information security standards. His work has encompassed sectors in aviation, manufacturing, food, hospitality, education, finance, research, software and transportation. He has diverse and significant experience working with accreditation agencies of ABET, ACBSP, AACSB, WASC, CAA, EFQM and NCEAC. Additionally, Dr. Tariq has operational experience in incubators, research labs, government research projects, private sector startups, program creation and management at various industrial and academic levels. He is Certified Higher Education Teacher from Harvard University, USA, Certified Online Educator from HMBSU, Certified Six Sigma Master Black Belt and has been awarded PFHEA, SMIEEE, and CMBE.

Ahmet Yıldız holds a master's degree in communication and social transformation and is currently pursuing his doctoral studies in communication sciences. As a lecturer at Harran University Siverek Vocational School, he conducts research in the fields of communication studies, society, mass communication, and digital communication. He aims to shed light on social change through interdisciplinary and mixed-method approaches. He is currently serving as an associate professor at Fırat University's Faculty of Communication, having completed his master's degree in General Sociology and Methodology and his doctoral education in the same field. His research interests focus on sociology, cultural sociology, communication sociology, and social change. In his research, he adopts interdisciplinary methodological approaches that combine qualitative interviews, surveys, content and discourse analysis, ethnographic/field studies, and theoretical-conceptual analysis.

Index

A

B

C

D

E

G

H

I

L

M

N

O

P

Q

R

S

T

V

W

Y

www.ingramcontent.com/pod-product-compliance
Ingram Content Group UK Ltd.
Pitfield, Milton Keynes, MK11 3LW, UK
UKHW050949290926
15470UKWH00005B/1728